S0-BRV-991

HANDBOOK OF GROUP INTERVENTION FOR CHILDREN AND FAMILIES

HANDBOOK OF GROUP INTERVENTION FOR CHILDREN AND FAMILIES

Edited by

KAREN CALLAN STOIBER
University of Wisconsin–Milwaukee

THOMAS R. KRATOCHWILL
University of Wisconsin–Madison

Allyn and Bacon
Boston London Toronto Sydney Tokyo Singapore

Series editor: Carla F. Daves
Series editorial assistant: Susan Hutchinson
Marketing manager: Joyce Nilsen
Advertising manager: Anne Morrison
Manufacturing buyer: Suzanne Lareau

A Viacom Company
Needham Heights, MA 02194

Internet: www.abacon.com
America Online: keyword: College Online

Library of Congress Cataloging-in-Publication Data

Handbook of group intervention for children and families / edited by
Karen Callan Stoiber, Thomas R. Kratochwill.
p. cm.
ISBN 0-205-15695-9
1. Group psychotherapy for children. 2. Group psychotherapy for teenagers. 3. Family psychotherapy. I. Stoiber, Karen Callan,
II. Kratochwill, Thomas R.
RJ505.G7H37 1998
618.92'89152--dc21 97-36966
CIP

Printed in the United States of America
10 9 8 7 6 5 4 3 2 1 02 01 00 99 98

To my husband, Greg, who will
always hold a special place in my heart
and who creatively tolerated
many "single-parent" weekends and evenings.

To my children—Lucas, Leah, Zachary,
and Andrew—for their remarkable patience
while I worked on this project.

K. C. S.

To my wife, Carol, and my son, Tyler,
for their support
of my professional activities.

To the loving memory of my father,
Rudy Kratochwill,
who died during my work on this book.

T. R. K.

CONTENTS

PREFACE

Our own work as well as collaboration with students and practitioners made us aware of the need for a book that addresses group approaches for prevention and intervention. A primary goal in bringing together broad-based empirical structures for group work is reflective of the changing forces affecting the mental health and health care professions. The challenge to mental health and health care professionals is to develop effective approaches to prevention and intervention that can be applied efficiently and systematically. This book is responsive to the increasing appreciation of group prevention and intervention and to the newly created needs of mental health and health care professionals to develop competence in group work. Although the field of applied clinical practice may not yet be in a position to offer an integrated theory of group prevention and intervention, it seems that knowledge is advanced sufficiently to provide necessary guidance and direction.

Handbook of Group Intervention for Children and Families is intended for three critical audiences. The first is students and practitioners who will benefit from an up-to-date summary of existing research on group prevention and intervention work. The book should be highly relevant for university-related courses, professional schools, and practicing clinicians. Many of these individuals may be involved in conducting prevention and intervention groups. The book's focus on specific activities and strategies for group prevention and intervention should also be beneficial to them in designing, implementing, and evaluating group practices. The second audience consists of those at the organizational level—program developers, administrators, community agency staff, and grant organization professionals. These individuals are typically policymakers in determining future directives for mental health and health promotion. Our third intended audience is researchers and program evaluators, who, through their collaboration with practitioners, will assist in moving us to the next level of developing "best practices" in group prevention and intervention. Hence, we hope that this book will be a resource both for those working directly and indirectly in group prevention and intervention practices.

The chapters that follow are grouped into three sections. Chapters 1 through 4 provide an overview or conceptual orientation for the practice of group prevention and intervention, with attention directed at specific considerations for school and community settings. Chapter 4 specifically addresses research and design issues in evaluating group approaches to prevention and intervention. Chapters 5 through 14 address specific types of problems, disorders, or issues—depression, anger and violence, divorce, peer rejection, loss and grief, substance abuse, children of alcoholics, mild disorders, traumatic stress disorders, and cultural diversity. The concerns and specific disorders discussed in the second section are not exhaustive of the possible targets for group prevention and intervention. However, the topics are representative of the types of groups being emphasized in school and community settings. The models of prevention and intervention presented in these chapters should provide a framework for thinking about and implementing other need-specific groups.

Family- and parent-focused groups for addressing a broad range of needs are presented in the third section. Chapters 15 through 21 draw on social, cognitive, behavioral, and developmental theory to delineate meaningful ways of structuring groups for enhancing parenting, parent/child relationships, and home/school collaboration. Some chapters include strategies that have applicability for addressing psychosocial problems such as adolescent pregnancy, child abuse, and at-risk vulnerability. Particular group interventions for parents of children with developmental disabilities are discussed in two chapters. Consideration is given to parents and families more generally in chapters that offer suggestions for facilitating multiple family group therapy and conflict resolution between parents and schools.

Each chapter is structured in a similar manner to provide consistency in organization. The initial section defines the problem (e.g., depression, child abuse) or focus (e.g., groups in the schools, multiple family groups) being addressed in the chapter. Salient or distinguishing features of the problem or situation are provided as well as a rationale for group approaches. A critical review of the empirical literature describing group work in the specific area is offered, highlighting limitations and central findings that have specific implications for structuring and implementing groups. Each chapter also includes details about strategies or activities that have been shown to be effective for prevention and intervention. The objective of this component is to provide for the reader a real sense of the group process. Finally, the chapters conclude with comments about future directions for research and practice. Attention is given to possible issues that need to be considered to improve the quality and effectiveness of groups as well as suggestions for the next steps in guiding continued efforts.

We feel appreciative of those students and practitioners who have pointed out the advantages in developing this book. The process of editing this comprehensive volume has given us an incredible opportunity to consider possibilities for our own development as professionals, trainers, and group facilitators. By outlining steps for improving group practices, perhaps this book will help others develop competencies in group facilitation. The thoughtful involvement in groups by our readers holds promise for the field of mental health. The broad focus of this book is intended to be appealing to psychologists, counselors, social workers, and other mental health and health care professionals working in school and community settings. We believe it is profitable for all of us to promote the health of children, adolescents, and families. The current work is offered as a step in moving us toward using validated group approaches in reaching this goal. If this book encourages the reader to discover ways to meet the challenge of unmet mental health needs, then it has served its purpose well.

We noted in the beginning of this Preface an appreciation to students and practitioners who provided the impetus for developing this book. We are grateful to Sue Hutchinson and Mylan Jaixen, who assisted us in the preparation of this manuscript. In addition, we wish to acknowledge the constant support and encouragement of our editor, Carla Daves. Our appreciation also goes to the following reviewers for their comments on the manuscript: Jan N. Hughes, Texas A&M University, and Deborah Tharinger, The University of Texas at Austin. We also want to acknowledge the enduring support from our families, which was sustained over many months.

ABOUT THE CONTRIBUTORS

Arthur J. Anderson is a Ph.D. candidate in the School Psychology Training Program in the Department of Educational Psychology at the University of Wisconsin–Milwaukee. He completed his predoctoral internship at the Ethan Allen School for Boys and the South Oaks School for Girls, which are residential centers for delinquent youths. His research interests include risk behaviors in adolescents and adolescent pregnancy. He is currently employed as a school psychologist by the Shorewood School District in Wisconsin.

Sandra T. Azar, Ph.D., is an associate professor and director of the Clinical Training Program at the Frances L. Hiatt School of Psychology at Clark University in Worcester, MA. She has published numerous articles and chapters in the area of child abuse and parent training. Azar has acted as director of a group parent training program for abusive and neglectful parents and conducts research in the areas of high-risk parenting, cognitive processes in child maltreatment, and legal issues and parenting evaluations.

Lisa Blum is a doctoral candidate at the Graduate School of Applied and Professional Psychology at Rutgers University. She has worked as a program consultant to teachers implementing Elias and Clabby's Social Problem Solving/ Social Decision Making Curriculum in the elementary grades. She specializes in prevention work with children and families.

Susan J. Breton, M.A., is currently a graduate student in the Clinical Psychology Program at the Frances L. Hiatt School of Psychology at Clark University in Worcester, MA. She has a B.A. from Bennington College and an M.A. in developmental psychology from Wesleyan University. Her research interests include gender differences in aggression and cognitive behavioral approaches to conduct disorders in children and adolescents.

Cindy Carlson, Ph. D., is professor of educational psychology at the University of Texas at Austin. She received her doctorate from Indiana University, completed an APA-approved clinical psychology internship at the University of Tennessee College of Medicine, and is a licensed psychologist. She is a Fellow in the American Psychological Association and a recent Notable Scholar at the University of British Columbia. Carlson's research interests focus on connections between the family, school, and peer ecological systems in child development, family-school linkages in early adolescence, and multicultural issues in the transition from elementary to middle school.

Sandra L. Christenson, Ph.D., is an associate professor of educational and child psychology and coordinator of the School Psychology Program at the University of Minnesota. She is the director of several applied research projects aimed at increasing the academic and social competence of students by increasing home/school/community partnerships. Christenson was the 1992 recipient of the Lightner Witmer Award from APA for scholarship and early career contributions to the field of school psychology.

Roseanne Clark, Ph.D., is an assistant professor and director of the Parent-Infant and Early Childhood Clinic in the Department of Psychiatry at the University of Wisconsin Medical School–Madison. She has developed parent group and dyadic intervention approaches and has consulted to numerous early intervention programs. In addition, she developed the Parent-Child Early Relational Assessment, an instrument used to measure the affective and behavioral quality of parent-child relationships. Clark's interests include assessment and treatment of parent-child early relational disturbances, infant mental health, maternal depression, and maternal employment characteristics and family functioning.

Margaret Dempsey, Ph.D., is an assistant professor of school psychology in the Department of Psychology, Tulane University. She completed her predoctoral internship in Pediatric Psychology at Michigan State University. Dempsey's primary interests are in coping, emotional regulation, social development, and family issues. Her current research focuses on coping with the transition from elementary to middle school in inner-city high-risk students.

Stewart W. Ehly, Ph.D., is professor and director of training for the School Psychology Program in the Division of Psychological and Quantitative Foundations at the University of Iowa. He is the author of three books (including *Peer Tutoring for Individualized Instruction* and *Individual and Group Counseling in Schools*) and more than 90 other publications.

Maurice J. Elias, Ph.D., is professor of psychology at Rutgers University, and co-founder of the Consortium on the School-Based Promotion of Social Competence. His school-based life skills development and problem behavior prevention programs have been recognized by the National Mental Health Association and the U.S. Department of Education's National Diffusion Network and National Education Goals Panel.

Giselle B. Esquivel, Ph.D., is associate professor in the School Psychology Program at Fordham University. She directs the Bilingual School Psychology Program and is the current chair of the Division of Psychological and Educational Services in the Graduate School of Education.

Eva L. Feindler, Ph.D., is currently a professor of psychology at the Long Island University doctoral program in clinical psychology. As coordinator of the Specialty Track in Family Violence and as director of the Psychological Services Clinic, she is directly involved in programs to help children and families manage their anger and resolve conflict. She has authored several books and numerous articles on parent and child anger, its assessment and treatment, and has conducted professional training workshops across the United States and Canada. Feindler has served an appointed term on the New York State Board for Psychology and on the Board of the Nassau County Psychological Association, and was the program coordinator for the Association for the Advancement of Behavior Therapy Conference in 1995. She also served on the APA Commission on Violence and Youth from 1992 to 1995 and on the APA Task Force on Violence and the Family.

Marian C. Fish, Ph.D., is professor of school psychology at Queens College, where she is the coordinator of the Graduate Program in School Psychology. In addition, she serves on the doctoral faculty of the Ph.D. Program in Educational Psychology at the Graduate Center of the City University of New York. Fish received her B.S. degree from Cornell University, and her M.A. and Ph.D. degrees from Teachers College, Columbia University. Her interests include a family orientation to school psychology, family-school relationships, and interventions with parents of children with disabilities. She is coauthor of a recent book, *Handbook of School-Based Interventions: Resolving Student Problems and Promoting Healthy Educational Environments.* Her current research involves the development of the Classroom Systems Observation Scale, which uses a systems approach to classroom assessment and intervention.

Peter T. Gager, M.S., is a graduate student in clinical psychology at Rutgers University. He has published articles in the areas of prevention, special education, multiculturalism, identity, and social competence.

Enedina García-Vázquez, Ph.D., teaches in the Counseling and Educational Psychology Department in the College of Education at New Mexico State University. She is the training coordinator of the school psychology program. García-Vázquez has published manuscripts on peer tutoring, effects of language use, acculturation and psychological factors, skin color and community interest, and mentoring. Her current research focuses on the development of an acculturation instrument for adolescents and the effects of acculturation on psychological factors and academic success.

Maribeth Gettinger, Ph.D., has been on the faculty in the School Psychology Program at the University of Wisconsin–Madison since 1980. She is also currently the director of Research and Training at the Waisman Center Early Childhood Program. Her teaching and research interests include early childhood special education and classroom learning.

Janet F. Gillespie, Ph.D., is assistant professor of psychology at the State University of New York College at Brockport. She received her Ph.D. in child-clinical and community psychology from Southern Illinois University at Carbondale. Her research interests are in the areas of school-based preventive interventions, social problem solving, social support, and high-risk youths and their families.

Marlene Miziker Gonet, Ph.D., works as a substance abuse prevention counselor with Ann Arbor Public Schools in Michigan. In addition, she teaches graduate courses on substance abuse counseling at Eastern Michigan University in Ypsilanti. She received both her M.A. in Education and M.S.W. from the University of Michigan. Since 1974, she has taught in Cleveland Public Schools, has worked as a clinical social worker at a juvenile correctional facility, and has practiced as a family therapist in a residential treatment program for chemically dependent adolescents. She also provides consultation and training to schools and adolescent treatment programs. Gonet is the author of *Counseling the Adolescent Substance Abuser: School-Based Intervention and Prevention* (Sage).

Patricia A. Graczyk is a doctoral student in the School and Clinical Psychology Programs at Northern Illinois University. She was formally a practicing school psychologist in both the public and private sectors. Her major research interests are in child and adolescent peer relationships, social problem-solving skills, and internalizing disorders.

Kristen Waters Guetschow is a doctoral student in the School Psychology Program in the Department of Educational Psychology at the University of Wisconsin–Madison. Her research and clinical interests include early childhood intervention and parent involvement in schools.

Blair Bowen Hickey is a Ph.D. candidate in the School Psychology Training Program in the Department of Educational Psychology at the University of Texas at Austin. She completed her predoctoral internship at Cypress-Fairbanks ISD in Houston, Texas. Her dissertation research is on the self-schematic processing of adolescents diagnosed with a depressive disorder.

Julie A. Hirsch is a doctoral candidate of the School Psychology Program at the University of Minnesota. Her professional interests include promoting school engagement for at-risk youths, family- and community-based interventions for deliquent children, and family/school/community partnerships.

Lisa Hunter, M.S., is a doctoral candidate in clinical psychology at Rutgers University She is currently completing a predoctoral internship at the Yale Child Study Center. Her research interests include violence prevention, multicultural education, and school-based action research.

Madinah Ikhlas, M.A., is a graduate student in the Ph.D. program in clinical psychology at Kent State University. She received her bachelor's and master's degrees in psychology from the State University of New York (SUNY), College at Brockport. She has completed externships in research at SUNY Brockport and at the University of Rochester's Mt. Hope Family center. Her research interests are in the areas of developmental psychopathology and resilience in children.

Neil Kalter, Ph.D., is professor of psychology in the Department of Psychology and in the Department of Psychiatry at the University of Michigan. He is former director of the University of Michigan Center for the Child and Family, which was established under his leadership. He also maintains a private practice in Ann Arbor. Kalter has been involved actively in supervising and teaching child and family assessment treatment since receiving his doctorate in Clinical Psychology at the University of Michigan. He serves as a consulting editor for the *American Journal of Orthopsychiatry* and on the editorial board of the *Journal of Child and Family Studies.* Kalter is a nationally recognized authority on the effects of divorce on the trajectory of children's development.

Mary Kopala, Ph.D., received her M.Ed. in counseling and her Ph.D. in counseling psychology from Pennsylvania State University. She has taught at Fordham University and is associate professor of counseling at Hunter College of the City University of New York. Kopala is widely published in numerous professional journals and has contributed work to several published texts. She has also worked as a clinician and has provided direct services to clients at the University of Delaware, Drexel University, and Georgia State University.

Jeffrey S. Kress, M.S., is a graduate student in clinical psychology at Rutgers University. He has recently completed his internship in Clinical/Community Psychology at the University of Medicine and Dentistry of New Jersey. He is interested in social competence promotion and the implementation of school-based preventive programs. He is also involved in action-research in the area of religious identity development in adolescents.

Cynthia Kurowski, Ph.D., received her doctorate in the School Psychology Training Program in the Department of Educational Psychology at the University of Texas at Austin. Her research interests include problem solving and coping in adolescents. Kurowski completed her predoctoral internship at The Astor Home for Children in New York City.

Lisa Reiss Miller, M.A., is currently a doctoral student in clinical psychology at the Frances L. Hiatt School of Psychology at Clark University in Worcester, MA. She has an A.B. from Harvard University. Her interests include the study of attributional processes in parenting and pediatric neuropsychology.

Scott A. Napolitano, Ph.D., is an adjunct faculty member at the University of Nebraska at Lincoln where he teaches courses in developmental neuropsychology. He completed his postdoctoral training in pediatric neuropsychology at Children's Medical Center of Dallas. Napolitano is a pediatric neuropsychologist in private practice in Lincoln, Nebraska.

Bonnie K. Nastasi, Ph.D., is director and associate professor in the School Psychology Programs at the State University of New York at Albany. Her research interests include the promotion of mental health and prevention of health risks in children, youths, and young adults. She consults nationally and internationally with schools and community agencies regarding development and evaluation of primary prevention programs. She has coauthored a book titled *School Interventions for Children of Alcoholics.* Nastasi is associate editor of *School Psychology Review* and a member of the editorial boards for *Journal of Educational Psychology* and *Journal of School Psychology.*

Andrew Paulson, Ph.D., is a psychologist in private practice. He is a clinical instructor and provides supervision for psychology interns in the Parent-Infant and Early Childhood Clinic in the Department of Psychiatry. In addition, he provides consultation to a number of agencies serving families with young children age birth to 3 years old.

Sheldon Rose, Ph.D., is professor of social work at the University of Wisconsin–Madison. He received his Ph. D. from the University of Amsterdam (Holland) in social psychology and his master's degree in social work from Washington University in St. Louis. He has carried out extensive research on the effectiveness of various family and group approaches to the treatment of both children and adults in groups. He has written eight books and numerous articles in this area. He is also coauthor of training manuals for family therapists, leaders of children's groups, stress management groups, assertive training groups, and pain management groups. Rose serves on the editorial board of many journals in psychology and social work. His present research is on damaging group experiences.

Maria Scalley attended Adelphi University, where she received her B.A. in psychology and M.A. in applied psychology. She is presently a candidate for Psy.D. in clinical psychology at Long Island University/C. W. Post Campus and has earned an M.S. in applied psychology in 1992. She is currently completing her predoctoral internship at the Pederson-Krag Center in Huntington, NY. Scalley has special interests in working with children, adolescents, families, and persons with developmental disabilities. Her dissertation work explores HIV/AIDS education among health care professionals who provide services to the developmentally disabled.

Diane Smith Schowalter is a doctoral candidate in school psychology at the University of Wisconsin–Milwaukee. She received her M.S. in educational psychology from the University of Wisconsin and her B.A. from St. Olaf College. She has practiced in clinic, school, and college settings, specializing in work with children, adolescents, and adults with learning and attention disorders. Schowalter has presented at National Association of School Psychology and National Learning Disabilities Association conferences.

Mary E. Seidl, M.S., is currently a school psychologist in Monroe, Wisconsin, and has been a staff member of the Parent-Infant and Early Childhood Clinic. Her areas of interest include assessment of infants and young children, therapeutic group interventions for preschool and school-age children, and facilitating home-school collaboration.

Dawn Sommer is a Ph.D. candidate in the School Psychology Training Program in the Department of Educational Psychology at the University of Texas at Austin. She is currently completing her predoctoral internship at Mendota Mental Health Institute in Madison, Wisconsin. Her dissertation research is on the relationships between childhood sexual abuse, cognitive style, and depression.

Kevin D. Stark, Ph.D., is an associate professor and program director of the School Psychology Training Program in the Department of Educational Psychology at the University of Texas at Austin. His research interests are in the areas of depressive disorders in children and adolescents, cognitive-behavioral intervention for depressed youths, and family influences on internalizing disorders in youths. Stark is a licensed psychologist in private practice in Austin, Texas.

Susan Swearer, Ph.D., is an assistant professor in the School Psychology Training Program in the Department of Educational Psychology at the University of Nebraska at Lincoln. She has worked as a licensed professional counselor at Children's Medical Center of Dallas and completed her predoctoral internship training at Father Flanagan's Boys' Home (Boys Town). Swearer's research interests include the comorbidity of psychological disorders in children and adolescents; cognitive, behavioral, and family factors that influence depression and conduct disorder in youths; and interventions with youths.

Gregory A. Waas, Ph.D., is an associate professor of psychology and director of the School Psychology Program at Northern Illinois University. He has published widely in the areas of children's peer relationships, social and personality development, and children's social cognition.

ministrative trust surrounding school-based professionals meetings with community professionals during school time) is also expressed in several chapters. In summary, the joint focus on school and community in this book attempts to address the greater heterogeneity, complexity, and diversity characterizing individuals being served in a wide variety of settings.

CONSIDERATIONS FOR GROUP PREVENTION AND INTERVENTION WORK

As mental health school professionals' time precludes them from intervening directly with all students, the appeal of group approaches has grown. Yet, group counseling and therapy should be provided only by those individuals with appropriate clinical preparation and competencies. Traditionally, therapy has been conducted by specially trained professionals from the field of psychology and social work. It is our belief, however, that some prevention and intervention groups can be implemented effectively by individuals with less extensive psychological background, such as teachers, paraprofessionals, and parents. These individuals may be especially well suited as co-facilitators. The inclusion of paraprofessionals also extends the number of people who can provide mental health services, especially after this task has been accomplished under the close supervision of a mental health care professional.

In this book, many chapters give particular attention to the empirical basis of groups. However, even the best designed prevention and intervention groups can go awry when the group facilitator lacks the understanding and skills necessary to be aware of and meet the needs of individual group participants. Unfortunately, many mental health professionals have not been able to keep pace with the growing sentiment for group-oriented social and psychological services. Illustrative of this point are school psychologists' reports of lacking sufficient training and supervised experience in group therapy and counseling (Huebner, 1993). Similarly, although both school-based and community-based psychologists, counselors, and social workers often play primary roles in the design of group counseling programs, they generally receive limited preservice instruction on treatment development and evaluation (Kazdin, 1990).

The skills needed to implement groups effectively are diverse in type and developmental in form. Group facilitators need to have well-developed capacities in the areas of empathy, listening, collaboration, confronting, and interpreting. Although similar competencies are needed for individual counseling and therapy, knowledge and skill in their use is more complex when one needs continually to focus and refocus attention on affective, emotional, and behavioral indicators across several individuals. The group facilitator should monitor the development and progress of each group participant, which frames what and how questions are asked and processed, guides observations, and informs when and how to proceed. An ongoing, conscious effort to attend to all group participants is extremely demanding work. Similar to other areas of mental health competence, group facilitation develops with deliberate reflective practice, explicit skill refinement, continuous monitoring, and careful supervision. Mental health professionals in the school and community must be aware of their own levels of competence so as to resist entering unethical boundaries of their professional practices.

Determining whether a child is best suited to group therapy also requires thoughtful consideration. An analysis of the child—including nature and severity of the problem, capacity to work in a group, emotional stability, and group interactive skills—should be conducted. For example, a child who is experiencing a crisis (e.g., recent death of a parent or family divorce) may be too psychologically volatile to tolerate or participate in a group (Tharinger & Stafford, 1995).

A contemporary challenge for school- and community-based mental health workers is to concurrently realize their own capacities and to respond in the best interests of children and families. We have selected authors who provide empirically supported guidelines for developing competence in group prevention and intervention. Furthermore, contributors demonstrate effective, efficient, and innovative strategies for preventing and intervening with children, adolescents, and families.

CURRENT TRENDS IN GROUP APPROACHES TO PREVENTION AND INTERVENTION

Inspection of the table of contents for this book reveals a variety of social and behavioral problems that received little attention a decade ago, especially in the schools. The expansion of concerns include, for example, child abuse, drug and alcohol abuse, adolescent pregnancy, divorce, and social rejection. In addition, schools and community programs are now drawing on different paradigms, structures, and individuals for understanding children's problems and issues. The formation of parent/school/community partnerships is widely affecting decisions related to prevention and intervention procedures and plans. For example, parents today have a more active voice in determining school-based interventions than in previous decades (Christenson & Conoley, 1992; Vickers & Minke, 1997). Furthermore, targets for understanding children and targets of intervention now include social and environmental systems, such as the family and the classroom (Fuchs & Fuchs, 1994; Glenwick & Jason, 1993). For example, knowledge of the social needs of children with disabilities has provided a theoretical basis for inclusive education practices wherein children with and without disabilities share classrooms and peers. This change is illustrative of how new educational policies create specific directives for prevention and intervention practices involving classroom-based groups.

Perhaps the most remarkable change affecting group therapeutic applications during the past decade is the prevention movement. Rather than waiting for problems to emerge and become crystallized, school and community prevention efforts have arose. A philosophy of prevention began to take roots in community psychology in the 1960s and 1970s (Albee, 1967; Levine & Perkins, 1987). The inadequacy of traditional human service delivery systems in schools has awakened an interest in school-based prevention during more recent years (Hightower, Johnson, & Haffey, 1995). A prevention perspective is reflective of the need to broaden the *targets* to include social and environmental factors. A paradigm shift toward prevention also alters the *time point* at which services occur. Finally, the *agents of change* may shift to parents and teachers rather than children or adolescents. Although definitions of prevention may sometimes vary, there is general agreement in the desirability of intervening proactively prior to the onset of disorders. Hence, a goal of prevention is to enhance person and environmental systems before intense therapy and remediation are required. Group approaches to prevention make sense because a broader spectrum of individuals and environments can be reached than are possible with individual person-centered interventions.

Through the inclusion of prevention groups in this book, we hope to address a wider range of health and mental health issues than would be possible through solely an intervention focus. The prevention emphasis in this book is consistent with the U.S. Department of Health and Human Services' recent endorsement in (1) promoting healthy lifestyles as a way to combat many of America's social ills and (2) discouraging health-endangering behaviors as a means to control burgeoning social difficulties and the high cost of mental health care (United States Department of Health and Human Services, 1991).

REFERENCES

Achenbach, T. M., Howell, C. T., Quay, H. C., & Conners, C. K. (1991). National survey of problems and competencies among four- to sixteen-year-olds. *Monographs of the Society for Research in Child Development, 56* (3, Serial No. 225).

Albee, G. W. (1967). The relation of conceptual models to manpower needs. In E. L. Cowen, E. A. Gardner, & M. Zax (Eds.), *Emergent approaches to mental health problems* (pp. 63–73). New York: Appleton-Century-Crofts.

Business & Health. (1993, September). The state of health care in America (Special Issue).

Carlson, C., Paavola, J., & Talley, R. (1995). Historical, current, and future models of schools as health care delivery settings. *School Psychology Quarterly, 10,* 184–202.

Christenson, S. L., & Conoley, J. C. (Eds.). (1992). *Home-school collaboration: Enhancing children's academic and social competence.* Silver Spring, MD: National Association of School Psychologists.

Cobb, C. T. (1995). Defining, implementing, and evaluating educational outcomes. In A. Thomas & J. Grimes (Eds.), *Best practices in school psychology III* (pp. 325–336). Washington, DC: National Association of School Psychologists.

DeMers, S. T. (1995). Emerging perspectives on the role of psychologists in the delivery of health and mental health services in schools. *School Psychology Quarterly, 10,* 179–183.

Doll, B. (1996). Prevalence of psychiatric disorders in children and youth: An agenda for advocacy by school psychology. *School Psychology Quarterly, 11,* 20–46.

Dryfoos, J. G. (1994). *Full-service schools.* San Francisco: Jossey-Bass.

Fawcett, S. B., Paine, A. L., Francisco, V. T., & Vliet, M. (1993). Promoting health through community development. In D. S. Glenwick & L. A. Jason (Eds.), *Promoting health and mental health in children, youth, and families* (pp. 233–255). New York: Springer.

Fuchs, D., & Fuchs, L. S. (1994). Inclusive schools movement and the radicalization of special education reform. *Exceptional Children, 60,* 294–309.

Glenwick, D. S., & Jason, L. A. (1993). *Promoting health and mental health in children, youth, and families.* New York: Springer.

Hightower, A. D., Johnson, D., & Haffey, W. G. (1995). Adopting a prevention program. In A. Thomas & J. Grimes (Eds.), *Best practices in school psychology III* (pp. 311–324). Washington, DC: National Association of School Psychologists.

Huebner, E. S. (1993). Psychologists in secondary schools in the 1990s: Current functions, training, and job satisfaction. *School Psychology Quarterly, 8,* 50–56.

Kahn, S. (1994). Children's therapy groups: Case studies of prevention, reparation, and protection through children's play. *Journal of Child and Adolescent Group Therapy, 4,* 47–60.

Kazdin, A. E. (1990). Psychotherapy for children and adolescents. *Annual Review of Psychology, 41,* 21–54.

Kazdin, A. E. (1993). Psychotherapy for children and adolescents: Current progress and future research directions. *American Psychologist, 48,* 644–657.

Knitzer, J. (1992). *Unclaimed children: The failure of public responsibility to children and adolescents in need of mental health services.* Washington, DC: Children's Defense Fund.

Knitzer, J., Steinberg, Z., & Fleisch, B. (1990). *At the schoolhouse door: An examination of programs and policies for children with behavioral and emotional problems.* New York: Bank Street College of Education.

Kratochwill, T. R., & Morris, R. J. (Eds.). (1993). *Handbook of psychotherapy with children and adolescents.* Boston: Allyn and Bacon.

Kymissis, P., & Halperin, D. (Eds.). (1996). *Group therapy with children and adolescents.* Washington, DC: American Psychiatric Press.

Levine, M., & Perkins, D. V. (1987). *Principles of community psychology: Perspectives and applications.* New York: Oxford University Press.

McDermott, P. A., & Weiss, R. V. (1995). A normative typology of healthy, subclinical, and clinical behavior styles among American children and adolescents. *Psychological Assessment, 7,* 162–170.

Minke, K. M., & Bear, G. G. (1997). Introduction: Children's needs and school psychology's response. In G. Bear, K. Minke, & A. Thomas (Eds.), *Children's needs II: Development, problems, and alternatives* (pp. ix–xv). Bethesda, MD: National Association of School Psychologists.

Pagliocca, P. M., & Sandoval, S. R. (1995). Best practices in counseling programs for secondary students. In A. Thomas & J. Grimes (Eds.), *Best practices in school psychology III* (pp. 917–929). Washington, DC: National Association of School Psychologists.

Pallas, A., Natriello, G., & McDill, E. (1989). The changing nature of the disadvantaged population: Current dimensions and future trends. *Educational Researcher, 18,* 16–22.

Reister, A., & Kraft, I. (Eds.). (1986). *Child group psychotherapy: Future tense* (American Group Psychotherapy Association Monograph Series No. 3). Madison, CT: International Universities Press.

Sandoval, J., & Davis, J. M. (1992). Applications of social psychology to school counseling and therapy. In F. J. Medway & T. P. Cafferty (Eds.), *School psychology: A social psychological perspective* (pp. 245–268). Hillsdale, NJ: Erlbaum.

Sugar, M. (1991). Planning group therapy for children. *Journal of Child and Adolescent Group Therapy, 1,* 5–14.

Tarnowski, K. J., & Blechman, E. A. (1991). Introduction to the special issue: Disadvantaged children and families. *American Psychologist, 20,* 338–339.

Tharinger, D. (1995). Roles for psychologists in emerging models of school-related health and mental health services. *School Psychology Quarterly, 10,* 203–216.

Tharinger, D., & Stafford, M. (1995). Best practices in individual counseling of elementary-age students. In A. Thomas & J. Grimes (Eds.), *Best practices in school psychology III* (pp. 893–907). Washington, DC: National Association of School Psychologists.

Tuckman, J. P. (1995). Short-term groups with children: The yellow brick road to healthy development. *Journal of Child and Adolescent Group Therapy, 5,* 3–17.

Tuttman, S. (Ed.). (1991). *Psychoanalytic group therapy and therapy: Essays in honor of Saul Schliedlinger* (American Group Psychotherapy Association Monograph Series No. 7) . Madison, CT: International Universities Press.

Tuma, J. M. (1989). Mental health services for children: The state of the art. *American Psychologist, 44*, 188–199.

United States Department of Health and Human Services. (1991). *Healthy people 2000: National health promotion and disease prevention objectives* (DHSS Publication No. PHS 91-50213). Washington, DC: U.S. Government Printing Office.

Vickers, H. S., & Minke, K. M. (1997). Family systems and the family-school connection. In G. Bear, K. Minke, & A. Thomas (Eds.), *Children's needs II: Development, problems, and alternatives* (pp. 547–558). Bethesda, MD: National Association of School Psychologists.

Zill, N. (1992, August). *Trends in family life and children's school performance.* Paper presented at the annual meeting of the American Sociological Association, Pittsburgh, PA.

CHAPTER 2

GROUPS IN THE SCHOOL CONTEXT

Stewart W. Ehly, UNIVERSITY OF IOWA
Enedina García-Vázquez, UNIVERSITY OF NEW MEXICO

Professionals who work or plan to work directly with children and adolescents experiencing psychological and behavioral difficulties—such as mental health counselors, school psychologists, and school social workers—confront an ever-changing array of challenges in providing services. Schools and community agencies are seeking guidance from service providers on how best to respond to the diverse problems experienced by children and adolescents (Natriello, McDill, & Pallas, 1990). Problems in the home, troubles with law-enforcement officials, drug use, suicide, and friction with peers are just a few of the difficulties that children and adolescents present to the professionals that provide mental health-related services. The public's perceptions of violence in schools and communities, the perceived breakdown of family life, and broad concerns about the adequacy of this nation's response to the needs of all children are echoed by a popular media seemingly intent on highlighting (if not manufacturing) problems in society.

In the classroom, teachers are on the front line working with children and adolescents. Yet few teachers would view their core responsibilities to intervene to assist students to deal with the problems each confronts. Instead, schools rely on community-based and in-house services, provided by school and community service providers, to extend remedial and preventive interventions to students. Such services are based on assumptions, often untested, about what works best within the educational system and community (Skrtic, 1991b). Within a typical school district, children are served by special education and other specialized programs that reflect a commitment to individualized attention and the overall provision of services in a least restrictive environment. Available evidence suggests that group interventions could be used, in addition to individualized services, to expand the overall network of services available in the schools and those community agencies that service children and adolescents.

While weighing the merits of appropriate interventions with children and adolescents, support professionals must consider the resources and limitations of the setting in which students spend several hours each week day—the school. The next section will consider the condition of U.S. education and the demand for interventions that support the work of the classroom teacher.

U.S. SCHOOLS AND THEIR STUDENTS

Public attention on the condition of schools has been intense in recent years. Annual polls conducted by Phi Delta Kappa and the Gallup organization (Elam, Rose, & Gallup, 1991) attest to a consensus that schools are in disarray, children are in danger of not learning (if not in actual physical danger from attending school), and teachers are prepared poorly for the diversity of children found in many schools. Surprisingly, parents express general satisfaction with the schools that their children attend. The opinion of many parents is that although their local schools are doing fine, other school districts are struggling, other children's teachers are inadequately prepared, and other principals have lost control of the academic process within schools.

Cuban (1990) has noted that concerns about schools have been expressed every decade over the past century. Parents have voiced dissatisfaction with the quality and outcomes of the educational process. During the current century, schools have been served by an array of support professionals, such as counselors, social workers, and school psychologists. Such professionals are well prepared for their responsibilities (e.g., see Bardon's [1989] description of the skills offered by school psychologists). Yet with the growth of the support professions, schools continue to struggle in their mission to serve all children.

Perkinson (1968), writing initially on the impact on schools of Lyndon Johnson's Great Society (and in two revisions on reforms since that time), argued that Americans always have high expectations for public schools. Expectations that the teacher attend to more than reading, writing, and arithmetic have been present for decades. Yet with every demand placed on schools to address a societal concern (producing reforms in the mission of schools or expectation of teachers), evidence suggests that schools are best suited for their role in the education of children, and struggle to meet society's broader expectations. Sarason (1971, 1982) offers a related perspective on the difficulty schools have in confronting and responding to calls for change, and how they have accommodated demands to reform or restructure (Sarason, 1990).

In a report by the National Assessment of Educational Progress (Mullis, Owen, & Phillips, 1990), an interesting conclusion is offered: Schools today are producing students roughly equivalent in skills to the graduates of 20 years ago. Goodlad (1990), in his Study of the Education of Educators, proposes that schools and their teachers must be ready to meet the needs of children using strategies and tactics that emerge from the best available evidence about children, the learning process, and the means by which schools, as organizations, can be structured to provide an optimum environment for the multiple responsibilities of education.

Milofsky (1986) has written that teachers experience difficulty in meeting demands, created by the expectations of students, parents, and the school administration. Consider the following:

1. *Undermanning.* Too few professionals are available to confront the total demand for services. Service providers, by their successes over the years in serving clients, have heightened expectations for service, further straining the system.
2. *Undersupport.* Low pay, chronic shortages of support, and increases in responsibility add to the strain on professionals.
3. *Client acceptance.* The priorities of children and their parents may not match those of the school and support professionals. The professional, to convince students and parents of the merits of an intervention approach, may become involved with persuading the client or family to assume values or beliefs of the service organization.
4. *Imperfection of technologies.* The options available to practitioners are not foolproof or guaranteed to work. Clients, in approaching the school, may present problems with few indications of the best way to proceed in using existing school services.
5. *Indivisibility of work.* Teachers and support professionals have varying degrees of autonomy to make important decisions about clients.

Professionals, in considering intervention options, face many choices for addressing the academic and behavioral needs of students. When group interventions are examined, professionals quickly discover that research on the relative merits of group options is limited. There is a lack of convincing evidence on the validity of many group interventions with children of differing characteristics. Few firm conclusions can be drawn regarding the influence of gender, socioeconomic status (SES), or cultural and linguistic variations on the outcomes of interventions.

GROUP PROCESS

An important consideration in the development and implementation of group interventions is process. The counseling literature contains frequent analysis of group process. This section examines that literature to highlight segments that could prove relevant in understanding and evaluating other forms of group intervention.

The processes that occur in groups have been interpreted from a stage model perspective. Like other stage models (i.e., ethnic identity development), there has been considerable debate as to whether all stages will be experienced sequentially or if an individual can experience the stages more than once. In counseling, the disagreement focuses on the same issue: Are the stages linear or cyclical? Despite disagreement, many stage models have been proposed.

Rogers (1972) discusses six stages that serve as guideposts for the process in groups (Marshak & Seligman, 1993). Typically in *Stage I*, a sense of confusion may be experienced by participants because the group leader allows group members to determine goals and how the group will proceed. Direct leadership is minimal in many therapeutic groups. However, the purpose of the group and the extent to which the leader will be directive will determine how pronounced Stage I will be. In *Stage II*, some resistance to personal expression and exploration may be evident. The extent to which group members discuss feelings and perceptions at this stage is dependent on their comfort and the focus of the group. In educational groups, members may be more comfortable at this stage to express and explore issues. At *Stage III*, self-disclosure is typically about past experiences and others outside of the group, such as friends and family members (Marshak & Seligman, 1993). As the group progresses, expression of negative feelings and attacks on the group leader may occur. *Stage IV* is marked by negative expressions but the emphasis is on present cognitions and emotions affecting group members.

In the last two stages, discussions and self-expression are more in-depth and meaningful, leading to a more cohesive group. One major difference between the last two stages is that in *Stage V*, meaningful information is derived from discussion of feelings about people outside the group, while in *Stage VI*, members express what they feel about themselves and other members within the group.

According to Corey (1995), groups develop in four stages. However, similarities between Rogers's (1972) and Corey's (1995) approaches are evident. For Corey (1995), the initial stage, *Stage 1*, involves orientation and exploration. Members learn how the group will function, define goals, clarify expectations, and determine their fit in the group (Corey, 1995). Primary tasks involve establishing an identity within the group and determining the extent to which to become involved. Establishing and maintaining trust becomes critical at the early stage. Additionally, the leader's role helps to set the tone for the group. The leader can assist the group by modeling group norms, helping to identify goals, dividing responsibility, and structuring.

Stage 2 involves dealing with resistance and enabling members to work through their anxiety, resistance, and conflict. During this transition phase, a struggle for power may ensue and control becomes a central issue. Challenging the leader may occur during this stage. The goal during Stage 2 is to help members recognize and deal with resistance. The leader's role is to facilitate the transition by providing encouragement as well as challenge to the members. During the first two stages, leaders are very active and confrontations with group members may be necessary (Corey, 1995). However, to maintain trust, confrontations need to be conducted with sensitivity and respect.

In the last stages, groups work toward becoming more cohesive. In *Stage 3,* cohesion is developed and the group becomes more productive. This stage is characterized by activities that promote in-depth exploration leading to change. When the group becomes cohesive, a trust among members is enhanced. The members become less dependent on the leader and more concerned about each other. The emphasis is on the "here and now." In order to move from cohesion to productivity, however, several factors must be addressed during group time. Trust and acceptance, empathy and caring, hope, self-disclosure, and freedom to experiment need to be in place. At the same time, members must establish a commitment to change and allow for intimacy to occur. Through this stage, cognitive restructuring is needed for change. Catharsis at this stage can be very therapeutic (Corey, 1995) but needs to be seen as part of the process and not the end product. Using confrontation can be part of this process; however, this needs to be done in a way that helps members work through problems. Maintaining dignity is critical and the goal is to enhance communication rather than close it (Corey, 1995).

The final stage, *Stage 4*, centers on consolidation and termination. In consolidation, members synthesize and examine their learning in the group. Integrating information and making connections to their outside environments are critical. Summarizing information and interpreting the experience create the link for members to understand the whole group experience. At this time, members deal with achieving closure to the group experience. Although termination is discussed in the early sessions, it is at this stage that experience of termination becomes intense. Members need the opportunity to discuss feelings of sadness that may be felt but also how closure and ending relationships is part of the entire group experience. Overall, during this stage, several tasks are completed, including dealing with feelings, examining the effects of the group on oneself, giving and receiving feedback, completing unfinished business, and carrying the learning further (Corey, 1995).

Although group sessions conclude with the termination stage, Corey (1995) proposes a follow-up session or individual sessions to obtain evaluative information. At the last working session, group members can agree on a time for the follow-up session. The benefits of follow-up sessions include obtaining evaluative information and monitoring progress of group members. Members may have a more realistic picture of the group's impact following termination. The follow-up session can be critical because it maximizes the benefits of the group experience and provides accountability (Corey, 1995). Corey also suggests that individual follow-up sessions be conducted with each of the members. Twenty-minute sessions can help the leader determine what progress toward goals has been made and identify resources for more individually guided therapeutic interventions. Other benefits include demonstrating concern toward the individual, assessing effectiveness of the group experience, and soliciting information about interest in future group experiences.

We have presented a brief summary of the stages of group process, but it is essential that the reader understand the complexity as well as the benefits of conducting groups. In keeping with ethical codes that provide guidelines on professional competency, additional training through courses or supervised experiences is recommended. Marshak and Seligman (1993) suggest that leaders be well grounded in psychological theory to understand human development. Leaders well versed in individual therapy have skills, such as microcounseling skills (e.g., perception checks, reflection of feelings), that can be effective in groups, but courses in group dynamics are recommended, as are experiences with groups (Marshak & Seligman, 1993).

CONSIDERATIONS IN DEVELOPING GROUPS

Establishing a Purpose

Within the school setting, we will consider the type of groups that are typically formed. Some will have goals that are therapeutic, educational, or both. The group's agenda will be influenced by the purpose of the group and the developmental levels of the participants. In schools, given that the leader is older than the students and represents an authority figure, students may look frequently to the leader for direction and structure. With groups involving elementary school children, the leader often will be very structured and directive.

In the schools, the reasons for developing and implementing groups reflect student and teacher needs. A group of students may present with similar difficulties that could be effectively addressed in a group. One example is students who may be experiencing academic difficulties accompanied by difficulties with self-esteem. A group could be developed to help enhance self-esteem, while academic needs are met on an individual basis. Once the purpose has been established, the group leader can determine the session content for the overall group (e.g., self-esteem vs. social skills) but the goals will determine what changes and roles the members will seek.

Typically, the goals for a group are determined by its members (Marshak & Seligman, 1993). Groups developed in schools will be influenced as well by the developmental levels of student members. Young elementary students may be able to verbalize general ideas of what they would like to accomplish in the group but not with the same sophistication as some high school students. In either case, the leader has to make an assessment of the extent to which he or she will be directive in determining goals for the group. As a result, for a group to be effective, preplanning and preparation is crucial (Corey, 1995).

Screening for the Group: Pregroup Interview

Even though student and teacher needs determine the type of groups that will be formed in schools, whether the students are likely to benefit from the planned activities should be assessed. For the self-esteem group mentioned earlier, a student with a severe self-esteem disorder, and who is clinically depressed, would not be well served by a group format. Students can be assessed for the severity of their presenting problems and considerations of treatment modalities explored before students are guided toward group counseling. Generally, individuals who are self-centered, hostile and aggressive, in extreme crisis, suicidal, or have sociopathic personalities need to be excluded from groups (Corey, 1995).

In addition, the group member is typically provided an opportunity to determine if the group is right for him or her. In the initial interview, the potential group member is encouraged to ask questions about the group. In schools, the students may have less input to influence decisions relating to group membership. Because of their age and the manner in which schools are run, students may have limited opportunity to accept or reject the recommendations of teachers, counselors, and parents. The professional, however, must remain concerned about the issue of informed and voluntary consent.

In counseling, the question of including involuntary members has been addressed. Yalom (1985) notes that members need to be highly motivated to benefit from the group experience. However, involuntary members should not be excluded arbitrarily. With appropriate member preparation and orientation, an involuntary client could make some changes in the group and benefit from group membership (Corey, 1995). In the schools, there is the potential to have many involuntary members because decisions about group participation are often made without the involvement of the student. What we have found is that preparation of students and outlining the benefits of their participation have been effective in alleviating many of the fears that students have about participating in a group. However, in some cases, extreme resistance was expressed and other forms of intervention were recommended.

Voluntary or involuntary, the basic question to ask about a potential group member is whether the student's membership will be compatible with others or be counterproductive (Corey, 1995). Whether an individual is included or not, the decision needs to be made within the context of the group's purpose.

Composition of the Group

The question of heterogeneity or homogeneity of groups often arises in the planning stages. Again, a decision of who to include will be dependent on the purpose of the group. However, there are some basic considerations that can be addressed by the group leader. Often, homogeneous groups are beneficial for students experiencing a common interest or problem (Corey, 1995). With a group that is similar on one dimension, such as having an alcoholic parent, students can vary on other dimensions, such as age. In this case, the leader must decide whether to include younger and older children of alcoholics.

For most groups focusing on a common problem, a homogeneous grouping tends to be productive (Corey, 1995). With an adolescent population, students will have certain needs that younger children may not. A group for adolescents will provide members with the opportunity to explore issues that are relevant to the population. They may be able to explore developmental and identity issues. At the same time, a group of ethnic minority adolescents would be able to explore ethnic identity development issues, specifically the role of culture in identity development. The students would be able to receive and give support to others experiencing similar concerns.

At other times, a heterogeneous grouping may be useful or important. If the goal is to replicate life outside of school, including students at different developmental levels would be important. For example, some younger students might benefit from feedback from older students about social skills. The younger student would be able to practice skills while the older would provide role models for appropriate social skills. The purpose of the group will influence whether a heterogeneous or homogenous grouping is used.

Other Organizational Variables

Opinions about the limits of group size have varied but most agree that for adult groups the number should not exceed 12 (Marshak & Seligman, 1993) but that 8 members with one leader is good (Corey, 1995). Decisions on group size are influenced by the nature of the group, the ages of potential group members, the leaders' expertise, and the type of problems (Corey, 1995). Marshak and Seligman (1993) provide similar suggestions but add that with a group that is too large, there is the potential for factionalism and lack of in-depth interactions. Students who are quiet may be lost in the group and those with attention difficulties may disrupt the group. Groups for children may need to be as small as 3 or 4. Ultimately, a group should be large enough not to lose the sense of the group and small enough for sufficient interactions (Corey, 1995).

Once a group size decision has been made, the leader needs to determine the frequency and duration of meetings. In schools, frequency may not be a problem except for school personnel who are assigned to the school only on certain days of the week. Given the academic year for schools, meeting every week may be possible. On the other hand, the frequency and duration of the sessions may be more difficult at the elementary level, where subjects are taught in shorter time periods or infused throughout the day. Finding an appropriate time to meet with a group of students may take some negotiation with school personnel. In terms of the total number of sessions, the length of the academic year does not pose a problem unless a group is implemented late in the school year. Whatever the decision on frequency and duration of sessions, leader preparation and planning will be critical.

Typically, counseling groups meet once a week for about two hours but groups for children and adolescents can meet more frequently and for shorter periods (Corey, 1995). Again, type of group, members, and the constraints of the schools need to be considered in making decisions about the frequency and duration of meetings.

Group members need to be prepared for the work together but what does the preparation entail? Corey (1995) suggests that members discuss the group process and the importance of the members' investment in the group. Members are asked to identify overall goals and session goals such as determining the type of information, personal issues, and self-disclosure they will be willing to share before each session.

Group norms also need to be discussed prior to the start of the group. These norms include regular attendance, punctuality, creating a supportive rather than a nonaccepting environment, verbalization of concerns, and assurance that the group's interactions are related to the group's goals (Yalom, 1985).

Members can discuss the importance of the emotions that might be experienced in the group and that these are usually a result of self-disclosure. Members must be willing to interact to make the experience meaningful and for the group to work. Empathy, caring, and warmth will contribute to a cathartic experience and may be felt throughout the group process. At the same time, members may feel anger, hostility, and other intense emotions. Fears about the group process or member involvement could be addressed in the preparation phase, as well.

Issues Affecting Groups in Schools

The most common groups in the schools are academic and behavioral in nature. Groups to enhance study skills and social skills are common. However, other forms can be identified, such as support groups for students from divorced families or students experiencing the grieving process. With the conditions in broader society, groups are needed that help children deal with dysfunctional families (children of alcoholics, incest survivors, and sexual and physical abuse). In addition, as more children with special needs are mainstreamed into the classroom, it may be important to prepare children with disabilities and others for regular classrooms. However, when groups are formed, consideration needs to be given to other issues relating to diversity, such as gender, age, and type of surrounding community.

In preparing students with disabilities for regular classrooms, classroom-based social interaction interventions for young children with disabilities have yielded positive results (Odom, McConnell, & Chandler, 1994). These interventions can be child-specific or peer-mediated interventions and can be used in a group format to train peers or teach the child with disabilities. At the same time, these interventions can be effective in a classroomwide variation. Even students with emotion/behavioral problems benefit from training in crisis management (Gilliam, 1993), which can be accomplished in small groups or whole-class format.

Other students benefit from groups, as well. In schools today, there is a growing need to intervene through preventive means with students experiencing conflict. Peer mediation in schools is fast becoming a preventive approach to handle students' conflict (Cutrona & Guerin, 1994). With serious crime on the rise among youths between ages 10 and 17, schools are finding that peer mediation provides an effective way to address the conflicts that students experience in schools. In light of this need for more attention to help students resolve problems, training groups for the peer mediators can be an effective and preventive approach to solving problems.

Individuals from ethnic minority backgrounds have generally not availed themselves of mental health services (Sue & Zane, 1987). Groups could be an effective method for mental health service delivery for these populations. At the same time, mental health providers have not modified the manner in which they advertise services to minority populations. With rapidly changing demographics in the United States, teachers and support professionals are asked to work with students from cultural backgrounds different from theirs. The need for cross-cultural contact has been evident for some time, but the sheer increase in the diversity of students has forced schools to expand and improve the quantity and quality of their services to every student. Unfortunately, researchers have not focused much attention on interventions and strategies with ethnic minority populations. As a result, few citations are found that can inform professionals about effective groups with minority populations.

Bowman (1993), in her search for literature on career intervention strategies and ethnic minority students, labeled available information disappointing. She indicated that group interventions may be very effective with ethnic minority students because many come from a group orientation rather than an individualistic perspective. Whereas this is true of many ethnic minority students (Sue & Sue, 1990), Bowman fails to account for type or degree of acculturation. Individuals who are bicultural or highly acculturated may react differently to groups than those who are less adapted to the Western world view.

Bowman (1993) raises other issues relating to assessment of cultural similarity and dissimilarity. The literature on racial identity development has shown that clients show a preference for counselors of the same ethnicity. In addition, group leaders need to examine their own biases, both negative and positive, and the impact of these biases on group process. Stereotypes need to be identified so that these do not interfere with any aspect of group process. It is important to note that when developing groups dealing with career issues, career decisions may be made by the family in conjunction with the individual. Bowman (1993) emphasized that using race- and sex-appropriate role models helps to promote awareness of new occupational options. At times, the professional will elect to present information in the member's first language. However, although an individual has an ethnically or linguistically diverse background, presenting concerns need not be related to cultural, linguistic, or identity issues.

Bowman reported that ethnic group members supported an expanded focus on career development in the schools. She found that students wanted more help with choosing a career, developing job skills for noncollege-bound students, locating placements for graduates as well as students who chose other options, using occupational information, developing interviewing skills, and preparing students for college (Bowman, 1993).

Overall, groups formed with ethnic minority individuals can be effective. Like any other group, consideration needs to be given to the purpose of the group. Becoming more multicultural in one's perspective is a life-long, dynamic process, and will increase competence in working with diverse individuals. More detailed information on group interventions with culturally and linguistically diverse students can be found in Chapter 14 of this book.

GROUP PREVENTION OPTIONS WITHIN SCHOOL SETTINGS

Group interventions can also serve a prevention function. Perlmutter, Vayda, and Woodburn (1982) echo Caplan's (1974) earlier goals for such activities. Examples provided by Perlmutter and associates (1982) are as follows: first level or primary prevention (e.g., working with the school to develop a drug abuse-prevention program, developing a program for teachers to sensitize them to the problems of single-parent families); second level or secondary prevention (e.g., a program at a school for children with disabilities to offer psychological first aid to those who are emotionally upset); and third level or tertiary prevention (e.g., a program to assist former inpatients to attend their first appointment for follow-up care).

Each level of prevention can be implemented within groups, some large and loosely structured, others small and well organized. Many first-level prevention activities found in schools are implemented to address perceived widespread needs within the community. Drug prevention and self-esteem programs in elementary and middle schools are structured around the assumptions of prevention. Stone and Bradley (1994) note that such programs will have limited success if efforts are "superficial, short term, and periodic" (p. 258). Prevention requires a "comprehensive effort extending across the year and involving all members of the school community—students, teachers, support personnel, and parents." Prevention programs can be infused into the curriculum so that all children have the opportunity to experience prevention themes and activities. Classroom teachers thus have an important role in many, if not most, first-level prevention programs.

Schools that engage in second-level prevention programs target so-called risk factors, such as drug abuse, child abuse and neglect, and suicidal behavior. Such prevention programs can be very intense for students and school staff, and involve much smaller groups than would be possible within a first-level prevention effort. Muro and Kottman (1995) note that special training is required of school personnel who function within services targeting risk factors; classroom teachers, who can have an important role in other forms of prevention, seldom have the time and preparation necessary to be key providers within more difficult prevention efforts. School support personnel, such as school psychologists, counselors, and social workers, assume major responsibility for the more demanding forms of prevention programs. Healy-Romanello (1993) provides an example of support group for bereaved children, during which children are guided to address their feelings and resolve areas of their grief.

Third-level prevention programs are characterized frequently by collaboration between the school and community agencies and facilities that had been caring for the student. Programs are individu-

Pugach and Johnson (1995) encourage professionals to refine the skills required to work with and support groups. Identifying several formats for groups (conversational, instructional, decision making, problem solving, and discovery), they emphasize the importance of the facilitator role. That person must be able to "organize group activities, create the communicative environment, and synthesize outcomes" (pp. 116–117). The facilitator works to maintain an atmosphere within which all participants can feel encouraged to participate. The role of the facilitator will change over the life of the group, providing structure, content, support, encouragement, and guidance as necessary.

When groups experience difficulty, Pugach and Johnson support the following actions for facilitators:

1. Skillful conflict resolution and arbitration
2. Willingness to deal simultaneously with issues while fostering comfort and flexibility
3. Establishing true group rapport
4. Projecting concern for group members
5. Facilitating group interactions and maintaining cohesion
6. Promoting a spirit of unity as a group

Clearly, the work of the facilitator involves the synthesis of instructional, counseling, disciplinarian, and cheerleader roles! Training in group work, especially for conflict resolution and therapeutic agendas, can be extensive before the professional is adept at addressing a broad array of intervention goals.

An important area of competency relates to the professional's competency in successfully establishing contact with students and parents who differ in multicultural characteristics. Rotheram-Borus (1993) proposes that the delivery of group interventions is influenced not only by multicultural factors such as language and ethnicity but also by the domain most affected by the intervention—school, home, neighborhood, or church.

As noted earlier, the multiculturally competent practitioner is sensitive to personal limitations while engaging in services to students. Pedersen (1988) proposes the following goals for educators: (1) be familiar with the customs, language, and history of the cultures represented among students; (2) be able to locate information on students' cultures and understand the implications of cultural data on service planning; and (3) be competent in developing school activities that contribute to the academic and social development of every student. Several skills combine to affect the ultimate impact of the practitioner on students from linguistic and racial/ethnic minorities. The ethical professional remains open to the needs of every student and pursues the goal of providing the best possible services to address individual and group needs.

CLOSING COMMENTS

This chapter has explored issues affecting the planning and implementation of group interventions within schools. Children and adolescents experiencing difficulty in meeting academic and behavioral goals can profit from involvement in group interventions. The professional committed to serving students in school and community agencies is well aware of group interventions that work, and only needs the time and tools to develop programs.

The chapters in this book, and studies cited from the broader literature, provide important information to assist professionals' understanding of how children can be served best within the school context. Group interventions are attractive to many educators and support professionals because all parties recognize that students seldom experience difficulties in isolation from their peers. Working with several students within an intervention has appeal, if only for the savings of time and energy that at first seem obvious.

Yet what may appear obvious or commonsensical can misdirect the efforts of educators, parents, and support professionals. Group intervention should be approached with the knowledge that individual children may not benefit in a group setting or may experience more immediate or longer-lasting gains when served one-to-one by the professional.

The future application of group interventions within schools will be influenced by forces both within and outside the control of school professionals. The good news is that professionals, through their individual efforts, can shape the agenda of local school service delivery. The status quo within an educational agency will support creativity and energy in pursuit of children's growth and development. As professionals engage in group forms of intervention, their representatives at local, state, and national levels will represent and promote services that are effective.

The bad news, of course, is that schools are under the scrutiny and influence of competing groups of stakeholders. The general public, which has limited access to day-to-day operations within schools, cannot express support for activities outside of their experience and influence. A step further removed from the broad community are critics of schools who envision a narrow agenda on academics, with resources limited to strategies that ensure mastery of basic skills. Readers do not need to be reminded of the intense debate being waged on public schools that could eliminate funding for many intervention-oriented projects that were developed with the support of federal education grant funds.

The school of the future has not been an object of consensus. Within education circles, multiple visions of schools have been proposed and piloted (e.g., Dryfoos, 1994; Holtzman, 1992). Whether current efforts to enrich academic and interpersonal outcomes for children proceed to include group interventions will depend on the efforts and will of the professional community and the goodwill and openness of the citizenry in support of their designated caregivers within schools.

The authors support activities that involve professionals in efforts to enhance and refine their understanding of students and the means by which children and adolescents are educated. Service responsibilities to students help keep professional sights on the immediate and long-term consequences of interventions. Each professional can contribute to our intervention knowledge base by implementing *and* evaluating interventions with children and adolescents.

Selecting a group intervention in a given situation will be influenced by such factors as

1. The urgency of the situation (in general, group approaches require more preparation time)
2. The goals of the school's special services program (group interventions can be attractive components of a school's overall strategy for addressing student needs)
3. The input of students, parents, and school staff (services that address school and community's priorities and needs will be appealing to consumers, especially if outcomes can be documented and discussed)

Group interventions with children and adolescents succeed when they reflect the interests of students, educators, and parents. Professionals are attracted to interventions that are perceived as effective as well as supportive of the mission of the school. A service plan that integrates individual and group approaches to interventions will be able to provide a broad range of programs that can match student needs with a proven potential for development.

REFERENCES

Bardon, J. I. (1989). The school psychologist as an applied educational psychologist. In R. C. D'Amato & R. S. Dean (Eds.), *The school psychologist in nontraditional settings: Integrating clients, services, and settings* (pp. 1–32). Hillsdale, NJ: Erlbaum.

Bayles, M. D. (1981). *Professional ethics*. Belmont, CA: Wadsworth.

Bowman, S. L. (1993). Career intervention strategies for ethnic minorities. *The Career Development Quarterly*, *42*, 14–25.

Caplan, G. (1974). *Support systems and community mental health: Lectures on concept development*. New York: Behavioral Publications.

Cohen, P. A., Kulik, J. A., & Kulik, C. C. (1982). Educational outcomes of tutoring: A meta-analysis of findings. *American Educational Research Journal*, *19*, 237–248.

Conoley, J. C., & Haynes, G. (1992). An ecological approach to intervention. In R. C. D'Amato & B. A. Rothlisberg (Eds.), *Psychological perspectives on intervention: A case study approach to prescriptions for change* (pp. 177–189). New York: Longman.

Corey, G. (1995). *Theory and practice of group counseling* (4th ed.). Pacific Grove, CA: Brooks/Cole.

Corsini, R. J. (1984). *Current psychotherapies* (3rd ed.). Itasca, IL: Peacock.

Cuban, L. (1990). Reforming again, again, and again.*Educational Researcher*, *19*(1), 3–13.

Cutrona, C., & Guerin, D. (1994). Confronting conflict peacefully. *Educational Horizons*, Winter, 95–104.

D'Amato, R. C., & Rothlisberg, B. A. (Eds.) (1992). *Psychological perspectives on intervention: A case study approach to prescriptions for change*. New York: Longman.

Davis, J. M., & Hartsough, C. S. (1992). Assessing psychosocial environment in mental health consultation groups. *Psychology in the Schools*, *29*, 224–229.

Dombalis, A. O., & Erchul, W. P. (1987). Multiple family group therapy: A review of its applicability to the practice of school psychology. *School Psychology Review*, *16*(4), 487–497.

Dryfoos, J. G. (1994). *Full-service school: A revolution in health and social services for children, youth, and families*. San Francisco: Jossey-Bass.

Ehly, S., & Dustin, R. (1989). *Individual and group counseling in schools*. New York: Guilford.

Ehly, S. W., & Larsen, S. C. (1980). *Peer tutoring for individualized instruction*. Boston: Allyn and Bacon.

Elam, S. M., Rose, L. C., & Gallup, A. M. (1991). The 23rd annual Gallup Poll of the public's attitudes toward the public schools. *Phi Delta Kappan*, *73*(1), 41–56.

Elliott, S. N. (1988). Acceptability of behavioral treatments in educational settings. In J. C. Witt, S. N. Elliott, & F. M. Gresham (Eds.), *Handbook of behavior therapy in education* (pp. 121–150). New York: Plenum.

Gilliam, J. E. (1993). Crisis management for students with emotional/behavioral problems. *Intervention in School and Clinic*, *28*(4), 224–230.

Goodlad, J. I. (1990). Better teachers for our nation's schools. *Phi Delta Kappan*, *73*(3), 185–194.

Healy-Romanello, M. A. (1993). The invisible griever: Support groups for bereaved children. In J. E. Zins & M. J. Elias (Eds.), *Promoting student success through group interventions*. New York: Haworth.

Holtzman, W. H. (Ed.). (1992). *School of the future*. Austin, TX: American Psychological Association and the Hogg Foundation.

Johnson, D., & Johnson, R. (1978). Cooperative, competitive and individualistic learning. *Journal of Research and Development in Education*, *12*(1), 3–15.

Johnson, D., Maruyama, G., Johnson, R., Nelson, D., & Skon, L. (1981). The effects of cooperative, competitive and individualistic goal structures on achievement: A meta-analysis. *Psychological Bulletin*, *89*, 47–62.

Maher, C. A., & Zins, J. E. (Eds.) (1987). *Psychoeducational interventions in schools: Methods and procedures for enhancing student competence*. New York: Pergamon.

Marshak, L. E., & Seligman, M. (1993). *Counseling persons with physical disabilities: Theoretical and clinical perspectives*. Austin, TX: Pro-Ed.

Mathias, C. E. (1992). Touching the lives of children: Consultative interventions that work. *Elementary School Guidance & Counseling*, *26*, 190–201.

McConnell, S. R. (1990). Best practices in evaluating educational programs. In A. Thomas & J. Grimes (Eds.), *Best practices in school psychology II* (pp. 353–370). Washington, DC: National Association of School Psychologists.

Melaragno, R. J. (1976). *Tutoring with students. A handbook for establishing tutorial programs in schools*. Englewood Cliffs, NJ: Educational Technology Publications.

Miller, J. A., & Peterson, D. W. (1987). Peer-influenced academic interventions. In C. A. Maher & J. E. Zins (Eds.), *Psychoeducational interventions in schools: Methods and procedures for enhancing student competence* (pp. 81–100). New York: Pergamon.

Milofsky, C. D. (1986). Special education and social control. In J. G. Richardson (Ed.), *Handbook of theory and research for the sociology of education* (pp. 173–202). New York: Greenwood. 173–202.

Mullis, I. V. S., Owen, E. H., & Phillips, G. W. (1990). *America's challenge: Accelerating academic achievement, A summary of findings from 20 years of NAEP*. Washington, DC: U. S. Department of Education.

Muro, J. J., & Kottman, T. (1995). *Guidance and counseling in the elementary and middle schools: A practical approach*. Madison, WI: Brown & Benchmark.

Nastasi, B. K., & Clements, D. H. (1991). Research on cooperative learning: Implications for practice. *School Psychology Review*, *20*, 110–131.

Natriello, G., McDill, E. L., & Pallas, A. M. (1990). *School disadvantaged children: Racing against catastrophe*. New York: Teachers College Press.

Odom, S., McConnell, S. R., & Chandler, L. K. (1994). Acceptability and feasibility of classroom-based social interaction interventions for young children with disabilities. *Exceptional Children*, *60*(3), 226–236.

O'Donnell, A., & Kelly, J. (1994). Learning from peers: Beyond the rhetoric of positive results. *Educational Psychology Review*, *6*(4), 321–349.

Patterson, C. H. (1986). *Theories of counseling and psychotherapy* (4th ed.). New York: Harper and Row.

Pedersen, P. (1988). *A handbook for developing multicultural awareness*. Alexandria, VA: American Association for Counseling and Development.

Perkinson, H. J. (1968). *The imperfect panacea: American faith in education*. New York: Random House.

Perlmutter, F. D., Vayda, A. M., & Woodburn, P. K. (1982). An instrument for differentiating programs in prevention: Primary, secondary, and tertiary. In F. D. Perlmutter (Ed.), *New directions for mental health services: Mental health promotion and primary prevention, No. 13*. San Francisco: Jossey-Bass.

Phillips, B. W. (Ed.) (1980). *Management of behavior in the classroom: A handbook of psychological strategies*. Los Angeles: Western Psychological Services.

Prout, H. T., & Brown, D. T. (Eds.). (1983). *Counseling and psychotherapy with children and adolescents: Theory and practice for school and clinic settings*. Tampa, FL: Mariner.

Pugach, M. C., & Johnson, L. J. (1995). *Collaborative practitioners, collaborative schools*. Denver: Love.

Reimers, T. M., Wacker, D. P., & Koeppl, G. (1987). Acceptability of behavioral intervention: A review of the literature. *School Psychology Review, 16*, 212–227.

Reppucci, N. D., & Haugaard, J. J. (1989). Prevention of child sexual abuse: Myth or reality. *American Psychologist, 44*, 1266–1275.

Reynolds, C. R., Gutkin, T. B., Elliott, S. N., & Witt, J. C. (1984). *School psychology: Essentials of theory and practice*. New York: Wiley.

Rogers, C. R. (1972). The process of the basic encounter group. In R. C. Diedrich & H. A. Dye (Eds.), *Group procedures* (pp. 185–211). Boston: Houghton-Mifflin.

Rotheram-Borus, M. J. (1993). Multicultural issues in the delivery of group interventions. In J. E. Zins & M. J. Elias (Eds.), *Promoting student success through group interventions*. New York: Haworth.

Sarason, S. B. (1971; 1982). *The culture of the school and the problem of change*. Boston: Allyn and Bacon.

Sarason, S. B. (1990). *The predictable failure of educational reform*. San Francisco: Jossey-Bass.

Schön, D. A. (1983). *The reflective practitioner*. New York: Basic Books.

Schön, D. A. (1987). *Educating the reflective practitioner*. San Francisco: Jossey-Bass.

Skrtic, T. M. (1991a). *Behind special education: A critical analysis of professional culture and school organization*. Denver: Love.

Skrtic, T. M. (1991b). The special education paradox: Equity as the way to excellence. *Harvard Educational Review, 61*(2), 148–206.

Slavin, R. E. (1983). *Cooperative learning*. London: Longman.

Slavin, R. E., Karweit, N. L., & Madden, N. A. (1989). *Effective programs for students at risk*. Boston: Allyn and Bacon.

Sockett, H. (1990). Accountability, trust, and ethical codes of practice. In J. I. Goodlad, R. Soder, & K. A. Sirotnik (Eds.), *The moral dimensions of teaching* (pp. 224–250). San Francisco: Jossey-Bass.

Stone, L. A., & Bradley, F. O. (1994). *Foundations of elementary and middle school counseling*. White Plains, NY: Longman.

Strain, P. S. (Ed.) (1981). *The utilization of classroom peers as behavior change agents*. New York: Plenum.

Strike, K. A. (1990). The legal and moral responsibility of teachers. In J. I. Goodlad, R. Soder, & K. A. Sirotnik (Eds.), *The moral dimensions of teaching* (pp. 188–223). San Francisco: Jossey-Bass.

Sue, D. W., & Sue, D. (1990). *Counseling the culturally different: Theory and practice* (2nd ed.). New York: Wiley.

Sue, S., & Zane, N. (1987). The role of culture and cultural techniques in psychotherapy: A critique and reformulation. *American Psychologist, 42*, 37–45.

Witt, J. C., & Elliott, S. N. (1985). Acceptability of classroom management strategies. In T. R. Kratochwill (Ed.), *Advances in school psychology: Vol. 4* (pp. 251–288). Hillsdale, NJ: Erlbaum.

Yalom, I. D. (1985). *The theory and practice of group psychotherapy* (3rd ed.). New York: Basic Books.

Zins, J. E., Curtis, M. J., Graden, J., & Ponti, C. R. (1988). *Helping students succeed in the regular classroom: A guide for developing intervention assistance programs*. San Francisco: Jossey-Bass.

ventive interventions. Furthermore, interventions in the community are likely to target specific unmet treatment needs relating to concerns that are populationwide (e.g., child abuse and neglect). Finally, a community mental health perspective assumes practice in "natural settings" and indigenous communities, rather than institutional settings far removed from clients' daily lives.

In the reality of implementation, community mental health center (CMHC) practice has fallen short of these ideals. Prevention experts (e.g., Hightower & Braden, 1991; Winett, Riley, King, & Altman, 1989) note that services at CMHCs have, for the most part, remained restricted to provision of outpatient treatment for existing psychopathology. Nonetheless, the preceding characteristics suggest that community-based settings retain considerable potential in being well suited to provide group therapy. CMHCs are likely to receive referrals from large groups of clients with similar presenting problems, and their clients, although from similar catchment areas, are not likely to be personally acquainted with each other prior to a group's forming. Also, community mental health centers frequently house other services, thus the clients arriving there for group therapy do not automatically have to self-identify as "patients" in a medical setting.

Moreover, access to treatment in a community setting may be essential for the child who is not enrolled in school or whose school's counseling services do not include group interventions. Surveys have long indicated that the mental health needs of children enrolled in U.S. schools are inadequately served by the resources presently available (Alpert, 1985; Gesten & Jason, 1987). Kovacs and Lohr (1995) cite 1989 Institute of Medicine statistics indicating that 12% of children and adolescents have a "diagnosable" emotional or behavioral disorder at any given time. Other reports (e.g., Glidewell & Swallow, 1969) have placed that estimate at up to one-third. Furthermore, community settings (including schools) that deal with children's concerns may currently have the most intimate knowledge of the scope of problems (e.g., drug abuse and adolescent pregnancy) in the community today.

Finally, it should be noted that community mental health centers, diverse as they are, are just one setting in which group therapy for children or parents may be effective. For example, a 1982 survey of settings for implementation of a group-oriented parent skills training package found that these groups were conducted not only in mental health centers but also in Head Start centers, schools, and hospitals (American Guidance Service, 1982).

The other advantages of groups based in community settings pertain directly to the value of the group process and the presence of the peer group itself. Group treatment for children has long been seen as valuable by virtue of its incorporation of a focus on children's peer relations, which have been repeatedly shown to be predictive of both achievement and adjustment in later adolescence and adulthood (see Waas & Graczyk in Chapter 8 of this book). Relevant to this, groups provide greater opportunities for the learning and practicing of new social skills as well as the potential for peer reinforcement (Rose & LeCroy, 1985). The advantages of group therapy apply to groups regardless of the reason for referral, although group therapy may be most beneficial to children with certain diagnoses. These would include deficits in peer skills, such as the ability to resist peer group pressure (Kraft, 1989); those whose treatment may require role-playing or rehearsal of new skills (Goldstein, 1986); or family problems where mutual sharing of feelings and addressing each other may have therapeutic benefit (Arnold & Estreicher, 1985). An additional advantage of the group approach is that clients feel less threatened by an adult therapist when contact with the adult is in the context of a peer group (Toseland & Siporin, 1986). Kraft notes that in adolescent groups, both peer support and peer confrontation may occur, the latter less likely to be perceived as criticism than when delivered by group leaders.

Unique advantages of parent group therapy have been enumerated by Arnold, Rowe, and Tolbert (1978). These authors viewed the positive features as including peer support, opportunities for venting feelings and engaging in vicarious learning and reality testing, and an experience that they call "blessings." The concept of "blessings" was meant to convey the realization by parents that their situation, by comparison, is better than that of some others. These "blessings by comparison/contrast" are thought to decrease demoralization, a concept similar to Yalom's (1995) "instillation of hope." Gaines (1986) reviewed methods of "parallel" group psychotherapy for parents of children being seen in groups. Among the advantages of a "parallel" parents' group are improved attendance by both parents and children in their respective groups; a decreased sense of isolation; emotional support; and the opportunity for "reality checks" for parents to see their child's behavior problems in context and in comparison to others.

GOALS OF GROUPS IN COMMUNITY SETTINGS

A survey of the literature reveals a commonality of goals in community-based child, adolescent, and parent therapy groups. These goals can be enumerated based on their similarity across age groups and presenting problems, and classified into three major categories: (1) goals relating to teaching cognitive, verbal, or behavioral skills (such as question asking, compliment giving, or self-statements); (2) goals relating to addressing developmental issues or states of awareness (such as self-monitoring angry feelings or awareness of loneliness or depression); and (3) goals relating to providing information that serves an educational and/or therapeutic function. These goals are congruent with traditional conceptions of the nature and value of group psychotherapy (Yalom, 1995). Examples of each goal should illuminate their definitions.

The first goal of training skills is perhaps best framed by again noting the frequency of children's referrals to groups as a result of peer difficulties. That groups afford opportunities for improvement of social and interactional skills, including the ability to communicate with others, has been stressed by many authors (Hazel, Sherman, Schumaker, & Sheldon, 1985; Polyson & Kimball, 1993; Schamess, 1986). Some social skills groups have as their goals the modification of young clients' aggressive and oppositional tendencies, but children need not already show disturbance to be referred for social skills groups. Many groups that focus on social skills are preventive in nature. Practicing adaptive, peer-to-peer communicative and/or behavioral skills is a major objective of these, as well (Weissberg, Caplan, & Sivo, 1989).

When the group focus is intervention and prevention of substance abuse, the skills taught may be those of refusal assertiveness or negotiation of peer pressure through social problem solving (Botvin & Tortu, 1988). Groups dealing with adolescent pregnancy prevention also stress assertiveness, as well as the teaching of decision-making skills (Robinson, Watkins-Ferrell, Davis-Scott, & Ruch-Ross, 1993). Groups formed to promote effective parenting frequently focus on instruction in child management skills and discipline and in improved verbal communication (Dangel & Polster, 1988). Groups for maltreating parents also stress skills training in appropriate disciplinary practices (Wolfe & St. Pierre, 1989).

The second goal relating to developmental issues has been addressed in various ways in community groups. The mere fact of a group's existence, for an age period, may have developmental implications; for example, adolescent groups may inherently involve issues of identity formation. Transition and adaptation to new developmental periods (e.g., role transitions) has also been addressed, both with adolescents and younger children. Although preadolescence may be less characterized by role confusion than the adolescent years, younger clients may also need the comfort of a shared similarity to group members—for example, when the role transition is to that of being a child from a divorced family. Stated somewhat differently, if the child's referral to a group involves painful events with which other children share familiarity (e.g., parental divorce, death), then group treatment may be one avenue to prevent children from feeling alone and isolated with the problem.

Self-awareness, such as in the form of realization of internal states (e.g., anger, dependency) that promote or maintain maladaptive behavior, is also a possible manifestation of this goal. Group programs for aggressive children frequently feature a goal of improved awareness of inner states that relate to anger arousal, including its cognitive, physiological, and affective signs (Goldstein, Glick, Reiner, Zimmerman, & Coultry, 1987; Lochman, White, & Wayland, 1991). Wolfe and St.

Pierre (1989) have written of the goal of desensitization to feelings of overarousal in improving abusive parents' capacities to deal calmly with aversive situations with their children.

Finally, groups' potential cathartic function has been noted as a goal for many years. MacLennan (1986) has identified a primary goal of children's "crisis" groups as the expression of feelings and the recovery of a sense of safety. Examples of this include groups for children who are survivors of a natural disaster or groups in shelters for domestic violence.

The third major goal is to provide information that serves an educational and/or therapeutic function. Child abuse and neglect interventions often stress education about child development, appropriate expectations for children, and childrearing responsibilities (Wolfe, Sandler, & Kaufman, 1981). Groups formed to deal with issues of adolescent sexuality usually incorporate an educational component—for example, information about AIDS and sexually transmitted diseases, contraception, and "safe sex" (Crockett & Chopak, 1993). Finally, numerous substance-abuse intervention and prevention programs have included an educational component. It has been noted that, in the case of alcohol use, adolescents may not intentionally mean to be self-destructive but rather may simply not know what amount of alcohol is dangerous (Pittman, 1987).

GUIDELINES FOR SUCCESSFUL IMPLEMENTATION OF COMMUNITY-BASED GROUPS

This section reviews techniques used in implementation of community-based groups, including information on the composition of groups and characteristics of members, the temporal sequence and duration of groups, and specific treatment strategies and processes that have been useful as reported by group therapists. Again, these groups are described based on the referral reasons ("morbidities") that were described earlier. Table 3.1 provides an outline for this section by summarizing the most frequently described therapeutic strategies for groups reviewed in this chapter. Most of the therapeutic techniques can be classified into three categories: didactic-descriptive, interactive-interpersonal, and internal-cognitive.

The first element of the categorization of group techniques is similar to that of Hazel and colleagues (1985), who organized frequently used methods of training social skills for adolescents into categories of descriptive procedures, modeling, and behavioral rehearsal. *Didactic-descriptive* procedures refer to those in which the role of the group leader (professional or paraprofessional) is primary in imparting information or educational techniques to group members. *Interactive-interpersonal* strategies are those that rely on the presence of peers for feedback and participation in learning, trying (rehearsal), and revising (feedback) the execution of new skills in the *in vivo* atmosphere of the group. Finally, *internal-cognitive* techniques refer to the group members' learning and practicing skills that relate to cognitive states, to one's own communication style, or to personal attitudes and attributes that can be modified when coexistent with the possibility of feedback from group members.

Common specific therapeutic techniques and strategies (e.g., assertiveness skills) within each type of skill category are depicted in Table 3.1 along with the type of group. To explain this table, we will briefly overview the groups summarized therein. This section will also include points relevant to the number of clients accommodated in a group at one time; the temporal sequence of sessions; and the gender, cultural, and socioeconomic factors that have been identified as influencing the formation and functioning of community-based groups.

Group Programs Addressing the "New Morbidities"

Substance Abuse

The majority of substance-abuse intervention and prevention programs attempt to modify clients' behavior by influencing knowledge of drugs and alcohol, attitudes toward drug use, and/or interper-

Table 3.1 Techniques Utilized in Community-Based Groups by Age and Level of Intervention

	PREVENTIVE ----------					---------- INTERVENTIVE
POPULATION	DESCRIPTIVE	INTERACTIVE	COGNITIVE	DESCRIPTIVE	INTERACTIVE	COGNITIVE
Children	a,b Teach about drug effects, provide information.	g, h Teach social skills such as helping, sharing, and play.	j Teach social problem-solving skills.	l Teach specific feelings identification.	u, v Sociorecreational games, symbolic play, group process.	Relaxation training, self-monitoring.
Adolescents	c,d,e,f Life-skills training to teach preparenting skills, AIDS awareness.	i Teach social skills preventive (e.g., "skill-streaming" [modeling, role-plays, feedback, transfer training] and refusal assertiveness)	k Teach social problem-solving skills.	m, n, o Provide contraception information, teach for knowledge of addictions.	w, x Utilize empathy, confrontation, role-playing, and skillstreaming.	z, z2, z3 Teach anger "triggers," cues, anger reducers, and 12-Step philosophy.
Parents				p, q, r, s, t Teach safe, effective disciplinary skills. Explain domestic violence issues (e.g., escalation of child behavior). Teach development in infancy and early childhood.	y Utilize sharing, empathy, and confrontation.	z4 Desensitization and anger management.

a Blau, 1986; b Botvin & Tortu, 1988; c Robinson, Watkins-Ferrell, Davis-Scott, & Ruch-Ross 1993; d Kirby, Barth, Leland, & Fetro, 1991; e St. Lawrence, Brasfield, Jefferson, Alleyne, O'Bannon, & Shirley, 1995; f St. Lawrence, Jefferson, Alleyne, & Brasfield, 1995; g Durlak, 1977; h Mannarino, Michelson, Beck, & Figueroa, 1982; i Goldstein, Sprafkin, Gershaw, & Klein, 1980; j Weissberg & Allen, 1986; k St. Lawrence et al., 1995; l Weissberg & Allen, 1986; m Blau, 1986; n Botvin & Tortu, 1988; o Robinson et al., 1993; p Dangel & Polster, 1988; q Mt. Hope Family Center, 1990; r Webster-Stratton, 1994; s Wolfe & St. Pierre, 1989; t Wolfe, Sandler, & Kaufman, 1981; u Schiffer, 1984; v Slavson & Schiffer, 1975; w Dennison, 1988; x Goldstein et al., 1980; y Arnold, Rowe & Tolbert, 1978; z Goldstein et al., 1987; z2 Lochman, White, & Wayland, 1991; z3 Ross, 1994; z4 Wolfe & St. Pierre, 1989.

sonal variables such as self-esteem. Schinke and colleagues' 1991 classification of techniques used in substance-abuse prevention programs included approaches that stress one of the following five methods: (1) the provision of information, intended to increase knowledge of drugs; (2) "affective education" designed to increase self-esteem; (3) the provision of alternative activities to drug use, intended to reduce boredom and alienation; (4) skills training focusing on increasing ability for decision making, anxiety reduction, and assertiveness skills; and (5) "psychosocial resistance skills" to promote awareness of cultural influence and pressure to drink or use drugs.

Thus, the didactic-descriptive procedures most commonly used in these programs include education about characteristics of substance abuse and addiction and also didactic approaches to define assertiveness and demonstrate assertiveness skills such as refusal (Nay & Ross, 1993). Primary interactive-interpersonal procedures employed include role-playing, which has been described by Ross (1994) and others (e.g., Blau, 1986). Blau's multilevel treatment package included an assertiveness training component in which role-playing was utilized to train peer resistance skills and refusal assertiveness for temptation to try drugs and alcohol.

Schinke, Botvin, and Orlandi (1991) also reviewed residential-setting treatment programs for adolescents with substance-abuse problems. Three were presented, all of which rely on interactional procedures of group discussion and group process to encourage self-examination and behavior change. The basis for these groups is often a 12-step model, originated by Alcoholics Anonymous (AA). The philosophy and basic tenets of the Twelve Steps and AA as a self-help, peer-support program have been reviewed elsewhere (e.g., McCrady, 1994). Briefly, the Twelve-Step recommendations for an inner-directedness in attitude change would qualify as internal-cognitive based on our classification.

Botvin's Life Skills Training Program is a preventive intervention that has been proven effective in preventing youths from beginning substance use. This school-based program treated children in whole classrooms at a time and used a combination of information (didactic-descriptive), communications training, social skills and assertiveness training (interactive), and internal-cognitive approaches such as self-image improvement and techniques for coping with anxiety. The Life Skills Program was designed for use with seventh-graders, with "booster sessions" in eighth and ninth grades, and has documented positive results. Outcome data reported by Botvin and Dusenbury (1989) revealed significant decreases in smoking onset, drinking, and marijuana use for children enrolled in the program.

Adolescent Sexual Activity

Group programs that deal with early, unprotected sexual activity among adolescents have focused on two major areas: prevention of adolescent pregnancy and prevention of sexually transmitted diseases (STDs). Several authors (e.g., Brooks-Gunn & Paikoff, 1993; Crockett & Chopak, 1993; Robinson et al., 1993; Stoiber and colleagues in Chapter 16 of this book) have reviewed programs created to deal with this "new morbidity." Inspection of the therapeutic characteristics of these programs reveals numerous common elements that can be classified into didactic-descriptive, interactional-interpersonal, and internal-cognitive training components. One example in Chicago is the Teens Learning to Cope (TLC) Program, which has achieved success. The group elements of this program include a small-group, participatory format, with groups held during available times in the classroom schedules of the students participating. Robinson and associates (1993) describe TLC groups of 8 to 10 members in same-gender groups with weekly meetings led by doctoral students in psychology. Didactic-descriptive procedures were followed via the provision of information on pregnancy and contraception; decision-making and communication skills were imparted via behavioral rehearsal in an interactional-interpersonal format.

Crockett and Chopak (1993) reviewed the Self Program in Baltimore, Maryland (Zabin, Hirsch, Smith, Streett, & Hardy, 1986a, 1986b); the School/Community Program for Sexual Risk Reduction among Teens (Vincent, Clearie, & Schlucter, 1987), and the Reducing the Risk Program in California. Both interactive-interpersonal and internal-cognitive elements are found in the Reducing the Risk Program, described as including social learning theory, "inoculation" against social pressure, and cognitive-behavioral theory to teach one to set explicit personal norms (e.g., against unprotected intercourse) (Kirby, Barth, Leland, & Fetro's study, as cited by Crockett & Chopak, 1993).

Child Abuse and Neglect and Promotion of Effective Parenting

Groups for intervention in and prevention of child abuse and neglect, and the promotion of effective parenting, have been implemented in many forms over the past 20 years. Didactic-descriptive approaches have often been utilized, as research suggests that abusive and neglectful parents may hold inappropriate notions of their roles as parents and of child development (Wolfe & St. Pierre, 1989). Accordingly, topics presented by group leaders have included the nature of child behavior problems and emotional disturbance (e.g., Arnold et al., 1978), principles of normal child development (Arnold et al., 1978; Wolfe et al., 1981), developmental and psychosocial issues associated with adulthood and being a parent (Mt. Hope Family Center, 1990; Webster-Stratton, 1994), and principles of behavior management and disciplinary techniques with children (Dangel & Polster, 1988).

Finally, techniques to facilitate healthy parent/child communication have frequently been presented by therapists leading parenting groups. One of the oldest programs to feature the teaching of principles of parent/child communication is the Parent Effectiveness Training Program (P.E.T.; Gordon, 1970, 1976). Despite the popularity of P.E.T. in its 1970s heyday, its long-term effectiveness is still debated (e.g., Rinn & Markle's 1977 study, as cited in Forehand, Walley, & Furey, 1984).

One behaviorally oriented program for training parenting skills that has been extremely successful is the WINNING Program of Dangel and Polster (1988). Their behaviorally oriented parent training groups are held weekly for eight weeks. Skills trained include basic behavior modification concepts of reinforcement (via praise, attention, rewards, and privileges), punishment (via time-out, response cost, and physical punishment) and other methods of improving child compliance with instructions, and maintenance of change. The program is described by Dangel and Polster as having been implemented with approximately 3,000 families over the last 15 years; outcome data are positive.

Parent groups have also frequently used interpersonal approaches, specifically modeling, as a part of therapy. Usually, this type of training has involved *in vivo* modeling, role-play, and rehearsal to supplement presentations by group leaders and manuals instructive of child behavior modification (Forehand & McMahon, 1981). Webster-Stratton (1994) has reported success with a parent group intervention using videotaped modeling.

The third area of concentration for parenting groups has also been interactional (i.e., focusing on group process as well as skill rehearsal). Arnold and associates (1978) note that many of the aspects of any group therapy, particularly for adults, can also be helpful for groups with parents. These include basics such as having group members introduce themselves to each other, having group members share something of their situation and reason for referral, having all group members take part in goal setting and definition for the group, and promoting group cohesion by encouraging input from all present.

Anger Control

Common characteristics in therapeutic techniques for dealing with anger and antisocial behavior in children and adolescents can similarly be classified into the three categories mentioned. In their successful Aggression Replacement Training Program (ART) Goldstein and colleagues (1987) use treatment components that they label "structured learning," "anger control training," and "moral education." The structured learning component incorporates a similar, basic sequence for all skills taught: modeling of the skill by the group leader, clients' role-playing of the skill in front of the entire group, receiving of feedback on one's role-play performance from all group members, and "transfer training," or applying the skill in various real-world situations that evoke temptation to use aggressive responses. Thus, Aggression Replacement Training utilizes both didactic-descriptive methods and interactive ones.

The Anger Coping Program of Lochman and associates (1991) incorporates similar techniques, via its adoption of group socialization games aimed at helping clients resist temptation to be aggressive. In one example, children take turns at a tower-building task using dominoes, while other group members deliberately try to distract the "builder" by taunting. There is also an internal-cognitive focus in both programs: Group leaders teach clients awareness of bodily signals of anger (e.g., increased muscle tension and pulse rate, blood rushing to one's face). This is followed by training self-management skills such as personal "anger reducers" (e.g., counting, self-calming) that can be utilized anywhere. In the Anger Coping Program, self-monitoring strategies are presented to increase awareness of environmental "triggers" for anger and individual differences in physiological responses. Furthermore, Aggression Replacement Training adds a unique internal-cognitive element in the form of training in moral reasoning, provided through brainstorming and group discussion of moral dilemmas.

GENDER AND ETHNIC COMPOSITION OF GROUPS IN COMMUNITY SETTINGS

The question of heterogeneity versus homogeneity in group composition is an issue when treating children and adolescents, as with any population. There have been recommendations for both same-gender and mixed-gender groups of children, depending on the nature of clients' reasons for referral. Classic texts such as those by Slavson and Schiffer (1975) and Schiffer (1984) make these determinations based on developmental concerns stemming from a psychoanalytic perspective and generally recommend same-gender groups. More recently, Reid (1987) recommended that both boys and girls be included in child therapy groups, with an age range of 5 to 12 years. The rationale for this diverse composition, according to Reid, stems from children's natural environments, where heterogeneity is often the norm.

It is important to note that traditional child therapy groups tend to be mixed in terms of presenting problem. When a group is homogeneous with respect to referral reason (e.g., aggressive behavior, substance abuse), several authors have provided different recommendations for group composition. Ross (1994) recommends a group size of five to eight for chemically dependent adolescents in recovery. Finch and colleagues (1993) recommend that in the case of treatment of antisocial adolescents, no more than four clients be included in a group if there is to be just one adult therapist present as group leader. For elementary school-aged aggressive children, the recommendation is for no more than five per group. Sugar (1991) recommends a maximum of five to seven children for any type of elementary-aged group. In the case of adolescent groups, Dennison (1988) states that no more than eight per group be included, as larger sizes may mean that there is not adequate time to address members' individualized needs. Finally, Finch, Nelson, and Moss (1993) note that regardless of age, group composition is aided when at least one relatively less-disturbed client is included to serve as a positive model in group activities. Ross (1994) recommends including numerous clients who are "further along in their recovery" (p. 159).

The issue of ethnic composition of groups has also been addressed. Koss-Chiono and Vargas (1992) acknowledge that the therapist/client relationship can be affected by the ethnicity of each. Rotheram-Borus and Tsemberis (1989), writing about implementation of social competency training programs, caution that programs implemented with ethnic minority individuals must be sensitive to cultural differences. They note that the norms for behavior as seen by the majority culture may be at odds with minority culture. This caution is relevant to child and adolescent therapy group provision, as most of social skills training is accomplished in a group format.

Kernberg and Chazan (1991) recommend against inclusion of a lone group member from a different ethnic group or race due to the potential for stigmatization of the child by other group members. These authors also recommend against inclusion of group members who are much older or younger than others, or inclusion of a single group member who has a pronounced physical disability.

TEMPORAL SEQUENCE OF GROUPS

Weekly group meetings have long been the norm in mental health services provision and remain the most frequently employed temporal sequence for groups in a community setting. This finding spans referral reason, age of clients, and the group "mission," whether preventive or interventive. For example, weekly, 45- to 60-minute group sessions are utilized in traditional, activity/play group child therapy (Slavson & Schiffer, 1975); psychodynamically oriented psychotherapy groups for adolescents (Azima, 1989); humanistic, group process-oriented groups for adolescents (Dennison, 1988); childhood anger control training programs (Finch et al., 1993; Goldstein et al., 1987); groups for adolescent mothers (Robinson et al., 1993); groups for teenagers for prevention of early sexual behavior (Robinson et al., 1993); and groups for prevention of child abuse and neglect (Wolfe et al., 1981).

CONTRAINDICATIONS FOR GROUP THERAPY

Slavson and Schiffer (1975) specified contraindications for traditional child therapy groups as including psychotic children, children in "severe anxiety states" (Slavson & Schiffer, 1975, p. 110), children who are extremely aggressive, and children with difficulties in "ego development." More recently, authors such as Kernberg and Chazan (1991) give contraindications for inclusion in therapy groups for young children who show antisocial behavior. They recommend against inclusion in groups of children with attention deficit disorder and seriously depressed children whose needs for individual attention cannot be met in groups. Sugar (1991, 1993) also stresses the importance of not including a child who is so much an isolate that his or her needs will not be served by a group.

EFFECTIVENESS OF COMMUNITY-BASED GROUPS

Research on the effectiveness of community-based groups for children, adolescents, and parents is a vital issue for many reasons. The need to develop the most cost- and time-effective forms of mental health treatment has become more important than ever, given the current state of health care provision in this country, and treating clients in groups often is cited for that reason (Sleek, 1995). High-quality outcome research, however, remains difficult to fund and accomplish. Community-based practitioners often do not have the resources needed to conduct effective program evaluation. Federal grant funding for such interventions, which could guarantee incorporation of an evaluation component, has decreased over the last decade. Numerous group programs have reported outcome data in various levels of detail, yet the overall state of knowledge of effectiveness is still debated. Some classic reviews of the effectiveness of child psychotherapy include group treatment among the therapies reviewed but do not distinguish its unique effectiveness (e.g., Casey & Berman, 1985).

It is important to note that any consistent examination of the effectiveness of community-based groups must be based on a certain type of program for a certain referral reason. Substance-abuse intervention programs have reported mixed results, depending on the clinical history of the clients (Ross, 1994). Kovacs and Lohr (1995) note that clinical knowledge of treatment of children's aggressive behavior, compared to other types of groups, perhaps is the area in which clinicians have learned the most in recent years. Obviously, one must also acknowledge the probability that successful programs exist but remain unknown in the scholarly literature, as full-time clinicians and practitioners in community settings often are not able to take time to publish their results.

Feindler and Ecton (1986) reported anecdotal data on over 300 adolescents completing a group-based anger control intervention at a children's center. In the majority of cases, former clients remained symptom free after treatment, as judged by clinical reports of independent living, improved self-control, and nonrecidivism for aggressive acts. For group interventive and preventive interventions for substance abuse, it is known that the method of mere information dissemination is *not* effective (Botvin & Tortu, 1988; Schinke et al., 1991). This also appears to be the case for adolescent sexuality programs that rely on information alone (Brooks-Gunn & Paikoff, 1993; Stoiber and colleagues in Chapter 16 of this book; Zabin & Hayward, 1993). Walker and Mitchell (1988) reviewed the literature on evaluation of adolescent pregnancy support programs. They concluded that, overall, studies in that area do not employ program evaluation strategies adequate to actually detect the short- and long-term effects of such programs. Among the shortcomings these authors note is the lack of control groups (i.e., adolescents in similar environments who have not become pregnant).

There has also been work published on the effectiveness of groups for primary prevention. One excellent example is the edited volume of Price, Cowen, Lorion, and Ramos-McKay (1988), which presented effective, community-based programs that included rigorous program evaluation and research components. Inclusion of a program in their book was dependent on the program's meeting stringent criteria both for implementation and evaluation. Necessary features included a clear description of the preventive intervention itself, including detailed information on the services provided and their timing and duration. Also required was a clear specification of outcome, results, and follow-up. Because the majority of programs detailed in the book do not consist primarily of group therapy provision, the only example presented in this chapter is the Life Skills Training (LST) Program previously cited. The key here appears to be the multimodal effort of LST in training not just for substance-abuse prevention but for generalized, "real-world" social competencies, as well. Primary prevention efforts for substance abuse that do not ensure generalizability to other critical "life skills," whether delivered in a group or whole-classroom format, have been criticized as ineffective as already mentioned. The widely implemented Drug Abuse Resistance Education, or D.A.R.E., utilized throughout the United States, consists of law-enforcement personnel delivering didactic-type warnings by visiting schools. D.A.R.E. has received significant funding but has apparently had little measurable preventive impact (Ennett, Tobler, Ringwalt, & Flewelling, 1994).

The *Journal of Community Psychology* published a special issue on research-based substance-abuse prevention programs in 1992. A community-based group substance-abuse prevention/intervention program in that volume is noted here for its effectiveness. Super II (Bruce & Emshoff, 1992) was based in Atlanta and designed to prevent drug abuse in 11- to 17-year-olds. The adolescents and their parents attended seven two-hour group sessions separately that included educational, experiential, and social skills building activities. The groups were implemented in various community service agencies such as Boys' Clubs, Girls' Clubs, Salvation Army sites, and parks and recreational centers. Findings were superior to those of other drug-abuse treatment and prevention programs not based in community settings. Finally, in a later special issue of the same journal, Kim, Crutchfield, Williams, and Hepler (1994) articulated guidelines for disseminating information from drug prevention programs. They warn that publishing the results of programs achieving only minimal gains may actually harm rather than help if this serves to continue funding for unsuccessful efforts.

ISSUES OF TRAINING FOR GROUPS CONDUCTED IN COMMUNITY SETTINGS

Yalom (1995) suggests four essential elements that should be included in a comprehensive training program for group therapists. First, a trainee should have the opportunity to observe an experienced therapist conducting group sessions. Second, first-hand group experience during one's training is important; therapists hoping to conduct group therapy should not concentrate solely on individual therapy provision during graduate training. Third, trainees should receive close supervision of their initial groups. Finally, Yalom stresses that fledgling group therapists should also have some personal experience of psychotherapy.

Dies (1974, 1980, cited in Kymissis, Licamele, Boots, & Kessler, 1991) asked practicing psychotherapists to evaluate 12 training techniques and rank them from most to least helpful. The first 4 items were connected to supervision, the following 3 to experience, the next 3 to observational learning, and the final 2 items to didactic teaching. Active participation was preferred instead of procedures where the trainee was removed from group involvement.

Working with adolescents requires different group organizational strategies than those used with adults (Carrol & Wiggins, 1990). Phelan (1974) suggests that adolescent and adult groups are different in that adolescents' therapists will, in essence, function as "teachers" and "parents" in addition to being in a counselor role. Thus, knowledge of developmental principles is vital to successful implementation of child and adolescent groups, in community settings or elsewhere. Adolescents are trying to free themselves from their caregivers, establish sex roles/sexual identities, explore careers, and determine their feelings toward relationships, work, and leisure. Thus, for them, in particular, the peer group will exert a key influence on group members altering their attitudes or changing their behavior. A group leader for this developmental period would have to be aware of and sensitive to these pressures.

Group therapists must also be sensitive to the multifaceted nature of children's spheres of development. Familiarity with techniques of collaboration between various community agencies is important. Next to the family, the school probably has the greatest influence on many children. The belief that it is desirable to work with the child, the family, and the school organization in the context of their larger social environment is becoming more popular (Sherman et al., 1994).

Contact with the school to establish collaboration does not have to be limited to individual cases. Some steps that community agency workers and therapists can use to establish a working relationship when beginning groups are (1) learning about current practices by meeting with school staff and mentioning interest in collaboration and (2) offering a variety of services (e.g., a family/school liason) (Sherman et al., 1994). Evident in school structure are feelings of territoriality that are present in many social organizations. The extent of these feelings vary, depending on a variety of factors, including the organization's level of general well-being. It is paramount that the outside therapist be aware of this and express respect for the integrity of the school in addition to having knowledge of the services it offers (Sherman et al., 1994). In community-based settings, this may be even more important. Trickett and Birman (1989) note the vital importance of familiarity with a setting's ecology prior to attempts to intervene within the setting.

REFERENCES

Alpert, J. L. (1985). Change within a profession: Change, future, prevention, and school psychology. *American Psychologist, 40,* 1112–1121.

American Guidance Service. (1982). *Effective Parenting: A Newsletter for STEP Sponsors and Leaders, 6.*

Arnold, L. E., & Estreicher, D. (1985). *Parent-child group therapy: Building self-esteem in a cognitive-behavioral group.* Lexington, MA: Lexington Books.

Arnold, L. E., Rowe, M., & Tolbert, H. A. (1978). Parents' groups. In L. E. Arnold (Ed.), *Helping parents help their children* (pp. 114–125). New York: Bruner-Mazel.

Axline, V. M. (1969). *Play therapy.* New York: Ballantine Books.

Azima, F. J. C. (1989). Confrontation, empathy, and interpretation issues in adolescent group psychotherapy. In F. J. C. Azima & L. H. Richmond (Eds.), *Adolescent group psychotherapy* (pp. 3–19). Madison, CT: International Universities Press.

Blau, G. M. (1986). *Drug and alcohol abuse prevention: Utility and effectiveness with rural fifth grade students.* Unpublished master's thesis, Auburn University.

Bloom, B. (1973). *Community mental health: A historical and critical analysis.* Morristown, NJ: General Learning Press.

Botvin, G. J., & Dusenbury, L. (1989). Substance abuse prevention and the promotion of competence. In L. A. Bond & B. E. Compas (Vol. Eds.) & G. W. Albee & J. M. Joffe (Series Eds.), *Primary prevention and promotion in the schools* (pp. 146–178). Newbury Park, CA: Sage.

Botvin, G. J., & Tortu, S. (1988). Preventing adolescent substance abuse through life skills training. In R. H. Price, E. L. Cowen, R. P. Lorion, & J. Ramos-McKay

(Eds.), *Fourteen ounces of prevention: A casebook for practitioners* (pp. 98–110). Washington, DC: American Psychological Association.

Brooks-Gunn, J., & Paikoff, R. L. (1993). "Sex is a gamble, kissing is a game": Adolescent sexuality and health promotion. In S. G. Millstein, A. C. Petersen, & E. O. Nightingale (Eds.), *Promoting the health of adolescents* (pp. 180–208). New York: Oxford University Press.

Bruce, C., & Emshoff, J. (1992). The SUPER II program: An early intervention program. *Journal of Community Psychology, OSAP Special Issue*, 10–21.

Campbell, D. T., & Stanley, J. C. (1966). *Experimental and quasi-experimental designs for research*. Chicago: Rand McNally.

Caplan, G. (1964). *Principles of preventive psychiatry*. New York: Basic Books.

Carrol, M. R., & Wiggins, J. (1990). *Elements of group counseling: Back to the basics*. Denver: Love.

Casey, R. J., & Berman, J. S. (1985). The outcome of psychotherapy with children. *Psychological Bulletin, 98*, 388–400.

Cowen, E. L. (1977). Baby-steps toward primary prevention. *American Journal of Community Psychology, 5*, 1–22.

Cowen, E. L. (1980). The wooing of primary prevention. *American Journal of Community Psychology, 8*, 258–284.

Cowen, E. L. (1983). Primary prevention in mental health: Past, present, and future. In R. D. Felner, L. A. Jason, J. N. Moritsugu, & S. S. Farber (Eds.), *Preventive psychology: Theory, research and practice* (pp. 11–25). Elmsford, NY: Pergamon.

Cowen, E. L., & Hightower, A. D. (1990). The Primary Mental Health Project: Alternative approaches in school-based prevention interventions. In T. B. Gutkin & C. R. Reynolds (Eds.), *The handbook of school psychology* (2nd ed., pp. 775–794). New York: Wiley.

Crockett, L. J., & Chopak, J. S. (1993). Pregnancy prevention in early adolescence: A developmental perspective. In R. M. Lerner (Ed.), *Early adolescence: Perspectives on research, policy, and intervention* (pp. 315–334). Hillsdale, NJ: Erlbaum.

Dangel, R. F., & Polster, R. A. (1988). *Teaching child management skills*. New York: Pergamon.

Dennison, S. T. (1988). *Activities for adolescents in therapy: A handbook of facilitating guidelines and planning ideas for group therapy with troubled adolescents*. Springfield, IL: Charles C. Thomas.

Dies, R. R., & Riester, A. E. (1986). Research on child group therapy: Present status and future directions. In A. E. Riester & I. A. Kraft (Eds.), *Child group psychotherapy: Future tense* (pp. 173–220). Madison, CT: International Universities Press.

Dryfoos, J. G. (1994). *Full-service schools: A revolution in mental health and social services for children, youth and families*. San Francisco: Jossey-Bass.

Duffy, K. G., & Wong, F. Y. (1996). *Community psychology*. Boston: Allyn and Bacon.

Durlak, J. A. (1995). *School-based prevention programs for children and adolescents*. Thousand Oaks, CA: Sage.

Durlak, J. A., & Jason, L. A. (1984). Preventive programs for school-aged children and adolescents. In M. C. Roberts & L. Peterson (Eds.), *Prevention of problems in childhood: Psychological research and applications* (pp. 103–132). New York: Wiley.

Ennett, S. T., Tobler, N. S., Ringwalt, C. L., & Flewelling, R. L. (1994). How effective is drug abuse resistance education? A meta-analysis of Project DARE outcome evaluations. *American Journal of Public Health, 84*, 1394–1400.

Feindler, E. L., & Ecton, R. B. (1986). *Adolescent anger control: Cognitive-behavioral techniques*. New York: Pergamon.

Felner, R. D., & Adan, A. M. (1988). The school transitional environment project: An ecological intervention and evaluation. In R. H. Price, E. L. Cowen, R. P. Lorion, & J. Ramos-McKay (Eds.), *Fourteen ounces of prevention: A casebook for practitioners* (pp. 111–122). Washington, DC: American Psychological Association.

Finch, A. J., Jr., Nelson, W. M., III, & Moss, J. H. (1993). Childhood aggression: Cognitive-behavioral strategies and interventions. In A. J. Finch, Jr., W. M. Nelson, III, & E. S. Ott (Eds.), *Cognitive-behavioral procedures with children and adolescents: A practical guide* (pp. 148–205). Boston: Allyn and Bacon.

Forehand, R. L., & McMahon, R. J. (1981). *Helping the noncompliant child: A clinician's guide to parent training*. New York: Guilford.

Forehand, R. L., Walley, P. B., & Furey, W. M. (1984). Prevention in the home: Parent and family. In M. C. Roberts & L. Peterson (Eds.), *Prevention of problems in childhood: Psychological research and applications* (pp. 342–368). New York: Wiley.

Gaines, T. (1986). Applications of child group therapy. In A. E. Riester & I. A. Kraft (Eds.), *Child group psychotherapy: Future tense* (pp. 103–122). Madison, CT: International Universities Press.

Gesten, E. L., & Jason, L. A. (1987). Social and community interventions. *Annual Review of Psychology, 38*, 427–460.

Ginott, H. (1961). *Group psychotherapy with children: The theory and practice of play therapy*. New York: McGraw-Hill.

Glidewell, J. C., & Swallow, C. S. (1969). *The prevalence of maladjustment in elementary schools.* (Report prepared for the Joint Commission on Mental Health).

Goldstein, A. P. (1986). Psychological skill training and the aggressive adolescent. In S. J. Apter & A. P. Goldstein (Eds.), *Youth violence: Programs and prospects* (pp. 89–119). New York: Pergamon.

Goldstein, A. P., Glick, B., Reiner, S., Zimmerman, D., & Coultry, T. M. (1987). *Aggression replacement training: A comprehensive intervention for aggressive youth*. Champaign, IL: Research Press.

Goldstein, A. P., Sprafkin, R. P., Gershaw, N. J., & Klein, P. (1980). *Skillstreaming the adolescent: A structured learning approach to teaching prosocial skills*. Champaign, IL: Research Press.

Gordon, T. (1970). *P.E.T., Parent Effectiveness Training: The tested new way to raise responsible children*. New York: Wyden.

Gordon, T. (1976). *P.E.T. in action*. New York: Wyden.

Gullotta, T. P., Adams, G. R., & Montemayor, R. (1995). *Substance misuse in adolescence*. Newbury Park, CA: Sage.

Hazel, J. S., Sherman, J. A., Schumaker, J. B., & Sheldon, J. (1985). Group social skills training with adolescents. In D. Upper & S. M. Ross (Eds.), *Handbook of behavioral group therapy* (pp. 203–246). New York: Plenum.

Hightower, A. D., & Braden, J. (1991). Prevention. In T. R. Kratochwill & R. J. Morris (Eds.), *The practice of child therapy* (2nd ed., pp. 410–458). New York: Pergamon.

Hobbs, N. (1964). Mental health's third revolution. *American Journal of Orthopsychiatry*, *34*, 822–833.

Institute of Medicine. (1994). *Reducing risks for mental disorder: Frontiers for preventive intervention research*. Washington, DC: National Academy Press.

Johnson, J. H., Jason, L. A., & Betts, D. M. (1990). Promoting social competencies through educational efforts. In T. P. Gullotta, G. R. Adams, & R. Montemayor (Vol. Eds.), *Developing social competency in adolescence* (pp. 139–168). Thousand Oaks, CA: Sage.

Kernberg, P. F., & Chazan, S. E. (1991). *Children with conduct disorders: A psychotherapy manual*. New York: Basic Books.

Kim, S., Crutchfield, C., Williams, C., & Hepler, N. (1994). An innovative and unconventional approach to program evaluation in the field of substance abuse prevention: A threshold-gating approach using single system evaluation designs. *Journal of Community Psychology, CSAP Special Issue*, 61–78.

Kirby, D., Barth, R. P., Leland, N., & Fetro, J. V. (1991). A norms and skills based sex education curriculum: Its impact upon sexual risk-taking behavior. *Family Planning Perspectives*, *23*, 253–263.

Koss-Chiono, J. D., & Vargas, L. A. (1992). Through the cultural looking glass: A model for understanding culturally responsive psychotherapies. In L. A. Vargas & J. D. Koss-Chiono (Eds.), *Working with culture: Psychotherapeutic interventions with ethnic minority children and adolescents* (pp. 1–22). San Francisco: Jossey-Bass.

Kovacs, M., & Lohr, W. D. (1995). Research on psychotherapy with children and adolescents: An overview of evolving trends and current issues. *Journal of Abnormal Child Psychology*, *23*, 11–30.

Kraft, I. A. (1989). A selective overview. In F. J. C. Azima & L. H. Richmond (Eds.), *Adolescent group psychotherapy* (pp. 55–68). Madison, CT: International Universities Press.

Kraft, I. A., & Riester, A. E. (1986). Past as prologue to the future in child group psychotherapy practice. In A. E. Riester & I. A. Kraft (Eds.), *Child group psychotherapy: Future tense* (pp. 3–6). Madison, CT: International Universities Press.

Kratochwill, T. R., & Morris, R. J. (1993). *Handbook of psychotherapy with children and adolescents*. Boston: Allyn and Bacon.

Kymissis, P., Licamele, W. L., Boots, S., & Kessler, E. (1991). Training in child and adolescent group therapy: Two surveys and a model. *Group*, *15*, 163–167.

Lawson, G. W., & Lawson, A. W. (1992). *Adolescent substance abuse: Etiology, treatment and prevention*. Gaithersburg, MD: Aspen.

Lochman, J. E., White, K. J., & Wayland, K. K. (1991). Cognitive-behavioral assessment and treatment with aggressive children. In P. Kendall (Ed.), *Child and adolescent therapy: Cognitive-behavioral procedures* (pp. 25–65). New York: Guilford.

MacLennan, B. W. (1986). Child group psychotherapy in special settings. In A. E. Riester & I. A. Kraft (Eds.), *Child group psychotherapy: Future tense* (pp. 83–102). Madison, CT: International Universities Press.

McCrady, B. S. (1994). Alcoholics anonymous and behavior therapy: Can habits be treated as diseases? Can diseases be treated as habits? *Journal of Consulting and Clinical Psychology*, *62*, 1159–1166.

Mt. Hope Family Center. (1990). Mt. Hope Family Center Parent Group Program. Rochester, NY: Author.

Nay, W. R., & Ross, G. R. (1993). Cognitive-behavioral

CHAPTER 4

THE ROLE OF RESEARCH IN GROUP THERAPY WITH CHILDREN AND ADOLESCENTS

Sheldon Rose, UNIVERSITY OF WISCONSIN–MADISON

At present, there is an unfortunate dichotomy between research and the practice of group therapy with children and adolescence. Yet, if one examines the nature of research and its purposes, one will find a close connection between research and the needs of the group therapist. After all, research is a systematic way of answering questions to which practitioners are looking for answers. Research methods involve formulating a problem, developing and describing research design about the way data are to be collected and interpreted, presenting the researcher's findings, and analyzing the meaning of those findings. It should be noted how similar research theory is to the assessment-intervention therapy paradigm. The group therapist can facilitate having his or her questions answered in at least two ways: as a critical consumer of the research of others and by applying research methods to his or her own practice in order to answer questions. The purpose of this chapter is to describe major considerations in carrying out these two roles.

Group therapy is a highly complex endeavor. As a target of research, one must consider a variety of factors. These include the population being served, the targets of intervention, the type of interventions, the intensity of treatment, the composition of the group, the characteristics of the group therapist, the patterns of group interaction, the demands of the sponsoring agency, the material and psychological resources of the members, the concerns of significant others of the group members, and the type of outcomes one can expect from group therapy. The basic questions most research is designed to answer are threefold: What kinds of group intervention packages are most effective? How does each of the preceding variables separately and in interaction contribute to outcome? What characteristics of those children/youths or their parents can best utilize a given model of group therapy or a particular intervention? In addition, questions about optimal group conditions such as size and coleadership should be considered.

How does the group therapist find answers to the questions that these complex tasks stimulate? To begin, one certainly should draw on clinical experience and intervention theory. Another way is to explore the available research on group interventions. The third possibility is to make use of research methods, either as an independent researcher or a collaborator in a research project designed to answer the questions of concern. In most cases when a practitioner does research, he or she works with others. As a research collaborator, the first role of the group therapist is the careful definition of goals, either those used by the organization that is offering a treatment program or those that the clients have developed for themselves with the help of the group and therapist. Only in those approaches oriented toward helping the client or the group as a whole to achieve goals can outcomes be readily evaluated. Thus, at the very least, the group therapist can contribute to the research process by the careful formulation of goals for and with the participants, parents, and/or teachers.

The group therapist may facilitate the research process in many other ways. As a member of the research team, he or she can inform the research specialists of what information would be most useful for the clinician. He or she can also advise the researcher of the practical implication of therapy models, which may point to relevant outcome measures. As an expert in the therapeutic role, this individual can assist in the development of a treatment manual, a prerequisite for outcome research. The group therapist can also be instrumental in the formulation of questions the research is designed to answer. It is her or his questions that are the most relevant to the field. Ethical issues sometimes arise in carrying out research. The group therapist, usually sensitive to such issues, can advise the researcher as to what is appropriate or questionable. He or she has particular importance in preexperimental pilot studies. Often, he or she will observe phenomena, undetected by the researcher, that might be a source of error. Finally, the practitioner can serve as experimental or control therapist for the youth groups or serve as a supervisor and/or trainer of the therapists. However, group therapists can be only as effective as they are knowledgeable about the research task, research methods, research design, and the population being served. One of the most important areas in which practitioners should become familiar is how to access a body of measures that can be used to determine the outcome of a given treatment or to determine characteristics of group process that impinge on outcome.

MEASUREMENT PROCEDURES FOR INDIVIDUALS

Group therapists can use a number of measurement procedures to evaluate the outcome of their practice. The most common ones are checklists and rating scales by parents and teachers, self-rating checklists and inventories, self monitoring, extra-group observations by others, role-play tests, sociometric tests, goal attainment scaling, knowledge tests, and social impact measures. Most of these measures can be used equally well to evaluate the outcome of individual and family treatment as well as parent training, and are not specific to group conditions although specific uses in groups will be pointed out. Each of these measures will be described briefly as they have been used in evaluation of outcomes as the result of group interventions with children and parents.

Parent/Teacher Ratings of Child Behavior

At times, significant others, such as parents or teachers, may fill out standardized rating scales or practitioner-designed scales to assess or determine progress of group members. The advantages of ratings of children and adolescents by teachers and parents include the following (Piacentini, 1993):

1. Rating scales form a standardized format for the collection of data, thereby reducing the subjectivity inherent in judgments by observers.
2. Rating scales and checklists draw on the informant's past experience with the child, thereby minimizing day-to-day variability noted in direct observations.
3. Rating scales are efficient and economical to use in terms of time and cost.
4. Rating scales are sensitive to revealing situations that are relatively rare (e.g., fire setting).
5. Rating scales permit a broad analysis of problems or an in-depth analysis of specific areas such as depression, conduct disorders, or hyperactivity.

6. Rating scales provide quantifiable information regarding the severity and frequency of both positive and negative behaviors and other attributes.

For these reasons, most research that evaluates outcomes in group therapy, in addition to other measures, employs some form of rating scales of children by parents, teachers, or other significant individuals.

Some rating scales are general (broad-band scales) and help in the process of identifying and differentiating a wide range of problems. One of the most commonly used broad-band scales is the Children Behavioral Rating Checklist (CBCL; Achenbach, 1991; Achenbach & Edelbrock, 1983). The CBCL is designed to assess in a standardized format the social competencies and behavior problems of children ages 4 through 16 as reported by their parents or others who know them well (Achenbach, 1991). Social competence is assessed by up to 40 questions measuring the amount and/or quality of the child's involvement in sports, nonsport activities, organizations, chores or jobs, friendships, family, and school. The behavior problems section lists many childhood problems, the frequency of which parents are asked to rate. Space is also provided for parents to list and rate items that are not specifically included in the checklist. Test-retest reliability for nonreferred samples that Achenbach (1991) reported is generally very high. Achenbach (1991) also presents "stability" data comparing checklists completed before treatment began with those obtained 6 and 17 months later. Overall, the behavior-problem scores appear to be reasonably stable and yet almost all show posttreatment decreases in problem behaviors, which indicates sensitivity for clinical use.

In addition, scales to be rated by parents or teacher are available for more specific or narrow-band behavioral problems. The Conner's Parent Scale and the Teacher Rating Scale (Conners, 1990; Rosenberg & Beck, 1986) are used with parents or teachers when hyperactivity is being evaluated. The Eyberg Child Behavior Inventory (Eyberg, 1980; Eyberg & Robinson, 1983) is commonly used when the presenting problem is in the area of conduct disorders for children ages 2 to 17. Some 36 items are rated on two dimensions: a seven-point frequency scale and a yes-no scale indicating whether the behavior is a problem.

In the treatment of depression, the most frequently used rating scale is the Children's Depression Inventory (Kovacs, 1981). Versions for children and parents exist. Both consist of 27 items that assess behavioral, cognitive, and affective manifestations of depression. Though parental agreement is high, child/parent agreement is quite low. Test-retest reliability is moderately acceptable.

Self-Report Strategies

Self-report is a method that requires the subject to describe his or her response to a set of statements or questions (Reynolds, 1993). The statement or question may ask for a response about the subject's mental state, the degree of agreement with a given belief, or a choice between two or more personal performance possibilities in a given situation. Self-report has a number of advantages. Foremost is the fact that for internal phenomena, such as cognitions or mental state, the best observer is the client. His or her unique perspective is an important part of any assessment of a given individual. Self-report instruments enable the client to report systematically on behaviors, beliefs, expectations, or internal emotional states related to a specific target or to a general problem area. The specific checklist or rating scale used depends on the theme of the group or on the specific target problem the client has identified.

According to Reynolds (1993), a number of issues impinge on the effective use self-report measures. One of these is developmental issues. Obviously, the same questions or statements cannot be presented to 7-year-old children as to middle-school youths. Self-monitoring skill level, reading comprehension, physical and cognitive development, and other factors are quite different from one stage of development to the next. A second concern is the willingness of a child or adolescent to self-disclose. Furthermore, there is almost no way of monitoring the accuracy of responses. Many children and adolescents answer the questions so as to place themselves in the best light (Kazdin, 1992, p.

238). This has been referred to as a *social desirability error*. A third issue is the strength of such psychometric properties as reliability, validity, and normative information. All too often in the use of nonstandardized self-reports, these psychometric properties are overlooked.

Rating the Group Experience

One type of self-rating scale is the Post Session Questionnaire (PSQ) in which participants rate their own responses to each group session. These are in the form of 6 to 12 questions administered to all the members and the therapist at the end of every session. There are two major purposes for this action. The first is to gain information as to how members evaluate the various components of the each session and general "consumer" satisfaction with the program. Second, the practitioner can estimate how well various group factors are perceived by the youths and how the therapist's perception is at variance with that of the members. No one questionnaire is appropriate for every group. The post-session questionnaire in Figure 4.1 was developed for a general therapy group of adolescents in a day treatment program for adjudicated adolescents.

Self-Monitoring

Self-monitoring requires the client to record his or her own behavior or thoughts or feelings at specified intervals or under specific conditions in a systematic manner. Self-monitoring may involve the client in either tallying his or her behavior as it occurs or rating his or her overt or covert behavior (e.g., degree of anxiety) periodically (e.g., every four hours or once a day at noon). Of all the measurement procedures, self-monitoring is the most "reactive," although reviews of studies of the reactivity of self-monitoring procedures are inconsistent (Shapiro & Cole, 1993). That is, this procedure may or may not independently affect outcome. In fact, self-monitoring is sufficiently reactive to be considered a self-control intervention strategy. This is less a problem for the practitioner than for the researcher, for whom the interpretation of the results is confounded. If self-monitoring is carried out systematically, the results of self-monitoring may contribute to, as well as measure, the ongoing and final outcome of group therapy.

Overt behaviors may also be self-monitored, especially when the frequency of a given behavior indicates the severity of the problem. It has been observed that children more reliably record positive behaviors than negative behaviors. For example, in a group of conduct-disordered children, the youths agreed to tally each time they ignored or walked away from a "challenge" from other children. In a social skills group, young children were asked to count the number of people they have asked to play with them in a week. In an anger control group, adolescents have recorded the frequency with which they used calming procedures, such as counting to 10 or using deep breathing (instead of episodes of their verbal and physical abuse of others). Parents have been asked to count the number of times they used such procedures as time-out, positive reinforcement, and asking for clarification. Examples of overt behaviors monitored by group members in self-control groups include the number of low-calorie foods eaten, the number of occasions the individual refused to have a drink offered by others, and the number of minutes spent in prosocial recreational activities.

The group therapist can readily model the process of self-observation. For example, one therapist informed the group that he was monitoring his own sarcastic statements that he occasionally used when he did not agree with someone. In a group exercise, the members were then encouraged, in pairs, to provide each other with diverse examples and then to describe these to the group as a whole. The others then commented on the appropriateness of the behavior selected to be monitored. (Was it important? Was it doable? Could someone check on it? Was it clearly defined?) In addition, the group provided an opportunity for practicing self-observation with ample feedback from the youths' peers as to the accuracy of their self-monitoring activity. The group also lends itself to monitoring self-observations. Because each member must report publicly to the group the results of his or her observations, group pressure usually exists to carry out the assignment and to be as accurate as possible in the recording. Some group therapists provide incentives for monitoring by reserving an extra portion of group

Figure 4.1 Example of Postsession Questionnaire

1. How useful was this session?

   1-----------2-----------3-----------4-----------5-----------6-----------7-----------8-----------9
   not at all very little somewhat quite a bit extremely

2. How actively involved were the members in today's session?

   1-----------2-----------3-----------4-----------5-----------6-----------7-----------8-----------9
   not at all very little somewhat quite a bit extremely

3. How helpful were members to each other during this session?

   1-----------2-----------3-----------4-----------5-----------6-----------7-----------8-----------9
   not at all very little somewhat quite a bit extremely

4. How much did the members reveal about themselves (their real thoughts, feelings, motivations, and or concerns) during this session?

   1-----------2-----------3-----------4-----------5-----------6-----------7-----------8-----------9
   not at all very little somewhat quite a bit extremely

5. How bored or tired looking were the members during this session?

   1-----------2-----------3-----------4-----------5-----------6-----------7-----------8-----------9
   not at all very little somewhat quite a bit extremely

6. How close did the members feel to each other during this session?

   1-----------2-----------3-----------4-----------5-----------6-----------7-----------8-----------9
   not at all very little somewhat quite a bit extremely

7. How upset or angry were the members during this session?

   1-----------2-----------3-----------4-----------5-----------6-----------7-----------8-----------9
   not at all very little somewhat quite a bit extremely

8. How task oriented were the members during this session?

   1-----------2-----------3-----------4-----------5-----------6-----------7-----------8-----------9
   not at all very little somewhat quite a bit extremely

9. How much did the members control the content and direction of this session?

   1-----------2-----------3-----------4-----------5-----------6-----------7-----------8-----------9
   not at all very little somewhat quite a bit extremely

10. How much conflict was there during this session?

    1-----------2-----------3-----------4-----------5-----------6-----------7-----------8-----------9
    not at all very little somewhat quite a bit extremely

11. How anxious were you during this session?

    1-----------2-----------3-----------4-----------5-----------6-----------7-----------8-----------9
    not at all very little somewhat quite a bit extremely

time for recreation if all the youths successfully complete their ongoing monitoring assignments. Such self-reported high-frequency behaviors can be readily used in time-series research designs (described later).

Observations Outside the Group

The major problem of rating scales and checklists is their failure to take into account the situational variability of most behavior. A great deal of variation of responses by diverse raters on checklists and rating scales can be attributed to the absence of or vague anchor points and the range of time frames during which the behavior occurred. In the children groups, the behaviors to be observed are usually discussed with the members, who may coach their parents in the monitoring process. One group of parents agreed to have the children monitor one parental behavior—which, in most cases, was "yelling"—in exchange for their monitoring one behavior of the child. Not only did this yield an excellent monitoring result but it was also highly therapeutic for the family interactive process.

With younger children, it is possible to monitor their in-group behavior. (Older children have sometimes objected to the presence of an observer taking notes in the group.) In unstructured group events for young children, the behavior tends to replicate behaviors in other unstructured situations and thus provide a meaningful sample of behavior from the real world. However, as soon as any control or structure is placed on the children, the behavior may no longer be typical of behavior found outside the group, and subsequently the researcher must reconsider whether the observations are worth the extensive effort.

In-Group Observational Tools

In order to get a picture of group phenomena, data can also be collected through direct observation of members interacting with each other. There are many different types of observational systems, ranging from simple to highly complex. Because the simple systems have proven to be quite useful and require minimum observer training, they seem to be the most useful to investigate process in the group. The observers are often colleagues who wish to learn the group method, and observing gives them a function in the group. Students who wish to learn about the treatment method may also be employed as observers. Occasionally, when using some of the simpler techniques described here, members of the group have served on a rotating basis as observer.

Of these simpler observation systems, the most commonly used is a fixed interval system of recording who is talking. This system provides the frequency of participation of each of the members and the therapist, from which one can calculate the distribution of participation among the members and the ratio of member to therapist participation. These data correlate highly with outcome in assertive training groups (Rose, 1981). In this method, data are recorded every 30 seconds on who is speaking. Shorter time periods may be used, depending on the skill of the observers.

The major use of observation by group therapists has been individualized categories rather than general observations on everyone. For example, data have been collected by observers on participation in role-playing, off-task behavior, positive reinforcement or praise, and criticism or other negative categories. The specific category to be observed depends on the therapist's preassessment of frequently appearing behaviors in the group and specific research question. If, for example, the group therapist has noted informally that there is too much off-task behavior, it becomes useful to observe systematically on-task and off-task behavior for several meetings. In this case, the observers would be trained to identify off-task behavior and then record on a stopwatch all behavior that is off task. As soon as all off-task behavior stops, the stopwatch is stopped. Using this method, a group indicator of off-task behavior has been created, but not an indication of who is being off task. Another commonly observed behavior has been interruptions of others, especially in groups where aggressive and shy clients are mixed. If one person is speaking and another begins, the act of the second is regarded as an interruption.

Role-Play Tests

Observation of complex interactive behavior in the real world would be an ideal way of obtaining information about a client's success in manifesting goal behavior in situations where it counts. However, because of the limitations cited earlier, observations are rarely used in group treatment as the major source of information. Often, important events such as fights or serious arguments do not occur in the presence of the observer.

One possible substitute for observation of problem events as they occur in the real world is the standardized role-play test. Role-play tests simulate clients' real-life problem situations but the events are controlled by the researcher. The tester presents the client with a description of a number of situations, one at a time, generally 6 to 24 in total. The tester asks the client to imagine being in a given situation and to respond just as if the client were in that situation. The role-played responses are recorded, often on video- or audiotape to facilitate evaluation of the client's responses. The client's responses are evaluated according to some criteria—for example, social appropriateness, probable effectiveness of the response, and long-term consequences of the response. Using the results of the role-play test, the group therapist can determine which type of situations are difficult for the client. In addition, the group therapist can compare the results of a pregroup role-play test with the results of a later one to evaluate the youth's progress.

Role-play tests are most effective when the target response is (at least in part) a response to an interactive situation. Most targets of change in groups fall into this category. Some examples for which the role-play test is suitable are the following: dealing with persons in authority, with persons who impose on the client, with persons the client would like to know better, with asking other people for help, with requesting one's rights, with informal socializing with others, with interviewing or being interviewed, with racist or sexist remarks, with expressing feelings appropriately, and with receiving and giving feedback. In parent groups, skills in reinforcing children, setting limits, solving problems, and giving time-outs are amenable to observation in a role-play test.

Role-play tests also have major limitations. Role-play skill can be confounded with the behavioral skills the test is designed to measure. The extent to which improvement on skills in a role-play test really reflects changes in real-life performance is unclear and has not been empirically established. If role-playing is used as part of intervention, the tests are reactive. For these reasons, other tests should also be used to evaluate outcome in addition to role-play tests. (See Bellack, Hersen, & Turner [1978] for further criticism of the role-play tests.)

Goal Attainment Scaling (GAS)

Goal attainment scaling (Kiresuk, Smith, & Cardillo, 1994) is another procedure commonly used in group therapy, both for defining and determining the level of attainment of individual as well as group goals. Goal definition and goal measurement permit individualization within a standardized format. Goals of group therapy for each individual are selected prior to treatment or during the first two group sessions. These goals are stated in observable and highly specific terms, in terms of realistic levels of achievement, in common sense language, and on a five-point scale ranging from much less than expected outcome to much better than expected outcome.

Group attainment scaling can also be used in group therapy as a way of determining whether group goals are achieved. Group goals usually refer to a change in process such as broader participation, greater cohesion, increase in on-task behavior, greater decision making by members, or reduction of in-group conflict. Group goals cannot be determined immediately. They are best determined when a problem is identified, usually by means of the postsession questionnaire, observations, or group discussions. The best judges for rating the group are a combination of the members and the leader after which the group attempts to come to a consensus.

There are a number of limitations of GAS. (See, for example, Seaberg & Gillespie [1977] for details.) In particular, validity and reliability data have not been especially impressive. Also, conceptual clarity and consistency across studies can often be questioned and major scaling problems have not been resolved. In using the GAS, one must, indeed, proceed with caution in interpreting one's results. In spite of these limitations, GAS remains a useful clinical tool in establishing individualized and group goals and in evaluating their achievement. It is a method for involving youths and their parents in determining their own goals. Thus, the goals tend to be clinically relevant. Also, it is an excellent means of clarifying the specific purposes of treatment. Moreover, few alternatives appear to be available that permit both individualization and standardization for purposes of comparison across groups and across members.

Sociometric Strategies

A number of sociometric measures exist to determine the level of interpersonal liking in groups. The most commonly used is the roster and rating scale sociometric measure (Gottman, Gonso, & Schuler, 1976) in which all children rate each class member on a five-point Likert-type scale on such a question as "How much do you like to play with this person in school?" In several studies, sociometric tests have been used to evaluate outcomes because the goal to increase social skills was met sufficiently well that it had an impact on the relationship of the child to his or her peers. In one study, Edleson and Rose (1981) found that the children in the group social skills training did significantly better in raising their social status than children in the control group on the roster and rating scale method. Hepler and Rose (1988), using a peer nominations method in which the participants "nominated" those they would like most to go camping with, demonstrated that students in the treatment group showed significant improvement on a sociometric rating. Low-status children in the treatment group ($n = 5$) showed significant improvement on negative peer nominations at follow-up.

It should be noted that in both studies the authors were not interested in the pattern of interpersonal attraction in the therapy group but rather in the classroom because a therapy group is only a temporary social phenomenon. Though useful, the sociometric procedures are time consuming and require cooperation of the school and the teachers involved. Some teachers have objected to the use of sociometric devices because the teachers believed the sociometric method by asking children to rate each other in a classroom fixes a permanent social status for each child. However, no evidence of this phenomenon has been observed.

Social Impact Measures

Social impact measures refer to phenomena assessed outside the clinical setting and of importance to the community at large (Kazdin, 1992, p. 361). Examples of social impact measures include whether delinquents are working or in school, arrest records, pregnancy, health problems, and passing grades in school. The initial intent in organizing groups is to address or change social behaviors, but often social impact measures are ignored. The importance of a study is enhanced if such measures are included. These data are obtained directly through observation, in-depth interviews with significant others, and examination of public records.

Knowledge Tests

Whenever information is presented to group members about such topics as drug and alcohol abuse and how it affects the body, it is useful to develop a knowledge test to determine whether the information presented was actually learned. Though not sufficient in itself for determining the major outcomes of therapy, the information test is a valuable adjunct for evaluating one's teaching methods.

Additional Procedures for Collecting Group Data

The purpose of group data collection is to identify dimensions of the group structure, group processes, group performance, and group problems. Insofar as these attributes interfere with or enhance the achievement of individual treatment goals, they are formulated in such a way that the group therapist can eventually act on the information. It should be noted that many of these group data collection procedures provide information as to how individuals respond to the group. As such, these group data also facilitate individual assessment.

There are many different procedures used in collecting data in small groups. To describe most structures and processes, data can be collected on a regular basis throughout the history of the group. Because these data collection procedures are used by group therapists as part of the ongoing assessment process, only those procedures are presented that are minimally intrusive in the treatment process and relatively inexpensive to administer.

A number of procedures for capturing group phenomena have been discussed in the earlier sections. These include the postsession questionnaire, in-group observation, and group goal attainment scaling (GGAS). Three other strategies include (1) obtaining rates of extra-group task completion, (2) attendance and promptness, and (3) rate of dropouts.

The rate of task completion refers to the percentage of extra-group tasks negotiated with each youth at one session and completed and reported on at a later session. Because each client negotiates separate sets of tasks, the group rate is estimated as the average individual rate of completion. This rate has been shown to correlate highly and significantly with behavioral change, as indicated by the findings on a role-play test with adults in assertive training groups (Rose, 1981). The rate of task completion has been used as an index of ongoing session-by-session productivity (Rose & Edleson, 1987) because an extra-group task is a product of the preparation to carry out that task at the previous meeting. Only if that assignment is actually carried out can one consider it an indicator of positive productivity. Low weekly rates of extra-group task completion is a major group problem and usually requires group consideration as soon as it is detected.

The more time spent in a treatment situation, the greater the opportunity for learning. To estimate the group rate of attendance, the statistic used is either the percent of members attending a given meeting and/or the percent of total minutes attended of those that could be attended. For example, if a meeting of a four-person group is 60 minutes long, and one person is 10 minutes late, another leaves 5 minutes early, and a third is absent, then the ratio would be $(240 - 5 - 10 - 60)/240 = .69$. The general formula is $R = (MT - t - AT) / MT$, where R is the percentage of minutes all members are present in the group, M is the number of members in the group, T is time or length in minutes of a meeting, t is the total number of minutes late or leaving early for all members, and A is the number of persons absent.

This measure is useful primarily if attendance is voluntary, although even in groups with involuntary clients, such as the members of adjudicated delinquents on parole, irregularity of attendance is a strong indicator of low cohesion and/or disinterest. Resistance may also be indicated by a high level of lateness. Also, important reasons, such as illness of the client or a family member, and extreme weather conditions may influence the interpretation of the data.

The dropout rate refers to the percentage of youths who leave the group against the advice of the therapist or without soliciting that advice. Groups vary dramatically in their respective dropout rates. If the dropout rate in one group is comparatively high in comparing two different interventions, the mortality error will confound the interpretation. That is, the remaining sample is a self-selected and probably an excessively positive sample. The reasons youths drop out of therapy prematurely is also worthy of study to determine what the therapists might do differently to prevent clients from dropping out.

The collection of group data has primarily been for clinical purposes. The potential for including the findings of group data in evaluation of outcomes is promising. Theoretically, many of these processes—such as cohesion, establishment of pro-therapeutic norms, broad participation, dropping out of treatment, rate of attendance, and rates of homework completion—have been related to outcome. Some of these instruments should become standard procedures in all research processes so that norms can be established and the variance explained by group attributes can be determined.

EVALUATING DATA AND RESEARCH DESIGNS

One can distinguish at least two forms of data analysis: statistical and nonstatistical. The type of statistical plan depends on the nature and number of the comparisons being considered, the distribution and size of the sample, the significance levels that are acceptable, and the sources and size of error. In using statistical analysis, an experiment should have a statistical plan that is appropriate to the questions being asked and the data should meet the assumptions of the test.

Nonstatistical methods involve visual inspection of the data and are commonly used with time-series data (discussed later). When inspecting data visually, one should observe changes in the means of each condition or each subject over time, changes in level of the data, and/or changes in trends. Although useful especially in the early phases of research and in suggesting hypotheses, the rules of decision making are not consistent, and as result, decisions as to the interpretation of the data are often unreliable. Also, visual inspection can usually detect only strong differences.

Research Designs

Evaluations of any sort require a research design that is a logical strategy for collecting data and making inferences about levels of knowledge (Blythe, Tripodi, & Briar, 1994, p. 119). One of the major purposes of research design is to control for internal validity, the degree to which changes in the dependent variable can be attributed to the independent variable. The most commonly used, by far, and the most powerful design in terms of controlling for many of the threats to internal validity is the randomized pretest-posttest control group design.

RANDOMIZED PRETEST-POSTTEST CONTROL GROUP DESIGN

In outcome research, a randomized pretest-posttest control group design with a control group is referred to as the classic or true experimental design. A number of issues must be considered in the evaluation of clinical experimental research with groups or any other population. These issues include internal validity, external validity, power, and construct validity.

Internal Validity

Randomization of subjects in this design permits the assumption that threats to internal validity are equally distributed at known probability rates. This provides a formal benefit of allowing researchers to draw inferences from even faulty data, as the error is distributed by a known probability distribution. Thus, it can be assumed with randomization that subjects in all conditions experience maturation at the same rate, have similar historical influences, have the same amount of learning from the pretests, and are as likely to have test scores that regress to the mean with repeated measurement. Other threats to internal validity, such as differences in mortality (premature termination from the group), are not controlled but can be examined to see whether differences in dropouts in fact exist. There are few good ways of handling data of dropouts statistically, but the investigator should at least know the characteristics and test scores of those who drop out prematurely. Multiple treatment interference (Kazdin, 1992, p. 29) and the effect of previous treatment experience offers other alternative explanations for finding insignificant differences.

External Validity

External validity alludes to the degree to which the results of a study may be generalized across populations of clients, therapists, settings, and times. The reader can get an impression of external validity from a given study if a description of these parameters is available in the original report. (See Campbell & Stanley [1966] and Cook & Campbell [1979] for greater detail on internal and external validity.)

Power

In working with clinical groups and in the absence of funds to pay subjects, it is often difficult to recruit sufficient clients in clinical practice in order to get sufficient power needed to be able to reject null hypotheses. In most agencies, clients appropriate to any one modality tend to come in a few at a time. As a result of insufficient power, studies are carried out in which no significant differences were obtained or could have been obtained because of insufficient power. Thus, in the case of no differences, the reader should note whether there had been sufficient power to reject the null hypotheses in the first place. Prior to any experiment, power should be estimated based on the size of the expected results and the number of subjects the researcher expects to recruit. Even if the design was complete in all other ways, the negative findings would be less relevant if the sample was too small. (See Cohen [1988] for a more detailed discussion of power and the method of determining power for any given sample size and estimated expected differences.)

Construct Validity

Construct validity is the extent to which independent and dependent measures used by the researcher represents adequately the theoretical constructs that the research intends to investigate (Cook & Campbell, 1979). Among others, at least three questions must be considered in construct validity: (1) How well are treatment procedures described and implemented? (2) How specifically are the measurement procedures described? and (3) To what extent are multiple and meaningful measures used in the assessment of outcome? Although no single investigation is sufficient to establish construct validity, every study should be evaluated in terms of its contribution to it.

One excellent way of defining the treatment method is through the use of treatment manuals. Another way to establish adequate implementation is to check periodically whether the therapist in a given condition is actually doing what the instructions dictate. (See Kazdin [1992, pp. 204–206] for a further discussion of treatment integrity.) Otherwise, a negative result may be due to the fact that there was no essential difference between the conditions being compared.

Another way to improve construct validity is to enhance the clinical significance of the concepts used. Clinical significance refers to the practical value or importance of the effect of an intervention—that is, whether it makes any "real difference to the clients or to others" (Kazdin, 1992, p. 349). If most of the children in the experimental group improved by a few points on assertion inventory, and only a few did from the control group, the clinical change would be statistically significant but of little relevance for the therapist or the child. In analyzing the results, the group therapist should look at the relative size of the change and whether a large part of the client population has moved from a problematic frequency to one that is relatively adaptive.

Importance of the dependent measure should also be considered in determining clinical significance. Often, only rating scales, checklists, or self-reports are used as the dependent measures. Exclusive use of paper-and-pencil tests fails to eliminate the hypothesis that the subjects have merely improved their test-taking skills. Furthermore, such measures fail to demonstrate that the changes might generalize to performance in the real world under normal circumstances. The use of social impact data such as recidivism, dropping out of school, attendance at school, police contacts, and chores performed would supplement paper-and-pencil data and provide added clinical significance to statistical significance.

Even when social impact data are used, checklists and inventories need to be included to provide a variety of perspectives such as those of the child, therapy staff, and parents (Achenbach, 1991). Such multiple sources make it possible to document shared as well as diverse perceptions of the nature of the problem and sample a variety of situations perceived as problematic by diverse persons. Thus, multiple sources are likely to increase clinical significance.

EXAMPLES OF RANDOMIZED PRETEST-POSTTEST CONTROL GROUP DESIGN

In the remainder of this section, research on group therapy with children and youths will be briefly described and alternative ways of improving the design will be presented. In all of these studies, there were control or contrast groups; the subjects were randomly assigned to the treatment conditions; the concepts were, for the most part, well defined and well operationalized; in most cases the training is carefully explicated; and the background of the therapist is clearly indicated. In every example, some threats to internal validity have not been controlled. Some studies used only rating scales and self-report measures, which diminished their clinical relevance. One study used only a role-play test. Unfortunately, none of the studies appeared to evaluate the effect of group process, although in one study differences were observed. No studies were found that used the group as the unit of analysis, which is recommended to offset the interdependency of those clients mutually affecting outcomes in the same group. (The assumption of almost all statistical tests is that the data derived from each unit of analysis is independent from all other units.) Few deal with the issues of treatment integrity and clinical significance of the findings. In spite of all these potential errors, many of the studies have approximated the criteria for good research and only a few alternative hypotheses cannot be rejected. Based on the preceding discussion, some weaknesses and strengths with the research will be pointed out in the examples of randomized pretest-posttest control group designs.

Hawkins, Jenson, Catalano, and Wells (1991) tested a cognitive-behavioral skills training program in small groups with 141 incarcerated juvenile delinquents (aged 11 to 18 years). The adolescents were randomly assigned to an experimental skills training or normal institutional treatment group. The researchers used a randomized block design stratified by county of residence, race, and sex. A behavioral role-play inventory, the Adolescent Problem Situation Inventory, was used to assess the subjects' skill levels before and following the intervention.

Experimental subjects had significantly higher posttest scores than did control subjects in all 14 situations, which involved a range of situations, including avoidance of drug use, self-control, and social interaction and interpersonal problem solving. Generalization of skills to untrained role-play situations was found among experimental subjects. No evidence of interactive effects of gender, race, offense type, or pretreatment drug use on posttest skill level was found. The role-play tests were the only measures used as dependent variables. The absence of behavioral observations, rating scales, and social impact measures represents a limitation of this study. As a result, one cannot reject the alternative hypothesis that what the youths learned are solely role-play skills. The interpretations of the findings were further confounded by the addition of a case management program to the group treatment program.

Guerra and Slaby (1990) developed a 12 one-hour session intervention program, based on a model of social-cognitive development designed to remediate cognitive factors identified as correlates of aggression in an earlier study. The subjects were 120 male and female adolescents incarcerated for having committed one or more violent criminal acts (i.e., assault and battery, robber, rape, attempted murder, and murder). The subjects were equally divided by gender, ranged in age from 15 to 18 years, and randomly assigned (balanced by gender) to one of three experimental groups: cognitive mediation training (CMT), attention control (AC), and no-treatment control (NTC).

Compared with subjects in both control groups, subjects in the treatment group showed increased skills in solving social problems, decreased endorsement of beliefs supporting aggression, and decreased aggressive, impulsive, and inflexible behaviors, as rated by staff. Posttest aggression was directly related to change in cognitive factors. With respect to impact measures, no group differences were detected for the number of parole violators up to 24 months after release. The authors also controlled for any group attention by having an attention-group control as well as a no-treatment control. As in most studies, they did not consider group factors such as group cohesion, which probably was higher in the treatment groups than in the placebo groups where the youths did school work and could have provided another explanation of the findings. No attention was given to other group factors such as participation or the establishment of group norms, or subgrouping as contributors to outcome. Though youths were treated in groups, the individual was the unit analysis, which was a threat to the basic assumption of independence of data. The 12 brief one-hour sessions may have explained why there was no difference in parole violations, which may have required more therapy time and more focus. However, the limited number of sessions testifies to the strength of the program in demonstrating the other differences.

Dupper and Krishef (1993) evaluated the effects of a school-based social-cognitive skills training program for 35 sixth- and seventh-graders at risk for school suspension. Subjects were randomly assigned to a treatment or control group using a randomized pretest-posttest control group design. Scores from the Nowicki-Strickland (1973) Locus of Control Scale for Children and the Teacher's Self-Control Rating Scale were used to assess subjects' cognitive and behavioral changes before and immediately following the treatment program. There were significant differences between pretest and posttest scores from both measures for the treatment group but not the control group. However, there were no significant differences between the two conditions. The absence of social impact measures somewhat limits the relevance of the study. With an *N* of 35, there may have been insufficient power to reject the null hypothesis.

Omizo and Omizo (1987a) examined the effectiveness of a group counseling intervention on the self-concept and locus of control in children of divorce. In the original sample, 60 children (aged 9 to 12 years, 34 girls and 26 boys) of divorced parents were randomally assigned to either experimental and control conditions. Posttest results showed significantly greater levels of personal aspiration, less anxiety, a greater feeling of being accepted, and a greater sense of internal control for the subjects in the experimental groups. There were no social impact measures and the changes predicted were only in the area of internal psychological patterns. No follow-up measurement occurred to determine whether changes were maintained. Although attrition occurred for the experimental group, its significance was not examined. Unfortunately, attention was not given either to group process issues or to clinical significance of the findings.

Omizo and Omizo (1987b) studied the effects of group counseling emphasizing elimination of self-defeating behavior on the self-esteem and locus of control (LOC) of children with learning disabilities. The children, aged 12 to 15 years (52 boys and 8 girls) participated in a pretest/posttest control group design. The group program consisted of identifying and disputing self-defeating statements by looking at the consequences of those statements and recognizing the fears associated with giving up those statements. Guided imagery was also used. Posttest data indicated that experimental subjects felt better about themselves and had a more internal perception of LOC on some measures of the Locus of Control Inventory for Three Achievement Domains (LCITAD; Bradley et al., 1977) than did control subjects. Outcome data did not include either observation, behavioral, group process, or social impact measures.

Nonequivalent Control Group Design

In all the preceding research designs, the assumption is that the subjects have been randomly assigned to one of the various conditions of treatment. Sometimes, for ethical reasons, because of too small a sample or because of organizational concerns, randomization is not possible. When a similar group is chosen that does not receive the experimental intervention, the design incorporates a nonequivalent control group. It controls possible effects of history, maturation, and multiple treatment interference, but does not control for selection error. One can limit selection bias somewhat by matching subjects on relevant variables such as age, gender, and socioeconomic status. When this is not possible, a careful examination of the populations in each of the conditions needs to be made. If no pretest differences are noted between the experimental and nonequivalent control group, it strengthens the argument that no selection bias can be determined.

One example of a nonequivalent control group design was carried out by Hepler and Rose (1988). They investigated the effectiveness of a multicomponent group approach for improving the social skills of 40 children in two fifth-grade classrooms. One class received the treatment program while the other class served as a control group. Three skills were emphasized: (1) initiating and maintaining a conversation with peers, (2) joining an ongoing activity, and (3) including others in activities. The basic interventions were modeling, rehearsal, feedback, and homework. The measures administered were sociometric ratings using the peer nominations method, a role-play test, and a locus of control test.

Findings showed significant improvement among treatment subjects on sociometric ratings (follow-up) and the role-play test (posttest). Five low-status children in the treatment group showed significant improvement on negative peer nominations (follow-up) and the role-play test (posttest). The classrooms were randomly assigned to the two conditions but the children could not be randomly assigned. Thus, the control group had to be considered as a nonequivalent control condition. The interpretation of the results was confounded by the fact that different teachers led each of the classrooms and the composition of the two groups could not be considered homogenous. There was clearly a selection error and no discussion of clinical significance was presented. The sociometric test concerning classroom relationships could be considered an impact measure because it demonstrated the impact of the program in the perception of others and their relationships to the treatment subjects.

Case-Study Designs

Those designs that evaluate the success of an intervention have been characterized by Kazdin (1992) as case-study designs. Because of their flexibility and relative simplicity, they can be conducted by the informed group therapist without great cost, intrusion into therapy, and the assistance of a research specialist. They differ from narrative case studies in that data are systematically collected throughout and following treatment. While these designs are readily implemented, case-study designs are generally inadequate for making judgments about whether the group intervention is the cause of a positive change.

In case-study analysis, if the group therapist keeps detailed records of what is occurring in the group, what the therapist does, and what clients report they are doing outside of the group, it is possible to estimate progress of the members and to develop rich hypotheses. This estimation begins to cast light on the theories of practice that guide the practitioner. In such a study, one can consider a wide variety of variables that might impinge on outcome, including group process variables. Certainly, suggestions as to how the group might improve could evolve, which could in turn be tested in another group. A series of such groups could eventually lead to an impressive model. Much of developmental research (Thomas, 1984) has followed this paradigm. It should be noted that there are many types of case-study designs, and only a few are discussed here. (For more details, see Kazdin [1992].) The case-study design most readily available to the group therapist is the pretest-posttest design without a control group.

Pretest-Posttest Design

In the pretest-posttest design without a control group, data are gathered prior to the start (at baseline) and then again at the completion of intervention. It may be carried out with one subject or replicated, which, if results are consistent, adds to confidence in its findings and the population to which findings can be generalized. This design allows one to make a judgment as to the magnitude as well as the direction of change. The group therapist might use a follow-up measure to determine whether changes obtained immediately following treatment are maintained at follow-up.

The absence of a control group limits the control the investigator has over a number of alternative hypotheses that may explain any significant shifts in the data from pre- to posttesting. Because only a single measurement (observation or test) is taken before and after intervention, the sample of tests (observations) is limited. Interpretation of differences between pre- and posttreatment are particularly subject to being explained by historical events (e.g., being in an accident, a major earthquake in the area, losing one's job, the onset of migraines). At the very least, one should examine whether such events occurred during therapy.

Because there is no control group, no selection bias can be assumed nor are there differences in rate of mortality. However, characteristics of dropouts should be examined and the number and percentage about those children and adolescents who fail to make use of groups and either remain and suffer or drop out or are driven out. Case studies of failure should be published on a regular basis with an analysis of what went wrong and why, especially when these are data-based case studies. This is an area of research readily available to the practitioner. The best initial methods might be through the use of systematic interviews. Not all dropouts are dropping out because of their experience in the group.

Little is also known about salient characteristics of therapists who conduct children and youth groups successfully. It is possible within studies that are looking at the best outcomes to compare therapists with the best outcomes with those having the worst.

Group therapy with children or youths may be necessary but not sufficient to deal with the complex problems that many clients bring to the group. Often, it is necessary to consider supplementing the children's group with family therapy or parent training. After all, the group will end after several sessions, perhaps for a year duration, but the family will continue until the child leaves the home. Although there is research on both family therapy and parent training groups, combining group therapy for children with one or both of the family approaches may yield far more desired and generalized results. This would be an important topic to investigate.

Finally, most studies evaluate the contribution of group therapy to outcomes. Numerous other variables may contribute to outcome as well such as group process, family relationships and structure, other social supports, parent skill level, and education. Most of the studies cited in this chapter deal with only a few variables at a time. Large samples permit multivariate testing, which would permit one to look at the interactions among contributing variables. It may be possible that nonsignificant findings between experimental and control may interact with other variables, or, when other variables are controlled, be highly significant.

LIMITS OF RESEARCH

A number of problems emerge that may interfere with an efficient and effective research process. These problems often arise out of the fact that researchers as well as staff and clients cannot be treated as if they were objects in a test tube. Often, staff and clients are not adequately involved in the research planning process because the research specialist believes he or she is the expert. If a research design or measures are introduced without major orientation to the agency staff and without their commitment, it seems unlikely that the staff will fully cooperate.

Clients are rarely involved in the research process except as subjects. Human subjects ensure that the expectations of the research staff are explicit. But the clients often may be suspicious and concerned that they are being treated as objects. These concerns have to be dealt with if the research is going to succeed. Of course, involvement of staff and/or group members in the research process influences treatment and may confound the interpretation of the results.

In clinical studies, researchers are sometimes also program developers and have an investment in one particular outcome. They often believe that the experimental condition is better than a contrast or control condition before the experiment is completed. Many times, negative findings are too readily explained away in terms of inadequate training of therapists, too little power, and so on. One equally possible alternative is that, indeed, no differences exist between the experimental and the control groups. Although one cannot accept the null hypotheses based on one study, neither can the null hypothesis be ruled out when adequate levels of significance are not attained. Similarly, the bias of the investigator is more likely to yield positive results compatible with that bias. This may be one of the reasons why replication of many studies with positive results do not yield the same results as the original.

If working within the confines of an organization or agency, the researcher is obliged to develop a program that is compatible with the interests of that agency. Often, major compromises must be realized if research is to be carried out at all. If the program in place is being compared with a new experimental program, loyalties usually exist within the agency for the existing program. Reluctance to learn or try out the new program is also likely. Before research can be carried out in an agency, the relationship of the researcher must first be established and the significance of the research to the agency must be clearly communicated in a dialogue.

In the absence of large grants, the cost of doing good research or program evaluation may be prohibitive. Research designs must be restricted by the amount of funding available. Collecting data requires additional staff time that could be spent directly with the children. Keeping to the requirements of the research design may create great pressures among staff and the clients, as well.

Finally, research cannot answer all questions. Most studies can deal only with a few variables at a time. Even the most sophisticated multianalytic design cannot deal with all the important variables that influence outcomes in groups. The practice of therapists and the theories that guide their practice are as important as the research process itself. In fact, explication of these theories should precede the other research steps.

REFERENCES

Achenbach, T. M. (1991). *Manual for the Child Behavior Checklist/4-18 and 1991 Profile.* Burlington: Department of Psychiatry, University of Vermont.

Achenbach, T. M., & Edelbrock, C. S. (1983). *Manual for the Child Behavior Checklist and the Revised Child Behavior Profile.* Burlington, VT: University Associates in Psychiatry.

Bellack, A. S., Hersen, M., & Turner, S. M. (1978). Role-play tests for assessing social skill: Are they valid? *Behavior Therapy, 9,* 448–461.

Blythe, B., Tripodi, T., & Briar, S. (1994). *Direct practice research in human service agencies. New York: Columbia Press.*

Bradley, R. H., Stuck, G. B., Coop, R. H., & White, K. P. (1977). A new scale to assess locus of control in three achievement domains. *Psychological Reports, 41,* 656.

Campbell, D. T., & Stanley, J. C. (1966). *Experimental and quasi-experimental designs for research.* Skokie, IL: Rand McNally.

Cohen, J. (1988). *Statistical power analysis in the social sciences* (2nd ed.). Hillsdale, NJ: Lawrence Erlbaum.

Connors, C. K. (1990). *Conners' Rating Scales Manual, Conners' Teacher Rating Scales, Conners' Parent Rating Scales: Instruments for use with children and adolescents.* North Tonawanda, NY: Multi-Health Systems.

Cook, T. D., & Campbell, D. T. (1979). *Quasi-experimentation: Design and analysis issues for field settings.*. Chicago, IL: Rand McNally.

Denzin, N. K., & Lincoln, Y. S. (Eds.). (1994). *Handbook of qualitative research.* Thousand Oaks, CA: Sage.

Dupper, D. R., & Krishef, C. H. (1993). School-based social-cognitive skills training for middle school students with school behavior problems. *Children-and-Youth-Services-Review, 15,* 131–142.

Edleson, J. L., & Rose, S. D. (1981). Investigations into the efficacy of short term group social skill training for socially isolated children. *Child Behavior Therapy, 3,* 1–16.

Eyberg, S. M. (1980). Child behavior inventory. *Journal of Clinical Child Psychology, 9,* 29.

Eyberg, S. M., & Robinson, E. A. (1983). Conduct problem behavior: Standardization of a behavioral rating scale with adolescents. *Journal of Clinical Child Psychology, 12,* 347–354.

Gottman, J., Gonso, J., & Schuler, P. (1976). Teaching social skills to isolated children. *Journal of Abnormal Child Psychology, 4,* 179–197.

Guerra, N. G., & Slaby, R. G. (1990). Cognitive mediators of aggression in adolescent offenders: Intervention. *Developmental Psychology, 26,* 269–277.

Hartmann, D. P., & Hall, R. V. (1976). The changing criteria design. *Journal of Applied Behavior Analysis, 9, 527–532.*

Hawkins, J. D., Jenson, J. M., Catalano, R. F., & Wells, E. (1991). Effects of a skills training intervention with juvenile delinquents. *Research on Social Work Practice, 1,* 107–121.

Hepler, J. B., & Rose, S. D. (1988). Evaluation of a multi-component group approach for improving the social skills of elementary school children. *Journal of Social Service Research, 11,* 1–18.

Kaul, T., & Bednar, R. (1986). Experiential group research. In A. E. Bergin & S. L. Garfield (Eds.), *Handbook for psychotherapy and behavior change* (3rd ed.). New York: Wiley.

Kazdin, A. E. (1992). *Research design in clinical psychology* (2nd ed.). New York: Macmillan.

Kiresuk, T. J., Smith, A., & Cardillo, J. E. (Eds.). (1994). *Goal Attainment Scaling: Applications, theory, and measurement.* Hillsdale, NJ: Lawrence Erlbaum.

Kovacs, M. (1981). Rating scales to assess depression in school-aged children. *Acta Paedopsychiatrica, 46,* 305–315.

Nowicki, S., Jr., & Strickland, B. R. (1973). A locus of

control scale for children. *Journal of Consulting and Clinical Psychology, 40,* 148–154.

Omizo, M. M., & Omizo, S. A. (1987a). Group counseling with children of divorce: New findings. *Elementary School Guidance and Counseling, 22,* 46–52.

Omizo, M. M., & Omizo, S. A. (1987b). The effects of eliminating self-defeating behavior of learning-disabled children through group counseling. *School Counselor, 34,* 242–288.

Piacentini, J. (1993). Checklists and rating scales. In T. H. Ollendick & M. Hersen (Eds.), *Handbook of child and adolescent assessment.* Boston: Allyn and Bacon.

Reynolds, W. M. (1993). Self-report methodology. In T. H. Ollendick & M. Hersen (Eds.), *Handbook of child and adolescent assessment.* Boston: Allyn and Bacon.

Rose, S. D. (1981). How group variables relate to outcome in behavior group therapy. *Social Work Research and Abstracts, 17,* 25–29.

Rose, S. D., & Edleson, J. (1987). *Working with children and adolescents in groups.* San Francisco: Jossey-Bass.

Rose, S. D., Rearden, K., & Todar, K. (1994, May). *Some factors contributing to bad group experiences.* Paper presented at the Tenth Annual Symposium for Empirical Foundations of Group Work, Madison, WI.

Rosenberg, R. P., & Beck, S. (1986). Preferred assessment methods and treatment modalities for hyperactive children among clinical child and school psychologists. *Journal of Clinical Child Psychology, 15,* 142–147.

Schellenberg, T., Skok, R. L., and McLaughlin, T. F. (1991). The effects of contingent free time on homework completion in English with senior high school English students. *Child & Family Behavior Therapy, 13,* 1–11.

Seaberg, J., & Gillespie, D. (1977). Goal Attainment Scaling: A critique. *Social Work Research and Abstracts, 13,* 4–11.

Shapiro, E. S., & Cole, C. L. (1993). In T. H. Ollendick & M. Hersen, (Eds.), *Handbook of child and adolescent assessment.* New York: Pergamon.

Thomas, E. J. (1984). *Designing interventions for the helping professions.* Beverly Hills, CA: Sage.

CHAPTER 5

SCHOOL-BASED GROUP TREATMENT FOR DEPRESSIVE DISORDERS IN CHILDREN

Kevin D. Stark, UNIVERSITY OF TEXAS
Susan Swearer, UNIVERSITY OF TEXAS
Dawn Sommer, UNIVERSITY OF TEXAS
Blair Bowen Hickey, UNIVERSITY OF TEXAS
Scott Napolitano, UNIVERSITY OF TEXAS
Cynthia Kurowski, UNIVERSITY OF TEXAS
Margaret Dempsey, UNIVERSITY OF TEXAS

RATIONALE FOR GROUP INTERVENTION WITH DEPRESSED YOUTHS: SCOPE OF THE PROBLEM

Research indicates that a relatively large percentage of youths are experiencing a depressive disorder at any given point in time and the prevalence increases with age and dramatically increases at around the time of puberty. Much of the existing epidemiological research solely reports the prevalence of major depression and overlooks the prevalence of dysthymic disorder. Thus, these figures are an underestimate of the extent of the problem of depression in the general school population.

Why is it equally important to report the prevalence of dysthymic disorder? Research indicates that dysthymic disorder is a serious, long-lasting disturbance that places the youngster at risk for the later development of an episode of major depression and is quite resistant to treatment. It is associated with disturbances in social functioning, and, due to its lengthy duration (average of over three years), can produce social disturbances that may become structuralized (Kovacs, Gatsonis, Paulauskas, & Richards, 1989). When both cases of major depression and dysthymic disorder are considered, between 5 and 7% of the general school population from the fourth, fifth, sixth, and seventh grades may be experiencing a depressive disorder at any given time (Stark, 1990). This figure progressively increases through the junior and senior high grades until it reaches the adult level of approximately 10%. The current prevalence rate for younger elementary-aged children progressively decreases for each successive grade until kindergarten and preschool, where it is very uncommon and associated with extreme chaos or abuse in the home (Kashani, Ray, & Carlson, 1984).

fer from adolescents, and adolescent characteristics differ from those of adults. Furthermore, differences have been found between pre- and postpubertal cases, suggesting that particular physiological traits associated with depression have both a developmental and a neuromaturational basis (Riddle & Cho, 1988). Researchers have delineated several psychophysiological variables that may be implicated in childhood depressive disorders (Burke & Puig-Antich, 1990; Kalat, 1992; Shelton, Hollon, Purdon, & Loosen, 1991), including neurotransmitter systems, neuroendocrine dysfunction, and biological rhythms.

Age and puberty appear to affect most psychobiological markers of depressive disorders in children and adolescents (Burke & Puig-Antich, 1990; Puig-Antich, 1986). To date, there is no identified biological marker of depression that reliably separates depressed individuals from healthy or psychiatric controls (Cowen & Wood, 1991). Future research will continue to examine possible biological markers that are triggered via environmental stresses that influence the expression and progression of child and adolescent depression.

Integrated Model

As noted in previous sections, there is empirical support for the association of cognitive, behavioral, family, and biochemical variables with depression during childhood. Most of the existing research evaluates the association between one of these domains to depression. No research has explored the possible concurrent and relative contribution of these variables to depression in children. One study was designed to identify which cognitive, behavioral, and family variables, from among those associated with the predominant models of depression, would differentiate depressed from anxious and normal control children (Stark, Humphrey, Laurent, Livingston, & Christopher, 1993). Results of this study are described here and have implications for a model of childhood depression and for the treatment model that is discussed later.

It was hypothesized that variables from each of the cognitive, behavioral, and family domains would contribute to the differentiation of the diagnostic groups. It was predicted that a measure that assessed the child's sense of self would, relatively speaking, account for most of the between group variance. Based on the existing social skills research, it was predicted that less appropriate social skills and more inappropriate assertiveness would characterize the depressed subjects, and that the youngsters' depression was supported by maladaptive messages about the self, world, and future from parents and by a dysfunctional family environment.

Results indicated that a combination of seven variables from the cognitive, behavioral, and family domains contributed more to the differentiation of the diagnostic groups than the variables from any single domain. Two significant discriminant functions were identified that accounted for 91% of the between-group variability and that could be used to accurately predict the diagnostic group membership of 71% of the children. The first variable to enter the equation was the children's sense of self, world, and future (Cognitive Triad Inventory for Children: CTI-C; Kaslow et al., 1984), which was followed at the second step by a measure of depressive cognitions (Automatic Thoughts Questionnaire for Children: ATQ-C; Stark et al., 1993). This suggested that the different disorders were characterized by different self-reported cognitions. Further support for this notion was evident in the correlations between the predictor variables and the canonical discriminant functions. The children's ratings on both the CTI-C and ATQ-C were important contributors to the differentiation of the depressed and anxious children and control children, whereas the children's ratings on the CTI-C contributed to the differentiation of depressed children and anxious children. In general, children who had a depressive disorder reported more negative cognitions than anxious or control children.

Although the cognitive variables were the first to enter the equation and accounted for most of the between-group variance, the results indicated that the addition of variables from the behavioral and family domains added to the overall predictive ability of the discriminant functions. Within the behavioral domain, the children's ratings of the degree to which they exhibited impulsive and angry social behaviors differentiated the clinical groups. These social behaviors were especially important predictors for differentiating the depressed and anxious children from the control children. Four variables from the family domain entered the discriminant equation, including: (1) the children's perceptions of the messages that they receive about themselves, their world, and their future from their mothers; (2) the children's perceptions of the messages that they receive about themselves, their world, and their future from their fathers; (3) the quality of the relationships they have with other family members; and (4) the parents' style of managing their families. From reviewing the correlations between the predictor variables and the discriminant functions, it appears as though the children's perceptions of the messages they receive about themselves, their world, and their future from their fathers significantly contributes to the differentiation of depressed children from anxious children.

Implications for Treatment

Results of the research reviewed and the speculative model we have drawn from it have implications for the treatment of children with depressive disorders. It is apparent that the intervention should be a multifaceted one that includes family intervention, parent training, and interventions directed at the child. The family intervention should include the identification of verbal and behavioral interactions that send maladaptive, schema-consistent messages to the depressed child (Stark, Schmidt, Joiner, & Lux, in press b). In other words, the therapeutic question becomes: What are parents and/or other family members communicating to the child verbally and/or through their interactions that would lead to the development and maintenance of the child's negative view of the self, world, and future and other maladaptive schemata? Once the maladaptive interactions are identified, the therapist works with the family to change those interactions. This may take any of many forms, dependent on the therapist's training. From a cognitive-behavioral perspective, it may involve cognitive restructuring procedures to change the beliefs that underlie the participants' behavior, and teaching family members new ways of interacting through education, modeling, rehearsal, coaching, and feedback. Subsequently, a parent would be assigned the homework task of self-monitoring the occurrence of the maladaptive interactions as well as engagement in more adaptive interactions.

When working with the family, it is important to determine whether conflict exists (Forehand et al., 1988), and, if so, its source should be identified and plans should be developed for reducing it. The plans may include marital counseling (Kaslow, Rehm, & Siegel, 1984). Because a reduced rate of involvement in recreational activities was reported for families of depressed children (Stark et al., 1990), it may prove useful to include the scheduling of pleasant activities into the family therapy. Caution and monitoring should occur with this suggestion because it could create more opportunities for family conflict. The reduction in conflict and the engagement in more pleasant activities as a family could enhance the family's sense of cohesion. Research also suggests that it is important to promote the inclusion of the children in some of the important decisions being made by the family (Stark et al., 1990). However, a balance needs to be struck between encouraging the children to participate in the decision-making process and maintaining a sense of the parents functioning as the executive pair who are in charge (Grossman et al., 1983).

The results also have broader implications for parent training. Our results (Stark et al., in press b) argue for the inclusion of a component that teaches parents to be aware of the messages they are communicating to their children. Basic modules could include teaching parents how to communicate positive and realistic messages to their children about the children themselves, the world, and the future. The training should emphasize teaching the use of positive behavior management skills, because a positive approach would send the child positive messages about the self, whereas a punitive approach communicates to the child that he or she is a "bad person." Furthermore, guilt-inducing parental behaviors would lead to a sense of self as worthless, bad, and unlovable. Thus, a common theme throughout the parent training would be to teach the parents to ask themselves: What is the message I am sending to my child about himself or herself through my actions and verbal exchanges?

Results suggest that depression in children is associated with a distortion in self-evaluation rather than a deficiency in information processing (Kendall, Stark, & Adam, 1990). This suggests that an efficacious intervention would be one that teaches depressed children to identify their maladaptive cognitions and modify them or replace them with more adaptive ones. The cognitive restructuring should also be applied to the youngster's social schemata (Stark et al., in press a). In addition, depressed children could benefit from social skills training (Kazdin, 1989; Matson, 1989) accompanied by coping skills training designed to reduce aversive physical arousal. The content of the social skills training should be directed toward teaching the youngsters to behave in a less angry fashion. It would appear that bossiness, stubbornness, frequent complaining, and expressions of anger and jealousy are potential targets for intervention.

Cognitive restructuring interventions should be integrated with the skills training to simultaneously increase engagement in social interactions and coping with self-statements and to reduce negative expectations, negative self-evaluations, and other negative cognitions. In addition, because the comorbid depressed-anxious children reported thinking that others were "picking on them," perhaps reflecting the encoding disturbances noted by Prieto, Cole, and Tageson (1992), the children may need to be taught to more accurately monitor, perceive, and evaluate the behaviors and intentions of others. The children noted that they were quick to anger, felt jealous, became angry when someone else was successful, and felt lonely (Stark et al., in press b), suggesting that cognitive interventions and affective education (Stark, 1990) should be directed toward intervening with the affective nature of the disturbance. Furthermore, these interventions may need to teach children how to monitor their own expression of angry and irritable behavior, as well as encourage the children to engage in more appropriate behavior. Relaxation training could be incorporated into the treatment to help the youngsters cope with and minimize aversive physical arousal. A more detailed description of the group intervention for depressed children, which was designed to address these needs, is included in a later section of this chapter.

SPECIFIC INTERVENTION TECHNIQUES

In the following sections, procedures for remediating the previously mentioned disturbances in depression during childhood are described. The treatment procedures have been adapted from models for the treatment of depressed adults. The self-control procedures have been adapted from those developed by Rehm (e.g., Rehm, Kaslow, & Rabin, 1987); the behavioral procedures have been adapted from a variety of sources, most notably Beck and associates (1979) and Lewinsohn (e.g., Lewinsohn & Graf, 1973); and the cognitive procedures have been adapted from Beck (e.g., Beck, Rush, Shaw, & Emery, 1979). However, the procedures have been altered for children and the medium used to implement them has been changed so that it is engaging for children (see the appendix at the end of this chapter). In essence, the therapeutic rationale and coping skills are taught through "fun" activities. Based on the previously discussed multidimensional model of depression, additional treatment procedures for parents and the family have been integrated into the treatment program. Due to the focus of this book and space limitations, only the group intervention for children will be described. Interested readers are referred to Stark, Rouse, and Kurowski (1994) for a description of the parent training and family therapy procedures.

The intervention program begins with affective education. This component provides the children and group leader with a common language and understanding of depression. It also serves as the primary vehicle for helping the youngsters tune in to their emotions, behaviors, and the situations that provoke negative thoughts and feelings. Subsequently, the mood enhancement procedures of activity scheduling and mastery experiences are used to provide them with some means of controlling their emotions and consequently to provide the youngsters with some distance from their depressogenic thinking. At this point, the group leader uses a number of self-control and behavioral procedures to learn more about the children and to help them acquire additional skills for controlling their depressive symptoms.

The overall goal of treatment is change at the level of core schemata (the most central rules for deriving meaning from daily interactions). The cognitive restructuring procedures—and both directly and indirectly, all of the procedures described in this chapter—are used to produce this change. A variety of cognitive procedures are used throughout treatment as opportunities arise, and a number of sessions are devoted to teaching the youngsters how to independently use cognitive restructuring. Included among the cognitive procedures are cognitive restructuring, cognitive modeling, behavioral assignments, problem solving, and self-instructional training.

A number of rules are followed when using the cognitive procedures. The therapist begins by using the techniques in a tentative, probing fashion as he or she tests to see if the children are ready for cognitive change. In the beginning of treatment, the group leader is primarily responsible for identifying and restructuring the participants' thinking. As treatment progresses, the children are taught to identify their own maladaptive thoughts and schemata, and to restructure them. The group leader and children then progress from identifying and restructuring automatic thoughts to identifying themes in the children's thoughts that are reflective of depressogenic schemata or core schemata. Finally, the most powerful way to produce cognitive change is through behavioral assignments. Thus, whenever possible, the children are given enactive assignments that require action and provide the youngsters with concrete evidence that is contrary to a dysfunctional schema or consistent with an adaptive schema.

Throughout the group work, the group leader is consulting with the youngsters' parents and teachers to teach them how they can support the therapeutic efforts. In addition, concurrently, the parents are engaged in parent training. The goals of the training are to teach the parents (1) positive methods for managing their children's behavior, (2) noncoercive methods for disciplining their children, (3) personal anger management skills, (4) self-esteem enhancement procedures, (5) empathic listening, and (6) recreation. If it is evident that the family is dysfunctional, then family therapy is instituted immediately. After completion of the parent training sessions, the families who need additional assistance are engaged in family therapy. Those who do not need additional help are finished. The following skills are taught to the family during meetings: (1) how to more effectively communicate, (2) how to use family problem solving, (3) how to communicate positive messages and feelings, (4) how to use conflict resolution skills, and (5) how to change interactions that support maladaptive schemata.

Time Frame

The time frame for the treatment groups varies, depending on the population and the setting. In general, we try to limit the meeting time to one class period. In a middle or high school setting, this works quite well. It also is an appropriate time frame for older elementary school students. However, for children below the fifth grade, we shorten the meetings to 30 to 45 minutes. In the special education and day treatment classrooms, we allow the therapist greater flexibility in the length of each meeting. Typically, the meetings last between 60 to 90 minutes, with the longer meetings occurring with groups comprised of older and more mature participants.

The number of total meetings also varies. With regular education students, we plan on meeting 25 to 30 times over an academic semester. For youngsters in special education or day treatment, we plan on meeting with them for at least a semester, oftentimes more. Given the greater severity of their problems and the greater diversity in the problems they are experiencing (e.g., they may be victims of abuse, experiencing greater chaos in their families, have an impaired parent or sibling, etc.), we plan for more meetings to achieve the therapeutic objectives.

As alluded to earlier, the spacing of the meetings depends on the population and setting. For those children who are enrolled in regular education programs, we meet two times a week for four to six weeks and then cut back to once-a-week meetings. Based on the overall special education curriculum, we typically meet with special education students and day treatment students three to five times a week.

Structure of Sessions

There is some consistency to the structure of the sessions. Each meeting begins with an invitation to the youngsters to contribute their agenda items, which are merged with the therapists' agenda. The "game plan" is then set for the day. After setting the agenda, the group moves into a discussion of the therapeutic homework assigned during the previous meeting, which is followed by a brief reward interval during which time the youngsters who

group members can play a very potent role here as the pros and cons of short-term gains and long-term losses are discussed. As therapy progresses, the therapist's role is reduced. He or she can just ask probe or reminder questions as the children become increasingly responsible for completing the process for one another and for themselves.

The fifth step involves reviewing the possible solutions, choosing the one that is most consistent with goals, and enacting the plan. Sometimes, the depressed youngster's indecisiveness can interfere with this step. However, the supportive prodding of fellow group members can help the child make a good decision. The final step is evaluating progress toward goal attainment and the overall outcome of the chosen solution. If the outcome is a desirable one, the child self-reinforces. If the outcome is undesirable, the youngster reconsiders the possible solutions, chooses an alternative one, and enacts it. Although this step seems relatively straightforward, depressed youths need some help with evaluating the outcome of their actions as they will tend to look for and find information that suggests that their actions represent a personal failure or loss. Thus, once again, processing the results of attempts at using problem solving outside the group provides the depressed youngsters with more objective feedback.

Figure 5.4 Affective Education Sequence, Titles of Activities, and Primary Objectives by Session

2 Emotion Vocabulary
- Learn labels for emotions
- Recognition of internal cues associated with different emotions

3 Emotion Vocabulary II
- Recognition of cues associated with various emotions
- Link between thinking, behavior, and emotions
- Experienced along a continuum of intensity

4 Emotion Charades
- Overt cues associated with various emotions
- Internal cues associated with various emotions
- Link between thinking and emotions
- Introduction to coping

5 Emotion Password
- Link between thinking and emotions
- Coping

6 Emotion Statues
- Link between thinking and emotions
- Coping

7 Emotion Pictionary
- Coping
- Thoughts that interfere with coping
- Link between thinking and emotions
- Personal meaning of event and associated emotions
- Getting motivated to cope

8 Emotion Expression
- External cues
- Link to thinking
- Coping
- Thoughts that would prevent coping
- Motivation to cope
- Personal meaning of event and associated emotions

INTERVENING WITH THE MOOD DISTURBANCE

General Approach

Depressed youths experience a variety of mood disturbances. The first procedure used in the process of trying to improve mood is affective education. Affective education helps the youngsters gain an understanding of the relationship between thoughts, feelings, and behaviors. Thus, it helps them learn the cognitive-behavioral conceptualization of depression. Furthermore, it is used as a means of helping each youngster develop a sense of trust in fellow group members and a sense of group cohesion.

A series of games (see Figure 5.4) are used as the medium for teaching children about their emotions. The activities begin by teaching the children the basics about emotions and then building progressively on this knowledge. Progressively more complex skills are taught and finer distinctions between the emotions are made. As a result of participating in these games, the youngsters learn (1) the names for a variety of pleasant and unpleasant emotions; (2) that emotions are experienced along a continuum of intensity; (3) how to recognize when they are experiencing various emotions as well as signs of what others look like when they are experiencing these emotions; (4) the relationship between thoughts, feelings, and behavior; (5) skills for coping with aversive feelings; and (6) skills for extending the duration of pleasant feelings.

During Emotion Vocabulary, a set of cards is constructed so that each card has the name of an emotion on it. The number of emotion cards created and the sophistication of the emotions on the cards varies, depending on the age of the children. With younger and less mature participants, fewer cards with more basic emotions on them are used (e.g., scared, sad, happy). The game is played by placing the deck of cards in the middle of the table. Players take turns drawing cards from the deck. After selecting a card, the player states the name of the emotion and then describes how the emotion feels and what was happening the last time he or she felt that emotion. The game is played a number of times until the children have learned how each of the emotions is experienced.

The therapist starts to teach the children the cognitive-behavioral perspective during Emotion Vocabulary II. Through this game, the children begin to learn about the relationship between thought, behavior, and emotion. The deck of cards is once again used and the game is played in much the same way as the first one. However, this time, after drawing a card and reading it aloud, describing how it feels, and what was going on the last time they felt that way, the children also describe what a person who is feeling that emotion might be thinking and how that person might be behaving. The objective is to help the children see that their feelings are associated with what they are thinking or imagining.

During Emotion Charades, the link between thoughts, feelings, behaviors, and situations is strengthened, and the children learn how to identify the emotional state of others. Once again, the players take turns drawing cards from the deck, only this time they don't read the name of the emotion out loud. Rather, they read it to themselves and think about what a person who is feeling that emotion might look like and how that child might behave. Then the child acts out the expression of the emotion while the other players try to guess its name. Once an emotion is correctly identified, the player states what the actor did that clued him or her into the name of the emotion, what was happening the last time he or she felt that way, and what he or she might have been thinking at that time.

Emotion Password is played following the same rules as the television game show. A second deck of emotion cards is constructed. The group of children is divided into two teams. Each team has a player who reads the card and gives the clues and another player who tries to guess the name of the emotion (group members take turns in each role). The teams alternate taking turns, giving clues, and trying to identify the emotion. The point value declines with each missed guess by 1. If the teams are having a difficult time identifying the word and the point value has declined to zero, then the word is revealed to the players. After a word is correctly identified, the losing team can get 2 bonus points for a member describing the last time he or she felt that emotion, what it felt like, and what he or she was thinking.

During Emotion Statues, the players take turns being the statue, the sculptor, and the audience. The child who is the sculptor chooses a card from the deck and doesn't let the rest of the group know what it is. Then the sculptor works with the statue to shape his or her facial expression, posture, and so on, so that the other child looks like a person who is experiencing that emotion. Once the emotion is identified correctly, the player who guessed it states the cues that he or she used to identify the emotion, what he or she might might have been thinking, how he or she was behaving, and what was happening the last time he or she felt that emotion.

Emotion Pictionary is played in a similar fashion to the game Pictionary. Each group member takes a turn drawing a card from the deck of emotion cards. Without the other group members seeing the card, the youngster draws some representation of the emotion. The child might draw a "smiley face" to depict the emotion, sometimes the way the youngster scribbles and the end product might capture the emotion, and other times a picture that depicts a situation that is commonly associated with the emotion may be drawn to depict the emotion. The individual who correctly guesses the emotion states what he or she might have been thinking. If it is a positive emotion, suggestions for maintaining pleasant emotions are solicited from the group. If it is an unpleasant emotion, methods for coping with it are discussed.

Emotion Expression is the final activity. This time, after drawing a card from the deck, without divulging the name of the emotion, the actor tries to express the emotion auditorially, through noises that he or she makes. No words are used as the child tries to express the emotion. The player that identifies the emotion correctly describes the thoughts he or she had the last time he or she felt that way. In addition, methods for prolonging pleasant emotions and for coping with unpleasant emotions are discussed.

It is important to note that the games serve as a springboard to much useful therapeutic discussion. In fact, often more time is spent in discussions that spring from the games than in actually playing the games. The therapist has to be alert for opportunities to probe for more depth and for opportunities to connect thoughts and feelings. In addition, the situations that the youngsters describe can be used as opportunities to model problem solving. Furthermore, the discussion naturally lends itself to discussions about how to cope with unpleasant situations and emotions, and how to focus on and maintain pleasant emotions.

Altering Dysphoric Mood through Activity Scheduling

Activity scheduling is the purposeful scheduling of enjoyable and goal-directed activities into the children's day. Enactment of these activities is a powerful coping skill that can be used to moderate depressive affect (Beck et al., 1979). It helps the youngsters obtain reinforcement and combat the withdrawal, passivity, and sedentary and self-destructive life-style associated with an episode of depression. Pleasant activities seem to lift mood through providing the children with distraction from their negative thinking and it may lead to some cognitive restructuring as the children rediscover that life can be enjoyable.

Training children to use this coping procedure is relatively easy. The training procedure begins by helping the children recognize the relationship between engagement in pleasant activities and improvement in mood. Most children readily understand that they feel good when they do fun things. The next step involves identifying mood-enhancing activities. This can be accomplished through group discussions about fun things to do and construction of a list of enjoyable activities. In addition, the children can be asked to keep track of activities that they enjoyed doing between meetings. Once mood-enhancing activities have been identified, the children are instructed to do them on a regular basis, especially when they are starting to experience a decline in mood. For the less compliant or skillful youngsters, the group leader may want to add more structure. This can be accomplished by scheduling, on a weekly calendar, pleasant activities to be enacted each day. We have found that parental support for this schedule is a necessity for success.

Parental permission often is necessary for participation in the activities. Parental support through participation, provision of transportation and financial support, and supervision may be required for some activities. Finally, parents can help by reminding their child to follow the schedule. In addition, they can provide the child with gentle encouragement to get up and follow their schedule. Furthermore, when a parent notices that the youngster's mood is becoming worse, he or she can remind the child to cope by doing something pleasant.

The final step prior to sending the children off to implement an activity schedule is for the children and group to try to identify any impediments to carrying out the plans. As impediments are identified, problem solving is used to develop plans for overcoming the impediments. It also is important for the children to recognize that unforeseen impediments will make it difficult for the plan to be carried out as initially conceived. When something comes up, the children are instructed to try to "go with the flow" and alter their plans to include as many of the scheduled pleasant events as possible. Finally, the children are instructed to self-monitor completion of the activities.

Another class of activities that is important to work into the scheduling is mastery activities. These are activities that usually have some sort of instrumental value. By completing these tasks, the children gain a sense of accomplishment or mastery. When scheduling mastery activities with depressed children, it is important to recognize that the youngsters commonly feel overwhelmed by the thought of trying to complete the task. To combat this, the group therapist works with the children to break tasks down into manageable components. Subsequently, completion of the components is scheduled on a weekly calendar so that they can be manageably and successfully completed. After scheduling, the therapist and children try to identify any potential impediments to completing the tasks. Problem solving is used to develop plans for overcoming the impediments. Once again, parental support is helpful. Parents can remind the children to stay on schedule and they can be instructed to help the children complete the component tasks. Following completion of each component task, the parents are asked to reinforce the children and to help them recognize their success.

Interventions for Excessive Anxiety

Deep muscle relaxation is taught to the children as a skill that they can use to cope with anxious affect and the related symptoms that commonly co-occur with depression. The state of relaxation that is achieved through deep muscle relaxation is positive and peaceful and provides depressed youths with a respite from their anxious and dysphoric moods. Following the suggestions of Ollendick and Cerney (1981), we have modified the relaxation procedure for children. It often takes a number of sessions to teach children to relax, because each training session is shorter than that for adults to match the children's shorter attention span. In addition, before the actual training begins, children have to be taught the names and locations of various muscles (e.g., "biceps"). They also find the procedure somewhat more discomforting than adults, as the procedure seems to be "weird" or "mysterious," "like you're trying to hypnotize me." Consequently, more time is spent preparing the youngsters for the actual procedure by explaining what the therapist is going to do and say and how the children are expected to react and behave. In addition, we have found that it is useful to explain the whole procedure to the children's parents beforehand so that they don't misunderstand what goes on within the group.

During the training, the children are informed that relaxation, like any other skill, takes practice to learn and use effectively. When reading the relaxation script, we alter the standard protocol to include more visual cues (e.g., "Make your right leg tight like a stretched-out rubber band," "Now let your leg muscle go completely loose and wiggly like Jello"). It also is important to pay very close attention to adherence to the instructions. If the children appear to be having trouble following some of the directives, or are doing it incorrectly, then the group therapist has to deviate calmly from the script and help them get on track. In addition, the therapist can watch each child's physical responses and utilize them within the exercise (e.g., "Your arm may begin to twitch as you become more and more relaxed and let go of all your worries and tension"). After the children have successfully relaxed all muscle groups, an audiotape of the complete relaxation exercise is made for them and they are instructed to listen to it, preferably through a Walkman, on a daily basis. The participants identify times when they can listen to the tape without being disturbed and places where they can get comfortable and won't be disturbed. After each time that they complete the exercise, they are instructed to complete a relaxation exercise rating form. This is used to structure the homework exercise, which seems to enhance compliance, and to help demonstrate that they are able to attain a deeper level of relaxation as a result of practicing.

Once the children have clearly mastered the relaxation exercise and can achieve a deep, restful state of relaxation independently through listening to the tape, an abbreviated version of the tape is introduced and they are taught to use relaxation whenever they are just beginning to feel anxious or worried. Typically, this is accomplished by going to a quiet and comfortable spot to listen to the tape. The key to employing relaxation successfully as a coping skill seems to be helping the youngsters to identify the first signs of worry or anxiety and then using the relaxation before the anxiety becomes overwhelming. The affective education training helps the children identify early signs of anxiety and the situations in which it usually occurs. These signs and situations serve as cues that it is time to get out the relaxation tape and find a quiet spot to listen to it. The ultimate goal is to teach children to recognize where they are physically tense and then to use their own internal representation of the section of the tape related to those muscles to relax away the tension.

Cognitive Interventions

One of the ultimate goals of the treatment program is changing the dysfunctional schemata that give rise to the errors in information processing and depressogenic automatic thoughts that are associated with the dysfunctional emotions and behaviors. The class of procedures that are used to directly change depressogenic schemata and depressive cognitions are cognitive restructuring procedures. Included among these are (1) What's the evidence? (2) What's another way to look at it? (3) What if? and (4) behavioral experiments.

The group treatment model has some advantages for using cognitive therapy procedures. The interpersonal situations that arise provoke negative cognitions and changes in mood that can be used as markers to assess the individuals' cognitions. Once identified and verbalized, the depressive cognitions can be processed within the group, which helps the youngsters gain some distance from their thoughts. As the youngsters learn the principles of cognitive therapy, they help each other identify depressogenic thoughts when they occur. It is easier to identify such thoughts in another individual than to identify one's own depressive thoughts. Thus, the group provides the youngsters with an opportunity to begin identifying negative thoughts in a less threatening way, which provides them with practice that can be applied to their own thinking later. It also provides the youngsters with an opportunity to practice using the cognitive restructuring procedures on other depressogenic thoughts while learning how to apply them to their own thoughts.

The cognitive therapy procedures are used throughout treatment as opportunities arise. In addition, cognitive restructuring procedures are taught to the youngsters during a number of meetings. The progression in the training procedure is outlined in Figure 5.5. As treatment progresses, the group becomes increasingly responsible for identifying and restructuring each other's maladaptive cognitions, hence, the therapist becomes involved less directly and more of a coach.

Thus far, the overview of the cognitive restructuring procedures has described the restructuring of automatic thoughts. To restructure schemata, which is the ultimate goal of therapy because it produces an overall change in the way the child perceives himself or herself and the world, it is necessary for the therapist and children to identify schemata through watching for themes in the youngsters' automatic thoughts and through a number of other procedures outlined in Stark (1990). This identification process relies very heavily on the therapist's skills, as the procedure seems to be too demanding cognitively for children. However, once a schema is identified by the therapist, the therapist checks the validity of the schema with the child by asking the child if it fits. At this point, the discussion now turns to descriptions of the different cognitive restructuring procedures that we have found to be useful with depressed youths.

What's the Evidence?

What's the evidence? is a very useful technique that children readily understand. It involves asking children to find evidence that supports or refutes the youngster's automatic thoughts and the schemata underlying them. The first step involves defining the premise that encompasses a child's maladaptive thoughts. Once this has been defined, the therapist and group members work with a child to establish the evidence that is necessary to support or disconfirm the underlying premise. After agreeing on the necessary and sufficient evidence, the therapist, other group members, and child evaluate the existing evidence and establish a procedure for collecting additional evidence. Subsequently, the therapist and child review the evidence and process the outcome. As the youngsters become skillful at identifying maladaptive thoughts and schemata, the children are taught to use the procedure independently as the thoughts arise. It is important to note that it takes an extended period of time to teach children to do this (8 to 12 meetings).

Figure 5.5 Cognitive Interventions by Session

2 Assist participants in seeing link between thinking and emotions as examples arise.

3 Identify thoughts that are associated with emotions.
Note themes in participants' thinking.
Note distortions in participants' thinking.

4 Identify thoughts that are associated with emotions.
Note themes in participants' thinking.
Note distortions in participants' thinking.
Highlight impact of negative thinking.

5 Reconstruct thoughts and images associated with emotions that occurred between sessions—group members help.
Identify thoughts associated with emotions—activity.
Note negative schemata and processing errors.

6 Reconstruct thoughts associated with emotions that occurred between sessions.
Identify thoughts that are associated with emotions.
Observe for pessimism and negative self-evaluations.

7 Identify thoughts that interfere with using coping strategies, getting psyched to cope, and problem solving.
Identify group and individual thoughts that accompany emotions.
Introduce the idea that one's emotional reaction is related to the meaning of the event for the individual.
Develop self-statements for getting psyched up for problem solving.

8 Identify thoughts that interfere with participants trying to cope.
Identify negative thoughts associated with unpleasant emotions.

9 Identify and counter thoughts that interfere with coping.
Generate positive thoughts to encourage problem solving.

10 Identify and counter pessimistic thoughts.
Generate thoughts that interfere with coping and development of counters—activity.
Identify negative thoughts that occur during the meeting.

11 Identify participants' sense of self.

12 Further identify participants' sense of self.
Build a positive sense of self.

13 Identify negative thoughts and positive counters.
Rehearse key positive thoughts.

14 Introduce cognitive restructuring.
Help the participants learn how to tune in to their thoughts—activity.

15 Catch negative thoughts—activity.
Introduce the concept of the thought detective.
Discuss what to do when a negative thought is true.

16 Examples of using What's the evidence?—Practice book activity.
Identify common cues of negative thoughts.
Practice using What's the evidence?

17 Discuss cues to negative thoughts.
Introduce alternative interpretation—activity.
Practice generating alternative interpretation.

18 Extend understanding of alternative interpretation.
Identify negative expectations.
Identify when it is best to use What's the evidence? and What's another way to look at it?

19 Introduce What if?
Practice using What if?

20 Practice use of cognitive restructuring activity.
Establish personal standards.
Identify self-evaluative style.

21–25 Develop a sense of self-efficacy.

26 Rehearse the use of positive coping statements for being assertive.

27 Rehearse the use of positive coping statements for being assertive.

28 Rehearse the use of positive coping statements for being assertive.

What's Another Way to Look at It?

Alternative interpretations is a cognitive restructuring procedure used to broaden the focus of children's thinking. The therapist and group members collaboratively generate a number of plausible, more adaptive, and *realistic* interpretations for what has happened or for a particular belief, asking *What's another way to look at it?* Then they evaluate the evidence for the alternative interpretations and the most plausible one is chosen. Once again, the goal is to teach the children to do this on their own.

What If?

Depressed children often exaggerate the significance of a situation and/or predict unrealistically dire outcomes. *What If?* can be used to help them obtain a more realistic understanding of the meaning of the situation and to see that the probable outcome is not going to be as bad as predicted. When using *What If?* the therapist and eventually other group members acknowledge a child's distressing situation and help the youngster recognize exaggerated interpretations of the significance of the event. These exaggerations are then countered with evidence for a more realistic outcome.

Behavioral Experiments

Perhaps the most efficient way to change children's thinking is to strategically alter behaviors that serve as the base of evidence for the children's thoughts. The alteration in behavior and the resultant change in outcomes provide the children with immediate, direct, and concrete contradictory evidence for an existing maladaptive schema or supportive evidence for a new more adaptive schema. This process of assigning personal experiments requires creativity as the group therapist has to be able first to identify a maladaptive thought or schema, bring it to a child's recognition, work with the child to establish the necessary evidence to support or refute the thought or schema, and then devise a behavioral assignment that tests directly the validity of it. Furthermore, steps have to be taken to ensure that the experiment is actually carried out as planned. In some instances, role-playing ahead of time, imaginally walking through the assignment, or writing a contract may be used to promote compliance.

Intervening with Maladaptive Behavior

Social Skills Disturbances

As noted in an earlier section of this chapter, the social skills disturbance is a multifaceted one that requires a multicomponent intervention. The group therapy format naturally lends itself to intervening with the social disturbances of depressed youths. Each meeting serves as an opportunity to assess the participants' social knowledge, skills, and the impediments (cognitive and affective) to successful interpersonal relationships. In addition, the meetings provide the group therapist with an opportunity to observe and assess the reactions of the other group members to each child. Thus, the group interactions provide the therapist with a nearly complete picture of the participants' social interactions with peers. They also provide a partial picture of how the youngsters interact with adults. Consequently, the social interactions that take place during each meeting serve as ongoing "targets of opportunity" for intervention. As maladaptive social behaviors are observed, they are identified by the therapist, processed (impact on others and child's cognitions that underlie the behavior are discussed), and alternative appropriate behaviors are rehearsed.

Another effective medium for assessing and teaching social skills is games. Most of our social rules (e.g., taking turns, following rules, etc.) are incorporated into successful game playing and most games (excluding video games) represent a structured interpersonal interaction. Thus, the participants' behavioral deficits and excesses as well as their skills are readily apparent during game play. Games usually are engaging and lead to an elevation in mood, which is therapeutic in and of itself.

In addition to the spontaneous interventions, a number of meetings are designed to teach social skills specifically. In particular, emphasis is on teaching appropriate assertiveness as an alternative to the angry, impulsive, and sometimes isolative behaviors commonly associated with depression. Additional social skills that are taught in the content group format that is utilized in the self-contained classroom and day treatment programs are listed in Figure 5.6.

Assertiveness skills are taught through several procedures. We begin the training by using a series of cartoons that illustrate the differences between passive, assertive, and aggressive people. During the presentation of the cartoons, the behavioral characteristics of the cartoon characters are noted along with the reaction of others and results of their behaviors. The therapist and children then take turns role-playing the different behaviors portrayed in the cartoons. Once the children understand the difference between aggressive, assertive, and passive behaviors, and understand the advantages to acting assertively, the training begins with asking to do something enjoyable. The children are asked to provide examples of activities they would like to do with someone. Then the thoughts and images that they might have that prevent them from asking someone to do the activities are discussed. After these expectations are processed and alternative ways of thinking and problem solving are worked through, the group members role-play asking the person assertively to engage in the activity. The therapist and other members provide supportive feedback and coaching. During the role-plays, if a child indicates excess anxiety surrounding making the request, the group helps the youngster develop coping statements that can be used to decrease apprehension. Similar procedures are used to teach giving compliments and asking others to stop annoying behaviors.

Figure 5.6 Social Skills Taught during Group

Give positive feedback to peers.
Express feelings appropriately.
Use the five steps of problem solving when a problem occurs.
Use anger reducers to control anger.
Give compliments.
Accept compliments.
Refuse an unreasonable request from peers.
Follow your own lead (learning how to stay away from negative leaders and not engage in problem behavior).
Be a good listener.
- Maintain eye contact.
- Don't interrupt.
- Give feedback.
- Face the person.

Appropriately ask someone to change his or her behavior.
Express feelings using "I feel" statements.
Compliment yourself.
Use "I'm proud of myself because . . . " statements.
Respect peers.
Focus on yourself.
Express anger appropriately.
Interact with opposite-sex peers appropriately.
Apologize in an appropriate way.
Accept an apology in an appropriate way.
Compromise when there's a problem.
Respond appropriately to an accusation.
Say good-bye in an appropriate way.
Avoid feeding into negative behavior.
Ask appropriate questions to peers and staff.
Ask for help in an appropriate way.
Follow staff instructions (directions).

Self-Evaluation

The last therapeutic procedure to be used with the youngsters is self-evaluation training. Depressed children evaluate their performances, possessions, and personal qualities more negatively than nondepressed youths and their self-evaluations tend to be negatively distorted. In other words, they tend to be unrealistically and unreasonably negative in their self-evaluations. Children can be taught to evaluate themselves more reasonably and positively when it is realistic to do so. During this process, they learn to recognize their positive attributes, outcomes, and possessions.

The first step of the procedure is to identify the existence and nature of the disturbance. This can be accomplished through the group administration of the My Standards Questionnaire-Revised (Stark, 1990). This measure allows the therapist to determine whether the children set unrealistically stringent standards for their performance. Consequently, when they evaluate their performance relative to these standards, the outcome is inadequacy. When this is the case, cognitive restructuring procedures are used to help the children accept more reasonable standards. When a child sets realistic standards, but evaluates himself or herself negatively, cognitive restructuring and self-monitoring are used. The cognitive restructuring procedures of *What's the evidence?* and cognitive modeling may be used. Self-monitoring would be used as a means of solidifying the new self-evaluations as the child is instructed to self-monitor the evidence that supports it. Over the course of treatment, the therapist and children review the evidence with the child that supports the new self-evaluation.

In some instances, the children can benefit from change. The goal of self-evaluation training then becomes helping them translate personal standards into realistic goals, and then to develop and carry out plans for attaining the goals. Typically, this training occurs late in treatment, after the children have acquired the other coping skills and have gained some distance from their negative thinking, which allows them to make and recognize the changes. Following the translation process, the children prioritize the areas where they are working toward self-improvement. Initially, a plan is formulated for producing improvement in an area where success is probable. Problem solving is used to help develop their plans. The long-term goal is broken down into subgoals and problem solving is used to develop a plan that will lead to a subgoal and eventually goal attainment. Prior to enacting the plan, the children and therapist try to identify possible impediments to carrying out the plan. Once again, problem solving is used to develop contingency plans for overcoming the impediments. When the plans, including the contingency plans, have been developed, the children self-monitor progress toward change. Alterations in their plans are made along the way.

TREATMENT OUTCOME RESEARCH

The group therapy format has been utilized for the treatment of depressed youths. This mode of treatment has received practical as well as empirical support. In this section of the chapter, existing research that has evaluated group therapy for the treatment of depressed children and adolescents will be reviewed. The goal of the review is to identify effective group treatment strategies for these youngsters.

Several treatment outcome studies analyzing intervention packages of a cognitive-behavioral nature have been conducted with depressed children and adolescents. These studies typically combine several techniques—such as social skills training, problem-solving training, self-control training, and assertiveness skills training— into a larger treatment package. Overall, these studies provide support for the efficacy of such interventions for the treatment of depressed youths.

One of the first group treatment studies was conducted by Reynolds and Coates (1986). In this investigation with moderately depressed adolescents from a public school, the investigators compared cognitive-behavioral therapy (CBT), relaxation training, and a wait-list control, and found that the CBT and relaxation training groups reported a significantly greater decrease in depressive symptoms relative to youngsters in the wait-list condition (Reynolds & Coates, 1986). A variety of cognitive-behavioral and self-control procedures were taught to the youngsters in the CBT groups, including cognitive restructuring, pleasant activity scheduling, relaxation training, and guided imagery. The relaxation groups received training in progressive muscle relaxation and guided imagery as a means of coping with the distress associated with depressive symptoms. Children in both treatment conditions met twice a week for a total of 10 one-hour sessions.

Another study designed to extend and replicate the study by Reynolds and Coates (1986) has supported the efficacy of group cognitive-behavioral therapy and relaxation training for depressed adolescents in the schools. Cognitive-behavioral therapy, relaxation training, a self-modeling treatment, and a wait-list condition were compared to each other for the treatment of moderately to severely depressed adolescents in the schools (Kahn, Kehle, Jenson, & Clark, 1990). The three treatment groups were completed over 6 to 12 weeks. The cognitive-behavioral condition was based on Lewinsohn's Coping with Depression (CWD) course and emphasized the following skills: (1) self-reinforcement, (2) pleasant events scheduling, (3) social skills, (4) communication, (5) negotiation, and (6) problem solving.

Progressive relaxation skills and mental imagery were taught in the relaxation condition. Treatment folders, workbooks, and homework were utilized in both of these groups. The self-modeling group consisted of subjects learning and practicing "nondepressed" behaviors. These behaviors were videotaped and subjects were required to watch the video of themselves behaving in a nondepressed manner. Results suggest that cognitive-behavioral therapy, relaxation training, and self-modeling facilitate significant increases in self-esteem and decreases in depressive symptomatology.

The aforementioned studies have targeted depressed adolescents and preadolescents in the schools. Studies have also been conducted that examine the efficacy of group interventions for depressed elementary school students. Teaching self-control techniques and behavioral problem solving to depressed children also produced a decrease in depressive symptoms compared to a wait-list group (Stark, Reynolds, & Kaslow, 1987). In the self-control group, subjects were taught self-monitoring, self-evaluation, and self-consequating. The behavioral problem-solving group focused on self-monitoring, problem solving, and pleasant activity scheduling. Both group interventions were effective, with moderately depressed elementary school students as subjects in the two groups reporting significantly less depression at posttesting compared to a wait-list condition.

School-based group interventions for moderately depressed youths have effectively remediated depressive symptomatology. The preceding studies illustrate the efficacy of several cognitive-behavioral interventions delivered in a group format. Additionally, these interventions have been successful in elementary school, middle school, and high school.

Other cognitive-behavioral interventions such as social skills training, cognitive restructuring, and role-playing have also been found to remediate depressive symptoms in children and adolescents. A social skills training group that met for eight sessions was found to increase prosocial interactions of both aggressive and depressed children (Anderson, Rush, Ayllon, & Kandel, 1987). These authors utilized a basketball program that reinforced prosocial behaviors. The authors concluded that the "fun" format of the group helped to promote generalization of treatment.

A 10-week intervention program for depressed preadolescents compared the effectiveness of role-play and cognitive restructuring techniques (Butler, Miezitis, Friedman, & Cole, 1980). In the role-play condition, a social skill was taught and then the group members participated in a series of role-plays designed to target depressive symptomatology. The cognitive restructuring group focused on identifying negative automatic thoughts, teaching thought substitution, teaching listening skills, and teaching the relationship between thoughts and feelings. Homework assignments were utilized in both treatment conditions. A reduction in depressive symptomatology was found for both techniques; however, the change was most dramatic in the role-play condition.

Additional support exists for the efficacy of role-play techniques with depressed youth. A group designed to develop social competencies, self-evaluation skills, and affective expression reduced depressive symptomatology in adolescents (Reed, 1994). Goldstein's Structured Learning Therapy (SLT) was taught to 18 depressed adolescents. SLT teaches social competencies, appropriate affective expression, and self-evaluation skills. Groups met for 12 one-hour sessions and followed Goldstein's *Skillstreaming the Adolescent.* The treatment subjects demonstrated improvement in depressive symptomatology compared to the control subjects. However, when divided by gender, the female subjects' levels of depression remained unchanged. The author concluded that treatments for depression need to be modified to include gender differences evident in adolescence.

The studies detailed so far support the use of cognitive-behavioral group interventions with moderately depressed youngsters in the schools. A cognitive-behavioral group therapy program has been developed and published for use in the hospital setting. A Program for Innovative Self-Management (PRISM) has been developed that outlines a group therapy treatment utilizing cognitive-behavioral interventions for adolescents (Wexler, 1991). The 16-session program utilizes the following components: self-talk, self-soothing, assertiveness training, and relaxation training. The PRISM workbook is used to teach and reinforce cognitive-behavioral skills. To our knowledge, no treatment outcome studies on the effectiveness of the PRISM program have been conducted. Future research on group interventions should examine the use of these techniques with more severely depressed youngsters.

CONSIDERATIONS

Creating a Group

There are several important points to consider when creating a group for depressed youths, most of which are important considerations for children in general. First, various environmental concerns must be addressed. Specifically, the meeting site must be secured, which is not an easy task within a school. Often, space cannot be found or the space that is available is in a public location. This does not work well, as older elementary school youngsters and teenagers are very sensitive to appearances and often do not want their classmates to know that they are in therapy groups. Thus, the location must provide them with anonymity. The location also should provide the group members with privacy. Thus, the location should not be one in which other students or teachers are likely to interrupt. Furthermore, it should not be a room where other students will be walking by and looking in the windows regularly.

A regular meeting time should be established, but this often is quite difficult to accomplish. If a regular meeting time is established and it is during school hours, then the teachers from whose classes the youngsters are being pulled have to be open to the youngsters missing class. Those teachers will need to devise a system for the youngsters to get the class notes and homework assignments and to make up tests and quizzes. This often is not possible, so it becomes necessary to rotate the meeting time so that no single class is missed any more than any other.

In addition to environmental concerns, other factors can influence the group dynamics. One factor to consider when creating a group is the members' level of goodwill (Jacobs, Harvill, & Masson, 1988). Goodwill refers to the degree to which members attempt to be helpful rather than resistant, disruptive, or hostile. A high level of goodwill promotes commitment and trust. When creating a group, members' attitudes toward each other and the leader should be considered. Likewise, the leader's attitude toward group members should not be overlooked. Any negativity could hamper group effectiveness. Another consideration is whether group participation should be voluntary or mandatory. If participation is mandatory, group leaders must be prepared for negativity (Jacobs et al., 1988).

Groups progress through stages. During the planning stage, the group leader specifies goals, tentative objectives, and strategies for the group (Brown, 1994). With respect to the treatment of depressed youths, this stage has already been completed as highly structured treatment manuals have been constructed and can be used to guide the treatment process (Stark & Kendall, 1995). The group leader along with group members establish basic rules and guidelines for running the group. The objective of the rules is to create an environment that minimizes distractions from behavior management issues. In addition, the leader should address pertinent developmental issues when working with children and adolescents. In particular, the leader must take more responsibility and a more active role in groups of younger children. Moreover, age-appropriate materials should be chosen (Dinkmeyer & Muro, 1979; Jacobs et al., 1988). Another aspect of the planning stage involves the development of data collection strategies to evaluate ongoing progress (Brown, 1994).

Initially, members become acquainted with each other and the leader in an effort to promote the development of group cohesion. This task is often accomplished by means of "get-acquainted" exercises (Brown, 1994). Also during this stage, safety needs should be openly addressed. Furthermore, group and individual goals should be integrated to obtain a consensus regarding the overall group focus. In addition, the leader assists members in the identification of personal support systems (Brown, 1994). Most of these tasks can be accomplished during the first session, leaving other sessions for working and termination (Brown, 1994). One of the primary therapeutic goals at this stage is relief of symptoms (Brown, 1994).

During the working sessions, the group engages in purposeful activities directed at goal accomplishment (Brown, 1994; Jacobs et al., 1988). At this stage, the therapeutic goals involve learning new ways of relating to others through open communication and cooperation. As the working sessions progress, the therapeutic goals may evolve. During these later stages, members are encouraged to develop an understanding of the influences of the past on their present functioning (Brown, 1994). Members are also encouraged to openly express feelings and to develop self-understanding (Brown, 1994). Unfortunately, at times, the group must terminate prematurely with one member. During this member's final session, time is taken to focus on him or her. Specifically, the group reviews the exiting member's initial goals and provides him or her with feedback and encouragement (Brown, 1994).

Terminating with the group necessitates planning and should not be taken lightly. During the sessions leading up to the final meeting, the ground for termination is laid. Emphasis is placed on reviewing what has been learned and progress that has been made. Responsibility for improvement is placed with the children. Therapy is directed toward bringing all of the previously learned skills to bare on self-improvement. During the last session, the members review and summarize their individual group experiences and assess personal growth and change (George & Dustin, 1988).

Unique Characteristics

Working with a group of depressed youngsters poses a special problem for the mental health professional in the schools. Due to the disturbances that characterize the disorder, youngsters are often difficult to engage in the group process. In fact, they complain commonly that therapy is boring and a waste of time—a statement that is disheartening for the helping professional to hear. However, such statements are less a reflection on therapy and more a reflection of the nature of depressive disorders in children. Everything in their lives is boring, dark, and gloomy. Why should group therapy be any different?

Overall, the tone of the meetings can be quite negative or flat as the negativity of depressed youths spills out during group meetings. Many depressed youngsters are used to obtaining negative attention while others are experiencing anhedonia, which is the loss of the pleasure response, and thus do not experience pleasure in the group meetings. In general, anhedonic youths derive less pleasure from a restricted range of activities. They feel bored and disinterested much of the time and require a highly engaging activity to become interested in an activity. In addition, they lack a sense of humor, which contributes to an overall flat tone to the group. They may feel hopeless, which leads to a lack of effort and a *Why bother?* attitude toward participation in treatment. The groups tend to have a low energy level as the children are lethargic and experience excessive fatigue. The youngsters may be socially withdrawn, which leads to a failure to engage their peers, a defensive posture, and a minimum of spontaneous speech. They may have difficulty concentrating and get lost in a sea of negative thoughts. They may be indecisive, which leads to dependency on each other and the therapists. In general, the youngsters' behavior is characterized by negative attention seeking.

From the previous discussion it is evident that depressed youngsters are not engaged by the traditional group process of discussing issues, receiving feedback from peers, and confrontation. In fact, while the discussions lead to a failure to engage in treatment, the confrontation and feedback may simply confirm a negative self-image. Obviously, this would be counterproductive to the youngster's treatment. To overcome these counterproductive tendencies, we have modified the treatment format in a number of significant ways. First, and perhaps most importantly, we have attempted to create a set of engaging activities that convey the therapeutic lesson in a fun and concrete fashion. Whenever possible, the therapeutic principle is conveyed through an activity. The activities are designed to get the children motorically, emotionally, and cognitively involved. Experiencing enjoyment has therapeutic benefits in and of itself as it leads to an improvement in mood and outlook, and disconfirms the belief that life is devoid of pleasure. These activities have a therapeutic message embedded within them, and it is believed that the format leads to a more lasting impression.

The group meetings are content driven. In other words, the therapist's agenda is merged with the ongoing process to produce change rather than rely on the group process as the sole vehicle of change. Thus, there are specific therapeutic objectives for each meeting and the overall goal is to teach the youngsters a set of coping skills that they can apply to limit the impact of their depressive symptoms. In addition, the sessions are structured and move quickly to prevent boredom and to prevent the children from getting lost in negative thinking.

The treatment process across sessions should also be flexible and continue with increasing emphasis on homework. At the same time, within-session events such as discussion and role-play should become more related to experiences with homework and other real-life situations. New information and skill building should continue as needed to deal with the appropriate real-life situations. The treatment process should continue until ongoing therapist, parent, teacher, self-report, and observational evaluations indicate skill objectives are met and the children report satisfaction with progress. Additionally, assessment should indicate generalization of skills across settings, behaviors, and time, and the ability to generate new skills as needed.

Limitations

Limitations of the group treatment program described in the previous sections are organized around three areas: (1) limitations of the therapist, (2) impact of comorbidity, and (3) limitations in amount and breadth of existing research. To successfully implement the treatment program briefly described in the preceding paragraphs, the therapist must have a good understanding of cognitive-behavioral therapy as well as of depressive disorders during childhood. It is not possible to simply pick up one of the author's treatment manuals and successfully implement the treatment program. There clearly is an art to implementing the scientifically derived techniques. The art is often overlooked and seems to consist of an ability to blend what is happening in the children's lives with the treatment techniques and agenda for the meeting. This makes the therapy real for the youngsters. It also involves making the group meetings fun for everyone.

Engagement in the therapeutic process is a prerequisite to successful treatment. If the youngsters are not engaged in the treatment process, they will not benefit from it. The therapist must create an atmosphere that leaves the group members feeling safe, nurtured, and open to self-exploration. The therapist also has to think through group membership and be able to construct a group in which the members are compatible and at a similar level of social skillfulness and status. We have experienced some difficulties when group members were not compatible.

As the understanding of depressive disorders during childhood expands, it is becoming apparent that most depressed youths are experiencing additional psychopathology along with the depressive disorder. Common co-occurring disorders include anxiety disorders, conduct disorder, oppositional defiant disorder, and attention deficit hyperactivity disorder (ADHD). The impact of these co-occurring disorders on treatment is not known. It is suspected that the co-occurrence of anxiety disorders does not complicate the clinical picture and that the co-occurrence of a disruptive behavior disorder significantly complicates the clinical picture and may make the youngsters less amenable to change. Another complicating factor that limits the impact of the intervention is the environment within which the youngster lives. Often, a depressed youngster has a parent who is experiencing a depressive disorder or some other psychological disturbance. In addition, the youngsters may come from an abusive or neglectful environment. The co-occurrence of abuse appears to significantly limit the impact of the intervention and adjustments must be made to deal with the impact of the abuse. The presence of sexual abuse appears to create the need for a modified intervention that concurrently addresses this issue.

The treatment of depressive disorders can be a lengthy process that requires a good deal of the mental health professional's time—time that he or she often does not have. To date, it is not possible to tell how long the intervention program must last to achieve maximum therapeutic gains. Our experience suggests that this varies greatly from youngster to youngster. Some depressed youths seem to respond very quickly to the nonspecifics of group therapy and improve quite quickly; others require an extensive intervention program.

It also is important to note that the aforementioned intervention is designed for the depressed youngster who is not suicidal. Due to the potentially infectious nature of suicidal ideation and behavior and the volatility of these youngsters, we do not treat them within a group format. In fact, we do not believe that it is ethical to treat such youngsters within a group format while they are actively suicidal. Individual therapy along with ongoing psychiatric consultation is necessary for successful prevention and intervention with suicidal youths.

SUGGESTIONS FOR RESEARCH AND PRACTICE

It should be apparent from the preceding discussion of the existing treatment outcome research, that a great deal of treatment outcome research remains to be completed. To date, research has essentially demonstrated that group interventions of a cognitive-behavioral nature are effective with moderately depressed youngsters within school settings and somewhat effective with depressed inpatients. However, much additional research remains to be completed before it is possible to conclude that psychosocial interventions are an effective means of treating depressed youths. Once this is apparent, it will be important to complete dismantling studies to identify the necessary and sufficient components to treatment. One related area is the necessity of including parent training, family therapy, and teacher consultation components along with the child intervention.

The impact of comorbidity on treatment outcome is an important area to explore. Are certain developmental issues predictors of treatment outcome? What is the ideal time frame for treatment? In other words, does most of the improvement occur within a certain limited number of sessions with any additional sessions producing negligible change? What is the impact of the new medications on depressive disorders in children? How does their impact compare to that of psychosocial interventions alone, and to a combination of psychosocial and medication treatments? At this time, the number of questions that remain to be addressed through research far exceeds the amount of information that has been empirically derived.

APPENDIX: SESSION-BY-SESSION OUTLINE OF GROUP TREATMENT FOR DEPRESSED YOUTHS

Session 1

Objective 1: Introduce therapist(s) and participants.
Objective 2: Shape accurate expectations.
Objective 3: Set rules for group.
Objective 4: Assess current severity of depressive symptoms.

Session 2

Objective 1: Set the expectation that group members will contribute to the agenda of each meeting.
Objective 2: Build group cohesion and establish labels for emotions.
Objective 3: Give the participants a basis for setting their own goals for treatment.

Session 3

Objective 1: Discuss the participants' concerns. Try to work their concerns into the rest of the agenda.
Objective 2: Continue to build group cohesion. Help the children learn to recognize their emotions and build an understanding of the relationship between thinking, feeling, and behaving.
Objective 3: Introduce the group to problem solving.

Session 4

Once again, emphasize the cues that they used to identify their emotions. Check to see if the list expanded. Ask for examples of problems they came across and emphasize the identification of cues that problems exist. Probe for internal and external cues. Also emphasize the thought-feeling-behavior relationship.

Objective 1: Extend participants' understanding of the mood-thought-behavior relationship.
Objective 2: Extend participants' understanding of problem solving.
Objective 3: Begin to link mood and engagement in pleasant events.
Objective 4: Create individualized pleasant events scales.

Session 5

Discuss the variety of emotions that the children experienced. Try to emphasize cues that helped them recognize that they were facing a problem.
Objective 1: Extend mood-behavior-thought relationship.
Objective 2: Extend pleasant events schedule.
Objective 3: Teach the children how to self-monitor pleasant events.
Objective 4: Extend participants' understanding of how to use problem solving.

Session 6

Emphasize that an unpleasant emotion is a problem to be solved. Emphasize recognition of cues that a problem exists.
Objective 1: Extend mood-behavior-thought relationship and group cohesion.
Objective 2: Personalize and clarify the tie between events, thoughts, and feelings.
Objective 3: Increase engagement in pleasant events.
Objective 4: Personalize problem solving.

Session 7

Emphasize the use of problem solving to cope with unpleasant emotions.
Objective 1: Extend the mood-behavior-event-thought relationship.
Objective 2: Increase engagement in pleasant events.
Objective 3: Improve problem-solving skills.
Objective 4: Extend activity scheduling to mastery tasks.
Objective 5: Fill in graphs of mood and events.

Session 8

Emphasize the use of nonevaluative solution generation (brainstorming) to solve the problems.
Objective 1: Extend ability to recognize emotions.
Objective 2: Extend problem solving to interpersonal situations.
Fill in Mood and Activity Graphs.

Session 9

Discuss attempts to cope with unpleasant emotions and interpersonal problems.
Objective 1: Extend problem-solving skills.

Session 10

Review success with problem-solving, coping with emotions, mastery activities, and pleasant events. Once again, special emphasis should be placed on consequential thinking. Special attention would be paid to looking at long-term consequences.
Objective 1: Introduce relaxation training.
Complete Mood and Activity Graphs.

Session 11

Emphasis is placed on evaluating progress toward long-term goals in particular.
Objective 1: Review and extend problem solving.
Objective 2: Extend relaxation skill. Complete the relaxation exercise in a similar fashion to last week.
Objective 3: Complete Mood and Activity Graphs.

Session 12

Emphasis is on self-evaluation during problem solving and looking at long-term consequences of actions and choices.
Objective 1: Continue to work on self-evaluation during problem solving.
Objective 2: Improve relaxation skill.
Objective 3: Complete Mood and Activity Graphs.

Session 13

Objective 1: Extend relaxation and problem solving.
Objective 2: Extend spontaneous use of problem solving.
Objective 3: Complete Mood and Activity Graphs.

Session 14

Objective 1: Comment on relaxation and problem solving.
Objective 2: Introduce cognitive restructuring.
Objective 3: Help children learn how to tune in to their thoughts.

Session 15

Emphasize the use of self-reinforcing and coping statements.
Objective 1: Practice catching thoughts.
Objective 2: Introduce to cognitive restructuring.

Session 16

Pay particular attention to use of problem solving in interpersonal situations and using self-reinforcing comments for successful use of problem solving. What were the clues that helped them catch their negative thoughts?
Objective 1: Improve understanding of how to use cognitive restructuring.
Objective 2: Improve the children's ability to catch their own thoughts.
Objective 3: Personalize the cognitive restructuring procedure.
Objective 4: Discuss what to do when a negative thought is true.

Session 17

Pay particular attention to the children's ability to catch their thoughts and their use of What's the evidence? and problem solving.
Objective 1: Introduce alternative interpretation.
Objective 2: Demonstrate how this concept can be employed with thoughts.
Objective 3: Tie this concept to the children's own thoughts about various situations.
Objective 4: Introduce a revised self-monitoring of the use of cognitive restructuring procedures homework sheet.

Session 18

Check on how the children are doing at catching their thoughts.
Objective 1: Extend children's understanding of alternative interpretation.
Objective 2: Illustrate notion of negative expectations and have fun.
Objective 3: Bring together all three cognitive restructuring procedures covered so far.

Session 19

Discuss how the children did at trying to use What's the evidence? and What's another way to look at it? Also check on how the children are doing with trying to cope with unpleasant emotions.
Objective 1: Extend children's ability to use cognitive restructuring.
Objective 2: Introduce What if? = What is going to happen?

Session 20

Objective 1: Review coping procedures.
Objective 2: Use cognitive restructuring procedures as a group whenever a negative thought is identified.
Objective 3: Introduce assertiveness.
Objective 4: Rehearse positive preparatory self-statements.

Session 21

Objective 1: Extend assertiveness skills to giving compliments.
Objective 2: Role-play giving compliments to family and friends.
Objective 3: Generate coping statements.

Session 22

Objective 1: Practice assertiveness training (telling people that they are doing something you don't like).
Objective 2: Develop coping statements.

Session 23

Objective 1: Establish standards in a concrete manner.
Objective 2: Introduce self-evaluation.
Objective 3: Demonstrate relationship of self-evaluation to ourselves.
Objective 4: Identify an area for self-improvement.

Session 24

Objective 1: Establish goals.
Objective 2: Break the goals into subgoals.
Objective 3: Help the participants start working toward self-improvement.

Session 25

Objective 1: Continue to work toward self-improvement.
Objective 2: Use problem solving and cognitive restructuring to facilitate change.

Sessions 26 to 28

Content of the sessions is the same as Session 23.

Session 29

Objective 1: Begin preparing for termination.

REFERENCES

Abramson, L. Y., Metalsky, G. I., & Alloy, L. B. (1989). Hopelessness depression: A theory-based subtype of depression. *Psychological Review, 96,* 358–372.

Abramson, L. Y., Seligman, M. E. P., & Teasdale, J. (1978). Learned helplessness in humans: Critique and reformulation. *Journal of Abnormal Psychology, 87,* 49–74.

Akiskal, H. S., & McKinney, W. T. (1975). Overview of recent research in depression: Integration of ten conceptual models into a comprehensive clinical frame. *Archives of General Psychiatry, 32,* 285–305.

Anderson, C. G., Rush, D., Ayllon, T., & Kandel, H. (1987). Training and generalization of social skills with problem children. *Journal of Child and Adolescent Psychotherapy, 4,* 294–298.

Arieti, S., & Bemporad, J. R. (1980). The psychological organization of depression. *American Journal of Psychiatry, 137,* 1360–1365.

Asarnow, J. R. & Bates, S. (1988). Depression in child psychiatric inpatients: Cognitive and attributional patterns. *Journal of Abnormal Child Psychology, 16,* 601–615.

Baron, R. M., & Kenny, D. A. (1986). The moderator-mediator variable distinction in social psychological research: Conceptual, strategic, and statistical considerations. *Journal of Personality and Social Psychology, 51,* 1173–1182.

Beck, A. T. (1967). *Depression: Clinical, experimental and theoretical aspects.* New York: Hoeber.

Beck, A. T., Rush, A. J., Shaw, B. F., & Emery, G. (1979). *Cognitive therapy of depression* New York: Guilford.

Bedrosian, R. C. (1989). Treating depression and suicidal wishes within the family context. In N. Epstein, S. E. Schlesinger, & W. Dryden (Eds.), *Cognitive-behavioral therapy with families* (pp. 292–324). New York: Brunner/Mazel.

Brown, N. W. (1994). *Group counseling for elementary and middle school children.* Westport, CT: Praeger.

Burbach, D. J., & Borduin, C. M. (1986). Parent-child relations and the etiology of depression: A review of methods and findings. *Clinical Psychology Review, 6,* 133–153.

Burke, P., & Puig-Antich, J. (1990). Psychobiology of childhood depression. In M. Lewis & S. M. Miller (Eds.), *Handbook of developmental psychopathology* (pp. 327–339). New York: Plenum.

Butler, L., Miezits, S., Friedman, R., & Cole, E. (1980). The effect of two school-based intervention programs on depressive symptoms in preadolescents. *American Educational Research Journal, 17,* 111–119.

Clarkin, J. F., Haas, G. L., & Glick, I. D. (1988). *Affective disorders and the family: Assessment and treatment.* New York: Guilford.

Cole, D., & Turner, J., Jr. (1993). Models of cognitive mediation and moderation in child depression. *Journal of Abnormal Psychology, 102,* 271–281.

Cowen, P. J., & Wood, A. J. (1991). Biological markers of depression. *Psychological Medicine, 21,* 831–836.

Coyne, J. C. (1976). Toward an interactional description of depression. *Psychiatry, 39,* 28–40.

Dinkmeyer, D. C., & Muro, J. J. (1979). *Group counseling: Theory and practice* (2nd ed.). Itasca, IL: Peacock.

Dixon, J. F., & Ahrens, A. H. (1992). Stress and attributional style as predictors of self-reported depression in children. *Cognitive Therapy and Research, 16,* 623–634.

Downey, G., & Coyne, J. C. (1990). Children of depressed parents: An integative review. *Psychological Bulletin, 108,* 50–76.

Forehand, R., Brody, G., Slotkin, J., Fauber, R., McCombs, A., & Long, N. (1988). Young adolescent and maternal depression: Assessment, interrelations, and predictors. *Journal of Consulting and Clinical Psychology, 56,* 422–426.

George, R. L., & Dustin, D. (1988). *Group counseling theory and practice.* Englewood Cliffs, NJ: Prentice Hall.

Gershon, E. S., Hamovit, J., Guroff, J. J., Dibble, E., Leckman, J. F., Sceery, W., Targum, S. D., Nurnberger, J. I., Goldin, L. R., & Bunney, W. E. (1982). A family study of schizoaffective, bipolar I, bipolar II, unipolar and normal control probands. *Archives of General Psychiatry, 39,* 1157–1167.

Goodwin, F. (1982). *Depression and manic-depressive illness.* Bethesda, MD: National Institute of Health.

Grossman, J. A., Poznanski, E. O., & Banegas, M. E. (1983). Lunch: Time to study family interactions. *Journal of Psychosocial Nursing and Mental Health Services, 21,* 19–22.

Hammen, C. (1991). *Depression runs in families: The social context of risk and resilience in children of depressed mothers.* New York: Springer-Verlag.

Hammen, C., Adrian, C., & Hiroto, D. (1988). A longitudinal test of the attributional vulnerability model in children at risk for depression. *British Journal of Clinical Psychology, 27,* 37–46.

Jacobs, E. E., Harvill, R. L., & Masson, R. L. (1988). *Group counseling strategies and skills.* Pacific Grove, CA: Brooks/Cole.

Kahn, J. S., Kehle, T. J., Jenson, W. R., & Clark, E. (1990). Comparison of cognitive-behavioral, relaxation, and self-modeling interventions for depression among middle-school students. *School Psychology Review, 19,* 196–211.

Kalat, J. W. (1992). *Biological psychology.* Belmont, CA: Wadsworth.

Kashani, J. H., Ray, J. S., & Carlson, G. A. (1984). Depression and depressive-like states in preschool-age children in a child development unit. *American Journal of Psychiatry, 141,* 1397–1402.

Kaslow, N. J., Rehm, L. P., & Siegel, A. W. (1984). Social-cognitive and cognitive correlates of depression in children. *Journal of Abnormal Child Psychology, 12,* 605–620.

Kazdin, A. E. (1989). Childhood depression. In E. J. Mash & R. A. Barkley (Eds.), *Treatment of childhood disorders* (pp. 135–166). New York: Guilford.

Kazdin, A. E., Esveldt-Dawson, K., Sherick, R. B., & Colbus, D. (1985). Assessment of overt behavior and childhood depression among psychiatrically disturbed children. *Journal of Consulting and Clinical Psychology, 53,* 201–210.

Kendall, P. C. (1981). Cognitive-behavioral interventions with children. In B. B. Lahey & A. E. Kazdin (Eds.), *Advances in clinical child psychology* (Vol. 4). New York: Plenum.

Kendall, P. C., Stark, K. D., & Adam, T. (1990). Cognitive deficit or cognitive distortion in childhood depression. *Journal of Abnormal Child Psychology, 18,* 255–270.

Kennedy, E., Spence, S. H., & Hensley, R. (1989). An examination of the relationship between childhood depression and social competence amongst primary school children. *Journal of Child Psychology and Psychiatry, 30,* 561–573.

Kovacs, M., Gatsonis, C., Paulauskas, S. L., & Richards, C. (1989). Depressive disorders in childhood: IV. A longitudinal study of comorbidity with and risk for anxiety disorders. *Archives of General Psychiatry, 46,* 776–782.

Lewinsohn, P. M. (1975). The behavioral study and treatment of depression. In M. Hersen, R. M. Eisler, & P. M. Miller (Eds.), *Progress in behavior modification* (Vol. 1, pp. 16–64). New York: Academic Press.

Lewinsohn, P. M., & Graf, M. (1973). Pleasant activities and depression. *Journal of Consulting and Clinical Psychology, 41,* 261–268.

Matson, J. L. (1989). *Treating depression in children and adolescents.* New York: Pergamon.

Matson, J. L., & Ollendick, T. H. (1988). *Enhancing children's social skills: Assessment and training.* New York: Pergamon.

Mendlewicz, J., & Rainer, J. D. (1977). Adoption study supporting genetic transmission in manic-depressive illness. *Nature, 268,* 327–329.

Mullins, L. L., Peterson, L., Wonderlich, S. A., & Reaven, N. M. (1986). The influence of depressive symptomatology in children on the social responses and perceptions of adults. *Journal of Clinical Child Psychology, 15,* 233–240.

Nolen-Hoeksema, S., Girgus, J. S., & Seligman, M. E. P. (1986). Learned helplessness in children: A longitudinal study of depression, achievement, and explanatory style. *Journal of Personality and Social Psychology, 51,* 435–442.

Ollendick, T. H., & Cerney, J. A. (1981). *Clinical behavior therapy with children.* New York: Plenum.

Poznanski, E. O., & Zrull, J. (1970). Childhood depression: Clinical characteristics of overtly depressed children. *Archives of General Psychiatry, 23,* 8–15.

Preston, J., & Johnson, J. J. (1993). *Clinical psychol-pharmacology made ridiculously simple* (pp. 2–13). Miami: Medmaster.

Price, J. (1968). The genetics of depressive behavior. *British Journal of Psychiatry.* Special Publication #2.

Prieto, S. L., Cole, D. A., & Tageson, C. W. (1992). Depressive self-schemas in clinic and nonclinic children. *Cognitive Therapy and Research, 16,* 521–534.

Puig-Antich, J. (1986). Psychobiological markers: Effects of age and puberty. In M. Rutter, C. Izard, & P. B. Read (Eds.), *Depression in young people* (pp. 341–381). New York: Guilford Press.

Puig-Antich, J., Lukens, E., Davies, M., Goetz, D., Brennan-Quattrock, J., & Todak, G. (1985). Psychosocial functioning in prepubertal major depressive disorders: I. Interpersonal relationships during the depressive episode. *Archives of General Psychiatry, 42,* 500–507.

Reed, M. K. (1994). Social skills training to reduce depression in adolescents. *Adolescence, 29,* 293–302.

Rehm, L. P., Kaslow, N. J., & Rabin, A. S. (1987). Cognitive and behavioral targets in a self-control therapy program for depression. *Journal of Consulting and Clinical Psychology, 55,* 60–67.

Reynolds, W. M., & Coates, K. I. (1986). A comparison of cognitive-behavioral therapy and relaxation training for the treatment of depression in adolescents. *Journal of Consulting and Clinical Psychology, 54,* 653–660.

Riddle, M. A., & Cho, S. C. (1988). Biological aspects of adolescent depression. In G. R. Adams, R. Montemayor, & T. P. Gullotta (Eds.), *Biology of adolescent behavior and development* (pp. 223–249). London: Sage.

Shelton, R. C., Hollon, S. D., Purdon, S. E., & Loosen, P. T. (1991). Biological and psychological aspects of depression. *Behavior Therapy, 22,* 201–228.

Stark, K. D. (1990). *The treatment of depression during childhood: A school-based program.* New York: Guilford.

Stark, K. D., & Brookman, C. (1992). Childhood depression: Theory and family-school intervention. In M. J. Fine & C. Carlson (Eds.), *Family-school intervention: A systems perspective* (pp. 247–271). Boston: Allyn and Bacon.

Stark, K. D., Humphrey, L. L., Crook, K., & Lewis, K. (1990). Perceived family environments of depressed and anxious children: Child's and maternal figure's perspectives. *Journal of Abnormal Child Psychology, 18,* 527–547.

Stark, K., Humphrey, L., Laurent, J., Livingston, R., & Christopher, J. (1993). Cognitive, behavioral, and family factors in the differentiation of depressive and anxiety disorders during childhood. *Journal of Consulting and Clinical Psychology, 61,* 878–886.

Stark, K. D., & Kendall, P. C. (1996). *Treating depressed children: Therapist manual for "Action."* Ardmore, PA: Workbook Publishing.

Stark, K. D., Linn, J. D., MacGuire, M., & Kaslow, N. J. (in press a). The social functioning of depressed and anxious children: Social skills, social knowledge, automatic thoughts, and physical arousal. *Journal of Clinical Child Psychology.*

Stark, K. D., Reynolds, W. M., & Kaslow, N. J. (1987). A comparison of the relative efficacy of self-control therapy and a behavioral problem-solving therapy for depression in children. *Journal of Abnormal Child Psychology, 15,* 91–113.

Stark, K. D., Rouse, L., & Kurowski, C. (1994). Psychological treatment approaches for depression in children. In W. R. Reynolds & H. F. Johnston (Eds.), *Handbook of depression in children and adolescents* (pp. 275–307). New York: Plenum.

Stark, K. D., Rouse, L., & Livingston, R. (1991). Treatment of depression during childhood and adolescents: Cognitive-behavioral procedures for the individual and family. In P. C. Kendall (Ed.), *Child and adolescent therapy: Cognitive-behavioral procedures* (pp. 165–208). New York: Guilford.

Stark, K. D., Schmidt, K., Joiner, T. E., & Lux, M. G. (in press b). Depressive cognitive triad: Relationship to severity of depressive symptoms in children, parents' cognitive triad, and perceived parental messages about the child him- or herself, the world, and the future. *Journal of Abnormal Child Psychology.*

Tems, C., Stewart, S., Skinner, J., Jr., Hughes, C., & Emslie, G. (1993). Cognitive distortions in depressed children and adolescents: Are they state dependent or trait like? *Journal of Clinical Child Psychology, 22* (3), 316–326.

Tsuang, M. T., & Farone, S. V. (1990). *The genetics of mood disorders.* Baltimore: Johns Hopkins University Press.

Venzke, R. C., Farnum, M. K., & Kremer, B. J. (1987). Childhood depression: Identifying children and adolescents in need of mental health services. *American Mental Health Counselors Association Journal, 9,* 28–37.

Wexler, D. B. (1991). *The adolescent self: Strategies for self-management, self-soothing, and self-esteem in adolescents.* New York: W. W. Norton.

CHAPTER 6

ADOLESCENT ANGER-MANAGEMENT GROUPS FOR VIOLENCE REDUCTION

Eva L. Feindler, LONG ISLAND UNIVERSITY, C. W. POST CAMPUS
Maria Scalley, LONG ISLAND UNIVERSITY, C. W. POST CAMPUS

RATIONALE FOR PREVENTING AND INTERVENING WITH YOUTH VIOLENCE

The Problem of Violence

Numerous sources of national data indicate that rates for youth violence in the United States have increased steadily over the past two decades. For example, of those persons arrested for violent crimes in 1990 (i.e., murder, manslaughter, forcible rape, aggravated assault), 23,060 were under age 15 and 1,270 were younger than age 10 (Goldstein, 1992). Further, in the United States, homicide is the second-leading cause of death for all teens and *the leading* cause for African-American teens (Cohall, Mayer, Cohall, & Walter, 1991; Prothrow-Stith & Weissman, 1991). Youths are exposed to violence in the community, in the media, in their own families, and in their schools. Not only are youths victimized at high rates (almost 1 in 15 teenagers was the victim of a violent crime in 1989; Cohall et al., 1991) but they are witnesses, as well. One study reviewed in the 1993 report by the Commission on Youth Violence sponsored by the American Psychological Association indicated that 73% of the eighth graders from Chicago reported seeing someone shot, stabbed, robbed, or killed.

Increases in the perpetration of violence by youths has been seen in both the community and the school. Perhaps the increase in homicide and violent crime among adolescents is related to the resurgence of gang activities (Cohall et al., 1991). According to a review by Goldstein and Glick (1994), delinquent gangs are located in almost all 50 states and are not limited to urban areas. Gang violence seems to be related to maintaining control over three major resources: drugs, territory, and guns. Competition for drug markets, ownership and occupancy rights, and access to a variety of weapons to use in attack and defense of resources all provide the bases for increased violence by gang members (Goldstein & Glick, 1994).

Interpersonal violence rates have also escalated during the last decade in both elementary and secondary school settings. Many school districts report 20 to 30% increases in assaults on students and school staff, harassment, and larceny (Goldstein, 1992). The National Adolescent School Health Survey indicated that one-half of the boys and one-third of the girls had been in at least one fight during the school year and about 13 to 15% of students had been robbed at least once (Cohall et al., 1991). Although most students direct aggression toward other students, the level of assaults on teachers is great enough to result in the development of a "battered teacher syndrome" of persistent stress reactions (Goldstein, 1992).

Finally, many more youths are taking weapons to school either for assault or protection (Webster, Gainer, & Champion, 1993). Goldstein (1992) reported that an estimated 270,000 students carry handguns to school one or more times a year. Further, 41% of boys and 24% of girls said in the School Health Survey that they could easily obtain a gun if they needed one (Cohall et al., 1991). Certainly, the availability of weapons to students who are at risk for aggressive behavior problems escalates the lethality of each interpersonal conflict.

Etiological Factors Related to Youth Violence

Numerous individual and contextual factors occur across the span of a child's development into adulthood that help to explain how patterns of aggression are acquired and maintained. A review of these factors that place children at risk for becoming violent will help to identify at-risk youths and to plan appropriate prevention and intervention programs.

Individual Risk Factors

Biological factors, such as a difficult or uninhibited temperament and the tendency toward impulsivity, will influence not only the child's self-regulation but also his or her interactions with the environments early and other's reactions to him or her (Pepler & Slaby, 1994). Further, there are individual social-cognitive factors as well as psychological skills deficiencies that determine a child's susceptibility to developing aggressive response patterns.

Social-cognitive theory maintains that an aggressive response is not inevitable, but is being contingent on specific thoughts and patterns of processing information about the world (Dodge & Crick, 1990). In fact, the continuity of aggression across developmental phases of a child's life seems related directly to internal and habitual patterns of cognition that support and maintain the individual's use of aggression in interpersonal contexts. For example, a child's perception and appraisal of a potentially aggressive event figures importantly into how that child reacts. Children and adolescents who display angry temper outbursts often accompanied by aggression tend to have difficulties encoding appropriate social cues, make hostile-biased attributions about intentionality of provocation, display an egocentric perspective, and invoke a set of beliefs that endorse aggressive behavior and external blame (Lochman & Lenhart, 1993). In a review of these distortions in social information processing, Feindler (1990b) indicated that aggressive youths misperceive neutral events as intentional, foreseeable, and direct attacks and that this interpretation justifies their aggressive responding. Nonaggressive or competent performance in social conflict situations would necessitate the appropriate encoding and interpretation of cues, response decision making and enactment, and self-control over impulses and intense affective reactions. Youths with deficiencies in these areas are at risk for developing aggressive behavior patterns.

Family Risk Factors

Most theoretical models that have attempted to explain the development of aggressive behavior in children point to the role of early experience. In their review of the influences of parent behavior and social cognition on the development of angry and aggressive behavior patterns, Lochman and Lenhart (1993) indicated that aversive parenting practices and marital aggression witnessed by children are quite influential. Patterson, DeBaryshe, and Ramsey (1989) have indicated that a child's temperament can interact with poor parental discipline exchanges, which may lay the foundation for misperception tendencies and cognitive distortions noted in aggressive children. From the parent perspective, three key variables combine to result in ineffective parent discipline and monitoring and to provide models for the development of aggressive responses: (1) a lack of parental social and child-management skills; (2) aggressive parental behavior and beliefs and child traits such as having a difficult temperament; and (3) disruptive stressors such as marital conflict, financial difficulties, or substance use.

Loeber (1982) enumerated several social and family variables that may predict the development of delinquent behavior patterns: poor parental supervision, lack of parent involvement, poor disciplinary methods, parental rejection, parental criminality and aggressiveness, marital problems, parental absence, poor parental health, composite family handicaps, and low socioeconomic status. Because of separation and divorce, nearly half of all adolescents can expect to live with a single parent at some time. Hence, many adolescents must endure shifting home environments and frequent changes in schools and communities due to increased family mobility (Straus, 1994). All of these family factors can lead to inadequate socialization of the child, who then may fail to assimilate to behavioral norms and societal expectations which, in turn, may result in peer rejection. Unfortunately, peer rejection introduces further problems. As these at-risk youths seek acceptance by a peer group, they tend to affiliate with those where antisocial and aggressive behavior is acceptable and reinforced. A developmental perspective on aggressive behavior suggests that individual and family risk factors will combine with a number of other influences to produce stable patterns of aggression.

School Influences

Pepler and Slaby (1994) review several characteristics of school environments that may contribute to violence: (1) a relatively high number of students occupying a limited amount of space; (2) difficulties avoiding confrontation; (3) the imposition of behavioral routines and conformity, which contribute to feelings of anger and resentment, and (4) poor building design allowing unsupervised "causality zones" such as lavatories, locker-rooms, and so forth (Goldstein, 1992). Other school variables that can lead to student violence include limited support services being available to troubled students who are on the fringes of school life, the nature of leadership, and the type of governance in the school. Goldstein (1992) reported that a firm, fair, consistent principal-leadership style has been associated with low levels of student aggression, whereas arbitrary leadership and severe disciplinary actions characterize schools with high levels of aggression.

Aggressive youths in school typically are poor achievers and may suffer from low self-esteem, frustration associated with learning disabilities, and truancy. These negative behavior patterns are likely to be bothersome to teachers, staff, and peers, setting up negative social perceptions, poor interactions, and rejection at school (Pepler & Slaby, 1994). Although it is unclear whether these school contextual factors are purely causal or simply contributory, there is sufficient agreement that all of the characteristics just described influence the development of patterns of aggression in youths and must be considered in any etiological formulation.

Peer Influences

Children who have developed aversive and aggressive behavior patterns at home are likely to enter school and the social world of their peers and emit a similar interpersonal response. Aggression is highly correlated with rejection, leading to further isolation and poor social skills development (Pepler & Slaby, 1994). Further, youths who are targets of rejection may also become targets of cycles of bullying and victimization in the school (Olweus, 1994). Because establishing and maintaining healthy peer relationships emerges as a critical developmental task related to good interpersonal adjustment, youths who are rejected due to their aggressive behavior patterns tend to develop other deviant behaviors and become associated with deviant peers, perhaps in the form of delinquent gangs (Pepler & Slaby, 1994). Obviously, then, a social context with fewer positive peer interactions becomes the training ground for more frequent and intense aggression and the problem of violence in our schools and communities is exacerbated.

The social skills deficiencies identified in aggressive youths may be the result of negative social experiences, may reflect deficits in specific areas such as assertiveness, communication, and problem solving, and are also linked to the individual social-cognitive factors described earlier (Feindler, 1995). Children and adolescents who become angry in response to perceived provocation resort to temper outbursts and aggressive behavior if they are unable to express frustration and concern verbally, to generate alternate nonaggressive solutions to interpersonal problems, and/or to respond in an appropriate prosocial manner. Clearly, peer influences via socialization experiences are very important in understanding the development and maintenance of aggressive behavior.

Other Influences

Sociocultural, community, and media factors are other influences that expose youths to violence. Straus (1994) suggested that urban, poor, minority youths are at greatest risk of being perpetrators, witnesses, or victims of violence. Researchers have noted that social risk factors such as unemployment, high population density, poverty, and substance abuse are associated with being both victims and perpetrators of violent crimes. Further, population demographics indicate that these risk factors are overrepresented among members of ethnic minority groups (Sampson & Lauritsen, 1994). The combination of social, community, and ethnic factors reflects inequity, racism, and discrimination that may place certain youth at greater risk. Without educational and vocational success, minority youths cannot enter the mainstream path to social and economic resources. Lacking a sense of future stability, at-risk youths have little reason to value their own lives (Prothrow-Stith & Weissman, 1991).

In addition to sociocultural and community issues that place youths at risk for the development of violent behavior patterns, the U.S. culture provides unremitting exposure to violent role models through its mass media. Newspapers, books, comics, radio, music videos, movies, and especially television, all offer a heavy diet of violence that research indicates contributes substantially to both the acquisition of aggressive behavior and the instigation of its actual enactment (Goldstein, 1992). At-risk youths who are frequently disengaged from both educational and social activities, may in fact spend more time watching television and witnessing more reporting of actual violence as well as fictional violence. Goldstein (1992) asserted that this type of media bombardment leads to a substantial decrease in sensitivity, concern, and revulsion toward violence among the general viewing audience. In addition to the direct modeling experiences, this violence exposure cycle also sets up subtle reinforcement systems that maintain repertoires of aggressive behavior.

RATIONALE FOR GROUPS FOR INTERVENING WITH YOUTH VIOLENCE

Although there appears to be a dearth of sound empirical studies of adolescent group psychotherapy, the clear importance of peer relationships and the devaluation of parent and adult authority figures in this developmental stage may make group therapy a more viable option than individual therapy (Cramer-Azima & Richmond, 1989). Grounded in the separation-individuation and achievement of autonomy tasks of adolescent development, group interventions, in general, seem more suited for the adolescent. Corder (1994) suggested that groups offer (1) opportunities for development of peer attachments and empathy with others, (2) perceived protection by the group from adult domination as the adolescent struggles toward independence from parental authority, and (3) a safe environment for youths to give and receive feedback concerning identity issues, life goals, and relationships with others.

The therapeutic goals for effective psychodynamic group psychotherapy, outlined by Didato (1974) several decades ago, still seem appropriate to include in designing interventions for violence prevention and reduction. These goals were to (1) increase the youth's capacity to experience powerful affective responses (positive and negative) without acting them out, (2) increase the youths capacity for empathy and perspective taking, (3) strengthen identification with the therapist as a positive role model, and (4) encourage new behavioral patterns in helping the group resolve intragroup conflict through nonphysical, verbal means.

What makes a group approach seem most appropriate, however, is the opportunity for reeducative, social learning experiences. Cognitive-behavioral research on aggressive youths have focused on a well-identified set of cognitive-mediational deficiencies and distortions in social information processing that are clearly related to the development and maintenance of aggressive behavior patterns. Levels of aggression in adolescents appear related to low levels of problem-solving skills, high endorsement of beliefs supporting aggression, overattribution of hostile intentions, misinterpretation of peer social cues, poor social decision making, poor consequential thinking, and poor interpersonal negotiation skills (Dodge & Crick, 1990; Feindler, 1990a; Guerra & Slaby, 1990). Further, delinquent and aggressive youths are considered deficient in empathy and perspective taking—qualities that correlate negatively with aggressiveness (Goldstein & Glick, 1994a).

Because these social-cognitive responses are crucial both to aggressive and nonaggressive responding and because interpersonal violence must, by its very nature, occur within a social context, the effectiveness of violence-reduction interventions would be enhanced through the use of a group approach. Straus (1994) reported that successful interventions with adolescents coping with violence recognize the peer group as a powerful source of support and connection. Not only can the group context provide training in verbalizing feelings associated with aggression in an acceptable manner but it can also arrange practice opportunities for the development of appropriate peer interactions during conflict and provocation. Finally, since peer feedback may be the most important source of social reinforcement for adolescents, the group would provide structured training and opportunities for peer feedback for newly acquired skills of anger management and nonaggressive responding (Corder, 1994). Group anger-management interventions, then, have the advantage of multiple models and sources of feedback, increased probability of spontaneous and naturalistic provocations, and greater opportunities for direct prompting and reinforcement for prosocial response to peer conflict (Feindler, 1990a).

REVIEW OF RESEARCH SUPPORTING USE OF ANGER MANAGEMENT FOR VIOLENCE REDUCTION

Recent attention to interventions in the prevention of violence and the treatment of youthful perpetrators and victims of violence has been widespread in both the mental health and educational arenas. Clearly, the development and maintenance of aggressive and antisocial behavior problems in youths is a complex and interactional process and multimodal efforts seem most effective. Two phenomena underlie the development of comprehensive anger-management programs. First, cognitive processes such as attributions, coding of social cues, decision-making and consequential-thinking skills, and self-statements have been shown to play a critical role in the development of affective states (i.e., namely anger) that result in aggressive responses to provocation (Wells & Miller, 1993). Second, social and interpersonal problem-solving skills deficiencies are documented as characterizing antisocial youths (Feindler & Guttman, 1994).

Cognitive-behavioral anger-management programs have been developed for use in various settings with a variety of populations to prevent or reduce interpersonal violence. Traditional behavioral approaches to aggression management have been criticized for a failure to address the intense emotional arousal that may accompany impulsive and explosive behavior (Feindler, 1990a). Although aggression can certainly occur in the absence of anger arousal, theorists generally agree that anger can act as a determinant of aggressive behavior and will influence the cognitive processes used to mediate one's response to a perceived provocation. Ample research (see Dodge & Crick, 1990; Waas & Graczyk in Chapter 8 of this book) has demonstrated that an individual's appraisal of situational events as provocation stimuli influences the magnitude of aggressive behavior and that aggressive youths have an anger-inducent hostile attribution bias.

Additionally, the early work by Novaco (1975) conceptualized anger as an affective stress reaction and emphasized the physiological arousal component of anger, which can potentiate impulsive and aggressive behavior. More recent clinicians have described a failure to notice an improvement in clients' interpersonal relationships even though verbal or physical aggression was eliminated from their response repertoires (DiGuiseppe, Tafrate, & Eckhardt, 1994). DiGuiseppe and colleagues (1994) attribute the continued dysfunction and lack of prosocial behavior to residual anger that needs

real-life situations that are currently affecting the lives of the students and to enhance the effectiveness of the intervention via practice and generalization. The techniques are adapted from Feindler and Guttman (1994) and Feindler and Ecton (1986).

Week 1

Didactic: Students are oriented to the group, introduced to facilitators and to each other, and a rationale for the program is provided. They also help construct a set of rules for the group, addressing issues such as participation, confidentiality, listening while others speak, and arriving to the group on time. These are designed to help the group run more effectively and to control disruptive behaviors. Following a general presentation of the behavioral conceptualization of anger, the first session focuses on the physiological arousal that accompanies anger reaction. Students identify their own physiological cues that signal anger arousal and use these cues to prompt a need for anger management. (Cues may include increased heart rate, increased galvanic skin response, and muscle tension.) Students are taught *deep breathing as a means to reduce physiological tension,* redirect their attention away from provoking stimuli toward internal control, and provide a time delay to review their choices before responding.

Finally, students are introduced to the "point system," which will be utilized throughout the group intervention. Students earn points as reinforcers for each homework assignment they complete, for each role-play in which they participate, and for each game in the curriculum that their team wins. At the end of the intervention, the names of the three students with the highest number of points will enter a drawing for a prize.

Exercises

1. Have all students think of a situation in which they were very angry and have them list the physiological and other cues they noticed at the time.
2. Model for students how to use deep breathing when they first recognize they are getting angry.
3. Have students provoke each other and practice using deep breathing to control their response.
4. Practice diaphragmatic breathing by telling students to imagine they have a balloon in their stomachs that they must blow up without moving the rest of their bodies.
5. Introduce the hassle log (see Figure 6.1). Explain how to fill it out using a hypothetical example. Provide a rationale for its use. Explain positive consequences for students who complete the logs (a point will be earned for each completed log). Students who complete logs will also be eligible to participate as actors in role-plays.

Week 2

Didactic: Introduce the concept of ABC's (antecedents, behavior, and consequences) and highlight the sequential analysis of angry interactions. Discuss problematic situations in terms of the situational variables (environment, physiological states), triggers (anger-provoking antecedent event), behavioral reaction, and consequences. Triggers are those events or stimuli (usually external) that evoke an angry response, including aggressive cognitions and behavior. Focus on and explain the direct and indirect nature of a trigger and teach students how to recognize their anger in terms of negative self-statements and physiological cues.

Exercises

1. Divide students into two teams to play "Trigger Finger." Have each team come up with a list of antecedents or external triggers that usually result in an angry reaction. The team with the longest list wins. The exercise may be restricted to a particular context such as school, home, social setting, or whatever.
2. Model how internal triggers in the form of negative self-statements can heighten a conflict. Have students provoke each other and have individual students relate to the group the negative self-statement they generated in response to the trigger. Discuss the effects of a combined internal and external trigger.

Figure 6.1 Hassle Log

Name:________________________ Date: __________ Time:__________

Where were you?	___ Home	___School	___ Outside	___Car/Bus	___Other
What happened?	___ Teased	___Told to do something	___ Someone stole from me		
	___ Someone started a fight with me		___ I did something wrong		
	___ Other ____________________				
Who was that somebody?	___ Friend	___ Sibling	___Another student	___ Parent	
	___ Teacher	___ Another adult	___ Therapist/Counselor		
	___ Other ____________________				
What did you do?	___ Hit back	___ Ran away	___ Cried	___ Ignored	
	___ Broke something	___ Was restrained	___ Told adult	___ Yelled	
	___ Walked away calmly	___ Talked it out	___ Told friend		
	___ Other ____________________				
How did you handle yourself?	___ Poorly	___ Not so well	___ OK	___ Good	___ Great
How angry were you?	___ Burning mad	___ Really angry	___ Moderately angry		
	___ Mildly angry	___ Not angry at all			

Notes:____

____

3. Have students compete in teams to develop lists of both positive and negative consequences for the provoker (i.e., What's the payoff for the one with the trigger finger?). The facilitators should supply a vignette of a provocative situation.
4. Facilitators role-play a provocative event from external trigger to internal trigger to actual response to outcome (i.e., a student thinks a peer or an adult is lying with regard to something that has been promised). Have students identify antecedents, behaviors, and consequences.
5. Have two students role-play a provocative event of their choice and have the group identify antecedents, behaviors, and consequences.

Week 3

Didactic: Teach students the concept of *refuting aggressive beliefs.* Explain that the beliefs one has about why people act in certain ways can lead one to think they are acting aggressively or nonaggressively. Illustrate the difference between aggressive and nonaggressive interpretations of situations and how nonaggressive interpretations of situations will help in controlling one's anger. Introduce the concept of *automatic thoughts* as habitual distorted beliefs that typically accompany anger arousal (DiGuiseppe et al., 1994). Focus on predominant themes: (1) rejection and disapproval by others; (2) purposeful action by others to insult, frustrate, or harm them; and (3) deservingness and unfairness.

Exercises

1. Introduce "All the Reasons Why" by giving students a problematic situation (i.e., someone passed you in the hall and puts her foot out, causing you to trip) and having them generate a list of attributions about why this happened. (Students will probably generate a list of nega-

tive attributions that reflect their bias to interpret events as intentional, hostile, and personal). Move on to step 2.

2. Now have students generate alternative, nonaggressive interpretations of the same situation. Encourage nonintentional, nonhostile, and impersonal attributions. Move on to step 3.
3. Have students engage in a debate as to whether each of the nonaggressive attributions is a plausible explanation.
4. Introduce "Challenge the Belief" by presenting students with several hypothetical conflict situations. For each situation, have students identify the automatic thoughts that occur *between* the provocation trigger and the student's responses.

   For example:

   "He has no right to treat me that way."
   "She's not giving me the respect she should."
   "He's always trying to get me in trouble."

Then ask students to challenge these thoughts by asking for evidence or facts that prove them to be true. Students may debate whether the "evidence" presented is sufficient to support the automatic thought.

Week 4

Didactic: Introduce the topic of assertiveness as an alternative to aggression. Students should discuss definitions of appropriate social behavior and distinguish between assertive, aggressive, and submissive responses. Teach the students to utilize the following four assertion techniques in situations that require quick action and/or when they feel they are being manipulated by another.

1. *Broken Record:* A calm monotone repetition of the student's request of another person is given without any increased volume or threatening gestures.
2. *Empathic Assertion:* Student acknowledges the other person's feeling state while continuing to assert his or her own request.
3. *Escalating Assertion:* Student's responses increase in assertiveness to receive a desired outcome and may include the forewarning of a contingency to be implemented for noncompliance.
4. *Fogging:* Students use this response to short-circuit an aggressive conflict by confusing the provoker with an apparent agreement of a personal criticism or attack.

Exercises

1. Have students sit in a circle and make a request for behavior change by another student (e.g., Give me your belt; Turn off the lights). Assign a technique to each student to demonstrate assertive responses to use when attempting to affect the situation. Students should practice broken record, empathic assertion, and escalating assertion. Facilitators might try this with both reasonable and unreasonable requests (e.g., Go smack that teacher) and ask students what they experienced as different in their internal and external responses.
2. The facilitators now provoke the students. They may choose any of the four techniques for their response and they must identify the technique they have used.
3. Introduce "Circle of Criticism." Have each student make a criticism to the person on his or her right to which they must respond with a "fog" (either an apparent agreement such as "I know you think so" or a "thanks for the compliment"). Continue around the circle several times.

Week 5

Didactic: Introduce the concept of *self-guiding speech* and the use of reminders to guide students' behaviors and help them react differently to perceived provocations. Reminders help students to think before they act, thereby increasing their options for an appropriate response. Students are instructed to "stop," "pause," "kickback," "chill out," and generate other *reminders* specific to the situation at hand. These might include a focus on one's own ability to handle anger ("I'm not gonna lose my cool over this") or a deemphasis of the provoker/provocation ("This guy isn't even worth my attention"). Reminders may be practiced aloud, but ideally they are used internally during provocation as cognitive responses designed to reduce anger arousal.

Exercises

1. Have students generate a list of reminders that they might use in a pressure situation—for example, "slow down," "take a deep breath," and "ignore this."
2. To participate in "It's Hot in the Middle," have students write the best reminders on index cards. With one student in the center of a circle, have the others provoke him or her. This student must respond aloud with the reminder on the card he or she has chosen. Discuss optimal times to use external reminders and how they enhance anger management.

Week 6

Didactic: Teach students to use *reminders in a covert way* so that they may delay reacting to a direct provocation. The emphasis should be on appropriate timing so that the reminder does not occur too early or too late.

Exercises

1. Have a student in the middle of a circle use self-generated covert reminders to deflect provocations. Ask the student to give feedback on which reminders he or she used and how this affected his or her anger control.
2. Have two students role-play a provocative situation in which they must utilize any of the anger-control techniques they have learned. Conduct a brief review of all anger-management techniques practiced thus far. The observing students should make note of all of the techniques they observe.
3. Students can use *Reminder* index cards throughout the week to cue themselves for this cognitive strategy.

Week 7

Didactic: Introduce the topic of *thinking ahead* as a means to help students identify future negative consequences of a present situation. Students are likely to focus on the immediate consequences of their anger rather than the longer-term social consequences (i.e., venting pent-up anger or intimidating another so as to get compliance to their request vs. serious damage in their relationships or reputations [DiGuiseppe et al., 1994]). Explain that consequences can be overt or covert, short or long term, and internal or external. Thinking of consequences in advance can help them substitute an alternative behavior, thereby eliminating the possibility of the negative consequence. Encourage students to elaborate on the burdensome aspects of having a reputation of an aggressive student.

Exercises

1. Have two teams of students generate a list of negative consequences for aggressive behavior. Then have them order the list from the least to most negative consequence. The team with the longer list wins.
2. Have students role-play a provoking event and identify the course of action they would normally have taken. Then have students use reminders (aloud) of negative consequences to substitute an alternative behavior. They should identify the alternative response to provocation they chose and the group can discuss the positive consequences of this choice.

Week 8

Didactic: Introduce the concept of self-evaluation as a means for students to provide themselves with-immediate feedback on how they have handled a conflict situation. These can also be referred to as *after reminders* because they should help guide and reinforce behavior. After reminders can be positive or negative. However, negative ones should be framed in terms of a coping statement. Explain that coping statements can be used before, during, and after a conflict to "remind" and help guide behavior.

Exercises

1. Have students develop lists of positive feedback statements and coping statements they might offer themselves for conflicts avoided,

conflicts resolved, or conflicts that have escalated.

2. Have students role-play provocative incidents while utilizing all of the skills they have learned to date. Have the observing students record and discuss the skills that were used.
3. Have a student stand in the middle of a circle while other students provoke him or her. Have the student explain the strategies used to control his or her anger. Also have the youngstser generate a positive self-evaluative statement regarding his or her performance. Ask the group to give positive feedback, as well.

Week 9

Didactic: Introduce the idea of *problem-solving training* as making choices between anger-control alternatives based on characteristics of the conflict situation. Emphasize the importance of "stop, pause, and think" and have students ask themselves the following series of questions that reflect social problem-solving skills (Slaby & Guerra, 1988):

a. *Problem Definition:* "What is the problem?"
b. *Goal Selection:* "If you were to solve the problem, what would be your goal?"
c. *Number of Facts:* "Would you need any more information?"
d. *Number of Solutions:* "What are all the ways you think you can solve this problem?"
e. *Best Solutions:* "What do you think is the very best solution?"
f. *Second-Best Solution:* "What do you think is the second-best solution?"
g. *Number of Consequences:* "What are all the things that might happen if you did this?"
h. *Evaluate the solution:* "How did it work?"

Not only do these statements represent the sequence of problem-solving strategies best incorporated into anger management training but they can also serve as additional internal reminders that will help the students manage their anger arousal.

Exercises

1. Have students generate solutions to a problem to which there are few or no solutions. This tactic will help students differentiate between situations that have few solutions and those with many alternatives. Use a variety of problem situations previously raised by group members.
2. Present the group with a scenario and have them identify the problem. Then break into teams to generate alternative solutions. Have them come back into one group to discuss the positive and negative consequences of all the possible solutions that they generated and then choose one solution. Help the students determine the effectiveness of that solution.

Week 10

Didactic: Review for students the various skills taught during the program. Discuss the various situational and personal elements that would help them determine which skill to use in which interpersonal situation. Introduce the idea of *barbs.* A barb is a provocative statement (usually a false accusation) given to the student that gives him or her the opportunity to practice skills outside the training situation (Kaufman & Wagner, 1972; Tisdelle & St. Lawrence, 1988). Barbs can be given by fellow group members and staff members. They should, at first, be given with a warning, "I'm going to barb you," then warnings can be faded out. The person delivering the barb should note the student's response and give both positive and constructive feedback. Finally, provide the members of the group with feedback regarding their cooperation, performance, and enthusiasm in the program. Focus on their motivation for change and any observable changes in behavior. Also have each student review his or her own participation. Have them give positive self-evaluative statements to themselves and reinforce observed changes in each other. Encourage students to discuss situations in which their newly learned anger-management skills may not be effective or might even serve to provoke others around them. Prepare students for this possible sense of failing or frustration and discuss coping strategies for these situations. At this time, make appropriate referrals for any students continuing to exhibit difficulty controlling their anger.

Exercises

1. Place on an index card each of the 10 skills (deep breathing, ABC analysis, refuting aggressive beliefs, broken record, empathic assertion, escalating assertion, fogging, reminders, thinking ahead, and problem solving) taught in the program. Each student selects one card at random. After a few moments to think, each student will (a) define/describe the strategy, (b) demonstrate the strategy, and (c) give examples of the best time/situation to implement the strategy.
2. Ask students to describe in detail several conflict situations that have occurred in their own lives. Have students choose another index card. Have each student role-play a scene incorporating a technique he or she has chosen. Observing students should try to identify the technique(s) the role-player is using.
3. The names of the three students who have accumulated the most session points should be put in a hat. The winner's name is drawn from the hat and receives a prize (i.e., gift certificate to a record store).

Illustrative Use of the Program

The format of the curriculum allows for students to bring to the group current issues and problems that are impacting their lives. By discussing and role-playing various scenarios, students learn to adapt their new skills to their present, real-life problems. For example, one young woman in the group shared a scenario where her supervisor at a fast-food restaurant made a hurtful comment toward her. Her response to the hurtful comment was typical for her in provocative situations; she ran out and cried. By bringing this scenario to the group, she was able to explore other ways she might have handled the situation. In acting out a role-play, she tried out a variety of alternative respones to her supervisor's comment. In this particular scenario, the following responses were practiced:

1. *Deep Breathing:* The student takes time to think about what is happening.
2. *Refuting Aggressive Beliefs:* The student comes up with a nonaggressive interpretation as to why her supervisor made that particular statement. (e.g., "She was having a bad day," "Someone upset her," and "She didn't really mean it," etc.).
3. *Empathic Assertion:* The student acknowledges the feelings of the supervisor while standing up for her own rights. (e.g., "You seem to be in a bad mood, but I really wish you wouldn't speak to me like that" or "I know you're upset, but that is no reason to insult me").
4. *Fogging:* The student short-circuits the conflict by introducing humor to the situation and by pretending to agree with the provoker (e.g., "I know you think so" or "Thanks so much").

Another case example involved a young woman and a faculty member who continuously provoked her and many other students. A role-play of situations involving this faculty member gave facilitators a sense of the difficulty in getting along with him. Because the faculty person would be instrumental in the decision to graduate this student, it was decided through role-play that some of the responses involving overt assertiveness may not be appropriate for resolving the situation. Rather than respond angrily, as she previously had, the student utilized a fogging statement the next time she was presented with difficulty from this faculty member (e.g., "I know I'm your favorite student"). She later reported that the faculty member was given a different sample of behavior of the student, which may not fit into his previous assumptions about her and would likely influence his behavior toward her in the future.

ADDITIONAL CONSIDERATIONS WHEN IMPLEMENTING ANGER-CONTROL GROUP INTERVENTIONS

Probably the most important consideration in the application of an anger-control intervention in an agency or school is the support of that institution in its implementation. Without it, an intervention may never get off the ground. This is particularly relevant when a therapist is acting as an outside consultant to the school/agency for the sole purpose of conducting such a group intervention. Although the use of an outside therapist may be preferable with regard to confidentiality and other boundary issues, it may be essential to enlist the involvement of at least one school staff member (even if you already have a co-therapist) who can coordinate the group.

Of great importance in school programs is the leader's ability to relate well to other school personnel, especially administrators and teachers (Berkowitz, 1989). Such internal issues as scheduling, room assignments, and time frame can be worked out in advance by that individual. He or she can also act as a staff observer who can subsequently help students maintain the gains they have made in the group by prompting them to practice those skills. Additionally, by observing the implementation of the intervention, this staff member may now be qualified to apply this intervention to future groups of students.

Another important consideration is the identification of any separate agenda of the school/agency that may interfere with the successful implementation of the group. For example, school administrators may want their eight most aggressive youths to participate in the intervention without considering their appropriateness for the program. Because the success of the intervention relies heavily on members' participation and practice, it is essential that the screening process be conducted by the mental health professional in advance of the group, and that blind referrals are not accepted. Decisions for inclusion/exclusion should be based on information obtained in the screening. An inappropriate group member may undermine the effectiveness of the intervention for the entire group. Ideally, a group should be composed of voluntary individuals who have given their informed consent to participate in the intervention. Often, referrals for treatment of anger and aggression come from someone other than the clients themselves, which makes it more difficult to form a therapeutic alliance (DiGuiseppe et al., 1994).

Students must be mature enough to be task focused, to participate in group discussions, and to relate the philosophy of anger-management training to their lives. Beliefs about anger and aggression and students' attitudes toward changing their anger and aggressive response patterns should be assessed (DiGuiseppe et al., 1994). Parents may also need to be informed and may request an overview presentation prior to the start of the program. This step may actually be crucial in the generalization and maintenance of behavior change because parent discipline practices and parent social cognition may influence the development of the students' anger responses directly (Lochman & Lenhart, 1993). Students' participation (or lack thereof) should not be reflected in their grades, ability to graduate, or participation in any other activity, which may conflict with perspectives held by others at the school. Therefore, careful planning and open communication with school officials are essential to establish an atmosphere in which both parties can reach an agreement with regard to their specific agendas.

Because the ultimate purpose of this group is the reduction of violence through increased anger management and conflict-resolution skills, one must consider seriously the role of violence in the lives of the group members. Violence may be perceived as the only resource for problem solving for a number of the members prior to the group, and many of them may continue to engage in acts of aggression. They may often bring accounts of such violence or intended violence to the group and express profound justification for such aggressive behavior patterns. The therapists must consider the ethical principles under which their profession operates and makes decisions about what their responsibilities are in each individual case. They should consult with a colleague or supervisor who can help them to objectively assess the situation and make a decision about what action, if any, should be taken. Limits to confidentiality concerning group members' self-disclosure may be of concern, should members describe their intentions to harm others.

A final issue refers to the possible need for ongoing or concurrent treatment. Although anger-management skills are helpful in the reduction of aggressive responding, most aggressive youths require other forms of therapeutic intervention. During the course of the group intervention, therapists may identify a student or students for whom they wish to recommend individual therapy. Some students may require individual treatment after the termination of the group. Therapists should be prepared with resources for making referrals as needed throughout the group process. Additionally, a post-consultation session with each of the individual members and their interested parents can be set up after the termination of the group to assess how group members are doing and to identify any needs for ongoing treatment or support.

Relationships among administrators, teachers, and students may be both sources of support and conflict and may interact with the group content and the group dynamics (Berkowitz, 1989). All therapeutic groups should discuss the issue of confidentiality and come to some agreement about how to handle information revealed/shared in group meetings. It may be difficult for students to create a boundary between what occurs in the group and what occurs the remainder of the day. They therefore may be confused about what exactly is confidential material. Discussion in advance can help group members recognize the difficulties associated with confidentiality and provide them with strategies to ensure that certain material is held confidential. Without some effort to ensure confidentiality, the majority of teenage group members will not participate verbally for fear of rumor spreading, teasing, or perhaps retribution. Confidentiality must favor the adolescent to gain trust and to establish and maintain therapeutic alliance (Cramer-Azima & Richmond, 1989).

Finally, related to confidentiality is the issue of privacy. Unlike mental health settings, school staff do not necessarily recognize the need for privacy. Group sessions frequently take place in a classroom and sessions may be interrupted by the random entry and exit of staff members.

Teachers or other school personnel may ask for feedback from leaders on specific group members. Privacy is important for adolescents and the lack of it may undermine their participation in the group. It is probably best to address this issue with school officials/staff prior to the onset of the group and to select the site for group meetings carefully. Perhaps there is a group room or lounge that can be reserved for uninterrupted group meetings.

LIMITATIONS OF THE GROUP INTERVENTION APPROACH IN SCHOOLS

Because the described program has been specifically designed for easy implementation in a school-like setting, the advantages far outweigh the limitations. However, there are a few limitations that need to be taken into consideration so that their impact on the efficacy of the group be minimized. The first limitation is a time factor. When conducting a group in a school setting, one must conform to the existing class schedule, in which class periods usually run approximately 35 to 45 minutes long. This is not a problem for most groups, as this is usually enough time to present, discuss, and practice curriculum material. However, for groups of older or more verbal students, one may need up to 90 minutes to present the material and address any concerns or questions of the students. One may not be able to change this, yet being aware of the time constraint may be important for both therapists and students to ensure that the time allotted is used wisely. Certainly, the anger-management program can be extended beyond the 10-week protocol described here.

Another manifestation of the time factor is that groups must also adhere to the school calendar. School holidays and recesses interfere with the flow of the group process from week to week. Ideally, one should schedule the 10-week program to fit into a block of time with the fewest interruptions and at a time of year when students are most motivated (clearly not the last two months of the academic year!).

A second limitation refers to confidentiality. A school intervention group, rather than being held in a separate unit, is conducted in the school setting. This necessarily limits both anonymity and privacy. It is important to emphasize the need for privacy to all involved and to request that interruptions be kept to a minimum. In any case, a sign can be posted on the door that the group is in session. This serves as a reminder for staff members to knock or come back later. Finally, a policy concerning specific feedback to staff, teachers, and parents needs to be outlined. We suggest minimal feedback concerning general compliance and group attendance and urge the students themselves to share their observations privately with interested parties.

IMPLICATIONS FOR FUTURE RESEARCH AND PRACTICE

The program described here is easily adapted for violence-reduction intervention in the high school setting and incorporates a group psychoeducational format seen to be effective and cost efficient. Although there are sufficient published reports of the success of anger-management training for aggressive youth in both institutional and educational settings, there are several clinical issues yet to be fully understood.

First, much work needs to be done on assessment of anger difficulties for both individual behavior change as well as program evaluation. Feindler (1990b) suggested that a comprehensive assessment strategy that helps to delineate clearly which cognitive distortions and deficiencies exist and which social skills are present or absent would be best. Further, a multimodal approach would help to clarify which type of anger-control problem a youth presents with (i.e., physiological arousal, predominant social/communication skills deficit, etc.) and would help to obtain data from other sources in other contexts (i.e., school performance, parental ratings, and peer evaluations). Ideally, a comprehensive individual assessment package would also help direct treatment planning. (See Feindler [1995] for an individualized case assessment linked to individualized anger management.)

In addition to measures reflecting skill acquisition, data are needed on generalization and maintenance of anger-management skills to the natural environment. Best practices for getting observational data on actual aggressive behavior toward peers, parents, school personnel, and others have yet to be determined. Nonetheless, to evaluate rigorously a violence-reduction program, these outcome data will be critical in determining effectiveness.

A second clinical issue has to do with the multicomponent approach of anger management. Feindler (1990b) summarizes that there are five basic components of anger-control training: (1) arousal reduction, (2) cognitive change, (3) behavioral skills development, (4) moral reasoning development, and (5) appropriate anger expression; and at least six modalities in which intervention can be provided: (1) individual therapy, (2) group skills training, (3) family anger management, (4) dyadic anger management-training, (5) parent-only anger management, and (6) classroom anger management/affective education. Which of these therapeutic components and in which modalities treatment would be most effective, or for which types of agressive adolescents, is a complicated query. Only with careful assessments and program evaluations of different components and in different contexts will therapists begin to understand the answers.

Tagged to this is the question of multisystematic treatment of antisocial youths. Recent theories (Tolan et al., 1995) suggest that the convergence of risk factors in the development of aggressive behavior patterns points to the need for multicomponent, multicontext interventions. Further, they summarize that the most promising prevention and intervention programs focus on changing individuals, the influence of close interpersonal relations, and the contexts of development (Tolan et al., 1995). Given the psychoeducational skills-training approach herein described as adapted to the school setting, we wonder which additional component of training would augment the effects of the anger-management approach. We would suggest, at the very least, teacher and parent anger-management groups to be adjunctive as well as a schoolwide effort at reinforcing nonviolent methods of interpersonal problem solving.

A final clinical issue worth exploring is the use of the group intervention approach with an aggressive population in a "captive" context such as the school. Numerous questions concerning group composition can be answered only through sound research efforts. Given the developmental changes occurring during the adolescent years, at just what ages group treatment is more viable needs to be determined. Other factors such as gender, socioeconomic status, and academic functioning level can also influence the heterogeneity or homogeneity of group membership. The ideal composition of a high school anger-management group still needs exploration.

In summary, anger management for violence reduction represents a promising avenue for school and community intervention. We hope as more programs are developed and evaluated in various contexts that our knowledge about effectiveness of various techniques, influential group intervention factors, and methods of measurement of individual and group change will all become more sophisticated and even more effective. The youths of today are surrounded by the violence in our culture, in our homes, and in our relationships. Working with communities and schools will help us in our fight to protect our children from growing up violent.

REFERENCES

Berkowitz, I. H. (1989). Application of group therapy in secondary schools. In F. J. Cramer-Azima & L. H. Richmond (Eds.), *Adolescent group psychotherapy,* Monograph Series (American Group Psychotherapy Association). Madison, CT: International Universities Press.

Brigham, T. A., Hopper, C., Hill, B., De Armes, A., & Newsom, P. (1985). A self-management program for disruptive adolescents in the school: A clinical replication analysis. *Behavior Therapy, 16,* 99–115.

Cohall, A. T., Mayer, R., Cohall, K., & Walter, H. (1991). Teen violence: The new mortality. *Contemporary Pediatrics, 8,* 76–86.

Corder, B. F. (1994). *Structural adolescent psychotherapy groups.* Sarasota, FL: Professional Resource Press.

Cramer-Azima, F. J. and Richmond, L. H. (Eds.). (1989). *Adolescent group psychotherapy,* Madison, CT: International Universities Press.

Dangel, R. F., Deschner, J. P., & Rasp, R. R. (1989). Anger control training for adolescents in residential treatment. *Behavior Modification, 13,* 447–458.

Didato, S. V. (1974). Delinquents in group therapy. In C. Sanger & H. S. Kaplan (Eds.), *Progress in group and family therapy.* New York: Brunner/ Mazel.

DiGuiseppe, R., Tafrate, R., & Eckhardt, C. (1994). Critical issues in the treatment of anger. *Cognitive and Behavioral Practice, 1,* 111–132.

Dodge, K. A., & Crick, N. R. (1990). Social information-processing bases of aggressive behavior in children. *Personality and Social Psychology Bulletin, 16*(1), 8–22.

Feindler, E. L. (1990a). Adolescent anger control: Review and critique. In M. Hersen, R. M. Eisler, & P. M. Miller (Eds.), *Progress in behavior modification* (Vol. 26, pp. 11–59). Newbury Park, CA: Sage.

Feindler, E. L. (1990b). Cognitive strategies in anger control interventions for children and adolescents. In P. C. Kendall (Ed.), *Child and adolescent therapy: Cognitive-behavioral procedures* (pp. 66–97). New York: Guilford.

Feindler, E. L. (1995). An ideal treatment package for children and adolescents with anger disorders. In H. Kassinove (Ed.), *Anger disorders: Definition, diagnosis and treatment* (pp. 173–195). Washington DC: Taylor and Francis.

Feindler, E. L., & Ecton, R. (1986). *Adolescent anger control: Cognitive-behavioral techniques.* New York: Pergamon.

Feindler, E. L., Ecton, R., Kingsley, D., & Dubey, D. (1986). Group anger control training for institutionalized psychiatric male adolescents. *Behavior Therapy, 17,* 109–123.

Feindler, E. L., & Guttman, J. (1994). Cognitive-behavioral anger control training for groups of adolescents: A treatment manual. In C.W. LeCroix (Ed.), *Handbook of child and adolescent treatment manuals.* New York: Lexington Books.

Feindler, E. L., Marriott, S., & Iwata, M. (1984). Group anger control training for junior high school delinquents. *Cognitive Therapy and Research, 8*(3), 229–311.

Filipczak, J., Archer, M., & Friedman, R. M. (1980). In-school social skills training: Use with disruptive adolescents. *Behavior Modification, 4,* 243–263.

Goldstein, A. P. (1992). *School violence: Its community context and potential solutions.* Testimony presented to Subcommittee on Elementary, Secondary and Vocational Education, Committee on Education and Labor, U.S. House of Representatives, May 4.

Goldstein, A. P., & Glick, B. (1994a). *The prosocial gang: Implementing aggression replacement training.* Thousand Oaks, CA: Sage.

Goldstein, A. P., & Glick, B. (1994b). Aggression replacement training: Curriculum and evaluation. *Simulation and Gaming, 25*(1), 9–26.

Guerra, N. G., & Slaby, R. G. (1990). Cognitive mediators of aggression in adolescent offenders: 2. Intervention. *Developmental Psychology, 26,* 269–277.

Hains, A. A., & Szyjakowski, M. (1990). A cognitive stress-reduction intervention program for adolescents. *Journal of Counseling Psychology, 37*(1), 79–84.

Kaufman, L. M., & Wagner, B. R. (1972). Barb: A systematic treatment technology for temper control disorders. *Behavior Therapy, 3,* 84–90.

Kirkland, K. D., Thelen, M. H., & Miller, D. (1982). Group assertion training with adolescents. *Child and Family Behavior Therapy, 4,* 1–12.

Larson, J. D. (1990). Cognitive-behavioral group therapy with delinquent adolescents: A cooperative approach with the juvenile court. *Journal of Offender Rehabilitation, 16,* 47–64.

Larson, J. D. (1992). Anger and aggression management techniques through the Think First Curriculum. *Journal of Offender Rehabilitation, 18,* 101–117.

Lochman, J. E., & Lenhart, L. A. (1993). Anger coping intervention for aggressive children: Conceptual models and outcome effects. *Clinical Psychology Review, 13,* 785–805.

Loeber, R. (1982). The stability of antisocial and delinquent child behavior: A review. *Child Development, 53,* 1431–1446.

Long, S. J., & Sherer, M. (1984). Social skills training with juvenile offenders. *Child and Family Behavior Therapy, 6*(4), 1–11.

Novaco, R. W. (1975). *Anger control: The development and evaluation of an experimental treatment.* Lexington, MA: D. C. Heath.

Olweus, D. (1994). Bullying at school: Basic facts and effects of school based intervention programs. *Journal of Child Psychology and Psychiatry, 35,* 1171–1190.

Patterson, G. R., DeBaryshe, B., & Ramsey, E. (1989). A developmental perspective of antisocial behavior. *American Psychologist, 44,* 329–335.

Pepler, D. J., & Slaby, R. G. (1994). Theoretical and developmental perspectives on youth and violence. In L. Eron, J. Gentry, & P. Schlegel (Eds.), *Reason to hope: A psychosocial perspective on violence and youth.* Washington, DC: American Psychological Association.

Prothrow-Stith, D., & Weissman, M. (1991). *Deadly consequences.* New York: HarperCollins.

Sampson, R. J., & Lauritsen, P. (1994). Violent victimization and offending: Individual, situational and community-level risk factors. In A. R. Reiss, Jr. & J. Roth (Eds.), *Understanding and preventing violence: Social influences* (Vol. 3, pp. 1–114). Washington, DC: National Academy Press.

Schlichter, K. J., & Horan, J. J. (1981). Effects of stress inoculation on the anger and aggression management skills of institutionalized juvenile delinquents. *Cognitive Therapy and Research, 5,* 359–365.

Slaby, R. G., & Guerra, N. G. (1988). Cognitive mediators of aggression in adolescent offenders: 1. Assessment . *Developmental Psychology, 24,* 580–588.

Snyder, J., & White, M. (1979). The use of cognitive self-instruction in the treatment of behaviorally disturbed adolescents. *Behavior Therapy, 10,* 227–235.

Straus, M. B. (1994). *Violence in the lives of adolescents.* New York: W. W. Norton.

Tisdelle, D. A., & St. Lawrence, J. S. (1988). Adolescent interpersonal problem solving: Social validation and generalization. *Behavior Therapy, 19,* 171–182.

Tolan, P. H., Guerra, N. G., & Kendall, P. C. (1995). A developmental-ecological perspective on antisocial behavior in children and adolescents: Toward a unified risk and intervention framework. *Journal of Consulting and Clinical Psychology, 63*(4), 579–584.

Webster, D. W., Gainer, P. S., & Champion, H. R. (1993). Weapon carrying among inner city junior high school students: Defensive behavior vs. aggressive delinquency. *American Journal of Public Health, 83*(111), 1604–1608.

Wells, D., & Miller, M. J. (1993). Adolescent affective aggression: An intervention model. *Adolescence, 28*(112), 781–791.

CHAPTER 7

GROUP INTERVENTIONS FOR CHILDREN OF DIVORCE

Neil Kalter, UNIVERSITY OF MICHIGAN

The dramatic rise in the divorce rate in the United States between 1960 and 1980 is well documented. During this period, the divorce rate increased from 9.2 divorces per 1,000 marriages to 22.6 per 1,000 in 1981 (Cherlin, 1981). Correspondingly, the proportion of children who experienced parental divorce soared from below 10% in the years just prior to 1960 to approximately 30% in 1980 (Furstenberg, Nord, Peterson, & Zill, 1983). Recent projections indicate that over 40% of children born in the United States in the 1970s and 1980s will see their parents divorce (Hernandez, 1988). The sheer number of youngsters affected is impressive; since 1973, there have been over one million new children of divorce each year (National Center for Health Statistics, 1990). Though the rate of divorce has leveled off and even declined slightly since the early 1980s, it has been stable for the past five years (National Center for Health Statistics, 1995). There is no indication that there will be a significant drop in the incidence of divorce or the percentage of children affected in the foreseeable future.

EFFECTS OF DIVORCE ON CHILDREN

These figures reveal dramatic changes in the landscape of the American family. However, by themselves, they would draw little interest from those social scientists, educators, and clinicians whose main focus is the developmental trajectory and well-being of children. What has provoked great concern is the increasing awareness that parental divorce is associated with substantial difficulties for many of the youngsters touched by it.

There is considerable agreement among professionals that divorce constitutes an immediate and major disequilibrium in the lives of children. The *short-term effects*—usually defined as occurring within two to three years of the decisive parental separation—have been carefully studied for nearly two decades. Accumulated findings indicate that all domains of children's development are vulnerable to significant disruption in the wake of divorce. *Emotional adjustment difficulties*—often referred to as internalizing problems such as anxiety, depression, low self-esteem, regressive loss of developmental achievements, inhibitions, and somatic complaints—are greater, on average, in the immediate aftermath of divorce than for children from intact families. *Behavioral difficulties*—typically described as externalizing problems such as being oppositional, defiant, aggressive, and involved in substance abuse—are also more prevalent among youngsters in the period soon after their parents' separation than they are for children whose parents never have divorced. Investigators have reported that following divorce, children additionally evidence greater *social problems* with peers, including social isolation and aggression, than youngsters whose parents have not divorced. Finally, greater *academic difficulties* differentiate children whose parents have separated recently from their counterparts living in intact families (Chase-Lansdale & Hetherington, 1990; Guidubaldi 1988; Hetherington, Stanley-Hagan, & Anderson, 1989; Wallerstein, 1991).

Although these findings are reason enough for concern about the effects of divorce on youngsters, even more disturbing are the results of studies aimed at investigating the *long-term effects* of parental divorce on children. There have been fewer efforts in this direction, but a consensus is beginning to emerge. Studies that differ substantially in their conceptual models, research methods, sample characteristics, and sample size are reaching similar conclusions about the long-term impact that divorce can have on the offspring. It appears that at least a substantial minority of children of divorce either suffer for many years following their parents' separation or develop divorce-related difficulties long after the decisive parental separation. Problems in emotional and behavioral adjustment, academic progress, and social and intimate relationships have been found (Amato & Keith, 1991; Chase-Lansdale & Hetherington, 1990; Wallerstein, 1991; Zill, Morrison, & Coiro, 1993).

Increasingly, researchers have focused on the pivotal parameters of the divorce experience for children that contribute to their vulnerability to both short- and long-term divorce-related sequelae. These factors can be grouped into four clusters: characteristics of each parent, characteristics of the child, the relationship between the parents, and the postdivorce family form and relationships. Each will be discussed briefly in turn.

The primary characteristics of parents that have been associated with how children adjust to divorce are their mental health and economic resources. The more emotionally well-adjusted parents are, especially the parent with whom the child spends most time, the better youngsters do (e.g., Kalter, Kloner, Schreier, & Okla, 1989). Similarly, when parents are reasonably secure economically, they are less distressed and children evidence fewer adjustment problems (e.g., Emery, Hetherington, & DiLalla, 1984; Guidubaldi, 1988), though this seems to be a less powerful relationship than the former.

Individual characteristics of youngsters have been strongly predictive of their adaptation to parental divorce. These include the age of the child at the time of the marital rupture, the age of the child at the time the assessment is conducted (which taken together define the time since the parental separation), and the child's gender. Children who are preschoolers when their parents divorce have a more difficult time than older children, in the short run (e.g., Wallerstein & Kelly, 1980), but may evidence the best adjustment many years after divorce (Wallerstein, 1987). In a similar vein, a youngster's current age and the time since the divorce are predictive of child adjustment: The older the child and the greater the distance from the marital dissolution, the better adjusted the child tends to be (Chase-Lansdale & Hetherington, 1990). Gender has been linked to child outcome, as well: Boys appear to fare more poorly than girls in preadolescent years (Zaslow, 1988, 1989). However, in adolescence and adulthood, this gender difference becomes less pronounced as female offspring increasingly display significant problems (Chase-Lansdale & Hetherington, 1990; Kalter, 1990; Wallerstein, 1991).

The quality of the relationship between divorcing and divorced parents repeatedly has been found to affect the adjustment of youngsters. Hostility between parents is powerfully related to how children cope with divorce and its aftermath (e.g., Emery, 1982). Children whose parents are at war tend to display the full range of adjustment problems (e.g., Chase-Lansdale & Hetherington, 1990). Conversely, youngsters whose parents are not antagonistic toward one another and, further, who can cooperate and develop constructive co-parenting relationships, are more likely to fare well in the face of divorce (e.g., Ahrons, 1981; Wallerstein & Kelly, 1980).

Postdivorce family that form relationships are crucial to children's well-being in the short- and long-run aftermath of divorce. Living in a single-mother-headed household, is by far the most common immediate postdivorce family form, appears to benefit girls until adolescence regardless of the recency of the divorce, whereas boys evidence significant difficulties in this family structure. On the other hand, mother/stepfather families, the most frequently observed family form in the long run after divorce, seem to be more conducive to healthy development for boys than for girls (e.g., Chase-Lansdale & Hetherington, 1990). Joint physical custody, single-father headed households, and primary residence in a father/stepmother home are family forms that, taken together, account for a distinct minority of postdivorce arrangements, and consequently they have been less extensively studied.

Family relationships, apart from family structure, are seen by many investigators as crucial to determining how children grow up in the aftermath of divorce. The quality of the youngster's relationship with each parent, the relationship with his or her stepparent(s), the relationship between spouses in a remarried family, and the role relationships and dynamics in single-parent and remarried families have received considerable attention in the research and clinical literature.

The more available parents are to the child, the more emotionally positive the parent/child and stepparent/child relationship, the better the communication between spouses in a remarried family, and the clearer and more appropriate the family roles, the better youngsters fare (Bray & Berger, 1993; Camara & Resnick, 1989; Chase-Lansdale & Hetherington, 1990; Wallerstein & Kelly, 1980).

Though there is now a voluminous body of research investigating the effects of divorce on children and attempting to discover and refine predictors of child adjustment, the great majority of these efforts point to what adults need to prevent or ameliorate, not the mechanisms by which they come about. As Chase-Lansdale and Hetherington (1990) note in their thoughtful and comprehensive review of this literature, "There is more evidence for outcomes than for processes" (p. 134). There has been considerably less attention paid to developing explanatory models for the processes that underlie these associations.

Attempts to conceptualize the ways in which marital disruption and postdivorce life experiences affect the developmental trajectory of childhood can be grouped into three broad domains: developmental-transactional focuses on interpersonal behaviors, especially among family members; developmentally focused psychodynamic theory takes the inner world of the child—affects, fantasies, conflicts, and self-image—as the major locus of adjustment issues; and cognitive-behavioral focuses on the connection between children's perceptions and understanding of events and feelings and the behaviors that flow from these cognitions. Each framework provides explanations for the mechanisms through which divorce-related phenomena affect the adaptation and adjustment of youngsters. And each has implications for intervening on behalf of children whose parents divorce.

The *developmental-transactional* work is most centrally associated with Hetherington and colleagues (e.g., Hetherington, 1993; Hetherington, Cox, & Cox, 1985; Emery, Hetherington, & Di-Lalla, 1984;) but also includes the contributions of Bray (e.g., Bray & Berger, 1993) and Camara (e.g., Camara & Resnick, 1989). In this perspective, it is the divorce-induced altered roles and relationships within the family (single parent and remarried) that are paramount in determining what effects divorce will have on the youngsters involved. Examples include such factors as the overburdened single mother whose parenting style becomes more controlling and less nurturant, especially toward sons; the lack of significant experience and contact many youngsters have with a noncustodial father and the anxiety and awkwardness many children then feel in other relationships with males; the stress of having to share their mother with a new stepfather that girls especially feel when their mother remarries; and the new availability of a male role model as well as a buffer to the mother/son relationship that a mother's remarriage brings. Though this framework is not systemic in the ways in which many family theorists think (e.g., Hoffman, 1981; Walsh, 1993), it approximates a structural family systems approach.

The implications of the developmental-transactional model for interventions on behalf of children seem to be parent education regarding changing family role relationships as a preventive intervention and family therapy as a treatment modality. However, as Grych and Fincham (1992) note in their review of interventions for children of divorce, "Despite the emphasis on family factors in basic research, less has been written about parent-oriented interventions than child-focused interventions and little data exist concerning the efficacy of such programs" (p. 442). In fact, in this review of a handful of such interventions, there was little evidence for their effectiveness.

Psychodynamic theory applied developmentally to the divorce experience for children emphasizes the interior of a youngster's life when confronting divorce events and issues. This includes attention to inner conflicts and defenses, fantasies, feelings, and the internalization of the child's views of each parent as well as the relationship between parents (Wallerstein, 1991). In this perspective, divorce engenders conflicts such as which parent to align with emotionally, loyalty conflicts between feelings toward a stepparent and the parent of the same sex as the stepparent, and conflicts over powerful ambivalent feelings toward parents who are loved yet have disappointed the child and, as seen through the child's eyes, have made life more difficult by divorcing. The resolution of such conflicts can result in successful adaptation to divorce and its aftermath. However, they may trigger maladaptive defenses that create great internal distress—such as anxiety, guilt, and depression—or that propel the youngster toward acting out conflicts by becoming aggressive, destructive, and generally self-defeating. Similarly, the internalization of one's view of each parent, and their relationship, can lead to a good postdivorce adjustment or a repetition of parental choices and behaviors that are maladaptive (Kalter, 1987, 1990; Wallerstein, 1985, 1987, 1991; Wallerstein & Kelly, 1980).

The implications for intervention of the psychodynamic approach point in the direction of individual child psychotherapy and parent guidance, with a focus on internal conflicts and their observable expressions. It also suggests preventive approaches with children that seek to reduce the need for certain defenses by interfering with the formation of specific inner conflicts. In fact, Wallerstein's Center for the Family in Transition has been engaged in such treatment and preventive interventions with children and their parents for over two decades. Kalter's treatment efforts (e.g., Kalter, 1984) and group preventive intervention (e.g., Kalter & Schreier, 1993) are informed by developmentally focused psychodynamic and, as we shall see next, cognitive-behavioral conceptual frameworks.

The *cognitive-behavioral* perspective addresses the ways in which children think about and understand divorce, their resulting feelings about it, and their reactions to it. Central to this framework is attention to children misinterpreting the causes of and responsibility for divorce in self-blaming ways and their considerable distress over the many changes and stresses associated with divorce (Kurdek, 1988). These factors then result in negative perceptions of self, anxiety, and anger toward parents, which collectively result in interferences in maintaining healthy self-esteem; developing impulse control, communication skills, and social skills; and increasing the capacity to attend to academic tasks (Kalter, 1990; Kurdek, 1988; Pedro-Carroll & Cowan, 1985; Stolberg & Mahler, 1994). The focus here is very much child centered and on children's responses—cognitive, affective, and behavioral—to the vicissitudes of parental divorce.

The implications for intervention are quite clear: Children are the primary locus of prevention and therapeutic efforts. The three most systematically developed and researched preventive intervention/therapeutic programs, which also are among the most widely used, have been derived, to some degree, from this perspective. They are the Children's Support Group (CSG; Stolberg & Cullen, 1983), the Children of Divorce Intervention Program (CODIP; Pedro-Carroll & Cowan, 1985), and the Developmental Facilitation Group model (DFG; Kalter, Pickar, & Lesowitz, 1984). A notable exception is the Banana Splits program developed by Elizabeth McGonagle, one of the earliest and surely the most used support groups for children of divorce. However, it has not been systematically evaluated nor has it even been published descriptively in the professional literature.

RATIONALE FOR GROUP INTERVENTIONS WITH CHILDREN OF DIVORCE

As the foregoing section indicates, there are several possibilities for intervening on behalf of children of divorce. Any intervention may be directed either at *preventing* the emergence of youngsters' problems or *treating* the existence of difficulties already in evidence. However, as Stolberg and Mahler (1994) point out, this distinction may not hold in actual practice. Many children enrolled in prevention programs manifest developmental difficulties, often within the range of being clincally significant (Garvin, Kalter, & Leber, 1991; Stolberg & Mahler, 1994). Conversely, modalities typically associated with treatment (e.g., child and family therapy, parent guidance) can be used prior to the onset of observable symptoms. Brief interventions using these traditional treatment formats can serve as effective methods for preventing mental health problems and maintaining a youngster on a healthy developmental course (Kalter, 1990). Whether the aim is to prevent or treat divorce-related problems, the *target of the intervention* may vary.

Though group-based interventions are probably more palatable and therefore more likely to be used by parents and children, the target for such an intervention still must be chosen. Should groups be offered to youngsters, to parents, or to families? Though reasonable arguments can be made for each, at this time there are conceptually based as well as practical reasons for directing more resources toward groups for children than for parents or families.

A group format for parents and families makes sense, theoretically. Parents and families can profit from becoming aware of the kinds of child difficulties, parenting styles, sources of conflict, and coping strategies that characterize families during the extended divorce process. Participants in parent- and family-focused group interventions can have their concerns normalized, place their situations in the context of what others are confronting, and learn from one another methods for coping with the stresses that attend divorce. Unfortunately, a major difficulty with these sorts of groups is that only a small proportion of eligible people choose to participate. Even among those who enroll in such groups, attendance tends to be sporadic. Whether it is feelings of uneasiness or shyness over discussing personal issues with strangers, guilt, shame, or anxiety over the nature of their circumstances, or simply the time constraints and scheduling complexities in single-parent and remarried families, the great majority of separated and divorced parents do not avail themselves of this kind of service.

Groups for youngsters whose parents have parted have three clear practical advantages over individual child interventions and group interventions for parents and families. First, children's groups are more cost effective than seeing children one at a time. Second, parents seem more willing to permit their children to be in a divorce-focused group than attend groups for parents or families. Third, children are more willing to participate in groups than in individual or family therapy. These factors result in far more children being reached when children's groups are used.

There are also important conceptually and clinically based reasons for conducting groups for children of divorce. First, being in a group permits youngsters to interact with peers around divorce-related issues. Although most children are aware that some, perhaps many, of their classmates' and friends' parents are divorced, few know that they share with their peers similar feelings, thoughts, worries, and ongoing family conflicts. In the course of divorce groups for children, members become thoroughly aware of the fact that, in so many ways, they are not alone or different. This is not simply due to their heightened sensitivity to the fact that other youngsters' parents have divorced, too. Rather, it is through a keen sense that their *inner reactions* to divorce are widely shared and understandable that they can begin to feel normal. This, in itself, can reduce feelings of stress and isolation and enhance self-esteem.

A second and related advantage to children's groups is that they are a source of peer support (Kalter, Schaefer, Lesowitz, Alpern, & Pickar, 1988; Pedro-Carroll & Cowan, 1985). As children progress developmentally, they are increasingly embedded in a peer culture whose values, relationships, and feedback are crucial to one's evolving sense of self. As youngsters listen to one another, resonate to each other's concerns, and express understanding and support toward group members, they come to experience themselves in more positive ways. Further, support groups are especially important when traditional family sources of support are less available. When children find it difficult, if not impossible, to turn to their parents, precisely because so much divorce-related conflict and distress for youngsters directly involves one or both parents, it is tremendously helpful to have peers and group leaders available (Kalter et al., 1988).

Third, groups provide children with a sense of safety in numbers. In individual and family approaches, youngsters often feel very much on the spot: They either are the sole focus of attention or are in the position of voicing private concerns in front of parents and siblings. Though youngsters can and do comfortably and productively settle into individual and family therapy, it usually takes considerably longer than time-limited interventions typically conducted. On the other hand, a group format allows children to listen to others rather than always being the central focus, and gives them a feeling of being only one of several participants who are commenting on and self-disclosing feelings, ideas, and experiences relevant to divorce.

Collectively, these advantages to groups for children whose parents have separated or divorced, in conjunction with the barriers to entering into and participating openly in individual or family therapy, and the difficulties recruiting parents for parent- and family-focused interventions, underscore the merits of groups for children of divorce. Though no one approach is right for all youngsters, or even for the same child at different ages and whose family is at different stages of the divorce process, group interventions offer a large percentage of youngsters an opportunity to confront and come to grips with their reactions to divorce. And, of course, many of these interventions are not mutually exclusive; children can participate in more than one intervention either simultaneously or sequentially.

EFFICACY OF GROUPS FOR CHILDREN OF DIVORCE

Quantitative data regarding the effectiveness of group interventions for children of divorce are mixed. While some reviews are quite positive (e.g., Farmer & Galaris, 1993), others are less so. Grych and Fincham (1992) find that such interventions "have limited empirical support" (p. 440) and Lee, Picard, and Blaine (1994) state that they "have produced only modest gains" (p. 3) for reducing the adverse impact of divorce on children. These findings have led some reviewers (Grych & Fincham, 1992; Lee et al., 1994) to urge that greater emphasis be placed on parent-focused interventions, especially because the source of many children's difficulties with divorce is strongly related to parent behavior and parenting styles. When taken in the context of the finding that parent-oriented programs have demonstrated considerably less effectiveness in helping children of divorce than groups for children (Grych & Fincham, 1992) and that there are considerable difficulties involving parents in such services, their suggestion seems more wish related than grounded in reality.

Why are formal, quantitatively based evaluations of the efficacy of groups for children of divorce at variance with the impressions of parents, teachers, group leaders, and the children themselves? Though qualitative data often are presumed to be less rigorous and valid than objective measures, and there are certainly problems with qualitative data, there are good methodological reasons for obtaining only modest evidence for the effectiveness of this kind of intervention.

First, most group interventions for children of divorce have a preventive thrust. As a result, many participants are not selected because they are evidencing significant psychopathology. The aim of these interventions is to reduce the emergence of divorce-related difficulties some time in the future. If these interventions work, one should see a control group's problems increasing over time while the target group who received the service maintains a relatively constant level of difficulties. Figure 7.1 illustrates this result.

If the intervention occurs at time T and the immediate postintervention evaluation occurs at $T + 1$, there may be little difference between children who have participated in the intervention and those who have not. At $T + 2$, say 6 to 12 months after the intervention, the difference may reach a modest level, and at $T + 3$, perhaps two to four years after the intervention, the groups can be quite different. However, because use of a wait-list control group is by far the most common assessment design (Lee et al., 1994), it is difficult to obtain data bearing on long-term efficacy. To do so would delay service to the control group for an intolerably long period. The result is that most studies of chil-

Figure 7.1 Results of Successful Preventive Intervention

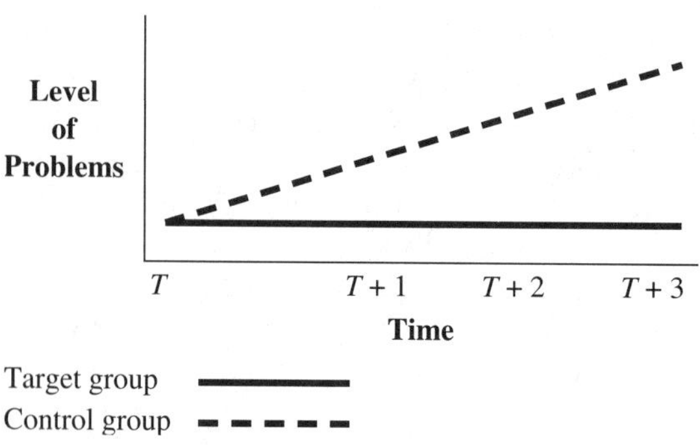

dren of divorce interventions conduct analyses immediately after the intervention (at $T + 1$) and a few wait as long as 6 to 12 months after the groups end (at $T + 2$). It would be unlikely for preventive interventions to show more than modest results in such a foreshortened time frame.

In fact, it is rare for reported results to correspond to what is depicted in Figure 7.1. Nearly all findings reviewed by Lee and associates (1994) could be described by Figure 7.2, which reflects a successful treatment paradigm, not a preventive intervention. Here, the control group's problems remain constant over time while the treated group's difficulties initially decline and then are maintained in the long run. It is easier to detect intervention-related effects in the short run when the group being studied evidences clinically significant difficulties prior to treatment (Lee et al., 1994). Thus, though most groups for children of divorce are conceptualized as primarily *preventive* interventions, they yield modest short-term *treatment* effects even though most group participants and control group youngsters do not manifest clinically significant problems. As much as a "modest" effect is surprisingly positive! And prevention effects are rarely assessed at all, due to the short time frame used in nearly all studies.

A second reason for only modest results, relates to group interventions typically being offered to youngsters who differ substantially on many dimensions relevant to postdivorce adjustment. Children participating in the same group may include boys and girls, with up to a four-year age difference, whose parents separated recently or many years in the past, who live in single-parent or remarried families, who have warring or cooperative parents, and who may enjoy excellent or poor relationships with their parents and perhaps stepparents. Each of these variables—gender, current age, time since divorce, marital status of parents, relationship between parents, and parent/child relationships—has been associated significantly with postdivorce adjustment. Most sample sizes in outcome research for children of divorce groups are simply not large enough to take into consideration statistically these subgroups, let alone combinations of them. Instead, only aggregate data are reported, though some investigators have included gender and/or age as factors in data analyses (e.g., Pedro-Carroll & Cowan, 1985; Kalter, 1988). Diversity on so many dimensions characterizing children and their divorce experience can easily mask the clear-cut efficacy of these groups for sizable subgroups of youngsters.

Despite these formidable methodological obstacles to finding decisive quantitative evidence for the effectiveness of these groups, the three programs that have been most rigorously developed and assessed (i.e., CODIP, CSG, and DFG), and are among the most widely used, have shown promising results. Research on each will be reviewed briefly.

The Children of Divorce Intervention Project (CODIP) has perhaps been the most thoroughly evaluated children's divorce group model (e.g., Alpert-Gillis, Pedro-Carroll, & Cowan, 1989; Pedro-Carroll & Cowan, 1985, 1987; Pedro-

Figure 7.2 Results of Successful Treatment

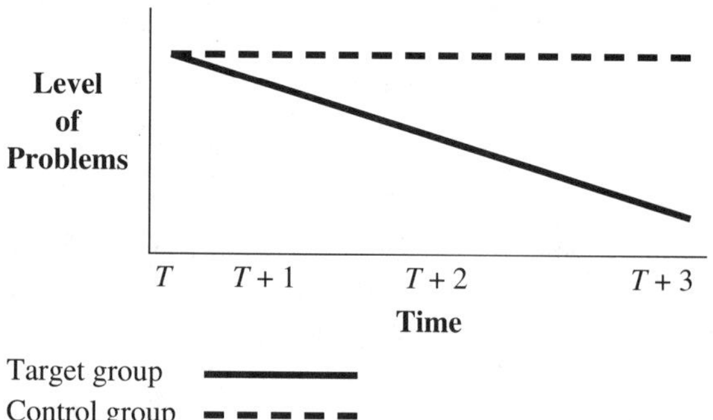

Carroll, Cowan, Hightower, & Guare, 1986) with among the best results (Grych & Fincham, 1992; Lee et al., 1994). Pedro-Carroll and colleagues have demonstrated that teachers, parents, group leaders, and child participants report significant improvements for children in areas such as acting-out behavior, shy-anxious behavior, peer sociability, learning competence, and anxiety, when compared to wait-list controls. Further, after the intervention, youngsters who have been in these groups more closely resemble children from never-divorced families.

The Children's Support Group model (CSG) also has been evaluated rigorously (e.g., Stolberg & Garrison, 1985; Stolberg & Mahler, 1994) with promising findings. Children who have participated in the intervention show enhanced self-esteem and reductions in anxiety and in internalizing (emotional) and externalizing (behavior) problems according to parent and child reports when compared to a no-intervention control group. Stolberg's use of a no-intervention rather than a wait-list or delayed service control design permitted him to examine longer-term (one-year) effects of his intervention than is usually the case. It is interesting to note that some outcome measures (e.g., internalizing problems) showed an immediate postintervention improvement that was maintained substantially after one year. Other measures (e.g., externalizing problems) evidenced continued improvement from preintervention to postintervention up to one year follow-up, and still other measures (e.g., adaptive functioning at school, happiness) showed gains only at the one-year mark (Stolberg & Mahler, 1994). The authors claim that their findings suggest that the CSG model is a treatment, not a preventive, intervention because so many of the youngsters in their sample (nearly 50%) had behaviors that were rated in the clinically significant range. And, in fact, many of their findings approximate the treatment effect pattern displayed in Figure 7.2, presented earlier. However, some of their results also indicate a prevention effect.

The Developmental Facilitation Group model (DFG) has been evaluated descriptively as well as formally using delayed-service and no-treatment control groups and standardized, quantitative, assessments of child outcome variables. Findings for short-term evaluations parallel those found by Pedro-Carroll and Stolberg (Kalter, 1988). However, an evaluation using a no-treatment control group conducted four years after intervention provides evidence for long-term prevention and treatment effects. Rubin (1990) found that 15 of 37 standardized quantitative variables favored the intervention group to a statistically significant degree and another seven measures showed a trend in that direction. Equally compelling was the finding that youngsters who had not been in the intervention group made substantially more use of mental health services than those who had participated (54% versus 14%), yet the group graduates were significantly better adjusted on a wide range of standardized measures.

CHARACTERISTICS OF MODEL CHILDREN OF DIVORCE GROUPS

These three children of divorce intervention group models share many characteristics. All are time limited, ranging from 8 to 14 sessions, restrict the age of the participants in a single group to an appropriate developmental range, and are conducted primarily in schools, though are used in other settings, as well. Each focuses on children's feelings, thoughts, and coping strategies vis-à-vis divorce-related events and experiences, and each attempts to foster peer support and understanding. However, distinctions among these three models are also noteworthy. Both CODIP and CSG focus on general cognitive skill building using similar techniques. This includes recognizing and labeling feelings, use of self-statements, and a focus on developing clear problem-solving strategies for dealing effectively with one's feelings, especially anger. CODIP, however, makes greater use of indirect communication methods such as role-play and filmstrips than does CSG. It is not surprising that these two models have so much in common; CODIP is essentially a modification of CSG (Pedro-Carroll & Cowan, 1985).

The DFG model, developed independently of the other two, makes greater use of indirect methods of communication (e.g., drawing, group storytelling, puppet play, role-play), and focuses more extensively on specific divorce-related experiences, thoughts, and feelings. In some ways, it is more tailored to divorce issues and life experiences, whereas CODIP and CSG have more generalized components. However, DFG does lend itself to uses with other populations; a translation of it to a model for intervention groups for bereaved youngsters recently has been completed (Lohnes & Kalter, 1994). The remainder of this chapter will focus on the DFG model.

DEVELOPMENTAL FACILITATION GROUPS FOR CHILDREN OF DIVORCE

The DFG model is intended to help youngsters confront and cope adaptively with the burdensome misconceptions, difficult feelings, and problematic family interactions that are so often elements in the complex and ongoing divorce mosaic. Cognitively based sources of distress and subsequent divorce-related difficulties include beliefs that the child is responsible for the divorce, for ongoing animosities between parents, and for a parent not staying significantly involved with him or her. These self-blaming beliefs are corrosive to a child's valued sense of self and can lead to lowered self-esteem, depression, or the action defenses against such painful affects (Kalter, 1987, 1990). Further, cognitive confusion over why the divorce is occurring and what the postdivorce arrangements will be creates powerful feelings of helplessness and anxiety in many youngsters.

Emotional conflicts also take their toll on healthy child development. Loyalty conflicts over which parent to align with, divisions in feelings toward a stepparent and the parent of the same sex as the stepparent, and painful ambivalence toward parents can create both internalizing emotional problems as well as externalizing behavior difficulties.

Conflictual family interactions may result in children developing a wide range of internalizing and externalizing problems. Being caught in the middle of angry, warring parents, becoming a primary caregiver to siblings and/or a distressed parent, and having to adapt to a parent dating and possibly remarrying tend to tax the inner resources of youngsters and may then lead to maladaptive efforts to deal with their distress.

All of these sources of difficulty—cognitive, intrapsychic, and transactional—can also interfere significantly with a child's academic progress and social relationships. Broadly stated, the goal of the DFG model is to reduce the intensity and number of these negative outcomes.

SPECIFIC AIMS OF THE DEVELOPMENTAL FACILITATION GROUP MODEL

There are five specific aims of the DFG. First, we seek to *normalize* children's status as coming from a divorced family as well as their reactions to divorce. When children of divorce come together in groups, they can see directly that they are not alone. Even more important, however, is the process of children sharing privately held, rarely voiced feelings, questions, and worries about divorce that permits youngsters to understand that their inner concerns are not bad, wrong, or silly, but are widely shared.

Second, we try to *clarify* divorce-related issues that can be upsetting and/or confusing to children. These cognitively based sources of distress are addressed by leaders providing information and by seeing other youngsters wrestle with them. It is interesting to observe group members who steadfastly believe that they were in some way responsible for their parents' divorce, nonetheless find similar ideas held by other group members to be nonsensical. They often gradually come to see that their beliefs are just as ill-founded as those of their peers.

Third, we attempt to provide a safe place for children to *experience and understand* emotionally painful reactions to their parents' divorce. The accepting and supportive atmosphere of the group, the articulation of rarely if ever spoken conflicts, and the comfort afforded by "safety in numbers" encourages youngsters to become more aware of and examine their feelings and experiences.

Fourth, we seek to promote the *development of coping skills* to better manage troublesome feelings and family interactions common to parental divorce. Children share ideas for what to do or say in various situations, and group leaders reinforce adaptive strategies and explain why other approaches are usually less useful.

Finally, we encourage and attempt to foster *increased communication between children and parents.* Leaders explain that parents can help best when they know what is troubling their children. New and less threatening styles of conveying information to parents are presented and often practiced within the group.

TECHNIQUES FOR CONDUCTING DEVELOPMENTAL FACILITATION GROUPS

In a time-limited intervention, it is crucial that important issues are assured coverage. The luxury afforded by open-ended interventions to wait patiently for important themes to arise and unfold gradually is not available in short-term work. Instead, structure is needed.

The DFG creates structure by addressing *specific themes* that the clinical and research literature indicates are both common and important in the course of the extended divorce process. Further, we order these themes according to the *temporal sequence* that many children experience. For example, the theme of predivorce parent arguments appears early, followed by the parents' decision to divorce and tell their children about it. Custody and visitation issues appear next, and then parent dating, remarriage, and stepfamily relationships come later in the sequence of sessions. We have found that the unfolding of key divorce events in this naturally occurring order gives children a pronounced sense of coherence to their experience of the intervention.

The conceptual heart of the DFG is the twin use of displacement activities and universalizing statements. *Displacement activities* are well known to child therapists. Puppet play, drawing, the use of dolls and action figures, and talking about imaginary youngsters and families are facets of traditional play therapy. These displacement activities are used to present pivotal divorce themes initially within the safety of a "one step removed" format. It permits group members to talk about, observe, and gain understandings about their private feelings and thoughts. Directly addressing painful and conflict-laden concerns (e.g., "How did you feel when your parents told you they were getting a divorce?" "Whose fault do you think the divorce was?") most typically is met with defensive and unrevealing responses such as shrugs, "I don't know," "Okay, I guess," and silence. Particularly verbal and compliant youngsters may parrot adult-approved "party-line" statements such as one third-grader's explanation for her parents' divorce: "The reason for the divorce was that my mom and dad just developed different interests and grew apart."

Responses to displacements stand in sharp contrast to these defensive reactions. Initially presenting difficult issues in the middle distance afforded by displacement techniques, such as discussing the feelings and thoughts of an imaginary character in a story about a family in which a divorce is taking place, permits children to begin to explore their ideas and feelings about their own life circumstances. As group members discuss an imaginary child's reactions to divorce, they are in fact actively sharing some of their own concerns and experiences, though cloaked by the displacement activity. This becomes clear surprisingly quickly as youngsters begin spontaneously to describe their own family's interactions as well as their inner experiences of them.

Universalizing statements are the primary vehicles for leaders to communicate important information to the group in a manner that makes it possible for children to hear and use of this knowledge. Such statements are essentially generalized comments such as, "It seems like most kids whose parents split up have worries about what's going to happen next?" and "A lot of fifth- and sixth-graders have some pretty big angry feelings toward their parents about the divorce." Statements cast in these ways allow leaders to discuss key divorce-related events and experiences without putting group members on the spot, without provoking defensive responses or withdrawal from discussion, while simultaneously normalizing the events and reactions being addressed. Together, displacement activities and universalizing statements provide an engaging, nonthreatening vehicle for helping youngsters confront, discuss, and cope with their distress and concerns about divorce.

FORMAT FOR DEVELOPMENTAL FACILITATION GROUPS

Developmental facilitation groups have been *conducted in a variety of settings,* including public and private elementary and secondary schools, community mental health centers, churches and synagogues, and outpatient mental health clinics. They have been used in over 2,500 sites representing 43 states and three Canadian provinces. School-based groups account for over 80% of these sites and have the advantages of easy access for children, the presence of a ready-made peer group, and increased regularity of attendance by group members who are not dependent on parents for arranging transportation to and from sessions.

The *composition* of these groups is mixed with respect to time since divorce, current living arrangements, gender, and, to a lesser extent, grade. We have found it useful to include youngsters from all stages of the extended divorce process. Children whose parents recently have separated can see from interacting with "veterans" of divorce that there is indeed life after the initial disruption of parental separation. And they can begin to anticipate what kinds of events and experiences may very well be in store for them. Conversely, youngsters whose parents separated years ago can return to earlier divorce events and their reactions to them, thus gaining an opportunity to rework old conflicts and develop new, adaptive understandings of their family's history.

Diversity with respect to living arrangements provides different perspectives for youngsters. Children who live in a single-parent home learn from their peers who have acquired a stepparent (and perhaps, step- and/or half-siblings, as well) about the advantages and challenges to each kind of home. This reduces children's tendencies to idealize or denigrate their own or others' circumstances, and permits group members to place their own situation in a broader context. Further, it allows youngsters whose primary custodial parent has not remarried to begin to anticipate this possible transition while those living in a remarried household can revisit older issues that attended life in a single-parent home.

Having boys and girls in a group also helps youngsters understand and appreciate different perspectives. Although we have conducted same-gendered groups, the absence of often thought-provoking differences in how the sexes experience various divorce issues makes for a less richly elaborated sense of each child's thoughts and feelings.

While variation on the foregoing dimensions tends to enrich our intervention, we have restricted the range of developmental levels represented in any single group. Through nearly 20 years of experimenting with these formats, we have come to the conclusion that cross-age groups are useful, but only when members are within roughly two to three years of one another. Youngsters more than three years apart differ substantially in their cognitive abilities, the nature of their relationships with parents, and their peer group. When group members are more than three years apart, we have found that any given discussion seems irrelevant to some proportion of the group, and thus many children lose interest in actively participating. Sometimes it seems akin to teaching math to children who are three or more grades apart: It is difficult to know which topics need coverage, how to present material, and at what pace to conduct the class. Further, substantial variation in age within a group tends to reduce group cohesion, may intimidate younger members, and infantalize older participants.

We have chosen a male/female *co-leader* format for several reasons. First, it is helpful in a mixed-gender group for each child to have a same-sexed co-leader available as a potential role model. Second, many children seem to feel that an adult of the same gender will have a special understanding of them. Third, as children observe the co-leaders working together and respecting one another, they are exposed to a model for a positive relationship between a man and woman, an experience many children of divorce have not had. And, on practical grounds, it is helpful to have co-leaders: role-playing is made easier by having co-leaders play gender-consonant roles (e.g., a female group leader playing mother or stepmother); and, as expectable management issues arise (e.g., children giggling, becoming restless, poking each other), one leader can attend to those group members while the other leader continues to work with the main body of the group. A serendipitous aspect of using a co-leader model is that it lends itself to training new leaders; an experienced leader paired with a novice can provide hands-on training, modeling, and direct supervision.

It is useful to note here what the *leader qualifications* are for conducting these groups. We have had special services personnel co-lead groups in schools. In other settings, psychologists, psychiatrists, and social workers, as well as trainees in these disciplines, and members of the clergy have conducted groups. Generally, adults who are sensitive to youngsters and are comfortable with them can carry out this intervention. It is especially helpful if at least one co-leader has an understanding of child development, be it from an educational, clinical, or childrearing perspective. The overwhelming majority of group leaders have told us that the session-by-session implementation manuals (Kalter & Associates, 1985, 1988, 1993) are sufficiently detailed, clear, and filled with examples that they quickly feel a sense of mastery when leading these groups.

THE DEVELOPMENTAL FACILITATION GROUP MODULES

The DFG intervention consists of three modules: the Early Elementary School-Age intervention (Kalter & Associates, 1988), intended for children in grades 1 through 3, or roughly 6 to 8 years old; the Later Elementary School-Age groups (Kalter & Associates, 1985), developed for children in grades 4 through 6, or about 9 to 11 years old; and the Early Adolescent module for youngsters in grades 7 through 9 who are usually between 12 and 14 years old. Though there are important differences among these three modules with respect to some of the substantive issues that are emphasized, the methods used to help youngsters deal with divorce, and the pace of the groups, there are three centrally important, overarching similarities that link them. These commonalties, described in greater detail earlier, are the temporal organization of the themes across sessions, the use of displacement activities and universalizing statements, and the five aims of the DFG. It is these three components that define the essence of the DFG model across all modules.

In order to illustrate this model, sessions from each module will be described in detail. These sample sessions are intended simultaneously to capture distinctive qualities of each module while illuminating key differences among them. A brief overview of the themes covered in each session across the three modules is given in Table 7.1.

The Early Elementary School Module (Ages 6 to 8)

The Early Elementary School module relies more heavily on concrete methods for representing ideas, feelings, and family interactions than do the other two modules. Drawing and puppet play, two activities not found in either of the other two interventions, are used throughout this module. These visually concrete displacement activities help young children better understand divorce-related concepts and enable them to differentiate more clearly the imaginary quality of role-play by group leaders of conflictual family situations from the reality of leaders as caring, helpful adults.

Children in early elementary school also tend to react in developmentally expectable ways to key divorce issues. For example, hostility between parents tends to elicit primarily feelings of anxiety, confusion, and sadness, and anger secondarily. Parent dating often evokes rivalrous feelings toward the parent's partner, fears of losing the parent to him or her, and distress over having to give up cherished wishes that the parents reconcile and get back together. Leaders need to be aware of these common reactions so that they can be sensitive to them when they arise and articulate them when they are conspicuous by their absence.

The following sessions illustrate the techniques and substantive emphases that characterize the Early Elementary School module.

Table 7.1 Session Themes for the Three DFG Modules

SESSION	EARLY ELEMENTARY SCHOOL	LATER ELEMENTARY SCHOOL	EARLY ADOLESCENT
1	Introduction to the Group and Drawing Family Pictures	Introduction to the Group and Group Storytelling	Introduction to the Group
2	Family Pictures and Group Storytelling	Predivorce Fighting between Parents	Group Storytelling
3	Fighting between Parents	Parents Tell the Children about Intention to Divorce	Predivorce Fighting between Parents
4	Parents Tell Children about Plans to Divorce	Custody Issues	Coping with Hostilities between Parents
5	First Visit with Father Following Separation	Visiting and Parent Dating Issues	Parents Tell Children about Plans to Divorce
6	Postdivorce Visiting Issues	The Possibility of Remarriage	Custody Issues
7	Postdivorce Visiting Issues and Parent Dating	The Divorce Newspaper	Custody Issues
8	Remarriage and Stepfamily Issues	Group-Ending Party	Visiting and Parent Dating Issues
9	The Divorce Newspaper		Remarriage and Stepfamily Issues
10	Group-Ending Party		Stepparents and Discipline
11			The Divorce Newspaper
12			Group-Ending Party

Session 1: Introduction to the Group

The aims of this session are to introduce the children and leaders to one another, to identify the rules and focus of the group, and to begin to clarify the concept of divorce. The session starts with the leaders and children seated in a circle. Leaders introduce themselves and note that the group will be about "divorce and how kids feel and think about it." The leaders also tell the children that the group will be meeting once a week for about 50 minutes, and that there will be a total of 10 sessions. Next, leaders suggest an icebreaker activity called "The Name Game," which youngsters this age usually enjoy. This begins with a group leader asking for a volunteer to say his or her name. The next youngster in the circle (to the left or right) says his or her name and the name of the first child. This activity passes around the circle with each member, including the leaders, saying his or her name and those of everyone who has come before.

Then leaders state, "It's important for us to have some rules so that our group can go better." The leaders introduce the four group rules: (1) no interrupting one another, (2) no put-downs, (3) anyone can "pass" rather than talk, and (4) confidentiality. The latter usually has to be explained (often by referring to it as the "top-secret" rule) to these young children.

Leaders then tape a large sheet of newsprint to the wall and tell the group that they are going to draw a picture labeled "Family Before Divorce." One of the leaders facilitates the discussion about this while the other draws the various family members and pets that the group members describe. Usually, youngsters come up with a family composed of a mother, father, two or three children, a baby, and an assortment of pets. The leader who is drawing this on the newsprint sheet also labels the figures and places them in a drawing of a house. This is done on the left half of the sheet. Then the leaders say, "Now we're going to draw a picture what this family might look like after a divorce." A leader draws a line down the middle of the sheet of newsprint and titles the righthand side "Family After Divorce." Usually, this consists of the original house and a smaller house or apartment. Initially, it is common for the mother, girls, baby, and cat to be placed together in the original house and for the father, boys, and dog to be in the smaller, second house.

Finally, participants are given their own sheet of paper with a line drawn vertically down the middle. Leaders tell the children that now they are going to draw a picture of their own family before and after divorce. The group leaders circulate around the room, assisting the children. One common occurrence has been the tendency of youngsters to focus on the "Before" drawing and have difficulty moving to the "After" drawing. Leaders can then say, "It seems like kids sometimes try to remember what it was like before the divorce and have a harder time thinking about what it's been like since the divorce happened." This universalized statement helps articulate many children's longing for the idealized predivorce family, and their less positive feelings about their current, postdivorce family situation.

As leaders circulate in the group, they can quietly help group members label and write in the relationship name of some of the postdivorce family figures. Thus, terms such as *stepfather, stepsister,* and *half-brother* often emerge. Leaders can also say to the whole group, "After divorce, parents sometimes get married again. Then there are new kinds of names for people in your family, like *step*father, and *half*-sister. Who can tell us what those names mean?"

This session begins to clarify the meaning of divorce-related concepts, including what divorce, itself, is about. Drawings help these young children understand difficult ideas, while providing a comfortable, familiar activity for group members to engage in during this first session.

Session 8: Remarriage and Stepfamilies

This session aims to provide a forum for discussing remarriage and the idea of a blended family, along with the relationships it brings. The session begins with a puppet play about a mother telling her children that she is planing to marry John, the man whom she has been dating. The female leader uses the mother puppet and the children take turns using the boy and girl puppets. Typically, following mother's thoughtful and gentle announcement of her plans, the children heatedly express numerous criticisms of John (e.g., "He's gross!" "He's really ugly") and of mother's intention to marry him (e.g., "We don't need a new dad," "John's around too much already").

Leaders then call a time-out and ask the group what the children in the play are thinking and feeling. Often, group members amplify the critical comments they made in the puppet play. The leaders can then ask, "Why do you suppose kids are so dead-set against their mom getting married?" Concerns we have heard include: "If she gets married, she won't spend hardly any time with her kids," "The kids don't want a stepdad, they already have a dad," and "If she marries John, she can't get married back to their dad." Leaders can then use universalized statements to articulate the children's competitive feelings toward a stepfather for the mother's time and affection, loyalty feelings toward their father that are a barrier to a positive relationship with a stepfather, and remarriage as an interference in children's wishes for parental reconciliation. An example is: "It sure sounds like lots of kids are worried that if their mom gets remarried she won't spend as much time with her kids and maybe won't even love them as much as she used to." As this is discussed, leaders can correct this fantasy and lower anxiety by saying, "But that's not how it works. Moms keep loving their kids after they get married even if they spend a little less time doing things just with them."

Similar universalized statements are used to articulate other worries and wishes and provide corrective information and perspectives. We find that having children express their concerns and having group leaders articulating, clarifying, and normalizing them, while crucial to helping youngsters, is not enough. Learning specific coping skills is necessary to providing support to children of divorce.

The Early Elementary School module makes substantial use of the displacement activities of drawing and puppet play to represent key divorce events and issues. Children take to this format with ease and comfort, and most participate enthusiastically. Group leaders use these activities, along with universalized statements, to clarify concepts, normalize children's experiences, and direct youngsters to adaptive coping behaviors.

The Later Elementary School Module (Ages 9 to 11)

The Later Elementary School module also uses displacement activities. However, children of this age do best with role-playing, rather than puppet play or drawings, though these methods can also be effective with later elementary school-age youngsters. The cognitive abilities of 9- to 11-year-olds permit them to understand most divorce-related terms and concepts. Thus, there is less need for cognitive clarification of factual aspects of divorce. However, burdensome beliefs (e.g., that they were in some way responsible for the divorce and/or for reduced contact with a nonresident parent) and worries about the future (e.g., that remarriage will mean less love from a parent) still require considerable corrective cognitive input from leaders.

Children in later elementary school grades have characteristic reactions to centrally important divorce events and issues, though they also share some of the reactions of their younger peers. For example, hostility between parents elicits primarily anger and anxiety, and sadness only secondarily. Parent dating evokes feelings of rivalry and fears of losing their parent to his or her dating partner, just as it does in younger children, but anger at the parent (not simply criticisms of the parent's partner) is more common among this older group of children.

The following session describes the techniques and issues that characterize this intervention for later elementary school-age youngsters.

Session 5: Visiting and Dating Issues

The aims of this session are to permit feelings and thoughts about visits with the nonresident parent and parent dating to emerge. If there are group members in joint custody arrangements, leaders also phrase this as "going from one parent's home to the other's." Leaders articulate and normalize children's feelings about these divorce issues and discuss ways to cope with them.

This session follows one focusing on issues of custody (see Table 7.1), which made use of a courtroom scene as the major displacement activity. After a brief review of that session, leaders tell the children, "Today we're going to be talking about what it's like to go from one parent's home to the other parent's. Let's go around the circle and see what different kinds of schedules we have in our group." After custodial and transition arrangements are shared, leaders introduce the idea of a skit in which children are waiting to be picked up by their father to go to his home. The female co-leader plays the mother who is waiting with the children at her home, the male co-leader plays one of her sons, and one or two group members are chosen to be the other children who are also waiting for their father. Father is late, the children are anxiously awaiting his arrival, and mother is becoming increasingly angry. She reminds the children that "he has a lot of trouble being on time" and goes on to make other disparaging remarks about him.

The leaders use the stop-action format described earlier to elicit comments from the group about the father's lateness, mother's anger, and what the children in the play are thinking and feeling. Responses are incorporated into the skit and discussion permits leaders to address group members' concerns. In our groups, we often hear youngsters voice anger at the mother for badmouthing the father and anger as well as sadness over not feeling as special and important to their father as they wish. Group members also spontaneously share their own experiences with transitions.

Leaders use universalized statements to normalize and empathize with children's reactions and to correct self-blaming beliefs: "Most kids sort of hope that the divorce would stop the fighting and badmouthing between their parents. It makes kids mad and sad when parents are still angry at each other" and "A lot of kids feel that they don't see one of their parents enough. That makes kids unhappy. Sometimes even fifth- and sixth-graders get the idea that if they were only nicer, or did better at school, or something, then their dad (or mom) would spend more time with them. But that's not how it works. Sometimes it's hard for parents to do what any kid would want them to do, but that doesn't mean that parents don't care, and it doesn't mean that there's something wrong with the kids. Parents can have grown-up problems that make it hard for them to do what's best." These comments normalize children's thoughts and feelings and help reduce a sense of being unworthy without derogating parents.

The remaining two skits in this session deal with parent dating. One takes place at McDonald's and includes the father, played by the male co-leader, and his children, who are played by two or three group members. Father generously insists that the children order as much of whatever they would like, and chats with them about school and their friends. The skit is then stopped, and children are asked what they think is going on. Youngsters note father's indulgent behavior, but often are a bit suspicious of it. When the play is resumed, it is quickly brought to a conclusion with father suggesting that they rent a videotape for the evening, adding, "Since Mary (father's dating partner) and I are going out to a party tonight, I thought you'd like to have something special to do back at the apartment."

The children in the skit often become angry, saying things like, "You're going out with her *again?*" "Why can't you just watch the movie with us?" and "She's gross!" Father calmly tells his children that he likes Mary a lot and that he'll only be gone for a few hours. The skit ends and group discussion is invited. Usually, members are incensed; they now feel that father's generosity was a bribe to keep the children from becoming angry at him. They make disparaging remarks about Mary and, as is so often the case in this intervention, they spontaneously share their own experiences.

Leaders underscore the children's anger, but also say, "Maybe the children are so mad because they feel hurt and disappointed. Dad wants to be with his girlfriend, and they sort of wish that he'd spend all the time with them." In most groups, youngsters can quickly become aware of and acknowledge their underlying feeling of sadness. The tenor of the group becomes more subdued. Leaders can continue to use universalized statements to underscore the connection between anger at a parent and the sad, hurt feelings that give rise to it: "Kids usually feel angry when a parent starts to go out on dates. But that's because they feel jealous that their mom or dad wants to spend *some* time with a grown-up he or she cares about. And it can make them feel sad, too." In similar ways, worries about a parent transferring love away from children to a dating partner can be addressed. Leaders articulate this underlying worry and correct the belief that love is finite and in short supply; if a parent cares about a dating partner, it does *not* mean that he or she has less love for the children.

The final scene focuses on the children returning to their mother's home. The female co-leader plays the mother and two or three group members play the children. In this short skit, the mother grills the youngsters about their time with father. The children often talk about McDonald's and the huge amount of food they ordered. They also mention the video, taking that opportunity to tell mother about father's date with Mary. It is interesting to note how common it is for group members to be protective of mother when they mention father's girlfriend: "She's sort of mean" and "She's not really very pretty" are the sorts of things we hear.

As this skit is discussed, leaders reiterate the hurt feelings youngsters often have when a parent dates, and also note how protective of mother's feelings children want to be. Leaders can say, "Sounds like the children are worried that mom's feelings are going to be hurt, too." This concern about mother allows leaders to raise the issue of loyalty conflicts in a child's feelings toward a parent's dating partner and the other parent: "Sometimes kids think that it's *not* okay to like someone their parent is dating. They worry that it might hurt the other parent's feelings, like being disloyal." Members often respond with relief, and reveal that they have had similar worries. To cope with this conflict, the group is encouraged to tell a parent that they love him or her best, but to ask, "Is it is okay for me to have some fun with mom's boyfriend (or dad's girlfriend)?" Because some youngsters initially are uneasy about this, the group is given permission to say to a parent, "The divorce group said that it's real important to tell your parents about your feelings, especially one like this." With this support, many children are able to use this coping behavior.

The Early Adolescent Module (Ages 12 to 14)

The Early Adolescent module requires three significant modifications of the elementary school interventions. First, because teenagers are more likely to have stepparents and be sensitive to discipline and authority than their younger counterparts, there is a greater emphasis here on relationships within remarried families. Second, we have found that adolescents do not enthusiastically accept the leaders being completely in charge of structuring sessions; role-play that is guided primarily by leaders too often is met with a pronounced lack of interest and involvement. To be engaging, the skits in this module are first scripted, in broad strokes, by eliciting ideas from group members. Third, many of our teenage group members are put off by universalized statements. They seem a bit hurt and puzzled by references to "Lots of teenagers . . ." and "Most kids in middle school and high school. . . . " It was as if they wanted us to pay attention to them, not some other people we may know. Yet, as was the case with our younger group participants, they were defensively unresponsive to direct approaches. Our solution was a technique we came to call a "within-group universalized statement." Rather than referring to other teenagers or "kids," in general, we began comments with phrases such as, "It seems what most of the group is saying . . . " and "Sounds like pretty much everyone here today feels that . . . " to present ideas to groups of young adolescents.

The following session from the Early Adolescent module reflects these technical and substantive changes.

Session 4: Parent Fighting and Adolescent Coping

The aims of this session are to permit feelings and thoughts about parent fighting to emerge and be elaborated, to normalize these reactions, to correct beliefs about their responsibilities when parents fight, and to provide strategies for coping with interparental conflict.

This session follows the first session devoted to predivorce warfare between parents. In that session (Session 3), role-play very similar to what was reported earlier for Session 2 in the Later Elementary School module takes place. However, young adolescents' reactions to those skits are more intense than later elementary school-age children's. Far more than their younger counterparts, these teenagers experience powerful feelings of rage and maintain a firmly held conviction that it is incumbent on them to do something about their parents' hostilities because they feel they are old enough to take such action. These issues led us to develop a second session about parent fighting, but with a primary emphasis on coping strategies.

The session begins with a review of the prior session. Most group members vividly recall the role-play about parent fighting. The group is then told that in this meeting, the parent argument will continue. To engage the youngsters in this activity, leaders ask how they think the altercation will proceed. One leader writes the group's ideas on a large piece of newsprint taped to a wall. This pre–role-play scripting is required in all sessions as a way of actively involving adolescent group members in displacement activities. Frequently voiced scripting ideas include notions that the fight will include screaming and swearing, accusations of infidelity and drinking, and that it will ultimately lead to the parents separating and seeking a divorce.

After writing these scripting suggestions on the newsprint, the leaders begin the role-play with the female co-leader again playing the mother and the male co-leader playing the father. The group's suggestions for how the skit will unfold are incorporated into the role-play. The leaders, playing the warring parents, yell at each other, hurl accusations, throw threat of divorce at one another, and eventually, the father angrily exits. The role-play is then stopped, and leaders ask the group, "What's happening with Mr. and Mrs. X?" Usually, the members say that the fighting will get so out of hand next time that one parent will hurt or kill the other, that one parent, typically father, will abandon the family, that mother will become so depressed that she will not be able to care for her children, and that a divorce is certain to occur.

Group members spontaneously refer to events in their own families as this discussion continues. Using the within-group form of universalized statements, leaders empathize with and normalize the adolescents' concerns: "I think what a lot of you are saying is that it's pretty common to worry about parents' anger getting completely out of control and really hurting someone" and "Sounds like what this group is saying is that parents may get so caught up in their own feelings that they won't want to or be able to take care of their kids." Often, these comments lead group members to share their personal war stories and become increasingly open to expressing their anxieties about parental hostilities. Leaders continue to accept and normalize these feelings.

The remainder of the session is devoted to developing appropriate and adaptive coping strategies for dealing with ongoing, as well as remembered, acrimony between parents. Crucial to this process is leaders making connections between teenagers' urges to jump into the fray, often angrily, and the underlying painful feelings of helplessness mixed with a sense of responsibility that together give rise to their need to spring into action.

Leaders ask the group, "What can teenagers do when they see their parents fighting?" Typically, responses focus on angrily intervening (e.g., "I'd get my baseball bat and go after my dad if he kept it up," "I'd call my grandfather and tell him to bring his shotgun over"). Leaders empathize with the teenagers' anger as well as their need to take action. They also attempt to modulate these reactions by casting them against the reality of such situations: "It seems like a lot of you get real angry about parents fighting, and you think you're old enough and big enough so that you feel it's your job to do something. But when you think about it, it really doesn't make sense to get in the middle of a fight between parents. And it could easily make things worse instead of better. It's hard to walk away when you see your parents getting into it, but that's what really makes sense. That stuff is grown-up business between parents." This usually leads to ideas about what actually would happen if a teenager picked up a baseball bat or told his or her parents to "shut the hell up." Comments we have heard include: "My dad would go ballistic—it'd definitely get worse" and "My mom would probably just cry more and then scream at me." Leaders underscore the unhelpful outcomes to adolescents intervening directly in their parents' altercations.

When that principle is established, leaders can say, "So what can you really do? What makes sense? It feels crummy to just helplessly watch." Participants usually come up with ideas for extricating themselves from the situation. They suggest going to their room and listening to music, going to the basement to play video games, getting together with a friend or calling a friend on the telephone, and the like. These strategies are reinforced by the leaders: "This group's come up with some very good ideas for what to do to get away from the battlefield. That makes good sense. If you hang around, it just makes you feel angry and helpless. And getting in the middle is just asking for things to get worse." These comments relieve youngsters of the twin burden of feeling helpless and responsible at the same time. It gives them realistic alternatives to inappropriate action, or guilt over not taking action, which become acceptable through the leaders' support and agreement by their peers.

Communication with parents after an argument is strongly encouraged as a way to cope actively and adaptively with feelings stimulated by parental hostilities. It is interesting that despite their anger and bravado, most teenagers are extremely reluctant to approach parents with their feelings about parental animosities. Initially, when leaders ask, "What can you say to parents about their fighting after the argument is over, like the next day?" group members say that they can tell their parents, "You're acting like jerks" or to "knock it off." But when leaders invite the group to think about exactly when they would tell their parents such things or ask how their parents would probably respond, the group backs away from the idea of saying anything. Leaders can note this and empathize with the group: "It sure sounds like what you're all saying is that actually talking to parents about their fighting is very hard."

Leaders then introduce the idea of "I statements" as a way of safely telling parents how they feel and how they would like their parents to act. They can say to the group, "It's scary to think about telling parents what you feel and want, but that's because you don't know good and safe ways to do it. But there is a way that can work a lot of times; it's called using 'I statements.' Parents can usually hear 'I statements' and not get upset." Examples are then given: "*I* get worried that someone's going to get hurt when you and dad fight"; "*I* usually get yelled at after you and mom argue, and *I* feel bad about that"; and "*I* wish you and dad wouldn't fight so much. It's been five years since the divorce and *I* still get upset when you're angry at each other." Adolescents tend to accept this strategy, and leaders can also add that if a teenager is more comfortable writing these messages instead of directly telling parents, that works, too.

Explaining adolescents' anger and their urge to act in terms of underlying feelings of helplessness and a misplaced feeling of responsibility, in combination with a focus on adaptive coping strategies, provide teenagers with a marked sense of relief.

LIMITATIONS OF GROUP INTERVENTION APPROACHES

Though there is evidence that intervention groups for children of divorce can be helpful to youngsters, it is a far cry from a "silver bullet." Children who are in acutely stressful divorce circumstances or who are exposed to chronic divorce-related stresses over years will need a more tailored and clinically oriented intervention (i.e., individual or family therapy). Similarly, children who suffer from firmly entrenched divorce-related conflicts that have become part of the fabric of their personality (e.g., the highly aggressive, severely inhibited, seriously depressed, or significantly academically impaired child) are unlikely to profit substantially from a brief group intervention. But participating in such a group provides leaders with the opportunity to informally assess how a youngster is progressing developmentally. Recommendations to parents for additional help, such as therapy, may be more likely to be accepted when based on knowledge of the child and the implicit comparison to other children who have participated in such groups.

These interventions are also unlikely to be very useful to youngsters suffering from difficulties that are not related to their parents' divorce. At times, we have had children referred to our groups who had significant learning disabilities, biologically based affective disorders, pervasive developmental disorders, anxiety disorders, and conduct disorders, which were in no way associated with divorce or its aftermath. These youngsters had serious, long-standing problems; divorce just happened to have been a part of their family background. It is useful to keep in mind the sorts of difficulties divorce tends to engender in youngsters, as noted in the review section of this chapter, and those it does not.

DIRECTIONS FOR FUTURE RESEARCH

It would be particularly useful to clarify the distinction between treatment and preventive interventions, elaborated earlier. Confusion as to whether an intervention is geared to treating existing conditions (even those linked to the divorce experience) or preventing the emergence of difficulties at some time in the future has plagued outcome studies. The implications this conceptual clarification has for selecting group members, outcome measures, and the time frame for the evaluation are enormous. Some evidence exists for the presence of both treatment and prevention effects as a result of participating in these groups. Clearly distinguishing treatment and prevention would permit a more fine-grained analysis of which children profit from each and which do not.

Comparisons among different interventions would also be of value. Assessing interventions for children of divorce has been in its infancy. Thus, it has made sense to compare children who have had a particular intervention with wait-list or no-service control groups. While this should continue, it would be useful to compare the efficacy of alternative interventions within the same research project rather than indirectly across studies. A multisite investigation of the sort that has been used to assess various psychological and pharmacological therapies would be useful to evaluate comparatively these interventions.

REFERENCES

Ahrons, C. (1981). The continuing coparental relationship between divorced spouses. *American Journal of Orthopsychiatry, 51,* 415–428.

Alpert-Gillis, L. J., Pedro-Carroll, J. L., & Cowen, E. L. (1989). The children of divorce intervention program: Development, implementation, and evaluation of a program for young urban children. *Journal of Consulting and Clinical Psychology, 57,* 583–589.

Amato, P. R., & Keith, B. (1991). Parental divorce and the well-being of children: A meta-analysis. *Psychological Bulletin, 110,* 26–46.

Bray, J. H., & Berger, S. H. (1993). Developmental issues in stepfamilies research project: Family relationships and parent-child interactions. *Journal of Family Psychology, 7* , 76–90.

Camara, K. A., & Resnick, G. (1989). Styles of conflict resolution and co-operation between divorced parents: Effects on child behavior and adjustment. *American Journal of Orthopsychiatry, 59,* 560–575.

Chase-Lansdale, P. L., & Hetherington, E. M. (1990). The impact of divorce on life-span development: Short and long-term effects. In P. Baltes, D. L. Featherman, & R. M. Lerner (Eds.), *Life-span development and behavior* (Vol.10, pp. 105–150). Hillsdale, NJ: Lawrence Erlbaum.

Cherlin, A. (1981). *Marriage, divorce, remarriage.* Cambridge, MA: Harvard University Press.

Emery, R. E. (1982). Interparental conflict and the children of discord and divorce. *Psychological Bulletin, 92,* 310–330.

Emery, R. E., Hetherington, E. M., & DiLalla, L. (1984). Divorce, children, and social policy. In H. Stevenson & A. Siegel (Eds.), *Child development research and social policy* (Vol. 1, pp. 189–266). Chicago: University of Chicago Press.

Farmer, S., & Galaris, D. (1993). Support groups for children of divorce. *American Journal of Family Therapy, 21,* 40–50.

Furstenberg, F. F., Jr., Nord, C. W., Peterson, J. L., & Zill, N. (1983). The life course of children of divorce: Marital disruption and parental contact. *American Sociological Review,* 656–668.

Garvin, V., Kalter, N., & Leber, D. (1991).Children of divorce: Predictors of change following preventive intervention. *American Journal of Orthopsychiatry, 61,* 438–447.

Grych, J. H., & Fincham, F. D. (1992). Interventions for children of divorce: Toward greater integration of research and action. *Psychological Bulletin, 111,* 434–454.

Guidubaldi, J. (1988). Differences in children's divorce adjustment across grade level and gender: A report from the NASP-Kent State nationwide project. In S. A. Wolchik & P. Karoly (Eds.), *Children of divorce: Empirical perspectives on adjustment.* New York: Gardner.

Hernandez, D. J. (1988). The demographics of divorce and remarriage. In E. M. Hetherington & J. D. Arasteh (Eds.), *Impact of divorce, single parenting, and stepparenting on children.* (pp. 3–22). Hillsdale, NJ: Lawrence Erlbaum.

Hetherington, E. M. (1993). An overview of the Virginia longitudinal study of divorce and remarriage with a focus on early adolescence. *Journal of Family Psychology, 7,* 39–56.

Hetherington, E. M., Cox, M., & Cox, R. (1985). Long term effects of divorce and remarriage on the adjustment of children. *Journal of the American Academy of Child Psychiatry, 24,* 518–530.

Hetherington, E. M., Stanley-Hagan, M., & Anderson, E. R. (1989). Marital transitions: A child's perspective. *American Psychologist, 44,* 303–312.

Hoffman, L. (1981). *Foundations of family therapy.* New York: Basic Books.

Kalter, N. (1987). Long-term effects of divorce on children: A developmental vulnerability model. *American Journal of Orthopsychiatry, 57,* 587–600.

Kalter, N. (1988). *Developmental facilitation groups for children of divorce: Six-month and one-year outcomes.* Unpublished manuscript.

Kalter, N. (1990). *Growing up with divorce.* New York: The Free Press.

Kalter, N., & Associates (1985). *Time-limited developmental facilitation groups for children of divorce: The later elementary school model.* Ann Arbor, MI: The Family Styles Project.

Kalter, N., & Associates (1988). *Time-limited developmental facilitation groups for children of divorce: The early elementary school model.* Ann Arbor, MI: The Family Styles Project.

Kalter, N., & Associates (1993). *Time-limited develop-*

mental facilitation groups for children of divorce: The early adolescent model. Ann Arbor, MI: The Family Styles Project.

Kalter, N., Kloner, A., Schreier, S., & Okla, K. (1989). Predictors of children's postdivorce adjustment. *American Journal of Orthopsychiatry, 59,* 605–618.

Kalter, N., Pickar, J., & Lesowitz, M. (1984). School-based developmental facilitation groups for children of divorce: A preventive intervention. *American Journal of Orthopsychiatry, 54,* 613–623.

Kalter, N., Schaefer, M., Lesowitz, M., Alpern, D., & Pickar, J. (1988). School-based support groups for children of divorce: A model of a brief intervention. In B. H. Gottlieb (Ed.), *Marshalling social support* (pp. 165–185). Newbury Park, CA: Sage.

Kalter, N., & Schreier, S. (1993). School-based support groups for children of divorce. *Special Services in the Schools, 8,* 39–66.

Kurdek, L. A. (1988). Cognitive mediators of children's adjustment to divorce. In S. A. Wolchik & P. Karoly (Eds.), *Children of divorce: Empirical perspectives on adjustment.* New York: Gardner.

Lee, C. M., Picard, M., & Blaine, M. D. (1994). A methodological and substantive review of intervention outcome studies for families undergoing divorce. *Journal of Family Psychology, 8,* 3–15.

Lohnes, K., & Kalter, N. (1994). Support groups for parentally bereaved children. *American Journal of Orthopsychiatry, 64,*594–603.

National Center for Health Statistics. (1990). Advance report of final divorce statistics, 1987. *Monthly Vital Statistics Report* (Vol. 38, No.12, supp. 2). Hyattsville, MD: U.S. Public Health Service.

National Center for Health Statistics. (1995). Advance report of final divorce statistics, 1989 and 1990. *Monthly Vital Statistics Report* (Vol. 43, No. 9). Hyattsville, MD; U.S. Public Health Service.

Pedro-Carroll, J. L., & Cowen, E. L. (1985). The children of divorce intervention program: An investigation of the efficacy of a school-based prevention program. *Journal of Consulting and Clinical Psychology, 53,* 603–611.

Pedro-Carroll, J. L., & Cowen, E. L. (1987). The children of divorce intervention program: Implementation and evaluation of a time-limited approach. In J. Vincent (Ed.), *Advances in family intervention, assessment, and theory* (Vol. 4, pp. 281–307). Greenwich, CT: JAI Press.

Pedro-Carroll, J. L., Cowen, E. L., Hightower, A. D., & Guare, J. C. (1986). Preventive intervention with latency-aged children of divorce: A replication study. *American Journal of Community Psychology, 14,* 277–290.

Rubin, S. (1990). School-based groups for children of divorce: *A four-year follow-up evaluation.* Unpublished doctoral dissertation, University of Michigan, Ann Arbor.

Stolberg, A. L. & Cullen, P. M. (1983). Preventing psychopathology in children of divorce: The divorce adjustment project. In L. A. Kurdek (Ed.), *New directions for child development: Children and divorce* (pp. 71–81). San Francisco: Jossey-Bass.

Stolberg, A. L., & Garrison, K. M. (1985). Evaluating a primary prevention program for children of divorce. *American Journal of Community Psychology, 13,* 111–123.

Stolberg, A. L., & Mahler, J. L. (1994). Enhancing treatment gains in a school-based intervention for children of divorce through skill training, parental involvement, and transfer procedures. *Journal of Consulting and Clinical Psychology, 62,* 147–156.

Wallerstein, J. S. (1985). Children of divorce: Preliminary report of a ten-year follow-up of older children and adolescents. *Journal of the American Academy of Child Psychiatry, 24,* 545–553.

Wallerstein, J. S. (1987). Children of divorce: Report of a ten-year follow-up of early latency-age children. *American Journal of Orthopsychiatry, 57,* 199–211.

Wallerstein, J. S. (1991). The long-term effects of divorce on children: A review. *Journal of the American Academy of Child and Adolescent Psychiatry, 30,* 349–360.

Wallerstein, J. S., & Kelly, J. B. (1980). *Surviving the break-up.* New York: Basic Books.

Walsh, F. (1993). *Normal family processes* (2nd ed.). New York: Guilford.

Zaslow, M. J. (1988). Sex differences in children's response to parental divorce: 1. Research methodology and past divorce family forms. *American Journal of Orthopsychiatry, 58,* 355–378.

Zaslow, M. J. (1989). Sex differences in children's response to parental divorce: 2. Samples, variables, ages,and sources. *American Journal of Orthopsychiatry, 59,* 118–141.

Zill, N., Morrison, D. R., & Coiro, M. J. (1993). Long-term effects of parental divorce on parent-child relationships, adjustment, and achievement in young adulthood. *Journal of Family Psychology, 7,* 91–103.

CHAPTER 8

GROUP INTERVENTIONS FOR THE PEER-REJECTED CHILD

Gregory A. Waas, NORTHERN ILLINOIS UNIVERSITY
Patricia A. Graczyk, NORTHERN ILLINOIS UNIVERSITY

Both researchers and practitioners have long been keenly interested in elementary school-aged children (i.e., 6–12 years) who experience difficulty developing and maintaining positive relationships with their peers. This interest undoubtedly is due to several factors, including a large body of empirical research and clinical experience indicating that these children are at increased risk for a wide array of concurrent difficulties, as well as psychological and adjustment problems later in life. Although the precise causal linkages between peer rejection, concurrent symptomatology, and long-term adjustment problems is not clear, it is likely that the failure to establish positive peer relationships makes it more difficult for children to master important social and personal skills that are developed within the peer group context (e.g., Hartup, 1983).

Despite an emerging consensus that peer-rejected children are at risk, the most appropriate treatment intervention for this group remains unclear. A wide variety of intervention approaches has been utilized with these children, but none has been entirely satisfactory. Clearly, a number of factors contribute to this treatment difficulty. For example, the peer-rejected population is heterogeneous in terms of the causes of rejection. It is not surprising that a child who is rejected due to severe aggression might require a very different treatment approach than a child who is rejected due to extreme anxiety. A second important factor that makes treatment of these children difficult—one that is shared by all rejected children—is that peer rejection by definition is a social difficulty, involving the perceptions of peers as well as the rejected child's interpersonal behavior. An effective intervention, then, must not only focus on the rejected child but also change the way peers perceive the child.

A growing body of psychological research in the social, educational, clinical, and developmental areas suggests that group-oriented counseling interventions may be most powerful in ameliorating both the causes and effects of peer rejection. The efficacy of a group approach, however, may be significantly affected by the way the group is conceptualized and used in the therapy process. It is important to distinguish between two types of group-oriented interventions: (1) interventions conducted in groups and (2) group interventions. Frequently, both practitioners and researchers conduct *interventions in groups,* mainly for cost-effectiveness reasons. In these cases, a promising intervention is identified and applied to relevant groups of children to maximize the efficiency of treatment delivery. Such a strategy is certainly reasonable, especially for psychologists who confront an oversupply of potential clients and an acute shortage of time and resources. This kind of intervention typifies treatment-outcome studies involving peer-rejected children.

Although superficially similar to the first type of group approach, *group interventions* use the group context itself as a major therapeutic element. It is this second type of intervention that may be most useful in therapeutic work with peer-rejected children. After all, the core characteristic of these children is that they cannot create and maintain positive relationships with their peer group. The very nature of the adjustment difficulty they experience suggests that actively incorporating their peers into a group intervention may be a useful strategy in changing the rejected child's maladaptive behaviors and the negative pattern of social relationships that the child experiences.

In this chapter, we will provide an overview of the characteristics most commonly observed among peer-rejected children and review briefly the assessment procedures for identifying this at-risk group. A discussion of recent research that supports the use of group interventions with these children will follow, and a heuristic of how psychologists, social workers, and other mental health professionals might conceptualize therapeutic work with peer-rejected children will be provided. Finally, we will review group-oriented interventions that may be particularly useful with these children and describe how a group approach can evolve naturally into a consultative framework to promote generalization and maintenance of treatment gains.

DEFINITION AND CHARACTERISTICS

Peer rejection has been defined and operationalized in numerous ways over the years, but most definitions include at least two components as being central to the identification of this group of children. First, peer-rejected children are those individuals who have few, if any, positive friendships (e.g., Dubow & Cappas, 1988; Parker & Asher, 1993). They are seldom chosen as favored playmates by peers when sociometric procedures are completed, and they frequently are ostracized by peers during free-play activities in the classroom, on the playground, or in the neighborhood. In distinction from neglected children, who frequently are left out by peers as well, socially rejected children also are actively disliked by peers (e.g., Bierman, 1989). It is this insidious combination of factors, few positive relationships plus many negative relationships, that uniquely identifies this at-risk group.

An extensive and growing body of research indicates that socially rejected children tend to be inept in their interactions with peers, displaying a variety of socially inappropriate behaviors. For example, when attempting to enter an ongoing group activity, peer-rejected children tend to engage in more high-risk tactics such as attention seeking and disruptive behaviors, whereas nonrejected children use more group-oriented statements and engage in behaviors that are more consistent with the group activity (Dodge, Schlundt, Schocken, & Delugach, 1983; Putallaz & Wasserman, 1989). By far, the most frequently cited characteristic of peer-rejected children is aggression (e.g., Asher, 1990; Newcomb, Bukowski, & Pattee, 1993), but they also are viewed by peers as bossy, explosive, immature, and attention seeking (Dubow, 1988). Conversely, they demonstrate significantly less prosocial behavior than other children, such as leadership and cooperation (Dubow & Cappas, 1988). In addition to negative externalizing behaviors, however, these children also are viewed by peers as being oversensitive, sad, and socially isolated (Boivin, Thomassin, & Alain, 1989; Cantrell & Prinz, 1985). Indeed, rejected children report more loneliness and higher levels of stress (Crick & Ladd, 1993; Parkhurst & Asher, 1992).

The peer milieu, however, is not the only arena in which peer-rejected children experience difficulties. Both parents and teachers view them as demonstrating significantly more behavioral difficulties than their nonrejected peers. At home, these children are viewed as hyperactive, disruptive, and withdrawn (French & Waas, 1985). Teachers describe them as inattentive, overactive, nervous, and demonstrating significant academic difficulties and task-inappropriate behavior (Cantrell & Prinz, 1985; French & Waas, 1985).

Peer-rejected children also have been shown to be significantly different from nonrejected peers in the social-cognitive domain. When evaluating social situations, they underutilize relevant interpersonal information (Dozier, 1988) and they are more likely to attribute hostile intent in ambiguous interpersonal encounters (e.g., Dodge, 1980; Dodge & Somberg, 1987). They view aggressive behavior in a more favorable light as a strategy to use in interpersonal encounters and are more interested in the instrumental outcomes of social interactions than relational outcomes (Crick & Ladd, 1990). For example, whereas most children view the goals of a game as winning and having fun, rejected children are more likely to focus exclusively on winning, regardless of the negative impact this may have on their relationship with playmates (Renshaw & Asher, 1983).

In addition to the concurrent difficulties these children experience, peer-rejected children also are at greater risk for a variety of difficulties later in life. Of those individuals who have experienced adjustment difficulties in adulthood, 28 to 78% of them have a history of peer-relationship difficulties as children (Parker & Asher, 1987). Peer-rejected children are more likely to engage in adolescent and adult criminal behavior, drop out of school, develop mental health disorders, and attempt suicide (Kupersmidt, Coie, & Dodge, 1990; Parker & Asher, 1987). Such negative longitudinal outcomes underscore the importance of identifying this group of at-risk children and developing effective interventions for them.

ASSESSMENT OF PEER REJECTION

The two most common procedures for identifying socially rejected children are peer ratings and peer nominations (Asher & Dodge, 1986; Kennedy, 1988). Peer ratings provide an index of the child's general level of social acceptance among his or her peers. In this procedure, each child is given a listing of all same-sex members of the class or grade and instructed to rate how much he or she likes to be friends with or play/work with every other peer in the class. Peer-rejected children are defined as those children who receive the lowest average rating scores in the class.

A second common procedure for assessing peer rejection involves the use of peer nominations. In this procedure, children are provided a listing of all same-sex members of the class or grade and asked to identify the two or three children they most like to work or play with and the same number of children they least like. Rejected children are those individuals who receive the fewest positive nominations and a high number of negative nominations. The nomination method provides a frequency index of the child's positive and negative peer relationships.

Although the use of rating and nomination procedures provide important screening information about a child's general level of social acceptance, it is critical to collect additional data on the specific behaviors and characteristics of a child that contribute to his or her peer rejection (Coie, 1985; Coie & Koeppl, 1990). As has been shown, peer-rejected children exhibit a wide variety of difficulties and may be socially rejected for a wide variety of reasons. To the extent that different psychological and social problems require different therapeutic approaches, it is inappropriate to intervene with all peer-rejected children in the same way.

Unfortunately, the treatment-outcome literature is replete with studies in which peer-rejected children are identified, and a standardized treatment regimen is applied without additional assessment being conducted to ensure that a match exists between the intervention used and the needs of the child. Failure to achieve such a match may be an important contributor to the inconsistent outcomes reported in the treatment literature (e.g., Bierman, Miller, & Stabb, 1987; Coie & Krehbiel, 1984). Indeed, Akhtar and Bradley (1991) suggested that the use of an overly standardized approach in social skills training represents a major problem with many interventions.

A detailed review of the extensive literature on sociometrics, direct observation procedures, interview approaches, and parent/teacher ratings involved in the comprehensive assessment of peer-rejected children is beyond the scope of this chapter. However, the interested reader is referred to several excellent discussions of these assessment procedures (e.g., Gresham & Reschly, 1988; Hops & Lewin, 1984; Kennedy, 1988; Shapiro & Kratochwill, 1988).

RATIONALE FOR GROUP INTERVENTION: EMERGING RESEARCH

A growing body of converging evidence is beginning to show that peer rejection is not the result of only deficient social skills on the part of the rejected child, but that peer rejection also is developed and maintained by the way that others think about and evaluate the rejected child (e.g., Hymel, 1986; Waas & Honer, 1990). Baldwin (1992) has called these ways of thinking about other persons "relational schemas." Individuals use these relational schemas to form working models of their interpersonal relationships, which serve as cognitive maps to help them navigate their social world.

If, for example, an individual frequently suffers insult from a second person following a disagreement, the individual may develop a relational schema that includes himself or herself as victim, the other person as verbally aggressive, and a script involving disagreement leading to insult. This script will likely be activated when the individual is in the presence of the insulting other, causing the individual to expect such insults and to behave accordingly (e.g., with aloofness or defensiveness). If an interaction pattern is repeated frequently, a social script may become automatic and could even be applied to inappropriate social circumstances (Smith & Lerner, 1986). In our example, the individual may become defensive in expectation of the other person's insults, even when the other person has no intention of insulting the individual.

Once such negative relational schemas are established about a rejected child, they have a self-fulfilling effect on future interactions with the child and are resistant to change. For example, it is now clear that, in addition to exhibiting deficient social skills, rejected children also tend to have a negative reputation among their peers that biases the way other children think about them and act toward them. Dodge (1980) reported that a child's reputation (aggressive vs. nonaggressive) was an important factor in determining how classmates evaluated his or her social behaviors, and that the use of reputation in making evaluations about a peer tended to increase with age.

Consistent with these findings, Coie and Kupersmidt (1983) reported results from an observation study in which children were observed during free-play sessions. They noted that after six half-hour sessions, children rated socially rejected peers as more aggressive than other children in the group when, in fact, the rejected peers had engaged in no more aggressive exchanges than their playmates. Further, although peer-rejected children did exhibit higher rates of inappropriate solitary behavior, this pattern was observed only after their rejected status had been established within the play group.

These studies are suggestive of a negative cycle in which peer rejection increases deviant behavior on the part of the child, which in turn contributes to further rejection by the child's peers. This negative cycle results in both the rejected child and his or her peers developing rigid beliefs (i.e., negative relational schemas) about how the other child behaves, and these beliefs in turn affect how each child interacts with the other. For example, a child who maintains a relational schema that a rejected peer is aggressive and socially incompetent will likely seek confirmation of these negative beliefs and will tend to behave in a manner that is consistent with these beliefs (e.g., ostracism and social rejection).

This relational aspect of peer rejection may partly be responsible for the inconsistent findings relating to social skills training with socially rejected children. Frequently, the use of social skills training procedures has resulted in improved performance of the social skill trained, but has not resulted in greater social acceptance among the child's peers (e.g., Bierman et al., 1987; Coie & Krehbiel, 1984). Often, these children continue to have few friends and remain rejected by most of their classmates.

It appears that training new social skills alone may not always be powerful enough to change relational schemas among the rejected child's peers. Therefore, in addition to training relevant social and cognitive skills, designers of interventions for peer-rejected children must attempt to break this cycle by changing the biased relational schemas that rejected children have toward others and other children have toward the rejected child. The use of a group format in the treatment of these children may provide a useful context within which such change can begin to take place. Finally, in order to facilitate the generalization and maintenance of group therapy effects, consultative interventions with teachers and parents are recommended. A general heuristic of this treatment approach is presented in Figure 8.1.

GROUP INTERVENTION: PRACTICE

Based on the emerging research relevant to peer rejection, we advocate that group interventions involving these children focus on two major components: (1) teaching new social skills that are relevant to the development of positive peer relationships and (2) structuring interactions within the group to facilitate the modification of negative relational schemas. These components are discussed separately for conceptual clarity, but in practice each component often takes place simultaneously within the group. The first part of the model involves training new skills that have been identified during the assessment phase as being most relevant to the participating children.

Figure 8.1 Heuristic for Group Intervention with Peer-Rejected Children

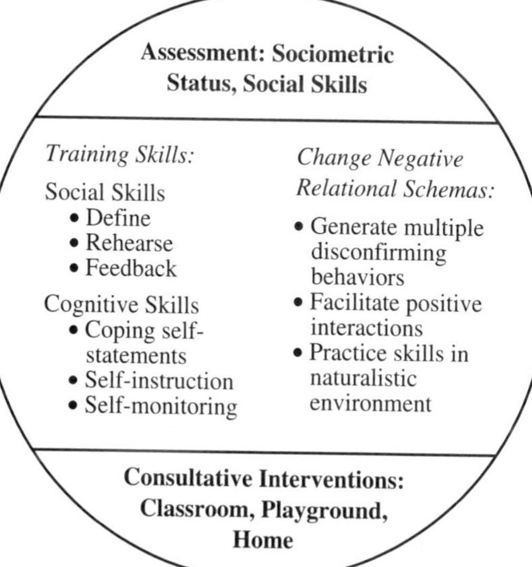

Teaching New Social Skills

The development of effective social skills is critical to children achieving and sustaining positive peer relationships. Some of the most common skills included in treatment intervention studies with peer-rejected children are listed in Table 8.1. Many of these skills can be taught most effectively through a social-learning methodology. In summary, this approach involves developing children's understanding of skill concepts, promoting skill performance, and fostering skill maintenance (e.g., Cartledge & Milburn, 1986; Ladd & Mize, 1983). Throughout this process, a group setting provides a powerful context within which social skills can be developed and practiced.

The first step in the skill-building process is introducing the skill concept and increasing the group members' motivation for learning the skill. For rejected children, who often have a poor understanding of the causal connection between inappropriate behavior (e.g., aggression) and the negative consequences associated with peer rejection (e.g., loneliness), it is important to point out explicitly the benefits of learning better social skills (Kazdin, 1988). Although the group leader should structure this discussion, other children in the group can play an important role in increasing participants' motivation for learning a given skill. Peers within the group can serve as a "reality check" for each other's perception of the consequences of a behavior and can provide group members relevant examples of the benefits of learning a particular social skill.

Whereas group discussion provides therapy participants with language-based information about the targeted skill, modeling frequently is used in the skill-building stage to provide visual information on how to perform the skill. In modeling procedures, a child learns the target skill by watching others perform the component behaviors of the skill under various conditions. A major advantage of social skill modeling is that observers are shown how behaviors are integrated and sequenced to re-

Table 8.1 Common Targets of Intervention with Peer-Rejected Children

SOCIAL-SKILL DOMAIN	SAMPLE TREATMENT-OUTCOME STUDIES
Communication/Cooperation	
Sharing information about self	Bierman, 1986; Bierman & Furman, 1984; Kolko, Loar, & Sturnick, 1990
Asking questions	Bierman, 1986; Ladd, 1981; LaGreca & Santogrossi, 1980
Giving support	Bretzing & Caterino, 1984; Cole & Krehbiel, 1984; Gresham & Nagle, 1980
Sharing/taking turns	Bierman, Miller, Stabb, 1897; Kolko et al., 1990; Oden & Asher, 1977
Dealing with Conflict	
Teasing	Pepler, King, & Byrd, 1991; Kettlewell & Kausch, 1982; Schneider, 1991
Aggression	Coie, Underwood, & Lochman, 1991; Lochman, 1992; Pepler et al., 1991
Negotiation skills	Coie et al., 1991; Kettlewell & Kausch, 1982; Schneider, 1991
Social Cognitive Skills	
Alternative solutions	Coie et al., 1991; Pepler et al., 1991; Stiefvater, Kurdek, & Allik, 1986
Evaluating consequences	Hudley & Graham, 1993; Vaughn & Lancelotta, 1990; Yu, Harris, Solovitz, & Franklin, 1986
Selecting best solution	Hudley & Graham 1993; Pepler et al., 1991; Omizo, Hershberger, Omizo, 1988
Self-monitoring	Pepler et al., 1991; Tanner & Holliman, 1988; Rotherman, 1982

sult in successful performance (Elliott & Gresham, 1993).

A group format provides the opportunity for children to observe a variety of models, which promotes generalization of the trained skills and provides a wide sampling of behavioral solutions for group members to evaluate. For example, the therapist may initially model the target skill, providing group members with a performance criterion toward which to strive. Group members then may take turns attempting to implement the skill. In this process, the therapist serves as a mastery model and other group members function as multiple approximations of the mastery criterion.

Within the social-learning model, the skill is developed further by having group members identify relevant and irrelevant attributes of the skill concept and generate both positive and negative exemplars of the skill. In a group working on compliment giving, each child might be assigned to think of both a positive and negative example of a compliment. Fellow group members would then take turns role-playing the positive and negative suggestions and the natural consequences of each example. Alternatively, a game-like activity might be developed in which attributes of the skills are printed on cards, and each group member randomly selects a card for evaluation. Such embellishments as a game board, dice, and penalties could be incorporated to maintain interest in the activity.

Perhaps the central component of social skills training is the promotion of skill performance through guided rehearsal, feedback, reinforcement, and practice (Cartledge & Milburn, 1986; Ladd &

Mize, 1983). As with learning the skill concept, each group member should be involved actively in all phases of the skill performance stage. Not only will such involvement enhance motivation and peer relations within the group but also the use of peers during role-playing and feedback activities will maximize the modeling effect of these exercises.

Guided rehearsal is a structured form of role-playing in which a particular skill (e.g., entering an ongoing activity) is rehearsed under supervision. The goal of guided rehearsal is to help children replace maladaptive responses with more appropriate ones through repeated practice. Supervision typically involves coaching children on the specific behaviors required to perform the skill successfully, as well as highlighting the relevant social cues occurring in a particular interaction. Such supervised practice is particularly helpful to many rejected children, who have difficulty utilizing social cues and social feedback in an effective fashion.

Bandura (1977) suggested that covert and verbal forms of rehearsal might be usefully combined with role-playing. For example, after discussing with the group possible strategies for entering an ongoing activity (e.g., walk up close to the participants, express an interest in the activity, request entry), children may be asked to imagine carrying out their plan. Group members might then verbally rehearse the strategies and discuss possible outcomes of their efforts, as well as plan possible responses to alternative outcomes. They may then repeatedly perform the overt behaviors involved in the skill until they are able to perform them in a fluid and competent fashion. Group members can take turns role-playing various situations involving a given skill, with other members of the group filling the different roles of the situation.

Because many rejected children have difficulty understanding other people's feelings and actions, assuming different roles within a role-play exercise may facilitate development of their ability to understand another person's viewpoint and enhance their level of empathy. Initially, role-play situations should be identical to those rehearsed covertly and verbally, but after sufficient practice, variations of the situation can be introduced to increase the challenge and enhance generalization of the new skill.

Feedback is a natural extension of the role-playing process that involves a *post-hoc* analysis of the actor's performance of the skill. Under the guidance of the group leader, other children can provide important verbal feedback about a group member's use of a particular skill. As a part of keeping all children actively involved in the activities, the group leader might assign one or more children in the group to serve as "referee" or "advisor" to the role-player. Both they and the role-player might be asked to answer each of the following: (1) What did the actor want to happen? (2) What did they try? (3) Did it work? (4) What might they do differently next time? Additional questions might revolve around how each participant in the role-played situation would feel and probable short-term and long-term consequences (Cartledge & Milburn, 1986). The use of fellow group members to give role-players feedback on their performance is not only an effective method of evaluation but it is also an important part of building a sense of cohesiveness among group members (George & Dustin, 1988).

A second form of feedback involves the tangible reinforcement of an appropriately performed skill. Bierman and colleagues (1987) reported on a token reinforcement procedure used in two of three treatment conditions designed to increase prosocial behavior in peer-rejected boys. In both conditions, skills were introduced and group members were provided with various activities in which to practice the targeted skills. Whenever a child demonstrated a targeted skill, the coach praised his performance, labeled the skill, and placed a token in a cup with the child's name on it. At the end of each session, children were allowed to exchange their tokens for a snack. Bierman and colleagues (1987) reported that children involved in the reinforcement conditions exhibited improved and sustained positive peer interactions.

Providing group members with the opportunity to practice newly learned skills under less structured, less closely supervised conditions is an important part of training for generalization and maintenance (Cartledge & Milburn, 1986; Ladd & Mize, 1983). The group setting provides an ideal opportunity for such practice to occur through activities such as independent role-play practice, therapeutic games, structured activities, and free play. For example, Bierman and Furman (1984) coached children in self-expression (e.g., sharing information about self and feelings), questioning (e.g., asking others about themselves and feelings), and leadership bids (e.g., giving advice, invitations). Children then were given opportunities to practice the skills through role-playing and a structured activity in which children made videotapes of group members engaged in the target skills. Alternatively, Bretzing and Caterino (1984) used psychological board games such as "Roll-a-Roll" or "Social Security" as supplemental activities to encourage children's practice of targeted skills. Similarly, Yu, Harris, Solovitz, and Franklin (1986) utilized group crossword puzzles and drawing projects to provide children with additional practice.

Another way to enhance the power of such interventions and increase the likelihood that children will use newly learned skills in the naturalistic environment is to encourage children to share actual incidents in their lives. Edelson and Rose (1982), for example, began each group session by having children describe recent problematic encounters with peers outside the therapy session and critique their own performance in that situation. These actual situations served as the foci for group training activities, which included brainstorming of alternative solutions, response selection, modeling of responses, rehearsal, coaching, and group feedback.

Teaching Cognitive Skills

Cognitive-behavioral procedures also have been widely used with peer-rejected children and are directly applicable to a group format. Whereas behavioral skill training is used primarily to build specific social skills thought to be important to peer acceptance, cognitive-behavioral procedures are used primarily to decrease impulsive (often inappropriate) responding, facilitate a more reflective approach to thinking about a given problem, and increase the child's self-monitoring and self-reinforcement.

One commonly used cognitive intervention with children is self-instructional training. This procedure addresses a number of social problem-solving skills that often are difficult for peer-rejected children, including the generation of alternative solutions, examination of consequences, and remaining focused on the problem task. Self-instructional training involves the group members and therapist working together to generate a series of questions the child can ask himself or herself to help work through the problem-solving process (e.g., Kendall & Braswell, 1985; Meichenbaum, 1985). Questions such as What is the problem? What are all the ways to solve it? What might happen? and Which one should I choose? typically are developed, rehearsed, and used by the child in various practice situations.

Within a group setting, the therapist would instruct the group members on the basic content and sequence of the self-instructional questions, but children should be encouraged to work among themselves to formulate the precise wording of the questions. Such group involvement will enhance the children's sense of "ownership" of the statements generated, make the statements more meaningful to them, and increase the likelihood that group members will actually use the problem-solving steps when confronted with a social dilemma.

Coping self-statements are designed to help children control their level of emotional arousal and decrease impulsive responding when they are upset. This procedure involves the therapist and children working together to identify especially problematic situations (e.g., being denied participation in a playground game), and then collaboratively developing self-statements that the child can use to help maintain self-control (e.g., "That's okay, I don't have to get mad. I'll look around and find something else to do"). As with social skills training, the use of coping statements is developed through modeling, coaching, and practice. (See Bernard & Joyce [1984] for review.) Other types of arousal-reducing procedures, such as progressive relaxation, often are used in conjunction with coping self-statements (e.g., Lochman, 1992).

A third common target of cognitive procedures is the child's self-monitoring of emotional arousal and awareness of situations that lead to such arousal. One common technique is the "feeling thermometer." Children use a large drawn illustration of a thermometer to label the different degrees of an emotion they experience in different situations and then explore the consequences associated with the different levels of the emotion. For example, children learn to identify specific situations that lead to different levels of anger and then practice strategies (e.g., coping statements, relaxation, alternative behaviors) to lower the intensity of inappropriate levels of anger. Several other activities have been developed to increase children's self-monitoring skills (Bernard & Joyce, 1984; Linscott & DiGiuseppe, 1994).

As with the social skills training procedures, when teaching cognitive skills to groups of children, it is important to involve all group members during each stage of the intervention process. From a group-management perspective, this is important in order to maintain the children's attention and minimize disruptive behavior. More importantly, from a social-learning perspective, the strategic use of group members will enhance intervention efficacy in several ways. Group members will serve as powerful models for each other during rehearsal, child coaches will increase their own understanding of the skill being taught when assigned to give feedback, comments from peers may be more persuasive than adult commentary, and practice scenarios involving group members will more closely approximate the child's actual social environment.

The Use of Homework

A natural extension of activities conducted in the therapy group is the practice of newly learned social and cognitive skills in the natural environment. A common method of increasing such generalization is through the assignment of homework to group participants. Typically, homework assignments consist of tasks that have already been practiced and discussed in the therapy group and that the children have demonstrated proficiency at carrying out the assignment. Because the natural environment provides none of the structure and support associated with the therapy group, it is critical for the therapist to plan explicitly and carefully with the group members all aspects of the assignment. Children's motivation for completing the assignment should be assessed and, if needed, enhanced. Edelson and Rose (1982) began each group session with a review of homework assignments and awarded points to children who completed the assignment. In addition, each component of the assignment should be reviewed with the child and potential problems discussed.

Particular attention should be paid to the targeting of appropriate others when the assignment requires the child to interact socially. Initially, other group members may serve as participants. Fellow group members represent a relatively "safe" target in that they already have a positive relationship with the child and can assist the child in carrying out the assignment. Family members also may be appropriate targets. Additionally, careful consideration should be given to targeting appropriate situations for skill practice. For example, a child will likely be more successful practicing requests for peer assistance during cooperative group activities than during individual seatwork. The strategic identification of target situations and individuals for homework assignments will provide the highest likelihood for successful completion and positive interactions. Planning for such success will enhance the chances of maintenance and generalization of the newly learned skill.

Changing Relational Schemas

The second component of the group therapy process involves the use of the group itself to target negative relational schemas that both the peer-rejected child and his or her peers have developed. Such negative relational schemas are likely developed by the rejected child as a result of the high frequency of conflictive interactions in which he or she has been engaged. Other children, as well, tend to develop negative relational schemas of the rejected child based on their direct experience with the child or observations and general reputation of the rejected child. Such schemas are likely to result in an increasingly negative reputation of the child, leading peers to direct additional rejecting behaviors toward him or her (Coie & Kupersmidt, 1983; Hymel, 1986; Waas & Honer, 1990). A vicious cycle involving inappropriate behavior on the part of the rejected child, negative relational schemas, and rejecting behavior on the part of peers is quickly formed. The group therapy format, by involving members of the rejected child's peer group, provides a context within which such negative relational schemas and negative reputational bias can be modified.

Price and Dodge (1989) suggested that direct reputation change will most likely occur if the peer group observes the rejected child performing highly salient reputation-disconfirming behaviors. For example, a rejected child who has a reputation for aggressive behavior might be included in activities that demand high levels of cooperation and sharing among peers. Such an intervention would be highly salient to peers and would likely be a powerful intervention for modifying the rejected child's reputation for aggression. Price and Dodge noted that the rejected child must be allowed to perform a large number of these disconfirming behaviors in order for peers to accept them as part of the rejected child's behavioral repertoire. A group setting provides a rich context in which activities that promote such behaviors can be designed and implemented.

The literature on stereotypes also offers possible intervention strategies for changing a child's reputation among his or her peers. In discussing the modification of negative stereotypes, Cook (1985) suggested that favorable change in attitudes will result when there is personal contact with members of a disliked group, provided that certain conditions are met. Applied to the domain of children's peer relations, these conditions include (1) all members of the group should enjoy equal status, and the norms of the group should promote a sense of equality among members; (2) the attributes of the rejected children in the group must disconfirm prevailing stereotypes; (3) cooperation among group members in the achievement of joint goals should be encouraged; and (4) rejected children should be allowed to communicate personal information about themselves so they are perceived as unique individuals and not as stereotypes.

There are a number of different approaches that one might take in attempting to accomplish the objective of changing the negative relational schemas that children have developed about the rejected child. At the outset, however, it is important to note that whatever specific tactic is used, the focus of the intervention strategy should be explicitly aimed at changing the negative pattern of interactions that has developed between the rejected child and his or her peers. Research in developmental and social psychology suggests that children's direct participation in positive activities with the rejected child (which disconfirm the child's negative reputation) likely will be most successful at improving rejected children's sociometric status (Hymel, 1986; Waas, 1991).

One method of accomplishing this objective is to combine traditional social skills training with group involvement in a positive, cooperative task. A cooperative task involves children working together to achieve a common goal that demands interdependence and prosocial behaviors among group members. Bierman and Furman (1984), for example, had children work together in small groups of three to make films of students involved in friendly interactions. While the children were engaged in this activity, the therapist monitored their interactions, provided reinforcing comments, gave feedback to group members, and made suggestions on the social skills they were being taught.

It is important to note the important strategic elements that comprised this apparently simple activity. First, the objective of the activity (i.e., making a video about friendship interactions) ensured that the social skills being taught in the group would be practiced. Additionally, the structured nature of the activity, combined with the close monitoring by the therapist, ensured that the rejected children were involved in multiple disconfirming behaviors—in this case, positive social interactions—that contributed to breaking the negative reputational cycle associated with peer rejection. Finally, the activity itself was attractive to the children and contributed to maintaining their interest and motivation.

Bierman and Furman (1984) reported that children in a treatment condition involving only social skills training increased skill acquisition and skillful social interactions with peers; however, they did not achieve sociometric change. Only children in a combined condition, involving both social skills training and the peer-involvement tasks, exhibited both skill-acquisition gains and improved sociometric status among peer partners.

Other researchers (e.g., Bretzing & Caterino, 1984; Yu et al., 1986) have used various types of games to accomplish this dual goal of social skills practice and involvement in cooperative tasks (dominoes, picture-drawing games, tic-tac-toe, Monopoly, etc.). More important than the particular activity chosen, however, is the way the therapist structures the activity. First, it is critical that the children are given the opportunity to practice newly learned skills. To this end, the therapist may need to provide explicit cues for using the skill, suggestions and feedback on the child's performance of the skill, and reinforcement for skill enactment. Additionally, the therapist needs to structure the activities so that the target skills are practiced to mastery. Finally, it will be important to plan and monitor activities so that potential conflict among group members is minimized.

Failure to monitor and structure group activities to enhance the potential for reputation change likely will end in the all too common result of unimproved sociometric status. Vaughn and Lancelotta (1990), for example, examined the effect of social skills training with low-status second-, third-, and fourth-grade children who were paired either with high-status peers or without high-status peers. They reported little support for the peer-pairing strategy as an improvement over social skills training alone. They noted, however, that little effort was made to systematically structure the group activities to take advantage of the peer-pairing condition: "It could be that the interaction between the low-status and high-status students did not sufficiently engage them in cooperative efforts that involve joint interest and mutual support" (p. 186). Vaughn and Lancelotta hypothesized that increased interdependence, collaboration, and group processing among the children may have resulted in improved perceptions by peers.

There are virtually an infinite number of possible activities that could be used to provide group members with the opportunity to practice newly learned social skills and engage in positive social interactions. It will be important for therapists to identify activities that fit their specific circumstances. For example, groups held in facilities with art supplies may be art centered. Groups held in a school setting may have access to a gymnasium and thus may involve many sports-oriented activities. Groups held during the noon hour might include eating lunch together. Whatever activity one chooses, however, it is important to maximize the opportunity for practice and the likelihood that participants will be involved in positive interactions.

Regardless of how carefully one structures group activities to promote cooperation and positive interaction among members, conflicts are bound to occur. During these periods, the therapist may need to establish a signal (e.g., "Time Out!") to stop ongoing activities and allow the group to reflect on interactions that have just occurred. This may involve having each participant review the interaction from his or her own perspective and the therapist assisting children to understand the personal validity of differing perspectives. Group members then may brainstorm alternative solutions to the conflict and role-play the most promising ones. It will be important for therapists to monitor carefully the level of conflict within the group in order to preserve the possibility of changing negative relational schemas to more positive ones, while at the same time allowing for interpersonally relevant interactions to occur.

Other Group Considerations

In this chapter, we have advocated a dual focus in group work with peer-rejected children: social skills training and changing negative relational schemas. Implicit in such an approach are a number of issues related to basic group therapy characteristics that must be considered. A comprehensive discussion of such general therapy issues is beyond the scope of this chapter, but the interested reader is referred to several valuable texts that discuss these issues in greater detail (e.g., George & Dustin, 1988; Rose & Edleson, 1987; Yalom, 1995). Nevertheless, issues such as group composition, size, and behavioral rules are particularly relevant to the approach advocated in this chapter.

Group Composition

The issue of group composition is relevant to any therapy group, but is particularly relevant when structuring the group to change a child's negative pattern of social interactions and poor reputation. When determining group membership, it is useful to include only those children who have potential for contributing to group cohesiveness and are not likely to exhibit behaviors that are so deviant as to be disruptive to group functioning (George & Dustin, 1988; Rose & Edelson, 1987).

To these ends, Rose and Edelson (1987) suggested that each member of the group should be able to identify at least one other member who is not too much different in terms of social skills, social background, or presenting problem. George and Dustin (1988) noted that group cohesiveness will be maximized by children who share commonalities with each other and who are attracted to the group leader and their fellow group members. Conversely, the inclusion of children who are actively antagonistic toward other members of the group will likely undermine group cohesiveness and should, therefore, be avoided. Because one of the major therapeutic objectives when working with socially rejected children is to improve their peer relationships outside the therapy group, the inclusion of nonrejected children, or peer models, might be considered (Bierman, 1989).

Group Size

Closely related to the issue of group composition is the question of group size. Significant variability exists in the treatment literature regarding the number of children included in therapy groups, with 3 to 10 children most often included. Larger groups have a number of advantages over smaller groups, including more children who can serve as role models for any given social skill or behavior, a greater chance that each member of the group will identify with a fellow member, a larger group of children with whom each member can practice newly learned skills, and a more extensive social network with which to begin the process of changing the rejected child's negative reputation.

Although larger groups carry with them some important advantages, they also have a number of risks associated with them. For example, as the group membership increases, the therapist will find it more difficult to provide individual attention to each child. Planning activities that are engaging to all children and actively involve all members will be more difficult. In larger groups, it will be easier for some children to be off task or simply disengaged and passive. Therapists also will find it more difficult to monitor and structure group activities to facilitate cooperative interactions within the group. Because many peer-rejected children exhibit aggressive behaviors, failure to provide such structure likely will lead to conflict. One way of minimizing the disadvantages associated with larger groups is to recruit a co-therapist or assistant to help plan and carry out group activities.

Behavioral Program

In many social skills groups, therapists utilize a behavioral program to promote conformity with group rules, cooperation among group members, and the completion of group activities. For example, Bierman and associates (1987) utilized both a reinforcement and a response-cost procedure in which children were provided a token whenever a targeted skill was demonstrated. However, members lost the opportunity to earn tokens for a brief amount of time whenever they violated a group rule (e.g., no yelling). Schneider and Byrne (1987) also used a combination of reinforcement and response cost in their study of severely behavior-disordered children placed in residential care and a day program. Children were provided a set amount of tokens at the beginning of each treatment session. Throughout the session, children earned additional tokens for demonstrating appropriate behaviors and lost tokens for inappropriate behaviors. At the end of each session, tokens were used to earn toys or privileges. In these studies, the use of a token system served as feedback and positive reinforcement for newly learned social skills, but it also helped to curtail severe, uncontrolled conflict that might undermine group cohesiveness and motivation.

EXTENDING THE GROUP: CONSULTATIVE INTERVENTIONS

An important adjunct to group therapy is extending group interventions to the naturalistic environment (e.g., home, supervised playground, classroom) by structuring activities that will facilitate positive interactions between the rejected child and his or her peers. Such environmental structuring will maximize the probability that therapeutic gains are generalized and maintained. Psychologists and other mental health providers who are located in school settings are ideally positioned to provide such services because school is the major arena for social interaction for most children (e.g., Hartup, 1983). For therapists who work outside the school setting, it will be important to establish a cooperative relationship with school personnel so that the positive effects of group intervention can be maximized and extended to the school. Finally, it will be necessary for all therapists to consult closely with the child's parents to enhance overall treatment efficacy.

One method of extending the impact of group therapy is to utilize the child's peers to facilitate and maintain change that has occurred within the therapy group. Odom and Strain (1984) identified three types of such peer-mediated interventions in which peers serve as behavior change agents: (1) peer-proximity interventions involve placing socially competent and incompetent children together during activities (Bierman & Furman, 1984); (2) peer prompting and reinforcement interventions involve teaching peers to prompt and reinforce target peers for engaging in specified social behaviors (Goldstein & Ferrell, 1987); and (3) peer-initiation procedures involve training a peer to initiate social interactions with the target child (Odom & Strain, 1986).

An extension of peer-mediated strategies involves attempting to improve the rejected child's social network. For example, Haring and Breen (1992) had teachers identify one or two students who had positive contacts with a severely disabled target student (i.e., autistic, moderately retarded). These students were assigned to interact with the rejected child during specified 5-minute transition periods throughout the day and during the 30-minute lunch period. Groups met once a week, during which the previous week was reviewed, specific social skills (greeting, response to greetings, conversation, etc.) were trained and rehearsed, and members discussed their satisfaction with the program. During the group meetings, pizza and soda were provided by the adult instructor. Haring and Breen (1992) reported that after approximately three weeks of the intervention, target students' interactions increased and student peers' ratings of friendship improved.

Less formal social-network interventions might be implemented through consultation with parents and teachers. At the most simple level, this might involve assisting the teacher in monitoring and strategically manipulating the membership of small classroom work groups. For instance, pairing an amiable higher-status child with a lower-status child to work on a structured task that has a low risk for conflict (i.e., it is not too difficult, does not require extensive negotiation between participants, etc.) will facilitate the target child's social skills development and increase his or her positive interactions with others. Sasso and Rude (1987) reported that training high-status children to interact with severely disabled children resulted in untrained nonhandicapped students increasing positive social interactions with a target child.

The use of cooperative groups can also be used to help rejected children improve their relations with students outside the therapy group. Cooperative group-learning techniques involve small groups of students working together toward a common goal. The structure of these groups may vary on several dimensions, and it will be important for the therapist and teacher/parent to collaboratively determine the best structure for promoting reputation change. Nastasi and Clements (1991) suggested that the type of subject matter (e.g., basic skills, narrative, conceptual) and the degree to which children are interdependent are important strategic considerations when forming cooperative groups. Cooperative group structure also may differ on whether rewards and grades are given to the entire group or to individuals, and whether groups are competing with each other, are cooperative with other groups, or are independent.

Very little research has been conducted that evaluates systematically these factors in terms of their impact on social interactions and peer evaluations. It will be important for both practitioners and researchers to identify group variables that maximize the probability of positive interactions among group members and minimize the potential for conflict (cf. Bohlmeyer & Burke, 1987; Nastasi & Clements, 1991).

ESSENTIAL GUIDELINES AND SAMPLE FORMAT

Because of the heterogeneous nature of the peer-rejected group, there is no standardized set of modules that can be provided for group sessions. It is expected, however, that most groups will involve both rejected and nonrejected children, and sessions will consist of both building social skills activities as well as experiential activities designed to modify negative peer relational schemas. The precise composition of the group, social skills to be targeted, and session activities, however, should be determined by the therapist's ongoing hypotheses about participants' specific needs and which intervention tactics are most likely to address those needs.

Provided next are sample formats for two different types of sessions: one focusing on the development of negotiation skills and the other focusing on enhancing positive interactions among group members.

Social Skills Sessions

During sessions devoted to social skills training, the therapist would start the group by describing the social skill to be focused on during the group meeting (e.g., negotiation skills) and helping participants recognize situations in which such skills would be beneficial (e.g., when they are disagreeing with peers and find themselves becoming angry or upset). In the example involving negotiation skills, the therapist would lead a discussion about the advantages of employing negotiation skills in conflictive situations as well as the disadvantages of not using them. Group participants would be encouraged to discuss situations in which they had successfully employed negotiation skills (i.e., positive exemplars) and situations in which negotiation skills would have been helpful but were not employed, thus resulting in negative outcomes (i.e., negative exemplars).

The therapist would next describe the steps involved in the negotiation process. These steps would include such activities as looking the other person in the eye, asking to discuss the disagreement with the intent of trying to work things out, expressing one's viewpoint in a clear and relaxed manner, listening carefully to the other person's viewpoint and his or her ideas for possible solutions, proposing a compromise, and arriving at a mutually acceptable solution. Group members would review each step of the negotiation process to ensure their understanding of it. Using situations generated by the group or provided by the therapist, the therapist would then model these steps. Finally, group members would role-play various parts in conflictive situations and provide one another with constructive feedback about their performance in resolving the social problems.

Because disagreements typically involve emotional arousal, the therapist may also employ interventions targeted at increasing group members' awareness of their emotions and ameliorating their self-control abilities. For instance, group members may be encouraged to recognize signs that they are becoming angry or upset in order to cue themselves to implement coping self-statements (e.g., "Stay calm. I can negotiate this"). Self-statements would be used to control arousal before engaging in the steps involved in the negotiation process. As with other social skills, the therapist would model these skills and provide group members with opportunities to engage in role-play and feedback activities. Throughout the session, group members would also be awarded token reinforcements for participating in role-plays and giving one another constructive feedback. Tokens would be recorded on a group chart at the end of each session and periodically exchanged for back-up rewards (e.g., school supplies).

Toward the end of each session, a homework assignment typically would be given to provide group members with practice in applying negotiation skills in actual conflictive situations during the upcoming week. For example, participants may be asked to identify those situations during the next week that likely will require the use of self-statements and negotiation skills. Additionally, plans would be made for participants to check in with each other at lunch every day to review and reinforce one another for negotiating rather than fighting.

Group Interaction Sessions

As discussed previously, the goals of sessions devoted to group interaction are twofold: to allow group members additional opportunities to practice newly acquired skills and to enhance positive interactions among group members in order to change negative relational schemas. At the beginning of such sessions, the homework assignment from the previous group meeting would be reviewed and group members would be given reinforcement for completion of the assignment. A game or other activity would then be introduced that would allow for the practice of newly trained skills in a less structured, less supervised setting.

In the case of negotiation skills, a game such as Monopoly would be introduced and members would be encouraged to practice negotiating skills within the framework of the game. In order to minimize the likelihood of inappropriate behavior, group members would also be reminded of provisions already in place to control disputes, such as a signal for time out. Such planning would allow the therapist to preempt severe conflict and utilize disagreements as an opportunity for group members to practice the newly learned negotiation skills. At times, the therapist may find it necessary to stop a negative interaction and actively coach participants through the negotiation process. Throughout the group activity, the therapist would reinforce participants for implementing negotiation skills appropriately.

Finally, to facilitate practice, generalization, and maintenance of newly learned negotiation skills, the therapist would inform teachers of the negotiation procedures presented in the group. Teachers would then be encouraged to look for opportunities to reinforce group members' efforts at negotiating, to coach them through real-life situations in which such skills are applicable, and to provide them with optimal opportunities in which to practice new social skills. This might involve discussing with the teacher upcoming cooperative activities in the classroom and to identify specific peers with whom the rejected child can positively interact. Periodic checking in with the teacher will give the therapist the opportunity to match school activities with therapy goals and provide important information on the generalization of treatment gains.

CONCLUSIONS AND FUTURE DIRECTIONS

Effective intervention with peer-rejected children is an important but difficult task. Children who comprise this at-risk group are heterogeneous, and peer rejection itself is a complex process involving both individual and social variables. Intervention efforts directed at these children should address both the behavioral and psychological needs of the child, as well as the negative reputational cycle that often exists between the child and his or her peers. It is argued that group interventions may be the most appropriate therapeutic format for accomplishing these goals, and that consultative interventions provide a natural extension of such group efforts. However, there is a relative dearth of treatment studies that explicitly apply such a comprehensive approach. Future research efforts will need to begin the important task of combining strategies in order to maximize the impact of intervention efforts.

As has been noted, there is an emerging body of cogent research in the social, educational, and developmental psychology domains that underscore the importance of adopting a broader therapeutic perspective when intervening with peer-rejected children. Additional research is needed, however, in a number of areas. For example, it is necessary to more clearly identify the types of social information and processes that children use in forming reputational evaluations about their peers, and, most relevant to the treatment of rejected children, identify the types of interventions that are most efficacious in changing negative reputational evaluations. Such issues as the role of the teacher versus peers in changing children's negative evaluations, the most strategic age to intervene, the best combination of traditional social skills training procedures and strategies designed to change negative relational schemas, and the best ways to combine consultative interventions with group therapy interventions all are important areas for future research.

In order to maximize the progress in our work with children who experience severe peer relationship difficulties, however, both researchers and practitioners will need to become more interdisciplinary in their analyses of the peer-rejection phenomenon and the interventions utilized when working with this group of at-risk children. The conceptualization of peer rejection as a multicomponential problem involving both psychological and social factors represents a first step in this endeavor.

REFERENCES

Akhtar, N., & Bradley, E. J. (1991). Social information processing deficits of aggressive children: Present findings and implications for social skills training. *Clinical Psychology Review, 11,* 621–644.

Asher, S. R. (1990). Recent advances in the study of peer rejection. In S. R. Asher & J. D. Coie (Eds.), *Peer rejection in childhood* (pp. 3–14). New York: Cambridge University Press.

Asher, S. R., & Dodge, K. A. (1986). Identifying children who are rejected by their peers. *Developmental Psychology, 22,* 444–449.

Baldwin, M. W. (1992). Relational schemas and the processing of social information. *Psychological Bulletin, 112,* 461–484.

Bandura, A. (1977). *Social learning theory.* Englewood Cliffs, NJ: Prentice Hall.

Bernard, M. E., & Joyce, M. R. (1984). *Rational-emotive therapy with children and adolescents.* New York: Wiley.

Bierman, K. L. (1989). Improving the peer relationships of rejected children. In B. B. Lahey & A. E. Kazdin (Eds.), *Advances in clinical child psychology* (Vol. 12, pp. 53–84). New York: Plenum.

Bierman, K. L., & Furman, W. (1984). The effects of social skills training and peer involvement on the social adjustment of preadolescents. *Child Development, 55,* 151–162.

Bierman, K. L., Miller, C. M., & Stabb, S. (1987). Improving the social behavior and peer acceptance of rejected boys: Effects of social skill training with instructions and prohibitions. *Journal of Consulting and Clinical Psychology, 55,* 194–200.

Bohlmeyer, E. M., & Burke, J. P. (1987). Selecting cooperative learning techniques: A consultative strategy guide. *School Psychology Review, 16,* 36–49.

Boivin, M., Thomassin, L., & Alain, M. (1989). Peer rejection and self-perception among early elementary school children: Aggressive rejectees vs. withdrawn rejectees. In B. Schneider, J. Nadel, G. Attili, & R. Weissberg (Eds.), *Social competence in developmental perspective* (pp. 392–394). Norwell, MA: Kluwer Academic.

Bretzing, B. H., & Caterino, L. C. (1984). Group counseling with elementary students. *School Psychology Review, 13,* 515–518.

Cantrell, V. L., & Prinz, R. J. (1985). Multiple perspectives and rejected, neglected, and accepted children: Relation between sociometric status and behavioral characteristics. *Journal of Consulting and Clinical Psychology, 53,* 884–889.

Cartledge, G., & Milburn, J. F. (Eds.). (1986). *Teaching social skills to children* (2nd ed.). New York: Pergamon.

Coie, J. D. (1985). Fitting social skills intervention to the target group. In B. H. Schneider, K. H. Rubin, & J. E. Ledingham (Eds.), *Children's peer relations: Issues in assessment and intervention* (pp. 141–156). New York: Springer-Verlag.

Coie, J. D., & Koeppl, G. K. (1990). Adapting intervention to the problems of aggressive and disruptive rejected children. In S. R. Asher & J. D. Coie (Eds.), *Peer rejection in childhood* (pp. 309–337). New York: Cambridge University Press.

Coie, J. D., & Krehbiel, G. (1984). Effects of academic tutoring on the social status of low-achieving, socially rejected children. *Child Development, 55,* 1465–1478.

Coie, J. D., & Kupersmidt, J. B. (1983). A behavioral analysis of emerging social status in boys' groups. *Child Development, 54,* 1400–1416.

Coie, J. D., Underwood, M., & Lochman, J. E. (1991). Programmatic intervention with aggressive children in the school setting. In D. J. Pepler & K. H. Rubin (Eds.), *Development and treatment of childhood aggression* (pp. 389–410). Toronto: Erlbaum.

Cook, S. W. (1985). Experimenting of social issues. *American Psychologist, 40,* 452–460.

Crick, N. R., & Ladd, G. W. (1990). Children's perceptions of their peer experiences: Attributions, loneliness, social anxiety, and social avoidance. *Developmental Psychology, 29,* 244–254.

Dodge, K. A. (1980). Social cognition and children's aggressive behavior. *Child Development, 51,* 162–170.

Dodge, K. A., Schlundt, D. C., Schocken, I., & Delugach, J. D. (1983). Social competence and children's sociometric status: The role of peer group entry strategies. *Merrill-Palmer Quarterly, 29,* 309–336.

Dodge, K. A., & Somberg, D. R. (1987). Hostile attributional biases among aggressive boys are exacerbated under conditions of threats to the self. *Child Development, 58,* 213–224.

Dozier, M. (1988). Rejected children's processing of interpersonal information. *Journal of Abnormal Child Psychology, 16,* 141–149.

Dubow, E. F. (1988). Aggressive behavior and peer social status of elementary school children. *Aggressive Behavior, 14,* 315–324.

Dubow, E. F., & Cappas, C. L. (1988). Peer social status and reports of children's adjustment by their teachers, by their peers, and by their self-ratings. *Journal of School Psychology, 26,* 69–75.

Edelson, J. L., & Rose, S. D. (1982). Investigations into the efficacy of short-term group social skills training for socially isolated children. *Child Behavior Therapy, 3,* 1–16.

Elliott, S. N., & Gresham, F. M. (1993). Social skills interventions for children. *Behavior Modification, 17,* 287–313.

French, D. C., & Waas, G. A. (1985). Behavior problems of peer-neglected and peer-rejected elementary-age children: Parent and peer perspectives. *Child Development, 56,* 246–252.

George, R. L., & Dustin, D. (1988). *Group counseling.* Englewood Cliffs, NJ: Prentice Hall.

Goldstein, H., & Ferrell, D. R. (1987). Augmenting communicative interaction between handicapped and nonhandicapped preschool children. *Journal of Speech and Hearing Disorders, 52,* 200–211.

Gresham, F. M., & Nagle, R. J. (1980). Social skills training with children: Responsiveness to modeling and coaching as a function of peer orientation. *Journal of Consulting and Clinical Psychology, 48,* 718–729.

Gresham, F. M., & Reschly, D. J. (1988). Issues in the conceptualization, classification, and assessment of social skills in the mildly handicapped. In T. R. Kratochwill (Ed.), *Advances in school psychology* (Vol. 6, pp. 203–247). Hillsdale, NJ: Lawrence Erlbaum.

Haring, T. G., & Breen, C. G. (1992). A peer-mediated social network intervention to enhance the social integration of persons with moderate and severe disabilities. *Journal of Applied Behavior Analysis, 25,* 319–333.

Hartup, W. W. (1983). Peer relations. In E. M. Hetherington (Ed.) & P. H. Mussen (Series Ed.), *Handbook of child psychology: Vol. 4. Socialization, personality, and social development* (pp. 103–196). New York: Wiley.

Hops, H., & Lewin, L. (1984). Peer sociometric forms. In T. H. Ollendick & M. Hersen (Eds.), *Child behavioral assessment: Principles and procedures* (pp. 124–147). Elmsford, NY: Pergamon.

Hudley, C., & Graham, S. (1993). An attributional intervention to reduce peer-directed aggression among African-American boys. *Child Development, 64,* 124–138.

Hymel, S. (1986). Interpretations of peer behavior: Affective bias in childhood and adolescence. *Child Development, 57,* 431–445.

Kazdin, A. E. (1988). *Child psychotherapy.* New York: Pergamon.

Kendall, P. C., & Braswell, L. (1985). *Cognitive-behavioral therapy for impulsive children.* New York: Guilford.

Kennedy, J. H. (1988). Issues in the identification of socially incompetent children. *School Psychology Review, 17,* 276–288.

Kettlewell, P. W., & Kausch, D. F. (1983). The generalization of the effect of a cognitive-behavioral reatment program for aggressive children. *Journal of Abnormal Child Psychology, 11,* 101–114.

Kolko, D. J., Loar, L. L., & Sturnick, D. (1990). Inpatient social-cognitive skills training groups with conduct disordered and attention deficit disordered children. *Journal of Child Psychology and Psychiatry, 31,* 737–748.

Kupersmidt, J. B., Coie, J. D., & Dodge, K. A. (1990). The role of poor peer relationships in the development of disorder. In S. R. Asher & J. D. Coie (Eds.), *Peer rejection in childhood* (pp. 274–305). New York: Cambridge University Press.

Ladd, G. W. (1981). Effectiveness of a social learning method for enhancing children's social interaction and peer acceptance. *Child Development, 52,* 171–178.

Ladd, G. W., & Mize, J. (1983). A cognitive-social learning model of social-skill training. *Psychological Review, 90,* 127–157.

Linscott, J., & DiGiuseppe, R. (1994). Rational emotive therapy with children. In C. W. LeCroy (Ed.), *Handbook of child and adolescent treatment manuals* (pp. 5–40). New York: Lexington Books.

Lochman, J. E. (1992). Cognitive-behavioral intervention with aggressive boys: Three-year follow-up and preventive effects. *Journal of Consulting and Clinical Psychology, 60,* 426–432.

Meichenbaum, D. H. (1985). *Stress-innoculation training.* New York: Pergamon.

Nastasi, B. K., & Clements, D. H. (1991). Research on cooperative learning: Implications for practice. *School Psychology Review, 20,* 110–131.

Newcomb, A. F., Bukowski, W. M., & Pattee, L. (1993). Children's peer relations: A meta-analytic review of popular, rejected, neglected, controversial, and average sociometric status. *Psychological Bulletin, 113,* 99–128.

Odom, S. L., & Strain, P. S. (1984). Peer-mediated approaches to promoting children's social interaction: A review. *American Journal of Orthopsychiatry, 54,* 544–557.

Odom, S. L., & Strain, P. S. (1986). A comparison of peer-initiation and teacher-antecedent interventions for promoting reciprocal social interaction of autistic preschoolers. *Journal of Applied Behavior Analysis, 19,* 59–71.

Parker, J. G., & Asher, S. R. (1987). Peer relations and later personal adjustment: Are low-accepted children at risk? *Psychological Bulletin, 102,* 357–389.

Parker, J. G., & Asher, S. R. (1993). Friendship and friendship quality in middle childhood: Links with peer group acceptance and feelings of loneliness and social dissatisfaction. *Developmental Psychology, 29,* 611–621.

Parkhurst, J. T., & Asher, S. R. (1992). Peer rejection in middle school: Subgroup differences in behavior, loneliness, and interpersonal concerns. *Developmental Psychology, 28,* 231–241.

Price, J. M., & Dodge, K. A. (1989). Peers' contributions to children's social maladjustment. In T. J. Berndt & G. W. Ladd (Eds.), *Peer relationships in child development* (pp. 341–370). New York: Wiley.

Putallaz, M., & Wasserman, A. (1989). Children's naturalistic entry behavior and sociometric status: A developmental perspective. *Developmental Psychology, 25,* 297–305.

Renshaw, P. D., & Asher, S. R. (1983). Children's goals and strategies for social interaction. *Merrill-Palmer Quarterly, 29,* 353–374.

Rose, S. D., & Edleson, J. L. (1987). *Working with children and adolescents in groups.* San Francisco: Jossey-Bass.

Sasso, G. M., & Rude, H. A. (1987). Unprogrammed effects of training high-status peers to interact with severely handicapped children. *Journal of Applied Behavior Analysis, 20,* 35–44.

Schneider, B. (1991). A comparison of skill-building and desensitization strategies for intervention with aggressive children. *Aggressive Behavior, 17,* 301–311.

Schneider, B., & Byrne, B. M. (1987). Individualizing social skills training for behavior-disordered children. *Journal of Consulting and Clinical Psychology, 55,* 444–445.

Shapiro, E. S., & Kratochwill, T. R. (Eds.). (1988). *Behavioral assessment in schools.* New York: Guilford.

Smith, E. R., & Lerner, M. (1986). Development of automatism of social judgments. *Journal of Personality and Social Psychology, 50,* 246–259.

Vaughn, S., & Lancelotta, G. X. (1990). Teaching interpersonal social skills to poorly accepted students: Peer pairing versus non-peer-pairing. *Journal of School Psychology, 28,* 189–202.

Waas, G. A. (1991). Social information and the development of children's peer evaluations. *Merrill-Palmer Quarterly, 37,* 407–424.

Waas, G. A., & Honer, S. A. (1990). Situational attributions and dispositional inferences: The development of peer reputation. *Merrill-Palmer Quarterly, 36,* 239–260.

Yalom, I. D. (1995). *The theory and practice of group psychotherapy* (4th ed.). New York: Basic Books.

Yu, P., Harris, G. E., Solovitz, B. L., & Franklin, J. L. (1986). A social problem-solving intervention for children at high risk for later psychopathology. *Journal of Clinical Child Psychology, 15,* 30–40.

CHAPTER 9

LOSS AND GRIEF GROUPS

Merle A. Keitel, FORDHAM UNIVERSITY
Mary Kopala, HUNTER COLLEGE
Lisa Robin, PROJECT RENEWAL, NEW YORK CITY

RATIONALE FOR A GROUP APPROACH

Research suggests that social support helps bereaved individuals (Gray, 1988). Immediately following a death, friends and family may rally around the bereaved; however, within a few weeks, this support often disappears or diminishes. Members of the immediate family may be emotionally unavailable to each other because they are coping with their own grief. Consequently, professionals represent a necessary resource for supporting and intervening with grieving individuals.

Children may be especially vulnerable and frightened, in particular when they lose a primary caregiver (Siegel, Mesagno, & Christ, 1990). Children may wonder who will take care of them and what other life changes might ensue, such as with whom they will reside, whether they will change schools, and so on. The surviving parent or caregiver may be psychologically devastated by the loss and unable to care for children adequately. Similarly, when a child has died in a family, parents may be unable to provide their surviving children with support. Witnessing their parents exhibiting intense emotions for the first time can be quite distressing for surviving siblings. Children may not ask for help because they fear burdening their parents, and they may not know how to talk about the death. Bereavement groups are one mechanism for children to get social support without relying on their parents.

Children are often not given permission by their parents to talk about death. Many parents avoid talking about death because it evokes fears about their own mortality. Furthermore, discussions of death may elicit intense emotions. To protect themselves from having to witness their children's pain, parents may prohibit their children from actively grieving. Parents may also attempt to protect their children by prohibiting their attendance at the funeral, forbidding discussions of the deceased, and cutting off any expression of feelings, such as crying, with empty reassurances and platitudes. In the extreme, parents may not inform their children of the death. Limiting children's involvement in the mourning process may contribute to children believing that death is a taboo topic. Groups may counteract avoidance tendencies toward death by providing a forum for sharing feelings and for talking about the death experience and the deceased.

FACTORS THAT MAY AFFECT THE GRIEF RESPONSE

Many factors determine how much pain an individual experiences in response to a loss. People grieve many types of losses through, for example, divorce or death. They may lose (or be severely neglected by) a loved one due to substance abuse or psychosis. They may move to new neighborhoods, lose their jobs, or relinquish familiar roles to assume new roles (e.g., marriage results in surrendering one's identity as a single person). Children may experience grief reactions to all of these losses, but grief is likely to be most intense when a loved one dies. This chapter will therefore focus on responses of children and adolescents who experience the death of someone close to them.

Who died is a critical factor in understanding the reaction of the bereaved. The loss of a parent or primary caregiver has been discussed in the literature as a traumatic event (Moore & Herlihy, 1993). Other losses, however, may evoke strong grief reactions. For example, the death of a pet or a grandparent, which is likely to be the first loss a child experiences, may be significant. Children may also lose friends, school mates, aunts and uncles, or teachers. All losses may provoke a grief response, but the closer the relationship the child or adolescent has had with the deceased (particularly the loss of a parent or caregiver), the more intense and long lasting will be the grieving process.

When a parent dies, the child yearns to "recover" the parent and at the same time is angry at the parent for leaving. The child defends against his or her feelings toward the lost parent in various ways, with the net result being that these feelings and desires are not conscious. This defensive process occurs at an accelerated rate in children and so children have no opportunity to express yearning and reproachment after the death.

Similarly, the loss of a parent during adolescence may interfere with the adolescent's maturation. Adolescence represents a natural transition period of separation from the parent. As with toddlers or younger children, separation-individuation is facilitated by the presence of a stable object (i.e., the parent or primary caregiver). When a parent dies, the adolescent can no longer engage in the necessary process of alternately approaching and distancing himself or herself from the parent. Without the safety of the stable object, it is more difficult for adolescents to successfully separate from the deceased caregiver and resolve their grief.

The way someone died may also affect the grieving process. Sudden deaths have been found to be more difficult for adults to grieve than are anticipated deaths, but the findings for children are less clear. When death is anticipated, individuals have an opportunity to prepare so that grieving can begin prior to the death. Watching a loved one deteriorate from an illness may afford time to prepare for the death, but is very painful, nonetheless.

The cause of death may also affect the response of the bereaved. Death by murder, suicide, and AIDS, for example, may complicate the grieving process because of the stigma. Bereaved individuals may be reluctant to reach out to others because they fear negative responses. Violent deaths, particularly when they are witnessed by the child or adolescent, may lead to posttraumatic stress disorder. (For a thorough discussion, see Kopala & Keitel in Chapter 13 of this book.)

The age of the child at the time of the death also has an impact on the grief response. Children's understanding of death changes as they mature. Nagy (1948) theorized that until age 5, children view death as reversible. They do not see death as inevitable nor as resulting from cessation of bodily functions. From ages 5 to 9, children see death as avoidable and due to external forces, but as irreversible if it "gets you." After age 9, children understand that death is universal, inevitable, and irreversible (Nagy, 1948).

Children's cognitive understanding of death, and the subconcepts of death in particular, have received a great deal of empirical attention and general support (Prichard & Epting, 1992). The research is inconsistent, however, regarding how these subconcepts are labeled and which subconcepts are included for study. Subconcepts of death are irreversibility (the dead never come back to life), cessation or finality (biological functions cease and the dead cannot sense, feel emotions, or think), causality (understanding the objective causes of death), and inevitability (all living things die and ultimately so will the child) (Lazar & Torney-Purta, 1991; Orbach, Gross, Glaubman, & Berman, 1985).

The relationship between age and understanding of death is mediated by other variables. For children of high cognitive abilities, anxiety can interfere with their understanding of death. Orbach and colleagues (1985) suggested that highly anxious, intelligent children defend against fears evoked by death by failing to understand the meaning of death, although their equally intelligent but less anxious peers do understand the meaning of death.

Lazar and Torney-Purta's (1991) longitudinal study of young children found that the subconcepts of irreversibility and inevitability develop before the other subconcepts of death, and that children must understand one or the other of these before they can understand cessation or causality. Children's reasoning differed regarding deaths of humans versus animals. The majority (60%) of 7-year-old children mastered the subconcept of cessation with regard to human death.

The emotional status of parents or caregivers is also related to the well-being of the bereaved child. Children of depressed widows, in particular, have been found to have high rates of behavioral disturbances (Van Eerdewegh, Clayton, & Van Eerdewegh, 1985). Rosen (1986) suggested that when a sibling dies, the surviving siblings must deal with their own feelings as well as the feelings of their bereaved parents.

The family environment may also help determine the child or adolescent's bereavement reaction. Children in families that are dysfunctional or where marital discord exists may develop "pathological bereavement." Furthermore, the more conflict in the relationship between the child and the deceased parent, the more difficulty the child may have coping with the death (Elizur & Kaffman, 1983).

CHARACTERISTICS AND SYMPTOMS OF BEREAVED CHILDREN

Children respond to loss in a variety of ways. In the case of divorce, they may experience depression (Schilling, Koh, Abramovitz, & Gilbert, 1992), anger, anxiety, or sadness (Kelly & Wallerstein, 1976). Children of divorce may exhibit loss of appetite, acting-out behavior, difficulty sleeping, lack of concentration, and poorer grades. Similarly, in a study of 35 bereaved children ages 2 to 8, 92% showed behavioral disturbances within a few weeks of the death of a parent (Raphael, 1982). *Behavioral disturbance* was defined as two or more of the following symptoms: "high anxiety, exaggerated separation responses, clinging behavior, excessive crying, marked aggressive behavior, sleep disturbances, and disorders of eating and toileting" (Black & Urbanowicz, 1987, pp. 467–468). Only seven of the children were symptomatic prior to the death of the parent.

Van Eerdewegh and colleagues (1985) studied 105 bereaved children between the ages of 2 and 17 and compared them to 80 matched controls. Initially (i.e., at one month after the death of a parent), 70% of bereaved children were sad, crying, or irritable, and 11% had a depressive syndrome compared with 4% of the controls. Sleep difficulties, poor appetite, and withdrawn behavior were more frequent in the bereaved children than in the controls. Later, 13 months after the death, the bereaved children were reassessed and found to have decreased school performance and minor depressive symptoms.

Harris (1991) conducted semistructured interviews and administered standardized measures to 11 bereaved adolescents. Teacher reports and parent interviews provided additional information. Similar to Van Eerdewegh and associates (1985), Harris found that six weeks after a parent's death, teens exhibited impaired school performance, strained peer relations, sleep disturbances, and intense emotional, cognitive, physical, and behavioral reactions. Finally, adults who had lost their siblings during adolescence retrospectively reported survivor guilt and negative feelings about how they dealt with their sibling's death (Fanos & Nickerson, 1991).

Grief may manifest itself differently at different ages. In children who were psychiatric patients, affective responses were characterized more by anxiety and negativism (Cheifetz, Stavrakakis, & Lester, 1989), whereas adolescents tended to be depressed.

GROUP INTERVENTIONS FOR BEREAVED CHILDREN AND ADOLESCENTS

Primary prevention of problems related to loss includes psychoeducation and death education with nonbereaved individuals, whereas intervention for bereaved individuals consists of individual, group, or family counseling or psychotherapy. Bereavement groups may help to facilitate the grieving process and thus prevent problems from developing or remediate existing problems resulting from the loss. Groups can be instrumental in preventing or alleviating minor problems that children exhibit in the early stages of the grieving process. When children do not do the grief work they need to do for themselves (e.g., their families do not allow grief to be expressed) and do not receive professional intervention, they run the risk of developing complicated bereavement. Intervention is most effective, therefore, when it occurs soon after a loss.

Groups for bereaved children and adolescents usually do not attempt to change personality or resolve interpersonal problems. The purpose of such groups is mainly to alleviate suffering related to loss through members' mutual support. Gray (1988) found that 40% of the adolescents she interviewed who had participated in grief groups found it helpful to be taught the distinction between therapy and support before commencement of their groups. Masterman also emphasized this difference when training bereavement group leaders (Masterman & Reams, 1988).

Nonetheless, some support groups may be incidentally therapeutic. For instance, Zambelli and DeRosa (1992) found that for children who had interpersonal difficulties before becoming bereaved, the support group had a therapeutic effect. In these cases, the boys' fathers reported decreased peer-related problems toward the end of the group. In addition, their social functioning within the group improved.

For children with more severe problems, a therapy group may be used. Madonna and Chandler (1986) described a therapy group for four preadolescent boys who were exhibiting socially dysfunctional behaviors as the result of incomplete paternal bereavement due to loss through death or divorce. The therapists reported that the boys were able to manage their anger better after the group and that their symptomatic behavior decreased.

Loss and grief groups are commonly conducted in schools by school psychologists, counselors, and/or social workers. Groups conducted in schools tend to focus on prevention or remediation of less severe problems. Special death education presentations may be given in the classroom as well in order to provide all children with information about grief and mourning. Children who are identified as having serious or long-standing problems are likely to be referred for individual or group psychotherapy. Bereavement groups in schools typically include only students and not their family members because school policies endorse a separation of home and school (Carlson & Fullmer, 1993).

Bereavement groups are also provided in hospices, hospitals, social service agencies, and satellite locations such as churches by counselors, psychologists, social workers, art therapists, family therapists, and pastoral counselors. Members of these groups may include children or adolescents with varying degrees of dysfunction or may target children or adolescents who are experiencing more severe grief reactions.

Groups in nonschool settings may be composed solely of children or adolescents who experienced a loss or may include parents and other significant family members. Mental health professionals who conduct multifamily groups should be skilled in both group and family counseling or psychotherapy.

Disadvantages of combining children and their grieving parents in the same group are that children may feel inhibited about expressing their feelings because they (1) fear burdening their surviving parent, (2) may be angry at the surviving parent and may be reluctant to alienate the only caregiver they have, and/or (3) feel guilty expressing anger toward the deceased parent in the presence of the surviving parent. Another disadvantage of including grieving parents in groups is that children may be unable to handle their parent's displays of grief (e.g., crying). Furthermore, adolescents who are in the process of separation-individuation and are rebelling against authority may be reluctant to discuss anything openly with their parents. Finally, surviving parents who have not resolved or are not working on their own issues related to death, and the current loss in particular, may actually impede their children's grieving.

On the other hand, grieving parents may be most helpful to their children in group counseling when the parents are working to resolve their grief in a healthy manner, and already have a strong, positive relationship with their children. These parents can be role models and can demonstrate appropriate ways to express their grief as well as their coping mechanisms. Parents can help children to understand their pain as an appropriate reaction to loss. Parents can share accurate facts about the death and help to diminish irrational fears in children that they were somehow responsible for the death. However, this is not to say that parents must be "perfect" in order to participate effectively in multifamily groups. When parents respond during group in ineffective and even harmful ways, the group counselor can intervene directly, by teaching or modeling for the parents more appropriate responses. Families that demonstrate severely dysfunctional interactions could be referred for family therapy.

SPECIFIC TECHNIQUES

Various techniques are used in bereavement groups for children, adolescents, and/or their family members. The majority of the techniques are also employed in individual and family counseling. All therapeutic work with young people necessitates an understanding of cognitive and emotional development. The majority of the techniques presented here can be adapted to suit the developmental needs of group members. For example, play activities are useful for young children because they may not be able to verbalize their feelings; psychoeducational approaches—including mini-lessons, coping skills training, and discussion of feelings and thoughts about the death—may be more appropriate for older children and adolescents; and bibliotherapy and art therapy may be suitable for children of all ages (Harmey & Price, 1992).

Play Activities

Play activities include structured and unstructured play with dolls, toy soldiers, stuffed animals, puppets, and so on, as well as arts and crafts activities and structured games. Such activities allow children to communicate when they do not have the verbal skills to express their thoughts and feelings directly. Play activities are also useful for children who defend themselves by using excessive verbalizations that do not relate to their feelings regarding the loss. Counselors can introduce play to develop nonverbal communications (Carey, 1990) so that children can indirectly express thoughts and feelings that are difficult to articulate, thus reducing their anxiety and conflict (Lubetsky, 1989).

When children express their fears and feelings through play activities, particularly nondirective play, they tend not to become overwhelmed and can more easily take control of their fears (Lubetsky, 1989; Miller & Boe, 1990). Play activities allow children to work through conflicts and emotional issues in a safe environment, thereby allowing children to complete developmental tasks (Lubetsky, 1989). Play is typically reserved for use with younger children who have yet to reach a stage of cognitive and emotional development that enables verbal expression of feelings; however, art therapy and game play are also used with older children and adolescents. Play therapy, art therapy, and game play are discussed next.

Play Therapy

Play may be used to learn new or more adaptive behaviors, release tension, and foster communication. Group leaders may also observe members' play in order to formulate or refine diagnostic impressions. Play therapy activities that have been used include aggressive play techniques such as paper swordfights, pillow fights, arm wrestling (Madonna & Chandler, 1986), throwing paper airplanes at the end of sessions to relieve tension (Masterman & Reams, 1988), and placing personal messages to deceased parents in helium balloons and releasing them into the atmosphere (Tait & Depta, 1993).

Art Therapy

Art therapy is commonly employed with children, although Zambelli, Clark, Barile, and de Jong (1988) and Harmey and Price (1992) suggested that interventions that incorporate art are suitable for all ages. Children may be provided with any number of media (i.e., paint, crayons, clay, crafts, etc.) and are invited to begin using the materials individually.

Exercises may vary from session to session. For example, in early sessions, they may be used as icebreakers and means of identifying children's interests and concerns. This application of art therapy is usually open-ended, with the leader allowing members to create whatever comes to mind. Later sessions may involve more structured activities. For example, the leader may ask children to draw a picture related to the deceased (e.g., Zambelli & DeRosa, 1992).

There are many benefits to an art therapy approach. First, art is a means of communication in which children readily engage, and it is a form of symbolic communication that bypasses defenses children employ to "avoid discussing painful and frightening feelings" (Zambelli et al., 1988, p. 43). Second, art therapy helps children identify feelings and gain understanding. "The youngsters can consider their reactions to death in a concrete form without becoming overcome by their emotions" (Zambelli & DeRosa, 1992, p. 486). Third, children may increase self-esteem and self-efficacy through completed projects (Zambelli & DeRosa, 1992). Fourth, both the children's process of making art and their completed projects are diagnostic tools for the therapist or group leader. Fifth, engaging in art activities can be cathartic (Segal, 1984). Last, a key element of art therapy that is specific to groups pertains to the interaction among members that ensues when comparison and discussion of their projects takes place. Such discourse may promote a sense of togetherness.

Game Play

Game play refers to a leisure activity or game that addresses loss issues. Sometimes, the game is a variation of one children already know. For example, Zambelli and DeRosa (1992) described a variation of the card game Concentration. The objective of the game is altered so that points are earned by sharing memories. The person with the most points wins the game. This approach works for several reasons. First, the familiarity of a social activity promotes an environment wherein discussions of death are perceived by children as normal and therefore, acceptable. Also, children are able to express uncomfortable thoughts and feelings during the course of a game that would be embarrassing to verbalize in direct conversation. They feel the import or "reality" of their comments is diluted since "it is only a game" (Zambelli & DeRosa, 1992, p. 488). And third, individuals tend to strive to win in game play situations and thus will tolerate activities and discussions that they would typically avoid.

Psychoeducational Approaches

The importance of acquiring and integrating information in the mourning process has been discussed by some authors. Furman (1974) stated that in order for a child to mourn, there must be "understanding" of death. Similarly, Baker, Sedney, and Gross (1992) suggested that accurate information about death may provide a "foundation for the child's struggle to grasp the intellectual and emotional meaning of loss" (p. 106).

Clearly, psychoeducation may occur incidentally, during an art therapy or bibliotherapy session, for instance. In groups where members are at different stages in the grief process (which is often the case), more experienced youngsters may reveal survival skills and coping strategies that are integrated by their less experienced peers. Nonetheless, psychoeducational approaches are typically distinct components of programs.

Mini-Lessons

In a mini-lesson, the group facilitator presents information pertaining to relevant issues in grief work. The Kubler-Ross stages of grief or similar theories may be presented. Group members may acquire a shared, relevant vocabulary that facilitates expression of ideas and provides material for discussion through the duration of the group (Moore & Herlihy, 1993).

Brainstorming

Brainstorming is an exercise where children or adolescents are asked to contribute ideas as the facilitator writes them down on a chalkboard or easel. Hickey (1993) gave several examples of brainstorming used in a bereavement group with students in a junior high where a popular drug counselor died of a heart attack. The group facilitator asked the members to share their feelings in response to the death and what was difficult about not having the chance to say good-bye. Seeing their feelings and thoughts in black and white may help members to feel more in control and may also normalize their reactions.

Anonymous Questions

Another widely used exercise described by Gray (1988) involves each group member writing a question on a card and submitting it to the leader, who reads the questions aloud. Members may take turns answering the questions or the leader may answer them. This allows children or adolescents to ask questions they would not voice on their own in the group and affords an opportunity for acquiring information. Group members are often relieved to learn that many of their peers have the same questions they have.

Bibliotherapy

Special books with stories pertaining to death and grief issues are employed in age-appropriate groups. *The Fall of Freddie the Leaf* (Buscaglia, 1982) and *Saying Goodbye to Daddy* (Vigna, 1991) are two books that have been used for this purpose. Heath (1986) compiled an annotated bibliography of 23 books that were grouped by type of loss. Appropriate age ranges for each book were noted. In bibliotherapy, the facilitator may read a story aloud to the group and then invite members to express related thoughts and feelings verbally or through art (e.g., Zambelli & DeRosa, 1992). Through these exercises, children may learn age-appropriate information about death and the grieving process. In addition, children may identify with characters in books. Through identification, children's feelings of isolation are lessened (Zambelli & DeRosa, 1992). Finally, books allow children the safety of distance while helping them to identify their feelings.

Coping Skills Training

The value of effective coping skills in the grieving process is obvious. As children age, they develop coping mechanisms that enable them to deal with anxiety evoked by death and can thus eliminate defensive maneuvers that interfere with their understanding of death (Yalom, 1980). Developing coping mechanisms in children who are highly anxious can help them comprehend the meaning of death. Problem solving, relaxation techniques, and interpersonal communication skills are examples of skills that can be taught.

Sandler and associates (1992) used a four-step problem-solving model in a bereavement program with adults, although it appears to be suitable for use with older children and adolescents, as well. The steps were (1) defining the problem, (2) developing alternative solutions, (3) evaluating the solutions and selecting one, and (4) developing a plan to implement the selected solution.

For example, an adolescent male whose father has died may define the problem as needing more space to grieve alone and spend time with close friends. His mother may be lonely and wanting to spend all of her time with him. He feels guilty about "abandoning" her. A counselor can help him develop options for how to meet his own needs and still feel as though he is being sensitive to his mother's needs. Together, the counselor and group member can evaluate the pros and cons of each solution. Finally, a specific plan for implementing the solution would be developed. For instance, if the adolescent decides to share his feelings with his mother, the best time to have the conversation, and the tone and content of the conversation, can be discussed.

Relaxation techniques can be helpful to bereaved children and adolescents who experience generalized anxiety, stress caused by specific events related to the loss, and/or sleeping difficulties. Counselors can teach group members progressive muscle relaxation, deep breathing, and guided imagery to promote feelings of peace and well-being.

Interpersonal communication can be enhanced by listening and assertiveness skills. The group facilitators can teach children simple rules such as reflecting others' statements before stating their own opinions and how to use "I statements" as opposed to "blaming" statements. They can also teach children and adolescents how to articulate their own needs without impinging on the rights or needs of others.

GUIDELINES FOR CONDUCTING LOSS AND GRIEF GROUPS

Group size, duration of the group, and length of sessions appear to be somewhat standard across groups. Support group formats tend to be held for 6 to 10 weeks, whereas therapy groups may last as long as 6 months (e.g., Madonna & Chandler, 1986). Sessions tend to meet weekly and be 60 to 90 minutes long. A preferred group size is 6 to 8 members. Groups with very young children or with all members having severe problems may need to be smaller (e.g., Masterman & Reams, 1988; Madonna & Chandler, 1986).

Although groups may be heterogeneous or homogeneous on a wide range of variables, the overwhelming majority of bereavement groups for children and adolescents are heterogeneous with respect to sex. Age of members, type of bereavement suffered, and time elapsed since death tend to vary among group members. Other factors for group leaders to consider when forming groups are whether children know each other, culture, and before-death functioning in social and academic domains.

Groups consisting of participants with similar-aged cohorts are generally recommended. Younger children and adolescents are usually in separate groups; however, sometimes preadolescent children and adolescents are combined. Groups are usually heterogeneous with respect to recency of death. It is simply impractical to find youngsters who have all been bereaved for the same period of time or who are all in the same stage of the grief process. To complicate matters further, it is not clear how long each stage might take, so that two people who have been bereaved for the same amount of time may very well be working on different tasks.

Regarding the type of bereavement suffered, groups have been created for a variety of situations, including death of a father (e.g., Masterman & Reams, 1988), death of a parent (e.g., Moore & Herlihy, 1993), death of a classmate due to suicide (e.g., Alexander & Harman, 1988; Catone & Schatz, 1991), and death of a school counselor (Hickey, 1993). Harmey and Price's (1992) work with children bereaved by the death of a sibling suggested that members were able to identify with each other in spite of the fact that their siblings' deaths resulted from different causes. These researchers did suggest, however, that no member be different from all other members with respect to an important factor, such as being the only "surviving child" in the family.

Selection of members varies depending on the group setting. For example, groups conducted in schools may rely on information from teachers and school counselors to identify potential members, whereas groups conducted in agencies may rely on referrals from parents or other relatives. Letters of permission are sent to surviving caregivers. Individual screening interviews are generally conducted with prospective group members to determine "readiness" for group work, establish rapport, and introduce group rules.

GROUP ILLUSTRATIONS

Several groups are described that illustrate interventions with various age groups. Although the structure and content of the groups differ, they have common procedures.

Moore and Herlihy (1993) described a six-session open group for six to eight high school students grieving the loss of a parent. Students who had participated in previous years were permitted to attend and, in fact, often did.

The first session, "Sharing the Event," began with introductions and a recap of group rules and goals. Members were asked to participate by sharing information regarding the death. Students who had participated in previous years often volunteered to begin, thus modeling appropriate behavior for new members. The counselor often referred to impressions gained in the screening interviews as a basis for stimulating group process. For example, "How is your situation similar to Susan's?" is the type of question that would encourage communication among members. The authors noted that leaders need to be careful about violating confidentiality when asking such questions. Guided imagery or relaxation exercises were used to conclude the first group because the novelty of sharing was often stressful for students. Members were encouraged to use these exercises when they were feeling stress outside of the group.

The second session, "Stages of Grief," was primarily psychoeducational. Objective information about the grief process, including the work of Kubler-Ross, was presented in a mini-lesson format. Students were again assured that the stages of bereavement may actually vary from person to person and that it is "equally OK to be anywhere in the process" (Harmey & Price, 1992, p. 55). Worksheets were sometimes distributed to promote awareness of feelings and also to help students to recognize their progress.

The third session, "Events after the Death," consisted of open discussion about their loss. Common themes were funerals, the return to school after the death, interpersonal difficulties with non-bereaved peers, and positive experiences with non-bereaved peers. Curiously, humor often "surfaced" during this session. Students were taught that laughter was appropriate in the group and even a healthy part of the mourning process. Dreams also were explored; they tended to be a source of comfort for students, although some members did have nightmares and sad dreams.

In the fourth session, "The Changing Family Structure," salient issues included parental dating, new roles and responsibilities, and blended families. Special concerns were apparent for adolescents who were the oldest children, or the only boys or the only girls in their families. With regard to parental dating, students who accepted their parents' new relationships often helped less accepting students come to terms with this issue.

In the fifth session, "Family Rituals and Holidays," concerns about visiting the cemetery and celebrating holidays without the deceased were discussed. Other relevant issues that may arise in such a group are birthdays, anniversaries, and special milestones such as graduation. Special occasions tend to be difficult for bereaved people in that they are likely to miss the deceased most at these times.

Session six was used to facilitate termination of the group. Facilitators provided students with an opportunity to evaluate the program and make suggestions for improvement. Students commonly wished that the group would continue; however, Moore and Herlihy (1993) cautioned against this. They stated that members needed to "rest after weeks of intense emotion" and "get on with their own lives." Students were invited to meet with the counselor individually and were reminded that the group would be offered the following year.

Moore and Herlihy (1993) found that adolescents preferred interaction with peers in the familiar context of the school environment to individual counseling. They noted that several members revealed having been "taken for therapy" and "resenting it." Clearly, without a controlled study, it is impossible to determine whether preference for group over individual is a function of the recency of the loss, the appeal of congregating with peers, the familiarity of the school setting, or any combination of these.

Zambelli and associates (1988) described an interdisciplinary program for bereaved children that included work with parents. Children and adults were separated into two groups: a creative arts therapy group and a companion parent-support group, respectively. Zambelli and associates stated that feedback from both parents and children was "positive overall" (p. 47). Parents felt children were "more secure and expressive" and more skilled at managing grief-related anger after the group concluded. Children reported that meeting other bereaved children was helpful and that they enjoyed the creative arts. Some children commented that they did not like having to explain their art, which the authors suggested is a reflection of the difficulty some children have verbalizing feelings related to grief.

Overall, members felt the program "facilitated the grieving process." Zambelli and colleagues observed that the value of therapy increased when the intervention included all family members. Because parents who did not participate were less likely to fill out the evaluation forms and attend the follow-up family meetings, the authors could not make any definitive conclusions about the value of incorporating family members into the treatment.

Zambelli and DeRosa (1992) also described another bereavement support group, solely for children whose mothers had died of cancer. The authors observed that the four group members had better-developed coping and social skills at the end of the group. According to Zambelli and DeRosa, the members also appeared to have increased self-esteem, despite each child's scoring the same on pretest and posttest administrations of a self-concept scale.

Masterman and Reams (1988) developed a bereavement group for preschoolers aged 3 to 6 years as an outgrowth of a program for young widows. The group format was the same each week. Each session alternated periods of discussion and play.

Each week the group started by children showing a toy they brought from home. Children played with various toys and engaged in "rough and tumble play" with the leader. Early play sessions were unstructured, whereas later ones involved the leader directing play toward relevant themes. Common themes that emerged in children's play were guilt, anger, and powerlessness. The authors cautioned leaders against introducing new themes toward the middle or late part of the eight weeks because there may be insufficient time to work through them.

A discussion period during each session was based on a preplanned theme of the week, which was introduced to the children through the use of storytelling or puppet plays created and performed by the leader. Care was taken to foster children's identification with the characters in the hope that the children would learn the coping strategies implied in the story. For instance, one story about Rupert the Squirrel dealt with Rupert's fear that he made his dad die by being bad. In a conversation with his mother, Rupert learned that this is not possible; his father died because he was sick. After the story, the leader asked questions such as, "Did you ever feel like if you act real good then maybe your dad would come back?" (Masterman & Reams, 1988, p. 568).

The authors emphasized the importance of bearing in mind the limited cognitive abilities of preschoolers including, "attention span, vocabulary, making distinctions among concepts (especially relevant when dealing with feelings), grasping abstract concepts, and making connections the group leader has not explicitly stated. Therapeutic conclusions need to be stated in concrete terms and repeated a number of times" (Masterman & Reams, 1988, p. 568). The authors recommended using unusual character names, "funny voice tones," and "clumsy character movements" to keep children's interest and alleviate the seriousness of the subject (Masterman & Reams, 1988, p. 568).

Masterman and Reams (1988) also created a group for students 7 to 17 years old. This grouping of preadolescent and adolescent children is unusual. The authors defended this aspect of the program by stating it had not caused many problems and siblings could be in groups together.

Each of the eight weekly sessions was structured as follows: (1) 15 minutes for members to talk about their week since the last group, (2) 10 minutes of discussion related to homework assignments from the last group, (3) 25 minutes devoted to discussion of a preplanned topic, and (4) 10 minutes allowed for a game or exercise to close the session.

As just mentioned, the 25-minute segment of each weekly group focused on a specific topic. During Week 1, a "nonthreatening" game was played, leaders facilitated discussions of fears and ambivalence about being in the group, and the format for remaining sessions was presented. The second week, leaders shared their own experiences with grief and then the children were asked to tell about their experiences related to the death. In the third session, salient issues regarding last rites were discussed. Family changes due to the death and coping skills were explored during Week 4. In the fifth session, common grief reactions were discussed as well as topics such as afterlife and heaven. During Week 6, children's concerns about the future were acknowledged, including children's fears of their own death and the surviving parent's death, as well as issues related to blended families. The seventh session was devoted to preparing for group termination. The authors noted that leaving the group is another loss for the children. Leaders asked members about available supports outside the group and helped them to identify such resources. Finally, during the last session, informal evaluation was conducted by asking children, "What would you do the same or different if you were planning the next group?"

Of the play activities used to close the sessions, one was highlighted by the authors due to its popularity and success. Children made and threw paper airplanes. The authors suggested that the throwing of the airplanes was a release of tension built up during the preceding 25 minute discussion. Also, they noted that members often threw planes aggressively at the leader who was the same sex as the deceased and that "a direct hit usually results in gleeful laughter as the children express some of their forbidden anger at the deceased" (Masterman & Reams, 1988, p. 566). The authors used this activity to close their session; therefore, it is assumed that interpretation of the aggressive behavior was not offered. However, when working with adolescents, it may be beneficial to acknowledge aggressive behaviors and initiate discussion of the meaning of those behaviors.

LIMITATIONS OF GROUP INTERVENTIONS

Not all bereaved children will benefit from a group experience. Clearly, as discussed previously, group is not appropriate for all individuals (e.g., individuals who are psychotic, impulsive, or in crisis). However, in addition to these specific cases, there are other situations where a group intervention may not be the most effective treatment.

Researchers and clinicians have observed that the grief process consists of stages and/or tasks that need to be accomplished (Crenshaw, 1994; Kubler-Ross, 1968). Not all participants in the group will be at the same stage or ready to accomplish the same task at the same time. This makes it difficult for the leader to facilitate the group because the negotiation of different stages or the accomplishment of different tasks may require different interventions. Consequently, it may be most effective for treatment to be individually tailored so that task- or stage-appropriate interventions may be offered.

At the same time, there are benefits to participants being at different stages—for example, someone who has worked through much of his or her grief can give hope to others. The therapist must weigh the benefits against the costs in determining which approach will best meet each individual's needs.

Further, children or adolescents who have been assessed as "pathologically bereaved" may not function optimally in a group. Elizur and Kaffman (1983) outlined the following symptoms as constituting "pathological bereavement": "regressive overdependent behavior, manifold fears, separation anxiety, night sleep disorders, discipline problems, restlessness, learning difficulties, eating disorders, enuresis, aggressive or inhibited behavior, and social withdrawal" (p. 668). Children manifesting one or more of these problems that are associated with loss may require individual attention. Interpersonal problems such as shyness, isolation, and scapegoating may also interfere with children and adolescents having a successful group experience. Such children might work better in pairs rather than in group or individual counseling (Bluestone, 1991).

RECOMMENDATIONS FOR FUTURE RESEARCH AND PRACTICE

To say that there are many unanswered questions about bereavement and interventions for bereavement would be an understatement. The actual numbers of bereaved children are unavailable. The federal government does not even compile victim data for children under 12 years of age. The police do not collect information regarding the ages and numbers of survivors in a household where a death has occurred (Bureau of Justice Statistics, personal communication). Similarly, the United States Census does not publish statistics regarding the presence, ages, or number of surviving children of adults who have died due to illness. While data suggest that more violent crimes occur in cities, versus rural or suburban areas, again, the number of children who are bereaved as a result is not known.

Osterweis (1988) pointed out that little, if any, research has examined the potential negative impact of bereavement interventions. Almost all aspects of bereavement groups for children and adolescents need to be assessed. For example, are heterogeneous or homogeneous groups preferable with respect to age and gender of participant, and their relationship to the deceased? Does membership in a particular cultural or ethnic group affect responses to death and/or interventions? What is the optimal time for the intervention after the death? What is the optimal duration of the group? Should new members be allowed to enter at any stage of the group? How does the gender of the leader affect member progress? Are certain interventions more effective than others as applied to specific populations? Should the circumstances of the death and individual difference factors (e.g., coping styles, personality, intelligence) influence the choice of intervention strategies? Can peer pressure affect group members negatively?

Future studies designed to answer these questions require careful planning. First, group interventions should be based on theory and empirical data. Second, such interventions must be evaluated using scientific methods. Group interventions developed from theory and empirical evidence and rigorously evaluated are virtually nonexistent. A study by Sandler and associates (1992), however, evaluated a theoretically derived family bereavement program (as opposed to a group intervention) designed to prevent children from experiencing future problems as a result of the death of one of their parents. Random assignment to an intervention or control group, psychometrically sound standardized measures, and the use and monitoring of a standardized intervention protocol allowed for a more rigorous evaluation of the treatment than most other outcome studies. For a thorough discussion of developing preventive interventions for bereaved children based on theoretical and empirical foundations, the reader is referred to West and colleagues (1991).

For a meaningful body of knowledge relevant to bereavement to develop, future research must be systematic. This can be accomplished, in part, through the use of standardized treatment protocols and psychometrically sound assessments that allow for comparisons across studies; replication and extension studies are sorely needed.

REFERENCES

Alexander, J. C., & Harman, R. L. (1988). One counselor's intervention in the aftermath of a middle school student's suicide. A case study. *Journal of Counseling and Development, 66,* 283–285.

Baker, J. E., Sedney, M. A., & Gross, E. (1992). Psychological tasks for bereaved children. *American Journal of Orthopsychiatry, 62,* 105–116.

Black, D., & Urbanowicz, M. A. (1987). Family intervention with bereaved children. *Journal of Child Psychology and Psychiatry, 28,* 467–476.

Bluestone, J. (1991). School-based peer therapy to facilitate mourning in latency-age children following sudden parental death. In N. B. Webb (Ed.), *Play therapy with children in crisis* (pp. 254-275). New York: Guilford.

Buscaglia, L. (1982). *The fall of Freddie the leaf–a story of life for all ages.* New York: Holt, Rinehart and Winston.

Carey, L. (1990). Sandplay therapy with a troubled child. *The Arts in Psychotherapy, 17,* 197–209.

Carlson, J., & Fullmer, D. (1993). Family counseling/consultation: Principles for growth. In J. Carlson & J. Lewis (Eds.), *Counseling the adolescent: Individual, family and school interventions.* Denver: Love.

Catone, W. V., & Schatz, M. T. (1991). The crisis moment: A school's response to the event of suicide. *School Psychology International, 12,* 17–23.

Cheifetz, P. N., Stavrakakis, G., & Lester, E. P. (1989). Studies of the affective state in bereaved children. *Canadian Journal of Psychiatry, 34,* 688–692.

Crenshaw, D. A. (1994). Death and dying. In J. L. Ronch, W. Van Ornum, & N. C. Stillwell (Eds.), *The counseling source book: A practical reference on contemporary issues* (pp. 510–518). New York: Crossroad.

Elizur, E., & Kaffman, M. (1983). Factors influencing the severity of childhood bereavement reactions. *American Journal of Orthopsychiatry, 53,* 668–676.

Fanos, J. H., & Nickerson, B. G. (1991). Long-term effects of sibling death during adolescence. *Journal of Adolescent Research, 6,* 70–82.

Furman, E. (1974). *A child's parent dies: Studies in childhood bereavement.* New Haven, CT: Yale University Press.

Gray, R. E. (1988). The role of school counselors with bereaved teenagers: With and without peer support groups. *The School Counselor, 35,* 185–193.

Harmey, N., & Price, B. (1992). Groupwork with bereaved children. *Groupwork, 5,* 19–27.

Harris, E. S. (1991). Adolescent bereavement following

the death of a parent: An exploratory study. *Child Psychiatry and Human Development, 21,* 267–281.

Heath, C. P. (1986). Understanding death. *Techniques, 2,* 88–92.

Hickey, L. O. (1993). Death of a counselor: A bereavement group for junior high school students. In N. B. Webb (Ed.), *Helping bereaved children: A handbook for practitioners* (pp. 239–266). New York: Guilford.

Irizarry, C. (1992). Spirituality and the child: A grandparent's death. *Journal of Psychosocial Oncology, 10,* 39–58.

Kelly, J. B., & Wallerstein, J. S. (1976). The effects of parental divorce: Experiences of the child in early latency. *American Journal of Orthopsychiatry, 46,* 20–32.

Kubler-Ross, E. (1968). *On death and dying.* New York: Macmillan.

Lazar, A., & Torney-Purta, J. (1991). The development of the subconcepts of death in young children: A short-term longitudinal study. *Child Development, 62,* 1321–1333.

Lubetsky, M. (1989). The magic of fairy tales: Psychodynamic and developmental perspectives. *Child Psychiatry and Human Development 19* (4), 245–255.

Madonna, J. M., & Chandler, R. (1986). Aggressive play and bereavement in group therapy with latency-aged boys. *Journal of Child and Adolescent Psychotherapy, 3,* 109–114.

Masterman, S. H., & Reams, R. (1988). Support groups for bereaved preschool and school-age children. *American Journal of Orthopsychiatry,* 562–570.

Miller, C., & Boe, J. (1990). Tears into diamonds: Transformation of child psychic trauma through sandplay and storytelling. *The Arts in Psychotherapy, 17,* 247–257.

Moore, J., & Herlihy, B. (1993). Grief groups for students who have had a parent die. *School Counselor, 41,* 54–59.

Nagy, M. (1948). The child's theories concerning death. *Journal of Genetic Psychology, 73,* 3–27.

Orbach, I., Gross, Y., Glaubman, H., & Berman, D. (1985). Children's perception of death in humans and animals as a function of age, anxiety, and cognitive ability. *The Journal of Child Psychology and Psychiatry, 26,* 453–463.

Osterweis, M. (1988). Perceptions not yet matched by research. *Journal of Palliative Care, 4,* 78–80.

Prichard, S., & Epting, F. (1992). Children and death: New horizons in theory and measurement. *Omega, 24,* 271–288.

Raphael, B. (1982). The young child and the death of a parent. In C. M. Parkes & J. Stevenson-Hinde (Eds.), *The place of attachment in human behavior.* London: Tavistock.

Rosen, H. (1986). When a sibling dies. *International Journal of Family Psychiatry, 7,* 389–396.

Sandler, I. N., West, S. G., Baca, L., Pillow, D. R., Gersten, J. C., Rogosch, F., Virdin, L., Beals, J., Reynolds, K. D., Kallgren, C., Tein, J., Kriege, G., Cole, E., & Ramirez, R. (1992). Linking empirically based theory and evaluation: The family bereavement program. *American Journal of Community Psychology, 20,* 491–521.

Schilling, R. F., Koh, N., Abramovitz, F., & Gilbert, L. (1992). Bereavement groups for inner-city children. *Research on Social Work Practice, 2,* 405–419.

Segal, R. M. (1984). Helping children express grief through symbolic communication. *Social Casework: The Journal of Contemporary Social Work, 65,* 590–599.

Siegel, K., Mesagno, F., & Christ, G. (1990). A prevention program for bereaved children. *American Journal of Orthopsychiatry, 60,* 168–175.

Tait, D. C., & Depta, J. (1993). Play therapy group for bereaved children. In N. B. Webb (Ed.), *Helping bereaved children* (pp. 169–185). New York: Guilford.

Van Eerdewegh, M. M., Clayton, P. J., & Van Eerdewegh, P. (1985). The bereaved child: Variables influencing early psychopathology. *British Journal of Psychiatry, 147,* 188–194.

Vigna, J. (1991). *Saying goodbye to daddy.* Morton Grove, IL: Albert Whitman.

West, S. G., Sandler, I., Pillow, D. R., Baca, L., & Gersten, J. C. (1991). The use of structural equation modeling in generative research: Toward the design of a preventive intervention for bereaved children. *American Journal of Community Psychology, 19,* 459–480.

Yalom, I. D. (1980). *Existential psychotherapy.* New York: Basic Books.

Zambelli, G. C., Clark, E. J., Barile, L., & de Jong, A. F. (1988). An interdisciplinary approach to clinical intervention for childhood bereavement. *Death Studies, 12,* 41–50.

Zambelli, G. C., & DeRosa, A. P. (1992). Bereavement support groups for school-age children: Theory, intervention, and case example. *American Journal of Orthopsychiatry, 62,* 484–493.

CHAPTER 10

GROUPS FOR DRUG AND ALCOHOL ABUSE

Marlene Miziker Gonet, ANN ARBOR PUBLIC SCHOOLS

OVERVIEW OF THE PROBLEM

Adolescent substance use and abuse is a complicated multifaceted problem having a distinct social history with unusual trends of use and behavior. To be effective in working with young people who are using drugs, one needs to understand the adolescent's present substance-use patterns and their implications for the future. A review of the history on drug-use trends and patterns suggests that they are not constant. One must therefore continue to monitor how these trends and patterns are changing and reassess the ever-changing needs of young people. The former has been happening since 1975 under the Monitoring the Future project, a University of Michigan Institute for Social Research effort funded by a grant from the National Institute on Drug Abuse (Johnston, O'Malley, & Bachman, in preparation).

Alcohol and tobacco remain the most commonly used drugs by adolescents. While cigarette smoking has been declining among adults, it has been rising for adolescents. Episodes of heavy drinking are also common among adolescent youths. The most recent study by Johnston and associates (in preparation) found that when students were asked if they had five or more consecutive drinks on at least one occasion in the two weeks prior to the survey, 16 percent of eighth-graders, 25% of tenth-graders, and 30% of twelfth-graders responded affirmatively. In addition, 3.7% percent of seniors reported daily alcohol use.

The U.S. national average of lifetime marijuana use rates for high school seniors in 1995 was 36% (Johnston et al., in preparation), a decrease from the 50% rate in 1978, yet still an unacceptable high level. Of those students who indicated that they had tried marijuana, 2.4% reported daily use rate, indicating a number of young people with possible drug dependence.

Unfortunately, many of the drug prevention gains made in the 1980s are losing their impact. The most recent national data (Johnston et al., in preparation) suggest that drug use may be rising after more than a decade of steady decline. The increase in drug use among teens has several explanations. According to Lloyd Johnston (1996):

> *Among the most likely, in my opinion, is the fact that this most recent crop of youngster grew up in a period in which drug use rates were down substantially from what they had been 10 to 15 years earlier. This gave youngsters less opportunity to learn from other's mistakes and resulted in what I call "generational forgetting" of the hazards of drugs, as the process of generational replacement has taken place.*

ADOLESCENT DEVELOPMENT AND SUBSTANCE USE

A variety of detrimental effects have been associated with substance abuse, including negative consequences on physical, psychological, behavioral, and social functioning (Dryfoos, 1990). Significant problems have been reported for even the most commonly used substances—tobacco, alcohol, and marijuana. Clinicians working with adolescents involved with drugs are also aware that drug use negatively affects adolescent development. Adolescent smokers are prone to small airway dysfunction and a high incidence of coughing, phlegm production, wheezing, and other respiratory symptoms. While short-term use of cigarettes produces respiratory problems, long-term use increases the likelihood of cancer of the lungs, larynx, oral cavity, esophagus, pancreas, and bladder and has been linked to peptic ulcers, chronic bronchitis, emphysema, and cardiovascular disease (U.S. Department of Health and Human Services, 1982). Short-term use of alcohol places youths at greater risk for academic difficulties, automobile accidents and accidental death, delinquency problems, and suicide (Forman & Pfeiffer, 1997). Several serious health risks have been linked to long-term alcohol abuse, including cirrhosis of the liver and stomach cancer as well as psychiatric illness and impaired social functioning (Dryfoos, 1990). Consequences associated with short-term marijuana use include impaired psychomotor performance, impaired short-term memory, and psychological difficulties. Long-term consequences of marijuana use include serious health problems, job and marriage instability, psychiatric issues, and financial problems (Dryfoos, 1990).

At whatever age a young person begins a relationship with alcohol and other drugs, normal emotional and social development stops. This does not mean that development ceases with experimentation or the first time a young person becomes intoxicated. Rather, normal development ends when the young person develops an emotional bond with the drugs. For example, a 16-year-old may giggle inappropriately during group work, indicating the maturity level of a much younger person. A 17-year-old may have difficulty with abstract thinking. A 19-year-old may have difficulty developing intimate friendships and appear very narcissistic. In addition, not all learning stops when drug use begins. The drug use interferes with learning in that the adolescent users fail to move on to higher levels of functioning in their development. As Baumrind and Moselle (1985) explained:

> *Adolescents who become involved in the use of drugs may be able to effectively exercise previously acquired conceptual schemes, acquire new facts, and refine basic learning skills. Therefore their academic performance will not necessarily deteriorate, nor will they necessarily lose the ability to maintain smooth interpersonal relations with peers or adults. However, the transition to higher stages of social reasoning and associated patterns of social interaction, almost by definition, involve a process of overtaxing what were previously the adolescent's most comprehensively effective schemes of thought and action. Maximally efficient functioning is required in order to resolve the disequilibration that constitutes the impetus for developmental progress. Loss of optimal cortical tone due to drug use may be reflected in the failure to consolidate a higher and more complex stage of understanding, a process which requires full "presence of mind." (p. 53)*

The irony of the problem for the young person is that by using drugs in an attempt to promote independence and maturity, he or she is most likely keeping such growth from taking place.

The young person in trouble with alcohol or other drugs needs to remain dependent on parents to continue drug use. Herein lies an important paradox. It is humiliating for most older adolescents and young adults to admit an extreme dependence on their parents. Therefore, most adolescents with substance addictions deny dependency. Many young people transfer dependency needs to peers or other significant adults as they move toward independence. If they transfer dependency needs to drugs, however, they cannot achieve independence, and so they become mired in the dependency stage. One way to deny dependency on parents is to mask it by using drugs and mimicking perceived adultlike drinking behavior. Because drug use impedes emotional and psychosocial development, these young people never become truly independent. In fact, as the disease of addiction progresses, they become more dependent on their parents. The recognition of this condition and the humiliation that goes along with it may lead to continued drug use, and the same devastating and painful cycle continues. Thus, at the very time drug use produces the illusion of autonomy, it actually is immobilizing its young victim. Group therapy provides a means to interrupt this cycle by allowing young addicts to transfer their dependency needs from the drugs to their peer therapy group.

When young people turn to drugs to feel better about themselves, serious identity problems can ensue. Drug use often promotes a tendency to cover up one's true feelings. However, feelings are the key to who a person is. By being in touch with our feelings, we are in touch with ourselves. By having our feelings validated by others, our self-concept develops. By talking about and taking action on feelings of inadequacy, we begin to feel adequate. Drug use deters growth in this area. Drugs trick the mind into thinking that all is well and provide the user with a false sense of well-being. Such persons eventually lose touch with their true feelings about who they are or who they wish to become. Working through the confusion that precedes identity formation becomes simply impossible. A young person's perception of reality, and therefore of the self, becomes severely distorted.

One recovering young man explained how drug use affected his identity. He felt somehow "different" from others. He was struggling with where he fit into his world. However, he did not see any possibilities because he felt disconnected from the human race. He was in tremendous pain because of a difficult family situation. The first time he used a drug, he fell in love. He stated that for the first time in his life he "felt normal." For the first time since he could remember, there was a relief from emotional pain. However, the more he relied on drugs to ease his suffering, the worse his situation became. Eventually he was living on the street, thousands of miles from home, fighting to remain chronically intoxicated. He certainly did not "feel normal" any longer. This young man now believes that he was an addict from his first moment of use.

GROUP INTERVENTION MODELS

The fact that drug and alcohol abuse problems are tied closely to social relationships and interactions has pointed to the use of group counseling as a timely mechanism for treatment as well as prevention (Lewis, Dana, & Blevins, 1988). Group therapy is an effective means of working with substance-abuse issues and adolescents (Reister 1991, Duckert, Amundsen, & Johnson, 1992; Flores & Mahon, 1993). The use of groups with exclusively chemically dependent clients will maximize treatment efforts (Khantzian, 1985; & Fram, 1990). The group psychotherapy treatment modality has been so effective in that most drug rehabilitations use it as the core of their programs. One investigative study found the aspect of treatment that chemically dependent patients reported as being most beneficial to them was group counseling (Rootes, 1993).

Although there has been extensive research examining the effectiveness of treatment modalities in treating drug abuse, research examining the effectiveness of specific interventions and techniques used within the treatment modalities is minimal (Mejta, Naylor, & Maslar, 1994). For example, as of 1991, there were no systematic descriptions of group counseling/therapy approaches with drug abusers, nor were there any outcome studies examining the effectiveness of group counseling/therapy with drug abusers (Galanter, Castaneda, & Franco, 1991). However, group counseling and therapy remain frequent in the treatment of drug abuse.

Alcohol and drug problems have multiple causes and usually require multiple solutions. Within the substance-abuse field, there are three very distinct levels of response to all issues resulting from the use, abuse, and addiction to alcohol and other drugs. The primary response is *prevention*; the secondary, *intervention*; and the tertiary, *treatment* (Suski, 1992). Both schools and community agencies are recognizing the need for this three-pronged approach to drug-related problems. As a result, many schools and treatment agencies are incorporating drug prevention, intervention, and recovery groups in their counseling programs.

Prevention groups include education and activities that prevent or forestall the onset of drug use, abuse, and/or dependency as well as reduce the risk that individuals will develop problems as a result of substance use. The types of activities found in prevention groups often include education and information, self-esteem building, social skills enhancement, life skills development, problem-solving skills, and resistance skills training. The goal of these groups is to "inoculate" young people to the pressures to use drugs that they may encounter and to promote healthy life-styles and wellness. Wellness is a concept that uses a holistic, preventive approach toward the development of optimum human functioning (Myers, 1992).

Primary prevention strategies have contributed directly to the reductions realized in substance-abuse risk factors (Conyne, 1994). One rationale for the use of groups in implementing a primary prevention program is that the group experience often facilitates the development of a variety of therapeutic conditions (Adix, Kelly, & Rosenthal, 1984). Examples of successful prevention groups have been documented such as well-being groups (Tredinnick, 1993), friendship groups (Rosenthal, 1993), and general promotion of mental health (Carty, 1993). Tobler (1986) identified five types of substance prevention programs, all of which could be conducted in using peer or family groups: (1) knowledge-only programs that focus on information giving and use scare tactics; (2) affective-only programs that focus on social and emotional functioning and incorporate self-esteem, citizenship, and values clarification strategies; (3) peer-oriented groups that target interpersonal resistance skills, social skills, and coping mechanisms; (4) knowledge-plus-affective programs that are based on the notion that attitudes, values, and beliefs must change for behavior to change and emphasis is placed on decision-making skills; and (5) alternative-oriented programs that stress more healthful options such as recreational activities.

Multicomponent programs that focus on social influence and coping skills have been shown to be effective in deterring overall substance use as well as individual substance use (i.e., cigarette, alcohol, marijuana, other illicit drugs) (Tobler, 1986). For average or typical students, peer programs appear to be most effective for reducing substance use; however, alternative programs showed the greatest promise for specific high-risk populations, such as delinquents. Information-alone programs and one-shot or minimal group presentations have little or no effect on substance use. Although programs that emphasize resistance skills have demonstrated a short-term influence in deterring substance use, these outcomes often dissipate at two- or three-year follow-up. Programs showing the most promising, long-term effects incorporate either booster sessions or a multilevel approach that includes school-based group sessions, parent involvement, the media, and the community (Hawkins & Catalano, 1992). Recent reviews point to the general ineffectiveness of many school-based prevention programs, especially in reducing long-term substance use (Hansen, 1992; Meyer, 1995).

One comprehensive, multicomponent prevention program that has demonstrated success in preventing substance use among middle-school students is Project STAR (Students Taught Awareness and Resistance), developed by Mary Ann Pentz and colleagues (Pentz, Cormack, Flay, Hansen, & Johnson, 1986). The project, which has involved more than 100 middle schools across Kansas City and Indianapolis, has five major components.

1. A school-based curriculum focuses on resistance and other coping skills during 10 sessions. These sessions include role-plays and homework assignments that involve family members.
2. A parent program incorporates parent education in family communication and parent/student/principal groups formed to promote a drug-free environment.
3. A community-focused component targets community organizations and leaders who are trained in drug prevention, and is supported in developing task forces, mass media appeals, award ceremonies, and referral programs.
4. Health policy is addressed through creating neighborhood watches and networks against

drugs, enforcing drunk driving laws, and promoting antismoking policies by government officials.

5. Drug prevention is promoted through mass media activities, which include press kits, new features, commercials, and other television programs.

Evaluation results on 42 Kansas City schools indicated significantly lower cigarette, alcohol, and marijuana use by students and parents in Project STAR schools, compared to control schools (Pentz et al., 1989). At three-year follow-up, rates for tobacco and marijuana use remained significantly less in experimental than in control schools, and evidence suggested that the Project STAR program was effective with high-risk youths as well as with lower-risk youths (Johnson et al., 1990).

Intervention groups have been designed for individuals who are exhibiting high-risk behaviors for involvement with alcohol and other drugs, for using alcohol and other drugs, and for young people who are just beginning to get into trouble with their drug-use behavior. In a sense, the intervention response to substance abuse and its related issues can be regarded as an overlapping stage of response. That is, certain elements included in a well-rounded program of prevention may be interpreted as interventionary in nature, such as the education on high-risk drinking for the children of alcoholics (Suski, 1992). Groups designed to disrupt drug use of adolescents have also been established in both schools and treatment agencies. However, few strategies have been developed that would intervene into the social/cultural/environmental context before the drug-using behavior occurs. In general, school-based programs have been more effective in preventing substance abuse among low-risk or typical adolescents, but less effective in reducing drug use among those at greatest risk for abuse (Hansen, 1992; Meyer, 1995).

Initiation into use of illicit drugs other than marijuana seems to be predicted by poor parent/child relationships, parent and peer licit and illicit drug-using models, and feelings of depression (Hawkins & Catalano, 1992). At this point, intervention means referral to a treatment agency for individual, group, or family counseling. In addition, because the disease of addiction runs in families, most treatment centers now have group counseling for the young children of adults in their program as well as other affected family members. Many school districts currently have support groups for students with chemically dependent parents. (Groups for children of alcoholics is discussed extensively in Nastasi in Chapter 11 of this book.)

Support groups and group therapy with addicts have been established to help the chemically dependent person learn to maintain sobriety, develop a recovery program, and manage his or her life with the disease of chemical dependency (LaSalvia, 1993). Chemical dependency is a chronic disease; that is, once a person has the disease, he or she will have it for life. However, the disease is totally controllable with abstinence. Recovery for this disease includes the life-style changes necessary to promote and maintain abstinence. Thomas (1990) has stated that group therapy is the most effective and common treatment available for helping adolescents who abuse drugs or who have had other problems with the law. These groups may be therapy groups comprised totally of chemically dependent adolescents, multiple family groups in which family members of the addicted individuals comprise the group, and aftercare groups. Aftercare groups focus on addicts who have become drug free, have started the recovery process, and are working to maintain sobriety. Therapy and multiple family groups occur in treatment centers, whereas support groups or aftercare groups occur in both treatment centers and schools.

The most recognized example of support groups is likely Alcoholics Anonymous (AA), based on a Twelve-Step philosophy. Recent estimates indicate that as many as 75% of all inpatient, outpatient, and residential programs for adolescent treatment of abuse problems are based on the AA model (Lawson & Lawson, 1992). The primary purpose of these groups is to change substance-use behavior and to build social, educational, and vocational skills as well as the abusers' self-esteem and confidence. AA groups emphasize a belief in a power greater than oneself as integral to the group treatment. Many school-based intervention programs highly recommend that adolescent abusers participate in an AA-type community-based group. In fact, for those who attend AA meetings on a regular basis, it is the single-most powerful means of maintaining sobriety known (Alford, Koehler, & Leonard 1991; Cross, Morgan, Mooney, Martin, & Rafter, 1990; Sheeren, 1988). The AA "Preamble," read repeatedly at many AA meetings, provides a philosophy and a purpose:

> *Alcoholics Anonymous is a fellowship of men and women who share their experience, strength and hope with each other that they may solve their common problem and help others to recover from alcoholism.*
>
> *The only requirement for membership is a desire to stop drinking.*
>
> *There are no dues or fees for AA membership; we are self-supporting through our own contributions. AA is not allied with any sect, denomination, politics, organization, or institution; does not wish to engage in any controversy; neither endorses nor opposes any causes.*
>
> *Our primary purpose is to stay sober and help other alcoholics to achieve sobriety.*[1]

AA provides its members with a sense of belonging to an accepting and caring community. Within that community is tremendous support along with the Twelve Steps to help one learn to manage the impulse or urge to drink. The Twelve Steps are:

1. *We admitted we were powerless over alcohol—that our lives had become unmanageable.*
2. *Came to believe that a Power greater than ourselves could restore us to sanity.*
3. *Made a decision to turn our will and our lives over to the care of God as we understood Him.*
4. *Made a searching and fearless moral inventory of ourselves.*
5. *Admitted to God, to ourselves, and to another human being the exact nature of our wrongs.*
6. *Were entirely ready to have God remove all these defects of character.*
7. *Humbly asked Him to remove our shortcomings.*
8. *Made a list of all persons we had harmed, and became willing to make amends to them all.*
9. *Made direct amends to such people wherever possible, except when to do so would injure them or others.*
10. *Continued to take personal inventory and when we were wrong promptly admitted it.*
11. *Sought through prayer and meditation to improve our conscious contact with God as we understood Him, praying only for knowledge of His will for us and the power to carry on.*
12. *Having had a spiritual awakening as the result of these steps, we tried to carry this message to alcoholics and to practice these principles in all our affairs.*[2]

Many adolescents are not developmentally ready with the abstract reasoning skills necessary to incorporate such a Twelve-Step program. However, with simplification and an explanation from an understanding adult, they can do so. For example, the first three steps can be consolidated into "admitting you have a problem and need help." Simply stated, Steps 4 and 5 mean looking at the consequences of past behavior. All of the steps can be presented and used in a way to make them important and meaningful in the young person's life.

Alcoholics Anonymous is the parent of all Twelve-Step programs. It has grown to include all addicts and all polydrug users. However, Narcotics Anonymous (NA) and Cocaine Anonymous (CA) are available to provide similar Twelve Steps for addicts who feel they have special needs.

This chapter will focus on therapy and support groups for working with adolescents who are chemically dependent or in serious trouble with their drug use and on the road to addiction. Here, the terms *alcoholism, chemical dependency,* and *addiction* are used interchangeably for several reasons. First, because alcohol is the drug most commonly abused by both adults and adolescents, much of the research literature concentrates on alcohol. A great deal of what holds true for alcoholism applies similarly to addictions to other drugs, particularly those whose sedative-hypnotic effects resemble those of alcohol. Second, many young people are polydrug abusers: They are abusing or addicted to more than one drug. No longer is the question, To what drug are you addicted? More accurately, it is, What are your drugs of choice? Finally, much of the literature on adolescent drug use interchanges these terms.

DEFINING THE PROBLEM

Drawing the lines between adolescent drug use, abuse, and dependency is not always easy. Conceptualizing use patterns on a continuum with experimentation on one end and late stages of addiction on the other helps to illustrate that adolescent use levels vary. However, some adolescents who initially try drugs eventually develop the disease of addiction: an insidious, dangerous, and destructive disease that develops over time and will only get worse without intervention and treatment. The transition from use to abuse has been characterized by Clayton (1992) as occurring across five stages. The first stage is initiation, wherein a nonuser moves to being a user. The user makes a decision to continue use in the second stage. In Stage 3, the user escalates quantity, frequency, or both with a type of drug. During Stage 4, an individual's use extends to other drug types, and experimentation with simultaneous use of multiple drugs occurs. The fifth stage is characterized with regression, cessation, and relapse cycles that may repeat several times before an individual either is successful in discontinuing drug use or remains dependent. An individual's progression from one stage to another is influenced by family, social, psychological, and biogenetic factors as well as his or her involvement in prevention and intervention programs.

Defining dependency is a difficult task. In fact, the World Health Organization has been struggling with defining alcoholism/addiction for years (Keller, 1982). John Wallace (1986) has provided a practical definition of alcoholism that works equally well for any chemical addiction:

> *Alcoholism is a genetically influenced disease of the chemistry of the brain that is complicated by psychological and social factors. Hence, it is a biopsychosocial disease, one that involves biology, behavior, and sociocultural factors. The disease is characterized by inconsistent control over one's behavior while drinking and/or drinking behavior. A cardinal feature is continued compulsive use in the face of frequent negative psychological, biological, or social consequences of use. Alcoholism is a progressive, chronic and fatal disease. (p. 163)*

This definition is comprehensive in that it covers the three vital human conditions affected by the disease: a person's biology, psychology, and social environment. In addition, this definition includes three behaviors characterized by any drug dependence: (1) compulsion to use the drug, (2) loss of control over the drug, and (3) continued use of the drug despite adverse consequences. These basic behaviors are characteristic of any addiction, whether it is to nicotine, cocaine, marijuana, alcohol, or any other drug.

The compulsion to use a drug does not necessarily refer to frequency of the actual drug-using behavior. Rather, it suggests one's relationship to the drug—a psychological preoccupation with drug use. For example, a young person may make it through a week of classes without using drugs, but if this can only be accomplished by looking forward to the weekend and the opportunity to finally use, he or she exhibits compulsive use behavior. Hence, more and more of a student's time, energy, and money are spent thinking about being high and ensuring that a steady supply of drugs is available.

Loss of control over the drug, another characteristic of drug dependence, again does not necessarily refer to quantity or frequency. Rather, it refers to the loss of the user's ability to predict whether there will be control over using behavior. For example, a young person may go to a party and plan to have a couple of beers early in the evening, ensuring a clean and innocent look when a parent comes to drive him or her home. The plan works and is put into action at several subsequent parties. Eventually, however, the chemically dependent youth loses the ability to control intake—and the parent arrives to find son or daughter totally inebriated. The addicted person, then, has lost control not only over limited use but also over the ability to predict whether he or she would lose control.

Continued use despite negative consequences is another indicator of drug dependency. It is not how much and how often students use a drug, but instead, what happens to them when they do. Conflicts with school, parents, friends, and law-enforcement officers begin to develop. One may decide that it would be better to cut down or quit using altogether and may even succeed for a few weeks. However, the chemically dependent person eventually will continue use despite the negative consequences.

Group therapy provides the adolescent with peer associations that help in processing information and comparing experiences. As an addict, the young person eventually begins using drugs to medicate against feelings of tremendous shame, guilt, and a sense of worthlessness. Groups are a safe place where the individual addict can break through the pervasive sense of isolation, reduce shame by hearing the experiences of others, practice positive new behaviors and language, and develop effective problem-solving skills for daily living. When teenagers begin to understand addiction as a disease and their behaviors as symptomatic of that disease, shame and guilt begin to subside. The healing and recovery process then can begin.

Groups are also a place where young, newly sober addicts can talk about their ambivalence with recovery and receive feedback from other addicts who have a longer history of sobriety. As trust develops, members can promote recovery for each other by confronting sobriety-threatening thoughts and behaviors and thus support positive life-style changes.

PSYCHOLOGICAL DEFENSES AND ADDICTION

Chemically dependent adolescents are young people who, despite all outward appearances, are in a tremendous amount of pain. In an attempt to secure drugs, they have violated their personal value systems, often deeply hurting the people they love. They are experiencing severe negative consequences for their drug-using behavior. These adolescents have learned that the only thing they can rely on and trust is their drug. This state of addiction is so painful—and powerful—that chemically dependent adolescents develop a number of psychological defenses to protect themselves from misery. These defenses are not present simply because a young addict wants to continue to get high. By the time addiction sets in, most young addicts are using drugs just to feel normal. The defenses are there to keep young addicts from being overwhelmed by the emotional, physical, and spiritual destruction of the disease. Common defenses include denial, projection, avoidance and minimization, and rationalization.

Denial

Denial is the defense typically employed to guard against the pain of addiction. Denial, however, is not the same as lying. It is simply the afflicted person's belief system and perception of reality. What is obvious to everyone else becomes blocked out in the addict's mind. In fact, denial is often a thin thread holding the addict intact psychologically.

In the field of chemical dependency, denial is used differently from the more traditional sense of the term as a psychological defense mechanism. In chemical dependency, denial is meant to encompass all psychological defenses incorporated to protect and maintain the drug-using behavior.

Denial seems to go hand in hand with the disease of addiction. If one is working with addicts, one can expect client denial. The individual will attempt to convince the group that certain "problems" are resolved or minimize significant issues (Corey, 1990). Denial keeps addicts from seeing the problems that his or her drug use has caused them and to protect them from facing the fearsome reality of their addiction. Thus, another addict often is the person best qualified to help an addict see his or her problem and to alleviate the denial system. Because the denial system can be entrenched in an addict's personality and life-style, having several addicts gently confront and share their stories, while at the same time communicating hope and recovery, is the optimal way to interrupt denial and begin the treatment process. The group process ensures that the same message is repeated and exemplified by group member upon group member.

Projection

Projection is the tendency to place one's own undesirable or unwanted traits onto others. It is a way of externalizing self-hatred. Projection often takes the form of blaming others. Assimilative projection refers to the view that others share many of one's characteristics or participate in the same behavioral patterns. It is the assumption that others hold similar traits. Projection is a common defense of many addicts. Most teenage drug addicts believe that almost all students in their high school use drugs.

Assimilative projection is a defense that makes addicts excellent group member candidates. The belief that others share their attributes aids in fostering interactiveness and the development of compatibility within the group. Therefore, addicts are more likely to share shameful or embarrassing situations with other addicts than with group members who might not have similar character attributes. This sharing will promote group cohesion, which in turn can be used to exert pressure on new members to go along with the group norm.

Avoidance and Minimization

When addicts are in emotional pain, they seek to avoid and minimize conflict. Avoidance and minimization may take the form of conveniently forgetting or misunderstanding. The addict is often trying to escape from a problem or difficult situation. Sometimes it is difficult to believe that addicts want to avoid conflict because of their behavior. However, addicts tend not to be very adept at managing anger and confrontation, especially in interpersonal relationships.

Groups provide an arena where avoidance is difficult and minimization is challenged. Group members who have learned to recognize avoidance and minimization in themselves can then openly address these defense tactics when enacted by other group members. The group also provides an environment for addicts to learn how to face difficult issues and resolve conflict along with numerous opportunities to practice these skills.

Rationalization

Rationalization is an addict's attempt to make justifiable and plausible excuses to oneself or others for his or her irresponsible or socially unacceptable behavior. Chemically dependent adolescents seem to be masters at rationalization with a remarkable ability to explain the unfathomable. Addicts are in the best position to recognize and break apart another addict's faulty logic.

Defense System

The psychological defense system of young addicts make them excellent candidates for group work. Effective group intervention strategies are those designed to help the addict recognize these defenses that promote addictive-type thinking and behavior and replace them with healthy thinking and behavior. However, it is critical to understand that an addict uses these defenses as protection against dire feelings of shame, guilt, remorse, self-hatred, anger, and despair. These defenses will need to be worked with carefully and slowly because eventually an addict will be forced to face the reality of the consequences of his or her disease. It is only in a supportive, understanding, and genuine environment that the addict can even begin to look at his or her defenses. It is only after a foundation of hope and trust that an addict can begin to look at the hurt and pain that necessitate his or her defense system. The most effective way to provide a therapeutic environment is with a group consisting of other addicts.

Drug counseling tends to be more task oriented (Cook & Petersen, 1989), problem focused, and behaviorally oriented than traditional analytic methods of group therapy. A series of studies by Friedman and colleagues (Friedman & Glickman, 1986, 1987; Friedman et al., 1987) found increased treatment effectiveness in programs with experienced staff favoring practical problem-oriented approaches over psychoanalytic or confrontational therapies. Addicts need a direct approach focusing on the "here and now." The "here and now" focus is especially true with early interventions. If an addict does not have a strong base of recovery before dealing with anxiety-provoking, powerful, reflective, analytical work, the resulting emotional intensity and unease will set the stage for acute drug cravings and relapse.

The counselor or therapist may find that working with clients who are in trouble with their use of alcohol and other drugs is somewhat different from counseling other clients. The initial intent of the group process is not to help clients feel better, but rather to help them recognize that the genesis of their problem lies in the hurt, pain, and trouble stemming from their drug-using behavior. Thus, the connection between the clients' problems and their drug use must be developed slowly and maintained, while at the same time building a supportive alliance to the group. Directly confronting clients with their drug problems too early and too intensely may be perceived as threatening, thus undermining the development of cohesion within the group.

In addition, there may be an interplay between drug use and other issues. However, young addicts cannot address major life difficulties until they become drug free. The drug use may be the primary problem, may be clouding underlying questions, or may be exacerbating deeper concerns. The bottom line is that young people cannot work on emotional issues if they are using drugs to cover feelings or to help cope with and "solve" problems. A significant portion of group counseling is identifying, understanding, and managing feelings. This difficult work cannot be accomplished if drugs are used to ease the process. To grow and mature, young people need to experience the important developmental task of struggling with their feelings, which drug use inhibits and stunts.

Enabling

In traditional counseling practice, enabling refers to empowering the client by helping the client self-direct and problem solve. In traditional counseling, enabling has a positive connotation. In drug counseling, however, the term has come to describe behavior that allows another to remain free from responsibility in conduct and emotions, often indirectly permitting the drug-using behavior to continue. *Enabling* used in drug counseling connotes "We want to help you" rather than "We want to help you to help yourself."

The underlying message that results from enabling is: "You poor baby, you can't help it. Let us take care of it for you." This paternalistic message not only keeps young people from experiencing the consequences of their behavior but it also keeps them from taking charge of their lives. Hence, enabling undermines independence as well as beliefs of hope on which true independence is based. Addicts need to understand that they are responsible for their actions and then behave accordingly. Allowing young addicts through group intervention to experience the consequences of their conduct is a therapeutic gift. Helping chemically dependent adolescents take responsibility for their feelings and behaviors engenders respect toward them as worthwhile people. The underlying group message becomes: "We trust that you have the inner resources to deal with your problems. There are things that you can do to change your present situation and affect your future."

SPECIFIC CONSIDERATIONS FOR GROUPS FOR SUBSTANCE ABUSE

Adolescents who experience overindulgence, frequent use, and/or negative consequences due to their substance use are in need of treatment. There are strong indications in the literature that effective treatment programs must be comprehensive and should address (1) the substance-abuse problem, (2) underlying causes such as family dysfunction or poor peer relations, and (3) life-style changes during the transition to nonuse and aftercare. In addition to these three components, Kaminer (1994) emphasized that the concept of least restrictive environment should be considered when determining treatment options. In this respect, treatment options available within the school setting, when feasible, should be considered prior to more restrictive options such as inpatient treatment or partial hospitalization. Student assistance programs in which trained mental health professionals at the school provide interventions for students who have substance-abuse problems are available in some schools. Although treatment can occur on an individual basis, the most common treatment for drug and alcohol abuse both at school and community settings takes place within a group.

Group Facilitator's Belief System

Fundamental to any successful resolution of a client's drug problem is a group therapist or group facilitator's belief that there is hope for the young person to become drug free. One must truly believe that chemical dependency is a treatable disease and that addicts do get better. Without this underlying belief, therapists will not communicate hope to the group members. Drug use destroys and devastates the capacity for the vital kind of hope that is implicit in and necessary for any normal, healthy growth;

behind any growth is the hopeful notion, however subtle, that things will get better. As hope is transferred from group leader to each member, they can then reinforce that hope to each other, especially in times of stress.

Daley and Raskin (1991) developed a set of useful questions clinicians can ask themselves to determine potential biases or negative attitudes that might interfere with their projecting a sense of hope in the drug counseling relationship. These include the following:

1. *What substances have you used? What were the results?*
2. *What role do substances currently play in your life?*
3. *Does your religion influence your use or nonuse of alcohol or other drugs? If yes, how?*
4. *Have you personally known any drug addicts or alcoholics?*
5. *If you have known such people, how has their addiction affected your life?*
6. *Do you believe in addiction as a disease?*
7. *Do you think addiction is treatable?*
8. *Do you think an addicted person must "hit bottom" or admit to having a problem before he or she can be helped?*
9. *How do you feel about working with a client who is an alcoholic or a drug addict?*
10. *How do you feel about working with an alcoholic or drug addict who doesn't want help? (Daley & Raskin, 1991, p. 23)*

Developmental Group Therapy

Group therapy is directed by a trained therapist and takes place in an established treatment environment. In this setting, the group therapist works directly with group members, helping them to gain insight into their behaviors, thoughts, feelings, and actions. In addition, therapy helps the client move into and through the recovery process. The complexity of the rehabilitative process for the substance abuser or addict can be reduced conceptually to sets of needs that change relatively rapidly as a function of time from the onset of withdrawal symptoms (Pittman & Gerstein, 1984).

Recovery or *recovering* is the term used to indicate that someone has the disease of addiction in remission. Recovery is about learning to live life without the use of chemicals. It is more than just controlled abstinence, however. Much like treatment, recovery is a process. Abstinence is the foundation of recovery in that one cannot recover without it, yet abstinence alone is not enough. Recovery also must be the process of learning to live a productive, meaningful, and comfortable life without the use of chemicals.

Because recovery is developmental, treatment must be developmental, as well. It must be designed in phases moving a client from pretreatment, which prepares the client for the process, through aftercare and maintenance, which provides support for lifestyle changes while challenging behaviors that threaten sobriety. Again, treatment is a process, not an event.

An insightful and innovative model designed to promote such a continuum of care is the Adolescent Developmental Model of Recovery (ADMR), developed by Tammy Bell (1990). It is based on the work of Terrence T. Gorski, who developed the adult developmental model of recovery. Bell adapted this model for use with adolescents. The ADMR takes a client through six carefully developed phases. Effective group therapy will reflect the changing needs of group members as they work through these phases.

1. *Pretreatment.* This is the last stage of active use and the first stage in recovery. In the pretreatment phase, the user makes the connection between negative consequences and use, comes to an understanding of the loss of control over drugs, and recognizes that he or she might not be a social user.

Addicts are initially going to be ambivalent about giving up their drug use. In addition, many will be confused about what is happening to cause them to lose control over their lives. The group can provide education about the disease of addiction and help to remove guilt and shame by relating the message: "It's not your fault. No one starts using drugs with the goal of becoming an addict." In addition, group members can understand the ambivalence and help others to accept and work with it. The message here needs to be: "It's OK to be ambivalent but you don't have to act on it." This needs to be done in a curious, nonjudgmental, and empathic manner that is respectful of their fear and supportive of any expressed desire to change.

Because drug-using adolescents are often distrustful of adults, groups can be a powerful allurement for adolescents to participate and remain in treatment. A group of peers can provide a sense of belonging and an outlet to share experiences and explore thoughts and ideas. As young addicts develop trust within the group, they can then transfer their dependency needs from their relationship with the drugs to their relationship with the group.

2. *Stabilization.* Here, the craving cycle and drug-use preoccupation are interrupted. Detoxification takes place. This is when a young addict learns to live minute by minute without chemicals. Hope and motivation begin to replace despair and resistance.

This is the time when addicts are beginning to feel more fully the withdrawal effects of the drugs. Some effects are more subtle, whereas others (depending on the drug used and extensiveness of the use) will be more debilitating. It may take as long as six months for the body to truly rebound from the physical effects of the chemicals. Difficulties with memory, gross motor skills, and periods of free-floating anxiety will be experienced by the newly sober teenager. Having peers explain the withdrawal experience will help to normalize detoxification. Cravings for the drug can be openly acknowledged along with group discussion on management techniques. There will also be continued ambivalence about giving up the drug. Again, acknowledging the ambivalence and talking about it is crucial. One useful technique is to have more advanced group members express, "This may be true for you, but for me. . . . "

Creating and instilling structure is important to a young person whose life feels out of control. Newly recovering addicts need to learn new behaviors, expressions, and ways of organizing their thinking patterns and their lives. They need to establish healthy eating, sleeping, and exercise patterns. They need to remove all the drug paraphernalia from their daily routine. In addition, they need to learn how to schedule free time, resume old interests, and develop new interests. During the second treatment stage, chemically dependent adolescents are beginning a new identity as an addict and learning the framework for recovery. The group is an excellent forum to teach and model this behavior.

3. *Early Recovery.* The young addict begins to develop a sober-centered life-style. Comprehending the disease of addiction and developing a sobriety-centered value system are crucial. Attendance at AA meetings helps link the teenager with other addicts who have made the necessary life-style changes and who can teach him or her how to do the same. This is also the time when adolescents need to begin dealing with family-of-origin issues.

Teenagers need to be prepared for AA. Many adolescents are not developmentally ready with the abstract reasoning skills necessary to incorporate a Twelve-Step program. However, with simplification and an explanation from older group members or an understanding adult, they can do so. Also, it is frightening for a teenager to attend an AA meeting alone. Having a group member take a new member to the group can ease the transition and help orient him or her to the Twelve-Step program.

Group members at this stage should have a more stable base in recovery and the individual's personality is more clear, allowing a greater ability to understand and work with affect and relationship issues. Most adolescent treatment programs have a family component and it is often integrated into the treatment program at this point. Many treatment programs will include a multiple-family therapy group that will continue until the adolescent completes the program. This is important work because most adolescents will be returning home to live.

When working on family and relationship issues, the group should proceed with caution. Family-of-origin issues can be extremely anxiety provoking and the emerging feelings can be experienced as loss of control. Therefore, the shift from a behavioral approach to a more dynamic focus should be prudent.

4. *Middle Recovery.* During middle recovery, young addicts learn how to live in a drug-using society. As they develop healthy self-esteem, their identities broaden and they begin to view themselves as more than recovering addicts. This is also a time to learn age-appropriate social skills. Finally, they need to repair damage to family members, friends, and others to rebuild relationships and to set up a foundation for intimacy.

Recovering adolescents generally lack the skills needed to initiate healthy change. Therefore, in addition to social skills, they need to learn basic life skills such as clarifying personal values, communication skills, anxiety management, decision making, assertiveness training, and life-career planning. This is the time that the new skills developed in group are transferred to interactions with nonrecovering peers, family members, and other adults. The group provides a field to discuss successful as well as failed attempts. It also provides a niche to plan, rehearse, and anticipate new situations requiring new proficiency and competence.

5. *Late Stage.* Engaging in independent thoughts and actions, life goal planning, and healthy, intimate relationships is all part of the late-stage recovery phase. This stage generally takes place after the completion of an inpatient program. In this stage, the young addict learns truly to enjoy sober life.

By now, the young recovering addict, while remaining alcohol and drug free, will be integrating back into an alcohol- and drug-using culture. Steps to ensure abstinence and recovery while involved in daily living is an important task during this stage of group treatment. The skills developed in middle recovery now need to be expanded and implemented. Through group activities, role-playing, and modeling, young addicts can learn to deal with frustrations and conflicts when they apply these new skills to their everyday lives. In addition, the group provides a secure space for reality testing and appropriate modification of irrational thoughts and the resulting behaviors. Through experienced successes, the young addict can continue to build a more accurate self-image along with the achievement of personal life goals.

6. *Maintenance.* In this final phase, young addicts learn how to maintain a recovery program with continued growth and development. Looking toward future life problems, the addict learns how to cope without the use of chemicals. This is a time to make peace with the past. Maintaining a recovery program means never forgetting that sobriety is critical.

Many addicts in this phase will continue to be involved in AA or other Twelve-Step programs rather than group therapy. The school-based recovery group (described soon) provides another support group for young addicts in this phase. Group therapy is not a substitute for life; however, recovery will remain a part of a young addict's future.

Multiple-Family Therapy Groups

Multiple-family group therapy presents an unparalleled opportunity to promote recovery in young addicts. The use of multiple-family therapy groups in which members of different families are dealt with conjointly enhances the treatment effort. (See Carlson in Chapter 15 of this book.) Led by two or three co-therapists, these groups are composed of 3 to 10 multigenerational families sitting in a large circle. Each has an opportunity to share experiences and concerns, as well as to receive and offer help. Most multiple-family group sessions take place over a minimum of two hours. This unique group approach allows for families to identify with and learn from the conflicts and struggles of other families. In addition, families serve as facilitators of and support for growth and change in other family group members. This interplay also increases the network of supportive friendships for families otherwise feeling very much alone; it is especially useful as a resource for single-parent families and for isolated families.

Multiple-family therapy groups help addicts remain sober by improving family functioning and involvement in recovery (O'Shea & Phelps, 1985). Kosten, Hogan, Jalali, Steidl, and Kleber (1986) studied multiple-family therapy in an outpatient treatment program. They concluded that multiple-family therapy can help families of addicts progress from chaotic interactions to more stable family structures and from rigid to more flexible family functioning.

A School-Based Recovery Support Group Model

Perhaps the best way schools can help a recovering student is to provide a support group during the school day. A school-based support group helps a recovering adolescent learn to manage the loneliness, eases the transition from treatment to school, refocuses an interest in school, reinforces the aftercare program, and reduces the likelihood of relapse (Vik, Grizzle, & Brown, 1992). The model described here is a personal-problem oriented group that assumes that group members possess basic information about the disease of addiction.

The support group in the high school should not be an AA group. AA groups are ongoing in the community and always available. Moreover, anonymity is an objective of AA, and anonymity cannot be guaranteed in the school setting. When students miss class, they need to be excused, and other students and school staff will be able to observe which students attend the meetings. Nevertheless, AA should be a part of every student's recovery program, and the role of the school is to encourage AA attendance.

The Chemical Abuse Addiction Treatment Outcome Registry (CATOR) is a study that monitors adolescent treatment programs in an attempt to assess the characteristics and outcomes of adolescents who have entered chemical dependency programs. The CATOR database has conducted the most extensive outcome monitoring longitudinal data on 493 adolescents who have been in treatment. The study found a strong, positive relationship between the duration of postreatment involvement in AA and abstinence: 66% of recovering adolescents who remained in AA for the entire follow-up year reported total abstinence, compared with 11% of those who never attended (Harrison & Hoffmann, 1987).

The transition back to school after inpatient treatment is likely a frightening experience for a young addict. Often, school is the very place that most of the connection to drug-using peers and drug use occurred. School may not feel like a safe environment to the young addict, especially shortly after the warm, caring, and understanding treatment center that focused almost exclusively on the adolescent's needs. The support group may be the one safe place for young addicts. It is a place where they can find like-minded peers who have similar experiences, histories, and struggles. The support group is the one place young addicts can relax and talk about their recovery programs with others who understand the disease and the difficulties. In addition, the support group is a way for young addicts to make friendships with sober peers.

Most recovering students returning to high school participate in an out-of-school aftercare group. Aftercare reinforces the intensive skill building that many young addicts need to be successful in a sober life. A strong aftercare program is the key to preventing relapse. Students who are newly recovered and who are not in such a group should be encouraged to join one. An effective school-based support group will complement the work of aftercare groups. Therefore, group members need to be aware of each other's individual aftercare programs. In this way, members can support and encourage the maintenance of sobriety-enhancing behaviors.

School is not a place where many young addicts have experienced success, yet they must return to school to be successful in life and also as part of their aftercare program. A support group is a safe place for young, recovering students to share their concerns and problems around school. "How is school going for you?" is a question that group facilitators repeatedly should ask support group participants. In the school support group, school-related issues should take precedence over those that may be better addressed in the treatment setting. School-related issues generally include avoiding past drug-using friends, handling overheard peer drug-use talk, faring with cravings that occur in school, and making new friends who are not recovering but yet are not a threat to sobriety. Living down past reputations among teachers, experiencing academic success, keeping school and education a priority, organizing and completing homework, and balancing heavy schoolwork loads with competing AA meetings and aftercare programs are additional problems for the school support group to address.

Group Scheduling

In this model, the support group meets on a weekly basis during rotating class hours so that one class is never missed on a consistent basis. The first weekly group session meets during the first class hour, the second during the second hour of the day, the next during the third class hour of the day, and so forth. After completing the seven-hour day schedule, the routine repeats.

Students are responsible for informing their teachers about the group and making sure they are not missing an important test, lecture, or lab. On some occasions, students may attend another class that the teacher conducts for the same course; at other times, students need to decide between the support group or class. What remains crucial is that students take responsibility for their decisions, along with all make-up class work and assignments. If a conflict seems to be developing between the teacher and the student, the group facilitator may wish to intervene and quietly work out an understanding with the teacher. Some teachers do not understand the disease of addiction, the struggle recovering high school students are in, and the importance of relapse prevention. It is critical for teachers to understand that if a young, recovering student relapses, school instantly becomes irrelevant.

Food is available at each meeting because the presence of food symbolizes nurturing. A simple snack, such as popcorn or crackers, may be provided by either the group facilitators or group members. Never underestimate the significance of food to teenagers!

Group Membership

All members participating in the recovery support group must be attending AA meetings outside of school. This rule ensures that only students serious about their recovery will attend the group. The group's purpose is not to help drug-using teenagers with their drug problems. Asking recovering students to interact with actively using peers sets up the recovering student for relapse. Recovery support groups must be exclusively nondrug using. Some group members will experience slips or relapses, which must be addressed in the group. However, the underlying commitment is to abstinence and recovery, which maintains the strength of the group.

It is the role of the group leader to interview new members to explore their feelings about the group and to determine the appropriateness of their placement in this group.

Group Structure

Group time is divided equally among members. They begin with a "feelings check" in which they let others know how they are feeling in the "here and now." Often, the feelings check sets the stage for discussing either how things have been going for them in general or any special issues they may wish to present. Although group time is divided, sometimes someone may be in a crisis and the group may choose to focus on that individual member's current need. What is useful is that the group members make the decision about how to spend the group time. Occasionally, the group will be in the midst of an important discussion when the school bell rings to dismiss class. When this happens, the facilitator determines whether the group needs to continue. If the group continues into the next class hour, the facilitator will bring the group to a close when appropriate and send students back to class with a note to the teacher or a hall pass, depending on the system used in that particular school.

Occasionally, facilitators may have a concern about how the group is functioning, or they believe the group should discuss a special issue. Then the group facilitator should let members know that before regular discussions there is group business to be resolved. In this way, group-process needs can be interjected into a model that focuses primarily on individual members' needs.

Group Stages

Group counseling tends to move in phases in much the same way as individual counseling, treatment, and recovery. Although the recovery support group is an open, ongoing group, membership changes as students move into recovery, graduate, transfer schools, or relapse. Despite the fluid nature of the group, most school recovery groups have an early, middle, and late stage. Although most groups move through all three phases, individual groups may do so with different speeds and with distinctive styles.

Early or Formation Stage

The early phase usually begins at the start of the school year when the group is formed and staff and students are discovering newly recovering students and determining group membership. Blume (1985) has noted that in the open group the leader must take a more active role because he or she serves as the connecting thread and group historian. The newcomer in an open group often feels at a disadvantage compared to the "old-timers." It is the responsibility of the therapist to ensure that "in" jokes and references to sessions past are explained.

Specific group rules need to be established early on, agreed upon, and valued by group members. Concise yet clear group rules help set the stage for a structured and productive group environment. Often they include the following:

1. Any information shared in group is confidential. Maintaining confidentiality must be a top priority, for without it there can be no trust and subsequently no group. However, if someone relates life-threatening behavior, especially suicide, the group facilitator will need to break confidentiality and inform parents so that necessary help can be secured. In addition, by state law, any information about physical and or sexual abuse of a minor must be reported to protective services. If the group facilitator must break confidentiality, this must be discussed individually with the student involved.
2. Only one person at a time may speak. No side conversations should occur, because this behavior disrupts group interaction.
3. There will be no "put-downs." This does not mean that conflicts never may arise in the group. Aggressive, hurtful, or scapegoating behavior, however, is unacceptable because it interferes with acceptance of and respect for others.
4. Group participants are expected to be in group on time and ready to start.
5. There must be no glorifying of past drug-use experiences. AA calls this "stinking thinking," and it needs to be confronted at all times.
6. Each group member has a right to "pass" if he or she does not feel like talking or addressing a particularly difficult issue.

Generally, recovering students have had some past group experience and can determine what they would like their group rules to be. When members determine the rules, the rules are more likely to be followed. However, if members do not include the preceding rules, the group facilitator must be sure to include them.

In addition to group rules, the group must agree on group goals. This is relatively simple with a recovery group because the overall group goal has been established: to help members maintain sobriety and promote recovery. Changing attitudes and behaviors around alcohol and drug use will be impossible if young addicts continue their substance use. Responsibility for sobriety belongs to each group member.

The agreement of group goals and rules provides a common understanding that is essential in developing a cohesive group identity. However, chemically dependent adolescents often are placed in the school recovery group as a mandate of treatment. If the young addict has accepted the need for sobriety, inclusion in the group is appropriate. If the student has not yet accepted the need to remain sober, he or she initially may meet the group with resistance, acting out, and disruptiveness (Ramos & Richmond, 1991). If the student cannot accept the overall group goal of abstinence and recovery, he or she may not be appropriate for the group. However, if the addict remains in treatment and moves through the treatment process, his or her resistance to the group will subside. The addict's therapeutic relationship with the group facilitator, identification with other group members, and the group's interaction will contribute to positive, effective group involvement (Fram, 1990). In fact, groups with substance abusers have been found to be powerful inducements to continue treatment and accept treatment plans (Kofoed & Keys, 1988; Licarione, 1989).

The group process must allow time for establishing comfort among group members. If a member begins to self-disclose too early, before he or she or other group members are ready, this person may feel "exposed" and retreat from interaction as a means of self-protection. However, young people who have participated in AA or similar groups have learned to be extraordinarily honest and willing to share personal experiences. Recovering group members have an excellent starting point in that all have had problems with substance abuse. Sharing stories about treatment and how they became sober may help move the group-formation stage along.

Power and influence need to be equal among all group members. Certainly, some members will be more active and play a significant leader role in the group—especially the students with extended recovery programs. But the importance of each group member must be understood and valued; participation and leadership functions must be shared by all members to some degree. Conflict will be tolerable when every individual member is treated with respect and dignity by all members and group facilitators.

Anger is a feeling that often accompanies conflict. It is also a feeling that chemically dependent and high-risk adolescents do not manage well. Therefore, there may be a tendency for group members not to acknowledge their anger until it has reached heightened levels and become threatening to the group process. Several methods help group members deal effectively with anger. Anger should be expressed early on to prevent it from building into a "pressure cooker ready to explode." The group facilitator must never permit the escalation of conflict within the group.

Because extreme negative emotions may precipitate drinking in alcoholic patients, it is important to avoid ending the group session leaving individual members in a state of unresolved conflict (Blume, 1985). One technique to address conflict is to ask each member, at the closing of each group session, "Do you have any resentments over anything that happened here today?" Next, ask each member, "Do you have any appreciation toward anything that happened here today?" By mentioning resentments first, opportunities to address potential conflict are dealt with immediately. By discussing appreciation last, the group will end on a positive note.

The early stage of group development ends approximately at the time when members become comfortable interacting with one another. At this point, the group is compatible; its members appreciate each other and are responsive to the needs of group members, as well as interested and active in helping one another.

Middle Stage

The middle stage is where the "performance" of group members takes place—the time when the real work of group counseling happens. It is a highly interactive time; members should have familiarity with one another, along with a commitment to helping each other. Members have become interdependent and can engage in self-disclosure about personal concerns, issues, feelings, situations, and problems. Members will show solidarity by listening, providing feedback, giving, helping, and affirming. They also can use the group to share joy, happiness, and positive experiences, as well as to receive reinforcement and applause for their accomplishments.

Often, addicts use alcohol and other drugs to relieve a state of painful feelings. In the process of living without drugs, it becomes important for the addict to identify and label his or her emotional state in order to make an adequate response to his or her distress (Blume, 1985). In addition, the addict needs to learn new behaviors rather than past self-destructive behaviors. This group model provides an excellent forum for addicts to do this work. Because of their similar experiences, addicts tend to respond readily to other group members with empathetic responses. Empathy among group members can be drawn out easily with the simple question, "Has anyone here experienced a similar situation (feeling)?" Empathetic responses to the relating of personal history, experiences, and feelings help reduce the vast amount of shame and guilt caused by the disease of addiction.

The middle stage of group counseling is where much of the hard work of problem solving, experimenting with new roles and behaviors, and goal-directed activities take place. This work can be very intense and demanding. During the middle stage of group counseling, an activity to release stress and tension is helpful. A group task or ritual that group members choose can serve this purpose. Often, groups will do this task automatically. For example, I have found that after a group has had an intense session, the following meeting will almost always tend to be light, easy, and often even playful. This is a natural way for a group to manage stress and tension.

Late Stage: Closure and Termination

Groups have a beginning, a middle, and an end. The ending, or saying good-bye, is not always easy, especially for young people who have dealt with significant loss in their lives. For the drug-dependent adolescent, termination is the most difficult stage in the group process (Licarione, 1989). Therefore, the ending of this group must not be an abrupt, surprise event. It should be planned and fit into the natural flow of the process. Failure to address issues surrounding the ending of a group program will only add to the feelings of helplessness and loss that group members may have experienced in their lives. In addition, a graduation or closing ceremony helps provide closure for all group members.

Group closure should focus on how individuals can get their needs met outside group. Referrals to other support groups and/or individual counseling may therefore be appropriate. Reinforcement for maintaining new skills developed in groups and the means for practicing such skills are important. Such skills as asking for help, using group members for support on an informal basis, and/or using new behaviors learned in groups in other settings add to the continued growth and development of each group member.

Many young addicts have strong abandonment issues that add to their difficulties with termination. In addition is the fear that without their therapy or aftercare group, they will not be able to maintain sobriety. These concerns need to be addressed directly in the group. One way that many addicts solve this problem is to attend daily AA meetings until they feel stronger with their recovery program.

Group facilitators may choose to use an "ending exercise" to assist members with many feelings associated with termination. One exercise involves asking individual members to write a personal letter to the group about what they learned about their recovery or how the group experience added to their personal recovery program. After completing the letters, group members may wish to read them aloud and talk about their feelings.

Another closure exercise, sometimes referred to as "cat's cradle," involves all group members and a ball of yarn. Group members sit in a circle, and one person has the ball of yarn. The person with the yarn throws it to someone in the group and says something nice about that person or thanks him or her for some way that person has been of help. The person receiving the yarn cannot respond except with a thank you. The person receiving the yarn wraps it around one hand. It is then that person's turn to throw the yarn to another person and again express positive feelings and gratitude toward that person. That person responds with a thank you, wraps the yarn around one hand, and throws it to yet another group member. After all have received the yarn at least once, the exercise comes to a close. By this time all group members will be connected through the many strands of yarn. Members then pass around scissors and cut the yarn to separate themselves from each other. This act symbolizes that all group members are connected yet now must go their separate ways.

FUTURE RESEARCH AND PRACTICE

Literature identifying the application of effective modes of group intervention with adolescent substance abusers is scant. Because very few substance-abuse programs are designed specifically for adolescents, there are little outcome data regarding program effects (Kaminer, 1994). However, clinicians are seeking more effective treatment approaches for drug abuse to confront complex client needs, greater demand for their services, and reduced financial resources to provide these services (Mejta et al., 1994). Continued research focusing on differential effectiveness of group intervention models of adolescent drug-abuse treatment in controlled outcome studies is needed to gain scientific, technical, and clinical understanding.

Most authors on substance abuse and group work recognize the appropriateness of a developmental group process beginning with high structure and direction and frequently progressing to more open, interactive styles as the clients mature into them (Fuhrmann & Washington, 1984). The theoretical underpinnings of the approaches used at various levels of group development need to be explored.

Finally, research that empirically substantiates treatment techniques and treatment effectiveness needs to be expanded. According to Mejta and colleagues (1994):

> *In order to determine the relationship between techniques and effectiveness, a number of factors need to be considered: (a) the actual techniques utilized in counseling need to be described; (b) the empirical evidence regarding the effectiveness of these techniques needs to be explored; (c) factors contributing to or counterproductive to overall treatment effectiveness need to be determined; and (d) the assumptions underlying the theoretical model upon which the counseling is based need to be validated. (p. 67)*

This research needs to be developed with consideration to the special needs and characteristics of the substance-abusing/chemically dependent adolescent.

ENDNOTE

1. Copyright © by the AA Grapevine, Inc.; reprinted with permission. Permission to reprint this material does not imply any affiliation with or endorsement by the AA Grapevine, Inc.
2. The Twelve Steps are reprinted with permission of Alcoholics Anonymous World Services, Inc. Permission to reprint the Twelve Steps does not mean that AA has reviewed or approved the contents of this publication, nor that AA agrees with the views expressed herein. AA is a program of recovery from alcoholism only—use of the Twelve Steps in connection with programs and activities which are patterned after AA, but which address other problems, or in any other non-AA context, does not imply otherwise.

REFERENCES

Adix, R. S., Kelly, T., & Rosenthal, D. (1984). Substance abuse prevention: A developmental skills approach. *Journal for Specialists in Group Work, 9,* 32–43.

Alford, G. S., Koehler, R. A., & Leonard, J. (1991). Alcoholics Anonymous–Narcotics Anonymous model inpatient of chemically dependent adolescents: A 2-year outcome study. *Journal of Studies on Alcoholism, 52,* 118–126.

Baumrind, D., & Moselle, K. A. (1985). A developmental perspective on adolescent drug abuse. *Alcohol and substance abuse in adolescents.* New York: Haworth.

Bell, T. L. (1990). *Preventing adolescent relapse.* Independence, MO: Herald House/Independence.

Blume, S. B. (1985). Group psychotherapy in the treatment of alcoholism. In S. Zimber, J. Wallace, & S. B. Blume (Eds.), *Practical approaches to alcoholism psychotherapy* (pp. 7–107). New York: Plenum.

Carty, L. (1993). Group counseling and the promotion of mental health. *Journal for Specialists in Group Work, 18,* 29–39.

Clayton, R. R. (1992). Transitions in drug use: Risk and protective factors. In M. Glantz & R. Pickens (Eds.), *Vulnerability to drug abuse* (pp. 15–51). Washington, DC: American Psychological Association.

Conyne, R. K. (1994). Reviewing the primary prevention of substance abuse: Elements in successful approaches. In J. A. Lewis (Ed.), *Addictions: Concepts and strategies for treatment* (pp. 23–36). Gaithersburg, MD: Aspen.

Cook, P. S., & Petersen, R. C. (1989). Individualizing adolescent drug abuse treatment. In A. S. Friedman & G. M. Beschner (Eds.), *Treatment services for adolescent substance abusers.* Rockville, MD: National Institute on Drug Abuse.

Corey, G. (1990). *Theory and practice of group counseling* (3rd ed.). Pacific Grove, CA: Brooks/Cole.

Cross, G. M., Morgan, C. W., Mooney, A. J., Martin, C. A., & Rafter, J. A. (1990). Alcoholism treatment: A ten-year follow-up study. *Alcoholism, Clinical and Experimental Research, 14,* 169–173.

Daley, D. C., & Raskin, M. S. (1991). *Treating the chemically dependent and their families.* Newbury Park, CA: Sage.

Dryfoos, J. G. (1990). *Adolescents at risk: Prevalence and prevention.* New York: Oxford University Press.

Duckert, F., Amundsen, A., & Johnson, J. (1992). What happens to drinking after therapeutic intervention? *British Journal of Addiction, 87,* 1457–1467.

Flores P. J., & Mahon L. (1993). The treatment of addiction in group psychotherapy. *International Journal of Group Psychotherapy, 43,* 143–156.

Forman, S. G., & Pfeiffer, A. (1997). Substance use and abuse. In G. G. Bear, K. M. Minke, & A. Thomas (Eds.), *Children's needs II: Development, problems, and alternatives* (pp. 917–924). Bethesda, MD: National Association of School Psychologists.

Fram, D. H. (1990). Group methods in the treatment of

substance abusers. *Psychiatric Annals, 20* (7), 385–388.

Friedman, A. S., & Glickman, N. W. (1986). Program characteristics for successful treatment of adolescent drug abuse. *Journal of Nervous and Mental Disease, 174,* 669–678.

Friedman, A. S., & Glickman, N. W. (1987). Residential program characteristics for completion of treatment by adolescent drug abusers. *Journal of Nervous and Mental Disease, 175,* 419–424.

Friedman, A. S., Utada, A. T., Glickman, N. W., & Morrissey, M. R. (1987). Psychopathology as an antecedent to, and as a "consequence" of, substance use in adolescence. *Journal of Drug Education, 17,* 233–244.

Fuhrmann, B. S., & Washington, C. S. (1984). Substance abuse and group work: Tentative conclusions. *Journal for Specialists in Group Work, 9,* 62–63.

Galanter, M., Castaneda, R., & Franco, H. (1991). Group therapy and self-help groups. In R. J. Frances & S. I. Miller (Eds.), *Clinical textbook of addictive disorders* (pp. 431–451). New York: Guilford.

Hansen, W. (1992). School based substance abuse prevention: A review of the state of the art in curriculum, 1980-1990. *Health Education Research, 7,* 403–430.

Harrison, P. A., & Hoffmann, N. G. (1987). CATOR 1987 report: *Adolescent residential treatment: Intake and follow-up findings.* St. Paul, MN: Chemical Abuse/Addiction Treatment Outcome Registry, Ramsey Clinic.

Hawkins, J. D., & Catalano, R. R. (1992). *Communities that care: Action for drug abuse prevention.* San Francisco: Jossey Bass.

Johnson, C. A., Pentz, M., Weber, M., Dwyer, J., Baer, N., Mackinnon, D., & Hansen, W. (1990). Relative effectiveness of comprehensive community programming for drug abuse prevention with high-risk and low-risk adolescents. *Journal of Consulting and Clinical Psychology, 58,* 447–456.

Johnston, L. (1996). The rise of drug use among American teens continues in 1996. *News & Information Services,* December 19, University of Michigan, Ann Arbor.

Johnston, L., O'Malley, P. M., & Bachman, G. (in preparation). *National survey results on drug use from the Monitoring the Future study, 1975–1996: Vol. I. Secondary school students.* Rockville, MD: National Institute on Drug Abuse.

Kaminer, Y. K. (1994). *Adolescent substance abuse: A comprehensive guide to theory and practice.* New York: Plenum.

Keller, M. (1982). On defining alcoholism: With comment on some other relevant words. In E. L. Gomberg, H. White, & J. Carpenter (Eds.), *Alcohol, science, and society revisited* (pp. 119–133). Ann Arbor: University of Michigan Press.

Khantzian, E. J. (1985). Psychotherapeutic interventions with substance abusers—The clinical context. *Journal of Substance Abuse Treatment, 2,* 83-88.

Kofoed, L., & Keys, A. (1988). Using group therapy to persuade dual-diagnosis patients to seek substance abuse treatment. *Hospital and Community Psychiatry, 39*(11), 1209–1213.

Kosten, T. R., Hogan, I., Jalali, B., Steidl, J., & Kleber, H. (1986). The effect of multiple family therapy on addict family functioning: A pilot study. In B. Stimmel (Ed.), *Alcohol and substance abuse in women and children* (pp. 51–62). New York: Haworth.

La Salvia, T. A. (1993). Enhancing addiction treatment through psychoeducational groups. *Journal of Substance Abuse Treatment, 10,* 439–444.

Lawson, G. W., & Lawson, A. W. (1992). *Adolescent substance abuse: Etiology, treatment, and prevention.* Gaithersburg, MD: Aspen.

Lewis, J., Dana, R., & Blevins, G. (1988). *Substance abuse counseling: An individual approach.* Pacific Grove, CA: Brooks/Cole.

Licarione, M. (1989). Conducting group therapy with chemically dependent adolescents. *Treatment services for adolescent substance abusers.* (pp. 150–163). Rockville, MD: National Institute on Drug Abuse.

Mejta, C. L., Naylor, C. L., & Maslar, E. M. (1994). Drug abuse treatment: Approaches and effectiveness. In J. A. Lewis (Ed.), *Addictions: Concepts and strategies for treatment.* Gaithersburg, MD: Aspen.

Meyer, A. L. (1995). Minimization of substance use: What can be said at this point? In T. P. Gullotta, G. R. Adams, & R. Montemayor (Eds.), *Substance misuse in adolescence* (pp. 201–232). Newbury Park, CA: Sage.

Myers, J. E. (1992). Wellness throughout the life span. *Counseling and Human Development, 24,* 89–117.

O'Shea, M. D., & Phelps, R. (1985). Multiple family therapy: Current status and critical appraisal. *Family Process,* 24, 555–582.

Pentz, M. A., Cormack, C., Flay, B., Hansen, W., & Johnson, C. A. (1986). Balancing program and research integrity in community drug abuse prevention: Project STAR approach. *Journal of School Health, 56,* 389–393.

Pentz, M. A., Dwyer, J. H., Mackinnon, D. P., Flay, B. R., Hansen, W. B., Wang, E. Y. I., & Johnson, C. A. (1989). A multicommunity trial for primary prevention of adolescent drug abuse. *Journal of the American Medical Association, 261,* 3259–3266.

Pittman, J. F., & Gerstein, L. H. (1984). Graduated levels of group therapy for substance abuser. *Journal for Specialists in Group Work, 9,* 7–13.

Ramos, N., & Richmond, A. (1991). Adolescent group therapy in an inpatient facility. *Group, 15*(2), 81–88.

Reister, A. E. (1991). Group psychotherapy and the mosaic adolescent. *Journal of Child and Adolescent Group Therapy, 1,* 71–77.

Rootes, L. E. (1993). A comparison of staff and patient perspectives of substance abuse treatment and its effectiveness (Doctoral dissertation, The Union Institute, 1992). *Dissertation Abstracts International:* AAC 9303571.

Rosenthal, H. (1993). Friendship groups: An approach to helping friendless children. *Educational Psychology in Practice, 9,* 112–120.

Sheeren, M. (1988). The relationship between relapse and involvement in Alcoholics Anonymous. *Journal of Studies on Alcohol, 1,* 104–106.

Shoemaker, R. H., & Sherry, P. (1991). Postreatment factors influencing outcome of adolescent chemical dependency treatment. *Journal of Adolescent Chemical Dependency, 2,* 89–106.

Suski, P. J. (1992). Responding to substance abuse and its related issues. *Journal of Adolescent Chemical Dependency, 2,* 45–57.

Tobler, N. (1986). Meta-analysis of 143 adolescent drug prevention programs: Quantitative outcome results of program participants compared to a control or comparison group. *Journal of Drug Issues, 16*(4), 537–567.

Thoits, P. A. (1986). Social support as coping assistance. *Journal of Consulting and Clinical Psychology, 54,* 416–423.

Thomas, R. M. (1990). *Counseling and life-span development.* Newbury Park, CA: Sage.

Tredinnick, L. C. (1993). The effect of well-being groups. *School Social Work Journal, 17,* 22–29.

U.S. Department of Health and Human Services. (1982). *The health consequences of smoking: Cancer—A report of the Surgeon General* (DHHS Publication No. PHS 82-50179). Washington, DC: U.S. Government Printing Office.

Vik, P. W., Grizzle, K. L., & Brown, S. A. (1992). Social resource characteristics and adolescent substance abuse relapse. *Journal of Adolescent Chemical Dependency, 2,* 59–73.

Wallace, J. (1986). The other problems of alcoholics. *Journal of Substance Abuse Treatment, 3,* 163–171.

CHAPTER 11

GROUPS FOR PREVENTION AND INTERVENTION WITH CHILDREN OF ALCOHOLICS

Bonnie K. Nastasi, STATE UNIVERSITY OF NEW YORK AT ALBANY

It is estimated that 28 million persons within families are affected by alcohol, commonly referred to as *children of alcoholics,* or *COAs,* over 7 million of whom are school-aged children (Roosa, Gensheimer, Short, Ayers, & Shell, 1989). The use and abuse of alcohol in the adult population is prevalent. A 1990 national household survey conducted by the National Institute on Drug Abuse indicated that approximately 60% of young adults, ages 18 to 25, and 50% of adults over the age of 25 use alcohol (Drugs and Drug Abuse Education, 1990). Moreover, 38% of the adult population in the United States report a family history of alcoholism, among biological first-, second-, and/or third-degree relatives (Harford, 1992).

In the early 1990s, the multidisciplinary joint committee of the National Council on Alcoholism and Drug Dependence (NCADD) and the American Society of Addiction Medicine convened to research and establish a definition of alcoholism that met the criteria of scientific validity, clinical utility, and clarity for the general public (Morse & Falvin, 1992). They defined *alcoholism* as

> *a primary, chronic disease with genetic, psychosocial, and environmental factors influencing its development and manifestations. The disease is often progressive and fatal. It is characterized by impaired control over drinking, preoccupation with the drug alcohol, use of alcohol despite adverse consequences, and distortions in thinking, most notably denial. Each of these symptoms may be continuous or periodic. (p. 1013)*

Alcoholism also has been recognized as a family disease in which family members react to the dysfunctional behavior of an alcoholic by adopting complementary dysfunctional behaviors that both serve to support the alcoholism and maintain the family system (Brown, 1988). Without intervention, dysfunctional family patterns and individual maladaptive behaviors are likely to persist and be generalized to other interpersonal contexts.

PERSONAL/SOCIAL COMPETENCE

The theoretical basis for understanding COAs incorporates an ecological/developmental model of personal/social competence. Critical personal/social competencies include (1) self-efficacy and self-esteem, (2) interpersonal problem solving, and

(3) interpersonal interaction and relationship skills. These specific competencies are consistently included in definitions of personal/social competence (Nastasi & DeZolt, 1994) and have been linked to generalizable coping ability and resilience (Elias & Branden, 1988). In addition, common problems among COAs have been linked to deficiencies in these competencies (Nastasi & DeZolt). This section provides a description of the personal/social competence model proposed by Nastasi and DeZolt.

Self-Efficacy and Self-Esteem

Self-efficacy refers to perceived competence in specific domains of functioning (Harter, 1978, 1990; Schunk, 1990) and the sense of control over life events (Bandura, 1982). Harter (1990) delineates domains of perceived competence (e.g., cognitive, social) that vary across the life span and that influence global self-worth (*self-esteem* or general sense of personal value). Self-efficacy and perceived competence influence motivation (i.e., effectance or competence motivation) and attempts to interact with, master, or adapt to the environment; to engage in activities requiring specific competencies; to expend necessary effort for success; to cope with life stressors; and to persist despite failures. Success in these endeavors, along with positive social feedback about competencies, in turn enhance self-efficacy. Furthermore, the extent to which one's competencies are personally and socially valued influences development of self-worth, which in turn influences mental health status (e.g., likelihood of depression or delinquency; Harter & Marold, 1991). Thus, an individual who takes initiative and interacts successfully in social situations, for example, is likely to have a good sense of social competence. If these social competencies are important to the individual and to significant others (e.g., peers, parents), self-esteem is likely to be enhanced and occurrence of mental health problems (e.g., depression, delinquency) minimized.

Interpersonal Problem Solving

The process of problem solving involves defining the problem and selecting, applying, and evaluating solutions. In the model proposed by Nastasi and DeZolt (1994), interpersonal problem solving encompasses both individual and collaborative application of problem strategies to solve interpersonal or other real-life problems (see Table 11.1). Skillful interpersonal problem solvers are "able to work and play cooperatively with others, resolve interpersonal conflicts, and solve everyday problems in a variety of situations" (Nastasi & DeZolt, p. 13).

Table 11.1 Problem-Solving Steps Applied to Interpersonal and Collaborative Situations

STEPS OF INTERPERSONAL PROBLEM SOLVING	STEPS OF COLLABORATIVE PROBLEM SOLVING
1. Recognize feelings in self and others.	1. Each person states feelings.
2. Identify and define the problem.	2. Define and clarify the problem in terms of needs and views of each person.
3. Generate alternative solutions.	3. Brainstorm possible resolutions.
4. Consider the consequences of each solution, to self and others.	4. Consider how the resolutions meet the needs or integrate the views of participants.
5. Choose the "best" solution.	5. Choose the "best" resolution, seeking consensus or synthesis.
6. Implement the solution.	6. Implement the resolution.
7. Evaluate solution effectiveness.	7. Evaluate the resolution process.

Source: From *School Interventions for Children of Alcoholics* by B. K. Nastasi and D. M. DeZolt, 1994, New York: Guilford Press. Reprinted by permission.

Collaborative problem solvers, in particular, are skillful in communication, perspective taking, and negotiation.

Interpersonal Interaction and Relationship Skills

Interpersonal competence is critical for engaging in effective social interactions in a wide range of situations, developing and maintaining healthy interpersonal relationships (e.g., with peers, family), and promoting adaptation to daily challenges and life stressors (Nastasi & DeZolt, 1994). Specific skills include those relevant to initiating social contacts, communicating ideas and needs, prosocial responding (e.g., sharing, helping, emotional sensitivity), perspective taking, evaluating social cues (e.g., nonverbal behavior, social interactions), and exhibiting behaviors appropriate to the social context. Nastasi and DeZolt also use the concept of *caring* as the basis for defining interpersonal competence. Caring is defined as the "connection between human beings that reflects mutual receptivity and focuses on the interrelatedness of self and other" (Nastasi & DeZolt, p. 18; see also Gilligan, 1982; Zahn-Waxler, 1991). Interpersonal development is characterized by "increasing differentiation of self and other and a growing comprehension of the dynamics of social interaction" (Gilligan, p. 74).

Synergism

Development of personal/social competence has been described by Nastasi and DeZolt (1994) as a synergistic process, reflecting the complex interplay among self-efficacy and self-esteem, interpersonal problem solving, and interpersonal and relationship skills; and the interplay of these competencies with the multiple contexts the individual encounters across the life span (cf. developmental/ecological perspective of Bronfenbrenner, 1989). Thus, self-efficacy, interpersonal problem solving, and interpersonal skills influence each other and are influenced by interactions with environmental contexts, particularly family, peers, school, and community. In addition, early person/environment interactions and resulting personal/social competencies influence the nature and likelihood of subsequent interactions within similar contexts. Furthermore, healthy personal/social development requires environmental contexts in which individuals have opportunities to develop effective interpersonal problem solving and interaction skills (e.g., through modeling, instruction, and practice) and in which their personal competencies and characteristics are valued (cf. the concept of "ecological niche" in Bronfenbrenner, 1989).

Elias and Branden (1988) present two models for predicting mental health problems for individuals (person centered) and communities (environment centered). These models provide further support for an ecological/developmental model of mental health as well as a framework for examining the characteristics of COAs and their families. According to the person-centered model (originally proposed by the President's Commission on Mental Health, 1978, cited in Elias & Branden, 1988), the occurrence of mental health problems is a function of the individual's physical vulnerability to stress and the amount of stress experienced in relationship to self-esteem, coping ability, and social supports. Thus, the individual COA may be particularly vulnerable to alcoholism because of genetic predisposition (Anthenelli & Schuckit, 1990–91; Goodwin, 1988) in combination with stressors related to a parent's alcoholism (e.g., family conflict, poor parent/child relationships). However, the individual's self-esteem, coping skills (e.g., interpersonal problem solving) and use of available social supports (e.g., from peers, siblings, teachers, adult relatives) may mitigate the level of stress and facilitate healthy adaptation and development.

According to the environment-centered model (originally proposed by Elias, 1987), the incidence of mental health problems within a community (or other system; e.g., school, family) depends on the aggregate of environmental risk factors and stressors in relationship to the social resources, opportunities for connectedness, and socialization practices. Thus, despite the level of risk and stress related to parental alcoholism, the family (through some of its members) may provide an environment that facilitates healthy development through its socialization practices (e.g., that teach coping skills and enhance self-esteem), social resources, and opportunities for healthy relationships within the immediate and extended family. Similarly, the school or community may provide such a buffer by providing safe (stress- and risk-free) and supportive contexts (e.g., classroom, peer group, community youth program) that foster healthy psychological development. Research reviewed in subsequent sections suggests that family environment factors are important correlates and predictors of the adjustment of COAs. Similarly, social and emotional supports that teachers provide have been shown to play a critical role in the adaptation of resilient children (i.e., those who achieve successful life adjustment despite adverse circumstances; Anthony & Cohler, 1987; Garbarino, Dubrow, Kostelny, & Pardo, 1992). Thus, cultural contexts that provide opportunities for interpersonal interaction, social support, and development of personal/social competence may be critical to the development of resiliency in at-risk children and adolescents such as COAs.

CHARACTERISTICS OF CHILDREN AND FAMILIES AFFECTED BY ALCOHOL

Clinical data and empirical research (reviewed in this section) suggest that COAs, compared to the general population and to non-COAs, are at higher risk for mental health and life adjustment problems in childhood, adolescence, and adulthood. They also are at greater risk for developing alcoholism and other drug-related problems in adolescence and adulthood. Families with an alcoholic parent are more likely to be characterized by disharmony (e.g., spousal conflict), disruption (e.g., separation, divorce), physical and emotional abuse, poor parenting practices, and poor parent/child relationships. Furthermore, these family stressors have been shown to be related to the adjustment of COAs.

Characteristics of COAs

Most research on COAs has addressed questions regarding mental health problems or maladjustment, thus focusing more on pathology than competence (Barnard & Spoentgen, 1986; Nastasi & DeZolt, 1994). A limited amount of work has examined variables related to personal/social competence. The model of competence described earlier provides the framework for examining this work. In general, the research supports the at-risk status of COAs. They are less likely to develop personal/social competencies (self-efficacy and self-esteem, interpersonal problem solving, interpersonal and relationships skills) that mediate the effects of family environmental stressors. Furthermore, they are more likely to exhibit mental health problems from childhood through adulthood than the general population. As suggested by the person- and environment-centered models, the combination of high environmental stressors, low environmental support, and poorly developed personal/social competencies place them at greater risk for emotional and behavioral difficulties. In this section, research on personal/social competence and incidence of emotional and behavioral difficulties is reviewed.

Personal/Social Competence

Though limited in scope, the research on self-efficacy and self-esteem, interpersonal problem solving, and interpersonal and relationship skills suggests than COAs throughout the life span are less likely to develop these competencies that non-COAs. Adult COAs, compared to non-COAs, report higher levels of self-criticism, self-deprecation, and the need to control external and internal events; and lower levels of perceived personal power and positive self-regard, self-appraisal, and self-acceptance (Jarmas & Kazak, 1992; Slavkin, Heimberg, Winning, & McCaffrey, 1992). High school-aged COAs report lower self-esteem than non-COAs (Roosa, Sandler, Beals, & Short, 1988). Similarly, school-aged COAs and their parents undervalue students' academic competence (Johnson & Rolf, 1988).

The research on interpersonal problem solving and coping skills suggests that COAs may be ill-prepared for coping with interpersonal problems (Nastasi & DeZolt, 1994). For example, mothers of school-aged COAs (ages 5 to 17) reported higher levels of impatience and aggression consistent with a Type-A behavior pattern (Manning, Balson, & Xenakis, 1986). The Type-A behavior pattern is characterized by "a relatively chronic struggle to achieve a series of poorly defined goals in the shortest period of time possible" (Manning et al., p. 184), thus reflecting poor problem-solving skills related to goal setting and attainment.

Researchers typically have examined behavioral and social maladjustment that may reflect and/or be influenced by poor social competence (see next section). Direct examination of the interpersonal (social) competence of COAs, however, has received insufficient attention. In one study of 62 COAs (ages 6 to 16; Calder & Kostyniuk, 1989), parents rated COAs as less socially skillful and less well accepted than same-aged peers (on the Social Skills subscale of the Personality Inventory for Children, PIC; Wirt, Lachar, Klainedinst, & Seat, 1984). Furthermore, 5% of the COA group scored in the clinical range (two standard deviations above the mean) on this subscale.

In sum, research on personal/social competence of COAs suggests they may be ill-prepared to cope with life stressors and thus at risk for development of mental health problems. The next section presents an examination of the mental health status of COAs.

Behavioral, Academic/Occupational, and Health-Related Adjustment

Longitudinal and cross-sectional research provides consistent evidence that COAs, compared to non-COAs, are at greater risk for psychological and health-related problems from childhood through adulthood (for a review of research, see Nastasi & DeZolt, 1994). COAs exhibit more psychological difficulties characterized by depression, anxiety, somatic disorders, delinquency, substance abuse, and academic or work-related difficulties. As adults, they more often receive psychiatric diagnoses (Weintraub, 1990–91). As children and adolescents, they have higher rates of grade retention, school dropout, and referrals to school psychologists (National Institute on Alcohol Abuse and Alcoholism, 1990), and are overrepresented in clinical populations for internalized (e.g., depression) and externalized (e.g., delinquency) problems (Calder & Kostyniuk, 1989). Despite the higher incidence of problems and concerns, school-aged COAs do not necessarily receive special education services for learning or behavioral problems more often than non-COAs (Stern, Kendall, & Eberhard, 1991). Furthermore, COAs as a group do not present a distinct profile of maladjustment, and not all COAs are maladjusted (Calder & Kostyniuk, 1989).

Of particular relevance to drug prevention efforts in schools and communities is the notion of family transmission of alcoholism and other drug abuse. Research provides consistent support for the at-risk status of COAs with regard to alcoholism and drug dependence. Alcoholism among adult children of alcoholics (ACOAs) is three to five times greater than expected in the general population, as suggested by twin and adoption studies (Anthenelli & Schuckit, 1990–91; Goodwin, 1988) and by comparisons of ACOA and non-ACOA populations (Jarmas & Kazak, 1992). Furthermore, familial alcoholism is characterized by an intergenerational family history of alcoholism; that is, COAs are more likely than non-COAs to have a higher incidence of problem drinking or alcoholism among first- and second-degree relatives, particularly parents and grandparents (Perkins & Berkowitz, 1991). Those with both an alcoholic parent and alcoholic grandparent are at greatest risk for alcohol abuse (Perkins & Berkowitz, 1991). The next section examines more specifically the family environment in relationship to alcoholism and to the adjustment of COAs.

Characteristics of Families Affected by Alcoholism

Families affected by alcoholism and other substance abuse are more likely than those unaffected by substance abuse to be characterized by family disruption (e.g., separation and divorce) and disorganization, poor communication of thoughts and feelings, lack of cohesiveness, poor parental functioning, spousal and parent/child conflict, child abuse (physical, sexual, emotional), and other environmental stressors or negative life events such as exposure to the effects of parental drinking (Jarmas & Kazak, 1992; Roosa, Beals, Sandler, & Pillow, 1990). Furthermore, variations in these environmental factors have been found to account for variations in adjustment difficulties within the COA population. Indeed, some research suggests that family environmental factors, specifically disharmony (e.g., spousal and parent/child conflict, poor communication), may be critical for explaining adjustment or psychiatric problems experienced by COAs in childhood through adulthood (Stewart & Shamdasani, 1990). That is, the adjustment of COAs and non-COAs did not differ significantly when family disharmony was not reported. In addition, a review of research with the general population in the United States and other countries confirms the link between family disharmony and adjustment or psychiatric problems that continue into adulthood (Velleman, 1992).

In sum, research substantiates the claim that family dysfunction is an important correlate of acoholism and parental alcohol abuse and child/adolescent dysfunction. Considering the at-risk status of COAs for emotional and behavioral disorders, interventions with COAs and their families are critical. As suggested by the person- and environment-centered models of mental health, one might direct interventions toward the environmental source of stress, the personal competencies of the indiviudal (e.g., within the social environment). The approach described in this chapter uses the latter two alternatives as the foci of intervention. That is, group interventions for COAs are directed toward enhancing personal/social competencies and providing supportive adult and peer networks.

GROUP INTERVENTIONS AND TECHNIQUES

A social construction perspective of socialization and learning provides the basis for designing group-based interventions for COAs. The approach described in this chapter "is based on the premise that learning occurs as individuals within a specific socio-cultural context co-construct knowledge and norms of behavior" (Nastasi & DeZolt, 1994, p. 98). Interpersonal interaction and the coordination of divergent perspectives are critical to the development of both individuals and collective ideas and behaviors, and to the formation of group norms. Furthermore, it is through repeated opportunities for such exchanges that individual development and socialization are facilitated (cf. Rogoff, 1990; Vygotsky, 1978). Competence enhancement based on a social-constructivist (dialectical) model emulates the developmental process in which personal, interpersonal, and cultural development operate in a synergistic manner. Both peers and adults play essential roles as mediators or facilitators in this socialization process.

In this section, the social construction perspective is described in more detail. In addition, research verifying the effectiveness and critical features of group interventions is reviewed.

Social Construction

According to a social-constructivist perspective, interpersonal exchange is essential to the development of individual cognitions and behavior, and to the evolution and transmission of culture (Guisinger & Blatt, 1994; Rogoff, 1990; Vygotsky, 1978; Wertsch, 1991). Vygotsky, for example, suggests that new ways of thinking and behaving occur initially during social interactions in which more experienced or knowledgeable individuals mediate the person/environment interaction. With repeated exchanges in similar contexts, new ideas and behavior become internalized.

Furthermore, self-definition and relatedness are inextricably linked. Guisinger and Blatt (1994) characterize development of self-identity and relatedness as evolving in "an interactive, reciprocally balanced, mutually facilitating fashion from birth through senescence" (p. 108), such that development of mature self-definition is dependent on development of mature relationships, and vice versa. In a similar vein, Harter (1990) suggests that interpersonal relationships play a critical role in the development of self-perceived competence (or self-efficacy) and self-esteem. That is, perceived competence and self-worth are influenced by the extent to which significant others (e.g., parents, peers, teachers, friends) provide social feedback and support, and value the individual's competencies. Subsequently, one's self-efficacy regarding interpersonal skills influences the likelihood of initiating and maintaining interpersonal relationships (cf. Bandura, 1982, 1986). In this manner, the reciprocal process evolves.

An ideal dialectical exchange involves a co-constructive process in which "individuals face others who contradict their own intuitively derived concepts and points of view, and thereby create cognitive conflicts whose resolutions result in the construction of higher forms of reasoning" (Bearison, 1982, p. 203). Such exchanges require communication and negotiation of alternative perspectives, and commitment to the co-construction of ideas and norms (Nastasi & DeZolt, 1994). Dialectical exchanges are engendered by contexts in which dialogue, cognitive conflict between individuals, and conflict resolution through synthesis of divergent ideas are encouraged and valued. Educational environments that embody these features foster cognitive (e.g., higher-order thinking, problem solving, learning) and personal/social (e.g., self-esteem, self-efficacy, interpersonal skills) growth, and encourage acceptance and valuing of diversity. Such contexts are opportune for addressing the social/emotional needs of at-risk populations.

Review of Research on Group Interventions and Techniques

The empirical basis for group interventions and techniques comes from efficacy research on collaborative problem solving and group approaches to substance abuse education and prevention and personal/social competence enhancement. Each body of literature is summarized separately.

Collaborative Problem Solving

Collaborative problem solving, a type of cooperative learning, requires that participants work together to solve problems in simulated or real-life settings. Whether problems are assigned or self-selected, participants are responsible for defining the problem, generating alternative solutions, and selecting and implementing potentially effective solutions (see Table 11.1). Research conducted in academic contexts has indicated that collaborative problem solving is effective for enhancing interpersonal relations, competence motivation, and higher-level thinking (see Nastasi & Clements, 1991, for a review). Conditions for promoting these outcomes include (1) all participants are necessary for success and benefit from collaboration, (2) participants are individually accountable for contributions, (3) social support among participants is encouraged, and (4) participants evaluate and discuss group dynamics. In addition, certain types of interactions such as exchange of ideas and negotiation of perspectives are critical.

Nastasi and Clements (1991) have elucidated two types of interactions patterns that characterize collaborative problem solving: *reciprocal sense making,* whereby partners generate ideas and co-construct meaning through discourse, and *cognitive conflict and resolution,* whereby partners pose and resolve explicitly discrepant perspectives (cognitions, ideas). Group contexts that foster both reciprocal sense making and cognitive conflict resolution are characterized by (1) *self-directed collaborative problem solving* (participants work together to define and solve self-selected problems); (2) *conflicting perspectives* (participants are encouraged to pose alternative ideas and have access to information necessary for generating alternative problem solutions); and (3) *conflict resolution* (resolution of discrepant perspectives is requisite for successful problem solving; e.g., a single solution must be chosen) (Nastasi & Clements, 1992).

Critical features of collaborative exchanges characterized by reciprocal sense making include (1) consensus building, (2) exchange of ideas, (3) active participation, and (4) explication of thinking and solution strategies. Collaboration through reciprocal sense making, compared to engaging in competitive or individualistic learning activities, is more likely to enhance higher-level problem solving and transfer of learning, as well as effectance motivation, self-efficacy, self-esteem, and overall social/emotional well-being. Furthermore, collaboration that involves cognitive conflict and its resolution (i.e., posing and resolving discrepancies) may provide the optimal context for promoting both cognitive growth and effectance motivation, particularly when participants contribute equally to a process of conflict resolution, discuss the validity of ideas, and reach resolution through negotiation toward a compromise or synthesis. That is, it is not so much the occurrence of conflict but the *process of resolution* that is critical.

Features of collaborative contexts that are important for fostering self-efficacy and effectance motivation include modeling (e.g., by partner) of perceived competence, effectance motivation, and the process of goal attainment; providing/receiving social feedback; and engaging in cognitive conflict and its resolution (Nastasi & Clements, 1991; Nastasi & DeZolt, 1994). Participation in contexts in which individual competencies are socially valued may bolster self-esteem and personal/social adjustment (Harter, 1990; Harter & Marold, 1991). Furthermore, collaborative learning environments provide opportunities to learn and practice interpersonal skills and develop interpersonal relations.

Thus, collaborative problem-solving environments, if designed appropriately, offer valuable opportunities for fostering cognitive and personal/social development. The critical features of collaborative learning environments noted in this section provide the basis for creating and facilitating group interventions for COAs. Before describing these procedures, we examine the research on group-based prevention of substance abuse.

Substance Abuse Education and Prevention

Research on group approaches to substance (alcohol and other drugs) abuse education and prevention has examined the efficacy of school- and community-based interventions for influencing knowledge about drugs and their effects, attitudes related to drug use (e.g., beliefs, norms, self-efficacy), and behaviors that reflect the frequency and severity of drug use and personal/social competence (e.g., resistance skills, assertiveness). Early drug education and prevention efforts (1960s and 1970s) focused almost exclusively on knowledge and attitudes, with the assumption that behavioral changes would follow (Schinke, Botvin, & Orlandi, 1991). Efficacy research has failed to substantiate behavioral changes in drug use as a consequence of changing knowledge and attitudes (see also Bangert-Drowns, 1988). More recently (1980s and 1990s), prevention programming centered on developing generic protective skills and personal/social competencies (e.g., interpersonal skills, problem solving, resistance to social influence) has proven successful for enhancing target competencies as well as preventing or reducing drug use (for research reviews, see Dusenbury, Botvin, & James-Ortiz, 1990; Nastasi & DeZolt, 1994; Schinke et al., 1991). These programs characteristically target cognitive-behavioral components of personal/social functioning.

Programs that target resistance skills (i.e., fostering resistance to peer and media influences) incorporate knowledge acquisition and interpersonal skill (e.g., communication, assertiveness) training. Research has supported the efficacy of these approaches for enhancing knowledge, target interpersonal skills, and perceived competence for resisting social influence to use drugs; and for reducing or preventing initiation of drug use.

Building resistance to social influences (i.e., resistance skills) may be particularly important for COAs who are more likely than non-COAs to be exposed to models who use/abuse alcohol and who may be more easily influenced by such models. Male ACOAs in one experimental study (Chipperfield & Vogel-Sprott, 1988) altered their drinking behavior to conform to a live model (confederate) in a cocktail-testing task, in contrast to male non-ACOAs, who failed to significantly alter their behavior in response to the model. One prevention study (Baer, McLaughlin, Burnside, & Pokorny, 1988) showed resistance training to be more effective for adolescents who perceived strong modeling influences (i.e., approval of and actual drug use by parents or peers). In contrast, an intervention focused on decision making and attitudes toward drug use was more effective for those who perceived modeling influences to be weak. Although such research warrants replication, these studies speak to the importance of interpersonal skill building for COAs who are at greater risk than the general population for alcoholism and other drug dependence.

Contemporary substance use/abuse prevention programs have focused on building personal/social competencies such as coping skills, interpersonal and group interactive skills, self-efficacy, decision making, and problem solving (cf. the model of personal/social competence described earlier; Nastasi & DeZolt, 1994). Research supports the efficacy of these programs for enhancing drug-related knowledge and attitudes, developing personal/social competence, and reducing self-reported drug use (e.g., Botvin, Baker, Filazzola, & Botvin, 1990; Caplan, Weissberg, Grober, Sivo, Grady, & Jacoby, 1992). Short-term effects (immediately following intervention) are well substantiated although long-term effects on drug use are mixed. Factors that characterize programs with long-term gains (i.e., 1 to 2 years postintervention) are (1) use of peer leaders as program facilitators, (2) continued involvement of program developers (e.g., through co-facilitation, consultation, monitoring), and (3) use of booster or review sessions.

Research on the efficacy of group-based prevention programming within schools has focused primarily on the general population. Roosa and colleagues (Roosa, Gensheimer, Ayers, & Short, 1990) have designed and studied the efficacy of a school-based program targeting COAs (the Stress Management and Alcohol Awareness Program; SMAAP). The goals of the program include preventing adjustment difficulties through knowledge acquisition about alcoholism and its effects on the family, and enhancing coping skills and personal/social competence. COAs self-selected into and participated in an 8-week (1 hour/week) small-group intervention program that used a combination of strategies (discussion, didactic instruction, modeling and videotaped demonstrations, role-play, behavioral rehearsal, and homework). Consistent with program goals, SMAAP (in contrast to a no-treatment control condition) resulted in increased use of problem- and emotion-focused-coping strategies, which were correlated with teacher reports of adaptive classroom behavior. A unique aspect of the SMAAP program was the use of a systematic needs assessment to guide identification of participants and program goals.

In conclusion, research on substance-abuse prevention supports the use of group approaches that involve teaching resistance skills and personal/social competencies. Such approaches also hold promise for hindering adjustment difficulties through competence development. The next section provides a brief review of research on group interventions for developing personal/social competence in the general and at-risk populations.

Personal/Social Competence Enhancement

Research with the general population of children and adolescents corroborates the findings of substance-abuse prevention research regarding the benefit of cognitive-behavioral interventions for enhancing personal/social functioning. Group-based programs (e.g., small group or whole class) designed for general and specific at-risk populations have proven effective for enhancing cognitive and behavioral skill components of personal/social competence, including perspective taking, interpersonal cognitive problem solving, collaboration, interpersonal interaction skills, and conflict resolution (e.g., Goldstein, Reagles, & Amann, 1990; Weissberg, Caplan, & Harwood, 1991). The discrepancy between initial skill acquisition and generalization over time/context has plagued cognitive-behavioral social skills research. For example, extensive research by Goldstein and colleagues has documented high rates of skill acquisition, with greater than 90% of participants acquiring target skills (empathy, perspective taking, assertiveness, cooperation, negotiation, self-control, and conflict resolution), but only moderate levels of transfer (i.e., by 45 to 50% of participants) to real-world settings (Goldstein et al., 1990).

Research documenting generalization of program effects to real-life settings provide potential solutions and future directions. That is, extended training (e.g., longer program duration), booster sessions (periodic follow-up sessions), transfer training (e.g., through strategy explication and cueing or structured homework focused on applying target skills in real-life situations), and repeated opportunities for application in real-life contexts (e.g., through extended program implementation in the classroom) promote maintenance of initial program effects (Botvin et al., 1990; Goldstein et al., 1990; Lochman, 1992; Weissberg et al., 1991). Furthermore, the use of peer group facilitators and dyadic training (i.e., students learn and practice in pairs) seem critical to generalization of program effects across time and context (Botvin et al., 1990; D. W. Johnson, R. Johnson, Dudley, & Acikgoz, 1991). The role of peers may be especially critical in preventing substance abuse among adolescent COAs because of the powerful influence of peers on substance use (cf. Hawkins, Catalano, & Miller, 1992). Thus, co-construction of peer norms that are supportive of competence-promoting behaviors and antithetical to high-risk behaviors within a program that provides extended opportunities for learning and practice over time and context may be essential to preventive intervention with COAs.

GROUP INTERVENTIONS FOR COAS

This section presents information relevant to designing, implementing and evaluating group interventions for COAs that embody a social construction perspective (as described earlier). Specific techniques are described and practical and ethical issues are discussed.

Intervention Techniques

The intervention techniques described in this section are designed to facilitate the social construction of cognitions, behaviors, and peer norms that are favorable to the development of personal/social competence (self-efficacy and esteem, interpersonal problem solving, interpersonal interaction and relationship skills) of COAs as well as the general population of children and adolescents. Specific techniques include (1) social construction through resolution of dilemmas (i.e., cognitive conflicts), for knowledge and cognitive skill (e.g., decision making, reasoning, problem solving) acquisition; (2) use of story forms such as literature or film, as stimuli for problem solving and role-play; (3) collaborative problem solving, for skill application; and (4) group processing and individual journal writing, for reflection, self-monitoring and self-evaluation. Techniques are designed for use with dyads and small or large (e.g., whole-class) groups; and for use with the general population (e.g., as whole-class activity in the school setting) or the population of identified COAs who are at risk for maladjustment or identified as having emotional or behavioral disorders (e.g., small-group intervention in school or clinic setting). A description of each technique and the group facilitator's role with respect to the technique is provided in this section. Examples of activities are provided in the Appendix at the end of this chapter.

Social Construction

Technique. Social construction involves a dialectic process in which participants are presented with relevant hypothetical or real-life dilemmas (that represent or will likely induce conflicts of ideas or perspectives) and are encouraged to pose alternative perspectives and reach a mutually agreeable resolution. The primary criteria for resolution are viability (i.e., it can realistically be done), potential efficacy (it will likely solve the problem and lead to intended consequences), and consistency with norms of competence promotion (it will enhance the personal/social competence of the individual). As dilemmas are presented and discussed, participants are provided with information necessary to engage in informed decision making; the facilitator may provide the information directly through lecture and/or in response to questions, or indirectly through resource material (e.g., reference books). Reciprocal sense making and cognitive conflict resolution through negotiation and/or synthesis are crucial to the social construction process. Thus, participants should be encouraged to engage in consensus building through integration of compatible ideas (reciprocal sense making) and synthesis of discrepant ideas (conflict resolution).

To facilitate generalization, use dilemmas that are relevant to the real-life experiences of group members (e.g., have them generate the dilemmas). To encourage development of more generalized norms for personal and interpersonal functioning, present multiple dilemmas within multiple contexts. For example, present several dilemmas regarding making choices about alcohol use (e.g., whether to drink, drive, ride with an intoxicated person) across a number of contexts (e.g., with peers at a party, peers at a football game, a parent or sibling at home, a parent or sibling in a drinking establishment).

Facilitator's Role. The facilitator is responsible for selecting or guiding selection of dilemmas, presenting dilemmas, and providing necessary resources (e.g., information) and a format for discussion. Most importantly, the facilitator guides the implementation and evaluation of the dialectic process, particularly the use of reciprocal sense making and conflict resolution. In guiding implementation, the facilitator uses the techniques of scaffolding, explication, reflection, and modeling (described in a subsequent section on facilitator techniques). Evaluation of the dialectic process is conducted as a form of group processing (described in a subsequent section), in which the facilitator guides self-evaluation of individual participation and group dynamics. What is most critical is that the facilitator guides, rather than directs, the process of social construction. That is, the facilitator provides the necessary structure and guidance (i.e., scaffolding) for participants to construct their own ideas and behavioral standards for competence enhancement without imposing particular ideas or standards. If the process is successful, the necessary amount of structure and guidance diminishes, and ultimately, the group reaches an independent level of functioning.

Use of Story Forms

Technique. Story forms (literature, film, role-play, journal writing) are used to develop and practice interpersonal problem solving and interpersonal or relationship skills, and to foster self-efficacy and self-esteem. Specifically, stories provide models for emulation and social comparison; and hypothetical contexts for exploring emotions, discussing and solving interpersonal problems, and practicing interpersonal/relationship skills. Figure 11.1 provides a series of questions to guide the use of story. The story is discussed first in a depersonalized manner, focused on the experiences, feelings, thoughts, and behaviors of the characters. This first step thus focuses on story comprehension. Second, participants are encouraged to relate the characters' experiences to their own. Some participants may skip the first step and immediately relate the story to their own experiences; whether the first step is still implemented depends on the goals of the activity (i.e., solely personal/social or both academic and personal/social). Third, problem solving is applied to the dilemmas/problems faced by both the characters and participants. Nastasi and DeZolt (1994) provide a list of recommended books and films for participants, age 5 to adulthood.

Facilitator's Role. The facilitator selects or guides student selection of stories; in some instances, reads, presents, or guides presentation (e.g., guides role-play) of the story; and poses questions that guide analysis of the story and similar real-life experiences, from a problem-solving perspective (see

Figure 11.1 Using Story to Enhance Personal/Social Competence

Focus on the story in a *depersonalized* manner.

Reconstruct the story (characters, events).
- Who were the characters?
- What happened in the story?

Identify feelings and behavior of characters.
- How do you think she/he was feeling? How could you tell?
- What did she/he do?

Identify alternative behaviors.

What would happen if . . . ?

How else could she/he have handled the situation?

Focus on real-life experiences in a *personalized* manner.

How does this relate to your own experiences?

Have you ever encountered anything like this?

How did you feel?

What did you do?

Focus on *effectiveness of coping strategies* (depersonalized and personalized).

What was the problem the character encountered, or the goal the character was trying to reach?

How effective were the character's strategies for solving the problem, or reaching the goal?

How effective were your strategies in a similar situation?

What other strategies may have worked for the character? for you?

What might you do in the future in a similar situation? How effective are those strategies likely to be?

Source: From *School Interventions for Children of Alcoholics* by B. K. Nastasi and D. M. DeZolt, 1994, New York: Guilford Press. Reprinted by permission.

Figure 11.1). The facilitator uses the story context to assess and identify individual target skills, to facilitate and evaluate progress toward group and individual goals, and to guide application and generalization of target skills.

Collaborative Problem Solving

Technique. The essential characteristics of effective collaborative problem solving (for accomplishing academic/cognitive and social/emotional goals) are positive group interdependence, individual accountability, reciprocal sense making, cognitive conflict resolution through negotiation and synthesis, and processing of group dynamics (Nastasi & Clements, 1991). These features of group functioning are interrelated and also dependent on group norms.

Positive group interdependence is best accomplished when diverse skills are necessary and valued, roles are interdependent and clearly defined, contributions of each group member are necessary for goal attainment and when all group members participate actively, provide to and seek from each other support and constructive feedback, and criticize ideas rather than personal characteristics. Individual accountability and positive interdependence are closely linked, in that group norms consistent with positive group interdependence help to facilitate individual accountability. To ensure that each participant contributes to and benefits from the group process (e.g., understands concepts, masters skills, achieves individual and group goals), encourage participants to set individual goals with respect to beginning competence level, set group goals that take into account the needs and competencies of all members, identify and seek necessary information and other resources (within and outside of the group), and individually and collectively monitor the progress and understanding of all group members.

Reciprocal sense making is more likely to occur when group norms support both positive group interdependence and individual accountability. The optimal context for the co-construction of ideas that characterizes reciprocal sense making is one in which participants value diverse perspectives, willingly negotiate perspectives, and seek consensus. That is, they actively seek ideas from each other, attempt to ensure understanding (e.g., willingly explain ideas or seek clarification), and work toward resolutions that represent views of all members. Such an environment is fertile ground for cognitive conflict (explicit discrepancies of ideas) and resolution characterized by negotiation and synthesis. That is, when participants value multiple perspectives, the expression of alternative views is encouraged rather than avoided. Similarly, when participants seek to co-construct solutions to dilemmas/problems, negotiation and synthesis of discrepant views are more likely.

Facilitator's Role. The facilitator's role is similar to that regarding social construction. Using techniques of scaffolding, modeling, explication, and reflection (see subsequent section on facilitator techniques), the facilitator guides the social interaction of participants to encourage positive interdependence, individual accountability, and the co-construction of ideas through negotiation and synthesis. To allay anxiety about cognitive conflicts, emphasize the potential benefits of considering multiple views. Question and prompt participants to elicit alternative perspectives. The collaborative problem-solving model (Table 11.1) provides a framework for promoting the co-construction of ideas. Structure groups so that the participants' multiple interests and competencies are incorporated and their needs regarding competence building are addressed. Encourage conflict resolution through careful consideration of all presented ideas with the goal of accepting, through consensus, either the single-most viable and seemingly efficacious idea, a compromise among ideas, or the integration of several ideas. As suggested with regard to social construction, successful facilitation of the collaborative process results in decreasingly less reliance on the facilitator and increasing independence of the group.

Group Processing

Technique. Figures 11.2 through 11.4 provide questions and rating scales to guide discussion and evaluation of the group process. The purpose of processing is to encourage reflection, explication, and evaluation of both individual participation and overall group functioning. Participants are encour-

Goal: Fostering Conflict Resolution

Grade Level: High School

Materials:

Reference materials: Books, films, and media depictions (e.g., newspaper, magazine) of historical/current events.

Writing materials; props for role play (or materials to construct props).

Video production materials and supplies.

Integration into School Curriculum: Social Studies, Language Arts, Dramatic Arts, Health, Drug Education

Activity 1 (Social Construction):
Identify a conflict between individuals or groups (or issue with multiple perspectives) depicted in current events, literature, or history. Have participants in dyads or small groups develop portrayals of the event from the multiple perspectives of the parties involved, which they then present to the whole class (orally or in role-play or video). For example, participants portray events leading to the Emancipation Proclamation and rewrite the proclamation from several perspectives (e.g., a slave, a slave owner, an abolitionist, the U.S. President, a "free" person of color, a feminist, a journalist from South Africa). Using the steps of collaborative problem solving (see Table 11.1), guide the whole group in (1) making explicit the multiple views and inherent cognitive and social conflicts, and (2) negotiating a mutually agreeable resolution that addresses and/or integrates the views and interests of all parties. Facilitate the group's construction of definitions for key terms—*cognitive conflict, social conflict, conflict resolution (strategies and outcome), reciprocal sense making, collaborative problem solving, and social construction*—and identification of effective conflict resolution strategies. (This activity is likely to extend across several sessions.) Daily, participants respond individually to a question about collaborative problem solving (e.g., in journals; see Figure 11.2), and in dyads/groups evaluate their participation in the collaborative process (see Figure 11.3). Facilitate collaboration throughout whole-group and dyadic work, focusing on reciprocal sense making, cognitive and social conflict resolution through negotiation/synthesis, individual accountability, and positive group interdependence. Following the activity (daily and/or in total), guide group processing, emphasizing the importance of (1) collaborating to reach a mutual goal, (2) each person's contribution to the process, (3) ways in which they collaborated and resolved conflicts effectively, and (4) ways to improve collaboration and/or conflict resolution. Encourage participants to compare and contrast the collaborative and conflict resolution strategies they used in working together with those they constructed as an academic activity.

Activity 2 (Application):
As part of the alcohol education/prevention program, present a set of real-life social dilemmas (i.e., common dilemmas that involve social interaction and decision making in situations involving alcohol use or abuse and actual or anticipated conflict) for participants to solve in collaborative small groups, using the steps of collaborative problem solving (see Table 11.1). Small groups then present resolutions to the whole group orally or in role-play format. Guide discussion and social construction of behavioral norms for confronting such situations, by encouraging expression of alternative perspective/ solutions and negotiating toward consensus regarding viable alternatives (use guidelines for applying interpersonal problem solving, Figure 11.5). Make explicit how the preferred plan of action may vary depending on the specific conditions or situation. Encourage participants to develop a set of flexible guidelines for decision making and action rather a single solution or rule. Guide discussion and construction of definitions of key terms and relevant issues. Facilitate collaboration and group processing, using techniques described in Activity 1. Examples of dilemmas are:

1. Your friend is abusing alcohol. He or she gets drunk every weekend, insists on driving, and is verbally abusive to you. What would you do? What can you say/do to help your friend? And to protect yourself?
2. You arrive at a party and find out that alcohol is being served. What do you do?
3. Your father gets drunk every night and is verbally abusive to your mother, you, and your sib-

lings. You are the oldest and feel responsible for protecting your mother and siblings. What do you do?

For these dilemmas, focus discussion on key terms—*intoxication, alcohol abuse, alcoholism, family alcoholism, enabling, and assertiveness*—and relevant issues such as psychological effects of alcohol on self and others, individual responsibility for behavior while under the influence of alcohol, individual rights, social responsibility when intervening with someone who is abusing alcohol, protecting yourself in high-risk situations, seeking necessary resources (e.g., social support, professional assistance), and balancing the care for self and others.

Activity 3 (Generalization):
Encourage participants to apply interpersonal problem-solving steps to resolve their own real-life dilemmas or conflicts. In individual journals, have students describe their own experiences similar to the presented dilemmas, and apply the problem-solving steps (e.g., using format in Figure 11.5). Encourage subsequent discussion of individual experiences with the whole group, facilitating discussion of alternative perspectives and solutions.

Alternative/Supplement to Activity 3:
Facilitate application of collaborative problem solving to resolve conflicts that arise as participants work on collaborative academic or recreational activities.

Goal: Coping with Family Crises Related to Alcoholism

Grade Level: Middle School/Junior High

Materials:

Blume, J. (1972). *It's not the end of the world.* New York: Dell.

Blume, J. (1974). *The pain and the great one.* New York: Dell.

Blume, J. (1981). *Tiger eyes: A novel.* New York: Bradbury.

Blume, J. (1987). *Just as long as we're together.* New York: Dell.

Evans, B. A. (Producer), Gideon, R. (Producer), Schernman, A. (Producer), & Reiner, R. (Director). (1986). *Stand by me.* [Film]. RCA/Columbia Pictures. Based on the novela by Stephen King.

Hausman, M. (Producer), & Corr, E. (Director). (1986). *Desert bloom.* [Film]. RCA/Columbia Pictures.

Lots of kids like us. [Educational Film]. 28 minutes. (Consult film libraries in school district or regional drug education/prevention center.)

Morrison, T. (1970). *The bluest eye.* New York: Simon & Schuster.

Nixon, J. L. (1984). *The ghosts of now.* New York: Dell.

Ransom, C. F. (1988). *My sister the meanie.* New York: Scholastic.

Rylant, C. (1982). *When I was young in the mountains.* New York: Dutton.

Rylant, C. (1985). *A blue-eyed daisy.* New York: Bradbury.

Rylant, C. (1985). *The relatives came.* New York: Bradbury.

Shuler-Donner, L. (Producer), Donner, R. (Director), Douglas, M., Bieber, R., & Evans, D. M. (Exec. Producers). (1992). *Radio flyer.* [Film]. Columbia Pictures.

Smith, B. (1943). *A tree grows in Brooklyn.* Philadelphia: Blakiston. [Also on film].

Soft is the heart of a child. [Educational Film]. 28 minutes. (Consult film libraries in school district or regional drug education/prevention center)

Writing and drawing materials.

Integration into School Curriculum: Social Studies, Language Arts, Dramatic Arts, Health, Drug Education

Activity 1 (Social Construction):
Participants read or view stories that depict an array of family relationships and situations, and engage in discussion (see Figure 11.1) about families. Facilitate group construction of key terms—*family, familial relationships* (e.g., parent-parent, parent-

other adult/relative, parent-child, sibling-parent, sibling-sibling, child-other adult/relative)—and key concepts, diversity in family composition, caring and conflict resolution in families, building and maintaining family relationships. In dyads or small groups, participants write stories about ways family members display caring, build and maintain relationships, and/or resolve conflicts; and present (orally or through role play) stories to the whole group. Facilitate discussion of stories with emphasis on diversity in depictions of key terms and concepts; and encourage participants to generate/enact alternative scenarios. Facilitate reciprocal sense making, cognitive and social conflict resolution through negotiation/synthesis, individual accountability, and positive group interdependence during group work; and guide group processing, emphasizing the importance of (1) collaborating to reach a mutual goal, (2) each person's contribution to the process, (3) ways in which they collaborated effectively and exhibited caring for self and others, and (4) ways to improve collaboration and/or express caring to self/others. Note similarities and differences between peer (and facilitator/participant or teacher/student) and familial interactions and relationships.

Activity 2 (Application):
Present depictions of family alcoholism through books and films (see preceding list). Facilitate discussion and group construction of key terms—*alcoholism, family alcoholism,* and *enabling*—and concepts, characteristics of families affected by alcohol, experiences and difficulties of children of alcoholics. Guide group generation of lists of (1) strategies and resources for coping with family alcoholism and family crises; (2) resources available in schools and community; and (3) strategies for helping others in these situation (e.g., encouraging a friend to seek help from a relative or school counselor). Encourage participants to apply strategies from other personal/social competence lessons to family alcoholism and family crises (e.g., interpersonal problem solving, seeking and providing social support, caring for self and others).

Activity 3 (Generalization):
Participants describe in personal journals family crises they have encountered, using the guide for applying interpersonal problem solving (Figure 11.5). Guide discussion and role-playing of personal stories, focusing on feelings, problem definition, and generating and evaluating solution strategies. Encourage regular use of journals for recording and reflecting on family crises and efforts to cope, and for identification of COAs. Use ongoing group discussion to facilitate empathy and social support. Provide information about resources (e.g., relevant professional in school) for those who self-identify as COA or express any concerns about parental drinking. (This activity and the alternative/supplemental activity should be planned and conducted by or in collaboration with a professional with expertise in family alcoholism and therapeutic intervention—for example, school/clinical psychologist, school or drug counselor.)

Alternative/Supplement to Activity 3:
Have participants complete the *Children of Alcoholics Screening Test* (Jones, 1983) and/or the *Children of Alcoholics Life-Events Schedule* (Roosa, Sandler, Gehring, Beals, & Cappo, 1988), and provide scores and interpretation information. Provide information about resources (e.g., relevant professional in school) for those who self-identify as COA or express any concerns about parental drinking.

REFERENCES

Anthenelli, R. M., & Schuckit, M. A. (1990–91). Genetic studies of alcoholism. *The International Journal of the Addictions, 25*(1A), 81–94.

Anthony, E. J., & Cohler, B. J. (Eds.). (1987). *The invulnerable child.* New York: Guilford.

Baer, P. E., McLaughlin, R. J., Burnside, M. A., & Pokorny, A. D. (1988). Alcohol use and psychosocial outcome of two preventive classroom programs with seventh and tenth graders. *Journal of Drug Education, 18*(3), 171–184.

Bandura, A. (1982). Self-efficacy mechanism in human agency. *American Psychologist, 37,* 122–147.

Bandura, A. (1986). *Social foundations of thought and action: A social cognitive theory.* Englewood Cliffs, NJ: Prentice-Hall.

Bangert-Drowns, R. L. (1988). The effects of school-based substance abuse education—A meta-analysis. *Journal of Drug Education, 18*(3), 243–265.

Barnard, C. P., & Spoentgen, P. A. (1986). Children of alcoholics: Characteristics and treatment. *Alcoholism Treatment Quarterly, 3*(4), 47–64.

Bearison, D. J. (1982). New directions in studies of social interaction and cognitive growth. In F. C. Serafica (Ed.), *Social-cognitive development in context* (pp. 199–221). New York: Guilford.

Botvin, G. J., Baker, E., Filazzola, A. D., & Botvin, E. M. (1990). A cognitive-behavioral approach to substance abuse prevention: One-year follow-up. *Addictive Behaviors, 15*(1), 47–63.

Bronfenbrenner, U. (1989). Ecological systems theory. In R. Vasta (Ed.), *Annals of Child Development* (vol. 6, pp. 187–249). Greenwich, CT: JAI Press.

Brown, S. (1988). *Treating adult children of alcoholics: A developmental perspective.* New York: John Wiley.

Calder, P., & Kostyniuk, A. (1989). Personality profiles of children of alcoholics. *Professional Psychology: Research and Practice, 20*(6), 417–418.

Caplan, M., Weissberg, R. P., Grober, J. S., Sivo, P. J., Grady, K., & Jacoby, C. (1992). Social competence promotion with inner-city and suburban young adolescents: Effects on social adjustment and alcohol use. *Journal of Consulting and Clinical Psychology, 60*(1), 56–63.

Chipperfield, B., & Vogel-Sprott, M. (1988). Family history of problem drinking among young male social drinkers: Modeling effects on alcohol consumption. *Journal of Abnormal Psychology, 97*(4), 423–428.

Drugs and Drug Abuse Education. (1990, December). *XXI*(12).

Dusenbury, L., Botvin, G. J., & James-Ortiz, S. (1990). The primary prevention of adolescent substance abuse through the promotion of personal and social competence. *Prevention in Human Services, 7*(1), 201–224.

Elias, M. J. (1987). Establishing enduring prevention programs: Advancing the legacy of Swampscott. *American Journal of Community Psychology, 15,* 539–553.

Elias, M. J., & Branden, L. R. (1988). Primary prevention of behavioral and emotional problems in school-aged populations. *School Psychology Review, 17,* 581–592.

Garbarino, J., Dubrow, N., Kostelny, K., & Pardo, C. (1992). *Children in danger: Coping with the consequences of community violence.* San Francisco: Jossey-Bass.

Gilligan, C. (1982). *In a different voice: Psychological theory and women's development.* Cambridge, MA: Harvard University Press.

Goldstein, A. P., Reagles, K. W., & Amann, L. L. (1990). *Refusal skills: Preventing drug use in adolescents.* Champaign, IL: Research Press.

Goodwin, D. W. (1988). *Is alcoholism hereditary?* New York: Ballantine.

Guisinger, S., & Blatt, S. J. (1994). Individuality and relatedness: Evolution of a fundamental dialectic. *American Psychologist, 49*(2), 104–111.

Harford, T. C. (1992). Family history of alcoholism in the United States: Prevalence and demographic characteristics. *British Journal of Addiction, 87,* 931–935.

Harter, S. (1978). Effectance motivation reconsidered: Toward a developmental model. *Human Development, 21,* 34–64.

Harter, S. (1990). Causes, correlates, and the functional role of global self-worth: A life-span perspective. In R. J. Sternberg & J. Kolligan (Eds.), *Competence considered* (pp. 67–97). New Haven, CT: Yale University.

Harter, S., & Marold, D. B. (1991). A model of determinants and mediational role of self-worth: Implications for adolescent depression and suicidal ideation. In J. Strauss & G. R. Goethals (Eds.), *The self: Interdisciplinary approaches* (pp. 66–92). New York: Springer-Verlag.

Hawkins, J. D., Catalano, R. F., & Miller, J. Y. (1992). Risk and protective factors for alcohol and other drug problems in adolescence and early adulthood: Implications for substance abuse prevention. *Psychological Bulletin, 112*(1), 64–105.

Jarmas, A. L., & Kazak, A. E. (1992). Young adult children of alcoholic fathers: Depressive experiences, coping styles, and family systems. *Journal of Consulting and Clinical Psychology, 60*(2), 244–251.

Johnson, D. W., Johnson, R., Dudley, B., & Acikgoz, K. (1991). *Peer mediation: Effects of conflict resolution training on elementary school students.* Minneapolis, MN: Cooperative Learning Center.

Johnson, J. L., & Rolf, J. E. (1988). Cognitive functioning in children from alcoholic and nonalcoholic families. *British Journal of Addiction, 83,* 849–857.

Jones, J. W. (1983). *The Children of Alcoholics Screening Test (CAST): Test Manual.* Chicago: Camelot Unlimited.

Laurent, J., Hadler, J. R., & Stark, K. D. (1994). A multiple-stage screening procedure for the identification of childhood anxiety disorders. *School Psychology Quarterly, 9*(4), 239–255.

Lochman, J. E. (1992). Cognitive-behavioral intervention with aggressive boys: Three-year follow-up and preventive effects. *Journal of Consulting and Clinical Psychology, 60*(3), 426–432.

Manning, D. T., Balson, P. M., & Xenakis, S. (1986). The prevalence of type A personality in the children of alcoholics. *Alcoholism: Clinical and Experimental Research, 10*(2), 184–189.

Morse, R. M., & Falvin, D. K. (1992). The definition of alcoholism. *The Journal of the American Medical Association, 268*(2), 1012–1014.

Nastasi, B. K. (1995). Is early identification of children of alcoholics necessary for preventive intervention? Reaction to Havey & Dodd. *Journal of School Psychology, 33,* 327–335.

Nastasi, B. K., & Clements, D. H. (1991). Research on cooperative learning: Implications for practice. *School Psychology Review, 20,* 110–131.

Nastasi, B. K., & Clements, D. H. (1992). Social-cognitive behaviors and higher-order thinking in educational computer environments. *Learning and Instruction, 2,* 215–238.

Nastasi, B. K., & DeZolt, D. M. (1994). *School interventions for children of alcoholics.* New York: Guilford.

National Institute on Alcohol Abuse and Alcoholism. (1990, July). Children of alcoholics: Are they different? *Alcohol Alert,* pp. 1–4.

Perkins, H. W., & Berkowitz, A. D. (1991). Collegiate COAs and alcohol abuse: Problem drinking in relation to assessments of parent and grandparent alcoholism. *Journal of Counseling and Development, 69,* 237–240.

Reynolds, W. R. (1986). A model for the screening and identification of depressed children and adolescents in school settings. *Professional School Psychology, 1,* 117–130.

Rogoff, B. (1990). *Apprenticeship in thinking: Cognitive development in social context.* New York: Oxford University Press.

Roosa, M. W., Beals, J., Sandler, I. N., & Pillow, D. R. (1990). The role of risk and protective factors in predicting symptomatology in adolescent self-identified children of alcoholic parents. *American Journal of Community Psychology, 18*(5), 725–741.

Roosa, M. W., Gensheimer, L. K., Ayers, T. S., & Short, J. L. (1990). Development of a school-based prevention program for children in alcoholic families. *Journal of Primary Prevention, 11*(2), 119–141.

Roosa, M. W., Gensheimer, L. K., Short, J. L., Ayers, T. S., & Shell, R. (1989). A preventive intervention for children in alcoholic families: Results of a pilot study. *Family Relations, 38,* 295–300.

Roosa, M. W., Sandler, I. N., Beals, J., & Short, J. L. (1988). Risk status of adolescent children of problem-drinking parents. *American Journal of Community Psychology, 16*(2), 225–239.

Roosa, M. W., Sandler, I. N., Gehring, M., Beals, J., & Cappo, L. (1988). The Children of Alcoholics Life-Events Schedule: A stress scale for children of alcohol-abusing parents. *Journal of Studies on Alcohol, 49(5),* 422–429.

Schinke, S. P., Botvin, G. J., & Orlandi, M. A. (1991). *Substance abuse in children and adolescents: Evaluation and intervention.* Newbury Park, CA: Sage.

Schunk, D. H. (1990). Self-concept and school achievement. In C. Rogers & P. Kutnick (Eds.), *The social psychology of the primary school* (pp. 70–91). London: Rutledge.

Slavkin, S. L., Heimberg, R. G., Winning, C. D., & McCaffrey, R. J. (1992). Personal and parental problem drinking: Effects on problem-solving performance and self-appraisal. *Addictive Behaviors, 17,* 191–199.

Stern, R., Kendall, A., & Eberhard, P. (1991). Children of alcoholics in the schools: Where are they? Their representations in special education. *Psychology in the Schools, 28,* 116–123.

Velleman, R. (1992). Intergenerational effects—A review of environmentally oriented studies concerning the relationship between parental alcohol problems and family disharmony in the genesis of alcohol and other problems. II: The intergenerational effects of family disharmony. *The International Journal of the Addictions, 27*(4), 367–389.

Vygotsky, L. S. (1978). *Mind in society: The development of higher psychological processes.* Cambridge, MA: Harvard University Press.

Weintraub, S. A. (1990–91). Children and adolescents at risk for substance abuse and psychopathology. *The International Journal of the Addictions, 25*(4A), 481–494.

Weissberg, R. P., Caplan, M., & Harwood, R., L. (1991). Promoting competent young people in competence-enhancing environments: A systems-based perspective on primary prevention. *Journal of Consulting and Clinical Psychology, 59*(6), 830–841.

Wertsch, J. V. (1991). *Voices of the mind: A sociocultural approach to mediated action.* Cambridge, MA: Harvard University Press.

Wirt, R. D., Lachar, D., Klainedinst, J. K., & Seat, P. D. (1984). *Personality Inventory for Children.* Los Angeles: Western Psychological Services.

Zahn-Waxler, C. (1991). The case for empathy: A developmental perspective. *Psychological Inquiry, 2,* 155–158.

CHAPTER 12

GROUP INTERVENTIONS FOR STUDENTS WITH MILD DISORDERS: CLASSROOM INCLUSION APPROACHES

Maurice J. Elias, RUTGERS UNIVERSITY
Lisa Blum, RUTGERS UNIVERSITY
Peter T. Gager, RUTGERS UNIVERSITY
Lisa Hunter, RUTGERS UNIVERSITY
Jeffrey S. Kress, RUTGERS UNIVERSITY

The term *mild disabilities* (used interchangeably here with *mild disorders* and *mild handicaps*) is an umbrella term that refers broadly to children who have a variety of emotional, social, and behavioral problems, mild mental retardation, and a variety of learning disabilities (Wang, Reynolds, & Walberg, 1988). Often, this set of difficulties is referred to as *high-incidence disorders,* in contrast to *low-incidence* disorders such as severe intellectual disabilities (e.g., blindness, spinal bifida) (Fuchs & Fuchs, 1994).

Regardless of the specific disabilities included under this rubric, a commonality is that these children have difficulties with social relationships. Children with mild disabilities tend not to be accepted by their peers, and they display shortcomings in the way they interact with peers and adults. To an increasing degree, the education of children with mild disabilities in the mainstream has been identified as a priority in special education (McKleskey & Pacchiano, 1994; Waldron, 1997). This emphasis, which is referred to as the *inclusion approach,* follows recognition that singling these children out for intervention reduces opportunities for natural peer interaction and runs the risk of increasing their social isolation and stigma. Furthermore, categorizing these students and removing them from the mainstream may cause parents, teachers, and the students to lower their expectations and to lose confidence in the students' abilities (Waldron, 1997; Wang et al., 1988).

It is our view that widespread, effective intervention with children having mild disabilities must be based in the context of inclusive classrooms. Although inclusion can refer to a range of educational practices, it is defined generally as educating children with disabilities in classrooms with typically developing children for much or all of the school day (Stoiber, Gettinger, & Goetz, in press; Waldron, 1997). Inclusion is distinguished from mainstreaming. Whereas the concept of mainstreaming was based on the practice of allowing or permitting children with disabilities to be placed in regular education classrooms for which the child demonstrates age- or grade-appropriate skills, inclusion is based on acceptance and accommodation of learner diversity in general education classrooms (Waldron, 1997). Such an approach puts clinicians and other school professionals into the role of consultants, trainers, and co-therapists.

Many of the techniques to be described with regard to the mechanics of classroom-based interventions are equally applicable to small-group interventions in "pull-out" or clinical contexts. However, as will be discussed, there are additional features involved in moving the locus of intervention to the classroom that dramatically change the potency of what takes place. Further, a classroom-based model is necessary to reach the large number of children who otherwise are not likely to obtain needed services. Naturally, there remains an important role for group-based interventions for students with mild disorders, but we see this role as supplemental to a classroom-based intervention model.

A PERSPECTIVE ON INCLUSION

Inclusion, as we are defining it, takes as a central concern the establishment of common ground between all students, and the creation of an environment where all students feel that they belong and are encouraged to learn at their highest level. For the purposes of this chapter, we define *inclusion* as Schrag and Burnette (1994) have done in their recent review of literature on the subject. Inclusion is a controversial concept that states that a more unified and coordinated educational system is required to adequately serve *all* students, and that students with all degrees of disabilities should be educated in regular classrooms, with the required support services. However, inclusion is more than a plan for reforming classroom structure; it is also a philosophy:

> *Inclusion describes an educational context and a process that amount to much more than a "place" (e.g., the regular classroom). Inclusive schools do not just mainstream students—they include them.... Throughout all of the educational options is a philosophy of coordination and inclusion. This philosophy reflects a change in attitudes and values that celebrates diversity... [and] recognizes the importance of strong social relationship among children.... Within inclusive schools, there is a sense of community that values the abilities and limitations of all students and provides opportunities for students to develop a strong sense of self-worth, concern, and respect for others, as well as the ability to work interdependently. (Schrag & Burnette, 1994, p. 64)*

For inclusion to work, classes that are including students with disabilities must focus on the issues of self-worth, acceptance, respect for others, and friendship (Stainback, Stainback, East, & Sapon-Shevin, 1994).

In line with this focus, a principal goal of the inclusion movement is to enhance students' social competence and friendships and to change the attitudes of teachers and students without disabilities so that they better understand and are more accepting of others' differences (Fuchs & Fuchs, 1994). Among the most essential and reciprocal advantages derived from inclusion are that (1) social skills are developed schoolwide, (2) attitudes of nondisabled peers regarding students with disabilities can be impacted in a positive manner, and (3) friendships and positive relationships emerge from the mutual contact and sustained interaction (Fuchs & Fuchs, 1994).

FACTORS NECESSITATING CLASSROOM-BASED, INCLUSIVE GROUP APPROACHES

As MacMillan, Gresham, and Forness (1996) point out, research has not supported the assumption that mainstreamed students with disabilities will learn appropriate social behavior simply from interacting with nonclassified peers. In fact, research indicates that mainstreamed students, by and large, have low levels of social interaction in regular education settings. *Students with disabilities* may be identified as "different" on the basis of their behavior even before they are formally classified or segregated into special education programs (MacMillan et al.,

1996). These students are often treated with derision by their nonclassified peers, partly as a result of their deficits in social competence (Gartner & Lipsky, 1987). Research by Fox (1989) examined peer rejection among grade 4, 5, and 6 students classified as having learning disabilities. Mainstreaming was found to increase the risk of social rejection. Thus, one cannot assume that mainstreamed students will simply "pick up" proper social behavior from contact with typically developing peers. Active measures must be taken to promote social competence of most children with disabilities.

However, focusing solely on the social skills deficits of children with disabilities is only half the issue. Classified students often are confronted with stereotypes, preconceptions, and antagonistic and rejecting behavior from their nonclassified peers (Gresham, 1984). Blaming these negative behaviors on the deficits of the *classified* students, in effect, is analogous with "blaming the victim." Rather, nonclassified students are the children who lack self-control, empathy, and generally prosocial behavior. As such, it is apparent that focusing attention solely on the skills deficits of students with mild disorders does not go far enough.

These issues form the rationale for an inclusive group intervention that emphasizes all three of Fuchs and Fuchs' (1994) goals for inclusion. First, direct efforts must be made at improving social skills for *all* students through curriculum-based lessons in social skills and social-cognitive problem solving. Second, by bringing classified and nonclassified children together in a structured group setting to increase interpersonal awareness and empathy, an effective program aims at unraveling negative stereotypes between these two groups. The third goal area is directed toward providing a context for friendships to develop.

What Elias and Clabby (1992) described as second-generation social problem-solving programs meet the preceding criteria. These programs—delivered primarily in the form of teacher-led, group-based classroom lessons—focus on a variety of interpersonal skills, developmentally tailored to span years from pre-school through high school (Elias, 1997). Self-control, group participation, and social awareness skills are considered prerequisite skills for problem solving. Students learn a decision-making strategy for responding to a variety of everyday difficulties and choices that they face.

Finally, social problem-solving programs contain structured activities to ensure generalization of these skills to diverse academic and social situations. Social problem-solving programs are designed with a focus on the *promotion* of prosocial interaction and on fostering respect for diversity and positive social development for *all* students—both mainstreamed classified students and their typically developing peers. Classified students can benefit from direct instruction in appropriate social behavior and from *structured and guided* interaction with peers who, on the average, may be more skilled in these areas. Nonclassified students, through ongoing group interaction with classified students, gain an appreciation of learner diversity and learn ways to interact positively with a range of students.

EMPIRICAL EVIDENCE FOR SOCIAL PROBLEM SOLVING AND RELATED INTERVENTION APPROACHES

Within the school setting, social adjustment is being seen as equally important as academic skill development (Schloss, 1992). Programs that emphasize the development and use of social skills are especially promising for use in inclusive classrooms because they address issues that are relevant to both mildly disordered and nondisordered children. Therefore, social skill instruction, especially procedures incorporating social problem solving, has received extensive empirical study, including longitudinal research (Elias & Clabby, 1992). This section will review several of the most prominent social problem-solving programs.

Shure's (1992) ICPS—Interpersonal Cognitive Problem-Solving (or I Can Problem Solve)—has been evaluated over a period of 25 years and more recently in a 5-year longitudinal study. This curriculum is geared toward the promotion of mental health in kindergarten through sixth grades.

Designed with high-risk children in mind (i.e., those who are either impulsive [unable to wait, overly emotional, bossy to peers] or inhibited [overly shy, withdrawn, and passive rather than assertive]), the program includes a preproblem-solving phase (e.g., identifying feelings and perspective taking) followed by problem-solving training, both of which use games, stories, puppets, and role-playing. Across a number of empirical studies (summarized in Shure, 1992), gains in interpersonal as well as academic behavior, including a reduction in impulsive behavior, have been demonstrated; however, it is also clear that effects disappear in the absence of "booster" or follow-up sessions.

Similar to ICPS, Skillstreaming is a method of promoting social skills that emphasizes interpersonal and problem-solving skills. The Skillstreaming Curriculum aims at improving interpersonal communication in prosocial skills such as classroom survival, making friends, dealing with feelings, dealing with stress, alternatives to aggression, and planning (Miller, Midgett, & Wicks, 1992). Skillstreaming relies on modeling, role-playing, performance feedback, and transfer of training to promote prosocial skills (Goldstein, Sprafkin, Gershaw, & Klein, 1980). Research by Miller and associates (1992) examined the effects of Skillstreaming on a group of students with emotional disturbances. After using the curriculum for six weeks, teachers completed checksheets that examined their perceptions of each student's behavior in the areas of beginning social skills, advanced social skills, dealing with feelings, alternatives to aggression, dealing with stress, and planning skills. According to teacher ratings, after receiving the Skillstreaming Curriculum for six weeks, middle-school students had significantly improved their social skills in all examined areas.

Although these and similar programs have shown some success, it has become clear that results tend to be stronger, more generalizable, and enduring among programs that are ongoing and long term (Elias, Weissberg, & Associates, 1994). Thus, a "second generation" of social problem-solving programs has emerged with a dual emphasis on the integration of the program into the classroom structure and on continuity and reinforcement of skills.

Weissberg's Social Problem Solving (SPS) program integrates the affective, cognitive, and behavioral aspects of problem solving. Students are taught steps to use when responding to social challenges and problems. These steps are (1) Stop, calm down, and think before you act; (2) Say the problem and how you feel; (3) Set a positive goal; (4) Think of lots of solutions; (5) Think ahead to the consequences, and (6) Go ahead and try the best plan (Weissberg, Jackson, & Shriver, 1993). In a longitudinal study of the program, students who received SPS training were compared to students who did not receive the training. Results indicated that students receiving SPS training reported significant gains in their ability to generate more cooperative solutions to hypothetical problems and endorse assertive cooperative strategies to resolve interpersonal conflict (Elias & Weissberg, 1990).

Elias and Clabby's (1989) social problem-solving program has been studied since 1979. Validation of the program occurred with both nondisabled and mildly disabled students in mainstream settings, as well as in school-based and residential special education contexts. The scope of the program is multiyear and is intended to be integrated into all aspects of the school day in an ongoing manner. When compared to control groups, several major effects for children involved in the programs have been documented, including (1) greater sensitivity to others' feelings; (2) more observed prosocial behavior, as seen by their teachers; (3) being sought out more often by their peers for help with problems; (4) lower than expected levels of antisocial, self-destructive, and socially disordered behavior, even when followed up in high school; and (5) increased feelings of knowing more about their classmates. Additionally, data from the SPS program have been examined by the Program Effectiveness Panel of the U.S. Department of Education, and as a result, the project has been designated as a program of educational excellence by the U.S. Department of Education's National Diffusion Network (Elias & Clabby, 1992).

The Child Development Program (Battistich, Elias, & Branden-Muller, 1992) is another example of an effective SPS approach that seeks to have an impact on the school environment. The program was designed to create a caring and participatory school community in which children are given opportunities to learn about others' needs and perspectives, to collaborate with one another, and to engage in a variety of prosocial actions, all in balance with their own needs. Group activities include working in small cooperative groups toward common goals in academic and nonacademic tasks. Goals of fairness and consideration are reached through direct training in group interaction skills. Group discussions and meetings are also geared for increasing help and sensitivity toward other students, as well as understanding others' feelings, needs, and perspectives. Results from a longitudinal study comparing three suburban, middle-class elementary schools and three control schools using the Child Development Program had several important effects: increased spontaneous prosocial behavior (helpfulness, support, cooperation), higher student ratings of the extent to which the classroom was a "caring community," improved perspective-taking ability, greater peer acceptance, and decreased loneliness and social anxiety.

Finally, research confirms that an inclusion strategy is most effective when combined with a focus on social skills training, fostering of interpersonal relationships and use of cooperative learning within classrooms, and ongoing teacher efforts to build students' critical thinking and problem-solving skills (Scruggs, Mastropieri, & Sullivan, 1994). Moreover, there is little evidence that simple physical inclusion, without psychological inclusion, will benefit students with mild learning disorders (Stainback, Stainback, East, & Sapon-Shevin, 1994).

Thus, the intervention strategy of choice for this population is one that focuses on both the skills of the children and on their interpersonal learning environments. The following sections provide an introduction to applications of a social problem-solving approach that has particular promise for comprehensive, long-term effectiveness with mildly disabled students. (As noted earlier, the specific techniques presented all are applicable to non-classroom group interventions, as well.)

SPECIFIC INTERVENTION TECHNIQUES

SPS is carried out through classroom and group-based intervention approaches to improve the following capabilities of mildly disabled students and their classmates:

- To calm down and reorganize themselves when they are under stress such as negative peer pressure
- To develop their understanding of social situations and the feelings and perspectives of people in them
- To elaborate and clarify personally meaningful and prosocial goals
- To consider possible alternative actions and their consequences
- To plan detailed strategies for reaching their goals
- To understand and accept social decisions for which there are no alternatives, such as those related to drug use, illegal alcohol use, smoking, and the use of violence to resolve interpersonal disputes and conflicts

SPS interventions encompass three focal areas, which implementers can address sequentially or attempt to incorporate integratively, depending on the purpose of their work:

1. *Self-control and group participation and social awareness* targets self-control skills such as listening, following directions, resisting provocations, avoiding provoking others, and self-calming; and group participation and social awareness skills, such as how to select friends and show caring.
2. *Social decision making* consists of eight primary skill areas (or steps) identified as synthesizing a feasible, theoretically sound, and empirically supported decision-making and problem-solving strategy children can employ in their everyday lives (Elias & Clabby, 1992): (a) Notice signs of feelings in oneself and others; (b) Identify issues or problems; (c) Determine and select goals; (d) Generate alternative solutions; (e) Envision possible consequences; (f) Select your best solution; (g) Plan your actions and make a final check for obstacles; and (h)

Guide (Psychological Enterprises Incorporated, 1993). The software works by presenting to students the eight-step instructional strategy. It takes students through the eight-step problem-solving process, and, depending on the subroutine used, the focus is on how to avoid getting into trouble similar to the kind that they just did or how to decide on an action plan that will be used to tackle a health, peer, or academic problem that has been bothering them. The teacher's role is to serve as a guide or aid, to help students follow up on the action plans they generate, and to be available to deal with any questions students might have. The software allows individualized attention while using a process compatible with classroom curriculum procedures. In the vast majority of cases, Nigro found that referral to the Pupil Assistance Team/School Resource Committee for formal prereferral intervention consideration was not needed.

At other times, it will be necessary to have groups focused on particular problems that a group of children in the school share. Ongoing concerns in many schools are separation and divorce (Kalter & Schreier, 1993); children with attention deficit, hyperactivity, and related behavior problems (Braswell & Bloomquist, 1991); and social skills problems that do not allow students to participate in the behavioral rehearsal activities of social decision-making classes (Gresham & Elliot, 1993). In each of these instances, choices can be made to develop time-limited groups for students, to incorporate special modules within the social decision-making and problem-solving framework in the whole class, or to have individual or small-group tutorial meetings. Other areas where specialized groups have been found useful are groups for bereaved students, which unfortunately is all too common in urban areas (Healy-Romanello, 1993) and groups to develop adolescent leadership (Powell, 1993). The latter is especially important as a tool against dropout and disaffection, as well as developing teenagers as resources to their school, peers, and community.

Thus, there are significant roles to be played both in supporting teachers' application of SPS in the classroom and in working with such services as SPS Labs and specialized problem-solving groups.

Applications to Special Populations and Situations: Aggressive and Shy Children

There are two subgroups of mildly disordered children—aggressive children and shy children—that can benefit considerably from an inclusive SPS approach that gives them the opportunity to improve their social skills without being singled out. The data are clear that perpetuation of either of these behavioral patterns places children at long-term risk for a variety of psychological difficulties. Therefore, it is useful to review specific aspects of SPS that can be used in the inclusive classroom to assist these children.

Aggression in children has been related to a specific set of deficits in social problem-solving skills. Guerra and Slaby (1989) found that, in comparison to their nonaggressive peers, aggressive boys were more likely to define problems by viewing the intent of others as hostile, and to generate few consequences for aggressive solutions to a problem. Additionally, aggressive children, by definition, show a lack of self-control and a limited social response repertoire. A similar skills profile was found to characterize aggressive children as young as preschool age (Gouze, 1987).

The SPS program described here addresses the deficits and needs of aggressive children at several levels. As discussed, self-control skills form a central component of the Readiness Phase of the curriculum. Not only are skills in affective regulation and moderation taught directly in the form of the skill "Keep Calm," but efforts are taken to increase the prosocial skills repertoire of such students. New, prosocial behaviors can take the place of aggressive responses to problems and frustrations. Further, the social decision-making strategy emphasized in the Instructional Phase fosters generating possible solutions and consequences of these decisions. This provides an opportunity for the incorporation of newly acquired skills into consideration for use at situations where aggressive behaviors are common, as well as for the consideration of consequences of aggressive behaviors. These skills are "over-learned" and practiced in classroom lessons—before, not after, a child has the opportunity to use an inappropriately aggressive response.

The SPS program is also useful in situations where a student uses an aggressive response and finds himself or herself "in trouble." Curriculum materials are used to focus children's attention on the problem behavior and its consequences, on other behavioral options they had in this situation, and on the consequences of these alternate behaviors. This can be implemented by the classroom teacher, in conjunction with an in-class behavior management program. For example, the Problem Solving Diary is a procedure in which a worksheet is used to guide students through evaluating the consequences of their actions and planning alternative responses (Elias & Clabby, 1989). Blank diary sheets can be kept in a "cooling off" or "Keep Calm" area and used by students who are sent there for disruptive behavior. Alternatively, school personnel, such as social workers or crisis intervention personnel, can use these materials in response to a problem situation. Ultimately, however, the goal is to help children notice the earliest warning signs of their aggressive behavior and complete the diary sheets before they get into trouble. (A similar function is performed by having children go to an SPS Lab when they are feeling bothered by a situation that might escalate into aggressive incidents if left unattended.)

Further, as the SPS program targets all children without identifying any particular "problem children," students, as a group, can brainstorm ways to handle confrontation and other aggressive behaviors on the part of their peers. While not singling out any particular aggressive student, the class as a whole becomes involved in the prevention of such behaviors by learning and creating lists of nonaggressive responses to confrontation.

Unlike aggressive children who tend to disrupt the classroom, shy children often go unnoticed in the classroom. It is important for teachers to recognize shy children because shyness can lead to low self-esteem, difficulty in establishing interpersonal relationships, loneliness, and possible drug use (Garbe, 1990). Shy children lack the social skills necessary to initiate a conversation, join in a group, make new friends, ask questions, and so forth. These skills are important for all children, but especially vital for the shy child.

Since the interpersonal shortcomings of shy children are often linked to both cognitive-affective and social-behavioral factors, the SPS emphasis on understanding, thinking through, and acting in situations is particularly beneficial for shy children. Shy children can be encouraged to use FIG TESPN to help them deal with the various problems related to their shyness. Because FIG TESPN is a method that can be used by all children in a variety of situations, using this approach would benefit both shy and nonshy children. When discussing FIG TESPN in group situations, teachers can provide extra help for the shy child by using examples they are likely to experience (e.g., joining a group, making a new friend, asking for help).

The key skills involved in social approach behavior form the acronym BEST, a component of the SPS approach discussed earlier that can be structured to assist shy children. Shy children are often rejected by their peers because of their meek and passive manner. Encouraging children to be their BEST teaches them that they can use their body posture, eye contact, speech and tone of voice to come across as a confident person. These skills are especially important for the shy child.

Finally, Keep Calm is another aspect of the SPS approach that can be tailored to the shy child. Shy children often experience anxiety when they face situations that require them to speak up. These children—and their classmates—benefit from being taught how to use Keep Calm to lower their anxiety, thus enabling them to perform better.

FIG TESPN, Best, and Keep Calm all can be used by teachers in the classroom setting to assist shy children. It may be necessary, however, to coach shy children in these techniques on an individual basis so that they may gain confidence in their abilities. This might involve special prompts to remind them to use the skills in situations they are about to encounter. There may also be times when classroom instruction in the techniques could be supplemented by extra individual or small group help from an SPS-knowledgeable school counselor or psychologist.

In summary, this discussion of shy and aggressive children and event-triggered situations highlights the utility of the SPS program to address the

Table 13.1 Traumas That Have Been Found to Result in PTSD

TYPES OF TRAUMA	REFERENCES
Natural Disasters	
Hurricanes	Lonigan, Shannon, Finch, Daugherty, & Taylor, 1991
Fires	Jones & Ribbe, 1991; McFarlane, 1987
Earthquakes	Bradburn, 1991; Galante & Foa, 1986
Floods	Earls, Smith, Reich, & Jung, 1988
Accidents	
Vehicular (e.g., boat, train, bus, etc.)	Raphael, 1977; Toubiana, Milgram, Strich, & Edelstein, 1988; Yule, Udwin, & Murdoch, 1990
Nuclear	Dohrenwend, Dohrenwend, Warheit, Bartlett, Goldstein, Goldstein, & Martin, 1981
Violence	
Sexual/physical abuse	Famularo, Fenton, & Kinscherff, 1993
Atrocities of war	Chimienti, Nasr, & Khalifeh, 1989
Kidnapping	Terr, 1983
Acts of terrorism	Ochberg & Soskis, 1982
Other Violence	Pynoos & Nader, 1988a, 1988b

tic criteria to PTSD, but is used when symptoms occur within one month of exposure to the traumatic event and then remit. PTSD is diagnosed only if the symptoms persist past one month. Acute stress disorder would be treated in accordance with guidelines for early interventions and preventive group interventions detailed later in this chapter.

Both the *DSM-III-R* and *DSM-IV* distinguished between those events that are caused by nature versus those caused by human beings and suggest that events caused by human beings result in posttraumatic stress disorders that are lengthier and more severe (American Psychiatric Association, 1987; 1994). Human-induced violence such as rape, in particular, may result in a prolonged and serious PTSD reaction (Frederick, 1985). The *DSM-IV* also describes associated symptoms such as self-destructive behavior, shame, and despair that are frequently seen when the stressor was interpersonal in nature (e.g., sexual or physical abuse, torture, or being taken hostage). Although the *DSM-III-R* did not include specific criteria for diagnosis of PTSD in children, the *DSM-IV* includes specific notes regarding the behavior children may display, which can be different from adults. That is, children may experience nightmares, reenact the event through play, or engage in repetitive play that incorporates themes of the trauma. The *DSM-IV* does not, however, specify criteria for children of different ages. Later in this chapter, more specific developmental factors will be addressed.

SYMPTOMS

Cognitive, affective, behavioral, and physiological-somatic effects have been observed in children who have experienced some traumatic event. Some of these effects are consistent with *DSM-IV* criteria; others are not. Armsworth and Holaday (1993) cited self-abusive behaviors, lowered IQ, and negative body image, among others, as symptoms frequently observed in children and adolescents who have experienced some traumatic event, yet these symptoms are not specifically outlined in the *DSM-IV* criteria for PTSD. (See Table 13.2 for an extensive list of symptoms.)

Terr (1991) suggested that symptoms differ for those children suffering from Type I and Type II disorders. "Type I traumas do not appear to breed the massive denials, psychic numbings, self-anes-

Table 13.2 Symptoms of PTSD in Children

COGNITIVE SYMPTOMS	AFFECTIVE SYMPTOMS	BEHAVIORAL SYMPTOMS
Intrusive thoughts and images Recurring distressing dreams of the event Hallucinations Suppression of intrusive thoughts and images of the event Concentration difficulties Memory impairments Impaired intellectual functioning and potential academic decline Foreshortened sense of the future Negative body image Impaired self-concept	Labile affect (including anxiety, panic, fears, excessive worry, excessive crying and sadness, hopelessness about the future, generalized phobias, and anger) Survivor guilt	Angry and aggressive outbursts Regressive behaviors Self-destructive behaviors Inability to establish or maintain relationships Withdrawal and isolation Hyperalertness to danger Sleep disturbances Avoidance of situations, people, or objects that are reminders of the trauma Repetitive play (reenactment of aspects of the traumatic event) Separation and clinging behavior

Sources: Armsworth & Holaday, 1993; Eth & Pynoos, 1985; Pynoos & Nader, 1988b; Terr, 1985, 1991.

thesias, or personality problems that characterize the Type II disorders of childhood" (p. 14). Repression, identification with the aggressor, and aggression turned against the self are also more characteristic of Type II than Type I disorders.

Type I and Type II categories have not yet been validated; nevertheless, they make a useful distinction. Since Chapter 20 in this book (by Azar, Breton, & Reiss) is devoted entirely to groups for prevention of and intervention for child abuse, which may potentially result in a Type II disorder, we will focus on those cases that would be classified as Type I–PTSD (i.e., traumas that result from an acute stressor rather than repeated ordeals).

PTSD Symptoms According to Developmental Levels

When children are younger than 11 years of age, they are more vulnerable to trauma (Davidson & Smith, 1990). Symptoms of PTSD may also differ according to developmental levels. Very young children may have trouble differentiating fantasy from reality, thus increasing their distress. For example, children often daydream and have nightmares about the event and then incorporate aspects such as monsters into their memories of the actual event. Parents can help them clarify what is real. Preschoolers may not be able to identify their feelings. Those children who are able to identify their feelings are unlikely to verbalize them. Some youngsters may lack the vocabulary and language skills to describe their feelings, whereas others lack self-awareness (Joyner, 1991).

Lystad (1985) delineated age-specific responses to traumatic events. Preschoolers may engage in regressive behaviors, whereas elementary school-age children and adolescents are more likely to experience headaches and other physical and psychological symptoms. Adolescents who have suffered a trauma, according to Pynoos and Nader (1988a), may feel detached, ashamed, and guilty. Given their needs for peer acceptance, they are uncomfortable about these feelings and fear being viewed as abnormal. They may engage in self-destructive or aggressive behaviors (e.g., drug use, promiscuity, fighting). Dependent or counterdependent behavior may be manifested in a reluctance to leave home or a premature flight into adulthood. Table 13.3 lists symptoms according to developmental level.

Table 13. 3 Symptoms of PTSD in Different Age Groups

PRESCHOOLERS	ELEMENTARY	ADOLESCENTS
Crying	Physical Symptoms	Detachment
Thumb sucking	Depression	Shame
Clinging	Confusion	Guilt
Loss of bowel or bladder control	Inability to concentrate	Withdrawal from peers
Inability to be alone	Withdrawal from peers	Inability to concentrate
Fear of strangers	Fighting	Confusion
Confusion	Poor performance	Poor performance
Irritability	Fears about severe weather and lack of safety	Fighting
Immobility		Physical symptoms
		Depression

INTERVENTIONS

Discussion of Research

Group interventions for posttraumatic stress disorder appear to be of two types: (1) early intervention used to prevent the onset of PTSD and (2) interventions for those who suffer from PTSD. However, the effectiveness of these *group approaches* has not been studied systematically. Robinson's evaluation studies of the effectiveness of early intervention strategies with emergency personnel (e.g., police, paramedics, etc.) found that participants believed the interventions to be helpful; Everly provided some evidence that interventions that occur within 24 to 72 hours of the event impede cognitive misinterpretations of the event and therefore prevent PTSD (cited in Mitchell, 1988, November).

Few studies have investigated the effectiveness of *group treatment* for children and adolescents suffering from PTSD. Much of the research about PTSD in children and adolescents has utilized the case study approach and has focused primarily on symptoms of the disorder in children. Relatively few studies have examined coping and treatment of PTSD in children (Benedek, 1985; Garmezy, 1988), although Saigh (1987, 1989) completed a number of single-case intensive studies with children and adolescents aged 10 to 14. He found that *in vivo* flooding successfully effected positive changes in affective, cognitive, and behavioral functioning. Using a multiple baseline design in each of the experiments, positive changes were found on all variables after the introduction of *in vivo* flooding. In a similar multiple baseline design, a 6-year-old boy also showed positive changes in the same three areas (Saigh, 1986).

In the following section, group interventions that have been used with children and adolescents are described and interventions that have been used with individuals are adapted for group counseling with children. The reader should be aware that the effectiveness of the *group techniques* presented in the remainder of this chapter have not been empirically tested for children and adolescents exposed to trauma.

Early Intervention Methods

Early intervention is important not only because children and adolescents who experience trauma are vulnerable to posttraumatic stress disorder but also because they may develop severe problems in later life. For example, children who have been physically or sexually abused have an increased chance of becoming child abusers themselves or allowing child abuse to occur. Multiple personality disorder (Kluft, 1985) has been reported as one potential consequence of childhood trauma, although the validity of multiple personality disorder has been questioned. Children who have been raped may be victims of multiple rapes as adults (Terr, 1991). Feelings that the world is unsafe and that adults are unable to protect them may contribute to isolation and withdrawal from others. Rigid defenses that interfere with relationships and functioning may be used by traumatized children and adolescents. Early intervention, if well conceived and implemented, could prevent later problems and obviate the need for more extensive and costly remediation later in life.

Early intervention programs target individuals who have directly experienced a traumatic event as well as their family members and associates. The following section describes early intervention methods for adolescents and children over the age of 11, preschool children, and family members.

Diffusing and Critical Incident Stress Debriefing

Situational crises may result in the loss of possessions, jobs, significant others, home and community, status, bodily integrity (Raphael, 1986), and school activities and events. Actual loss or the threat of a loss following an event can result in psychological trauma. Left untreated, posttraumatic stress disorder can result. Critical incident stress debriefing (CISD) and diffusing are interventions that attempt to prevent the onset of posttraumatic stress disorder (Everly & Mitchell, 1992; Mitchell, 1988, November). They were developed for individuals who have been exposed to a traumatic event as part of their job, such as emergency workers. More recently, CISD has been applied to individuals who have experienced some trauma as a group (Bergmann & Queen, 1986; Flannery, Fulton, Tausch, & DeLoffi, 1991; Mitchell & Bray, 1990, cited in Wollman, 1993) and has been adapted for use with groups of children who have experienced a traumatic event (Toubiana, Milgram, Strich, & Edelstein, 1988).

Like other crisis intervention techniques, CISD and diffusing include group education about psychological responses to trauma and techniques for coping with stress (Wollman, 1993). These interventions are conducted by a mental health professional and two peers—that is, individuals who are emergency personnel but who were not involved in the event. It differs from other crisis interventions in that CISD and diffusing are used only with individuals who have shared a catastrophic life event outside typical experience and that would be distressing to most individuals. Consequently, the members of the group may be acquainted with each other. In other groups, individuals will not have shared the event (and therefore, they probably would not be acquainted) and they would be selected based on the type of event they had experienced—for example, rape (Wollman, 1993).

The primary goal of debriefing and diffusing is to reduce the stress that has resulted from the trauma and quickly return those individuals who have experienced the event to their previous level of functioning (Mitchell, 1988, November). In addition, the methods allow for the identification and referral of those individuals who may need additional help after the completion of the group intervention.

Crisis intervention techniques help individuals to better understand what has happened to them, to express their feelings, and to explore ways they have coped in the past. Diffusing and debriefing are similar except that diffusing is an intervention used immediately after the event (i.e., within 12 hours of the event) and is shorter in duration (approximately 30 to 60 minutes). If a diffusing is not conducted within 12 hours of the event, then the formal debriefing (CISD) is conducted anywhere from 3 days to 1 week after the event. Mitchell (1988, December) suggested that emergency personnel do not benefit from a formal debriefing "during the 24-hour period [following the event] because their reactions are too intense to absorb the important messages presented in a debriefing" (p. 45). However, if a diffusing is held first (primarily for support), individuals are more likely to share during the formal debriefing.

CISD consists of seven steps that occur during one session that lasts about three hours. Only individuals who participated in the event in some way are involved in the debriefing, except for the CISD team that consists of one mental health professional and two peers (i.e., emergency personnel who were not present at the event). Peers are included to give the team credibility, to ensure that participants feel understood, and to help the mental health professional better understand esoteric information. Prior to the debriefing, the CISD team learns as much as it can about the event through the careful reading of newspaper accounts, contacts with emergency personnel supervisors, and review of other media accounts.

At the beginning of the debriefing (the introductory phase), the mental health professional who facilitates the group introduces himself or herself, and then the peers introduce themselves. The facilitator then explains the debriefing process and issues of confidentiality. The facilitator might say, "The purpose of our meeting today is to allow each of you to talk about what happened. While I encourage you to participate, if you feel that you are not able to talk, that is OK." The facilitator then asks participants to describe what happened during the event. The facilitator might ask the participants, "Can you tell me what happened during the event?"

After this introduction, during the second phase (fact phase) only factual information is elicited. At this time, the facilitator asks, "What were you doing during the event?" and "What did you see?" Such questions allow the participants to get a complete picture of what was going on during the event.

During the third phase (thought phase), the facilitator urges the participants to describe their reactions to the group. Now the facilitator may ask, "What were you thinking about during the event?" or "What were your first thoughts as the event was happening?" Such questions help the group members begin to focus on the disturbing elements of the event.

During the fourth stage (the reaction phase), in order to shift the focus of the group from their thoughts about the event to their feelings about the event, the facilitator asks, "What part of the event was most traumatic for you?" or "What was the worst thing about the event for you?"

Phase 5 (symptom phase) focuses on the identification of individuals' symptoms of distress, and there is movement back to a cognitive level. Now the facilitator asks, "What kinds of things happened to you in the day after the event? What kinds of things are happening now? What kinds of symptoms are you experiencing?"

In phase 6 (teaching phase), the facilitator normalizes the participants' stress responses and educates the participants about coping and stress management. Individuals are encouraged to eat well and to maintain their exercise routine or begin such a routine if they do not have one. They are encouraged not to use substances to numb their feelings, and it is explained that such use may actually prolong their stress symptoms. Individuals are encouraged to talk about the event and spend time with friends, family, and other supportive people rather than withdraw or isolate themselves from others.

During the last phase (reentry phase), ambiguities are clarified and termination begins. The facilitator summarizes feelings and reactions expressed during the session, normalizes feelings, and emphasizes good coping skills. Further, the facilitator acknowledges that people may not feel normal for some time. Finally, handouts about expected symptoms and stress reduction methods are distributed.

Once the formal debriefing is completed, some social time is set aside for individuals to ask questions they may not have felt comfortable asking in the group and to make appropriate referrals for high-risk individuals. Finally, within 24 hours after the debriefing, if necessary, follow-up calls are made to high-risk individuals (Everly & Mitchell, 1992; Heidel, 1993).

The CISD model, designed for use with emergency personnel, can be applied to groups of older children and adolescents who have experienced a traumatic event. Further, the model can also be applied to individuals who are related or closely acquainted with those children or adolescents directly exposed to the stressor.

The concept of CISD and diffusing has been applied by several authors. Toubiana, Milgram, Strich, and Edelstein (1988) described a school bus accident in Israel in which 19 children and 3 adults were killed. Blom (1986) described an intervention used when a truck crane struck a pedestrian overpass adjacent to an elementary school. Six boys fell 15 feet to the pavement below while over 100 children watched from the playground. Thompson (1993) described a similar group intervention, which she termed posttraumatic loss debriefing, to be used for survivors of sudden loss such as school children who experience the sudden death of a classmate or teacher due to accident, suicide, or murder.

There is some evidence to support the efficacy of these interventions. For example, nine months after the intervention described by Toubiana and associates, a questionnaire that was administered to all the children indicated a marked decline in symptoms and no incidence of delayed stress. Research conducted seven months after the intervention described by Blom (1986) indicated that most individuals who responded to a follow-up questionnaire were functioning well. It should be noted that only 21 percent of the participants responded.

These interventions contained many of the same components as CISD, such as the distribution of accurate information about the event and normal responses to such a trauma, facilitation of emotions, short-term treatment focused on a return to pre-trauma functioning, education about coping strategies, and, finally, referral of individuals who required additional help. In addition, mental health professionals, teachers, school administrators, parents, community leaders, nurses, and physicians were included in the planning and/or the implementation of the program. However, these interventions differed from CISD in that they did not all occur immediately after the event, nor did they occur during one long session.

The CISD model was designed specifically for those who directly experienced the trauma; however, when working with children and adolescents, it is imperative that significant individuals in their social and family networks also be targeted. For this reason, group interventions for the prevention of PTSD in children and adolescents who directly experience a trauma, and other individuals who are affected, will be described. Responsibilities of professionals who can assist in the prevention effort will be detailed along with optimal times when these interventions should be delivered. The intervention described later is within a school context but it can be applied to other settings.

A preexisting policy statement on how to handle emergencies is critical to the timely implementation of crisis interventions. A written policy statement can help ensure that all necessary actions occur in a timely fashion, particularly because it may be difficult to think clearly in the aftermath of a tragedy. The following instructions may provide the basis for a policy and an intervention.

School administrators, after learning of a traumatic event, should share accurate information with teachers, parents, and students as soon as possible to prevent rumors from starting. Accurate information tends to decrease anxiety, whereas misinformation may foster undue stress. Each specific situation would dictate how this information would best be communicated. For example, making an announcement over the public address system or sharing information with teachers who in turn share the information with students may be appropriate in some situations. In other situations, the head administrator may wish to address the school community.

Administrators should excuse teachers and students who become too upset to remain in class and send them to mental health staff such as school social workers, counselors, or psychologists. When the school staff is not equipped to handle a crisis of this magnitude, experts should be immediately consulted. In some cases, it may be necessary to consult with police, physicians, nurses, and psychiatrists and other mental health workers. Administrators should instruct teachers to encourage all children to come to school to participate in individual and group activities to deal with the event, provide consultation for teachers on how to deal with their students, and praise teachers for keeping calm.

Mental health workers (e.g., social workers, psychologists, counselors) also play an important role. They can educate teachers on how to work with students and on how to manage their own anxiety. Relaxation exercises and stress management techniques may be helpful in this regard. They can remind teachers that it is important to take care of themselves if they are to be effective when working with their students.

These professionals should be prepared to provide support and empathy to parents of children involved in the traumatic event. Arrangements should be made for friends and relatives to join parents at the school so they can provide support while waiting for information about the children.

Mental health professionals and medical personnel should assess the presence of preexisting psychological or medical problems in children and adolescents who directly experienced the traumatic event as well as their family members in order to identify individuals who may need additional help. This can be done through interviewing of teachers, administrators, parents, and siblings. Appropriate referrals should be made.

Psychologists can enter the classrooms to conduct activities that encourage expression of feelings about the event such as discussion, writing poems, and drawing pictures. In addition, psychologists can hold individual sessions with students who are unable to remain in class.

During the week after the traumatic event, the nature of the intervention shifts. Individuals are now capable of assimilating information that would have been difficult for them to comprehend immediately after the event. More accurate assessments of psychological health can be made at this time.

Administrators and mental health workers can dispense information about the psychological impact of disasters to parents, teachers, and children not directly involved with the trauma during large group meetings. Such information would include stress symptoms, typical emotional reactions, and recommendations for coping, such as information about diet and exercise. The large group can then be divided into small group discussions where the mental health workers can promote the sharing of feelings and experiences and can help families cope with the event. At the same time, mental health professionals can continue to assess psychological functioning of individuals and family members in order to arrange for additional treatment where needed.

Those individuals who were directly involved in the traumatic event may be debriefed following the CISD model. Mental health workers could facilitate the group with teachers and children serving as peer co-facilitators. In the day after the debriefing, mental health workers should contact participants to ascertain their psychological state and offer additional group sessions or individual therapy if necessary.

An Early Intervention Play Group

One example of a play group for children (all under age 11) was described by Hofmann and Rogers (1991). Following the Santa Cruz earthquake, a play group in a shelter was conducted to (1) diffuse fear, (2) facilitate the expression of feelings about the trauma, and (3) give parents a break from children. The group was conducted by community volunteers and therapists from various mental health disciplines. Prior to the group, mental health professionals assessed children and families and one group therapist assessed the children's group needs.

Large tables were used to corner off a space that held the groups but allowed parents to watch. Some children were sensitive about being separated from their parents and this physical arrangement helped. The tables also served to divide the area from the chaotic setting of the shelter, and thus give some physical structure to the play area different from the rest of the shelter.

Further structure and focus were provided by establishing several ground rules (e.g., no drawing on another child's drawing without permission, no hitting or yelling, no talking while another child is talking, and asking permission to go to the bathroom) and having the children engage in specific tasks. For example, at first, each child was asked to introduce himself or herself. Children were asked their age, where they lived, and how they got to the shelter. Then the children were instructed to tell the story about what happened to them during the earthquake. They were asked where they were when the quake occurred and what their experience was. Since the children only responded briefly and mostly with visual images, the therapists asked them to draw pictures of what happened to them during the earthquake. The drawings helped to elicit more details of the event, so it was suggested that books of the pictures be made. In this way, the pictures had some continuity. When children felt that their pictures did not adequately portray what they intended, words were added to the pictures.

In order to shift more toward group play, children then shared the books with the group. This sharing led to discussion among the children, and, as a result, they began to bond. The Scribble Game further promoted group play and bonding. In this game, children sat in a circle. Each child was instructed to scribble on a large piece of paper and then pass the page to the next child in the circle in a counterclockwise fashion. Each successive child added his or her scribble to the page. Two categories of scribbles emerged: everyday images, such as fish or birds, and scary images such as monsters.

During the activities, the children were encouraged by the therapist to talk about their drawings through the use of *What?* and *How?* questions. For example, children were asked, "What is that?" or "How did that get into the picture?" *Why?* questions were avoided because they are difficult for children to answer.

Each group lasted for several hours at a time and were held morning, afternoon, and early evening, for the first four days the children were in the shelter. New children who joined the group were asked to draw pictures of their experience before they joined with the other children. Children who were very fearful were grouped together under the guidance of one therapist. They were involved with very structured activities such as board games where they could gain mastery over another or express their aggression in a nonpunitive way. Children who displayed less anxiety formed another group and played with other materials such as dolls, clay, cars, and so on.

By drawing their experiences and making their books, children were able to observe the other children at play while retaining control by being able to focus on their own books. Therapists were able to gather additional information about the children from their drawings. It is believed that unconscious feelings were projected on the paper during the Scribble Game, with scarier images suggesting a greater impact of the trauma on the child. Rules for behavior, the physical environment that was created, and the questioning techniques provided structure for the children. Children who displayed more anxiety gained some control by engaging in structured activities that allowed them to have mastery over others or express their aggression in a productive way.

Family Crisis Intervention

Family crisis intervention, similar to critical incident stress diffusing and debriefing, is preventive in nature, is implemented soon after the traumatic event occurs, and targets family members of traumatized individuals. Identification of dysfunctional family behavior that may interfere with the family's ability to cope with the crisis is the major focus of the intervention. Harris (1991) suggested a five-stage crisis intervention model to be used with traumatized families. The five stages include (1) making psychological contact, (2) exploring the dimensions of the problem, (3) examining possible solutions, (4) taking concrete action, and (5) follow-up.

Trust is built and rapport between family members and the therapist is established during the first stage of the intervention. The therapist encourages family members to express their feelings, concerns, and information about the event and their family. Similar to the beginning stage of individual or group therapy, the therapist gathers information about feelings and thoughts the family members have, corrects any misinformation that is voiced, and diffuses potentially explosive situations. If needed, the therapist may introduce stress management techniques.

During the second stage, each family member is encouraged to share his or her thoughts regarding the event, the victim, and the family's reaction to the event and the victim. Further, members are encouraged to identify and share what they see as the family's strengths and weaknesses in coping with the event and its aftermath. Therapists intervene during this stage by correcting misinformation and/or misperceptions and by facilitating positive communication among family members. Under stress, some family members could blame each other or the victim; and the therapist, however, would discourage this type of dysfunctional reaction. Helping the family members to pull together so they can more adequately support the victim is a critical focus of this second stage.

In the third stage, with the permission of the victim, the therapist explains the symptoms the victim has experienced and how he or she has been coping with the event. Further, the therapist explains how the family can help the victim recover. By matching the victim's problems with the identified strengths of specific family members as well as the family as a unit, the therapist aids the family in identifying ways it can promote the adjustment of the victim.

During the fourth stage, the therapist helps the family to identify systematic barriers and to brainstorm possible solutions. The therapist encourages the family members to confront and solve the problems experienced by both the victim and the family as a consequence of the event. Successful intervention during this stage empowers the family and enables them to see that they have the ability to help, as well as increases the credibility of the therapist. As problem-solving techniques are implemented by family members with the victim, the intervention comes to a close.

Plans for follow-up are then made at the discretion of the therapist or at the request of family. Such interventions could include continuing family therapy, referral to another therapist for continued family work, individual work for those family members who request additional therapy, support groups, or group therapy for individual family members. Additional sessions at the request of the family on an as-needed basis can also be encouraged by the therapist.

GROUP INTERVENTIONS FOR CHILDREN WITH PTSD AND ACUTE STRESS DISORDER

No generally accepted research study has established the superiority of any one group technique or treatment for trauma in children. Play therapy, psychodrama, psychotherapy, cognitive and behavioral therapies, and medication have all been used. Some therapists believe a combination of several of these is ideal (Webb, 1991). Play therapy and cognitive-behavioral techniques are especially conducive for use in groups.

Play Therapy with Children

Play therapy can be used within a group context to help children who have experienced a trauma express their feelings when it is too difficult for them to verbalize the horror of their experience. Many play therapy materials are available, including, but not limited to, craft materials (e.g., crayons, clay, etc.), dolls and puppets, storytelling, board games, sand, and photographs. Play therapy tends to be appropriate through age 11, although, according to Terr (1985), traumatized children will engage in play at older ages than nontraumatized children. The play of traumatized children is also less complex and imaginative than the play of nontraumatized children. When youngsters can talk about their anxieties, they are encouraged to do so, but play can serve as an escape when verbalizing becomes too frightening.

When traumatized children first begin therapy, it is critical to explain to them the reasons for their involvement in the group intervention. Judicious language should be used—that is, language that is easily understood by the children. The co-facilitators might say, "You may think you are responsible for what happened and that is why you are being sent to therapy every week, but the truth is you are not responsible and sometimes terrible things happen to children over which they have no control." The therapists can explain that they are there to talk to children about their feelings about what happened. It is often helpful to point out what other children have done in the playroom. Knowing that other children came for the same purpose and did fun things like playing with puppets, dolls, clay, and so on, helps to reduce anxiety. The presence of other children also helps to reduce anxiety and gives children an opportunity to develop socialization skills. During the first session, the children are encouraged to explore the playroom and play with any toys or materials they choose while the co-therapists observe. The therapists can show very young children pictures of different feelings to help them identify how they feel.

Some therapists believe that nondirective play that serves purely as a catharsis for the traumatized child could be healing. Many children are able to resolve their conflicts by repeatedly working and reworking their experiences through play. For example, a 9-year-old boy who experienced a near fatal car accident may play with a toy car and pretend that the car is crashing. During the play, he has control because he is the one manipulating the car. Also, by playing at crashing cars, he gets the opportunity to manage the feelings that this play awakens in him.

Playing itself can be healing without the therapist making explicit connections to the relationship between the play and the child's life, but when play is repetitive and/or secretive, it may not relieve the child's tensions. In this case, the therapist must help the child make connections between the play and the traumatic event. Terr (1983) recommended that children verbalize as well as play, and the therapist should direct the child to reenact the trauma using play materials that would help in the reenactment. Trauma-appropriate materials should be available; for example, in a play therapy group with seriously ill hospitalized children, there would be doctor and nurse dolls and puppets, stethoscopes, play needles, empty medicine bottles, and the like. Children may reenact the events as they happened or can be asked to act out a modified version of the event. The modified version could include the child telling the doctor all the things he or she did not like about what transpired. A doll can do the talking and share all the child's worries and fears. The therapist can make reassuring comments such as, "Of course the doll would feel this way, I think anybody would."

Art activities enable children to express their feelings about the trauma. The therapist can help the children talk about their pictures or other art projects. Children who are angry can act out aggressive feelings by pounding on modeling clay. Clay or play-doh (for younger children) are useful materials for play therapy groups because children can work individually or on a group project (Webb, 1991). One game that James (1989) calls the Clay Bombs Exercise is popular. The child first draws a picture of the person responsible for the accident, or the disease, or the particular natural disaster such as the flood. Then the child and therapist create about 10 "bombs" out of clay (balls should be smaller than a baseball). The child is instructed to stand across the room and yell out something to the picture as she or he throws the "bomb." The therapist can go first and say "I hate you for what you did to *Child's Name.*" The therapist and child take turns throwing the bombs, but the therapist has to be clear that it is the child's feelings that are being facilitated and not his or her own. James (1989) cautions that if the object of the bombs is a person for whom the child also has positive feelings or a psychological bond, these positive feelings should be fully explored before this exercise is conducted. This exercise is easily adapted for use in groups, with the children taking turns throwing the bombs. Children have the advantage of expressing their own feelings directly, but also listening to feelings of other group members. For an extensive list of techniques and exercises to use with traumatized children, see James (1989).

In children who suffered physical effects from traumas such as sexual or physical abuse, invasive medical procedures, fire, and so on, a sense of body integrity may need to be restored. Children who are burned or scarred or who felt their bodies betrayed them may no longer think of their bodies as friends. Movement, music, body awareness exercises, self-calming techniques, and sensorimotor play can be incorporated into group sessions. For example, children who are inhibited in their movements after the trauma can be helped by listening to music and expressing what they experience in the music; walking on tiptoe, jumping, spinning, skipping, acting like wind-up toy soldiers or ballerinas. These exercises could reduce muscle tension, improve coordination, and, since they're done in a group, decrease feelings of isolation (James, 1989).

It may also be helpful for therapists to recommend to parents that structured physical activity outside of sessions may help compensate for the very negative physical effect of the trauma in the child's memory. If children can successfully engage in athletic activities, they may be proud of their bodies and have an increased sense of control. Gymnastics, ballet, and karate are particularly good choices (James, 1989).

Further, children need to know that physical reactions such as urinating in one's pants, shaking, vomiting, and crying are commonly experienced by people when confronted by a very frightening event, and even adults such as police officers, fire fighters, teachers, and others. could have these responses. By explaining that these are normal responses, children begin to feel as if they are back in control and again may be more accepting of their bodies.

Groups for traumatized children should be time limited and end when the initial objectives have been met. It should be clearly explained to the children and their parents that future events may restimulate reactions to the initial trauma; for example, a significant loss, a developmental transition, or severe weather, may bring up old feelings. The group participants should understand that this is a typical reaction, and the reexperiencing of these feelings does not mean that the initial group intervention was not successful. Parents and children should be educated about the kinds of feelings to

ment difficulties. In addition, culturally different children, children of undocumented immigrant families, and youths from politically repressive and war-torn countries are at greater risk for emotional and behavioral problems (McIntyre, 1996). In contrast, culturally diverse children and their families tend to underutilize traditional mental health services or terminate therapy early, primarily due to a perception of these services as being incompatible with their culturally based assumptions about mental health issues and healing methods (Atkinson, Morten, & Sue, 1993). The unique needs presented by these children require interventions that are culturally appropriate or that consider the cultural and linguistic aspects of their experience.

Group intervention emerges as an effective treatment modality for culturally diverse children at risk because it is consistent with what happens to be a common aspect of their cultures—namely, a collective orientation and an emphasis on family and group values (Corey, 1995; Padilla, 1981; Shipp, 1983). The extended family and group members traditionally serve as support systems for these children and adolescents. For example, several American Indian group practices—including "sweat lodge" ceremonies for spiritual purification, "talking circle" as a time of sharing, "rites of passage" to signify critical changes, and other communal and seasonal celebrations (e.g. harvesting, planting)—have therapeutic value (Dufrene, & Coleman, 1992; Garrett & Osborne, 1995; Ho, 1992). When unemployment, the loss of extended family ties, migration or relocation to urban areas, intergenerational conflicts related to cultural clashes, and other stressful situations occur, there is a disruption of the family and group as resources, often leading to increased vulnerability to emotional problems (Huang & Ying, 1989; Powell, Yamamoto, Romero, & Morales, 1983). Group interventions, which emphasize cooperation, cohesiveness, and interdependence among group members, in much the same way that families and cultural group practices do, may provide an opportunity for children to deal with a number of these stress-related issues (Ho, 1992).

Although group interventions may be potentially effective and have cultural relevance, it is a modality often neglected in the mental health literature and in the provision of services, particularly in terms of its implementation with culturally and linguistically diverse children (Gibbs & Huang, 1989). There are issues related to the implementation of therapeutic groups that need to be explored, such as group composition, group goals, the role of the facilitator, and the group process itself. Cultural, class, and linguistic factors that serve as barriers in the counseling process need to be addressed (Sue & Sue, 1990). For example, differences in concepts of time and adherence to schedules, extent of emotional expressiveness, and styles of verbal and nonverbal communication are relevant factors to consider (Acosta & Cristo, 1981). Moreover, while recognizing the modal characteristics and heritage of each cultural group, it is important to be aware of differences across and within groups. In general, group interventions with culturally and linguistically diverse children should be developed and implemented based on a multicultural perspective.

Multicultural counseling provides a framework for understanding the role that culture has in influencing human behavior and interactions and, consequently, how culture can affect the counseling process (Pedersen, 1991). More specifically, a multicultural perspective offers a conceptual and empirically based structure for meeting the unique mental health needs presented by persons and families of culturally diverse backgrounds (Merta, 1995; Sue & Sue, 1990). Although traditionally, most multicultural counseling work has involved adults, attention has recently been given to the counseling needs of culturally diverse children and adolescents in the school setting (Baruth & Manning, 1991; Esquivel & Keitel, 1990; Lee, 1982; Pedersen & Carey, 1994; Thomason, 1995). Innovative group intervention techniques designed to be culturally sensitive or consistent with a multicultural model are also being implemented with culturally diverse children and adolescents (Canino & Spurlock, 1994; Costantino, Malgady, & Rogler, 1986; Ho, 1992). The primary purpose of multicultural group interventions is to remediate and prevent, in a culturally appropriate manner, the stressors and resulting adjustment problems experienced by culturally and linguistically diverse children and adolescents.

ETIOLOGICAL FACTORS

Stress in children has been related to mental health disorders (Garmezy & Rutter, 1983). Although there are a number of at-risk children who are resilient, epidemiological studies suggest that many children of immigrant and culturally diverse background are exposed to a number of stressors that make them potentially more vulnerable to problems in their psychological, social, behavioral, and academic functioning (Gibbs & Huang, 1989; Phinney & Rotheram, 1987). The effects of (1) poverty, (2) relocation or migration, (3) the acculturation process, and (4) school/community adjustment are among the most salient sources of stress for these children (Canino & Spurlock, 1994; Esquivel & Keitel, 1990; Kopala, Esquivel, & Baptiste, 1994).

Poverty

The socioeconomic status of families of immigrant children varies. Chinese Americans as a group have the highest median family income among ethnic minority groups. Chinese parents who come from Hong Kong and Taiwan, for example, tend to be highly educated and affluent (Chen, 1981). However, a substantial number of Chinese immigrant children come from the countryside and rural areas of China and have parents who are not well educated and have very limited skills and financial resources (Ho, 1992). A restricted economic situation can surround other immigrant groups, particularly those who come as refugees or without documentation, as well as for cultural groups within the United States (e.g., African American, American Indians) who have a history of slavery, conquest, or colonization (Ogbu, 1987).

The research literature documents the relation that exists between poverty and long-term problems in areas such as education, housing conditions, health care (e.g., prenatal, pediatric), and nutrition (Trueba, 1989). Moreover, poor urban areas are exposed to greater incidence of violence, crime, and substance abuse (Berlin, 1986; LaFombroise & Low, 1989). The negative effects of such conditions are compounded for children of racially diverse backgrounds, who have to deal with issues of discrimination and prejudice and may at times have limited resources for dealing with stressors that affect the quality of their life (Gibbs & Huang, 1989; Ponterotto & Pedersen, 1993).

RELOCATION AND MIGRATION

Relocation and migration have been identified as stressors for children (Garmezy & Rutter, 1983). Relocation is a special problem for American Indian children whose families have been moving in increasing numbers from reservations to urban areas seeking to find employment, although often unsuccessfully. The process of moving to even more uncertain situations has resulted in the disruption of families, the loss of extended family ties, and discontinuity with cultural traditions and social networks (LaFombroise & Low, 1989). The lack of a "cultural fit" between these families and the community in which they live is often a major source of stress (Boyce & Boyce, 1983).

The process of migration in itself does not necessarily result in negative psychological outcomes; in fact, immigrant children as a group do not show higher incidences of disorder than their native-born peers (Aronowitz, 1984). There are, however, circumstances associated with migration that may result in adjustment problems, manifested most frequently in behavioral disorders in children, and sex-role and identity conflicts in adolescents (Ho, 1992). Some factors that may affect the process of migration are the extent of loss and separation, the age and developmental stage of the child at the time of the move, the reasons for leaving, and the conditions in the native country. The above experiences are considered to be some of the "preflight" aspects of migration (Gonsalves, 1992).

Leaving the place of birth and encountering interpersonal losses, including the severance of extended family ties and friendships, can be difficult for families, especially when the move is permanent and conditions prevent them from visiting or returning. Very young children experience the loss indirectly, as it is transmitted to them by the reaction and psychological state (e.g., anxiety) of their parents, whereas older children and adolescents experience the loss more directly and as more significant (Ho, 1992; Huang & Ying, 1989). The migration process may be particularly difficult for adolescents because their developmental stage involves significant change and readjustment in almost every aspect of their lives. Tasks related to independence, peer relationships, and identity formation, which are central to adolescence, may be particularly aggravated by migration factors (Baruth & Manning, 1991).

Refugee children and families who experienced war in their country are particularly at risk of adjustment problems (Gonsalves, 1992). Kopala, Esquivel, and Susuki (1992) reviewed studies on the impact that war has on the psychological status of children. Many children are resilient and able to cope with exposure to war-related events (Saigh, 1985). However, children who have had more traumatic experiences, including, for example, the loss of their parents, are at high risk for academic problems, depression, low self-esteem, and somatic symptoms (Glasgow & Gouse, 1995; Ronstrom, 1989). The problem can be exacerbated for these children when they migrate because the supportive group bond formed in times of crisis and war is lost. The flight itself may be traumatic, depending on the conditions under which it occurs (Gonsalves, 1992). The resettlement period, at first, may be characterized by a repression of feelings, particularly for children from cultures that discourage the open expression of emotions or for whom having psychological reactions is considered shameful. Huang (1989) cites studies of Vietnamese children and adolescents who were in refugee camps. The initial denial and masked depression manifested by these youths in somatic symptoms, surfaced later in the form of acting out behaviors, depression and anxiety.

Acculturation

Acculturation has been defined as a process of change that occurs with the contact or interaction between two or more cultural systems. This process is not viewed as assimilation or blind adoption of the cultural patterns of the dominant culture, but rather as a continuum of adjustment to the requirements of the host country, while retaining those aspects of the native culture that are also viable and adaptive (Atkinson, Morten, & Sue, 1993). Although acculturation is not necessarily stressful in itself, many children and parents undergoing acculturation may have limited support systems or coping strategies to successfully mediate the task requirements involved in successive acculturative experiences.

The stages of acculturation have not been identified specifically for children, but have been described in terms of adult and family experiences. The process may involve at first adapting to physical aspects of the environment, such as climate, geography, and living. For example, families who come from rural or suburban areas have difficulty adapting to city life or to urban environments. Parents in these families may become overprotective and do not allow their children to socialize or play with other children in the community, thereby restricting an integral aspect of the acculturation process (De Vos, 1980). In turn, families who settle in rural areas may be more isolated from support systems.

During early stages of acculturation, children learn the language and the cultural roles of the dominant culture and begin to acculturate at a faster rate than their parents do. They are usually asked to act as mediators between the parent and the host country in such roles as interpreters or business transactors. This "parentified role" may be perceived as either negative or positive, depending on how the added responsibility is perceived by the child or adolescent (Gibbs & Huang, 1989).

At later stages in the migration history, greater intercultural and intergenerational conflicts emerge in families. Conflictual situations develop for adolescents and their parents when discrepancies occur between the traditional cultural values of the family and those from the host country (Chu & Sue, 1984; Esquivel & Keitel, 1990). For adolescent Latino girls, for example, the traditional female roles may make the normal identity development more difficult (Hardy-Fanta & Montana, 1982).

Although children from families who rigidify traditional values may face difficulties (Huang & Ying, 1989), it is important to recognize the positive effects of traditional cultural values, even those that appear as negative from a European American standard. For example, recent research suggests that the "authoritarian" parenting style assumed by Asian mothers is associated with a "training" ideology of support, nurturance, and direct guidance that is linked to academic success in children (Chao, 1994).

It appears that critical tasks in the acculturation process include the resolution of cultural conflicts and the integration of adaptive aspects of native and dominant cultures. Biculturalism has been associated with heightened mental health needs, whereas the development of a racial ethnic identity has been associated with positive outcomes in children and adolescents (Cross, 1987; Helms, 1994; Phinney, Lochner, & Murphy, 1990). A greater propensity toward negative adjustment tends to occur when an individual has a diffused racial/ethnic identity (Ponterotto & Pedersen, 1993).

School Adjustment

Difficulties experienced in the school setting are another major source of stress for immigrant and culturally diverse children. School adjustment difficulties have been related to factors such as poverty, violence, family conflicts, low self-esteem, and attitudes toward school and achievement. However, to a great extent, the school-related stress experienced by these children may be attributed to cultural discrepancies between the home and the school setting, and the limited understanding regarding their learning, behavioral and language characteristics.

Learning Characteristics

The generally low achievement level of children from culturally diverse groups has been reported as a source of stress associated with low self-esteem, dropping out of school, and special classroom placement. Chodzinski (1994) cites Casas's observation that the lower achievement of Latino students (e.g., Mexican Americans) begins early and increases as other stressors and socioeducational barriers increment. Although Chinese American children are stereotyped as the "model minority" and as being brighter and more conscientious, some recent immigrants have more limited English skills, present greater academic difficulties, and may be a greater disappointment to teachers (Huang & Ying, 1989). Academic stress is further experienced by immigrant youths who have had limited exposure to formal learning experiences in their native land and may have limited literacy skills in their own language.

Another area of difficulty relates to the limited attention given to the mismatch that occurs between a child's culturally based cognitive or learning style and expectations in the school learning environment, which can result in behavioral or emotional problems (McIntyre, 1996). American Indian children, for example, tend to show learning patterns that do not require verbal methods of instruction. The most critical aspects of their learning experience are attained through keen observation and nonverbal communication (Ho, 1992). An emphasis in our schools on verbal methods fosters the view in these children that the content of instruction is irrelevant or incongruous.

Behavioral Characteristics

Behavioral differences based on cultural values result in misunderstanding in the school setting. Behaviors that are taught and encouraged by the family based on cultural values may be discrepant with behavioral expectancies in the school culture (McIntyre, 1996). For example, Asian American children's tendency toward quiet behavior and deference to adults may be viewed as lacking initiative. For these children, verbal participation in the classroom may need to be solicited. Similarly, the general emphasis placed by American Indian culture on sharing and sensitivity in interpersonal relationships may be incompatible with a competitive attitude often expected in our schools.

Language Characteristics

Language differences may become barriers in interaction in the school setting. Non/verbal communication may vary in terms of personal and interpersonal space (proxemics) and physical movement (kinesics). *Proxemics* involves the physical distance that is perceived as safe and comfortable in social interaction, whereas *kinesics* includes bodily posture, gestures, facial expressions and eye contact. Cultures vary in the way social space is used and physical movement is expressed (Sue & Sue, 1990). For example, Latino children tend to be physically expressive, to stand close, and to touch one another while talking (Baruth & Manning, 1991), which are inconsistent with school practices that emphasize staying in line, keeping a distance, sitting up straight, and other prescriptions against kinesthetic expression. African American children, compared to children from other cultural backgrounds, tend to make less eye contact when spoken to, but more eye contact when speaking. Teachers may view children communicating in this manner as inattentive when spoken to and angry (intense staring) when speaking (Sue & Sue, 1990).

RESEARCH

Research on multicultural counseling has been described as limited in number, restricted mostly to laboratory experiments (or analogous situations) using quantitative methodologies, and lacking in a culturally meaningful theoretical or structural framework (Ponterotto & Casas, 1991). Likewise, a review of research on the implementation of group interventions with culturally diverse groups reveals at least three limitations: (1) an adult emphasis, (2) limited scope, and (3) lack of follow-up on outcomes. For example, group work with Latinos has mostly involved Puerto Rican and Mexican American adults in mental health settings; short-term interventions; use of dominant language (Spanish); and a focus on issues of cultural, marital, and family conflicts, and on stress-related symptoms.

The literature does provide, however, evidence of some attempts to implement and validate group interventions with culturally diverse children and youths. Most groups that are designed for culturally diverse children and youths focus on their unique characteristics and problems as well as critical aspects of their culture. Ethnotherapy, a technique developed to enhance ethnic identity with African Americans, was used by Klein (1976) in an encounter group with Jewish adolescents to increase pride in their heritage. More recent approaches to enhance ethnic identity development are described by Ponterotto and Pederson (1993). Groups have also been implemented to develop bicultural adjustment (e.g., Costantino et al., 1986), transitioning skills (Cardenas, Taylor, & Adelman, 1993; Glasgow & Gouse, 1995), and intercultural communication in school settings (e.g., Bilides, 1991; Cardenas et al., 1993). Canino and Spurlock (1994) suggest the clinical application of a stress theory model in which stressors, strengths, and vulnerabilities are assessed by a multidisciplinary team and considered in the development of a prevention or intervention plan.

Adolescent concerns have also been explored. A group intervention developed by Hardy-Fanta and Montana (1982) was successful in dealing with intergenerational conflicts and resulting behavioral problems of Latino adolescent girls whose parents had emigrated from Puerto Rico and other Caribbean and Central American Islands. The group intervention was conceptualized in terms of cultural conflicts experienced by Latino female adolescents around issues of identity formation, sexuality, and sex-role expectations. Fukuyama and Coleman (1992) developed an assertiveness training group, using a cognitive-behavioral approach, for Asian-Pacific American undergraduate students to deal with cultural issues affecting their self-expression. Two elements of Hardy-Fontana and Montana's group intervention, a time-limited basis and sensitivity to the interaction between developmental and cultural issues, were viewed as critical for the success of this group intervention.

Other group interventions have focused on the development of self-esteem in small group situations. Locke (1989) suggested group activities appropriate for African American children that foster self-esteem and validate cultural identity. Mitchum (1989) discussed pilot group interventions for Native American children that enhance group rather than individual self-esteem because these children do not respond to being praised or singled out as unique. Group interventions to deal with behavioral adjustment problems include Allen and Majidi-Abi's (1989) group for African American girls, using a combination of didactic and more active role-playing and problem-solving activities and Bobo's (1985) social skills training group for adolescents to address the harmful effects of alcohol abuse.

A common aspect of effective group interventions is that they are culturally sensitive (Inclan & Herron, 1989). Costantino and colleagues 1986) define culturally sensitive techniques as those which in some way validate, incorporate, or adapt relevant cultural aspects. One type of culturally sensitive approach makes counseling more accessible to the group in question—for example, by offering the services in the school or a community setting or by including bilingual interpreters and paraprofessionals (Acosta & Cristo, 1981). Another culturally sensitive modification to group interventions involves incorporating elements of the culture. For example, in a group situation, cultural aspects may be "mirrored" by including as leader an authoritative paternal figure and as co-leader a more nurturant maternal figure. Group interventions may also be modified by including indigeneous resources, parents, or extended family members (Kopala et al., 1994; Paniagua, 1994).

Although a culture-specific intervention should take cultural factors into account, it need not perpetuate those aspects of the culture that may be resulting in adjustment problems. For example, in some instances, the goal may be to develop greater assertiveness in adolescents who encounter interpersonal difficulties as a result of their submissive behaviors, even if these have a cultural basis. In a third approach, the therapeutic modality is in itself culture specific or based directly on elements of the culture. For example, cultural games or stories may be used as the therapeutic modality. A more detailed description of school-based and community-based interventions follows, which should illustrate the development and implementation of culturally sensitive group intervention techniques.

DESCRIPTION OF TECHNIQUES

Cuento Therapy

Cuento therapy is a culturally sensitive group intervention developed for Puerto Rican children (Costantino et al., 1986), but it may be modified for children of other culturally diverse backgrounds. This technique was targeted for at-risk children in elementary grades. *Cuento*, which means "story" in Spanish, is a therapeutic modality based on the storytelling technique. In this group intervention, the technique was adapted to incorporate the cultural values of the targeted children to increase their attention and identification with the content and characters and therefore facilitate the effectiveness of the intended outcome—namely, their bicultural adjustment. The rationale for introducing a cultural component was that the behavioral difficulties exhibited by culturally diverse children are often related to cultural discrepancies between the home and the school.

The cuentos consist of 40 folkstories representing values, feelings, and behaviors of Puerto Rican culture. The stories were selected by experts of Puerto Rican background from a more comprehensive list of stories from Puerto Rican folklore. Cuento therapy is considered to be a culturally sensitive technique in that it extracts from cultural elements (i.e., folktales) of the group in question (i.e., Puerto Rican) and uses these as the treatment modality. Two versions or modalities were developed from these folktales. One modality incorporated the cultural values and settings reflected in the original folktales. In the other modality, settings and themes were modified according to U.S. or mainstream culture. For example, a plantation was changed to an urban playground, and mango trees changed to apple trees. The U.S. version was intended to help children develop the values, roles, and skills of mainstream American culture as a way to facilitate their cultural adaptation and their ability to deal with stressful situations related to bicultural conflicts (Costantino et al., 1986).

Cuento therapy is implemented by the formation of 4 to 5 mother/child group dyads that are led by bilingual and bicultural psychotherapists. Mothers were chosen because in Puerto Rican culture the mother is the primary agent to teach and model social and moral behaviors. Therapists and mothers recount the cuentos bilingually, discuss the main themes, and role-play these with the children. Videotapes of these dramatizations are then played back by the leader and discussed with the group in terms of adaptive behaviors and consequences (Costantino et al., 1986). Cuento therapy was implemented in school classrooms after school hours, but it may also be implemented in mental health clinics and other community settings.

The therapeutic effectiveness of cuento therapy as a culturally sensitive group technique was validated, although no significant differences were found between the original and the bicultural modalities. Both versions of cuento therapy had greater effects on increased social judgment and long-term anxiety reduction than traditional art/play therapy and no treatment. The cultural modalities showed somewhat greater negative effects on aggressive behavior than the no-treatment control group, possibly because many of the stories contained themes involving adult punishment of the child protagonist's aggressive behavior. The authors suggest that in the replication of this technique, the modeling of aggression in the stories needs to be reduced (Malgady, Rogler, & Costantino, 1990). Cuento therapy may be a particularly appropriate group intervention for children whose culture follows an oral tradition or in which legends and folkstories are central for the transmission of spiritual, social, and moral values, as is the case in American Indian groups.

Hero-Heroine Modeling

The hero-heroine modeling intervention for adolescents is a similar group technique to cuento therapy, but uses biographical stories about prominent historical figures in the culture to foster ethnic identity, self-concept, and adaptive coping behavior for dealing with stressors of urban living (Malgady et al., 1990). Based on social learning theory, the achievement oriented and positively regarded adult figures serve as role models for adolescents. Like cuento therapy, this technique is culturally sensitive in that it incorporates features from the culture into the intervention.

The implementation of this technique consists of small groups of three to five students that may be led by a therapist, counselor, or school psychologist. Each group reads aloud a portion of the biography. The group leaders then analyze selected anecdotes taken from the biography and identify stressors and positive behaviors reflecting ethnic pride and adaptive coping strategies. Subsequent to this activity, the leaders ask questions focusing on the role model's conflicts, feelings, and ways of coping with obstacles. Group members are asked to offer their own personal experiences about similar incidents, as a means of facilitating their identification with the model. The leaders then reinforce those self-related behaviors that are consistent with the model's adaptive behaviors and encourage the group to explore and think of alternative adaptive responses. The group may also be involved in role-playing activities or skits elaborating the stories. At the end of the session, the group leaders summarize the problem situations and highlight adaptive coping strategies and facilitate the generation of options for maladaptive resolutions (Malgady et al., 1990).

This group technique was developed and researched with 90 Puerto Rican adolescents in eighth and ninth grades presenting behavior problems, which were not considered to be clinically significant. The rationale was that many of these youths come from single-family homes, where the father is absent, and they need role models for dealing with problems related to poverty, discrimination, and other stressors of urban life (Malgady et al., 1990).

Unitas

Unitas is a community-based group intervention developed primarily for children living in poor urban areas. It was founded by Edward Eismann in the South Bronx area of New York City, in an attempt to bring a culturally sensitive outreach program to Latino and African American children in that community, given the limited impact made by more traditional mental health services. Based on a combination of community, family systems, and interpersonal and psychosocial perspectives, the purpose of Unitas is to provide a surrogate family that serves as a supportive and healing community for these children. Many of the children who are referred formally by schools have or are at risk of developing behavioral and adjustment problems (i.e., excessive shyness or aggression). Most of these children have been neglected or abused and need a stable family structure. Other children are recruited by word of mouth or by the children in Unitas (Farber & Rogler, 1981).

Unitas uses the resources of indigeneous nonprofessionals in the form of local older adolescents and college students and some parishioners from neighborhood churches who are trained to form part of the surrogate or symbolic family. Each symbolic family consists of 10 to 15 youngsters between the ages of 5 and 14 and of adolescents who serve as their surrogate parents, aunts, or uncles. These families interact and meet informally on rooftops, schools, streets, clubhouses or tenement apartments in their own neighborhood (Procidano & Glenwick, 1985).

During the school year, the symbolic families meet one day a week in the gymnasium of a local parochial school to be involved in a large "circle meeting" mostly led by Eismann. These meetings usually involve group problem solving and discussion of ideas, role-playing, and the sharing of feelings and concerns. The topics discussed include how to deal with loss, how to make friends, or how to be kind to others. The circle ends with a summary, by the leader, of the themes that emerged and an exchange of hugs among the members of the families. All the children also participate in recreational activities and some are involved in individual therapy sessions. During the summer, the children have recreational programs in the street, which is closed off for that purpose, and meet late in the afternoon for circle discussions (Procidano & Glenwick, 1985).

Unitas has been evaluated as effective in providing the children with a strong support system, a mediator of stress that was also linked to problem solving in the study (Procidano & Glenwick, 1985). Exact replication of this approach is not viewed as feasable, given that the history of Unitas is unique and many of its features may be specific to the setting. However, Eismann (1982) provides a manual with a series of training procedures for replicating some aspects of the Unitas program in other settings. These components include group leadership skills, group communication and conflict resolution techniques, group dynamics, and large group discussion skills of a therapeutic community.

DISCUSSION OF GROUP TECHNIQUES

A sound theoretical framework for conceptualizing the research literature on multicultural or culturally sensitive group interventions is missing (Hurdle, 1991) and specific prescriptions may not be appropriate, given the diversity that exists among and within subgroups. However, the most commonly used and effective techniques for culturally diverse children are those based on ecological, social problem solving; social learning theories; and other models that are consistent with a reciprocal, systemic, and collectivist orientation (Brown, 1984). Moreover, group approaches with culturally diverse children and adolescents should include a developmental perspective, to address characteristic patterns of development based on different childrearing practices and the interaction between cultural and developmental issues (Baruth & Manning, 1991).

For example, the period of adolescence may be defined differently across cultures and the expectations for sex-role behaviors in adolescence may likewise vary. Since there are variations between and within cultural groups, including different levels of acculturation, a creative and flexible attitude is necessary for determining which approach provides the best fit for the group in question (Ho, 1992). For example, fantasy play and role-playing techniques, as well as more action-oriented arts, crafts, and recreational activities (Allen & Majdi-Abi, 1989; Lewis & Ford, 1991), have been equally effective with economically disadvantaged children. In general, the underlying factor that distinguishes effective group techniques with culturally diverse children and youths is that cultural relevance must become an integral and pervasive aspect of group development and implementation.

ROLE OF THE GROUP FACILITATOR

The ethnicity or race of counselors working with children from culturally diverse backgrounds has been examined. According to a "cultural compatibility" perspective, the counselor should be matched to the client(s) on the basis of ethnic/racial similarity (Paniagua, 1994). In general, children tend to resist therapists who are of different backgrounds than themselves, although they assign lower status to those who belong to ethnic minority groups (Ho, 1992). The group facilitator's bilingual proficiency is seen as important with linguistically diverse children (Delgado, 1983) and, obviously, more so for those who are limited English proficient or incipient bilingual. However, consistent with a "universalistic" perspective, the leader's multicultural counseling sensitivity and competence are more important characteristics than ethnic group membership (Baruth & Manning, 1991; Esquivel & Keitel, 1990; Paniagua, 1994).

Multicultural competence may be attained through successive stages of development involving awareness, knowledge, and expertise (Pedersen, 1988). The group facilitator attains cultural *awareness* by recognizing his or her own culturally based values, expectations, and behaviors and how these influence personal perceptions of and biases toward other cultures. In essence, the facilitator develops a multicultural perspective toward the counseling process.

The group facilitator also needs to have *knowledge* of the specific cultural characteristics of the children in the group and how these cultural patterns affect relationships and group interaction. For example, children from Asian American, American Indian, and Latino cultures tend to view and accord great hierarchical status to the leader as an authority figure (Chu & Sue, 1984). In response to these perceptions, the facilitator needs to play a more directive and active role at first and gradually model or set the tone for greater interaction and problem solving among the group members (Ho, 1992). In attaining knowledge about the culture, it may be helpful for the group facilitator to work with a "cultural consultant" or a person in the community (e.g. priest, social worker) who is familiar with the specific culture (Acosta & Cristo, 1981). These persons may also serve as mediators or co-leaders who provide culturally relevant information to strengthen the effectiveness of the intervention. Facilitators should also be sensitive to, and have knowledge of, ethical issues pertaining to group work with culturally diverse populations (Corey, 1995).

The development of *expertise* by the group facilitator requires a combination of clinical training and experience (Esquivel & Keitel, 1990). Expertise refers to the actual application of a multicultural perspective to practice and, in this case, to the development and implementation of a culturally sensitive group intervention. For example, an important skill required of the facilitator is the ability to ascertain the interrelation among age, developmental, personality, family, and cultural factors (e.g., migration history, level of acculturation) for the group in question and to adapt the intervention on the basis of these relations. This skill also requires flexibility on the part of the group facilitator. Ramirez (1991) emphasizes the need for counselors to have personality "flex" or the ability to match the cultural and cognitive styles of the client(s). For some groups, the facilitator needs to adopt a more formal style or extend the therapeutic role to that of adviser, educator, and advocate (Esquivel & Keitel, 1990; Inclan & Herron, 1989), whereas for other groups, a more personalized approach works better. The group facilitator is aware of cultural differences without stereotyping or losing sight of commonalities in human experience and the child's own uniqueness. The development of multicultural identity and expertise is considered to be a life-long personal and professional process (Sabnani, Ponterotto, & Borodovsky, 1991).

GROUP PROCESS

Group Selection

When forming a group, the facilitator should determine for whom a group intervention is appropriate and when it may be counterindicated by factors such as limited motivation to interact, lack of verbal facility, poor impulse control, or excessive need for attention (Ho, 1992). Although these criteria seem to apply across cultural groups, there are more culture-specific situations for ruling out group participation. For example, newly arrived immigrant children may feel intimidated by the type of group that requires direct expression of feelings and may, at first, benefit more from didactic or educational approaches (Ho, 1992).

Group Preparation

Sometimes the group facilitator or leader needs to develop greater familiarity and closeness with potential group members before presenting to them the idea of a group (Delgado, 1983). This focus is particularly important for Latino children, who tend to personalize experiences more and value personal closeness in most interactions. For example, Eismann initiated the concept of Unitas after spending a great deal of time interacting and learning from the children in their own setting (Farber & Rogler, 1981). It is also important to explore the expectations, verbal skills and styles of nonverbal communication, and emotional expression of the potential group members. These initial observations may help to define better the structure and nature of the group process. For example, children who show strength in verbal interpersonal styles will fit well in a group situation (Griggs & Dunn, 1989). However, children who rely more on nonverbal communication will be quiet and let others go first. Some children may not want to be singled out or praised and are hesitant to talk about their strengths in public based on cultural values (Baruth & Manning, 1991). It is important for the group facilitator to accommodate these differences in interactive style before initiating or encouraging change. For example, there may be a need to explore the attitudes of children or adolescents whose culture emphasizes deference before initiating or at the initial stages of an assertiveness training group.

Group Composition

Ho (1992) recommends a small group size of approximately six to eight members. However, the size may be determined partly by the characteristics of the group in question. Children and adolescents from cultures that emphasize verbal reserve may feel more comfortable in somewhat larger groups where they feel less pressured for direct or frequent interaction. Younger children tend to prefer same-sex groups because they feel less intimidated; adolescents, however, may do well with mixed-gender groups if the discussion of sexuality is not a cultural issue.

Heterogeneous grouping, or those groups that are mixed on the basis of race and ethnicity, seem to work well with children and adolescents, although they are counterproductive for adults because the latter tend to have difficulties dealing with issues of race and prejudice (Davis, 1984). Shipp (1983) found in a review of the literature that racially mixed groups are effective with African American adolescents with delinquency problems and high school and college students. Multicultual groups help to enhance diverse styles of interaction and problem-solving approaches and facilitate intercultural communication skills (Bilides, 1991; Gibbs, 1989, Ho, 1992; Inclan & Herron, 1989; Smith, Boulton, & Cowie, 1993). Homogeneous groups work better in situations in which the aim is to foster cultural awareness and ethnic identity.

Group Purpose and Goals

The major group intervention goals addressed in the literature include facilitating the acculturation process, reducing stress, enhancing coping skills and problem-solving strategies, fostering ethnic identity and biculturalism, and dealing with school-related behavioral and academic difficulties. Whenever possible, the goals should be clear and short term, because long-term goals may seem as impractical or inconsistent with the time concepts of some culturally diverse groups. In addition, group members should have input in the choice of goals (Ho, 1992).

Group Interaction

Group interaction is affected by cultural differences in verbal and emotional expression. It is important for some cultural groups to keep family problems confidential or to avoid disclosure of personal issues. Greater sensitivity to confrontation may be another critical factor to recognize in group interaction. Delgado (1983) suggests that the group leader not focus on pathology and emphasize the issue of confidentiality to facilitate greater participation and interaction.

Time and Termination

Some studies propose that group interventions with culturally diverse children and adolescents be brief in nature to deal successfully with the immediacy of the nature of problems experienced and to be consistent with an emphasis on present-time orientation (Delgado, 1983; Hardy-Fanta & Montana, 1982). Brief approaches may be extended with more long-term group interventions for those children who show an ability to benefit and readiness to continue with this type of intervention. The length and termination of the group intervention may be further affected by cultural factors involving the relative importance given to relationships versus task accomplishment. Leong (1992) suggests guidelines to prevent early termination of a group, at least by Asian American clients. In contrast, it may be more difficult to terminate the group with children who personalize relationships to a greater extent or who may have experienced traumatic losses in the past. Therefore, length of time and termination need to be considered in light of these issues (Ho, 1992).

LIMITATIONS

The major limitation of culturally sensitive group interventions with culturally diverse children, which may be seen more as a challenge, is the need to adapt to the complex variations involved across and within cultural groups, as well as to unique individual differences. Recognition, for example, that not all children from Asian American groups will be quiet in a group situation or will avoid eye contact and that personality, acculturation level, and other relevant factors may be more salient, should occur. While awareness of cultural differences should occur, it is also critical to avoid stereotyping. The complexity of a multicultural perspective in group interventions is accentuated by the limited research in this area and the lack of a more precise guiding framework.

SUGGESTIONS FOR RESEARCH AND PRACTICE

There is a need for more epidemiological studies and research on factors that affect the mental health of immigrant and culturally diverse children. It is important to study the unique stressors experienced by these children. Canino and Spurlock (1994) discuss the culture-specific manifestations of clinical syndromes in children and point to the lack of research in this area. However, research should not only focus on the problems and disorders that these children experience but also on their strengths and positive qualities. A promising approach in this area is the study of "invulnerable" children or of those children who are at risk of emotional disorders and yet are resilient and able to cope with stressful situations as a result of protective factors (Garmezy & Rutter, 1983). Greater understanding of effective coping skills (Anthony, 1987) and of the developmental process in attaining a bicultural identity (Phinney & Rotheram, 1987) will enhance the preventive components of group approaches.

In general, there is a need to develop, implement, and evaluate culturally sensitive group interventions in school and community settings. Ponterotto and Casas (1991) suggest that counseling interventions with ethnically and racially diverse groups be studied in their naturalistic context and include qualitative methods. This approach implies that the effectiveness of the group intervention is assessed not only in terms of outcomes but also as a real and formative process. Qualitative methodologies include naturalistic observations, interviewing techniques, and ethnographic studies. These approaches allow for a more holistic and in-depth perspective from which to explore the qualitative aspects and subtle nuances of cultural variations, often missed by purely quantitative studies. For example, there may not be differences in levels of social competence between a culturally diverse group and a more acculturated group. However, the ways in which social interactions are expressed may vary significantly between the two groups. These qualitative differences are of clinical significance in understanding group process and have implications for the implementation of group interventions with culturally diverse populations.

The ongoing group process may be studied in terms of the role of the facilitator, interactions among members, sources of conflict, and other group dynamics related to cultural factors. A microanalysis of videotaped sessions focusing on such areas as nonverbal behaviors, from both clinical and cultural perspectives, may provide useful feedback to the group facilitator. The developmental progression of the group may also be assessed based on multicultural stage models (Dillard, 1985; Casas & Vasquez, 1989). Quantitative and behavioral empirical methods may be supplemented with the preceding qualitative approaches to determine the relative effectiveness of different culturally sensitive techniques, or to compare different types of groups (e.g., culturally heterogeneous vs. homogeneous), or to assess other outcome data.

REFERENCES

Acosta, F. A., & Cristo, M. H. (1981). Development of a bilingual interpreter program: An alternative model for Spanish-speaking services. *Professional Psychology, 12,* 474–482.

Allen, L. R., & Majidi-Abi, S. (1989). Black American children. In J. T. Gibbs & L. N. Huang (Eds.), *Children of color: Psychological interventions with minority youth* (pp. 148–178). San Francisco: Jossey Bass.

Anthony, E. J. (1987). Risk, vulnerability, and resilience: An overview. In E. J. Anthony & B. J. Cohler (Eds.), *The invulnerable child* (pp. 3–48). New York: Guilford.

Aronowitz, M. (1984). The social and emotional adjustment of immigrant children: A review of the literature. *International Migration Review, 18,* 237–257.

Atkinson, D. R., Morten, G., & Sue, D. W. (1993). *Counseling American minorities:* A cross-cultural *perspective* (4th ed.). Dubuque, IA: Brown & Benchmark.

Baruth, L. G., & Manning, M. L. (1991). *Multicultural counseling and psychotherapy: A lifespan perspective.* New York: Merrill Macmillan.

Berlin, I. (1986). Psychopathology and its antecedents among American Indian Adolescents. *Advances in Clinical Psychology, 9,* 125–152.

Bilides, D. G. (1991). Race, color, ethnicity, and class:Issues of biculturalism in school-based adolescent counseling groups. *Social Work with Groups, 13,* 43–58.

Bobo, J. K. (1985). Preventing drug abuse among American Indian adolescents. In L. D. Gilchrest & S. P. Schinke (Eds.), *Preventing social and health problems through life skills training.* School of Social Work, University of Washington.

Boyce, W. T., & Boyce, J. C. (1983). Acculturation and changes in health among Navajo school students. *Social Sciences and Medicine, 17,* 219–226.

Bradley, S., & Skloman, L. (1975). Elective mutism in immigrant families. *Journal of the American Academy of Child Psychiatry, 14,* 510–514.

Brown, J. A. (1984). Group work with low-income black youths. *Social Work with Groups, 7*(3), 111–124.

Burke, A. W. (1984). The outcome of the multi-racial small group experience: Summary report. *International Journal of Social Psychiatry, 30,* 96–101.

Canino, I. A., & Spurlock, J. (1994). *Culturally diverse children and adolescents: Assessment, diagnosis, and treatment.* New York: Guilford.

Cardenas, J., Taylor, L., & Adelman, H. S. (1993). Transition support for immigrant students. *Journal of Multicultural Counseling and Development, 21*(4), 203–210.

Carrasquillo, A. (1995). *Language minority students in the mainstream classroom.* Clevedon, England: Multilingual Matters.

Casas, J. M., & Vasquez, M. J. T. (1989). Counseling Hispanics. In P. B. Pedersen, W. Lonner, J. Draguns, & J. E. Trimble (Eds.), *Counseling across cultures* (3rd ed., pp. 153–176). Honolulu: University of Hawaii Press.

Chao, R. K. (1994). Beyond parental control and authoritarian parenting style: Understanding Chinese parenting through the cultural notion of training. *Child Development, 65,* 111–119.

Chen, J. (1981). *The Chinese of America: From the beginnings to the present.* New York: Harper and Row.

Chin, J. L. (1983). Diagnostic considerations in working with Asian Americans. *American Journal of Orthopsychiatry, 53,* 100–109.

Chodzinski, R. T. (1994). Dropout intervention and prevention: Strategies for counselors. In P. Pedersen & J. C. Carey (Eds.), *Multiculututal counseling in schools: A practical handbook.* Boston: Allyn and Bacon.

Chu, J., & Sue, S. (1984). Asian/Pacific-Americans and group practice. In L. E. Davus (Ed.), *Ethnicity in social group work practice* (pp. 23–35). New York: Haworth Press.

Coladarci, T. (1983). High school dropout among Native Americans. *Journal of American Indian Education, 23,* 215–225.

Collier, C., & Hoover, J. (1987). *Cognitive learning strategies for minority handicapped students.* Lindale, TX: Hamilton.

Corey, G. (1995). *Theory and practice of group counseling.* Pacific Grove, CA: Brooks/Cole.

Costantino, G., Malgady, R. G., & Rogler, L. H. (1986). Cuento therapy: A culturally sensitive modality for Puerto Rican children. *Journal of Consulting and Clinical Psychology, 54*(5), 639–645.

Cross, W. E. (1987). A two-factor theory of black identity: Implications for the study of identity development in minority children. In J. S. Phinney & M. J. Rotheram (Eds.), *Children's ethnic socialization:*

Pluralism and development (pp. 117–133). Newbury Park, CA: Sage.

Cummins, J. (1984). *Bilingualism and special education: Issues in assessment and pedagogy*. Clevedon, Avon, England: Multilingual Matters.

Davis, L. E. (1984). Essential components of group work with Black Americans. *Social Work with Groups, 7(3),* 97–109.

De Vos, G. (1980). Ethnic adaptation and minority status. *Journal of Cross-Cultural Psychology, 11*(1), 101–124.

Delgado, M. (1983). Hispanics and psychotherapeutic groups. *International Journal of Group Psychotherapy, 33*(4), 507–520.

Delgado, M., & Humm-Delgado, D. (1984). Hispanics and group work: A review of the literature. *Social Work with Groups, 7*(3), 85–96.

Dillard, J. M. (1985). *Multicultural counseling* (pp. 285–316). Chicago: Nelson-Hall.

Dufrene, P. M., & Coleman, V. D. (1992). Counseling Native Americans: Guidelines for group process. Special Isssue: Group counseling with multicultural populations. *Journal for Specialists in Group Work, 17*(4), 229–234.

Dunn, R., Gemake, J., Jalali, F., & Zenhausern (1990). Cross-cultural differences in learning styles of elementary-age students from four ethnic backgrounds. *Journal of Multicultural Counseling and Development, 18*(2), 68–93.

Edwards, E. D., & Edwards, M. E. (1984). Group work practice with American Indians. *Social Work with Groups, 7*(3), 7–21.

Eismann, E. P. (1982). *Unitas: Building healing communities for children: A developmental and training manual*. Monograph No. 8. Bronx, NY: Hispanic Research Center, Fordham University.

Engel, M. (1984). Children and war. *Peabody Journal of Education, 61*(3), 71–90.

Esquivel, G. B., & Keitel, M. A. (1990). Counseling immigrant children in the schools. *Elementary school guidance and counseling, 24*(3), 213–221.

Farber, A., & Rogler, L. H. (1981). *Unitas: Hispanic and Black children in a healing community*. Monograph No. 6. Bronx, NY: Hispanic Research Center, Fordham University.

Fukuyama, M. A., & Coleman, M. C. (1992). A model for bicultural assertiveness training with Asian-Pacific American college students: A pilot study. *The Journal for Specialists in Group Work, 17*(4), 210–217.

Garmezy, N., & Rutter, M. (Eds.). (1983). *Stress, coping and development in children*. New York: McGraw-Hill.

Garrett, M. W., & Osborne, W. L. (1995). The Native American Sweat Lodge as metaphor for group work. *Journal for Specialists in Group Work, 20*(1), 33–39.

Gibbs, J. T. (1989). Black American adolescents. In J. T. Gibbs & L. Huang (Eds.), *Children of color: Psychological interventions with minority youth* (pp. 179–223). San Francisco: Jossey Bass.

Gibbs, J. T., & Huang, L. N. (1989). A conceptual framework for assessing and treating minority youth. In J. T. Gibbs & L. Huang (Eds.), *Children of color: Psychological interventions with minority youth* (pp. 1–29). San Francisco: Jossey-Bass.

Glasgow, G. F., & Gouse, S. J. (1995). Theme of rejection and abandonment in group work with Caribbean adolescents. *Social Work with Groups, 17*(4), 3–27.

Gonzalves, C. J. (1992). Psychological stages of the refugee process: A model for therapeutic interventions. *Professional Psychology: Research and Practice, 23*(5), 382–389.

Griggs, S. A., & Dunn, R. (1989). *Journal of Multicultural Counseling and Development, 17*(4), 146–155.

Hardy-Fanta, C., & Montana, P. (1982). The Hispanic female adolescent: A group therapy model. *International Journal of Group Psychotherapy, 32*(3), 351–366.

Helms, J. E. (1994). Racial identity in the school environment. In P. B. Pedersen & J. Carey (Eds.), *Multicultural counseling in schools*. Boston: Allyn and Bacon.

Herring, R. D. (1989). Counseling Native American children: Implications for elementary school counselors. *Elementary School Guidance and Counseling, 23,* 272–281.

Hisama, T. (1980). Minority group children and adolescent and behavior disorders: The case of Asian American children. *Behavior Disorders, 5*, 186–196.

Ho, M. K. (1992). *Minority children and adolescents in therapy*. Newbury Park, CA: Sage.

Hopstock, P., & Buccaro, B. (1993). *A review of analysis of estimates of LEP student population*. Arlington, VA: Development Associates.

Huang, L. N. (1989). Southeast Asian refugee children and adolescents. In J. T. Gibbs & L. N. Huang (Eds.), *Children of color: Psychological interventions with minority youth* (pp. 278–321). San Francisco: Jossey-Bass.

Huang, L. N., & Ying, Y. W. (1989). Chinese American children and adolescents. In J. T. Gibbs & L. N. Huang (Eds.), *Children of color: Psychological interventions with minority youth* (pp. 30–66). San Francisco: Jossey Bass.

Hurdle, D. E. (1991). The ethnic group experience. *Social Work with Groups, 13,* 59–69.

Inclan, J. E., & Herron, D. G. (1989). Puerto Rican adolescents. In J. T. Gibbs & L. N. Huang (Eds.), *Children of color: Psychological interventions with minority youth* (pp. 251–277). San Francisco: Jossey-Bass.

Klein, J. (1976). *Jewish identity and self-esteem*. New York: Institute on Pluralism and Group Identity.

Kopala, M., Esquivel, G. B., & Baptiste, L. (1994). Counseling approaches for immigrant children: Facilitating the acculturative process. *The School Counselor, 41*(5), 352–359.

Kopala, M., Esquivel, G. B., & Susuki, L. (1992). *The impact of war on children: Identification and intervention*. Ninth Annual Teachers College Winter Roundtable on Cross-Cultural Counseling and Psychotherapy, Columbia University, NY.

LaFromboise, T. D., & Low, K. G. (1989). American Indian children and adolescents. In J. T. Gibbs & L. N. Huang (Eds.), *Children of color: Psychological interventions with minority youth* (pp. 114–147). San Francisco: Jossey-Bass.

Lee C. C. (1982). The school counselor and the Black child: Critical roles and practices. *Journal of Non-White Concerns, 10,* 94–101.

Leong, F. F. T. L. (1992). Guidelines for minimizing premature termination among Asian American clients in group counseling. *Journal for Specialists in Group Work, 17*(4), 218–228.

Lewis, E. A., & Ford, B. (1991). The network utilization project: Incorporating traditional strengths of African-American families into group work practice. *Social Work with Groups, 13,* 7–21.

Locke, D. C. (1989). Fostering the self-esteem of African-American children. *Elementary School Guidance and Counseling, 23,* 254–259.

Malgady, R. G., Rogler, L. H., & Costantino, G. (1990). Hero/heroine modeling for Puerto Rican adolescents: A preventive mental health intervention. *Journal of Consulting and Clinical Psychology, 58*(4), 469–474.

Malgady, R. G., Rogler, L. H., & Costantino, G. (1990). Culturally sensitive psychotherapy for Puerto Rican children and adolescents: A program of treatment outcome research. *Journal of Consulting and Clinical Psychology, 58*(6), 704–712.

McGoldrick, P., Pearce, J. K., & Giordano, J. (Eds.). (1982). *Ethnicity and family therapy*. Cambridge, MA: Harvard University Press.

McIntyre, T. (1996). Guidelines for providing appropriate services to culturally diverse students with emotional and/or behavioral disorders. *Behavior Disorders, 21,* 137–144.

Merta, R. J. (1995). Group work: Multicultural perspectives. In J. G. Ponterotto, J. M. Casas, L. A. Susuki, & C. M. Alexander (Eds.), *Handbook of multicultural counseling*. Thousand Oaks, CA: Sage.

Mitchum, N. T. (1989). Increasing self-esteem in Native-American children. *Elementary School Guidance and Counseling, 23,* 265–271.

National Center for Education Statistics. (1993). *The condition of education*. Washington DC: Government Printing Office.

Ogbu, J. U. (1987). Variability in minority school performance: A problem in search of an explanation. *Anthropology and Education Quarterly, 18,* 312–334.

Ortiz, A. A., & Yates, J. R. (1983). Incidents of exceptionalities among Hispanics: Implications for manpower planning. *NABE Journal, 7*(3), 41–53.

Padilla, A. M. (1980). *Acculturation: Theory, models and some new findings*. Boulder, CO: Westview.

Padilla, A. M. (1981). Pluralistic counseling and psychotherapy for Hispanic Americans. In A. J. Marsella & P. B. Pedersen (Eds.), *Cross-cultural counseling and psychotherapy* (pp. 195–227). Elmsford, NY: Pergamon.

Paniagua, F. A. (1994). *Assessing and treating culturally diverse clients: A practical guide*. Thousand Oaks, CA: Sage.

Pedersen, P. (Ed.). (1988). *A handbook for developing multicultural awareness*. Alexandria, VA: American Association for Counseling and Development.

Pedersen, P. (1991). Multiculturalism as a generic approach to counseling. *Journal of Counseling and Development, 70*(1), 6–12.

Pedersen, P., & Carey, J. C. (1994). *Multicultural counseling in schools: A practical handbook*. Boston: Allyn and Bacon.

Phinney, J. S., Lochner, B. T., & Murphy, R. (1990). Ethnic identity development and psychological adjustment in adolescence. In A. R. Stiffman, & L. E. Davis (Eds.), *Ethnic issues in adolescent mental health* (pp. 53–72). Newbury Park, CA: Sage.

Phinney, J. S., & Rotheram, M. J. (1987). *Children's ethnic socialization: Pluralism and Development*. Newbury Park, CA: Sage.

Ponterotto, J. G., & Casas, J. M. (1991). *Handbook of racial/ethnic minority counseling research*. Springfield, IL: Charles C. Thomas.

Ponterotto, J. G., & Pedersen, P. B. (1993). *Preventing prejudice: A guide for counselors and educators*. Newbury Park, CA: Sage.

Powell, G. J., Yamamoto, J., Romero, A., & Morales, A. (Eds.) (1983). *The psychosocial development of minority group children*. New York: Brunner/Mazel.

Procidano, M. E., & Glenwick, D. S. (1985). *Unitas: Evaluating a preventive program for Hispanic and Black youth.* Monograph No. 13. Bronx, NY: Hispanic Research Center, Fordham University.

Ramirez, III, M. (1991). *Psychotherapy and* counseling *with minorities: A cognitive approach to individual differences*. Elmsford, NY: Pergamon.

Red Horse, Y. (1982). A cultural network model: Perspectives for adolescent services and paraprofessional training. In S. M. Manson (Ed.), *New directions in* prevention *among American Indian and Alaska Native communities* (pp. 173–185). Portland, OR: National Center for American Indian and Alaska Native Mental Health Research.

Ronstrom, A. (1989). Children in Central America: Victims of War. *Child Welfare, 68,* 145–153.

Rutter, M. (1983). Stress, coping and development: Some issues and some questions. In N. Garmezy & M. Rutter (Eds.), *Stress, coping and development in children*. New York: McGraw-Hill.

Sabnani, H. B., Ponterotto, J. G., & Borodovsky L. G. (1991). White racial identity development and cross-cultural counselor training: A stage model. *The Counseling Psychologist, 19*(1), 76–102.

Saigh, P. (1985). Adolescent anxiety following varying degrees of war exposure. *Journal of Clinical-Child Psychology, 14*(4), 311–314.

Sato, C. J. (1982). Ethnic styles in the classroom. In M. Hines & W. Rutherford (Eds.), *Selected papers from the annual conference of teachers of English to speakers of other language*. (ERIC Document Reproduction Services No. ED 223 979)

Shipp, P. L. (1983). Counseling Blacks: A group approach. *The Personnel and Guidance Journal,* 108–110.

Shuval, J. T. (1982). Migration and stress. In L. Goldberg & S. Breznitz (Eds.), *Handbook of stress: Theoretical and clinical aspects* (pp. 677–691). New York: The Free Press.

Sluzki, C. (1979). Migration and family conflict. *Family Process, 18*(4), 379–390.

Smilansky, S. (1982). The adjustment of elementary school children orphaned from their fathers. In C. D. Smith, P. K., Boulton, M. J., & Cowie, H. (1993). The impact of cooperative group work on ethnic relations in middle school. *School Psychology International, 14*(1), 21–42.

Spielberg, I. G. Sarason, & N. A. Milgram (Eds.), *Stress and anxiety* (Vol. 8). Washington DC: Hemisphere.

Sue, D. W., & Sue, D. (1990). *Counseling the culturally different: Theory and practice* (2nd ed.). New York: John Wiley & Sons.

Szapocznik, J., & Kurtines, W. (1980). Acculturation, biculturalism and adjustment among Cuban Americans. In A. Padilla (Ed.), *Acculturation: Theory models and some new findings* (pp. 139–159). Boulder, CO: Westview.

Thomason, T. C. (1995). Counseling Native American students. In C. L. Courtland (Ed.), *Counseling for diversity: A guide for school counselors and related professionals*. Boston: Allyn and Bacon.

Trueba, H. T. (1989). *Raising silent voices: Educating linguistic minorities for the 21st century*. New York: Newbury House.

CHAPTER 15

MULTIPLE FAMILY GROUP THERAPY

Cindy Carlson, UNIVERSITY OF TEXAS AT AUSTIN

In the contemporary milieu of dramatic change in the economic, social, and demographic structure of the nation, schools face unparalleled levels and severity of child and adolescent academic and mental health problems. Moreover, schools face these problems in this era of economic restraint with seriously limited resources. Multiple family group therapy (MFGT) was developed as a cost-effective treatment modality in response to a similar crisis of care for the severely mentally disturbed and their families, as resources for public inpatient treatment of this population were depleted. In short, MFGT was born of necessity; there were simply not enough therapists to go around (Benningfield, 1980). Both the clinical and cost advantages of the MFGT approach have begun to be recognized in outpatient treatment settings (O'Shea & Phelps, 1985), including schools (Dombalis & Erchul, 1987). This chapter will provide an overview of the MFGT approach to treatment, update previous reviews of this treatment method (i.e., Benningfield, 1980; Dombalis & Erchul, 1987; O'Shea & Phelps, 1985; Strelnick, 1977), and critically evaluate the applicability of this approach to the contemporary school setting.

O' Shea and Phelps (1985) have defined multiple family group therapy (MFGT) as

> *a deliberate, planful, psychosocial intervention with two or more families present in the same room with a trained therapist for all or most of the sessions. Each participating family should have two or more members that represent at least two generations in the family and are present for all or most of the sessions. Sessions should have an explicit focus on problems or concerns shared by all families in attendance. These focal problems should pertain directly or indirectly to cross-generational family interaction. Sessions should implicitly emphasize patterns in interfamilial interaction, as well as utilize actual or potential alliances among members of different families based on similarities of age, focal problem, or family role. (p. 573)*

Many multiple family therapy groups described in the literature do not meet this definition. Rather, there is a plethora of forms of MFGT that vary in terms of group membership, group focus, duration of treatment, open versus closed membership, as well as number and role of therapist/leaders. This diversity of settings and structures may be viewed as a pragmatic advantage of the treatment method. More specifically, MFGT is a method with considerable flexibility and adaptability. However, the failure to clarify the definition of MFGT has negatively affected the development of theory and research (O'Shea & Phelps, 1985).

HISTORICAL AND THEORETICAL BACKGROUND

Multiple family group therapy (MFGT) as a treatment method closely paralleled the development of family therapy. MFGT essentially combined emerging family therapy with established group therapy in both theory and practice (Benningfield, 1980). The primary impetus to the development of MFGT was observations across inpatient hospital settings that the quality of the patient's family relationships were a contributing factor in the course of their illness, combined with limited therapeutic resources to work with families (Benningfield, 1980). Thus, the perceived need to include families in patient treatment, combined with limited therapeutic resources for working with families, necessitated the development of a family-oriented therapeutic structure that would accommodate multiple families.

The pragmatic history of MFGT is captured clearly in the writing of its originator, H. P. Laqueur (1972). As noted by Laqueur, following the observation that patients returned from home visits in worse shape than they left, the hospital initiated family information sessions without the patients. These private meetings made the patients suspicious that the staff and families together were conspiring against them, so the hospital included the patients in the meetings. After the sheer numbers of persons attending the meetings became prohibitive, families were split up into small groups of family units. It was observed that not only was this expedient, but the interaction of several families seemed to produce faster behavioral change than did the treatment of individual families.

The unique history of MFGT as both a pragmatic solution to a presenting problem and a hybrid of existing group therapy practice with emerging family therapy has resulted in a therapeutic modality without a clear theoretical foundation. The merging of family systems theory with small group process theory has been articulated by Steinhauer (1987), and this theoretical integration may best approximate the theoretical base of MFGT. As noted by Steinhauer (1987), the study of family functioning has been approached from two distinct perspectives—that of the practicing family therapist, who viewed the family primarily from the perspective of general systems theory, and that of the social psychologist, who has studied family processes as they are similar to those governing ad hoc groups.

Working with the family as a small group, and by extension, conducting family group work, has its origins in the writing of John Bowlby, John Bell, Murray Bowen, and Robin Skynner (Steinhauer, 1987). Working with the family as a group originated in the work of John Bowlby, who published in 1949 an article describing the family as a group similar in dynamics to other structured groups. Bowlby introduced in this article the family concepts of homeostasis, scapegoating, triangulation, and individual symptoms as reflections of system pathology. Consistent with the psychoanalytic tradition, however, Bowlby recommended that the material generated in family group sessions be worked through in individual therapy.

John Bell was the first to apply small-group theory systematically to the natural group of the family. His treatment involved interviewing subgroups of the family in the presence of the larger family unit with the goal of creating new possibilities of action and communication. Murray Bowen considered family group therapy to be a good choice for inexperienced family therapists who might be more familiar with group therapy than family therapy techniques. Bowen, however, considered individual family therapy to be more powerful therapeutically in confronting pathological triangles and inadequate individual differentiation that he viewed to be at the root of severe family pathology. Robin Skynner provided the most developed approach to family group therapy—open systems group analytic family therapy (see Skynner, 1981). According to Skynner, the family can be viewed as representative of the following: (1) one subsystem within a network of larger and smaller systems; (2) an interface between the inner and outer worlds; and (3) an interface between the individual and the group. Thus, three levels are addressed in family group therapy: the intrapsychic, the intrapsychic-interpersonal interface, and the interpersonal subsystems.

The family as a small group functions as a problem-solving unit (Steinhauer, 1987). Problem solving requires clearly defined and allocated roles. Because roles are always reciprocal, families develop characteristic controlling mechanisms and leaders to regulate and accommodate change. Thus, intervention efforts targeted to the family as a small group tend to be problem-solving oriented with goals being the clarification of roles and the improvement of communication processes regarding roles and expectations.

The integration of group process theory with family systems theory poses significant theoretical challenges, as there are recognized distinctions between the family as a unit and an ad hoc group. First, the family is a kinship group consisting of at least some biologically related members that predisposes members toward biological similarity, as well as commitment, cohesion, and attachment. In addition, families contain at least two generations that guarantees differential power, roles, interests, and priorities among members. Also, families enter therapy with a shared past, present, and future, which both gives them a preexisting structure and equilibrium, but also greater affective intensity than is usually encountered in group therapy. Finally, whereas group therapy uses group process to change individuals, the goal of family therapy is to change the system. As noted by Steinhauer (1987), "In summary, then, general theories of group functioning can be applied to families but only by first considering the filtering or potentiating effects of the particular family's composition, common history, structure, and different motives" (pp. 81–82).

In summary, the early history and development of MFGT was strongly embedded in the psychoanalytically oriented group therapy tradition. However, as family systems theory emerged, systems conceptualizations were integrated with the more entrenched psychoanalytic group and individual therapy approach. The unique history of MFGT as a hybrid of group therapy and family therapy has resulted in little agreement regarding the essential and distinguishing features of MFGT. As noted by O'Shea and Phelps (1985), "Indeed, a consensus has yet to emerge as to whether the relative influence of group and family therapy components in MFT is or ought to be equal" (p. 567). Rather MFGT appears in as many different forms as there are forms of group therapy and schools of family therapy with no single school of therapy or theoretical framework as yet having established a clear proprietary right to MFGT. As such, MFGT may be viewed as being in an embryonic, preparadigmatic stage of development (O'Shea & Phelps, 1985).

CHARACTERISTICS OF MFGT

The primary defining feature of multiple family group therapy is that several families, or members from several families, meet together with a therapist/leader simultaneously. Beyond this defining characteristic, the therapeutic approach known as MFGT includes a variety of family groupings and considerable variation in duration and goals for treatment. MFGT has also been applied to diverse clinical and nonclinical populations across a variety of settings.

Confusion and ambiguity about the nature of multiple family group therapy is manifested most concretely in the nomenclature used to define this therapeutic modality (O'Shea & Phelps, 1985). The approach is variously termed MFT (multiple family therapy), MFGT (multiple family group therapy), MFG (multiple family group), and MFDG (multiple family discussion group), with the latter two abbreviations used to distinguish multiple family groups that are more consistent with psychoeducational discussion or support groups versus group therapy. The lack of consistency regarding designation of this therapeutic approach in not insignificant because how MFGT is denoted indicates whether one views and implements the approach as a variation of group therapy (MFGT), a variation of family therapy (MFT), or a supportive or psychoeducational, but not clinical, intervention (MFG, MFDG). In the following discussion, the term *MFGT* will customarily be used unless further differentiation is essential to the discussion.

Participants

The choice of participants in MFGT concerns multiple issues: (1) the types of families for whom MFGT is indicated, (2) which members of the nuclear or extended family should participate, and (3) how many families should participate. Each of these issues will be addressed respectively.

Multiple family therapy groups have been conducted with a considerable variety of identified patient problems. As noted in their review of the literature (O'Shea & Phelps, 1985), MFGT has most frequently been used as an adjunct to inpatient treatment of both psychotic and nonpsychotically disturbed adolescents and adults; it is also frequently used with the families of externalizing adolescents and with the families of drug abusers. There is evidence suggesting MFGT can be implemented successfully in outpatient settings with the families of preadolescent-aged children referred for a variety of problems, including social withdrawal, aggressiveness, and deterioration of academic performance (Hardcastle, 1977, cited in O'Shea & Phelps, 1985), as well as with the families of adolescents having cognitive disabilities as they negotiate the transition to adulthood (Parker, Hill, & Miller, 1987). Most recently, Gonzalez, Steinglass, and Reiss (1989) reported multiple family discussion groups (MFDG) have been successfully used with families facing any form of chronic illness among a family member.

Multiple family groups can be an especially useful therapeutic approach with low-income, urban, African American families with problems of alcoholism, adolescent acting-out, or life-cycle transition crises. In particular, MFGT is considered to be an effective treatment modality when the only available therapists are middle-class European Americans because it permits the change mechanism to be embedded more strongly within the families themselves than is possible in a traditional single-family therapy approach (Foley, 1982, cited in O'Shea & Phelps, 1985). Parker and associates (1987) found MFGT to be particularly appropriate for isolated families, families with rigid boundaries, and symbiotic families. These family types may all be viewed as having less permeable boundaries to direct therapeutic intervention. MFGT is considered to be contraindicated for chaotic families or actively psychotic family members, because being in touch with reality is important to participation (Parker et al., 1987). Laqueur (1972) also recommended that families with a vital secret that might lead to an explosive reaction be excluded from MFGT.

Although Laqueur (1972) recommended heterogeneous assignment of families on variables such as socioeconomic status, number of children, and other demographic factors, the majority of MFGT groups organize families based on some criteria of homogeneity related to the diagnosis or presenting problem of an identified patient family member. The criterion may be as broad as having a family member with a chronic illness or as narrow as having an adolescent substance abuser. Cassanso (1989a) also recommended homogeneity of age range of offspring within developmental stage as this permits the use of exercises appropriate to particular ages. Other clinicians/researchers arrive at the same conclusion regarding homogeneity by limiting their participating family members to those above age 12.

Although the label MFGT has been applied to therapeutic interventions that include only a single family member from multiple families, O'Shea and Phelps (1985) defined MFGT recently as requiring at least a two-generational family system, and this would appear to be the accepted standard of practice. It would also appear customary to include the identified patient, parents, and siblings in MFGT (e.g., Cassanso, 1989a, 1989b; Gonzalez et al., 1989; Parker et al., 1987). The inclusion of the identified patient in MFGT is viewed as particularly important, and provides a significant contrast between MFGT and support groups which often exclude the patient. Eliminating the identified patient from the MFGT is viewed as perpetuating or even amplifying the psychological distance and barriers that tend to exist between patients and other family members—barriers that may well serve as major impediments to successful coping (Gonzalez et al., 1989).

In a recent review of research, Cassanso (1989a) reported that the number of families included in MFGT ranged from 3 to 13. Most commonly, MFGT appears to be conducted with 4 to 6 families and with co-therapists conducting the session. Bowen (1972) found 4 families to be optimal, with 5 families too rushed to address each individual family's agenda.

In summary, MFGT, although historically quite varied in its structure, may currently be defined as an intervention applied to groups of four to six, two-generational family systems that include parents, siblings, and an identified patient. Efforts to provide some homogeneity of age range of identified patient and siblings may enhance group functioning and on-task behavior.

Treatment Goals

Because MFGT is most commonly used as an adjunct to individual treatment with a wide variety of identified patients and problems, treatment goals are similarly varied, reflecting the range of conditions. Overall, MFGT treatment goals tend to converge on the prevention of relapse and residual illness in the identified patient, and more recently to focus as well on facilitating the stress and coping of families with an identified patient family member. In no study reviewed was MFGT viewed as appropriate as the only treatment of genuine individual psychopathology.

Laqueur (1972) identified eight therapeutic goals for MFGT: (1) better functioning; (2) greater mutual liking and respect; (3) better acceptance of one another; (4) increased ability to enjoy day-to-day living; (5) greater capability for compassion, love, understanding, support, and cooperation among family members; (6) better insight and improved judgment; (7) greater openness to new information; and (8) more capable of building lasting and satisfying relationships with each other in the family and with the friends and environment. It should be noted that Laqueur's inpatient MFT groups typically lasted two to three years.

In contrast, the psycheducationally focused MFDGs, which are highly structured and limited to eight weekly sessions, have two main therapeutic goals (Gonzalez et al., 1989). The first goal is to impart information concerning the illness itself (i.e., its etiology, symptoms, expected course, environmental determinants, exacerbations, and conditions conducive to optimal quality of life with the disorder). Information is viewed as essential to increasing the family's capacity to cope constructively with the family member's illness as well as to anticipate difficulties and transitions. The second goal of the MFDG is to reframe the definition of and responsibility for the illness such that family members may be more motivated to engage in treatment and work toward altering the home environment to support the chronically ill family member. These researchers found that families typically feel guilty regarding the illness of a family member and doubtful about the adequacy of their interventions on the patient's behalf.

Duration and Stages of Treatment

MFGT ranges from a single day, primarily educational, intervention used as a preliminary to more intensive treatment to weekly meetings over a two- to three-year period as an ongoing adjunct to inpatient treatment. The more recent trend, paralleling mental health intervention in general, has been for MFGT to become more brief, focused, and psychoeducational. Parallel to brief family therapy, recent articles describing MFGT most commonly describe an intervention of 8 to 10 sessions (e.g., Cassanso, 1989a; Gonzalez et al., 1989). Sessions generally range from one and one-half to two hours in length and vary from weekly to monthly in frequency. Cassanso (1989b), in an empirical study of MFGT, however, concluded that more than 10 sessions may be optimal to extend the "work" phase of treatment.

Laqueur (1972) identified three phases of MFGT: initial interest, resistance, and working through. Laqueur noted that relief and a flight into health tended to affectively accompany Phase I, initial interest. Phase II, resistance, was associated with a fear of failure on the part of family members as they became more realistic about the difficulty of making quick changes. Significant attitude and behavior changes occurred in Phase III, working through, and were generally accompanied by greater confidence and openness on the part of family members. Gritzer and Okun (1983) identified three similar stages: anxiety and conflict over trust and disclosure; heightened activity by both the therapist and families toward goal achievement; and termination with accompanying denial, anger, relief, and self-appraisal. McFarlane (no date, cited in O'Shea & Phelps, 1985) identified four MFGT phases: (1) pregroup assembling of families and information, (2) fostering group cohesion and a therapeutic milieu, (3) modification of boundaries within and between families and active problem solving, and (4) evolution into a social support net-

1. Cases involving life-threatening or life-style-threatening physical or psychological debilitation.
2. Cases in which the nature of the presenting problem is such that any clinically responsible, appropriate treatment must include a substantial amount of specific, specialized, or technical information. In short, optimal treatment requires a didactic component together with a less structured, and more supportive intervention.
3. Cases in which social isolation characterizes both the index patient and family members, contributes in a major way to the maintenance or exacerbation of the symptoms or focal problem, or is implicated in deterioration of treatment effects.
4. Cases in which parental authority, responsibility, and role performance have broken down, been preempted by, been delegated to professionals, or been stymied by other factors such that parents need to be supported and encouraged to assume or maintain an executive role.
5. Cases with a poor prognosis or progressively deteriorating course and cases known to be resistant or refractory to treatment such that all previous treatments have failed and MFT cannot foreseeably make things worse.

As noted earlier in this chapter, MFGT is contraindicated for chaotic families, families with a psychotic or violent family member, and families with a secret that if revealed is expected to result in violence.

Applicability to Schools

Dombalis and Erchul (1987) concluded that MFGT was a promising approach for the practice of a family-oriented school psychology for multiple reasons. They noted that its most attractive features include its cost effectiveness and time effectiveness. In addition, these authors cite evidence of its effectiveness in improving the behavior and academic performance of students involved in MFGT groups. The learning or educational aspect of MFGT provides yet another advantage, given its congruence with the school agenda. Limitations cited by Dombalis and Erchul (1987) include the lack of objective, empirical research regarding the effectiveness of MFGT, the amount of training required to conduct MFGT groups, and the possible lack of support for such an intervention by school administrators, colleagues, or system resources, such as space.

Extrapolating from the literature reviewed in this chapter, it seems that a critical distinction related to the issue of applicability of MFGT to the school setting is the distinction between multiple family group therapy and multiple family discussion groups. Multiple family group therapy has a clear clinical emphasis. The primary purpose of such a group is the alteration of family relationships such that individual interventions with the index patient can be sustained in the home environment. Given the primary educational nature of the school setting, as well as clearly defined boundaries of privacy between home and school, such a clinically-oriented intervention as MFGT would appear inappropriate except for special populations, such as seriously emotionally disturbed children.

In contrast with the limited applicability of MFGT as described in much of this chapter to the school setting, there would appear to be great utility in the more recently developed psychoeducationally oriented multiple family discussion group (MFDG) (see Gonzalez et al., 1989). Recall that MFDG is a short-term, highly structured, eight-session intervention, primarily used in medical settings, with two main goals both directed toward enhancing the families resistance to stress and improving their coping. MFDG goals are (1) to impart information about the disorder and (2) to normalize and reframe the situation such that family members do not fear taking appropriate action. Moreover, MFDGs use a highly specified workshop format and training manual. The highly structured format and training manual facilitate efficient and rapid training of a therapist unfamiliar with the approach. This also increases the feasibility of having MFDGs led by mental health professionals with less family therapy training than is required in MFGT.

Second, the highly structured format of the MFDG allows it to be open to careful research study and replication. In summary, the more highly structured, psychoeducationally oriented MFDG format would appear to be superior to MFGT as a multiple family intervention applicable to the school setting. MFDG enhances therapist training, has a focus more consistent with the school environment, and is more amenable to program evaluation.

Multiple family discussion groups (MFDG) would appear useful to a variety of child/family/school problems. It will be recalled that MFDGs first provide information about the illness, next focus on individual family issues related to the illness, and finally examine how the illness affects family emotional life (Gonzalez et al., 1989). Use of the MFDG as described by Gonzalez and colleagues (1989) is very consistent with the new movement to place health clinics in school settings (see Carlson, Tharinger, DeMers, Paavola, & Bricklin, 1995). Also consistent with the illness framework, however, would be the organization of MFDGs around the various special education diagnoses given in schools using populations homogeneous by the developmental stages of elementary, middle, and high school. If teachers were to participate or co-lead such groups along with a mental health professional, it is likely that the home/school partnership would be greatly enhanced.

Leaving illness aside, MFDGs could also be organized around life or school transitions. School transitions most obviously involve the transition into school, between elementary to middle and middle to high school, or departure from school. Special groups within the school population may need greater assistance with these transitions. In addition, family life transitions unrelated to school may also form the basis for MFDGs. Critical transitions of separation/divorce, remarriage, or geographical move, in addition to those of illness noted earlier, are stressors for children and families that are often enacted in the school setting (see also Carlson, 1995). As noted by O'Shea and Phelps (1985), the use of MFGT would appear to be particularly useful for cases in which social isolation or mistrust of therapists characterizes the population. As such, MFDG may be a particularly useful intervention for use with single fathers, neglectful or abusive parents, and minority families experiencing school problems in a setting where the majority culture is different.

CONCLUSIONS

Multiple family group therapy (MFGT) is a unique form of group intervention that has been underutilized in outpatient settings but would appear to offer considerable promise for the school setting if appropriately modified and adapted. It is the opinion of this author that the form of multiple family group intervention most applicable to the school setting is the multiple family discussion group (MFDG). MFDG is a short-term (eight week), psychoeducationally oriented, family-focused intervention in which four to six families, including the identified problem children, come together to discuss issues related to the children's problem in a structured discussion format. MFDG was designed as an adjunct to the treatment of persons with chronic illnesses. Applied to the school setting, however, MFDG may be viewed broadly as an adjunct to the educational process such that children can optimally learn and achieve.

The advantages of multiple family group intervention, regardless of its form, are clear. It is a cost-effective and efficient method of treatment. Maximizing mental health professionals expertise across multiple families obviously is more cost effective than individual family therapy. Moreover, including a family-focused adjunctive treatment to the treatment of individual problems has been well supported in the literature as a means by which treatment gains are maintained and relapse is reduced. According to clinical reports, multiple family group interventions are also powerful methods of inducing change. The unique characteristics of multiple family groups facilitative of such change include, but are not limited to, the multiple direct and indirect learning opportunities available between the multiple members of the treatment system, the incorporation of the broader context of society in the form of multiple families into the treatment process, the inclusion of multiple generations within groups, and multiple sources of support and normalization.

Several limitations of MFGT, however, are noteworthy. These include the dearth of empirical support for this method of treatment, the considerable level of skill required of the MFGT leader/therapist, and possible lack of support from school administrators. It is the view of the author that each of these concerns is significantly reduced with the MFDG intervention when contrasted with the MFGT intervention. MFDG with its highly structured, psychoeducational approach provides a treatment more amenable to empirical validation, a training manual to facilitate development of group leader skills, and represents a format more consistent with the school educational environment. Given these strengths, MFDG would appear to offer a very pragmatic adjunctive or preventive treatment to a variety of school-related concerns experienced by children and families.

Clearly, however, research on the effectiveness of MFGT and MFDG is lacking. It is therefore viewed as imperative that mental health professionals and researchers who implement MFDGs in the schools do so with carefully developed treatment manuals and with adequate evaluation of the outcomes associated with this method of treatment. As noted by O'Shea and Phelps (1985), the dearth of empirical support for MFGT to date does not indicate that its yield, well documented by clinicians, is illusory or inflated. Rather, the fact that benefits are so consistently detected despite inadequate and unsophisticated research designs attests to the strength of MFGT, which renders it both deserving and long overdue for controlled, rigorous, scientific scrutiny.

REFERENCES

Benningfield, A. B. (1980). Multiple family therapy systems. In J. G. Howells (Ed.), *Advances in family psychiatry* (Vol. II, pp. 411–424). New York: International Universities Press.

Bowen, M. (1972). Principles and techniques of multiple family therapy. In A. Ferber, M. Mendelsohn, & A. Napier (Eds.), *The book of family therapy* (pp. 388–404). New York: Jason Aronson.

Carlson, C. I. (1995). Best practices for working with single-parent and stepparent families. In J. Grimes & A. Thomas (Eds.), *Best practices in school psychology manual* (Vol. III, pp. 1097–1110). Washington, DC: National Association of School Psychologists.

Carlson, C. I., Tharinger, D., DeMers, S., Paavola, J., & Bricklin, P. (1995). Health care reform and psychological practice in schools. *Professional Psychology: Research and Practice.*

Cassanso, D. R. (1989a). Multi-family group therapy in social work practice: I. *Social Work with Groups, 12*(1), 3–14.

Cassanso, D. R. (1989b). Research on patterns of interaction: II. *Social Work with Groups, 12*(1), 15–39.

Dombalis, A. O., & Erchul, W. P. (1987). Multiple family group therapy: A review of its applicability to the practice of school psychology. *School Psychology Review, 16*(4), 487–497.

Frager, S. (1985). Community-universality exercises in multiple family therapy. *Family Therapy, 12*(3), 245–251.

Gonzalez, S., Steinglass, P., & Reiss, D. (1989). Putting the illness in its place: Discussion groups for families with chronic medical illnesses. *Family Process, 28*(1), 69–87.

Gritzer, P. H., & Okun, H. S. (1983). Multiple family group therapy: A model for all families. In B. B. Wolman & G. Stricker (Eds.), *Handbook of family and marital therapy* (pp. 315–342). New York: Plenum.

Lansky, M. R., Bley, C. R., McVey, G. G., & Brotman, B. (1980). Multiple family groups in aftercare. In J. G. Howells (Ed.), *Advances in family psychiatry* (Vol. II, pp. 425–436). New York: International Universities Press.

Laqueur, H. P. (1972). Multiple family therapy. In A. Ferber, M. Mendelsohn, & A. Napier (Eds.), *The book of family therapy* (pp. 405–416). New York: Jason Aronson.

O'Shea, M. D., & Phelps, R. (1985). Multiple family therapy: Current status and critical appraisal. *Family Process, 25*, 555–582.

Parker, T., Hill, J. W., & Miller, G. (1987). Multiple family therapy: Evaluating a group experience for mentally retarded adolescents and their families. *Family Therapy, 14*(1), 43–51.

Skynner, A. C. R. (1981). An open systems group-analytic approach to family therapy. In A. S. Gurman & D. P. Kniskern (Eds.), *Handbook of family therapy* (pp. 39–84). New York: Brunner/Mazel.

Steinhauer, P. D. (1987). The family as a small group: The process model of family functioning. In T. Jacobs (Ed.), *Family interaction and psychopathology* (pp. 67–115). New York: Plenum.

Strelnick, A. H. (1977). Multiple family group therapy: A review of the literature. *Family Process, 16*, 307–325.

CHAPTER 16

GROUP PREVENTION AND INTERVENTION WITH PREGNANT AND PARENTING ADOLESCENTS

Karen Callan Stoiber, UNIVERSITY OF WISCONSIN–MILWAUKEE
Arthur J. Anderson, UNIVERSITY OF WISCONSIN–MILWAUKEE
Diane Smith Schowalter, UNIVERSITY OF WISCONSIN–MILWAUKEE

RATIONALE

A recent report by the Alan Guttmacher Institute (AGI, 1994) titled *Sex and America's Teenagers* provides compelling statistics on the incidence of adolescent pregnancy and parenting: More than one million adolescent women become pregnant each year, with nearly half of them (478,0000) becoming adolescent mothers. Another pattern related to adolescent pregnancy reported by AGI is a dramatic shift in adolescent and single mothers' choices to raise their children. Whereas in previous decades about 90% of single mothers relinquished their children, today, 90% of single mothers assume the responsibility of caregivers (AGI, 1994). It is not surprising that public concern regarding adolescent pregnancy and parenting has increased in recent years.

Several reasons support school- and community-based prevention and intervention efforts in adolescent pregnancy and parenting: (1) an increase in sexual activity among adolescents, (2) earlier developmental age being associated with initial sexual activity, (3) higher incidence of sexually transmitted diseases, and (4) long-term negative consequences for adolescent parents and their offspring. First, the likelihood of adolescents being sexually active or engaging in heterosexual intercourse has increased steadily over recent decades. The recent AGI report indicated that more than 50% of young women and 75% of young men are sexually active by their eighteenth birthdays. In contrast, during the 1950s, approximately 25% of America's female teens had engaged in sexual activity.

Second, at the same time that higher proportions of adolescents have experienced sexual activity, youths are initiating premarital intercourse at younger ages. To better understand the sexual behaviors of young adolescents, Stoiber and Good (in press) conducted a survey of 250 culturally diverse seventh- and eighth-grade students, who had an average age of 13.8 years. More than 35% of these male and 30% of female urban middle-school students reported being sexually active during the last year. Similarly, AGI (1994) reported that the greatest increase in adolescent births has occurred for teens aged 15 to 17 years, who show an increase of

learn to cope. Four aims of intervention groups for adolescent fathers are supported in the literature: (1) social support, (2) vocational/career development, (3) parent/child relationship, and (4) prevention of subsequent conceptions. First, support in dealing with their own complicated development as adolescents and with issues related to becoming parents is suggested. Important goals of intervention include (1) facilitating recognition and understanding of the sources and types of stress teenaged fathers experience and (2) developing problem-solving and coping strategies to deal with the probable stress related to adolescent fatherhood.

Second, intervention must directly address educational and vocational opportunities aimed at enhancing teenaged fathers' capacity to provide financial support for their child(ren). Kiselica and Sturmer (1993) indicated that research on adolescent fathers contradicts the myths that they do not typically contribute financially to the ongoing care of their children or sustain contact with the mothers and children. Because adolescent fathers, as a group, are more likely to have poor educational achievement and attainment, they represent a group at particular need for work- and career-focused intervention. A third component of teen father groups focuses on issues related to parenting, such as their knowledge of child development, parenting skills, and relationships with the mother and child. Most agree that males are less socialized than females in caregiving activities. Specific instruction and therapeutic discussions about issues such as nurturance, setting limits, and developing mutually satisfying parent/child relationships should be included in intervention groups. Finally, continued preventive emphasis should be given via thorough and accurate knowledge of contraception.

Group Interventions with Teenaged Fathers

Kiselica and Pfaller (1993) charge that there is a service bias against teenaged fathers. Both research studies on and intervention programs for adolescent fathers have typically focused on small, unrepresentative samples and have lacked adequate comparison groups and longitudinal data (Ruch-Ross, Jones, & Musick, 1992). Intervention programs for adolescent fathers, similar to those for adolescent mothers, have not been consistently and thoroughly evaluated to determine their effectiveness. It does seem clear, however, that the use of group interventions for adolescent fathers is theoretically and economically mandated, both within schools and communities.

Robinson (1988) described a program at the Young Men's Clinic at Columbia Presbyterian Hospital in New York as a "diamond in the rough." The clinic is located in a predominately Hispanic area of the city and coordinates its services with several other neighboring agencies. By using innovative means of attracting young men to the clinic, staff members go into the community with video cameras, film teenagers participating in sports, dance and other activities, and come to know them on a personal basis. The young men are then invited to the clinic to discuss topics concerning health and sexuality and to watch the videotapes.

Huey (1991), a former high school counselor in Decatur, Georgia, designed a group for teenaged fathers referred to as MALE (Maximizing A Life Experience). MALE groups focused on rights, responsibilities, and resources. The specific objectives for the group members were (1) learning more about themselves and their feelings about the pregnancies, (2) understanding their legal rights and responsibilities, (3) identifying and exploring present and future alternatives, (4) learning sound decision-making skills, (5) identifying resources, (6) accepting responsibility for the pregnancies, and (6) obtaining information on contraception. Huey (1991) planned nine one-hour sessions, and he incorporated the use of films and speakers from the local Legal Aid Society and Planned Parenthood.

The first session included an overview of the program, logistical information, a getting-acquainted activity, group and individual goal setting, and establishing ground rules. The second and third sessions used audiovisual resources to introduce discussions about values and attitudes concerning teen sexual activity and pregnancy and the importance of fathers having active roles in supporting unintended pregnancies. These two sessions also provided information concerning the legal rights and responsibilities of adolescent fathers. The fifth and sixth sessions provided information on reproductive biology, contraception, and sexually transmitted diseases, which included a trip to the local Planned Parenthood office. The seventh session focused on developing problem-solving and decision-making skills, which were practiced during the eighth session as each adolescent father confronted a personal problem related to adolescent fatherhood. The ninth session served as a wrap-up for the program and included a group evaluation and posttest. Informal evaluation by group members at the end of the nine-week session was extremely positive, and at one- and two-year follow-ups, all former members were contributing toward child support and none had fathered a second child.

Additional programs for teenaged fathers include instruction in infant care and child development at the Medical College of Pennsylvania Hospital and the Teen Indian Parents Program in Minneapolis, which provides instruction on parenting and child abuse and facilitates access to government assistance, housing, and employment. The Fatherhood Project in Portland, Oregon, matches young fathers to mentors in the community and also provides opportunities for peer support in ongoing groups.

LIMITATIONS

In general, classroom-based groups for preventing adolescent pregnancy seem to be appropriate for most middle-school and high school level students. However, the sensitive nature of information being discussed in classroom-based prevention groups is often more conducive to single-gender groups (i.e., separate groups for boys and girls). In addition, age considerations are suggested in designing pregnancy prevention programs. Younger students may not have the cognitive readiness to understand highly detailed information about human anatomy or condom use.

In planning more intensive prevention or intervention groups involving smaller numbers of adolescents (e.g., those having a mentoring or extensive career development component), consideration should be given to the group composition. Adolescents at 14 years of age have different developmental needs than those at 19 years of age. Similarly, language differences among participants should be considered in forming groups. Although a bilingual speaking facilitator is preferable for leading groups with adolescents having diverse language backgrounds (e.g., monolingual Spanish-speaking adolescents and monolingual English-speaking adolescents), our experience has been that it is extremely challenging to switch languages when focused on sensitive issues. Sexual experiences of participants is another consideration for forming prevention groups. Those students who are either sexually active or were sexually abused bring particular issues that may be difficult to address when combined with adolescents who are not sexually active. Group functioning can also be disrupted if participants are allowed to join the group at any time. Group cohesion can be difficult to achieve when there is great diversity due to age, background, sexual beliefs, or inconsistent attendance among group participants.

A final caveat is related to the mental health readiness and interactions styles of participants. Although many adolescents are very willing to engage in small-group discussion and activities, some may be resistive or reluctant. Also, some adolescents may have serious mental health issues that preclude them from benefitting from group interventions. Careful monitoring of participants' needs and capacities to function in the group setting should occur throughout group sessions. If an adolescent shows signs of serious distress or difficulty in the group, it is suggested that he or she receive individual therapeutic intervention.

SUGGESTIONS FOR RESEARCH AND PRACTICE

Increased attention to the evaluation of group approaches to adolescent pregnancy and parenting must occur both to understand what is happening through the group process as well as to understand important outcomes of the program. Treatment evaluation data are necessary, then, for determining whether targeted outcomes are being achieved and for determining how the program can be improved. The future direction of research in the area of adolescent pregnancy prevention and intervention will require several approaches.

First, any investigation of pregnancy prevention/intervention programs must be linked with adequate program evaluation designs. This is a necessary step to assess program outcomes effectively. Second, in addition to focusing on program outcomes, research efforts must focus more on the identification of important program elements or processes that take place within a group setting. Such information will provide researchers with a better understanding of why prevention programs work. Third, investigations must be longitudinal in nature to assess changes in attitudes or behaviors over time. Fourth, researchers must incorporate multiple program approaches in their design to permit comparison of program outcomes. The overall impact of, for example, sexuality curriculums, group presentations, contraceptive distribution approaches, and mentoring plans must be considered in relation to other program components. A comparative approach is necessary to gain a better understanding of the unique impact of each component while controlling for the effects of other components in a comprehensive program.

Finally, multiple specific outcomes, including both short-term and long-term effects on participants lives, should be evaluated. Multimodal evaluation strategies are needed to target individual characteristics of participants such as their knowledge about sexuality and reproduction, attitudes about pregnancy and parenting, risk behaviors, communication patterns with parents, decision-making ability, and self-esteem. In addition, programs should monitor other quality-of-life indicators, including the program's impact on academic achievement and educational attainment (rate of school attendance or school truancy, dropout, grade-point average, and rate of course failure), pregnancy rate, and pregnancy outcomes (incidence of low birth weight, whether adolescent remained in school).

More information would be helpful for determining ways that group approaches were not successful or failed to bring about desired changes. In addition, evaluations of group intervention programs with regard to specific demographic characteristics of participants should occur. For example, how might ethnicity or socioeconomic level influence program outcomes? Are differing program elements, such as including mentors or having a decision-making emphasis, more important for adolescents of differing ethnic or cultural backgrounds? Comparisons of group prevention and intervention strategies could occur between or among community contexts (suburban vs. rural vs. urban), social economic level, age (younger vs. older adolescents), and ethnicity. Although evaluation can be a daunting task, the complex nature and potentially detrimental outcomes of adolescent pregnancy delineate an equally, if not more daunting, mandate for evaluation activities of group adolescent pregnancy prevention and intervention programs.

APPENDIX A: HYPOTHETICAL CASE OF ADOLESCENT MOTHER GROUP PARTICIPANTS

The adolescent girls were referred to the intervention group through a variety of community agencies that provided services for adolescent mothers. All of the young women continued to remain in school, although some were clearly prone to absenteeism and at risk for dropping out of school. All participants were single mothers. Each was interviewed separately prior to the initiation of the adolescent mothers' group. The primary purpose of the interview was to make sure that each potential member demonstrated appropriate coping skills for group interactions and processes.

Description of Participants

Breanne was a very attractive European American 18-year-old who admitted to still being in love with the father of her child, a 15-month-old daughter named Brittany. Breanne virtually had no contact with her child's father for more than one year. However, she admitted to being "obsessed" with him and had not given up hopes that they would eventually be married. The father had moved to another state, which Breanne believes was motivated by his desire to get away from her and not pay paternity care costs. Breanne did not feel as though she had any friends. She lived in a small apartment with her daughter and revealed to being prone to "losing her temper" and throwing Brittany on the bed when she is too demanding.

Anna, a 16-year-old African American, lived with her parents, her 9-year-old brother and her 12-month-old daughter, Natasha. She attended school during the day and worked approximately 30 hours a week at a "quick-mart" gas station. Her parents cared for Natasha in their small two-bedroom home while Anna attended school and worked. She is unsure about the actual identity of the father of her daughter. She had been doing "speed" at a party and then had sexual relations with a few boys. Anna stated that she had just been "dumped" from her boyfriend and had resorted to drugs as a way to cope. She attested that the episode when she became pregnant was her first and last time that she used drugs. Anna suffered from depression and guilt related to taking drugs and not knowing who Natasha's father was. She reported usually spending 10 hours with her daughter each week, usually during the weekend. She often talked about wanting a better life for her daughter than the one she was experiencing.

Jody, a European American 17-year-old was the mother of a 2-year-old son, Christopher. She had concerns that her son did not feel as attached to her as to Christopher's grandmother. Jody's mother cared for Christopher while Jody attended school and went out with friends. He would tantrum when Jody would resume care for him. She revealed to having considerable difficulty "controlling" her son. Jody had recently tested positive for HIV. She purchased an answering machine because she hoped to capture "missed" phone calls from "guy friends" several years older than her that she met at bars and clubs. Jody stated that she tended to become very depressed when there were no phone messages from male acquaintances.

Tina was a soft-spoken, strikingly beautiful Hispanic American who was 18 years of age. She had signed a contract with a modeling agency but had to cancel due to her unintended pregnancy. She still has hopes of returning to a career as a model, but her agent has told her that she needs to lose 15 pounds of "baby weight" gained during her pregnancy. She ran away from home at 15 years of age and traveled to Florida with her boyfriend, who became the father of her son, Chad, now 30 months of age. She left him and then discovered that she was pregnant. She soon met another man, who lived with her in Florida until Chad was 2 years old. Chad believed this man was his father and called him "dada." Currently, neither Chad's natural father or substitute father has any contact with Chad. Due to financial constraints, Tina has moved back home with her parents and five siblings. She worries that she will grow to become like her mother, who argues constantly with her father but continues to live with him. When asked what makes her most proud about herself, Tina, replied "Nothing. I can't think of anything good about me."

Jenny, a 14-year-old European American single mother, is diagnosed as having a mild cognitive disability. She lives with her parents, who are also reported to have a history of learning and cognitive difficulties. Neither of Jenny's parents are currently employed; her family relies on welfare benefits. Her 9-month old son Daniel was born with medical complications, including congenital heart and lung problems that require him to be on a respirator. Based on reports from Jenny, she had been forced by Daniel's father to have sexual intercourse with him. However, because of Jenny's cognitive disability, it is difficult to determine the actual circumstances surrounding her pregnancy. She did not seek prenatal medical care until her fifth month. Jenny stated that having Daniel is the best thing that ever happened to her. She talks constantly about how cute he is. Both Jenny and her son appear to have poor hygiene. Jenny usually does not dress appropriately for the weather. For example, she will wear warm pants in July and short-sleeved shirts and no coat during the winter. Observations of Jenny with Daniel suggest that she has very little knowledge of how to care for him or how to interact with him. Jenny has unrealistic expectations of Daniel's development. Although Daniel is only 8 months old. Jenny has concerns about how much longer he will remain in diapers. Her closest friend is a 16-year-old cousin, who became pregnant about two months before Jenny.

APPENDIX B: SESSION-BY-SESSION OUTLINE OF GROUP TREATMENT OBJECTIVES FOR ADOLESCENT MOTHERS

Session One: Memories as Motivation for Being the Best Possible Parent

Objective 1: Build group cohesion by sharing plans for their own "wish day" (i.e., a day in which "anything is possible").

Objective 2: Develop an understanding of their childhood memories.

Objective 3: Begin to link current behaviors and beliefs to the memories being constructed by their children.

Objective 4: Establish group rules and obtain consensus on them across group participants.

Objective 5: Provide opportunities for developing pleasant mother/child memories.

Session Two: Communication Competence

Objective 1: Build group cohesion by sharing "I am most happy when. . . ."

Objective 2: Demonstrate essential characteristics of verbal and nonverbal communication.

Objective 3: Examine and interpret the meaning of verbal and nonverbal messages.

Objective 4: Help participants develop effective communication patterns.

Objective 5: Apply effective communication skills to parent/child interactions.

Session Three: Exploring Communication Patterns

Objective 1: Build group cohesion by sharing the best and worst thing that happened during the last week.

Objective 2: Introduce the concepts of assertive, aggressive, and passive communication styles.

Objective 3: Demonstrate and experience nonassertive, aggressive, and assertive communication styles.

Objective 4: Provide examples and opportunities for linking assertive responses to intimidating and challenging situations.

Objective 5: Increase adolescent mothers' positive relations with their children.

Session Four: Sexual Refusal and Pregnancy Prevention

Objective 1: Build group cohesion by participants sharing experiences when they refused to do something.

Objective 2: Explore different types of sexual harassment and sexual innuendos.

Objective 3: Recognize the signs of an abusive relationship.

Objective 4: Identify, practice, and become comfortable with various forms of refusal and sexual assertion.

Objective 5: Develop knowledge of contraception and reproductive health care.

Objective 6: Explore and practice ways to make the child feel safe with the mother.

Session Five: Reflective Decision Making Applied to Sexual Situations and Parenting Situations

Objective 1: Build group cohesion by sharing "The one thing I would change in my life is. . . ."

Objective 2: Introduce participants to steps in decision-making model.

Objective 3: Foster recognition of one's own values through personal, family, and friends values activity.

Objective 4: Practice using reflective decision making through dilemma case studies.

Objective 5: Increase shared decision making by parent/child dyads through play choices.

Session Six: Feeling Nurtured

Objective 1: Build group cohesion and feeling nurtured by participants sharing favorite foods and their feelings about how eating it can promote feeling nurtured.

Objective 2: Foster recognition of need for nurturance in the adolescent mothers' lives.

Objective 3: Construct ways to nurture friendships through "friendship bingo" exercise.

Objective 4: Examine behaviors and actions that promote nurturance of oneself.

Objective 5: Increase nurturance in parent/child relationship by engaging in feeding activities and game playing.

Session Seven: Understanding Love, Friendship, and Sexuality

Objective 1: Build group cohesion by participants sharing experiences when they felt special or loved.

Objective 2: Examine qualities and characteristics of different relationships (parent/child relationship, boyfriend/girlfriend relationships, girl-to-girl relationships).

Objective 3: Explore ways to promote satisfying relationships.

Objective 4: Help participants consider the role relationships play in determining how they feel and how they live.

Objective 5: Distinguish characteristics of healthy and unhealthy relationships.

Objective 6: Develop ways to promote healthy relationships and deal with unhealthy relationships.

Objective 7: Practice healthy relations with their children.

Session Eight: Goal Setting and Future Planning

Objective 1: Build group cohesion by sharing a goal that participants have set for themselves and a goal for their children.

Objective 2: Learn about the role of goal setting in planning for the future.

Objective 3: Describe models and approaches to goal attainment.

Objective 4: Explore how being a teen mother can affect goal setting and attainment.

Objective 5: Help participants set realistic personal goals for the next week.

Objective 6: Parent/child dyads role-play goals and dreams as a way to understand the meaning of goals.

Session Nine: Constructing Career Pathways

Objective 1: Build group cohesion by participants sharing the career they most value and their own career choice.

Objective 2: Assess whether participants were successful in achieving their personal goals for the last week and the reasons linked to goal outcomes.

Objective 3: Establish ways that participants can "reset" goals that were not attained successfully.

Objective 4: Help participants develop career goals by producing a "Me in five years movie."

Objective 5: Promote participants' decision-making responsibility through role-plays that focus on problems, issues, and successes via "critics' analysis" of "Me in ten years movie."

Session Ten: Staying on Track

Objective 1: Build group cohesion by participants sharing how being in the group has helped them.

Objective 2: Recognize the connection between decision making and goal setting.

Objective 3: Identify values related to career paths and employment though "values and employment" worksheet activity.

Objective 4: Generate methods and plans for "reality-checks" related to staying on career path.

Objective 5: Generate methods and plans for "reality-checks" related to enhancing parent/child relationship.

Objective 6: Increase participants' capacity to understand their impact as mothers and as role models on their children through imaginative play activities.

APPENDIX C: EXAMPLE OF SESSION PLANS AND ACTIVITIES FOR AN ADOLESCENT MOTHERS' INTERVENTION GROUP

Session Two Module: Communication Competence

Objective 1: Build group cohesion by sharing "I am most happy when. . . ."

A. Procedure: Begin the session by asking participants to complete the sentence "I am most happy when. . . ." Be sensitive to the responses given by participants, using reflective listening techniques. Help participants explore *why* and *how* this event or situation makes them feel happy.

B. Discussion Probes: In an attempt to extend participants' understanding of what makes them happy, follow with probes such as "What is it about. . . .that makes you feel so happy?" "Do you think this makes your child happy?" and so on. For some participants, you may need to urge them to think of a happy event. If they can't think of one, resist intrusive questions or probes. Rather, attempt to keep the mood light and suggest that one aim of the group is to help produce happy events in participants' lives, both as parents and as adolescents.

C. Communication Link: Ask participants if they can think of ways or signs that mean someone is happy. Probe about ways they make themselves feel happy. Ask participants what they do to make their children happy. Check with participants about how it feels when someone listens to them. Emphasize that listening is something that happens during group. Also, point out that listening is a way of showing respect or that you view them as valuable or important. Ask them about other ways that they show respect to others, including their children.

D. Time: 15–20 minutes

Objective 2: Demonstrate essential characteristics of verbal and nonverbal communication.

A. Procedure: Ask participants to form into dyads. Assign roles of designer and interviewer. Dyads should sit back to back. The designer then draws a picture that represents "being a good parent." After the designer has finished her picture, the interviewer asks questions about the picture. The interviewer should attempt to reproduce the designer's picture based on the information received through questioning. Dyad participants should compare pictures.

B. Discussion: Participants should discuss the following questions while in dyads: (1) How are our pictures alike? How are they different? (2) What made communication difficult in this exercise? (3) What questions made it easier for us to understand each other?

C. Communication Link: Bring participants back to a whole group. Ask them to share their pictures. Discuss what types of questions were most helpful for them. Engage in dialogue regarding what they learned about elements of effective communication from this activity.

D. Time: 15 minutes

Objective 3: Examine and interpret the meaning of verbal and nonverbal messages.

A. Procedure: Ask participants to form into triads. Assign roles of talker, listener, and observer. The talker should begin by talking for three minutes on topics related to being a teen mother (e.g., how her life has changed, what worries her most about being a teen mother, ways she has learned to cope). The listener should not interrupt during this time. The observer should take notes about the nonverbal feedback being given by the listener. After three minutes, reverse roles between talker and listener.

Again, the observer should take notes on nonverbal communication and provide feedback.

B. Discussion: Discuss the following questions in a large group: (1) What did I like about talking without interruptions? (2) What felt awkward? (3) How did it feel for the listeners not to be able to speak? (4) What types of nonverbal cues did the listeners use? (5) How did the feedback affect the second exchange? (6) What did I learn from this exercise? (7) What did I learn that I might consider when communicating with my child?

C. Communication Link: Based on the two exercises, make a list of communication facilitators and communication barriers. The group facilitator should consider the following lists and add these to the group's lists if necessary:

Communication Facilitators

Attempt to take the perspective of the other.
Don't ask too many questions.
Make efforts to keep communication open.
Don't offer advice if not requested.
Monitor giving and receiving of information.
Be clear about the message you are sending.
Make eye contact with the person you are addressing.
Be open to the view of others.

Communication Barriers

Being distracted by other events or behaviors.
Interrupting someone else while they are trying to speak.
Using slang or terms that the listener doesn't understand.
Daydreaming or mental preoccupation with something else.
Not paying attention to what is being said.
Not respecting the individual who is speaking.
Rehearsing your response while the other person is speaking.

D. Time: 20 minutes

Objective 4: Help participants recognize and develop effective communication patterns.

A. Procedure: Explain to participants that people are better communicators when they talk or share how they are feeling or what they would like. Emphasize the advantages of attempting to communicate feelings and thoughts, even unpleasant feelings and thoughts, rather than allowing them to "build up" or "fester." Explore with them the ways that they have reponded when someone calls them a name or says something hurtful toward them. Validate that a common response is to become angry or to speak critically about something or someone, either to another person or to direct it toward the person who has angered them. Share with participants that this exercise will give them practice in developing positive messages. Hand out one "I Messages" worksheet to each participant. Request participants to work in dyads or triads, and allow 5 to 10 minutes for participants to develop responses to scenarios. When they have finished constructing "I messages," ask for volunteers to role-play a situation. In the first role-play, they should use "you messages." In the second role-play, an "I message" response should be used. Facilitate feedback and other ideas for responses after each response. Possible probes include: "Was it easy or difficult to come up with that response?" "How did the first response make you feel?" "How did the second response ("I message") make you feel different?" "Can you think of a recent situation when you used a "you message"? and "How might you use 'I Messages'?"

Some Possible Scenarios

You are having trouble figuring the answer to a math problem. Your sister comments, "You must be really stupid. Math is my favorite subject."

You are leaving for school and your mother comments, "You never keep your room clean. I'm thinking of not taking care of your baby anymore unless you keep your room clean!"

You are feeding your infant mushed peas for the first time and the baby spits it out. Your little brother observes this and comments, "Your baby must not like you, otherwise she wouldn't be spitting food at you."

You need to go home right after school to take care of your baby. Your friend comments that you never want to do anything fun after school anymore.

Example

Your friend forgets to pick you up to go to the mall as planned. The next day at school she tells you what a great time she had there with another friend.

Angry Response: "You're a jerk! Can't you see that I'm already upset about you forgetting to take me along to the mall? I'll never trust you as a friend anymore!"

"I Message" Response: "I really am feeling upset about being left out. Could you please explain why you didn't take me along last night?"

B. Discussion Questions: Ask the following:

1. Is it difficult to express your needs when you are angry?
2. How does anger affect relationships? How does it affect your relationship with your friends? Your child?
3. Are there times when its OK to feel angry?
4. How are some ways that you can communicate feeling hurt without being unkind or mean?
5. Who can think of a situation involving your child when you felt angry? How are some ways to respond in a way that will not hurt your child?

C. Materials Needed: "I Messages" worksheet for each participant, pencils

D. Time: 20 minutes

Objective 5: Apply effective communication skills to parent/child interactions.

A. Procedure: Step One–Join adolescent mothers and their children. Provide each dyad with several healthy snacks that are appropriate for the child and mother (e.g., shaped crackers, raisins, cut-up fruit, etc.). First, have the parents present the snacks to the children. Instruct mothers that they should allow their children to choose a snack. Then they should observe their children eat the snack and imitate the nonverbal cues that the children show while eating the snack. Then the parent should choose a snack and use nonverbal cues to show they enjoy the snack. For children who are the appropriate age, encourage the mother to find ways of understanding what the child would like to eat.

Step Two–Give each parent/child dyad a ball to roll back and forth or a balloon to pass to each other. By engaging in this activity, the mother should automatically make some appropriate eye contact with her child. Encourage mothers to talk to their children while engaged in this activity (even if the child is not yet talking).

Step Three–Have parent/child dyads join into a circle and sing together, "If you're happy and you know it, show a smile." "If you're sad and you know it, show a frown." "If you're mad and you know it, say 'I feel mad.'" (etc.)

B. Materials Needed: Nutritious snacks, balls, balloons

C. Time: 15 minutes

APPENDIX D: GROUP PROCESS AND EVALUATION MEASURES

Group Process Questions for Evaluation of Individual Sessions

1. What did you most enjoy during group today?
2. What did you dislike or not enjoy during group today?
3. How did the group meet your needs today?
4. When did you feel most connected to the group?
5. When did you feel least connected to the group?
6. What made you feel most supported in the group?
7. Can you suggest a way the group might have been improved today?

Adolescent Parent Group Evaluation Survey

1. How would you rate the quality of the group meetings?

4	3	2	1
Excellent	Good	Fair	Poor

2. To what extent did the group sessions meet your needs?

4	3	2	1
Almost all my needs have been met.	Most of my needs have been met.	Only a few of my needs have been met.	None of my needs have been met.

3. Have the group meetings helped you deal more effectively with your problems?

4	3	2	1
Yes, they helped a great deal.	Yes, they helped somewhat.	No, they didn't help much.	No, they made matters worse.

4. If a teen friend were in need of similar support, would you recommend our parenting group to her?

1	2	3	4
No, definitely not	Probably not	I think so	Yes, definitely

5. How would you rate your learning of knowledge through the Parent Group Meetings?

1	2	3	4
Very high	Somewhat high	Somewhat low	Very low

6. How would you rate your skill development as a parent through the Parent Group?

1	2	3	4
Very high	Somewhat high	Somewhat low	Very low

7. How would you rate the support that you received through the Parent Group?

1	2	3	4
Very high	Somewhat high	Somewhat low	Very low

8. How would you rate the Parent Group in improving your relationship with your child?

1	2	3	4
Very high	Somewhat high	Somewhat low	Very low

9. How would you rate the Parent Group in helping you stay in school?

1	2	3	4
Very high	Somewhat high	Somewhat low	Very low

10. Would you like to continue with the Parent Group Meetings?

1	2	3	4
No, definitely not	Probably not	I think so	Yes, definitely

REFERENCES

Alan Guttmacher Institute. (1994). *Sex and America's teenagers*. New York: Author.

Allen, J., Philliber, S., & Hoggson, N. (1990). School-based prevention of teen-age pregnancy and school dropout: Process evaluation of the national replication of the Teen Outreach Program. *American Journal of Community Psychology, 18,* 505–524.

Archer, E., & Cahill, M. (1991). *Building life options*. Washington, DC: Academy for Educational Development.

Barth, R. (1989). *Reducing the risk: Building skills to prevent pregnancy*. Santa Cruz, CA: Network Publications.

Barth, R., Fetro, J., Leland, N., & Volkan, K. (1992). Preventing adolescent pregnancy with social and cognitive skills. *Journal of Adolescent Research, 7,* 208–232.

Bavolek, S. J. (1990). *Research and validation report of the nurturing programs.* Eau Claire, WI: Family Development Resources.

Bellingham, K., & Gillies, P. (1993). Evaluation of an AIDS education program for young adults. *Journal of Epidemiology and Community Health, 47,* 134–138.

Byrne, D., Kelley, K., & Fisher, W. A. (1993). Unwanted teenage pregnancies: Incidence, interpretation, and intervention. *Applied & Preventive Psychology, 2,* 101–113.

Centers for Disease Control. (1993, July 23). *Morbidity and Morality Weekly Report.* Atlanta: Author.

Christopher, S., & Roosa, M. (1990). An evaluation of an adolescent pregnancy prevention program: Is "just say no" enough? *Family Relations, 39,* 68–72.

Dawson, D. (1986). The effects of sex education on adolescent behavior. *Family Planning Perspectives, 18,* 162–170.

DeRidder, L. M. (1993). Teenage pregnancy: Etiology and educational interventions. *Educational Psychology Review, 5,* 87–101.

DiClemente, R. J. (1993). Preventing HIV/AIDS among adolescents: Schools as agents of behavior change. *Journal of the American Medical Association, 270,* 760–762.

Duggan, A. K., DeAngelis, C., & Hardy, J. B. (1991). Comprehensive versus traditional services for pregnant and parenting adolescents: A comparative analysis. In J. B. Hardy & L. S. Zabin (Eds.), *Adolescent pregnancy in an urban environment: Issues, programs and evaluation* (pp. 255–278). Washington, DC: The Urban Institute Press.

Eisen, M., Zellman, G., & McAlister, A. (1990). Evaluating the impact of a theory-based sexuality and contraceptive education program. *Family Planning Perspectives, 22,* 261–271.

Elster, A. B., & Lamb, M. E. (1986). *Adolescent fatherhood.* Hillsdale, NJ: Erlbaum.

Elster, A. B., & Panzarine, S. (1983). Teenage fathers: Stresses during gestation and early parenthood. *Clinical Pediatrics, 22,* 700–703.

Fisher, J. D., & Fisher, W. A. (1992). Changing AIDS risk behavior. *Psychological Bulletin, 111,* 455–474.

Forrest, J., & Silverman, J. (1989). What public school teachers teach about preventing pregnancy, AIDS, and sexually-transmitted diseases. *Family Planning Perspectives, 21,* 65–72.

Gordon, D. E. (1990). Formal operational thinking: The role of cognitive-developmental processes in adolescent decision-making about pregnancy and contraception. *American Journal of Orthopsychiatry, 60,* 346–356.

Harris, L. (1986). *American teens speak: Sex, myths, TV, and birth control.* New York: Planned Parenthood of America.

Harris, L. (1988). *Public attitudes toward teenage pregnancy, sex education, and birth control.* New York: Planned Parenthood of America.

Hayes, C. (Ed.). (1987). *Risking the future: Adolescent sexuality, pregnancy, and childbearing* (Vol. 1). Washington, DC: National Academy Press.

Howard, M., & McCabe, J. B. (1990). Helping teenagers postpone sexual involvement. *Family Planning Perspectives, 22,* 21–26.

Huey, W. C. (1991). *Counseling teenage fathers: The "maximizing a life experience" (MALE) group.* Ann Arbor, MI. (ERIC Document Reproduction Service No. ED 341 891)

Jorgensen, S., Potts, V., & Camp, B. (1993). Project Taking Charge: Six month follow-up of a pregnancy prevention program for early adolescents. *Family Relations, 42,* 401–406.

Kazdin, A. E. (1993). Adolescent mental health. *American Psychologist, 48,* 127–141.

Kenney, A. M., Guardado, S., & Brown, L. (1989). Sex education and AIDS education in the schools: What states and large school districts are doing. *Family Planning Perspectives, 21,* 56–64.

Kirby, D. (1992). School-based programs to reduce sexual risk-taking behaviors. *Journal of School Health, 62,* 280–287.

Kiselica, M., & Pfaller, J. (1993). Helping teenage parents: The independent and collaborative roles of counselor educators and school counselors. *Journal of Counseling and Development, 72,* 42–48.

Kiselica, M., & Sturmer, P. (1993). Is society giving teenage fathers a mixed message? *Youth and Society, 24,* 487–501.

Males, M. (1994). Poverty, rape, adult/teen sex: Why pregnancy prevention programs don't work. *Phi Delta Kappan, 54,* 407–410.

Marsiglio, W., & Mott, F. (1986). The impact of sex education on sexual activity, contraception use, and premature pregnancy among American teenagers. *Family Planning Perspectives, 18,* 151–162.

McAnarney, E., & Hendee, W. (1989). The prevention of adolescent pregnancy. *Journal of the American Medical Association, 262,* 78–82.

Miller, B. C., Card, J. J., Paikoff, R. L., & Peterson, J. L. (1992). *Preventing adolescent pregnancy: Model programs and evaluation.* Newbury Park, CA: Sage.

Miller, B. C., & Moore, K. A. (1990). Adolescent sexual behavior, pregnancy, and parenting: Research through the 1980's. *Journal of Marriage and the Family, 54,* 1025–1044.

Robinson, B. E. (1988). Teenage pregnancy from the father's perspective. *American Journal of Orthopsychiatry, 58,* 46–51.

Robinson, W. L., Watkins-Ferrell, P., Davis-Scott, P., & Ruch-Ross, H. S. (1993). Preventing teenage pregnancy. In D. S. Glenwick & L. A. Jason (Eds.), *Promoting health and mental health in children, youth, and families* (pp. 99–124). New York: Springer.

Roosa, M., & Christopher, S. (1990). Evaluation of an abstinence-only adolescent pregnancy prevention program: A replication. *Family Relations, 39,* 363–367.

Roosa, M., & Christopher, S. (1992). A response to Thiel and W. S. Bride: Scientific criticism or obstructionism? *Family Relations, 41,* 468–469.

Ruch-Ross, H. S., Jones, E., & Musick, J. (1992). Comparing outcomes in a statewide program for adolescent mothers with outcomes in a national sample. *Family Planning Perspectives, 24,* 66–96.

Sadler, L. S., & Catrone, C. (1983). The adolescent parent: A dual developmental crisis. *Journal of Adolescent Health Care, 4,* 100–105.

Schinke, S. P., Blythe, B. J., & Gilchrist, L. D. (1981). Cognitive-behavioral prevention of adolescent pregnancy. *Journal of Counseling Psychology, 28,* 451–454.

Schinke, S. P., Gordon, A. N., & Weston, R. E. (1990). Self-instruction to prevent HIV infection among African-American and Hispanic-American adolescents. *Journal of Consulting and Clinical Psychology, 58,* 432–436.

Small, S. A., & Luster, T. (1994). Adolescent sexual activity: An ecological, risk-factor approach. *Journal of Marriage and the Family, 56,* 181–192.

Sommer, K., Whitman, T. L., Borkowski, J. G., Schellenbach, C., Maxwell, S., & Keogh, D. (1993). Cognitive readiness and adolescent parenting. *Developmental Psychology, 29,* 389–398.

St. Lawrence, J. S., Brasfield, T. L., Jefferson, K. W., Alleyne, E., O'Bannon, R. E., & Shirley, A. (1995). Cognitive-behavioral intervention to reduce African American adolescents' risk for HIV infection. *Journal of Consulting and Clinical Psychological, 63,* 221–237.

Stoiber, K. C. (1995). Using research on adolescent pregnancy to construct prevention pathways. *The School Psychologist, 49,* 56–57.

Stoiber, K. C., & Anderson, A. J. (1996). Behavioral assessment of coping strategies in young children at-risk, developmentally delayed, and typically developing. *Early Education and Development, 7,* 25–42.

Stoiber, K. C., & Good, B. (in press). Risk and resiliency factors linked to problem behaviors in culturally-diverse urban adolescents. *School Psychology Review.*

Stoiber, K. C., & Houghton, T. G. (1993). The relationship of adolescent mothers' expectations, knowledge, and beliefs to their young children's coping behavior. *Infant Mental Health Journal, 14,* 61–79.

Stoiber, K. C., & Houghton, T. G. (1994). Adolescent mothers' cognitions and behaviors as at-risk indicators. *School Psychology Quarterly, 9,* 295–316.

Streett, R. (1991). Parenting education. In J. B. Hardy & L. S. Zabin (Eds.), *Adolescent pregnancy in an urban environment: Issues, programs and evaluation* (pp. 245–254). Washington, DC: The Urban Institute Press.

Stout, J, W., & Rivera, F. P. (1989). Schools and sex education: Does it work? *Pediatrics, 83,* 375–379.

Trad, P. V. (1994). Teenage pregnancy: Seeking patterns that promote family harmony. *The American Journal of Family Therapy, 22,* 42–56.

Walter, H. J., & Vaughn, R. D. (1993). AIDS risk reduction among a multiethnic sample of urban high school students. *Journal of the American Medical Association, 270,* 725–730.

Watkinson, L. C. (1991). Health education: Teaching the pregnant adolescent. In J. B. Hardy & L. S. Zabin (Eds.), *Adolescent pregnancy in an urban environment: Issues, programs and evaluation* (pp. 197–210). Washington, DC: The Urban Institute Press.

Windquist-Nord, C., Moore, K. A., Ruane-Morrison, D., Brown, B., & Myers, D. (1992). Consequences of teen-age parenting. *Journal of School Health, 62,* 310–319.

Zabin, L., Hirsch, M., Streett, R., Emerson, M., Smith, M., Hardy, J., & King, T. (1988). The Baltimore pregnancy prevention program for urban teenagers: How did it work? *Family Planning Perspectives, 20,* 182–192.

CHAPTER 17

FACILITATING PARTNERSHIPS AND CONFLICT RESOLUTION BETWEEN FAMILIES AND SCHOOLS

Sandra L. Christenson, UNIVERSITY OF MINNESOTA
Julie A. Hirsch, UNIVERSITY OF MINNESOTA

The eighth National Educational Goal states: "By the year 2000, every school will promote partnerships that will increase parent involvement and participation in promoting the social, emotional, and academic growth of children" (Goals 2000: Educate America Act, P.L. 103–227). Under the Improving America's Schools Act, P.L. 103–382, administrators must develop a policy specifying how they will consult parents while writing district plans to comply with new Title I mandates. As a result of this legislation, parents will have the opportunity to participate more and share responsibility for improved student achievement through parent/school compacts. These pieces of federal legislation have articulated a role for parents in planning state and local educational reform efforts. This role, according to Tony Wagner, president of the Institute of Responsive Education, is to ensure that parents "are not the passive, token 'yes' folks" (Hoff, 1994, p. 1). Implicit in these pieces of federal legislation is a recognition of what is known about the healthy development of children.

We know that both home and school are essential contexts for children's development (Okagaki & Sternberg, 1991); both parents and educators are vital, yet interdependent, socializing agents for children (Coleman, 1987); and the relationship between the microsystems of home and school is one variable that affects developmental outcomes for children (Bronfenbrenner, 1979). Thus, these facts should be the focus of psychologists' interventions (Christenson, Rounds, & Franklin, 1992). Research evidence strongly supports the home context as a major learning environment. Specifically, the importance of family variables in predicting a host of child outcomes (e.g., Rutter, 1985), academic achievement (Christenson, Rounds, & Gorney, 1992), and mean achievement for students in 37 states (Barton & Coley, 1992) has been documented. Home and school are conceived as overlapping spheres of influence (Epstein, 1992). Also, the seminal importance of consistency of influence and harmony between school and outside situations for children's development, first described in 1939 by Farris and Dunham, is recognized.

Schools must take the initiative for creating a climate of trust between families and schools. Barriers and misunderstandings exist for parents, educators, and the home/school relationship (Christenson, 1995a; Liontos, 1992). For example, parents may have negative attitudes about schools because of previous personal experiences, cultural and language barriers, and economic and emotional constraints. Schools and teachers may stereotype parents because of beliefs about at-risk populations, dwell on the hard-to-reach concept and parent apathy, and lack training in and funding for parent involvement. Limited time for communication, ritualized contacts, and differences in parent/professional perceptions are potential barriers for the home/school relationship.

New beliefs and principles help educators overcome the barriers. Liontos (1992) summarized the new beliefs about families and new principles for programs that characterize successful school "reaching out" efforts. New beliefs about families are (1) all families have strengths, (2) parents can learn ways to help their children if they are provided with the opportunity and necessary support, and (3) parents have important information and perspectives about their children. Principles underlying successful partnership programs are (1) a no-fault model where blame is not attributed to the family or school because there is not a single cause for the presenting concern, (2) a nondeficit approach where assets and strengths of individuals are emphasized, (3) the importance of empowerment where families are actively involved in decision making and choices for their personal lives, and (4) an ecological approach where there is recognition that the school environment influences the family and the family environment influences the school. Family/school partnership principles developed by the 42 schools in the League of Schools Reaching Out Project (Davies, Burch, & Johnson, 1992; cited in Ooms & Hara, 1991) provide a blueprint for creating a climate of trust between home and school. The nine principles are listed in Figure 17.1.

The elements of a collaborative partnership are not unrecognized by educators. However, even if home/school relationships are not of an adversarial nature, they may best be described by social distance or alienation (Lightfoot, 1978). Currently, home and school represent two microsystems that are used to operating autonomously, and this autonomy contributes a sense of social distance. Interventionists must understand that part of their task is to reorient parents and educators to the notion of shared responsibility (Seeley, 1991) and to the synergistic effect of the mesosystem of home and school on children's performance. Effective communication and problem solving are implied in the nine partnership principles listed in Figure 17.1. Putting the basic building blocks of a collaborative partnership together requires patience, desire, commitment, and a realistic sense of time (Knitzer & Yelton, 1989).

RELATIONSHIPS BETWEEN FAMILIES AND SCHOOLS

Relationships as rated by parents and teachers appear to be more positive than negative. Data from more than 2,000 parents and 1,000 teachers from the Metropolitan Life Survey of the American Teacher conducted in 1987 (cited by Olson, 1990) showed that 77% of parents and teachers rated the home/school relationship as good or excellent; only 7% of parents and 5% of teachers rated the relationship as poor. In addition, at least 60% of parents and teachers felt supported by each other; only 10% of parents and teachers reported poor support for each other. In a more recent national parent interview study on perceptions of home/school partnerships, Christenson, Hurley, Sheridan, and Fenstermacher (1994) found that 81% of 217 parents reported feeling very welcome or welcome at the school of their elementary- or secondary-aged child. Most parents described their contacts with school personnel as cooperative (93%) rather than conflicting (7%). A smaller percentage of parents described their contacts as mistrusting (11%), stressful (16%), or uncomfortable (16%).

These results reveal that home/school connections are less than optimal for a proportion, albeit small, of parents and teachers. In addition, 47% and 30% of parents indicated that their child's learning or behavior, respectively, had been a source of frequent and ongoing stress for the family. Olson (1990) cited that 19% of parents stated they felt awkward or reluctant to talk to school officials, whereas 55% of teachers said they felt uneasy or reluctant to approach parents to discuss their child. This mutual reluctance is at best a barrier for partnerships and at worst a stimulus for conflict and blame.

Figure 17.1 Partnership Principles for a Climate of Trust

1. Every aspect of the school building and general climate is open, helpful, and friendly to parents.
2. Communications with parents–whether about school policies and programs or about their own children–are frequent, clear, and two-way.
3. Parents are treated by teachers as collaborators in the educational process. Parents' own knowledge, expertise, and resources are valued as essential to their child's success in school.
4. The school recognizes its responsibility to forge a partnership with all families in the school, not simply those most easily available.
5. The school principal and other administrators actively express in words and deeds the philosophy of partnership with families.
6. The school encourages volunteer support and help from all parents by providing a wide variety of volunteer options, including those that can be done from home and during nonwork hours.
7. The school provides opportunities for parents to meet their own needs for information, advice, and peer support.
8. Parents' views and expertise are sought in developing policies and solving schoolwide problems; in some schools, parents are given important decision-making responsibilities at a policy level.
9. Schools recognize that they can best help parents provide a home environment conducive to children's learning if they facilitate their access to basic and supportive services.

Source: Family Impact Seminar, Washington, DC: American Association for Marriage and Family Therapy. Reprinted with permission.

Family/School Interactions

It is important to determine factors that facilitate or inhibit partnerships between schools and families. Power and Bartholomew (1987) offer a helpful categorization of family/school interaction patterns that is based on structural features of family and school systems, such as boundaries and hierarchies. They outline five family/school interaction patterns: avoidance, competitive, merged, one-way, or collaborative. The first four types are defined by either a rigid or diffuse boundary between home and school. Rigid boundaries reduce the cooperation between families and schools, whereas diffuse boundaries cause families and schools to perform one another's functions. In these situations, family/school interaction tends to result in conflicting relations. Even though parents and educators share common interests and tasks of socializing children to societal norms, it is often unclear which party is responsible for which task. Both families and educators may view their respective and the other's roles and responsibilities differently in meeting the needs of the developing child or youth. Due to the differing perspectives, which are often exacerbated by having information from only one context, conflicts and competition arise and can lead to alienation between the two systems.

Avoidant relations are defined by rigid boundaries that block communication between school and family. A lack of information sharing between the two primary systems of children's lives is harmful to development since it disrupts the functioning of the mesosystem (Bronfenbrenner, 1977). For example, consider the situation where Teresa was struggling in her fifth-grade reading class. The teacher asked Teresa's parents what they do to help Teresa improve her reading at home. Teresa's parents viewed the inquiry as intrusive and attempted to protect themselves from scrutiny by avoiding the discussion and assigning blame to the teacher. Teresa's teacher perceived the parents as unwilling to work with him and decided he would have to handle the situation by himself. Thus, a strict, rigid boundary between Teresa's teacher and family was established.

In a *competitive relationship*, the boundaries between home and school are diffuse, whereby each system exerts influence in the other system's domain. When school personnel and family members compete for dominant status within a hierarchy, conflicts can escalate to the point where the child is placed in a no-win position: failing to maintain the symmetrical transaction between home and school. Consider the following situation for Dawan. In the classroom, Dawan was very disruptive, often starting fights with other students and refusing to follow the teacher's directions. Dawan rarely completed his schoolwork and, as a result, was failing third grade. Dawan's teacher and mother met many times to discuss Dawan's school and family problems. Knowing Dawan's brother was very ill and his parents had less time to attend to Dawan, the teacher's solution was to allow Dawan to stop his schoolwork and sit in a corner of the classroom whenever he was upset. When he had "cooled down," which sometimes took as long as an hour, he and the teacher processed his outburst, and then he was permitted to return to class. Dawan's mother disagreed with this approach because he was missing too much schoolwork. She wanted the teacher to be harder on Dawan and require him to make up the work he missed during recess or after school. Both Dawan's mother and teacher agreed on finding a solution to his problem; however, in doing so, they encroached on each other's domain. Neither party was willing to back down from her position, and their relationships became competitive and hostile. While his mother and teacher were in conflict, Dawan received more attention; thus, he continued to act out in the classroom to maintain the increased attention at home and school.

A *merged relationship*, like the competitive relationship, is one in which the boundary between home and school is diffuse; however, the goals and purposes of each system become integrated. Feelings of suffocation or entrapment for children may occur because their needs are neglected. For example, both Ricky's teacher and mother were concerned about Ricky's increasingly poor attendance and absence from home for days at a time. Ricky's mother, as a single parent with three other boys to care for at home, was feeling overwhelmed. She was grateful that Ricky's teacher was willing to help prevent Ricky from dropping out of school and engaging in delinquent behavior. The teacher developed a hierarchical status in relation to Ricky's mother by undertaking more responsibility in managing Ricky's behavior, while his mother assumed less responsibility. As both systems merged in alliance against Ricky's behavior, Ricky felt more and more isolated, and his attendance problems increased.

The *one-way relationship* occurs when individuals in one system attempt to communicate with but are ignored by individuals in the other system. The one-way relationship, with its rigid boundaries, usually results in conflict because the initiating system will eventually become frustrated and either attack the other system or withdraw altogether. Again, the conflict that ensues creates more problems for the child, as in the case of Venesha. Venesha spent more time talking to her classmates than working on schoolwork. She had always been considered a very bright student, typically ahead of her classmates throughout her schooling. She was easily bored by the work her teacher gave her and tried to find other tasks to keep herself occupied, such as conversing with other students. Venesha's parents met with the teacher to request that Venesha be given more challenging assignments and additional homework. Venesha's teacher believed that the parents were pushing Venesha too hard and that her talking in class was in response to her parents' unrealistic expectations rather than boredom. The teacher explained her viewpoint and refused to adapt her teaching style. Venesha's parents became increasingly frustrated and appealed to the principal for Venesha to be assigned a new teacher. Their request was denied, so the parents felt their only alternative was to take the initiative to hire an after-school tutor for Venesha. In this one-way relationship, an agreement was not reached between home and school, and Venesha's parents assumed responsibility for the problem.

The fifth pattern of interaction, *collaborative*, involves neither rigid nor diffuse boundaries. Rather, in a collaborative relationship, a clear and flexible boundary exists where each partner defers to the other in each of their respective domains, according to circumstantial demands. Families and schools work together in a reciprocal and complementary fashion where parents and educators do not need to perform the same task or behavior to assist the child's school productivity. What is important is that the partners complement each other's efforts by working toward similar goals. For example, consider James, a fourth-grade student with a learning disability who had been in a full-day special education classroom since first grade. His teachers believed his math skills were strong enough to begin attending a regular education math class. A team meeting was held that included James's parents. The school staff was in favor of James transitioning to the regular math class, but his parents were hesitant. They were concerned about James's ability to function in a less supported setting and were afraid they were setting James up for failure. His parents were afraid that James, who is easily frustrated, would give up too easily in the new setting. After a long discussion, it was decided that James would be supported at school with a teaching aide in the math class until he felt comfortable on his own. At home, James would be supported by his parents, who would discuss with James his concerns and fears and encourage him not to give up. The team decided they would try the plan on a trial basis; the plan would be discontinued if either the team or James did not consider it effective. In this case, teachers and parents held common goals for James, and they collaborated on a solution to the problem. Each party felt comfortable sharing concerns, and neither party overstepped boundaries.

A major premise of this chapter is that conflict occurs when activities are incompatible (Tjosvold & Johnson, 1989), and blaming occurs when the incompatibility is not understood or left unresolved. Also, blame may imply that parents and educators hold a narrow conception of children's development. For example, in attempting to meet a child's needs, the teacher and parent focus only on one socialization context, either the home or school, but not the interaction between the two contexts. Examples of finger-pointing behavior between parents and teachers are provided in Table 17.1.

Blame between home and school often reflects a dysfunctional mesosystem that negatively affects the child. Consider DiCocco and Lott's (1982) description of four phases in the relationship between parents and teachers of a troubled child. Ask yourself: Is this situation descriptive of a troubled child or a troubled mesosystem? These phases demonstrate the development of conflict and how at each stage there is an opening for either the family or the school to act in a manner that prevents the conflict from escalating or causes the conflict to advance to the next stage.

The first phase occurs when there is the first sign of a problem. In this initial stage, there is an assumption that teachers will handle the student in school and the parents will handle the child at home. In the second phase, there is a shift in responsibility from teachers to parents; teachers believe that it is the parents' responsibility to make the child behave. In phase three, there is confusion about responsibility. A crisis has been reached where teachers and parents blame each other, and the child takes advantage of the situation by playing each party against the other. At this point, a mediator, such as a school psychologist, steps in and attempts to resolve the conflict. At the final phase, if a resolution has not been reached, both school personnel and the parents have relinquished responsibility and the child is removed from school. Failure to focus on the total learning environment for the child at home and the child at school provides the student with endless opportunities to increase inappropriate behavior.

To prevent blame, we encourage parents and educators to maintain a systemic orientation by focusing on a *problematic situation* that requires the attention, input, and responsibility of all partners rather than focusing on problematic behavior of an individual. Recognizing conditions that create and prevent conflict or blame will help educators in developing positive home/school relations, in addition to promoting consistent messages for the child as he or she traverses across family and school contexts.

CONDITIONS THAT CREATE CONFLICT

Conflict occurs when activities are incompatible (Tjosvold & Johnson, 1989); it is natural and noth-

Table 17.1 Examples of Parent/Teacher Finger-Pointing Behavior

PARENT STATEMENTS OF BLAME	TEACHER STATEMENTS OF BLAME
1. The teacher doesn't understand my child. My son has a unique learning style that requires attention that the teacher is unwilling to provide.	1. Parents are demanding. They don't realize that I have 29 other students and many other parents to deal with.
2. My daughter's teacher waits to call me until there's a problem. Doesn't he think I can be helpful before the problem arises? I know my child better than he does, yet no one has ever asked my opinion.	2. Some parents don't care enough about their children. How am I supposed to teach a student who has not been fed breakfast? Parents don't send their kids to school ready to learn.
3. Teachers act as if I know less than they do. I never know what goes on in my child's classroom. Don't they think I would understand?	3. Parents aren't understanding of my responsibilities and what a busy schedule I have. I teach six classes a day, which means I see 120 kids in a day. Parents expect me to keep track of their child and know his or her progress the second they call.
4. The teacher is too hard on my child. She singles him out to make him the example for the rest of the class.	4. I am a teacher, not a social worker. Yet I am expected to educate as well as handle my students' emotional needs.
5. The teacher treats me as if its my fault that my daughter is failing. The teacher expects me to teach my daughter at home; I work full time, I don't have time to do my job and hers, too.	5. Parents are hard to reach. They don't like me calling them at work, and I don't get paid to call them after 5:00 P.M.
6. Teachers treat parents as if they are a nuisance. I get the feeling I'm not an important part of my child's education.	6. Parents don't support my decisions. They undermine my instruction by questioning my judgment in front of their child.
7. The teacher never has time for my child. He gives all of his attention to the lower-level students; meanwhile, my child is not getting the education she deserves.	7. Most parents don't respect what I do—as if teaching is a less than prestigious profession. I bet most parents wouldn't last a day in my classroom.
8. Teachers are hard to reach. I always have to leave a message when I call the school. Sometimes it's days before they call back.	8. Parents aren't involved enough with their child's education. They don't even help their child with homework.

ing to be feared or avoided. For example, two individuals decide to meet for dinner in New York. One wants Italian food; the other wants Greek. They are experiencing conflict but not blame. The process of resolving different desires and understanding needs is key to circumventing blame and maintaining a personal relationship.

Conflict between home and school is not unidimensional; it occurs when individuals have different opinions about policies, practices, or program procedures. In describing the genesis of conflict, Margolis and Shapiro (1989) distinguish between pseudoconflict and substantive conflict. *Pseudoconflicts* are misunderstandings between parties, whereas *substantive conflicts* reflect disagreement between parties even when the parties accurately understand the other's perspective. While both types emanate from fear that individual needs will go unmet, conflicting perspectives do not need to result in a hostile transaction. According to Margolis and Shapiro (1989), "It is not disagreement that creates anger and its dysfunctional side effects, but *how* disagreement is handled" (p. 3, emphasis added). Therefore, our goal as interventionists is to prevent and/or manage conflict. Understanding that conflict simply arises from frustrating and socially tense situations (*ABCs of Scapegoating*, 1944), especially when personal perceptions and self-concepts are believed to be under attack, will assist educators in managing conflict effectively.

Conditions that contribute to conflict between schools and families stem from a number of

solving fashion. Finally, the impact of attitude on the success of interpersonal communication must be acknowledged. Positive expectations, openness to experience and ideas, and sincerity are some of the characteristics that contribute to the quality of the communication established.

Use of effective interpersonal communication skills and establishing two-way communication between home and school are described as major approaches for facilitating partnerships and preventing and/or handling pseudoconflict between home and school. Also, the use of active listening, assertive communication, negotiation, and blocking blame strategies are integral to the resolution of substantive conflict between families and schools.

Interpersonal Communication Skills

Defined as a process in which facts, opinions, or feelings are conveyed from one person or group to another person or group, communication is "much more complex than the definition implies" (Lombana, 1983, p. 42). The process relies on the accurate functioning of the sender, the message, and the receiver or "*expression* of an idea, a belief, a need, or a feeling by a speaker and the *assimilation* of this information by a listener in such a way that there is an almost perfect correspondence between what the speaker intended to say and what the listener understood" (DeBoer, 1986. p. 81). Communication involves both listening and expression; the use of effective skills is essential because the process yields the product (DeBoer, 1986).

In this section, deterrents to listening, passive listening, active listening, assertive communication, and conflict resolution skills are summarized. Much that has been written about communication skills focuses on those skills needed by educators to work effectively with parents (Lombana, 1983; Margolis & Brannigan, 1990) or by consultants to problem solve with teachers (DeBoer, 1986). Because the communication process is an exchange of information, the skills described in this section, and drawn from the work of the previous authors, apply to both parties in the partnership.

Deterrents to Listening

Listening, a learned skill and dynamic process that involves simultaneous processing of ideas and observable behaviors, is influenced by patterns of non-listening. DeBoer (1986) identified two deterrents to effective listening: the tendency by individuals to reject, evaluate, or contradict the message because of selective listening and the difficulty individuals have in acknowledging the perception of another individual. According to DeBoer (1986) and Margolis and Brannigan (1990), it is not necessary to agree with the content of the message, but empathy is essential. *Empathy* refers to the accurate understanding of the concerns, worries, proposed solutions, and perspective of the other individual. In other words, effective listening is dependent on the desire to listen; therefore, it is important for educators to create a context for conversation in which parents and educators feel relaxed, comfortable, and prepared. This is needed in all family/school group formats, including conferences, family/school meetings, and school-based management teams.

Passive Listening Skills

Passive listening, which is another term for attending, consists of physical attending and psychological attending. It is a prerequisite skill to active listening because it is a means of communicating interest, observing behaviors, and providing a framework that allows both parties to become active participants in the communication process. *Physical attending* refers to those behaviors by which individuals communicate that they are connected with other individuals, therefore, nonverbal behaviors, which are the conduit for emotional messages (DeBoer, 1986), are examples of physical attending.

Several nonverbal behaviors important for listening are illustrated in the FACES paradigm developed by Lombana and Pratt (1978). *FACES* refers to: face the person almost directly (F), approach by leaning slightly toward the person (A), compose yourself in this position (C), establish eye contact with the person (E), and space yourself two to four feet from the person(s). The degree of congruency between verbal ("I am interested in hearing what you have to say") and nonverbal (individual constantly glancing at the time) messages is essential to understanding what an individual is saying. DeBoer (1986) noted that 7% of information is communicated through words, 38% through voice pitch, intonation, and timing; and 55% through facial expressions and body language.

Psychological attending refers to giving the speaker undivided attention; therefore, the listener suspends judgments of the message, blocks out environmental distractions, and concentrates on the total message, which includes words, intonation, and body language sent by the speaker. It also refers to such facilitative skills as use of silence and responding. Lombana noted that individuals in general and educators in particular often have trouble with silence; the tendency is "to fill any vacuum with words" (1983, p. 65). Silence is used appropriately when it provides an individual who is expressing a problem or strong feeling with adequate time to pause and gather personal thoughts, reflect on previous comments, or engage in self-examination of feelings. Therefore, listeners must learn to be comfortable with silence and squelch the urge to comment on every statement made by the speaker. Finally, physical attending is enhanced by the use of appropriate responding skills by the listener. These include minimal encouragers, such as nodding of the head or phrases such as, "Yes, go on" and "Mm-hm," and the more complex skills of paraphrasing and clarifying. Passive attending skills are effective means of communicating interest and assisting an individual to express feelings; however, active listening is essential to engage in problem solving and conflict resolution.

Active Listening Skills

Listening is a vital ingredient for the quality of parent/educator relationships. Educators, in particular, need to assume a listening role when parents express a concern, share information, want help from an educator, or question school practices. Active listening has been described as total listening (DeBoer, 1986), empathic responding (Lombana, 1983), and empathic listening or understanding (Margolis & Brannigan, 1990). It includes such skills as "attending, responding, being non-judgmental, hearing the words, feelings, and thoughts expressed, hearing what is not being said, and hearing ourselves: our inner thoughts, feelings, insights, biases, and prejudices" (DeBoer, 1986, p. 87). Active listening communicates an acceptance of the individual, an understanding of what he or she is feeling, an understanding of the person's perspective of the situation; however, it should not be confused with agreement with the individual's perspective.

Active listening consists of three separate elements: understanding the situation from the other person's point of view, identifying and labeling the accompanying feelings that the person is expressing, and conveying understanding and acceptance. Lombana (1983) suggests that individuals formulate a response that contains the following elements: "You feel ____ because ____." To the statement, "What's the use of trying to help my kid?" an educator could say, "You feel really frustrated because you have tried many ways to change Tom's behavior."

The primary skill in active listening is reflecting. Other skills that facilitate understanding of perspectives between two parties include questioning and leading strategies. Guidelines for educators using questions include: (1) avoid the use of why questions because they conjure disapproval, judgment, and defensiveness; (2) limit the use of closed questions because the amount of information obtained is restricted and such an emphasis sets a tone of interview rather than problem-solving dialogue; (3) use open-ended questions to obtain truly necessary information; (4) ask questions that view the child's behavior contextually (e.g., "What happens when Joshua does . . . ?") (Fine & Clifford, 1992); and (5) phrase questions in the form of a statement (indirect question) to soften their interrogative quality. For example, Lombana (1983) suggests individuals say, "I'm interested in how your relationship got to this point" rather than "What happened to bring your relationship to this point?" (p. 69).

An important question is: What occurs as a result of active listening between parents and educators? Information sharing on more than a superficial level, gaining insight about the problem situation and an understanding of personal attitudes and feelings, and stronger communication were identified as benefits of active listening by Lombana (1983). Other benefits are dissipating parental anger, providing a better understanding of the problem, enhancing opportunities to generate solutions that are acceptable to parents (Margolis & Shapiro, 1989), and clarifying different positions so that compromises and integrations of positions can be made (Margolis & Brannigan, 1990).

In addition to listening, parents and educators must assume responsibility for clearly stating one's perspective. Both content (what is being stated) and process (how the message is communicated) must be considered to resolve pseudo- and substantive conflicts.

Assertive Communication

Lombana (1983) described three types of communication: passive, aggressive, and assertive; only assertive communication enables educators and parents to communicate thoughts, feelings, and needs to others effectively. In *passive* communication, feelings, opinions, or wishes are conveyed through body language, leaving the interpretation of the message primarily to the listener. In contrast, *assertive* communication involves the expression of ideas, thoughts, and feelings without attacking the listener and should be used when another person's behavior is creating a problem for an individual. According to Gordon (1974), "I messages" are an effective strategy for sending constructive messages because the sender communicates ownership of the problem. "I messages" have three components: description of the specific behavior that is unacceptable, effects or outcomes of the behavior, and true feelings about the behavior of the other person. The sender informs the listener of how his or her behavior is affecting the sender. In contrast, destructive messages for the relationship tend to place a negative focus on the other individual and emphasize what the individual did wrong through the use of "you messages."

Conflict Resolution Skills

Effective communication depends heavily on the use of active listening and assertive communication by both parents and educators. Regardless of the effectiveness of their communication, conflicts occur because individuals have different feelings and needs; individuals differ in their backgrounds, experiences, and viewpoints; and individuals interact in an ever-changing environment (Lombana, 1983). Blaming, however, does not need to occur. Conflict resolution must focus on both the specific problem to be resolved and the relationship between parties. Those engaging in conflict situations will find negotiating and use of blocking blame techniques essential skills to resolve the conflict *and* maintain the relationship between parties involved.

In *Getting to Yes: Negotiating Agreement without Giving In,* Fisher and Ury (1981) describe four elements of negotiation that are applicable to developing family/school partnerships: separate the person from the issue, focus on mutual interests, generate options prior to making decisions, and base final decisions on objective criteria. Negotiation leads to a win-win ("we vs. the problem") rather than a win-lose ("me vs. you") orientation. Unfortunately, sometimes the parent/educator relationship is influenced by the win-lose philosophy that permeates society. Approaching conflict as though it were a contest, with the goal of winning at all costs, perpetuates conflict and can weaken the parent/educator relationship. Negotiation skills are vitally important to prevent this situation.

First, the person, parent or educator, and the issue must be viewed separately; parents and educators must be viewed as "working together on the same side against the problem" (DeBoer, 1986, p. 21). They must attack the problem, not each other. The goals are to understand the perception and position of each party, and to accept the right of individuals to think differently. Persuasion rather than coercion—or education and logic rather than force—is recommended. Finally, acceptance between partners leads to feelings of worth and value, which encourages people to want to work together. Higher degrees of acceptance increase the likelihood that conflicts will be resolved. According to Fisher and Brown (1988), if one partner fails to use a behavior, the other partner should not give up, but rather continue because it is good for that person and the relationship.

With respect to the second element of negotiation—focus on mutual interests—parents and educators share a common interest: the education and development of children and youths. By focusing on how to promote the educational success of students (i.e., What is best for students ?), for example, parents and educators may find less need to defend a predetermined position through argument.

Collaboratively generating a variety of options before making a one-sided decision about problem resolution is a third element of negotiation. Obstacles that inhibit creative brainstorming of options include (1) premature judgment of a proposed solution, (2) a search for the best solution, (3) the belief that there are limited resources or options available, and (4) failure to see problems as a shared concern and shared responsibility for resolution (Fisher & Ury, 1981).

Finally, it is important to recognize that, under some situations, the interests of parents and educators conflict and may appear irreconcilable. The use of objective criteria to aid shared decision making—including research findings, ethical and fair standards, or expert judgment—increases the probability of achieving understanding between parties. Such an approach helps to maintain the relationship because the decision is not influenced by who is most tenacious in an argument.

The success of conflict resolution between parents and educators is influenced by the degree to which blocking blame techniques, which have been developed by Howard Weiss and colleagues on the Home-School Collaboration Project at the Ackerman Institute of Family Therapy, are employed (Weiss & Edwards, 1992). In Figure 17.2, descriptions and examples developed by Weiss for blocking blame between parents, teachers, and students are provided. The use of direct blocking, reframing, probing, refocusing, illustrating, validating, and agreeing by parents and educators when engaged in problem-solving dialogues about the student helps to maintain the focus on mutual responsibility for problem resolution.

Establishing Two-Way Communication

Effective communication is considered the foundation of all family involvement in education (Cale, 1993). According to Cale, good communication between parents and educators is needed to share information about children's progress, needs, and interests; establish shared goals for children's education; inform parents of what is expected in terms of student behavior and achievement; inform teachers of what parents expect relative to curriculum and discipline; inform parents of classroom activities and events; avoid misunderstandings; and help parents understand how to reinforce school instruction at home.

There are several characteristics of communication that facilitate a partnership and/or reduce the probability of pseudoconflict between families and schools. First, communication must be targeted to the general goal of improving students' educational success and development. Second, the content, method, and extent of communication should be developed to fit a specific purpose. For example, mass-produced print messages may be effective to provide most parents with general information on school policies and procedures; home visits or phone calls may be needed for some parents. In contrast, communicating about a controversial curriculum or school-based concerns for a child require face-to-face contact and parent/educator dialogue and discussion. Third, both frequency and content of the messages are important. According to McAfee (1993), home/school partnerships are dependent on communication of the right message: "*that mutual respect and interdependence of home, school, and community are essential to children's development*" (p. 21; italics added). Thus, the tone of the message, or whether parents are perceived as partners and peers in decision making, is as important as the frequency of contact between home and school. Both parents and educators may convey wrong messages such as, "School knows best,"

Figure 17.2 Techniques for Blocking Blame

Direct Blocking: Signaling that the purpose of the interaction is not to blame but to solve a problem. *Example*:

- Student: *Johnny always starts the fights—it's not my fault.*
- Teacher: *We're not here to find out who's to blame but to figure out how you and Johnny can get your work done instead of fighting.*

Reframing: Providing an alternate point of view about a set of facts which gives the facts a more positive, productive meaning. *Example*:

- Teacher: *These parents drive me nuts—all they're concerned about is whether their child is going to get into the top class. It starts in pre-kindergarten.*
- Teacher: *It sounds as if they're trying to be an advocate for their child's education and get them started off on the right track.*

Probing: Eliciting additional information to clarify the context leading to the blaming. *Example:*

- Student: *The teacher always picks on me.*
- Teacher: *I certainly don't intend to pick on you, David. What do you see me doing that makes you think I'm picking on you? Give me some examples.*

Refocusing: A statement which redirects the discussion from a non-productive or nonessential area to an area relevant to helping the student. *Example:*

- Parent: *Jose did great last year with Ms. Johnson. We think that Ms. Williams is just not as good a teacher.*
- Guidance Counselor: *I can see that you're very concerned that Jose has a good year this year, too.*

Illustrating: Giving concrete examples of areas of concern. *Example:*

- Parent: *He doesn't act that way at home. You just don't know how to deal with him.*
- Teacher: *What I've observed is that Johnny acts that way when he is with his friends. They enjoy talking with each other so much that they don't seem to be able to stop when it's time to get down to work.*

Validating: Recognizing the validity of another's perception or efforts. *Example:*

- Parent: *I know Jane needs me to spend more time with her—maybe I should quit going to school.*
- Principal: *I can understand your concern about spending time with Jane, but your going to school is also a positive role model for her. Let's see if there are other ways you could be helpful to her.*

Agreeing: Confirming someone's perception of a situation. *Example:*

- Teacher: *It really drives me nuts when people come in and think they can just take over the classroom.*
- Parent: *It would drive me nuts, too, if I thought someone was trying to take over something that I was responsible for.*

Source: Training handout from Howard M. Weiss, Center for Family-School Collaboration, Ackerman Institute for Family Therapy, New York, NY. Reprinted with permission.

"Parents must adapt to the school's agenda," or "School efforts are inadequate or inappropriate to meet the needs of our child." Fortunately, there are guidelines and specific practices that can be employed to establish and maintain two-way communication between home and school. Consider the following:

1. *Communication between home and school is characterized by a positive orientation rather than a deficit-based or crisis orientation.* With a positive orientation, all communication between parents and educators strives to focus on skill acquisition or goals rather than deficits or problems for the child, and is initiated at the first sign of problematic child behavior, whether it is observed in home or school contexts.

2. *Develop and publicize a regular, reliable home/school communication system that increases the potential for two-way communication* (McAfee, 1993). A major emphasis is placed on implementing communication strategies that reach all families. Therefore, the use of varied means (print; personal contact; technology; nonliterate symbol, such as a stop sign, to convey a need to talk to each other) and establishment of a routine phone calling/contact system will need to be available for parents and educators. McAfee rightly argues that "successful school-home communication begins where parents are—their interests, needs, and capabilities—not where the school wishes them to be" (1993, p. 28). With respect to increasing two-way communication, educators could provide parents with a list of important phone numbers; inform parents who, how, and when to contact at the first sign of a home-observed school performance concern; include as part of the communication system procedures that require a parent response or sign-off; use parent surveys, focus groups, or forums to obtain parent input, particularly on anticipated changes in school practices; make home visits for those parents who do not respond or attend school functions; and use *and* acknowledge use of information from parents when improving home/school communication and other practices.

3. *The focus of communication and dialogue between parents and educators is on children's performance vis-à-vis educational issues.* Emphasis is placed on frequent, systematic, and ongoing communication about children's school progress and completion of homework. The use of electronic technology (Bauch, 1990), school-to-home-to-school communications involving classroom activities (goals, materials) and progress (grades, effort, attitude), a suggested activity for parents (Ames, 1993), and a home/school notebook or assignment book for all students (Rioux & Berla, 1993) are means to achieve systematic communication. In addition, we contend that educators need to encourage parents to take responsibility for knowing the current and actual performance levels of their children. This can be accomplished by telling parents whom to contact if they are curious about their child's grades, assignment completion, attention, and participation in a course.

4. *Ensure that parents have the information they need to support their child's educational progress.* Sometimes educators mistakenly assume that school policies and procedures and the desired parent response are "obvious" to parents (McAfee, 1993). It has been shown that parents, particularly those who are more socially distant or alienated from schools, want their children to be successful in school, but do not assist their children because of a lack of information about school policies and procedures (Davies, 1991). The language of schooling (Christenson, 1995a), which must be communicated to *all* families, is an essential prerequisite of collaboration. Honest and clear communication is enhanced by parents and educators having similar information.

5. *Informal opportunities to communicate and build trust between home and school are created.* Referred to as climate-building activities by Weiss & Edwards (1992), several authors have noted the importance of informal social gatherings with food that provide opportunities for conversation as a way to initiate positive relationships between parents and educators (Comer, 1995; Swap, 1993). Swap (1993) describes several examples, including welcome-back-to-school events like multicultural potluck dinners, family member breakfasts, and holiday events; these activities have been described by Davies (1990, p. 42) as examples of the "essential lubrication for more serious intervention" and by Christenson (1995a) as ways of "finding friendly

faces in the crowd." Creating a welcoming atmosphere in school by greeting parents, displaying welcome signs, designating a parent center, providing for translators, and employing outreach workers (Swap, 1993) help to build trust.

Trust between parents and educators is not automatic; the value of implementing trust-building activities is that the notion of collaboration becomes the norm. Swap (1993) aptly contends, "If collaboration and open discussion of conflict are not normative, then it is difficult for individuals to risk authentic listening and sharing" (p. 90). The goal of trust building is more than helping parents feel comfortable at school or talking with educators. Most importantly, the goal is connection between parents and educators. A collaborative ethic is defined by the relationship as well as the completion of a task.

6. *All communication must underscore a shared responsibility between families and schools for educational outcomes.* Collaboration and partnership between home and school to promote students' school performance and development must be emphasized in communications. We contend that educators need to discuss the ecological theory of child development proposed by Bronfenbrenner (1979) and the socialization process described by Coleman (1987) with families. Many factors are associated with educational outcomes; therefore, the importance of partnership can be explained by summarizing the school and home factors, correlates of academic achievement, and the importance of congruent messages between these environments (Ysseldyke & Christenson, 1993; Norby, Thurlow, Christenson, & Ysseldyke, 1990).

PROBLEM-SOLVING APPROACHES

In this section, strategies for problem solving between home and school are described. Some of the approaches are relevant for building trust and partnerships between families and schools. Some are used for resolving conflict. All approaches require the use of effective communication skills and competency in problem solving. All are based on four principles:

1. School personnel view their relations with families as a means for preparing the child for success in school rather than as a mechanism for collecting information from parents that would help educators prepare the child (Powell, 1991). Thus, educators have moved beyond a focus on the components of the problem to a focus on the functional requirements for the development of a healthy, productive child (Christenson, 1995b; Powell, 1991) and on joint ownership of the responsibility for change and solution (Cronin, Slade, Bechtel, & Anderson, 1992).
2. Parents and educators recognize the child as the central purpose of their collaboration (Lightfoot, 1978). The collaborative relationship (Power & Bartholomew, 1987) establishes a clear boundary between home and school, but one in which parents and educators defer to each other in their respective domains, roles are flexible and change according to situational demands, and reciprocity is valued.
3. Discontinuities between home and school are not feared but are investigated and understood. Conflicts and differences are communicated openly and directly (Lightfoot, 1981; Swap, 1993). The communication system between home and school includes a mechanism for routinely sharing information on issues of mutual concern (Cronin et al., 1992).
4. The focus of professional helping shifts from diagnosis and treatment to development of a cooperative partnership with parents (Dunst & Trivette, 1987). Based on the principles of empowerment, the help seeker is viewed as capable and competent; opportunities need to be created to allow the competence to emerge. The help giver sees strengths of the client and facilitates problem solving to establish shared ownership for solution identification (deShazer, 1982; 1985).

Family/School Groups: Individual Focused

Descriptions of four approaches follow. Although the primary goal of these approaches is to create a partnership between families and schools to promote student competence, they also provide a forum for resolving pseudoconflict.

Family/School Problem-Solving Meeting

The purposes of the family/school meeting developed by Weiss and Edwards (1992) are to achieve a productive outcome for the child and to alter the interface between home and school so that a collaborative climate becomes the norm. This norm should not only apply to future interactions between parents and educators around a specific child but also to group problem solving, which allows educators and parents to mutually support each other to find solutions to schooling problems (e.g., school vandalism). The meeting follows a structured set of steps that maintain a focus on problem solving and nonblaming interactions.

Introduction and Overview, the first step, includes invitation of participants to attend the meeting and the introduction at the actual meeting. To maintain a systems-ecological approach, the student and key stakeholders in the student's life attend. The facilitator sets a nonblaming, problem-solving tone by communicating that (1) the purpose of the meeting is to discover how to provide the best school experience for the student, (2) all participants will have an opportunity to express their concerns, and (3) the desired outcome is a concrete plan of action to address a couple of mutually agreed upon concerns. This introduction signals, according to Weiss and Edwards, that the stakeholders' concerns are important and will be heard, the meeting is not a punishment, and the meeting has the clear purpose of action (not merely talk) for change. In addition, an appropriate boundary between home and school is underscored by maintaining a focus on school issues rather than family life issues.

In the second step, *Finding Facts,* participants describe one or two concerns, not a long list of worries or complaints. The facilitator probes for factors in the child's life that maintain the problem, situations when the problem does not occur, personal meanings participants have associated with described behaviors, and attempted solutions. Blocking blame techniques (see Figure 17.2) are employed to block blame between parents, teachers, and the student as they discuss the problematic situation. Throughout the *Finding Facts* step, the facilitator checks for consensus by highlighting areas of agreement around which parents, educators, and the student could work together.

Next, participants must decide on which concern they will work together to change; this is what is meant by *Determining a Decision.* The facilitator focuses the discussion toward which, of all things shared and discussed, will be most helpful to develop a plan of action. Participants *Arrive at Action* by delineating the roles and responsibilities of participants or who will do what, when, where, and how. The final step is a *Follow-Up Meeting,* which serves to hold participants accountable and provides a mechanism to routinely share information. If the outcome desired by participants was not achieved, no one is blamed; rather, the facilitator focuses discussion on constraints that prevented participants from implementing the plan and on development of a new plan.

Parent-Educator Problem Solving

The purposes of Parent-Educator Problem Solving (PEPS) are to create a partnership between parents and educators and to use the partnership as a vehicle for fostering an educative home environment, one in which congruence between home and school environments is achieved (Christenson, 1995a). PEPS, a modification of the family/school meeting described by Weiss and Edwards, was developed with parent and educator input and has been implemented in both suburban elementary and urban middle-school settings. The four steps in PEPS are: introduction, identification, selection, and implementation. While a structured sequence is followed by the facilitator, a relaxed conversational tone between parents and educators is sought.

Stage One: Introduction. In the introduction stage, the facilitator of the meeting builds rapport with parents, educators, and the student by discussing a positive school, school district, or community event and offering a positive comment that has been stated by an educator about the student. Also, the school-based concern is described. The facilitator expresses the concern about student performance using specific, observable, behavioral language that describes the actual behavior of the student, not an educator's inference or conclusion about the behavior.

Then the facilitator reframes the concern as a learning goal (i.e., what the student needs to learn or educators want to teach the student). The facilitator invites parents to help them achieve this goal by explaining that parents are important partners in school-based interventions and that student achievement is enhanced through family/school partnerships (Christenson, Rounds, & Gorney, 1992; Henderson & Berla, 1994).

If parents decide not to be active participants, the intervention to be employed by school personnel is described, parent input is sought, and parents' questions are answered. A way to maintain ongoing contact, usually through phone or home/school notes, is established. If parents agree to participate and become contributors to the solution, the remaining three stages are employed.

Stage Two: Identification. In the identification stage, concerns and perceptions of the participants that are related to the school-based concern are identified. Parents may describe other concerns, which are reframed and listed as learning goals, and recorded so they can be addressed. Next, participants identify mutual learning goals (i.e., desired student behavior). Learning goals for the student are listed and prioritized, and parents and educators select one to work on collaboratively. It is possible that parents and educators will work independently to address other goals. Information sharing about efforts to address these goals is encouraged and facilitated by establishing a contact system between home and school.

At this point, it is crucial for the facilitator to check for the understanding of participants. The facilitator accomplishes this by restating the learning goal as a discrepancy between actual and desired student behavior. The goal of the partnership is described as a common effort toward closing this discrepancy. The facilitator also asks whether there are other contributing factors in the child's life that must be shared to enhance the success of parents' and educators' efforts in supporting student learning.

Stage Three: Selection. In the selection stage, possibilities for solution are generated by brainstorming, listing all suggestions, and eliminating any evaluation of suggestions. The emphasis is on what parents, educators, and the student can do to enhance the probability that the learning goal will be achieved by the student. Next, participants indicate their choice of intervention for facilitating student progress toward the learning goal. The facilitator helps parents and educators identify necessary information or resources (such as the need for ongoing consultation) to support their implementation efforts.

Stage Four: Implementation. In the implementation stage, the solution plan is described by clearly stating the roles and responsibilities of participants and determining a time line for implementation and evaluation. The generated plan is implemented, during which time dialogue between home and school focuses on whether the plan is enhancing student performance. Modifications to the plan may be made as a result of this ongoing contact. The plan is considered successful if the discrepancy between actual and student behavior is closed. In these cases, all participants celebrate. If the plan is unsuccessful, no one is to blame; replanning occurs.

In the PEPS approach, parents are directly invited to be partners in supporting student learning. Parents overwhelmingly agree to be partners; however, without active follow-up by a designated case manager, implementation of the plan is low. It has been found that parents need information and support to follow through on the plan. The approach has been successful in addressing attendance and homework problems for elementary and middle-school students. Although no gains in student achievement have been attributed to the use of PEPS, parents and teachers rated home/school communication and interactions more favorably.

Solution-Oriented Family-School Meetings

Carlson, Hickman, and Horton (1992) have adopted the solution-oriented brief therapy approach (de Shazer, 1982) for use in schools through what they refer to as Solution-Oriented Family-School Meetings. The hallmark of the solution-oriented framework is a shift from problem resolution by analyzing in detail the problem to solution identification through an active search for solutions. Terminology of solution-oriented brief therapy is different; the word *difficulty* is used to replace *problem*, and *complaint* is used to signal that repeated efforts to resolve a difficulty have been unsuccessful because individuals get stuck in the way they view the difficulty and subsequently in the way they respond to the difficulty. At solution-oriented family/school meetings, the facilitator helps parents and educators construct solutions that fit personal constraints of the situation. Thus, the facilitator blocks blame between participants, encourages experimentation with different interventions, and maintains a positive orientation.

Techniques that change the viewing of a complaint include: (1) introducing uncertainty into the individual's viewpoint through reframing and normalizing and depathologizing the behavior of concern (O'Hanlon & Weiner-Davis, 1989); (2) increasing the controllability of a complaint through deconstruction; and (3) providing multiple solutions to the complaint through summarizing observations of child behavior in multiple contexts. Techniques for changing the response patterns surrounding the difficulty include: (1) focusing initial interview questions on exceptions to the complaint; (2) using interruption techniques that include altering frequency, intensity, duration, or sequence of the behavior (deShazer, 1988); and (3) focusing on resources, strengths, and abilities of the child, teacher, and parents.

An assumption underlying solution-oriented family/school meetings is that individuals involved in the home/school relationship (parents and educators) have the competencies and resources to handle the difficulty; however, they have gotten stuck in their view of the child's problem and in their efforts to change the child's behavior. As a result, child behavior appears stable, internal, and uncontrollable, parents and educators are frustrated and defeated, and blaming often is used to alleviate adult emotions. To resolve the complaint, 10 phases are followed by a facilitator during the family/school meeting in which the child is present. Consider the following:

Phase 1: Introduction. The facilitator (usually a school psychologist, counselor, or principal) introduces the participants and acknowledges the importance of multiple perspectives and active participation by all. In addition, a collaborative tone is set by noting the expertise of both parents and teachers and the good fortune of the student to have adults interested in his or her growth and development.

Phase 2: Explanation of the solution-oriented approach. The benefit of advance cognitive organizers, according to the authors, is to set the expectation that complaints are "dissolvable" and solutions are possible. The authors have found that the "norms for blaming and complaining in schools are so strong that some advance cognitive organizers are helpful" (Carlson et al., 1992, p. 201).

Phase 3: Joining. Joining is a necessary step toward building rapport and involves acknowledging each person's point of view through active listening and responding by mirroring a person's language. For example, if parents discuss an "attitude problem," the facilitator uses the word *attitude* in subsequent questions or reflective statements.

Phase 4: Negotiating a solvable complaint. The facilitator looks for similarities and differences across participants in their complaint and viewing of the problem. Participants are asked to provide a "video description" of their complaint (i.e., other participants can see the complaint in action as in a video recording) and to identify the strengths of the child and past solutions to the complaint. Exceptions to the difficulty or visualization of the future without the problem by parents and educators often point to possible solutions.

Phase 5: Establishing a solution goal. After a mutually agreed upon complaint is identified, participants identify an initial, positively oriented goal for change.

Phase 6: Gaining agreement on the smallest change in the direction of the goal. According to the authors, "Working toward the smallest change is an important shift in both the viewing and doing of the complaint within the social contexts of the child such that lasting change, which generally occurs in small increments, can be rewarded" (Carlson et al., 1992, p. 203). For example, the goal of taking a 10-minute walk each day will be more noticeable than will be the goal of losing 10 pounds.

two years of operation, team members found themselves engaged in finger-pointing behavior when a new issue was discussed. The encouraging news is that they quickly identified their unproductive behavior and focused common efforts toward a shared goal. They learned to listen, understand that different perspectives were acceptable, and create a plan that addressed the needs of students, families, and schools.

7. The final lesson, and perhaps most important, was that the partnership notion for student success in school had to be salient. The group facilitator was very persistent about ensuring that the goal of PATHS—partnerships for student learning—was dominant. Based on the experience with PATHS, Epstein's (1995) redefinition of "decision making to mean a process of partnership, of shared views and actions toward shared goals, not just a power struggle between conflicting ideas" (p. 705) is right on!

Parent/teacher action research teams, a tool for collective social problem solving, are considered especially relevant for schools and communities coping with complex social and educational problems (Palanki & Burch, 1995). Successful team process was characterized by negotiation and compromise and shifting discussion from complex rhetoric to specific and solvable problems. Among the identified benefits was the development of a constructive two-way communication process between families and school staff.

Workshops

In two school-based projects directed by the senior author, parents overwhelmingly agreed they needed information about ways to help their children be successful in school. This finding corroborates a conclusion from researchers examining family/school partnerships, which is "just about all families care about their children, want them to succeed, and are eager to obtain better information from schools and communities so as to remain good partners in their children's education" (Epstein, 1995, p. 703). According to Epstein, the challenge for educators is how to provide this information to all families who want it and need it. We know that the medium must be broader than print materials. Three examples of successful workshops with parents are described.

In the first example, parent groups were developed by identifying a group of students who had specific problems (e.g., poor task completion, behavior, attendance). Parents of the students were asked to help other parents and school personnel improve the student behavior observed in school. Parents whose children demonstrated the behavior met with two group leaders, a school psychologist and a social worker to discuss and share possible strategies for altering student behavior. Parents of students at an urban middle school in the Miami area were solicited for group participation in this fashion when their children were not completing assigned tasks in middle school. The approach was very successful in increasing the task completion rate for students whose parents were actively involved in the small-group sessions (Collins, Moles, & Cross, 1982). This approach focused on improving student performance for an identified problem and empowering parents to be part of the solution.

A second example is drawn from Comer's (1995) School Development Program. In this program, monthly seminars are provided on topics of mutual interest to parents and teachers and focus on acquisition of academic and social skills for students. Both parents and educators may attend the seminars, which provides the added benefit of placing parents and teachers in co-roles of teachers and learners.

In the third example, Goodman, Sutton, and Harkavy (1995) reported success in addressing parent-identified concerns (adolescent development, self-esteem, family communication, behavior management, peer pressure, sexuality, and substance abuse) in a series of six Saturday family workshops in an urban middle school. The majority of the 40 family members judged the workshops to be very helpful, the instructors to be very helpful, and their ability to care for their adolescent as greatly improved. In addition, the participants noted that it was valuable to exchange and share experiences in a caring and respectful setting. Goodman and associates (1995) concluded, "Many 'hard-to-reach' parents or middle school students will respond with enthusiasm and gratitude to opportunities for family-school collaboration. But in order to break through the layers of distrust and disillusionment built up over many frustrating years of hardship, extra and persistent efforts must be made. A successful program requires a great deal of organization; a skillful, experienced, enthusiastic staff; and a never-flagging attitude of care and respect" (p. 700). Once again, the seminal importance of connection with parents is illustrated.

These approaches are the antithesis of traditional parent education offerings where parents are referred to a specific course. They are proactive, link family/educator interaction to improving student performance, recognize the valuable input of parents' suggestions, and maintain the salience of partnership between home and school to promote the healthy development of children. Epstein (1995) has offered a helpful redefinition of *workshop*, which she suggests means "more than a meeting about a topic held at the school building at a particular time. Workshop may also mean making information about a topic available in a variety of forms that can be viewed, heard, or read anywhere, anytime, in varied forms" (p. 705). Content discussed in the three workshop examples could be disseminated through newsletters, videotapes, and consultation.

CONFLICT RESOLUTION STRATEGIES

There are times when parents and educators accurately understand each other's positions and continue to disagree. They both have needs they seek to satisfy. Also, conflict between individuals and systems often escalates because it is accompanied by intense feelings, such as anger, and/or the belief or fear that the other party will frustrate or impede satisfaction of a personal need. According to Margolis and Shapiro (1989), substantive conflict necessitates that structured problem solving follow trust building and empathic listening. In this section, strategies and guidelines for dealing with anger through empathic listening and trust building and resolving conflicts through structured problem solving are addressed. Specific application to parent/teacher conferences in which conflict is present follows.

Dealing with Anger

Issues underlying parental anger must be addressed rather than ignored because anger makes future cooperation more difficult, obscures reasons for the anger, increases the probability of increased interpersonal conflict, and affects program planning for students (Margolis & Brannigan, 1990). Several authors acknowledge that creating a receptive attitude in angry parents is not an easy task or fast process (Fine & Clifford, 1992; Lombana, 1993; Margolis & Brannigan, 1990). Strategies emphasize ways to help parents dissipate their anger and to begin to act in more rational and constructive ways. Educators cannot prevent angry parents; however, they can learn to manage anger and handle substantive conflict by behaving in specific ways. Although many suggestions for dealing with angry parents appear in the literature, we suggest five are essential for the home/school relationship: preserve the partnership, allow parents an opportunity to "vent," act as a problem solver, recognize the value of time, and employ a mediator.

First, conflict resolution should not be viewed as a win-lose or accommodative process, but rather as problem solving with an emphasis on achieving mutual satisfaction of parents', educators', and the student's needs (Margolis & Shapiro, 1987). Viewing the situation as an opportunity to improving existing conditions and operating with the belief that parents and educators can learn from the other help resolve disputes and enhance relationships (Margolis, 1991).

Second, listening is the key for dealing with aggressive, angry, or hostile parents. Effective listening requires educators to remain calm and attentive when parents are argumentative, encourage the exploration of critical concerns through the use of reflective statements on the most important aspects of parents' message, use open-ended questions to better understand parental concerns, explore concerns until pseudo-issues have been differentiated from critical, underlying concerns, and summarize points of agreement and disagreement (Margolis & Brannigan, 1990). According to Margolis (1990), the critical moment is immediately following the verbal attacks by an angry parent. He contends educators should listen to understand parents' positions and suggestions and explore their ideas as legitimate options. Hostile interactions are never pleasant and, admittedly, the goal is to restore equilibrium as quickly as possible.

Third, educators should adopt a problem-solving stance and behave in ways that facilitate the sharing of thoughts, ideas, feelings, and actions surrounding the problematic situation. Ways to stay on track when involved in an emotionally intense conference or verbal interchange include (1) Don't be afraid to explain that you have done some things differently or that you have made a mistake; (2) Recognize that you may not have the full picture or complete story—create an attitude of "We're here to work together"; (3) Maintain a focus on conflict resolution—emphasize present to future interactions by considering "What's going to happen from this point on?"; (4) Do not argue with parents or defend one's own or the school's position—explain perspectives, policies, or procedures; (5) Recognize that an acceptable compromise has not been found when an agreement is not reached; and (6) Keep language and vocabulary at the parents' level (Fine & Clifford, 1992).

Fourth, allocating sufficient time to resolve concerns and portray that parents' concerns have been heard and are understood is essential to conflict resolution. "Building trust in a climate of distrust takes time" (Margolis & Brannigan, 1990, p. 8). According to Margolis and Brannigan, trust building is an interactive process that is dependent on reciprocity, such as the sharing of ideas, information, feelings, and resources. They suggest that trust can be established with parents by behaving in trustworthy ways, including accepting parents as they are; sharing information and resources; focusing on parents' aspirations, concerns, and needs; keeping their word; discussing their objectives openly; and preparing for meetings. Too often, educators want to solve the problem quickly and in their way. They are too focused on *the* solutions rather than on the interaction process that can yield a sound product.

Fifth, in the event parent distrust of school personnel is extremely intense and intractable, a third party from outside the school, which the parents and school view as neutral, should be engaged to establish shared goals (Margolis & Shapiro, 1987) or to resolve conflicts in the home/school relationship in order to preserve student functioning (Lusterman, 1985).

Structured Problem Solving

Problem solving, essential to address substantive conflict, encourages cooperation between parents and educators and provides a systematic structure to assist parents and educators in identifying underlying concerns, generating manageable alternatives, enumerating their consequences, and selecting solutions that satisfy the needs of both parties (Margolis & Brannigan, 1990). The following two problem-solving sequences are very similar to the four individual-focused approaches. The difference in these approaches is the focus on disagreement between parties and the handling of the disagreement to avoid ongoing hostile interaction and blaming. Substantive conflict between parties must be acknowledged. It must be understood by parties that the focus of the problem solving is to resolve the disagreement or substantive conflict and to prevent more extreme measures of conflict resolution such as due process hearings or arbitration.

Margolis and Brannigan (1990) describe the steps in the IDEAL model developed by Bransford and Stein (1984) as *Identify* potential problems, *Define* and represent the problem, *Explore* prospective solutions, *Act* on agreed-upon solutions, *Look* at the effects. They note the model is structured, moving from understanding to solution seeking to evaluation, and recommend that the facilitator remain flexible and responsive to the needs of parents and educators engaged in the problem-solving process. Potential solutions must be generated without any consideration of merits or limitations because evaluation will only inhibit creativity and idea sharing.

Also, the use of several strategies to generate solutions is recommended. Strategies may include "brainstorming, dividing problems into parts, working backward from clearly defined end goals, developing analogs, investigating how others solved similar difficulties, and focusing on relevant but simpler circumstances" (Margolis & Brannigan, 1990, pp. 11–12). They advocate for participants to use criteria such as potential benefits and possible problems to evaluate suggested solutions and to provide a forum for parents and educators to educate the other about home or school viewpoints (Margolis, 1991).

Parents and educators strive to reach consensus, which means an idea is worth trying but may not be the preferred choice of parents and educators. In those situations where consensus is not reached, they recommend that parents and educators consider whether the problem was accurately identified, parents' and educators' needs were understood and addressed, hidden agendas were present, or differences in parent and educator values require resolution by an impartial third party, who is trusted by involved parties. Responsibilities and time lines should be provided in writing to involved parties, and a follow-up meeting to examine the effects of the plan should be scheduled. In this model, parents and educators decide together whether to continue, modify, or abandon the plan.

A five-stage conflict resolution process, illustrated by the acronym SOLVE, has been developed by Lombana and Pratt (1978; cited in Lombana, 1983, p. 76). The process occurs as follows:

1. S Share thoughts, feelings, and needs involved in the conflict.
2. O Obtain a list of all possible solutions to the conflict.
3. L Locate the best possible solution that will satisfy mutual needs.
4. V Validate the conflict resolution process by implementing the solution.
5. E Evaluate the implemented solution by following up on it.

SOLVE recognizes the needs and goals of both parties involved in the dispute and strives to maintain the parent-educator relationship. Active listening and assertive communication are used while the conflicting parties share their thoughts, feelings, and needs, and strive to understand those of the other party. Like IDEAL, brainstorming is used to generate a list of solutions to the substantive conflict identified. The authors have found a longer list provides greater likelihood that mutually satisfying solutions will be found. Both parties share in implementation of the plan.

In closing, IDEAL and SOLVE have been described as two examples of structured problem solving that are helpful conflict-resolution approaches. No studies examining efficacy of these approaches between families and school personnel were found. Although these approaches were developed with a focus on an individual student, it seems to us they are applicable to problem solving with small groups of parents and educators.

When All Else Fails

Margolis and Brannigan (1990) use the phrase *when all else fails* to convey that substantive conflict persists despite the use of trust building, structured problem solving, negotiation efforts, and creative mediation. The fundamental aspects of resolving disputes between parents and educators—arranging to discuss the issue as soon as possible; allowing sufficient time for problem-solving discussions; sharing information, feelings, and perceptions; listening to the point of view of the other party; and agreeing on definition of the problem—have been employed and yet parents and educators have different goals and continue to disagree about the nature of the problem (Margolis & Brannigan, 1990; Swap, 1993). In these situations, we suggest two options appear to be available to educators. They are to rediscuss the ownership of the problem or hold a formal due process hearing.

According to Kroth (1985, p. 129), "The first consideration in problem solving is to establish ownership of the problem. At first this may seem to be a clear-cut step, but parents and teachers tend to want to place the problem in the other's domain." Again, we contend blame exists when parents and educators, the significant adults in students' lives, fail to recognize the importance of partnership and shared responsibility for enhancing student progress and development. Swap (1993) recommends that educators need to be prepared to rethink their position. We contend that the following options, articulated by Swap (1993), are applicable to both parents and educators, and therefore could serve as the basis of conflict resolution training for both groups.

1. *Analyze feelings and rethink positions.* Ask: What factors are influencing your perception of the issue? Has the problem become the focus of a power struggle? What is in the best interests of the student?
2. *Reflect on the other's point of view.* Why might the teacher or parent take this point of view? What are his or her needs or interests?
3. *Check on the validity of your perceptions with a trusted colleague or friend.* What insights did you acquire?
4. *Meet again.* If another individual accompanies you to this meeting, state that in advance. Strive to keep all verbal and written communications friendly and understanding.
5. *Be prepared to negotiate a goal on which both parties can agree.* Be willing to consider several solutions to the complex problem. Review personal and common interests and needs.
6. *Involve a mediator.* Seek the help of a neutral third party. Introduce this avenue as a positive approach; do not use threats or convey hostility.

The probability of abolishing conflict is minuscule at best. Given the diversity of individuals' experiences, beliefs, and attitudes, there will always be the "when all else fails" situations. The legal system may be involved. In their work with child study team members, Margolis and Brannigan (1990) suggest that educators focus on maintaining the best possible relationship with parents while experiencing the tensions of a formal due process hearing. They suggest that educators can accomplish this by focusing on clearly defined issues rather than personalities, treating parents with respect, and using valid information when discussing recommendations. We encourage educators to emphasize the aforementioned characteristics of a working relationship developed by Fisher and Brown (1988).

Outcomes of Family/School Approaches

The primary basis for developing family/school partnerships resides in the extensive database demonstrating that family involvement in education is a correlate of positive academic outcomes for K–12 students (Barton & Coley, 1992; Henderson & Berla, 1994). The extent to which families create a home environment that encourages learning, communicates high, realistic expectations for children's achievement and future careers, and involves parents in their children's education at school and in the community is a stronger predictor of student achievement than income or social class (Henderson & Berla, 1994). In general, researchers have concluded that (1) the family makes critical contributions to student achievement; (2) efforts to improve academic and behavioral outcomes are more effective if they involve families; and (3) the more the relationship between family and school is comprehensive, long lasting, and well planned, the higher the student achievement (Henderson & Berla, 1994). When programs are designed to be full partnerships between home and school, student achievement not only improves but it also reaches levels that are standard for middle-class children (Comer & Haynes, 1991).

Despite the evidence for family involvement in education, systematic investigation of specific practices of partnership and the effects of a family/school partnership program on student outcomes is needed. We have a stronger conceptual than empirical base for implementing family/school partnership programs. While Epstein (1995) reports benefits for students, teachers, and parents for six types of involvement, the effects of implementing a partnership program at different schools, across grade levels, and for diverse populations of students, families, and teachers yet is unknown. In particular, a major question to be answered is: What are the effects of shared responsibility between home and school on educational and developmental outcomes for all students?

The use of effective communication, problem solving, and conflict resolution strategies between families and educators receives much attention in the literature as viable avenues for promoting positive outcomes for children. However, there is a lack of empirical support for these assertions. Intuitively, we know that effective communication and problem-solving tactics are "good things," however, we found little to no research that has examined the impact of these strategies on student performance or the conditions under which they are most effective. However, improving communication between home and school is the most frequently cited goal of partnership programs (Henderson & Berla, 1994; Rioux & Berla, 1993) and maintaining effective communication between home and school was one of three recommendations by the National Association of State Boards of Education (1992) for educational reform.

The empirical evidence for the use of effective communication strategies between families and educators in improving student performance is very limited. In a study of the school-to-home communication patterns, Ames (1993) found that parents whose children were in classrooms with teachers that were high users of school-to-home communications perceived their children as more motivated to learn than parents whose children were in low-use communication classrooms. The children's reports of their own motivation and competence were not directly related to the teachers' use of the school-to-home communication practices. Instead, the children's interest in learning was related to their perception of their parents' involvement in school. Children who reported higher levels of motivation and competence were children who held positive views of their parents' involvement. No empirical evidence was found for the use of effective communication strategies between families and educators in improving student achievement.

Empirical support exists for the use of problem solving and conflict resolution with children; however, less was found between families and schools. For example, effects of interpersonal problem-solving training on children has been shown to enhance students' problem-solving skills and behavioral adjustment (Elias, Rothbaum, & Gara, 1986; Spivack, Platt, & Shure, 1976). Also, we know that parents and teachers who are either involved in the training or support the use of the problem-solving skills are likely to enhance children's social competencies (Weissberg, Caplan, & Harwood, 1991). With the exception of efficacy data noted for the individual-focused, family-school, problem-solving approaches described previously, little empirical documentation for the effects of problem solving and conflict resolution between home and school exists. The effect of group-focused problem solving between families and schools on student outcomes, both when used to develop partnerships and resolve conflicts, needs to be systematically evaluated.

Role of the Group Facilitator

Trust between home and school is not automatic, and partnerships cannot be forced or mandated (Swap, 1993). A deliberate effort is needed to implement the communication and problem-solving strategies summarized in this chapter. The strategies are easy to understand but often difficult to implement. A facilitator is needed to provide the leadership required for successful implementation of family/school partnerships and use of strategies to resolve pseudo- and substantive conflict (Weiss & Edwards, 1992). The goal of the facilitator is to maintain a collaborative ethic between home and school for the educational benefit of students. To this end, roles for the group facilitator include trainer, facilitator, and consultant.

A family/school group facilitator trains educators and parents in effective communication skills and conflict-resolution strategies, facilitates individual- and group-focused problem-solving meetings, and consults with parents, teachers, and administrators to maintain treatment integrity for partnership interventions. A systemic orientation for understanding child behavior and development is underscored by the efforts of the facilitator who is interested in how change can be executed to develop a coordinated integrated partnership program rather than how inadequacies have developed in the family/school relationship.

GUIDELINES FOR INTERVENTIONISTS

A deliberate effort by mental health professionals and educators is needed to facilitate partnerships and resolve conflict between families and schools. We contend that the myriad of professionals—school psychologists, child clinical psychologists, social workers, counselors, special educators, child psychiatrists, and classroom teachers—who interface with families in assessment, consultation, or intervention-oriented activities must examine their practices to ensure that partnerships across systems are fostered and blame between systems is circumvented. We speculate that the approach, attitude, and action adopted by interventionists will influence the extent to which partnerships for student learning and development are attained.

Approach

The approach needed for facilitating partnerships between families and schools is based on a shared responsibility for educational and developmental outcomes for students across the grade levels. With this orientation, families and school personnel recognize that the total learning environment for students is comprised of school, home, and community contexts. No one individual has the big picture about the child, rather the picture is co-constructed by sharing between families and educators. Therefore, parents and educators recognize that for an accurate understanding of child behavior, adults must share their observations of children in different contexts. Because both home and school contexts influence the socialization of children and youths, families and school personnel stop operating in isolation to intervene.

Families and school personnel understand that the goal of the partnership is to promote the academic, social, and behavioral competence of students, and that there are positive benefits for students when they are provided with consistency of influence or a congruent message across home and school. Roles and responsibilities of families and school personnel for supporting student progress are negotiated and clarified. Communication between family and school is directed toward the degree to which their efforts are reaching the shared goal. The approach is mesosystemic; the relationship between home and school is valued, and therefore collaboration becomes the normative behavior for addressing concerns related to students.

Attitude

The attitude needed to facilitate partnerships between families and schools is that the *partnership is essential* and that *conflict is not pejorative*; it can be resolved and viewed as an opportunity for change. Blame must be circumvented; a constructive attitude is adopted to resolve conflicts between families and schools. Olson and Defrain (1994) discuss characteristics of constructive and destructive approaches to conflict resolution between couples. Borrowing from their classification system, we suggest the following characterize a constructive attitude for maintaining partnerships between families and schools:

1. Parents and educators agree it is OK to disagree and that they can work together despite differences.
2. Parents and educators believe each offers valuable contributions to solutions for student concerns.
3. Parents and educators are willing to communicate personal needs and concerns (e.g., constraints in their system) honestly and openly.
4. Parents and educators are willing to listen empathically to understand each other's position and perspective.
5. Parents and educators engage in solution-oriented and possibility thinking when addressing concerns about students.
6. Parents and educators are willing to consider several options to resolve concerns.
7. Parents and educators strive to establish an action plan that (a) satisfies the needs of parents, educators, their relationship, and the student and (b) addresses the constraints present in home and school contexts.

Assumptions about the behavior of another individual, which builds walls, are eliminated when individuals adopt a constructive attitude about partnerships and conflict resolution. Effective interpersonal communication, two-way communication, and problem solving between families and school personnel are aspects of a constructive attitude and build bridges between home and school.

Action

We recommend two actions. First, develop a collaborative ethic. A collaborative ethic—relationship and problem solving—between families and schools helps reduce conflict; trust is maximized and conflict is more easily handled without blaming. We speculate that the power for establishing a collaborative ethic lies in shared decision making. We recommend schools develop a home/school team to initiate an integrated, coordinated family/school partnership program with parent and educator input and design. The team sets the tone for trust and a positive attitude toward partnership. As the team plans, collaboration becomes the normative behavior. We speculate that it is shared governance that permits effective consultation across family and school systems to occur. For example, although sharing information between parents and educators is a commonly mentioned aspect of effective partnerships, it may be that sharing information and listening to each other is essential to shared decision making. Epstein's (1995) typology for family/school partnerships provides a structure and options for the team to decide how to proceed.

The team must be supported. To this end, training and trust-building activities can be initiated to address the three obstacles to a collaborative relationship identified by Moles (1993). Very importantly, schools would be wise to establish administrative support for partnerships with parents and employ a family/school coordinator to provide leadership—two prerequisites of successful partnership programs identified by the comprehensive work of Weiss and Edwards (1992) in the New York City schools.

The impact of approach and attitude on actions taken by families and schools in developing partnerships and resolving conflicts is acknowledged. *If* a mesosystemic orientation for understanding child-focused concerns is the approach adopted by families and school personnel, and *if* a collaborative and solution-oriented attitude permeates family/school interactions, *then* specific actions seem logical and automatic. In this situation, families and schools take time to build trust, resolve conflicts, and create partnerships. Interventionists allocate time to process elements, such as sharing information, needs, perspectives, and resources between the two systems.

Action is taken to develop a problem-solving structure in which key stakeholders focus on the problematic situation and on being unconditionally constructive (Fisher & Brown, 1988). Key stakeholders are committed to balance—or addressing the needs of parents, educators, and the student. Action is taken to block blame between individuals and across systems and contexts in the child's life. Action is taken to reduce the mutual reluctance parents and educators have toward communicating about the student. New norms are established, and may include (1) concerns about children are discussed sooner, not later; (2) pseudo- and substantive conflict is discussed openly and not avoided; and (3) action is taken to develop communication and problem-solving strategies that clarify the roles and responsibilities of families and schools vis-à-vis educational outcomes for students.

Second, research establishing the efficacy of family/school partnerships for enhancing student performance is needed. We know that family involvement in education is a correlate of academic achievement (Christenson et al., 1992; Henderson & Berla, 1994); successful programs are comprehensive, long lasting, and well planned (Henderson & Berla, 1994); benefits exist for all key stakeholders (Epstein, 1995); and schools have established and sustained partnerships with low-income families (Davies, Burch, & Johnson, 1992; Rioux & Berla, 1993). We still need to know what effect the shared responsibility for educational outcomes approach advocated in this chapter has for student outcomes. For whom and under what conditions is the effect positive? Also, systematic investigation of substantive conflict between home and school is needed.

In summary, we have described three components for facilitating partnerships and conflict resolution between families and schools: trust building, communication, and problem solving. We have summarized guidelines for interventionists in terms of a mesosystemic approach to understanding and supporting issues or concerns about students, a constructive attitude about partnerships, and action through teams that focus on the home/school partnership and home/school issues.

It seems that educators have a choice: Educate the child in the context of the school or educate the child in the context of his or her family and community, which includes the school. The first choice separates parents from the child's schooling. When conflicts arise, parents and educators are likely to blame one another because there are few, if any, built-in mechanisms for resolving conflict. In the second choice, parents and educators have formed a working alliance that prevents blaming and adversarial relationships from emerging and facilitates problem solving when conflicts occur. Admittedly, there will need to be a change in fundamental assumptions, practices, and relationships, both within schools and between schools and the community, for educators to select the second choice (Conley, 1991).

REFERENCES

ABCs of scapegoating. (1944). Cambridge, MA: Harvard University Press.

Alter, R. C. (1985). Parent-school communication: A selective review: *Canadian Journal of School Psychology, 8*(1), 103–110.

Ames, C. (1993). How school-to-home communications influence parent beliefs and perceptions. *Equity & Choice, 9*(3), 44–49.

Barton, P. E., & Coley, R. J. (1992). *American's smallest school: The family*. Policy Information Report. Princeton, NJ: Educational Testing Service.

Bauch, J. P. (1990). The TransParent School Model: New technology for parent involvement. *Educational Leadership, 47*(2), 32–35.

Beckman, L. (1973). Teachers' and observers' perceptions of causality for a child's performance. *Journal of Educational Psychology, 65*(2), 198–204.

Bransford, J. D., & Stein, B. S. (1984). *The ideal problem solver*. New York: W. H. Freeman.

Bronfenbrenner, U. (1977). Toward an experimental ecology of human development. *American Psychologist, 32*, 513–531.

Bronfenbrenner, U. (1979). *The ecology of human development*. Cambridge, MA: Harvard University Press.

Cale, L. B. (1993). Communication skills and strategies. In O. Moles (Ed.), *Building school-family partnerships for learning: Workshops for urban educators*. Washington, DC: Office of Research and Educational Improvement, U.S. Department of Education.

Canter, L., & Canter, M. (1991). *Parents on your side*. Santa Monica, CA: Lee Canter & Associates.

Carlson, C. I., Hickman, J., & Horton, C. B. (1992). From blame to solutions: Solution-oriented family-school consultation. In S. L. Christenson & J. C. Conoley (Eds.), *Home-school collaboration: Enhancing children's academic and social competence* (pp. 193–213). Silver Spring, MD: National Association of School Psychologists.

Chrispeels, J. A. (1987). The family as an educational resource. *Community Education Journal, 14*, 10–17.

Christenson, S. L. (1995a). Supporting home-school collaboration. In A. Thomas & J. Grimes (Eds.), *Best practices in school psychology III* (pp. 253–267). Silver Spring, MD: National Association of School Psychologists.

Christenson, S. L. (1995b). Families and schools: What is the role of the school psychologist? *School Psychology Quarterly, 10*(2), 118–132.

Christenson, S. L., Hurley, C., Sheridan, S., & Fenstermacher, K. (1994, March). *Which home-school partnership activities do parents prefer?* Annual meeting of National Association of School Psychologists, Seattle.

Christenson, S. L., Rounds, T., & Franklin, M. J. (1992). Home-school collaboration: Effects, issues, and opportunities. In S. L. Christenson & J. C. Conoley (Eds.), *Home-school collaboration: Enhancing children's academic and social competence* (pp. 19–51). Silver Spring, MD: National Association of School Psychologists.

Christenson, S. L., Rounds, T., & Gorney, D. (1992). Family factors and student achievement: An avenue to increase students' success. *School Psychology Quarterly, 7*(3), 178–206.

Cochran, M. (1987). The parental empowerment process: Building on family strengths. *Equity and Choice, 4*(1), 9–23.

Coleman, J. S. (1987). Families and schools. *Educational Researcher, 16*(6), 32–38.

Collins, C. H., Moles, O., & Cross, M. (1982). *The home-school connection: Selected partnership programs in large cities*. Boston: Institute for Responsive Education.

Comer, J. P. (1995). *School power: Implications of an intervention project*. New York: Free Press.

Comer, J. P., & Haynes, N.M. (1991). Parent involvement in schools: An ecological approach. *The Elementary School Journal, 91*(3), 271–278.

Conley, D. (1991). What is restructuring? Educators adapt to a changing world. *Equity and Choice, 7*(2 & 3), 46–55.

Cronin, M. E., Slade, D. L., Bechtel, C., & Anderson, P. (1992). Home-school partnerships: A cooperative approach to intervention. *Intervention in School and Clinic, 27*(5), 286–292.

Davies, D. (1991). Schools reaching out: Family, school, and community partnerships for student success. *Phi Delta Kappan, 72*(5), 376–382.

Davies, D., Burch, P., & Johnson, V. (1992, February). *A portrait of schools reaching out: Report of a survey of practices and policies of family-community-school collaboration. (No. 1).* Center on Families, Communities, Schools, and Children's Learning. Baltimore, MD: Johns Hopkins University.

DeBoer, A. L. (1986). *The art of consulting*. Chicago: Arcturus.

deShazer, S. (1982). *Patterns of brief family therapy*. New York: W. W. Norton.

deShazer, S. (1985). *Keys to solution*. New York: W. W. Norton.

deShazer, S. (1988). *Clues: Investigating solutions in brief therapy*. New York: W. W. Norton.

DiCocco, B. E., & Lott, E. B. (1982). Family-school strategies in dealing with the troubled child. *International Journal of Family Therapy, 4*(2), 98–106.

Dunst, C. J., Johanson, C., Rounds, T., Trivette, C. M., & Hamby, D. (1992). Characteristics of parent-professional relationships. In S. L. Christenson & J. C. Conoley (Eds.), *Home-school collaboration: Enhancing children's academic and social competence* (pp. 157–174). Silver Spring, MD: National Association of School Psychologists.

Dunst, C. J., & Paget, K. (1991). Parent-professional partnerships and family empowerment. In M. Fine (Ed.), *Collaboration with parents of exceptional children* (pp. 25–41). Brandon, VT: Clinical Psychology Publishing.

Dunst, C. J., & Trivette, C. M. (1987). Enabling and empowering families: Conceptual and intervention issues. *School Psychology Review, 16*(4), 443–456.

Elias, M. J., Rothbaum, P. A., & Gara, M. (1986). Social-cognitive problem solving in children: Assessing the knowledge and application of skills. *Journal of Applied Developmental Psychology, 7,* 77–94.

Epstein, J. L. (1987). Parent involvement: What research says to administrators. *Education and Urban Society, 19*(2), 119–136.

Epstein, J. L. (1992). School and family partnerships: Leadership roles for school psychologists. In S.L. Christenson & J.C. Conoley (Eds.), *Home-school collaboration: Enhancing children's academic and social competence* (pp. 499–515). Silver Spring, MD: National Association of School Psychologists.

Epstein, J. L. (1995). School/family/community partnerships: Caring for the children we school. *Phi Delta Kappan, 76*(9), 701–712.

Erchul, W. P. (1992). Social psychological perspectives on the school psychologist's involvement with parents. In F. J. Medway & T. P. Cafferty (Eds.), *School psychological perspective* (pp. 425–448). Hillsdale, NJ: Lawrence Erlbaum.

Farris, R., & Dunham, H. (1939). *Mental disorders in urban areas*. Chicago: University of Chicago Press.

Feiler, A., & Thomas, G. (Eds.). (1988). *Meeting special needs: An ecological perspective.* Oxford: Blackwell.

Fine, M. J. (1990). Facilitating home-school relationships: A family-oriented approach to collaborative consultation. *Journal of Educational and Psychological Consultation, 1*(2), 169–187.

Fine, M. J., & Clifford, R. (1992). *Parent-teacher conferences: Resolving conflicts.* Topeka, KS: Meninger Video Productions.

Fisher, L. (1986). Systems-based consultation with schools. In L. C. Wynne, S. H. McDaniel, & T. T. Weber (Eds.), *Systems consultation: A new perspective for family therapy* (pp. 342–256). New York: Guilford.

Fisher, R., & Brown, S. (1988). *Getting together: Building a relationship that gets to yes.* Boston: Houghton Mifflin.

Fisher, R., & Ury, W. (1981). *Getting to yes: Negotiating agreement without giving in.* Boston: Houghton Mifflin.

Friedson, E. (1970). *Professional dominance.* Chicago: Aldine.

Galloway, J., & Sheridan, S. M. (1994). Implementing scientific practices through case studies: Examples using home-school interventions and consultation. *Journal of School Psychology, 32*(4), 385–413

Goals 2000: Educate America Act (1994). *The National Education Goals Report.* Washington, DC: Government Printing Office.

Goodman, J. F., Sutton, V., & Harkavy, I. (1995). The effectiveness of family workshops in a middle school setting: Respect and caring make the difference. *Phi Delta Kappan, 76*(9), 694–700.

Gordon, T. (1974). *Teacher effectiveness training.* New York: Wyden.

Graden, J. L., & Bauer, A. M. (1992). Using a collaborative approach to support students and teachers in inclusive classrooms. In S. Stainback & W. Stainback (Eds.), *Teaching in the inclusive classroom: Curriculum design, adaptation, and delivery* (pp. 59–74). Baltimore, MD: Paul H. Brooks.

Guttmann, J. (1982). Pupils', teachers', and parents' causal attributions for problem behavior at school. *Journal of Special Education, 76,* 14–21.

Henderson, A. T. & Berla, N. (1994). *A new generation of evidence: The family is critical to student achieve-*

ment. Washington DC: National Committee for Citizens in Education

Hoff, D. (1994). New laws give schools change to fight. *Education Daily, 27*(230), 1.

Hulsebosch, P. L. (1989, April). *Significant others: Teachers' perspectives on relationships with parents.* Paper presented at the annual meeting of the American Educational Research Association, San Francisco.

Kagan, S. L. (1987). Home-school linkages: History's legacies and the family support movement. In S. L. Kagan, D. R. Powell, B. Weissbord, & E. F. Zigler (Eds.), *America's family support programs: Perspectives and prospects* (pp. 161–181). New Haven, CT: Yale University Press.

Katz, L. G. (1980). Mothering and teaching: Some significant distinctions. In L. G. Katz (Ed.), *Current topics in early childhood education* (pp. 47–63). Norwood, NJ: Ablex.

Knitzer, J., & Yelton, S. (1989). Interagency collaboration. In A. Algarin (Ed.), *Update: Improving services for emotionally disturbed children* (pp. 12–14). Tampa, FL: University of Florida, Florida Mental Health Institute.

Kroth, R. L. (1985). *Communicating with parents of exceptional children: Improving parent-teacher relationships* (2nd ed.). Denver: Love.

Leitch, L. M., & Tangri, S. S. (1988). Barriers to home-school collaboration. *Educational Horizons, 66*, 70–74.

Lightfoot, S. L. (1978). *Worlds apart.* New York: Basic Books.

Lightfoot, S. L. (1981). *Toward conflict resolution: Relationships between families and schools.* New York: Basic Books.

Liontos, S. B. (1992). *At risk families and schools: Becoming partners.* Eugene, OR: ERIC Clearinghouse on Educational Management, College of Education, University of Oregon.

Litwak, E., & Meyer, H. (1974). *School, family, and neighborhood: The theory and practice of school-community relations.* New York: Columbia University Press.

Lombana, J. H. (1983). *Home-school partnerships: Guidelines and strategies for educators.* New York: Grune & Stratton.

Lombana, J. H., & Pratt, P. A. (1978). *Communication skills for career success: A programmed textbook. Book 1: Overview and active listening.* Jacksonville, FL: University of North Florida.

Lusterman, D. D. (1985). An ecosystemic approach to family-school problems. *The American Journal of Family Therapy, 13*(1), 22–50.

Margolis, H. (1990, February). What to do when you're verbally attacked: The critical moment. *NASP Bulletin* (74), 34–38.

Margolis, H. (1991). Listening: The key to problem solving with angry parents. *School Psychology International, 12*, 329–347.

Margolis, H., & Brannigan, G. G. (1990). Strategies for resolving parent-school conflict. *Reading, Writing, and Learning Disabilities* (6), 1–23.

Margolis, H., & Shapiro, A. (1987). Systematically resolving parental conflict with the goal-output-process-input procedure. *High School Journal, 71*(2), 88–96.

Margolis, H., & Shapiro, A. (1989). Constructively avoiding the need for due process. *Special Services in the Schools, 4*, 145–157.

McAfee, D. (1993). Communication: The key to effective partnerships. In R. C. Burns (Ed.), *Parents & schools: From visitors to partners* (pp. 21–34). Washington, DC: National Education Association.

Moles, O. (1993). Collaboration between schools and disadvantaged parents: Obstacles and openings. In N. F. Chavkin (Ed.), *Families and schools in a pluralistic society* (pp. 21–49). Albany: State University of New York Press.

National Association of State Boards of Education. (1992). *Partners in educational improvement: Schools, parents, and the community.* Alexandria, VA: Author.

Norby, J. M., Thurlow, M. L., Christenson, S. L., & Ysseldyke, J. E. (1990). *The challenge of complex school problems.* Austin, TX: Pro-Ed.

O'Hanlon, W. H., & Weiner-Davis, M. (1989). *In search of solutions: A new direction in psychotherapy.* New York: Norton.

Okagaki, L., & Sternberg, R. J. (1991). *Directors of development: Influences on the development of children's thinking.* Hillsdale, NJ: Lawrence Erlbaum.

Olson, D. H., & Defrain, J. (1994). *Marriage and the family: Diversity and strengths.* Mountain View, CA: Mayfield.

Olson, L. (1990, April). Parents as partners: Redefining the social contract between parents and schools [special issue]. *Education Week, 9*(28), 17–24.

Ooms, T., & Hara, S. (1991). *The family-school partnership: A critical component of school reform.* The Family Impact Seminar, AAMFT, Washington, DC.

Palanki, A., & Burch, P. (1995, July). *In our hands: A multi-site parent-teacher action research project* (Research Report No. 30). Baltimore: Center on Families, Communities, Schools, and Children's Learning.

Peyton, J. V. (1994, October). *Collaborative family-school counseling: A non-deficit model.* Paper presented at the 1994 United Nations International Year of the Family Conference, Oakland.

Powell, D. R. (1991). How schools support families: Critical policy tensions. *The Elementary School Journal, 91*(3), 307–319.

Power, T. J., & Bartholomew, K. L. (1985). Getting uncaught in the middle: A case study in family-school system consultation. *School Psychology Review, 14*(2), 222–229.

Power, T. J., & Bartholomew, K. L. (1987). Family-school relationship patterns: An ecological assessment. *School Psychology Review, 16* (4), 498–512.

Rich, D. (1987). *Schools and families: Issues and actions.* Washington, DC: National Education Association.

Rioux, J. W., & Berla, N. (1993). *Innovations in parent involvement.* Princeton, NJ: Eye on Education.

Rogers, C. R., & Farason, R. E. (1957). *Active listening.* Chicago: University of Chicago Industrial Relations Center.

Rutter, J. (1985). Family and school influences on behavioral development. *Journal of Child Psychology and Psychiatry, 26*(3), 349–368.

Seeley, D. S. (1991). The major new case for choice is only half right. *Equity and Choice, 7*(1), 28–33.

Sheridan, S. M., & Colton, D. L. (1994). Conjoint behavioral consultation: A review and case study. *Journal of Educational and Psychological Consultation, 5*(3), 211–228.

Sheridan, S. M., & Kratochwill, T. R. (1992). Behavioral parent-teacher consultation: Conceptual and research considerations. *Journal of School Psychology, 30,* 117–139.

Sheridan, S. M., Kratochwill, T. R., & Bergan, J. R. (in press). *Conjoint behavioral consultation: A procedural manual.* New York: Plenum.

Sheridan, S. M., Kratochwill, T. R., & Elliott, S. (1990). Behavioral consultation with parents and teachers: Applications with socially withdrawn children. *School Psychology Review, 19,* 33–52.

Sinclair, M., Lam, S. F., Christenson, S. L., & Evelo, D. (1993). Action research in middle schools. *Equity and Choice, 10* (1), 23–24.

Spivack, G., Platt, J., & Shure, M. (1976). *The problem solving approach to adjustment.* San Francisco: Jossey-Bass.

Swap, S. M. (1993). *Developing home-school partnerships: From concepts to practice.* New York: Teachers College Press.

Thiabut, J. W., & Kelly, H. H. (1959). *The social psychology of groups.* New York: Wiley.

Tjosvold, D., & Johnson, D. W. (Eds.). (1989). *Productive conflict management: Perspectives for organization.* Edina, MN: Interaction Book Company.

Walberg, H. J. (1984). Families as partners in educational productivity. *Phi Delta Kappan, 65,* 397–400.

Weiss, H. M., & Edwards, M. E. (1992). The family-school collaboration project: Systemic interventions for school improvement. In S. L. Christenson & J. C. Conoley (Eds.), *Home–school collaboration: Enhancing children's academic and social competence* (pp. 215–243). Silver Spring, MD: National Association of School Psychologists.

Weissberg, R. P., Caplan, M., & Harwood, R. L. (1991). Promoting competent young people in competence-enhancing environments: A systems-based perspective on primary prevention. *Journal of Consulting and Clinical Psychology, 59*(6), 830–841.

Wolfendale, S. (1988). Psychologists working with parents: Context and skills. In R. C. Jones & T. Sayer (Eds.), *Management of the psychology of schooling* (pp. 158–166). New York: Falmer.

Ysseldyke, J. E., & Christenson, S. L. (1993). *TIES-II: The Instructional Environment System.* Longmont, CO: Sopris West.

Zill, N., & Nord, C. W. (1994). *Running in place.* Washington, DC: Child Trends.

CHAPTER 18

PARENT AND PARENT/CHILD GROUPS FOR YOUNG CHILDREN WITH DISABILITIES

Maribeth Gettinger, UNIVERSITY OF WISCONSIN–MADISON
Kristen Waters Guetschow, UNIVERSITY OF WISCONSIN–MADISON

RATIONALE

There are several reasons why group approaches are particularly well suited for parents of young children with disabilities. First, research has documented that parents of young children with disabilities experience significantly higher levels of stress than do parents of typically developing children (Murray, 1990). Parental stress may be periodic, usually increasing during critical transitions such as entry into school or initiation of a treatment program (Mori, 1983).

A family-centered model is based on the assumption that each family has unique strengths and resources that affect their ability to enhance their child's development and to cope with stressors in their lives. Within a family-centered perspective, professionals work in partnership with parents to identify family strengths and to address their concerns or needs. Although support for parents is obtained by working with specialists, early childhood professionals may not be parents of children with disabilities themselves. Therefore, a group approach to service delivery, which brings together other parents with similar experiences, is often effective in providing needed support for parents of children with disabilities. Research has shown that the degree of social comfort among parents is increased in the presence of others who have young children with disabilities (Seligman, 1993).

Parents of young children with disabilities share many common concerns and needs that can be addressed effectively through participation in groups. Groups provide parents with an opportunity to share their experiences with others who are able to empathize. Groups also provide a forum for an exchange of ideas and information among parents. Murray (1990) identified four common parental needs that can be met in groups. These include needs for information, social and emotional support, encouragement, and assistance in problem solving.

Parent groups may serve additional functions for parents of children with disabilities beyond addressing their specific needs. Groups can help increase confidence among parents, facilitate the development of realistic expectations for children, empower parents to make effective decisions, and encourage parents to work collaboratively with professionals (Murray, 1990). In addition, parent groups have the advantage over individual approaches of minimizing parents' sense of isolation (Lerner, 1992). In groups, parents understand they are not alone and they are able to establish a supportive context for problem solving. Finally, parent and parent/child groups allow parents to engage in helping others. According to Seligman (1993), it is important that parents are not always receiving help, but also have an opportunity to offer assistance to others.

CHARACTERISTICS OF PARENTS OF YOUNG CHILDREN WITH DISABILITIES

Parents of young children with disabilities are a diverse group. They may come from various cultural and socioeconomic backgrounds, and often have established their personal style of family functioning before the birth of the child. Because of this diversity, conclusions about social/emotional characteristics of parents of young children with disabilities may not generalize to all families. Nonetheless, it is helpful to understand research describing the common reactions, experiences, and mental health characteristics of parents subsequent to the birth of a child with disabilities.

Parent Reactions

Several theories have been developed to describe and explain "typical" parental reactions to the birth of a child with a disability. Gargiulo (1985) characterized parental reactions as representing three distinct stages. The primary phase includes reactions such as shock, disbelief, and denial. Parents may feel numb, experience feelings of helplessness, and may cry a great deal during this phase. Miezio (1983) suggested that talking with other parents of children with disabilities is helpful during this stage of coping because they "introduce the notions that joys are indeed possible for both the child and her parents" (p. 10).

The secondary phase involves feelings of ambivalence as parents attempt to cope with negative feelings, including possible rejection of the child, guilt, anger, shame, and embarrassment. Although the sources of negative feelings are numerous, the intensity of guilt and anger experienced by parents of children with disabilities exceeds that common to most parents (Upshur, 1991). Last, during the tertiary phase, parents begin to engage in adaptation, reorganization, and adjustment to parenting their child with disabilities. Within each phase parents may have unique reactions. Nonetheless, it is helpful for both professionals and parents to know that multiple reactions are typical and that feelings may change over time.

Parental reactions are not always negative. Many parents of young children with disabilities adjust to their special circumstances and experience life as fully as other parents. Poyadue (1993) identified acceptance as a common reaction among parents. Turnbull and Turnbull (1993) termed this reaction "cognitive coping," or thinking about a situation in ways that enhance parents' well-being. Cognitive coping reactions may include making downward comparisons ("We don't have it as bad as other families!"), considering positive outcomes of a situation or simply ignoring the negatives, attributing a meaningful and self-enhancing cause to the event, developing a sense of control or influence over the event, and finding humor in situations. Some parents believe that the challenges of raising a child with a disability actually enhance a marriage and bring spouses together (Wallinga, Paquio, & Skeen, 1987).

Family Needs, Stress, and Social Support

There is sufficient evidence that many parents experience considerable stress when they are coping with a child with a disability. Peterson (1987) delineated several sources of stress for parents of young children with disabilities. These include (1) financial burdens, (2) actual or perceived stigma, (3) time demands due to caregiving, (4) difficulties with basic caregiving tasks, (5) less time for sleep, (6) social isolation, (7) less time for personal and leisure activities, (8) difficulty with child behavior management, (9) interference with routine domestic responsibilities, and (10) general feelings of pessimism. In addition, factors such as waiting for the next developmental milestone to show evidence of delay, working through grief, coping with a possible loss of self-esteem, and finding appropriate child care often contribute to long-term parental stress.

Research shows that many families undergo a gradual process of accommodation subsequent to the birth of a child with disabilities. Accommodations may include changing jobs, adjusting work schedules, moving to a different residence, altering parenting styles with siblings, redistributing domestic chores, or adopting different beliefs or values (Gallimore, Weisner, Bernheimer, Guthrie, & Nihira, 1993). Certainly, such accommodations reflect positive and constructive reactions to having a child with disabilities. Despite the positive aspect of accommodation, however, Gallimore and associates (1993) cautioned that additional change may, in fact, lead to greater uncertainty and instability in a family's lives. Thus, too much accommodation on the part of a family to alleviate stress may not be appropriate.

Bailey, Blasco, and Simeonsson (1992) examined the needs of 400 families of young children with disabilities. Family needs were grouped into six types: Family and Social Support, Information, Finances, Explaining to Others, Child Care, and Professional Support. Bailey and colleagues (1992) found that mothers reported significantly more needs than did fathers, particularly in the areas of Family and Social Support, Explaining to Others, and Child Care. For all parents, having opportunities to meet with other families of children with disabilities was a prevalent need, although mothers expressed slightly more interest in these opportunities than did fathers.

Although families of young children with handicapping conditions report more stressful events overall than do families of typically developing children, stressors do not necessarily result in family dysfunction (Mahoney, O'Sullivan, & Robinson, 1992). Mahoney and colleagues (1992) administered the Family Environment Scale (FES; Moos, 1974) to 527 parents of young children with disabilities. Overall, characteristics of the family environments reported by parents with children with disabilities were comparable to those found in the general population. Differences that emerged were related to participation in recreational activities and religious affiliation. Specifically, families of young children with disabilities reported participating in fewer recreational activities and holding a stronger moral-religious orientation.

Social support appears to be a critical mediator of stress among parents of young children with disabilities. Trivette and Dunst (1992), for example, found that social support did not vary as a function of child's age, developmental status, or parental employment. The specific nature of social support did, however, vary as a function of marital status. Married mothers reported more support from their spouses and their spouses' parents and relatives than did single mothers. Single mothers, in contrast, reported relying more on support from community and social agencies.

Researchers have acknowledged the need to study the effects of socioeconomic variables on the development of young children with disabilities and their families. Landis (1992) examined socioeconomic variables in a small sample of 66 parents of young children with disabilities. The sample had a slightly greater proportion of single-parent families compared to the general population. Although a similar proportion of mothers in the sample worked outside the home compared to mothers in the general population, the majority of mothers of young children with disabilities worked only part time or had irregular shifts. The primary location for child care was in a home, often the mother's own home. Spouses assumed approximately half of the child care responsibilities while mothers worked.

Cultural variables have not been studied as extensively among families of young children with disabilities. Hanline and Daley (1992) examined the relationship between maternal perceptions of family coping and family strengths among Hispanic, African American, and Caucasian families of young children with disabilities. Across all three racial-ethnic groups, family strengths were predicted to a greater extent by coping strategies within the family than by outside support. Despite this similarity, each group exhibited a characteristic pattern of coping with the stress of having a young child with a disability. Thus, efforts to help parents enhance the development of their children should be sensitive to the diverse strengths and resources found in families with young children with disabilities.

There has been extensive research describing the various needs, stressors, and social support of families with young children with disabilities. Across the majority of studies, it appears that higher stress commonly experienced by parents (mainly mothers) is associated with an increase in caregiving responsibilities. It is also evident that social support, such as the type of support provided through participation in parent groups, can minimize parental stress.

SPECIFIC INTERVENTION TECHNIQUES: RESEARCH AND PRACTICE

A review of the social, psychological, and emotional variables associated with parenting a young child with special needs reveals the complexity of characteristics and problems among families. Approaches to conducting parent and parent/child groups are diverse and involve a range of different techniques. Although methods may vary, the ultimate goal of parent and parent/child groups is to facilitate simultaneously the development of the young child with disabilities and to assist parents in their adaptation to parenting their child. Therefore, groups are typically designed to provide knowledge, specific skills and strategies, as well as psychological support to families of young children with disabilities (Brinker, Seifer, & Samaroff, 1994).

Parent and parent/child groups are generally designed to serve either educative, therapeutic, or both educative and therapeutic functions. Groups that are primarily educative in purpose focus on providing parents with information about their child's disability as well as training in effective parenting skills. Parent groups that are essentially therapeutic in nature stress sharing and exploration of feelings, such as guilt or anger. In addition, such groups help parents to gain awareness of their own attitudes and patterns of behavior that might affect their child's development. The vast majority of parent groups described in the literature combine features of both educative and therapeutic groups.

Approaches to parent and parent/child groups, for either educative or therapeutic purposes, have evolved from several different theoretical perspectives. Approaches generally can be grouped into four broad categories: (1) interventions derived from models of stress and coping, (2) behavioral skills training, (3) parent support and counseling focusing on family strengths and resources, and (4) interventions focusing on parent/child interactions. In addition, a trend in recent years has been to develop parent groups designed specifically to meet the unique needs of fathers of children with disabilities. There are a number of positive effects that parents might achieve by participating in a group. In the literature, outcomes that have been reported tend to be primarily subjective (based on clinical judgment of group facilitators or subjective reports of parent satisfaction) and only occasionally objective. Research conclusions and practice guidelines related to each approach are described in the following sections.

The particular intervention approach for a parent group depends, in part, on the purpose of the group. Regardless of orientation or primary emphasis, there are several core elements that are common across parent and parent/child groups (Arnold, Rowe, & Tolbert, 1978). Most critical, perhaps, is the peer support afforded by parent groups. Group peer support can take several forms, including empathy, reassurance that a parent is not alone, or encouragement to make changes. Vicarious learning is another core element of parent groups. Parents often modify their own behaviors, beliefs, or attitudes when they hear how other parents have succeeded or handled situations similar to their own. Parent groups provide excellent opportunities for parents to learn from others.

Mutual helping, a third core element, is often more effective than help from one professional. Some parents, for example, report they can accept empathy, insight, or advice from other parents more readily than they can from one professional. Reality testing is a fourth element common across parent groups. Knowledge of developmental norms, for example, is critical for parents of young children with disabilities. Some parents experience relief and comfort from learning that another parent's child has problems similar to their own child's.

Similarly, some parents, without realizing it, may be overly indulgent or directive because they have a distorted impression of what their child developmentally is capable of achieving. During group sessions, parents have a chance to take a broader perspective and possibly acquire a better understanding of how children learn and develop.

Finally, as a fifth core element, groups foster the development of friendships among parents. Social isolation among parents of children with disabilities has been frequently documented. Groups offer parents the opportunity to meet other individuals who have shared similar experiences and are likely to understand how they feel.

Group Interventions Based on Stress and Coping Model

A variety of models have been proposed to explain the process of family adjustment to early childhood disabilities. One model that has had considerable appeal in recent years is a stress and coping model, which postulates that maladaptive family functioning occurs when a family is overwhelmed by the stressful demands of parenting a young child with a handicapping condition (Frey, Greenberg, & Fewell, 1989).

Parent groups based on a stress and coping model focus on parents' ability to handle the particular stressors with which they are faced. This approach departs from traditional early intervention programs that tend to focus on the developmental needs of the child rather than the adaptive capacities of families (Fewell & Vadasy, 1986). Many early childhood specialists recognize the subjective nature of parental stress and report that parents may react quite differently to the same situation (Gallagher, Peckham, & Cross, 1983). In fact, Frey and colleagues (1989) found that in a sample of 96 parents of young children with handicaps, parental beliefs and attitudes were the most powerful correlates of parenting stress and family adjustment. This finding lends strong support for the importance of cognitive appraisal. It also suggests that to be effective, group interventions designed to ameliorate parenting stress should target the development of adaptive beliefs and cognitions. For example, a potentially challenging task for parents of a young child with disabilities is to formulate appropriate standards of comparison for both the child and for themselves as parents. Therefore, effective group interventions should target the development of self-enhancing comparative frames of reference among parents. Standards of appraisal that are self-enhancing rather than self-deprecating are linked to coping efficacy and adaptive functioning (Taylor & Brown, 1988).

Singer, Irvin, and Hawkins (1988) evaluated the efficacy of a stress management group approach that incorporated a cognitive change component. The program was designed for parents of young children with severe handicapping conditions, including cognitive disability, autism, and neuromuscular disability. Specifically, their intervention incorporated three distinct treatment components: (1) self-monitoring of stressful events and physiological reactions to them, (2) muscle relaxation as an active coping response, and (3) systematic cognitive restructuring. Groups of 8 to 10 parents participated in two-hour sessions once a week for eight consecutive weeks. Group sessions were co-facilitated by a psychologist and special education teacher. During the sessions, parents were provided with in-home respite care for their children through a community respite care agency.

Each group session followed a standard format that included didactic instruction focusing on the targeted stress management skills, demonstration of skills, and discussion. Parents were assigned homework activities to facilitate their acquisition of skills through daily practice and to enhance generalization to home and community environments. Although parents were encouraged to talk about stressors in their lives during the group sessions and to discuss stress management skills, the emphasis was specifically on learning and applying skills rather than exploring feelings with group members.

The first treatment component, self-monitoring, consisted of training parents to recognize their personal symptoms of stress and to identify events associated with these symptoms. For example, as one assignment, parents were asked to evaluate their levels of stress three times during each day, and to identify events associated with high or low levels of stress. The second treatment component, relaxation, incorporated a variation of progressive muscle relaxation in which parents were taught to tense and release large muscle groups in a progressive manner. Parents were given taped recordings to guide their daily home practice in muscle relaxation. Finally, for the third cognitive restructuring component, parents were taught how to recognize thoughts associated with stress that are exaggerated or distorted, and to use self-talk to guide themselves to think in more realistic or rational terms.

All parents ($n = 18$) completed the State Trait Anxiety Inventory (Spielberger, Gorsuch, & Lushene, 1970), the Beck Depression Inventory (BDI; Beck, Ward, Mendelson, Mock, & Erbaugh, 1961), and a 14-item social validation measure to assess their satisfaction with the group procedures and their evaluation of the effectiveness of each treatment component (Kazdin & Matson, 1981). Overall, the stress management group procedure was effective in significantly reducing stress among parents (anxiety and depression) from pre- to postintervention. In addition, although the use of a multielement treatment approach did not permit an analysis of which components were successful, all three treatment components were perceived by parents as being helpful.

Interestingly, group approaches focusing on stress and coping have been shown to have variable effects on both family stress and children's development (Sameroff & Fiese, 1990). On one hand, some parents may be relieved that there are experts to help them facilitate the development of their child, thus increasing parental competence and reducing family stress (Stoneman, Brody, & Abbott, 1983). On the other hand, experts may serve to increase family stress by creating culturally atypical, time-consuming, difficult-to-schedule, socially challenging, or expensive demands on the resources of families (Brotherson & Goldstein, 1992).

Thus, professionals should consider whether asking parents to participate in groups may, in fact, impose additional stress on the family. Parents may view themselves from a deficit perspective, or be viewed by professionals as having deficits, if the focus in groups is primarily on stress. Often a respite program for parents that gives them a break from parenting may be just as helpful as groups designed to minimize stress through effective coping strategies (Gallagher et al., 1983).

Brinker and associates (1994) recently examined the relations among child development, parent stress, and parents' involvement in an early intervention group program. Based on a transactional model of child development, these authors theorized that changes in parents' functioning, through educational and stress reduction programs, may influence subsequent development and adaptation of both parents and child (Sameroff & Fiese, 1990). Brinker and associates (1994) examined maternal stress and children's developmental gains among 144 families of either middle or low socioeconomic status (SES). All parents participated in the Early Childhood Research and Intervention Program, which is a center-based early intervention program that offers services to young children with disabilities and their families (Seifer, Clark, & Sameroff, 1991). The program is both child and parent focused, and involves two-hour weekly sessions with parent/child groups and parent groups.

Using the Bayley Scales of Infant Development (Bayley, 1969) as an index of child development and an informal measure of parental stress, Brinker and colleagues (1994) found a complex three-way interaction among SES, level of parental stress, and participation in the group program. Specifically, participation by highly stressed, low-SES families was associated with fewer developmental gains in children, relative to similarly stressed low-SES families who did not participate and to low-SES families with low stress who did participate. In other words, participating in parent groups was related to subsequent parental stress and subsequent child development in different ways for different SES levels. This confirms the need for professionals to be cognizant of the highly diverse and individual nature of stress and coping among parents of young children with disabilities.

Behavioral Skills Training for Groups of Parents

Group approaches derived from models of stress and coping are based on the finding that parents of young children with disabilities are at risk for greater stress and adjustment difficulties than families with a child who is normally developing (Blacher, 1984b). This finding provides the rationale for group approaches that focus primarily on parents and their psychological needs. Behavioral parent training, on the other hand, represents a different perspective to group approaches—specifically, that intervention should address parents' needs for information and effective parenting skills. Friedlander and Watkins (1985) noted that a parent training model is based on the premise that parenting issues emerge from deficiencies in skills and information. Parents of young children with disabilities often experience greater difficulties in matters concerning care, management, and discipline than other parents do. Parent groups provide one context for acquiring skills and seeking constructive solutions to such problems.

The goal of behavioral skills training is to facilitate the acquisition of child management skills among parents. To achieve this goal, parents receive both didactic and experiential structured learning opportunities (Baker, 1989). *Didactic* learning opportunities are systematic instructional sessions designed to impart specific information and knowledge. *Experiential* learning opportunities are activities in which parents participate actively with their children in parent/child groups. In addition to including both parent and parent/child group formats, many behavioral skills training programs also use a dual approach that incorporates group training sessions as well as individual feedback or follow-up sessions. In a dual approach, parents participate as a group in training sessions; as a follow-up to each group session, feedback and assistance are provided to parents on an individual basis.

The primary goal of parent training groups is to provide a basic understanding of child management procedures and to introduce parents to a variety of child management and relationship-building techniques. Although targeted skills may vary across groups, common areas include application of natural and logical consequences, aspects of daily routines for living with children with disabilities, behavior management techniques, and differences between punishment and discipline techniques. Unlike counseling or parent support groups, parent training groups serve primarily an educative or information-dissemination function (Carlo, 1988).

One critisim of behavioral training approaches is that asking parents to carry out specific behavior management procedures may impose additional stress on parents. Baker, Landen, and Kashima (1991) explored the possibility of increased stress in a recent study of 49 families of children with cognitive disabilities who participated in an 11-session, parent training program. The program focused on both self-help skills (four group sessions) and behavior management techniques (four group sessions). The training program included three individual meetings for individualized assessment and feedback and eight parent group meetings distributed over a 16-week period. Group sessions were conducted with four to seven families and lasted about two hours.

Baker and colleagues (1991) found no evidence for adverse outcomes among participating families on psychological measures, including the BDI; the Questionnaire on Resources and Stress (QRS; Friedrich, Greenberg, & Crnic, 1983), which assesses stress and attitudes related to a child with delays; the Family Adaptive and Cohesive Environment Scale (FACES; Olson, McCubbin, Barnes, Larsen, Muxen, & Wilson, 1982), which assesses family adaptability and cohesion; and the Family Coping Strategies (F-COPES; Olson et al., 1982), which assesses strategies available to a family for coping with problems. Furthermore, parents showed positive gains in their knowledge and use of behavior management skills at home from pretesting to posttesting and at a one-year follow-up assessment.

The limited success that parents experience in generalizing their use of behavioral skills learned in training groups to home and community settings is a common weakness of behavioral training approaches. There are many theoretical and practical reasons why skills learned in group sessions may not transfer to home and community settings. In many treatment methods, programming for generalization is not always included. In addition, most everyday activities require that parents be actively engaged in behaviors that easily compete with parenting behaviors. Parents must frequently deal with competing demands for their attention in family settings. Similarly, community activities require parents to engage in behaviors that compete with parent/child social interactions. For example, parents who have successfully learned to give their child a choice of toys and to praise the child for appropriate play may simultaneously need to be cooking dinner or answering phone calls. A parent who is concentrating on grocery shopping may find it difficult to use child management procedures in responding to inappropriate behavior. Furthermore, in community settings, the stimulus conditions usually are not under the control of the parent to the extent that they are in home settings.

To address these problems, Sanders and Dadds (1982) developed an approach termed *proactive* or *planned activity training* in which parents learn to anticipate beforehand situations in which their attention will be diverted from their child. Parents learn to use proactive strategies for engaging the child in appropriate behaviors before they become occupied with other tasks. Using this procedure, Cordisco, Strain, and Depew (1988) demonstrated that, with varying amounts of coaching, parents of young children with disabilities can generalize the use of child management techniques from the group training setting to home settings. Similarly, Powers, Singer, Stevens, and Sowers (1992) found that through the provision of repeated in-home coaching paired with written prompts (laminated wallet size cards listing every step for each child management procedure), mothers were able to use child management techniques in both home and community settings.

These studies confirm that behavioral skills training must be expanded to meet the demands for effective parenting of young children with disabilities in new and authentic contexts. Whereas skill training may be appropriately given in groups, the amount, location, and type of training for generalization may need to be individualized to meet the unique situational demands of different parents.

Parent Support and Counseling Groups

Parents of young children who are at risk or have handicapping conditions are likely to be the most stable influence in the lives of their children. Given the importance of parents and the difficulties associated with parenting a child with disabilities, it is critical that interventions offer support for parents and build on family strengths and resources. This is the basic premise behind many group counseling approaches for parents (Fine & Gardner, 1991). Unlike approaches based on stress and coping models or behavioral skills training, supportive counseling approaches view parents from a strength perspective rather than a deficit model, and focus on restoration of adaptive capacities. The underpinnings of a family strength orientation are different from a deficit model; the latter implies that parents are somehow deficient in significant ways that affect their child (e.g., lacking child management skills).

Consistent with a strength model, Dunst and associates have advocated the concepts of empowerment and enablement in the provision of services to families of young children with disabilities (Dunst, Trivette, & Deal, 1988). The concept of *enabling* refers to "creating opportunities for competence to be displayed" (Dunst & Trivette, 1987, p. 445), and *empowerment* is reflected in parents perceiving themselves as being able to bring about positive change. According to Dunst and Trivette (1987), parents who feel empowered and are actively involved in making decisions concerning their children have a positive impact on themselves, their children, and other professionals.

Generally, parent groups that emphasize empowerment and enabling take a broad perspective to parent support by focusing on family life overall. According to Powell (1986), such approaches emphasize developing family strengths and resources rather than intervening to change what some might perceive as deficits in the family. By providing assistance to parents of young children with special needs, parent support groups facilitate growth for all family members. Many areas of assistance are typically generated by parent support groups. These include (1) providing emotional and psychological support; (2) offering opportunities for families to socialize; (3) sharing information about community resources, educational opportunities, and the like; and (4) serving as advocates on behalf of children with handicapping conditions (Powell, 1986).

Hallenbeck and Beernink (1989) outlined three basic goals of counseling or support groups for parents of young children with disabilities. Specifically, such groups (1) provide information and emotional support to parents of children in an informal setting, (2) foster better understanding of their

terproductive to both the individual and the group, groups should be fairly stringent in attendance requirements.

Although parent groups may adopt several formats, three key elements characterize the most successful parent groups: (1) designated times or opportunities for socializing, (2) more formal lecture or information presentation, and (3) informal sharing or discussing among parents. In addition, effective practices typically have involved (1) the use of two group co-facilitators, (2) inviting other professionals to give informational or special-topics lectures, and (3) incorporating a dual group focus, specifically providing information and skill development as well as allowing parents to openly discuss their reactions and emotional responses to having a child with disabilities in their family.

Limitations of Group Approach for Parents of Young Children with Disabilities

Despite the benefits that many parents of young children experience through participation in groups, there are some limitations to group approaches for this population. One limitation lies in the often ambiguous distinction between group education and group therapy. As noted earlier, the majority of parent groups combine features of both educative and therapeutic groups. Some parents welcome direct treatment or counseling for themselves; these parents function successfully in groups with a therapeutic focus, such as interventions geared toward stress reduction and coping. Other parents, however, resist the notion that they are experiencing stress or have other mental health needs, but are willing to accept information, education, or suggestions about parenting their child, such as training in child management strategies.

In practice, there tends to be an overlap between a therapeutic and educative orientation, with groups sometimes drifting more toward providing information and, at times, moving toward providing therapy or counseling. From a clinical perspective, this overlap may, at times, undermine group goals and group functioning, depending on parents' openness to either orientation. From a research standpoint, the ambiguity and overlap make it difficult to evaluate systematically the active treatment components and their effects on targeted outcomes.

McConkey (1985) identified several additional practical limitations or barriers to working with parents of young children with disabilities in groups. Perhaps one of the greatest challenges to successful group approaches is attendance. McConkey (1985) listed several common obstacles reported by parents that may prevent their attendance at group sessions, including lack of child care, transportation problems, reluctance about attending alone, and concerns that the groups will not be beneficial for themselves or their child. Furthermore, parents whose command of English is poor are unlikely to participate in parent groups unless the language barrier is surmounted (Gargiulo, 1985).

Finally, although group approaches are helpful for many parents of young children with disabilities, some parents may find that other forms of treatment or assistance are more facilitative. For example, there are parents who, for a variety of reasons, may actually have a negative effect on the group; their participation and comments may deter or inhibit the effectiveness of the group process overall. Furthermore, there are other parents for whom individual counseling or family therapy may be more appropriate. It is important during the individual pregroup interviews that professionals fully assess which intervention approach best fits the needs of parents. If a parent group does not seem appropriate, other forms of intervention should be explored as alternatives.

SUGGESTIONS FOR RESEARCH AND PRACTICE

Perhaps the most pressing research need is for longitudinal studies examining the progressive adaptation of young children with disabilities and their parents resulting from participation in parent and parent/child groups. Research in which parents of children with disabilities are followed from the time the children are identified through critical transition stages (e.g., from preschool to school programs) will add to our knowledge about family stress and the long-term benefits of parent groups.

Another direction for future research and practice is to develop and evaluate training programs designed to prepare professionals to work with parent and parent/child groups. Although family outreach and family-centered practices are mentioned with increasing frequency as part of the professional's role in early childhood service delivery, many professional preparation programs do not provide adequate coverage of parent and parent/child groups. If early childhood professionals are to become more active with parents of children with disabilities, training must be provided so that they are knowledgeable about family dynamics and adaptation to disability, communication techniques, facilitation skills, the nature of handicapping conditions among young children, and services provided by various community agencies and schools (Brantlinger, 1991). Effective facilitators need experience and training in group processes in general, and with parents of children with disabilities in particular. Training activities may include attending seminars concerning disability issues, co-facilitating parent groups with experienced professionals, and learning about strategies to elicit coping and problem solving among group members.

The literature on parent groups does mention several variables believed to influence parental reactions to the group process. These variables include: (1) SES, (2) additional support services parents are receiving, (3) presence of other children and spouse in the home, (4) previous births of typically developing children, (5) religiosity, and (6) prior information about their child's handicapping condition. Despite attention given to these individual variables, empirical research relating these variables to overall family functioning and to the degree to which parents benefit from participation in groups is lacking (Brinker et al., 1994).

Another concern raised by an examination of the existing literature is the lack of specification of the effect of severity of the child's disability on parental characteristics and participation in parent groups. For example, the adjustment reactions of parents of young children with a variety of disorders have been studied; however, one might question whether parents of a child with a severe, as opposed to mild, disability experience different reactions and outcomes through participation in parent and parent/child groups (Blacher, 1984a). Finally, other issues such as homogeneity of membership in groups, single versus married parents, and parents from different cultural backgrounds need to be studied.

REFERENCES

Arnold, L. E., Rowe, M., & Tolbert, H. A. (1978). Parents' groups. In L. E. Arnold (Ed.), *Helping parents help their children* (pp. 114–125). New York: Brunner/Mazel.

Bailey, D., Blasco, P., & Simeonsson, R. (1992). Needs expressed by mothers and fathers of young children with disabilities. *American Journal on Mental Retardation, 97*, 1–10.

Baker, B. L. (1989). *Parent training and developmental disabilities*. Washington, DC: American Association on Mental Retardation.

Baker, B. L., Landen, S. J., & Kashima, K. J. (1991). Effects of parent training on families of children with mental retardation: Increased burden or generalized benefit? *American Journal on Mental Retardation, 96*, 127–136.

Bayley, N. (1969). *The Bayley Scales of Infant Development*. New York: The Psychological Corporation.

Beck, A. T., Ward, C., Mendelson, M. J., Mock, J. C., & Erbaugh, J. (1961). An inventory for measuring depression. *Archives of General Psychiatry, 4*, 53–63.

Blacher, J. B. (1984a). Sequential stages of parental adjustment to the birth of a child with handicaps: Fact or artifact? *Mental Retardation, 22*, 55–67.

Blacher, J. B. (Ed.). (1984b). *Severely handicapped young children and their families: Research in review*. New York: Academic Press.

Brantlinger, E. (1991). Home-school partnerships that benefit children with special needs. *The Elementary School Journal, 91*, 249–259.

Bricker, D. D., Gentry, D., & Bailey, E. J. (1985). *Evaluation and programming system for infants and young children, assessment level 1: Developmentally 1 month to 3 years*. Eugene, OR: University of Oregon, Center on Human Development.

Brinker, R. P., Seifer, R., & Samaroff, A. J. (1994). Relations among maternal stress, cognitive development, and early intervention in middle- and low-SES infants with developmental disabilities. *American Journal on Mental Retardation, 98*, 463–480.

Brotherson, M. J., & Goldstein, B. L. (1992). Time as a resource and constraint for parents of young children with disabilities: Implications for early intervention services. *Topics in Early Childhood Special Education, 12*, 508–527.

Carlo, P. (1988). Implementing a parent involvement/

parent education program in a children's residential treatment center. *Child and Youth Care Quarterly, 17,* 195–206.

Cordisco, L. K., Strain, P. S., & Depew, N. (1988). Assessment for generalization of parenting skills in home settings. *Journal of the Association for Persons with Severe Handicaps, 13,* 202–210.

Dembo, M. H., Sweitzer, M., & Lawritzen, P. (1985). An evaluation of group parent education: Behavioral, P.E.T., and Adlerian programs. *Review of Educational Research, 55,* 155–200.

Dunst, C. J., & Trivette, C. M. (1987). Enabling and empowering families: Conceptual and intervention issues. *School Psychology Review, 16,* 443–456.

Dunst, C. J., Trivette, C. M., & Deal, A. G. (1988). *Enabling and empowering families: Principles and guidelines for practice.* Cambridge, MA: Brookline Books.

Fewell, R. R., & Vadasy, P. F. (Eds.). (1986). *Families of handicapped children.* Austin, TX: Pro-Ed.

Fine, M. J. (1991). The handicapped child and the family: Implications for professionals. In M. J. Fine (Ed.), *Collaboration with parents of exceptional children* (pp. 3–24). Brandon, VT: Clinical Psychology Publishing.

Fine, M. J., & Gardner, P. A. (1991). Counseling and education services for families: An empowerment perspective. *Elementary School Guidance and Counseling, 26,* 33–44.

Fine, M. J., & Henry, S. A. (1989). Professional issues in parent education. In M. J. Fine (Ed.), *The second handbook on parent education: Contemporary perspectives* (pp. 3–20). New York: Academic Press.

Frey, K. S., Greenberg, M. T., & Fewell, R. R. (1989). Stress and coping among parents of handicapped children: A multidimensional approach. *American Journal on Mental Retardation, 94,* 240–249.

Friedlander, S. R., & Watkins, E. C. (1985). Therapeutic aspects of support groups for parents of the mentally retarded. *International Journal of Group Psychotherapy, 35,* 65–78.

Friedrich, W. N., Greenberg, M. T., & Crnic, K. (1983). A short-form of the Questionnaire on Resources and Stress. *American Journal of Mental Deficiency, 88,* 41–48.

Gage, M. M., & Wishon, P. M. (1988). Establishing and maintaining parent-support groups. *Early Child Development and Care, 36,* 49–63.

Gallagher, J. J., Peckham, P., & Cross, A. H. (1983). Families of handicapped children: Sources of stress and its amelioration. *Exceptional Children, 51,* 10–19.

Gallimore, R., Weisner, T., Bernheimer, L., Guthrie, D., & Nihira, K. (1993). Family responses to young children with developmental delays: Accommodation activity in ecological and cultural context. *American Journal on Mental Retardation, 98,* 185–206.

Gargiulo, R. M. (1985). *Working with parents of exceptional children: Guide for professionals.* Boston: Houghton Mifflin.

Gargiulo, R. M., & Graves, S. B. (1991). Parental feelings: The forgotten component when working with parents of handicapped preschool children. *Childhood Education, 67,* 176–179.

Hallenbeck, M., & Beernink, M. (1989). Support program for parents of students with mild handicaps. *Teaching Exceptional Children, 22,* 44–47.

Hanline, M. F., & Daley, S. (1992). Family coping strategies and strengths in Hispanic, African-American, and Caucasian families of young children. *Topics in Early Childhood Special Education, 12,* 351–366.

Hornby, G., & Murray, R. (1983). Group programmes for parents of children with various handicaps. *Child Care Health and Development, 9,* 185–198.

Kazdin, A. E., & Matson, J. L. (1981). Social validation in mental retardation. *Applied Research in Mental Retardation, 2,* 39–54.

Lamb, M. E. (1986). *The father's role: Applied perspectives.* New York: Wiley.

Landis, L. (1992). Marital, employment, and childcare status of mothers with infants and toddlers with disabilities. *Topics in Early Childhood Special Education, 12,* 496–507.

Lerner, J. (1992). *Learning disabilities: Theories, diagnosis and teaching strategies* (6th ed.). Boston: Houghton Mifflin.

Levant, R. F. (1988). Education for fatherhood. In P. Bronstein & C. P. Cowan (Eds.), *Fatherhood today: Men's changing role in the family* (pp. 253–275). New York: Wiley.

Mahoney, G., O'Sullivan, P., & Robinson, C. (1992). The family environments of children with disabilities: Diverse but not so different. *Topics in Early Childhood Special Education, 12,* 386–402.

May, J. (1992). New horizons for fathers of children with disabilities. *Exceptional Parent, 22*(4), 40–44.

McBride, B. A. (1991). Parent education and support programs for fathers: Outcome effects on paternal involvement. *Early Child Development and Care, 67,* 73–85.

McBride, B. A., & McBride, R. J. (1990). The changing roles of fathers: Implications family life and parent educators. *Journal of Home Economics, 82,* 6–10.

McBride, B. A., & McBride, R. J. (1993). Parent education and support programs for fathers. *Childhood Education, 69*, 4–9.

McConkey, R. (1985). *Working with parents: A practical guide for teachers and therapists*. Cambridge, MA: Brookline.

Miezio, E. (1983). *Parenting children with disabilities: A professional source for physicians and guide for parents*. New York: Marcel, Dekker.

Moos, R. H. (1974). *The Family Environment Scale*. Palo Alto, CA: Consulting Psychologists.

Mori, A. (1983). *Families of children with special needs: Early intervention techniques for the practitioner*. Rockville, MD: Aspen.

Murray, J. (1990). Best practices in working with parents of handicapped children. In A. Thomas & J. Grimes (Eds.), *Best practices in school psychology—II* (pp. 823–836). Washington DC: National Association of School Psychologists.

Olson, D. H., McCubbin, H. I., Barnes, H., Larsen, A., Muxen, M., & Wilson, M. (1982). *Family inventories: Inventories used in a national survey of families across the family life cycle*. St. Paul, MN: University of Minnesota.

Peterson, N. (1987). *Early interventions for handicapped and at-risk children: An introduction to early childhood special education*. Denver: Love.

Powell, D. R. (1986). Parent education and support programs. *Young Children, 41*, 3–4.

Powers, L. E., Singer, G. H. S., Stevens, T., & Sowers, J. A. (1992). Behavioral parent training in home and community generalization settings. *Education and Training in Mental Retardation, 27*, 13–27.

Poyadue, F. (1993). Cognitive coping at parents helping parents. In A. Turnbull, J. Patterson, S. Behr, D. Murphy, J. Marquis, & M. Blue-Banning (Eds.), *Cognitive coping, families, and disability* (pp. 95–110). Baltimore, MD: Brookes.

Rose, B. (1990). Early childhood family education. *Day Care and Early Education, 17*, 27–29.

Sameroff, A. J., & Fiese, B. (1990). Transactional regulation and early intervention. In S. J. Meisels & J. P. Shonkoff (Eds.), *Handbook of early childhood intervention* (pp. 119–149). New York: Cambridge University Press.

Sanders, M. R., & Dadds, M. R. (1982). The effects of planned activities and child management procedures in parent training: An analysis of setting generality. *Behavior Therapy, 13*, 452–461.

Scott, S., & Doyle, P. (1984). Parent-to-parent support. *The Exceptional Parent, 14*, 1–2.

Seifer, R., Clark, G. N., & Sameroff, A. J. (1991). Positive effects of interaction coaching in infants with developmental disability and their mothers. *American Journal on Mental Retardation, 96*, 1–11.

Seligman, M. (1993). Group work with parents of children with disabilities. *The Journal of Specialists in Group Work, 18*, 115–126.

Singer, G. H. S., Irvin, L. K., & Hawkins, N. (1988). Stress management training for parents of children with severe handicaps. *Mental Retardation, 26*, 269–277.

Spiegel-McGill, P., Reed, D. J., Konig, C. S., & McGowan, P. A. (1990). Parent education: Easing the transition to preschoool. *Topics in Early Childhood Special Education, 9*(4), 66–77.

Speilberger, C. D., Gorsuch, R. L., & Lushene, R. C. (1970). *The State-Trait Anxiety Inventory*. Palo Alto, CA: Consulting Psychologists.

Stoneman, Z., Brody, G. H., & Abbott, D. (1983). In-home observations of young Down syndrome children with their mothers and fathers. *American Journal of Mental Deficiency, 87*, 591–600.

Taylor, S. E., & Brown, J. (1988). Illusion and well-being. Some social psychological contributions to a theory of mental health. *Psychological Bulletin, 103*, 193–210.

Trivette, C. & Dunst, C. (1992). Characteristics and influences of role division and social support among mothers of preschool children with disabilities. *Topics in Early Childhood Special Education, 12*, 367–385.

Turnbull, A., & Turnbull, H. R. (1993). Participatory research on cognitive coping: From concepts to research planning. In A. Turnbull, J. Patterson, S. Behr, D. Murphy, J. Marquis, & M. Blue-Banning, (Eds.), *Cognitive coping, families, and disability* (pp. 1–14). Baltimore, MD: Brookes.

Upshur, C. C. (1991). Families and the community service maze. In M. Seligman (Ed.), *The family with a handicapped child* (pp. 91–118). Boston: Allyn and Bacon.

Wallinga, C., Paquio, L., & Skeen, P. (1987). When a brother or sister is ill. *Psychology Today, 64*, 42–43.

Zeitlin, S., Williamson, G. G., & Rosenblatt, W. P. (1987). The coping with stress model: A counseling approach for families with a handicapped child. *Journal of Counseling and Development, 65*, 443–446.

CHAPTER 19

GROUPS FOR PARENTS OF SCHOOL-AGED CHILDREN WITH DISABILITIES

Marian C. Fish, QUEENS COLLEGE OF THE CITY UNIVERSITY OF NEW YORK

RATIONALE

The presence of a child with a disability in a family has an impact on family functioning. Although each family is unique, and family adaptation can vary dramatically, parents raising a child with a disability have many common experiences and stressors. Research has shown, for example, that daily care needs, socialization needs, finances, managing behavior, recreational opportunities, and future planning for the child are concerns identified by families with children with disabilities (Darling, 1991; Fish, 1995; Turnbull & Turnbull, 1990). Participation in parent groups provides a means of addressing these shared concerns.

A number of authors suggest that group approaches for parents of children with disabilities are beneficial because parents help provide education and support to each other. Information, support, encouragement, and assistance in problem solving have been identified as needs common to parents of children with disabilities (Murray, 1990). In a group, parents realize that they are not alone in having problems and may be more willing to try something new when they hear of the successful application by other parents (Wyckoff, 1980). Parents offer a wide array of coping behaviors from which other members learn (Meyerson, 1983). Parent groups provide participants with an opportunity to share experiences with group members that may generate feelings of support.

In contrast to individual or family therapy, feedback not only comes from the leader (i.e., therapist or facilitator) but also from peers (Meyerson, 1983). According to Seligman (1990), "Groups are an important resource for persons who are dispirited, lonely and isolated, poorly supported and misinformed about relevant information and services" (p. 161). Recent trends such as smaller family size, changing family structure (e.g., more single parents and working mothers), and isolation from other family members during childrearing years suggest that group interventions will become increasingly important for all parents (e.g., Clarke-Stewart, 1978; Combrinck-Graham, 1989), but perhaps especially needed by parents of children with disabilities.

Despite the additional demands families face when they have a child with a disability, there is little evidence suggesting these families are more pathological than other families (Hampson, Hulgus, Beavers, & Beavers, 1988). Most families with children having special needs are able to adjust and accommodate to the stress on the family system by mobilizing their resources and strengths, though they may want or need further information or support. Some families, however, experience chronic stress and family disruption and would benefit from therapeutic assistance (Seligman, 1990).

FUNCTIONS OF PARENT GROUPS

Groups for parents with a child with a disability generally serve educative/training or therapeutic functions or a combination of educative and therapeutic functions (Seligman, 1990). These models are not exclusive to parent groups of children with disabilities and are used with parents of typically developing children as well.

Educative/Training Groups

A group with an educative focus provides parents with both information and skills; it is based on the assumption that problems emerge when there are deficiencies in these areas (Friedlander & Watkins, 1985). The terms *parent education* and *parent training* are usually used interchangeably because information and skill development generally occur together (Fine, 1980). The goals of parent education are varied and can include understanding special issues related to a child's disability, learning or improving general parenting skills and how they might be adapted to the circumstances, learning effective coping skills, improving parent/child communication and/or identifying local and national resources. Educational/training groups tend to be rather structured, with both content and format predetermined; discussion is generally directed to the topic under consideration for that session (Meyerson, 1983).

Although parent education/training groups have been quite popular, there has been some criticism of the parent education movement by those who fear that parent education groups induce a sense of powerlessness and feelings of dependence in parents that can undermine parents' effectiveness with children (Dembo, Sweitzer, & Lauritzen, 1985). An opposite viewpoint asserts that much could be done to prevent handicaps through parent education courses introduced even before students become parents (Anastasiow, 1988).

Therapeutic Groups

Seligman (1990) noted that "parent groups that are essentially therapeutic in nature tend to stress the sharing and exploration of feelings" (e.g., guilt, frustration, anger) (p. 151). In therapeutic groups, there is usually more emphasis on understanding the etiology of behaviors and interactions and on dealing with personal issues. Therapy groups tend to be more open and flexible than educative groups.

Therapeutic parent groups move through fairly well-defined stages that are similar to other therapy groups (Meyerson, 1983). In the first stage, trust building for the leader and for the other parent members occurs. During this stage, there may be conflict, distrust, or disagreement on priorities, but eventually this leads to openness and willingness to share feelings. Dependency on the facilitator, who is seen as an authority, is common. During the second stage of the group, therapeutic "work" is done. In the words of Meyerson (1983), "Parents now more closely examine their own interactions and relationships and gain insight into the ways in which these contribute to the problems of their homelife" (p. 304). At the second stage, parent competence and confidence are enhanced. The final stage involves termination of the group and separation from group members.

The therapist must plan in advance for the diversity of reactions of group members, including anger that the group didn't do its job or sadness at leaving others with whom they have become close. Parents may feel abandoned by the therapist and scared of losing the support of the group. The therapist plays an important role in facilitating the process of separation by informing parents of additional resources available to them, encouraging continued member support of each other, and acknowledging their feelings (Meyerson, 1983).

Fine (1980) and Fine and Henry (1989) distinguished characteristics of parent education groups and parent therapy groups. First, the relationship between group facilitator and parents is usually more personal and in-depth in group therapy compared to the educator relationship wherein limited involvement with personal problems occurs. Following from this relationship, the interaction between group therapy members allows for confrontation and support, whereas it is more controlled in the education group. Therapy focuses on "personality change" (Dembo et al., 1985), but goals of education groups are more practical and may include behavior change, improved communication, or understanding child development. Finally, a parent education group is generally time limited (usually 6 to 10 sessions of one to two hours), whereas group therapy sessions are more often open ended. Despite these differences, lines between educational and therapeutic parent groups are often blurred, and the majority of parent groups described in the literature have features common to both (Seligman, 1990).

Intervention Techniques: Research and Practice

Parent groups vary in their theoretical base, content, instructional or therapeutic method and the degree to which their effectiveness is documented by research (Lee & Brage, 1989). The major theoretical models from which parent groups have evolved are (1) reflective, (2) Adlerian, (3) behavioral, (4) support and coping, and (5) stress management (Ehly, Conoley, & Rosenthal, 1985; Friedlander & Watkins, 1985; Medway, 1989). Despite the differing conceptual viewpoints, groups have common goals of providing information, support, encouragement, and assistance in problem solving to parents of children with disabilities, and ultimately enhancing both the development of the child within the family and the parent/child relationship.

Group Interventions Based on a Reflective Model

Parent groups with a reflective orientation evolved from Carl Rogers's client-centered therapy, a humanistic perspective emphasizing parent awareness, understanding, and acceptance of children's feelings. Communication techniques are taught in therapy to affect children's behavior and the parent/child interaction (Dembo et al., 1985; Medway, 1989). *Parent Effectiveness Training (P.E.T)* (Gordon, 1975) is the most widely used reflective program with typically developing children. The P.E.T. program assumes that the parent/child relationship is analogous to the therapist/client relationship. Parents need to provide an atmosphere of empathy, genuineness, and unconditional positive regard for children to grow and develop; this can be accomplished through accepting, supportive, and nonjudgmental behavior on the part of parents (Lee & Brage, 1989). Difficulties in communication stem from the use of 12 nonproductive verbal behaviors: ordering, threatening, moralizing, advising, ridiculing, arguing, criticizing, praising, diagnosing, sympathizing, probing, and withdrawing (Gordon, 1972), and specific communication techniques such as active listening, "I messages, silence," and a "no-lose" method of resolving conflicts involving negotiation are taught. The program usually consists of eight three-hour sessions held weekly. Instructional techniques used include lectures, readings, role-playing, and homework (Dembo et al., 1985).

Giannotti and Doyle (1982) investigated whether parent participation in the P.E.T. program would improve parent/child relationships and result in positive changes in the self-concepts of elementary school children with learning disabilities. Some 92 volunteer parents of 46 children participated in eight three-hour sessions that incorporated lectures and demonstrations (a cognitive component), discussion and role-playing (a group process component), and task analysis and practice of new responses (a behavioral component). Parent effectiveness in dealing with real parent/child situations was emphasized, as in a case where a boy complained to his parent about the easy work in the resource room that he hated. The parent responded that it really wasn't baby work, and that if he continued hating it, learning would be even more difficult. This response was discussed by the group and alternative responses were suggested. Because the child "owned" the problem, "active listening" by the parent would have been more appropriate than the parent response, which cut off further conversation and problem-solving activities.

Significant differences between the parents in the P.E.T. (experimental) group and a control group were reported on five parental attitudes of the Parent Attitude Survey. Parents in the P.E.T. group reported more confidence in themselves as parents, greater awareness of the effects of their behavior on children, a greater feeling of acceptance of their children, a greater understanding of their needs, and a greater willingness to trust their children than did parents in the control group. Similarly, on the Children's Report of Parental Behavior Inventory, children in the experimental group perceived their parents' behaviors as more accepting to them as individuals, less critical and rejecting of them, less neglectful of their needs, and more understanding of them than did children of parents in the control group. A greater increase in self-concept as measured on the Piers-Harris Children's Self-Concept Scale was reported for children with parents in the P.E.T. group than for those with parents in the control group.

Although the P.E.T. program resulted in positive changes, scores were still not as high as for parents and their nonhandicapped children. Since outcome measures used were self-report questionnaires, no information on actual behavior change is available nor is it clear which component(s) were responsible for change. Finally, the authors suggest that additional strategies such as teacher training and follow-up parental training used regularly would enhance the effectiveness of the program.

Group Approaches Based on an Adlerian Model

The Adlerian approach is based on the Individual Psychology theory of Alfred Adler and writings of Rudolf Dreikurs (c.f., Dreikurs & Soltz, 1964). Fundamental Adlerian tenets include (1) democratic rather than permissive and autocratic parenting, (2) purposive or goal-directed behavior (individuals strive to overcome perceived difficulties and move toward a goal), (3) encouragement, and (4) principles of logical consequences (Gamson, Hornstein, & Borden, 1989).

As applied in Dinkmeyer and McKay's (1976) *Systematic Training for Effective Parenting (S.T.E.P.)* program for typically developing children, parents learn to identify the four goals of misbehavior: gaining attention, power, revenge, and displays of inadequacy in order to effectively guide the child's behavior. Natural and logical consequences are emphasized as methods of discipline instead of reward and punishment techniques (Lee & Brage, 1989). Strategies used in S.T.E.P. and S.T.E.P./TEEN (Dinkmeyer & McKay, 1983) are adapted and modified from Dreikurs's ideas, but also incorporate communication strategies such as those described earlier in P.E.T., such as reflective listening, problem-solving techniques, and "I messages," and parents are taught to state how they feel about a child's specific behavior (Gamson, Hornstein, & Borden, 1989; Lee & Brage, 1989). The democratic approach attempts to solve conflicts by seeking new mutual agreements where everyone gains something from the decision (Thomas & Marchant, 1983). The S.T.E.P. program is generally presented in nine 2-hour sessions weekly.

Williams, Omizo, and Abrams (1984) evaluated the effects of S.T.E.P. on parental attitudes and locus of control of 38 learning disabled children ranging in age from 9 to 12 years. The parents participating in the S.T.E.P. group used booklets, cassette tapes, and posters and were taught principles pertinent to democratic parenting over the nine-week period. Results indicate that there were significant differences between the S.T.E.P. (experimental) group and the control group parents on three of five subscales of the Parent Attitude Survey. Parents in S.T.E.P. were more accepting and trusting, and perceived their own behavior as more of a causative factor in their children's behavior; these results were similar to the Giannotti and Doyle (1982) findings for the P.E.T. program. No differences were found in confidence in parenting ability and importance of communication between experimental and control groups.

Results from the Locus of Control Inventory for Three Achievement Domains, used to measure children's locus of control, indicate that children with learning disabilities in the experimental group were more internal in Success Social Domain, Success Physical Domain, Failure Intellectual Domain, and Failure Physical Domain than were control group children. This means, for example, that there was greater acceptance of responsibility for social success by those youngsters in the experimental group than those in the control group. The children in the experimental group perceived that events were consequences of their own actions and under their control. In sum, positive outcomes for parents and children seem to have resulted from parent participation in S.T.E.P, but again, all outcome measures were attitudinal.

Kottman and Wilborn (1992) compared Adlerian parent study groups led by school counselors with those led by trained parent leaders who received a six-week training program. Group participants were parents of elementary school-aged children. Again, five subscales on the Parent Attitude Survey were used to measure change pre- and postgroup participation. There were no significant differences in attitude change between the parent groups led by counselors and the parent groups led by parents on four attitudes: confidence, acceptance, understanding, and trust. On the fifth attitude, causation (recognition that their own behavior was a causative factor in their child's behavior), the counselor-led groups scored higher than the parent-led group, perhaps because causation is a more complex concept and requires a greater level of sophistication to teach. In sum, the results suggest that parent facilitators were effective in changing attitudes and that they should be encouraged to assist professionals as group facilitators in the future.

Popkin (1989) argues that the content of packaged programs such as S.T.E.P. and P.E.T. are not at issue; most programs are similar, promoting communication skills, encouragement, consequences, and addressing the developmental needs of the child. Rather, he supports the use of video-based training as a more effective delivery system for parenting education because it encourages group interaction, maximizes leader's strengths, is cost effective, and results in better retention of material in less time (Lee & Brage, 1989; Popkin, 1989). Popkin cites a 1984 study by Thomas and Thomas that concluded that the most efficient medium for presenting massive amounts of information and examples is videotape.

The instructional strategies using the democratic parenting model of *Active Parenting* include a behavioral component (modeling and practicing of effective parenting skills), a didactic component (reading and discussion), and a group process component (feedback, encouragement, and group exercises). Limited research, based on field test data only, is reported evaluating Active Parenting; 274 volunteer parents participated in Active Parenting offered in either a school, church, health care facility, or other community location (Popkin, 1983). Parents attended all six sessions and were given behavior checklists at the end to rate their parenting behaviors and their children's behavior before and after Active Parenting. Popkin (1983) indicates that 97% of parents reported positive changes in their own parenting, and 84% reported positive changes in their children's behavior. Of course, these results must be viewed with caution because no control group and no pretest measures were used.

Group Interventions Using a Behavioral Model

Behavioral programs involve the training of parents to act as therapists in their child's natural environment by applying the behavior management techniques learned in the parent training group; principles of learning such as the use of social and nonsocial reinforcers, shaping behavior, observation and recording procedures, reducing undesirable behavior, and increasing desirable behavior are taught.

Behavioral parent training for children with disabilities has a theoretical and empirical basis in the literature on aggression and challenging behavior in children—a quite different origin from that of the reflective and Adlerian groups that focused on typical child development (Newby, Fischer, & Roman, 1991). Early group work began with parents of children with autism, cognitive disability, and aggressive and oppositional behaviors such as tantrums. Research showed that parents of conduct-disordered children, for example, treated their children differently from the way that parents of normal children treated them (Patterson, 1986).

Patterson and colleagues at the Oregon Social Learning Center (Forehand & McMahon, 1981; Kozloff, 1979; Patterson, 1976) pioneered the use of techniques based on a social interactional model to treat boys referred for conduct problems in both the home and at school. Patterson's method was unique in that he focused on adults rather than children in effecting change in the childrens' problem behaviors. Results of his studies showed that parents could be trained in groups to successfully change their children's targeted behaviors, and that the behaviors remained changed at follow-up of as long as 12 months (c.f., Fleischman, 1981). In addition, these results generalized to other deviant behaviors. This seminal work isolated two critical aspects of a behavioral approach: (1) training parents to carefully observe and record the child's behavior and (2) training parents to reinforce the child's behavior appropriately.

Kramer (1990) reported that both researchers and parents have identified children's noncompliance as a major problem for parents. Noncompliance occurs when children refuse to comply with rules established by parents or when parents have not established rules; noncompliant behaviors can include whining, stealing, truancy, tantrums, not doing homework, headbanging, or ignoring parent requests. Because noncompliant behavior is a shared problem in almost all referrals, and a frequent parent complaint that often leads to parent/child negative interactions, current behavioral group parent training approaches generally focus on noncompliance and compliance as target behaviors in treatment. There is also evidence that noncompliant child behavior increases the likelihood of later more serious behavioral difficulties, but that when managed successfully, it can lead to improvement in overall psychosocial functioning (Anastopoulos & Barkley, 1990).

One of the most clearly described group parent training/counseling programs is Barkley's program discussed in *Defiant Children: A Clinician's Manual for Parent Training* (1987) (see also Anastopoulos & Barkley, 1990). The program teaches parents specialized contingency management techniques; in addition, when discussing Attention Deficit Hyperactivity Disorder (ADHD), Anastopoulos and Barkley recommend using cognitive therapy strategies to correct parents' faulty perceptions of themselves and of their children. More specifically, they suggest either incorporating them into the treatment systematically or providing separate counseling experiences.

Defiant Children is designed for parents of children between the ages of 3 and 11 (though current research is looking at applicability for use with adolescents from 12 to 17) who are challenged by child behavior problems, particularly noncompliance, having varied etiologies (e.g., functional behavior related to a disability). Defiant Children can be implemented either with individuals or in small groups. Because there is no evidence indicating superiority for group or individual-based approaches, Anastopoulos and Barkley (1990) suggested parents should choose the treatment mode. Several factors, however—such as scheduling constraints, intellectually slow parents, or parents who need particularly close supervision—may make individual treatment preferable. Parents with at least a high school education and low levels of personal and family stress are more likely to experience success with the program according to Barkley. In two-parent families, having both parents attend is considered optimal.

Newby and associates (1991) summarized the three goals of the program: (1) to improve parental management skills, (2) to increase parental knowledge of the causes of childhood misbehavior and the principles and concepts underlying the social learning of such behavior, and (3) to improve child compliance to commands and rules given by parents. Assessment procedures include interviews, parent and teacher questionnaires, and observations.

There is a 10-step core training program (Barkley, 1987). Additional sessions may be added when working with a specific disability such as ADHD. Generally, the program can be completed within 8 to 12 sessions, but flexibility of pace is desirable. In general, this program is similar in many ways to other behavioral parent group training programs. It uses sound instructional practices such as role-playing, behavioral rehearsal, video, modeling, and corrective feedback that require parents to be engaged in the process. Written handouts, homework assignments, home practice, and back-up strategies are included in the training. Competence must be demonstrated before new skills are introduced; contingencies for generalization are applied. Because there is little evidence to support the sole use of verbal approaches, such strategies are minimized.

In discussing the use of this program with parents of ADHD youngsters, Anastopoulos and Barkley (1990) noted several components that distinguish Defiant Children from more typical behavioral parent programs. These include a didactic lesson on ADHD to increase parental knowledge (i.e., that ADHD is an inborn, biological temperamental disposition with which we cope rather than cure) and the incorporation of cognitive therapy strategies to deal with parents' faulty perceptions that might interfere with their implementation of the program.

Little empirical support is available for the effectiveness of this program for parents of ADHD youngsters; however, parent group behavioral programs have been shown to be successful in teaching parenting skills to parents, resulting in positive behavior change in children with noncompliant, oppositional defiant, and conduct-disordered behaviors (c.f., Anastopoulus & Barkley, 1990; McMahon & Forehand, 1984). Patterson, DeBaryshe, and Ramsey (1989) indicate more positive outcomes working with children's antisocial behavior when children are younger at the time of parent training. A new, revised manual was published in 1997 (Barkley, 1997).

Other programs have been developed for parent training with a specific group—for example, Baker's (1983) cognitive-behavioral *Parents as Teachers* program aimed at parents of children with moderate to severe cognitive disabilities, ages 3 to 13. The first five sessions deal with teaching self-help skills, and parents learn how to set behavioral objectives, break skills down into components, and use contingent reinforcement. During one session, parents teach their child focusing in the group and receive feedback from the group facilitator. Strategies for behavior problem management and for behavior generalization are taught in later sessions.

Once again, role-playing, demonstrations, videotapes, and outside reading including the *Steps to Independence* series are used (Baker, 1983). Although little empirical verification of the effectiveness of this program is available, follow-up studies reported by Baker (1983) indicate that children maintained skill gains and developed additional skills. There are some limitations, however, as Baker (1989) reported that single-parent families had a lower completion rate than married parents, even when only one member of a married couple attended a group; this suggests that special attention be paid to developing techniques aimed at retention of single parents. Perhaps special videotapes, as discussed by Cunningham (1990), can be developed that reflect issues specific to single parents. Powers (1991) noted that despite the success of many behavioral training programs with parents of children with severe handicaps, there are some parents who do not benefit from the training. Negative parent training outcomes have been related to socioeconomic level, marital conflict, and parental depression (Powers, 1991).

Powers, Singer, Stevens, and Sowers (1992) note problems with generalization of new skills to home and community settings. They suggest procedures that go beyond regular contingency management training such as planned activities training to promote generalization. For this proactive strategy, parents are instructed to anticipate instances in which they are likely to have competing demands on their time and the child would be unlikely to keep busy. Behaviors from group training were generalized to other settings using planned activities training with coaching in a study by Cordisco, Strain, and Depew (1988).

In sum, there is considerable research support for the efficacy of behavioral parent training with parents of children with disabilities (Anastopoulos & Barkley, 1990). Children and parents are likely to benefit when parents are taught specific behavior management skills to be used on a daily basis (Baker, 1989). Additional strategies to address generalization and specific family issues may require more individualized treatment planning.

Parent Support Groups

According to Seligman (1990), support groups arose from the self-help movement and have three characteristics: (1) voluntary participation, (2) agreement on mutual self-help goals, and (3) peer leadership. Friedlander and Watkins (1985) describe their support group model as one in which the leader is inactive and parents helping parents is emphasized. The underpinnings of support groups stress the importance of social support to enhance functioning and to identify and build on family capabilities as a way of strengthening families (Dunst, Trivette, & Deal, 1988). A proactive stance toward families encourages focusing on family strengths and resources rather than on deficits (Dunst & Trivette, 1987). The concepts of enabling and empowering families through support groups offer parents opportunities to display their competence and to assume responsibility for bringing about change. For example, Carlo (1988) describes a parent support group program instituted in a children's residential treatment center that resulted in role reversal between parents and staff. Parents gained confidence and became actively contributing team members, and staff became more confident in the parents, giving them greater responsibility.

Nathanson's (1986) notes that although support groups share similar goals of providing social support and developing coping skills, their structure, leadership, sponsorships, and activities may vary. For example, support groups are sponsored in a variety of settings, including schools (Loewenstein, 1981), residential treatment centers (Carlo, 1988), and hospitals (Dreier & Lewis, 1991). Nathanson (1986) describes three basic types of support group leadership—parent led, parent/professional led, and professional led—and notes that choosing and delegating power may vary among these three leadership types.

Information is available for developing parent support programs (Pueschel, Bernier, & Gossler, 1989; Ripley & Rewers, 1989), and Nathanson (1986) provides guidelines for organizing and maintaining support groups specifically for parents of children with chronic illness and disabilities. She identifies a number of activities occurring in parent support groups, including (1) sharing mutual experiences, (2) providing information services for member parents, and (3) informing others of group needs. A typical supportive activity is visitation, where members of a group visit new parents, serving as a bridge for new families. Parent-to-parent phone networks are encouraged, especially for parents whose child's disability makes it difficult for them to attend meetings. Some groups serve as clearinghouses of information and may develop bibliographies, libraries, and files of information that can be disseminated. Almost all groups have a newsletter to inform members of the group's activities.

Parents of children with disabilities often have a limited social life and may find social events desirable. When with other families who have similar needs, parents are often more comfortable and relaxed about participating; there is no stigma from feeling different and no need to explain their child's condition. At the same time, parents may observe how other families handle their children as well as expectations other parents have for their children.

Parent groups have become an important source of power in facilitating medical, educational, and governmental systems toward improvements in areas such as research and treatment. Parent advocacy groups might focus on local change or on change in public policy at the national level.

There is growing recognition that support is needed not only by the mother of a child with a disability but also by other family members, especially fathers. Fathers have a unique set of needs that they bring to the parenting situation because they usually have little experience taking care of children before becoming parents (McBride, 1991). A growing number of father groups provide support, education, and greater involvement. An example of a fathers' support group is one described by May (1992). He identifies common themes to explain why fathers attend support groups. Interestingly, these reasons correspond closely to those reported by Nathanson (1986). Men attend because they feel safe, can let down their guard, are taken seriously, and know that confidentiality is observed. They are exposed to new information and feelings. They can relax, unwind, and make new friends. Finally, they participate because they know the other members understand their feelings and experiences.

Research evaluating fathers' groups is limited, especially for school-aged children. May (1992) cites research for young children that concludes that fathers' support groups can improve family communication; improve self-esteem; reduce stress, tension, depression, and fatigue; increase sharing of chores and responsibilities; enhance family support systems; and increase acceptance of the child and family harmony (c.f., Frey, Fewell, & Vadasy, 1989; Markowitz, 1984). Studies of programs for men of preschool-aged children and older have reported effectiveness in increasing fathers' perceptions of parenting competence and some forms of paternal involvement (McBride, 1990; 1991), in increasing communication skills with their children (Levant & Doyle, 1983), and in decreasing the amount of stress they experience in their parental roles (McBride, 1991). Surprisingly, results from Firestone, Kelly, and Fike (1980) found no differences between joint mother/father parent groups and mother-only groups using children's behavior as outcome measure, though both treatment groups were superior to the control group.

Attempting to address the unique needs of fathers, McBride (1991) investigated whether an intervention combining father discussion groups and joint father/child activities would affect parental feelings of competence and behavior. Some 30 fathers and their preschool-aged children met for two hours on 10 consecutive weeks in a parent education/play group program that included discussion for fathers on issues they selected during the first hour and joint father/child structured and nonstructured play activities for the second hour. Both interview and self-report data were collected and revealed that fathers who participated in the group program had greater involvement in childrearing activities on nonwork days and a greater sense of competence in parenting than control fathers. These positive findings suggest that continued efforts to develop and implement similar programs are warranted.

In addition to fathers, other family members such as siblings and grandparents may be the focus of support groups. Pearson and Sternberg (1986) described a mutual-help, school-based program *Living with a Handicapped Child* that had parent support groups and a unique component; sibling support groups. The two support groups met in adjacent rooms, with siblings ranging from ages 5 to 13. Each sibling group session began with a general question such as What do you like or dislike about your handicapped sibling? to spark discussion about feelings and family relationships. Siblings kept notebooks of drawings for discussion. Two recurring themes were identified: anger (due to a variety of reasons such as receiving less attention than the sibling) and a feeling of responsibility for the handicapped sibling. A research study on a grandparent support group by Vadasy, Fewell, and Meyer (cited in Turnbull & Turnbull, 1990) found that grandparents had many concerns and questions about their disabled grandchildren that they wanted to address, as well.

Turnbull and Turnbull (1990) describe an innovative parent group program called *Families Together,* which combines education/training, counseling, and support. What distinguishes this program is that entire families meet at weekend workshops extending from Saturday morning through Sunday noon. Approximately 18 families spend time on recreational activities, parent discussion groups, lectures, sibling discussion groups, and child activities. Participants reportedly benefit from the support, knowledge and recreational opportunities, which might otherwise be quite limited. Although the effectiveness of support groups has not been systematically evaluated, informal feedback and observations have generally suggested a positive response from the participants with positive attitude and behavior change.

Parent Groups Using a Stress Management Model

Although few studies address stress management for parents of children in the school-aged population, this model of group intervention has been widely used with families of young children. Frey, Greenberg, and Fewell (1989) suggest that alleviating stress in families through parent groups is effective in facilitating adaptive functioning. Stress management groups emphasize interventions to cope with stressors in family life rather than on typical development issues of childrearing.

Zeitlin, Williamson, and Rosenblatt (1987) describe a cognitive-behavioral model for coping with stress used with parents of children with disabilities under 3 years of age. According to Zeitlin and colleagues (1987), effective coping occurs when parents use their strengths and resources to manage tension-generating events. Strategies derived from a cognitive-behavioral perspective guide parents in a four-step process: (1) assessing the stressor-event and its meaning to them; (2) identifying internal and external resources (e.g., material, support, physical, and psychological status) so that they can decide on a coping effort; (3) acting on that decision through reappraisal or some type of coping; and (4) evaluating the effect of the coping behavior. Changing maladaptive beliefs and other faulty perceptions is key to this intervention.

A study of parents of school-aged children with severe developmental disabilities was conducted by Singer, Irvin, and Hawkins (1988) to determine the viability of an eight-session stress management group intervention. The self-management techniques taught included self-monitoring of stressful events and physiological reactions to them, muscle relaxation skills, and modification of cognitions associated with distress. These procedures are widely used in the cognitive-behavioral treatment of anxiety and depression. Parents reported that all three treatment components were helpful, with self-monitoring the most difficult for parents to complete reliably. Results indicated significant reductions in anxiety and depression that were greater for the experimental group than the control group. In sum, preliminary evidence suggests that stress management training is an effective intervention for parents of children with severe disabilities, although future studies should include the collection of follow-up data.

ROLE OF THE GROUP FACILITATOR

An effective group facilitator is essential for any parent training or therapy group. Although there is evidence that group leaders play an important role in facilitating positive change (Dembo et al., 1985), there is very limited research on what characteristics (e.g., personal, gender, marital status, experience as a parent with a child with a disability) might affect outcomes. It is not clear whether the sex of the leader is an important consideration (Seligman, 1993). Some research has recommended co-facilitation by a male and female therapist in groups with couples to model interactions more effectively (McConkey, 1985; Meyerson, 1983; Seligman, 1993).

Leadership roles vary depending on the type of group and phase of the group process and include teacher, facilitator, resource person, and model. Educative/training group leaders most often serve as teachers and facilitators of discussion (Seligman, 1993). In this capacity, they must be familiar with effective instructional strategies for adult learners. For example, Kramer (1990) notes that active involvement in the learning process through modeling, and interactive methods such as role-playing and behavioral rehearsal, has been shown to enhance learning, whereas verbal instructional methods have been shown to be among the least effective approaches.

Leaders of therapeutic groups tend to need a wide variety of interpersonal skills that include eliciting sharing and coping responses, confronting participant inconsistencies and psychological dynamics, and assisting participants in gaining insight (Seligman, 1993). In therapeutic groups, the leader should have knowledge of group processes and dynamics to facilitate and direct discussion. There is some empirical evidence that the leader must be well grounded in the theoretical orientation of the program. Specifically, when a therapist without prior experience in behavior therapy led Patterson's program, poor treatment outcomes resulted despite having a therapist who was carefully supervised and instructed in parent training principles (Newby, Fischer, & Roman, 1991).

Group leaders are frequently called on to be resource persons, particularly when working with parents of children with a specific disability. Leaders should have knowledge regarding diagnoses, prognoses and functional behavior, information about community resources, and an understanding of the psychological needs and strengths of parents and families. In a resource capacity, the leader functions as a natural "clearinghouse" of information about different types of services (Dunst et al., 1988).

Group facilitators serve as models for participants. When parenting issues are raised, for example, an effective facilitator will follow steps in problem solving as a model for parents to emulate in the future. Parents are encouraged to listen and respect the ideas of others and to consider alternative solutions.

Fine and Gardner (1994) identify five process skills that are crucial to successful collaboration with parents: (1) interpersonal skills such as positive reframing and demonstrating positive regard, (2) language skills (e.g., using *we* rather than *I*), (3) problem-solving skills, (4) taking into account family prerogatives, and (5) personalizing assessment.

In addition to the roles and skills just described, skill in selecting participants and in composing a viable group are useful to group leaders (Meyerson, 1983). Some type of screening procedure for training and therapy groups may prevent unsuitable participants from joining the group (Wyckoff, 1980). Interviews can often identify serious family dysfunction that would be treated better individually. Sometimes, pathology is not apparent immediately and begins to disrupt the group and the leader's authority. Providing parent(s) with an alternative resource for help is recommended in these cases.

Wyckoff (1980) reported that more homogeneous groups tend to be more successful, although there is virtually no data on the issue of homogeneity of parent characteristics on group intervention outcomes. Desirable characteristics of participants in a parent group might include responsiveness to training (in at least one of the parents), strong motivation to improve family interaction, predictable functioning, and sensitivity to the needs of other group members (Wyckoff, 1980).

In sum, May (1992) suggests that both professional and practical knowledge contribute to the effectiveness of a group leader. Professional training in group dynamics, interpersonal skills, and crisis intervention, for example, should be combined with knowledge of resources, referral services, and cultural considerations.

LIMITATIONS OF A GROUP APPROACH

There are situations where group approaches are less appropriate for parents of children with disabilities. For example, some parents are uncomfortable sharing feelings with "strangers" and may not be prepared to deal with emotional issues that arise. Parents may have specific family concerns and find a lack of responsiveness in a group situation. In these cases, parents would probably benefit from a more private situation such as individual or family therapy. Other parents may be disruptive in a group, challenging the leader or suggesting unacceptable practices. If these behaviors cannot be managed by the leader, alternative treatments should again be explored.

A number of practical problems arise that may preclude group participation, including scheduling conflicts, child care arrangements, and transportation obstacles that interfere with parents' ability to attend regularly as a full member. Often, a member's inconsistent attendance is a problem and detracts from the ongoing progress of the group.

Group participation requires adherence to specific ethical guidelines designed for group situations. Parents should be given information about the goals and methods of the group, about the qualifications of the leader, and about their freedom to participate or withdraw. If they find it difficult to follow the ethical constraints (e.g., they breach confidentiality), a different intervention approach should be recommended.

SUGGESTIONS FOR FUTURE RESEARCH AND PRACTICE

A number of issues should be considered in future research and practice with parent groups. First, available research is limited by methodological flaws, and information on family characteristics, leader characteristics, and the effect of program type and conceptualization is needed (Dembo et al., 1985; Helm & Kozloff, 1986). A number of design and measurement issues have been identified that apply to all group research, including the lack of randomization that increases the number of confounding variables, lack of control groups or use of inappropriate control groups, problems with statistical analysis such as the use of gain scores, and lack of objective appraisal of outcomes.

Helm and Kozloff (1986) question why observations rarely occur in the home to determine the extent to which training has generalized to this environment. They also note the absence of qualitative data that might provide information on parent explanations of their children's and their own behavior and parent expectations for their children. Information providing a greater understanding on how parents use training and how training has affected the family is also needed. Further, little research on parent groups is longitudinal. In general, Helm and Kozloff recommended that future research utilize control and experimental groups, document the process of change and use longitudinal designs that assess maintenance of behavior, assess family and leader characteristics, and focus on a functional behavioral repertoire.

Future research should consider the influence of family characteristics when developing groups—for example, cultural background and socioeconomic status. Values, customs, patterns of thought and/or language, including childrearing practices and parenting goals, vary significantly for different ethnic groups in U.S. society. The communication styles and discipline approaches of parents from a specific group would need to be understood and considered when determining the most appropriate therapeutic, educative, or support group approach. Similarly, there is evidence that socioeconomic status (SES) plays a role in parent/child interaction. Methods of therapy or training will probably vary depending on culture and SES. For example, mode of presentation (e.g., lecture, discussions, readings, role-playing, demonstration) and pace of presentation can be influenced by culture and SES. At this time, there is little or no research on the interaction of family characteristics and program format. Also, availability of groups for parents whose first language is not English might broaden the potential pool of participants.

An interesting issue is the conceptualization of the programs used in group approaches. Many are based on linear models of the family and reflect a unidirectional approach to family behavior—more specifically, the parent is conceptualized as the change agent and the child is the target of change. A shift in thinking following the seminal work of Bronfenbrenner (1979) and his ecological theory supports an interactional view of family members influencing each other, which underlies a systems approach as well. Both a systems and an interactional perspective emphasize the children's role in parent/child relationships. Cunningham's (1990) family-systems-oriented parenting program is based on a systemic orientation, but there is no research support as yet.

Finally, although the importance of working with families is clearly recognized, few professional preparation programs have incorporated group approaches into their training. It is clear that skilled and knowledgeable leaders are an important determinant in the success of parent groups, and this requires a knowledge base in areas just described, including group and family dynamics, interpersonal, skills and problem-solving approaches.

REFERENCES

Anastasiow, N. (1988). Should parenting education be mandatory? *Topics in Early Childhood Special Education, 8,* 60–72.

Anastopoulos, A., & Barkley, R. A. (1990). Counseling and training parents. In R. A. Barkley (Ed.), *Attention-deficit hyperactivity disorder: A handbook for diagnosis and treatment* (pp. 397–431). New York: Guilford.

Baker, B. L. (1983). Parents as teachers: Issues in training. In J. A. Mulick & S. M. Pueschel (Eds.), *Parent-professional partnerships in developmental disability services* (pp. 55–74). Cambridge, MA: Academic Guild Publishers.

Baker, B. L. (1989). *Parent training and developmental disabilities*. Washington, DC: American Association on Mental Retardation.

Barkley, R. B. (1997) *Defiant children: A clinician's manual for assessment and parent training.* (2nd ed.). New York: Guilford.

Barkley, R. B. (1987). *Defiant children: A clinican's manual for parent training*. New York: Guilford.

Bronfenbrenner, U. (1979). *The ecology of human development: Experiments by nature and design.* Cambridge, MA: Harvard University Press.

Carlo, P. (1988). Implementing a parent involvement/parent education program in a children's residential treatment center. *Child and Youth Care Quarterly, 17,* 195–206.

Clarke-Stewart, K. A. (1978). Popular primers for parents. *American Psychologist, 33,* 359–369.

Combrinck-Graham, L. (Ed.). (1989). *Children in family context: Perspectives on treatment.* New York: Guilford.

Cordisco, L.K ., Strain, P. S., & Depew, N. (1988). Assessment for generalization of parenting skills in home settings. *Journal of the Association for Persons with Severe Handicaps, 13,* 202–210.

Cunningham, C. E. (1990). A family systems approach to family training. In R. A. Barkley (Ed.), *Attention deficit hyperactivity disorder: A handbook for diagnosis and treatment* (pp. 432–461). New York: Guilford.

Darling, R. B. (1991). Initial and continuing adaptation to the birth of a disabled child. In M. Seligman (Ed.), *The family with a handicapped child* (pp. 55–89). Boston: Allyn and Bacon.

Dembo, M. H., Sweitzer, M., & Lauritzen, P. (1985). An evaluation of group parent education: Behavioral, PET, and Adlerian programs. *Review of Educational Research, 55,* 155–200.

Dinkmeyer, D., & McKay, G. (1976). *Systematic training for effective parenting.* Circle Pines, MN: American Guidance Service.

Dinkmeyer, D., & McKay, G. (1983). *Systematic training for effective parenting of teens (STEP/TEEN).* Circle Pines, MN: American Guidance Service.

Dreier, M. P., & Lewis, M. G. (1991). Support and psychoeducation for parents of hospitalized mentally ill children. *Health and Social Work, 16,* 11–18.

Dreikurs, R., & Soltz, V. (1964). *Children: The challenge.* New York: Hawthorn Books.

Dunst, C. J., & Trivette, C. M. (1987). Enabling and empowering families: Conceptual and intervention issues. *School Psychology Review, 16,* 443–456.

Dunst, C. J., Trivette, C. M., & Deal, A. G. (1988). *Enabling and empowering families: Principles and guidelines for practice.* Cambridge, MA: Brookline.

Ehly, S. W., Conoley, J. C., & Rosenthal, D. (1985). *Working with parents of exceptional children.* St. Louis: Times Mirror/College Publications.

Fine, M. J. (1980). The parent education movement: An introduction. In M. J. Fine (Ed.), *Handbook on parent education* (pp. 3–26). New York: Academic Press.

Fine, M. J., & Gardner, A. (1994). Collaborative consultation with families of children with special needs—Why bother? *Journal of Educational and Psychological Consultation, 5,* 283–308.

Fine, M. J., & Henry, S. A. (1989). Professional issues in parent education. In M. J. Fine (Ed.), *The second handbook on parent education* (pp. 3–20). New York: Academic Press.

Firestone, P., Kelly, M. J., & Fike, S. (1980). Are fathers necessary in parent training groups? *Journal of Clinical Child Psychology, 9,* 44–47.

Fish, M. C. (1995). Best practices in working with parents of children with disabilities. In A. Thomas & J. Grimes (Eds.), *Best practices in school psychology III.* Washington, DC: National Association of School Psychologists.

Fleischman, M. J. (1981). A replication of Patterson's "Intervention for boys with conduct problems." *Behavior Therapy, 12,* 115–122.

Forehand, R. L., & McMahon, R. J. (1981). *Helping the noncompliant child: A clinician's guide to parent training.* New York: Guilford.

Frey, K. S., Fewell, R., & Vadasy, P. (1989). Parental adjustment and changes in child outcome among families of young handicapped children. *Topics in Early Childhood Special Education, 9,* 38–57.

Frey, K. S., Greenberg, M. T., & Fewell, R. R. (1989). Stress and coping among parents of handicapped children: A multidimensional approach. *American Journal on Mental Retardation, 94,* 240–249.

Friedlander, S. R., & Watkins, E. C. (1985). Therapeutic aspects of support groups for parents of the mentally retarded. *International Journal of Group Psychotherapy, 35,* 65–78.

Gamson, B., Hornstein, H., & Borden, B. (1989). Adler-Dreikurs parent study group leadership training. In M. J. Fine (Ed.), *The second handbook of parent education* (pp. 279–302). New York: Academic Press.

Giannotti, T. J., & Doyle, R. E. (1982). The effectiveness of parental training on learning disabled children and their parents. *Elementary School Guidance and Counseling, 17,* 131–136.

Gordon, T. (1972). *Parent Effectiveness Training: Parent handbook.* Pasadena, CA: Effectiveness Training Associates.

Gordon, T. (1975). *P.E.T.: Parent Effectiveness Training.* New York: American Library.

Hampson, R. B., Hulgus, Y. F., Beavers, W. R., & Beavers, J. S. (1988). The assessment of competence in families with a retarded child. *Journal of Family Psychology, 2,* 32–53.

Helm, D. T., & Kozloff, M. A. (1986). Research on parent training: Shortcomings and remedies. *Journal of Autism and Developmental Disorders, 16,* 1–22.

Kottman, T., & Wilborn, B. L. (1992). Parents helping parents: Multiplying the counselor's effectiveness. *The School Counselor, 40,* 10–14.

Kozloff, M. (1979). *A program for families of children with learning and behavior problems.* New York: Wiley.

Kramer, J. J. (1990). Best practices in parent training. In A. Thomas & J. Grimes (Eds.), *Best practices in school psychology II* (pp. 519–530). Washington, DC: National Association of School Psychologists.

Lee, P. A., & Brage, D. G. (1989). Family life education and research: Toward a more positive approach. In M. J. Fine (Ed.), *The second handbook on parent education* (pp. 347–378). New York: Academic Press.

Levant, R. F., & Doyle, G. F. (1983). An evaluation of a parent education program for fathers of school-aged children. *Family Relations, 32,* 29–37.

Loewenstein, A. (1981). *TOPS Program: A school/mental health cooperative* (Grant No. G007903062). Washington, DC: Office of Special Education and Rehabilitative Services. (ERIC Document Reproduction Service No. ED 215 514)

McBride, B. A. (1990). The effects of a parent education/play group on father involvement in childrearing. *Family Relations, 39,* 250–256.

McBride, B. A. (1991). Parent education and support programs for fathers: Outcome effects on paternal involvement. *Early Child Development and Care, 67,* 73–85.

McConkey, R. (1985). *Working with parents: A practical guide for teachers and therapists.* Cambridge, MA: Brookline.

McMahon, R. J., & Forehand, R. (1984). Parent training for the noncompliant child: Treatment outcome, generalization, and adjunctive therapy procedures. In R. F. Dangel & R. A. Polster (Eds.), *Parent training: Foundations of research and practice* (pp. 298–328). New York: Guilford.

Markowitz, J. (1984). Participation of fathers in early childhood special education programs: An exploratory study. *Journal of the Division for Early Childhood, 8,* 119–131.

May, J. (1992). *Circles of care and understanding: Support programs for fathers of children with special needs.* Bethesda, MD: Association for the Care of Children's Health.

Medway, F. J. (1989). Measuring the effectiveness of parent education. In M. J. Fine (Ed.), *The second handbook on parent education* (pp. 237–255). New York: Academic Press.

Meyerson, R. C. (1983). Family and parent group therapy. In M. Seligman (Ed.), *The family with a handicapped child: Understanding and treatment* (pp. 285–308). New York: Grune & Stratton.

Murray, J. (1990). Best practices in working with parents of handicapped children. In A. Thomas & J. Grimes (Eds.), *Best practices in school psychology—II* (pp. 823–836). Washington, DC: National Association of School Psychologists.

Nathanson, M. N. (1986). *Organizing and maintaining support groups for parents of children with chronic illness and handicapping conditions.* Bethesda, MD: Association for the Care of Children's Health.

Newby, R. F., Fischer, M., & Roman, M. A. (1991). Parent training for families of children with ADHD. *School Psychology Review, 20,* 252–265.

Patterson, G. R. (1976). *Living with children: New methods for parents and teachers.* Champaign, IL: Research Press.

Patterson, G. R. (1986). Performance models for antisocial boys. *American Psychologist, 41,* 432–444.

Patterson, G. R., DeBaryshe, B. D., & Ramsey, E. (1989). A developmental perspective on antisocial behavior. *American Psychologist, 44,* 329–335.

Pearson, J. E., & Sternberg, A. (1986). A mutual-help project for families of handicapped children. *Journal of Counseling and Development, 65,* 213–215.

Popkin, M. H. (1983). *Active parenting.* Atlanta, GA: Active Parenting.

Popkin, M. H. (1989). Active parenting: A video-based program. In M. J. Fine (Ed.), *The second handbook of parent education* (pp. 77–98). New York: Academic Press.

Powers, M. D. (1991). Intervening with families of young children with severe handicaps: Contributions of a family systems approach. *School Psychology Quarterly, 6,* 131–146.

Powers, L. E., Singer, G. H. S., Stevens, T., & Sowers, J. (1992). Behavioral parent training in home and community generalization settings. *Education and Training in Mental Retardation, 27,* 13–27.

Pueschel, S. M., Bernier, J. C., & Gossler, S. J. (1989). Parents helping parents. *Exceptional Children, 19,* 56–59.

Ripley, S., & Rewers, C. (1989). *A parent's guide to accessing parent groups, community services and to keeping records.* Washington, DC: National Information Center for Handicapped Children and Youth (NICHY).

Seligman, M. (1990). Group approaches for parents of children with disabilities. In M. Seligman & L. E. Marshak (Eds.), *Group psychotherapy: Interventions with special populations.* (pp. 147–163). Boston: Allyn and Bacon.

Seligman, M. (1993). Group work with parents of children with disabilities. *The Journal for Specialists in Group Work, 18,* 115–126.

Singer, G. H. S., Irvin, L. K., & Hawkins, N. (1988). Stress management training for parents of children with severe handicaps. *Mental Retardation, 26,* 269–277.

Thomas, C. R., & Marchant, W. C. (1983). Basic principles of Adlerian family counseling. In O. C. Christensen & T. G. Schramski (Eds.), *Adlerian family counseling* (pp. 9–26). Minneapolis, MN: Educational Media Corporation.

Turnbull, A. P., & Turnbull, H. R. (1990). *Families, professionals, and exceptionality: A special partnership.* Columbus, OH: Merrill.

Williams, R. E., Omizo, M. M., & Abrams, B. C. (1984). Effects of STEP on parental attitudes and locus of control of their learning disabled children. *The School Counselor, 32,* 126–133.

Wyckoff, J. (1980). Parent education programs: Ready, set, go! In M. J. Fine (Ed.), *Handbook on parent education* (pp. 293–316). New York: Academic Press.

Zeitlin, S., Williamson, G. G., & Rosenblatt, W. P. (1987). The coping with stress model: A counseling approach for families with a handicapped child. *Journal of Counseling and Development, 65,* 443–446.

CHAPTER 20

COGNITIVE-BEHAVIORAL GROUP WORK AND PHYSICAL CHILD ABUSE: INTERVENTION AND PREVENTION

Sandra T. Azar, CLARK UNIVERSITY
Susan J. Breton, CLARK UNIVERSITY
Lisa Reiss Miller, CLARK UNIVERSITY

When the *battered child syndrome* was first identified over three decades ago, it was initially felt that few children were affected and that abusive parents were so disturbed that the best intervention was to remove children from the home. Abuse, however, was found to be more widespread than first thought and most abusers were not shown to be severely ill. Furthermore, foster care in some cases resulted in additional trauma to children. Consequently, efforts were directed at prevention and helping affected families stay intact.

Early treatment efforts, however, were not effective. Recidivism rates ranged from 20 to 70% (Cohn, 1979; Herrenkohl, Herrenkohl, Egolf, & Seech, 1979). In the last decade, our knowledge base has improved, fostering more complex etiological theories, a better understanding of outcomes in victims, and the beginnings of better intervention methods. This new knowledge base, which draws on social learning, developmental, and family systems theory, will be the focus of the first part of this chapter. We will then outline state-of-the-art strategies for intervening with abusive families and doing prevention. Our primary focus will be on perpetrators, since little empirical work on treating abused children exists and clearly, unless parental behavior changes, children will remain at risk. Nonetheless, we will highlight special issues and promising approaches in treating victims.

RATIONALE

Interpersonal skill deficits are a core disturbance in abusive parents, as well as a major outcome in victims. Thus, group treatment in which such skills can be modeled may be especially helpful. In addition, groups may act to counteract the social isolation that is common among abusive families and may diffuse the stigma of being labeled "inadequate." Similarly, for abused children, it may help them to feel less alone in their trauma experience (Steward,

Note: The writing of this chapter was supported by a NIMH FIRST Grant Award (NIMH Grant #MH46940) to the first author.

Farquhar, Dicharry, Glick, & Martin, 1986). Finally, groups provide opportunities for parents and children to experience alternative modes of interaction and to receive support for their efforts from others struggling with similar issues.

Empirical support for the use of group treatment and for treatment in general for this population, however, is quite limited, and thus the therapist considering such interventions should be very cautious. Recidivism rates are high and it is harder to monitor child risk in group settings. Children's trauma symptoms may also be more difficult to contain in groups as well.

SCOPE AND DEFINITION OF THE PROBLEM

Child abuse is a private event, and this makes defining its scope difficult. Prevalence and incidence figures vary considerably, depending on the definitions chosen and who is making the judgment. Physical abuse figures vary from 4.9 to 19 per 1,000, depending on who is surveyed (e.g., professionals [Burgdorf, 1988] or the general population [Gelles & Straus, 1987]). In 1994, 1,011,628 children were maltreated and 26% of these were physically abused (NCCAN, 1995). About 2,000 child and adolescent deaths occur annually due to maltreatment (McClain, Sacks, Froehlke, & Ewigman, 1993).

Operational definitions of physical abuse vary based on aspects of the act (e.g., its form, intensity, duration, frequency), its consequences (e.g., bruising), the perpetrator's intent, the child's age (e.g., being shaken is abusive for a baby, whereas for a teenager it might not be), and social norms (e.g., physical punishment as appropriate parental behavior) (Azar, Fantuzzo, & Twentyman, 1984). The heterogeneity in definitions makes it difficult to interpret and apply the treatment literature. Moreover, physical abuse often overlaps with other forms of maltreatment (neglect, sexual abuse, emotional abuse) and the phenomenology of the "disorder" may vary with the combinations present, and thus may call for different interventions.

In this chapter, abuse is considered a transactional problem nested within the broader context of a disturbed repertoire of parenting responses. It signals a breakdown of socialization processes, where parents function at the periphery of what is culturally considered normative parenting. Viewing abuse in this way suggests that any factor affecting caregiving adequacy should be the object of intervention, not just parental aggression. To address the abuse alone without addressing these other social and cognitive factors may only resolve the most "visible" symptom, without decreasing the negative consequences to the child in the long run.

Within this socialization framework, the constellation of problems of which abuse is a part manifests itself differently across development. Therapists must attend to the pattern of abuse (frequency, duration, chronicity in the time line of a child's life) and its associated features (e.g., poverty) across time, to intervene appropriately. For example, parents under financial stress who lose control with a colicky baby *one* time may require different treatment from a family in which a preschooler has been *consistently* subjected to battering and neglect. As a result, treatment may be much more difficult than in disorders with a more homogeneous presentation.

A COGNITIVE-BEHAVIORAL FRAMEWORK FOR UNDERSTANDING ABUSE

Understanding the etiology of abuse continues to be a complex task. Theory in this area has progressed through a number of "developmental" shifts (Azar, 1991a), with early models positing single causes (e.g., parent psychopathology) and later ones positing multiple causal factors, any one of which alone, or in combination, might result in abuse. The most recent abuse models, however, place greater emphasis on transactional factors. These models typically include a mix of transient and enduring factors that may be potentiating (increase risk) or compensatory (buffering or protective in nature) (Cicchetti & Rizley, 1981). When potentiating factors outweigh compensatory ones, then abuse is likely. Such models emphasize risk over time and link causal elements to child outcomes.

Wolfe (1987), for example, posited an escalation model whereby abusers increasingly rely on coercive responses to manage child behavior. Contextual and intrapersonal factors either hasten this escalation or slow it. This model, while useful, focuses on the abusive act alone, not the myriad of associated features that bode poorly for child outcome.

The model espoused in this chapter takes a broader perspective, placing abuse within a general model of parenting. It draws on cognitive-behavioral, family systems, and developmental theory (Azar, 1986, 1989; Azar & Siegel, 1990). The family in which abuse occurs is seen as a system embedded in a larger community context (e.g., available social supports, neighborhood use of violence, economic strain). Although the emphasis in intervention is on the skill deficits of individual family members, the interaction between these deficits and the context in which the family lives must also be considered.

In this model, social-cognitive disturbances are posited as core. All parents are seen as possessing a set of schema regarding children, childrearing, and relationships with others. In at-risk parents, these schema are not well articulated enough and are biased such that they increase risk for violence and other maladaptive responses, as well as result in a negative social context. Social cognitive problems (unrealistic expectations, poor problem solving, negative attributional bias) are seen as driving a set of skill deficits (poor parenting, stress management, anger control, and social skills) that increase risk for poor parent/child transactions and violence.

Schema act as filters through which social information is interpreted (Fiske & Taylor, 1991). Schemas grow out of experiences in one's family/cultural context. Thus, some individuals' schema, through a set of unusual or overly narrow experiences, can come to vary to a greater or lesser extent from those of the larger culture (e.g., be inappropriate in content) and result in maladaptive responding. Nowhere are such interpretive processes more important than in parenting. Because children's language capacities are diminished relative to that of adults, children are less able to communicate the intent of their actions. Parents must fill in this gap by supplying their own interpretations of child behavior and generating and attempting response alternatives until the correct one is found.

Schema aid parents in deciding when and how to intervene in child behavior (e.g., discipline, redirect, ignore, provide nourishment). *Optimal* parents approach children with standards that are developmentally sensitive (i.e., schema that are complex enough to allow for the child's skill level and a wide array of responses). They operate in the *zone of proximal development* (Rogoff & Wertsch, 1984), just slightly above the child's skill level so as to be still within his or her developmental reach, and yet discrepant enough to pull the child to the next developmental level. In addition, these interpretations allow parents a "developmental out" when confronted with difficult behavior (e.g., "She's only 2; she doesn't know any better"), enabling them to stifle negative affective reactions and facilitate consistent socialization. Without this flexibility, parents may come to misattribute negative intent to developmentally appropriate behavior (e.g., "He's trying to get to me"), increasing frustration and risk.

Although context clearly affects both parents' and children's behavior (e.g., social support level), parents' social-cognitive skills reciprocally play a role in determining the nature of the environment. That is, the same social-cognitive difficulties (e.g., inappropriate expectations, negative attributional bias toward others) that operate in parent/child transactions may also negatively influence the availability of social supports and physical resources, thus limiting compensatory factors that might reduce risk of abuse.

Studies support the validity of this transactional parenting model; Table 20.1 summarizes the findings. Presented next are implications for transactions within abusive families across development.

FACTORS DISTINGUISHING ABUSIVE PARENTS

Based on the model just described, abusive parents manifest *social-cognitive problems* that are seen as the root of a myriad of crucial skill deficits. Abusive parents show evidence of maladaptive schema regarding children and parent/child transactions, such as believing that a 2-year-old can comfort them when they are upset, or that a 4-year-old knows enough not to embarrass a parent in a grocery store (Azar, Robinson, Hekimian, & Twentyman, 1984; Azar & Rohrbeck, 1986). Abusive parents have a negative attributional bias in interpreting child behavior, assigning more responsibility to their children for negative outcomes (Lar-

Table 20.1 Skill Deficits in Parents That May Increase the Risk of Abuse at Different Points in Children's Development and the Outcomes Observed among Abused Children and Adolescents

AGE	PARENT PROBLEM AREA	CHILD PROBLEM AREAS
I. Infancy and Toddlerhood	• Insensitive and noncontingent responsiveness • Poor ability to tolerate stresses, such as prolonged crying, sleep problems, and feeding difficulties • Failures to engage in behaviors that foster language, social, and emotional development • Lack of attention to safety issues and health needs/ knowledge deficit • Expectancies that infants and toddlers are able to judge perspective, are capable of intentional provoking behavior, and can provide the parent comfort • Deficits in skills to comfort/soothe child, utilize distraction, redirect, and manage the environment as a means to reduce aversive child behavior and manage child behavior	• Attachment problems and health-related difficulties, such as undernourishment, low birth weight, prematurity, and physical trauma (e.g., shaken baby syndrome) • Lags in toilet training, motor skills, speech and language development, and socialization
II. Early and Middle Childhood	• Inconsistent and indiscriminant use of discipline • Overuse of physical strategies to manage behavior • Lack of use of optimal socialization strategies (such as explanation) • General lack of interaction • A negative bias in overlabeling child behavior as evidence of misbehavior (even developmentally appropriate behavior) • Poor ability to deal with stress of self-regulation problems in children (e.g., noncompliance) • Unrealistic expectations of children's perspective-taking abilities, self-regulation skill, ability to place parental needs ahead of their own, engage in self-care, and other household duties	• High levels of noncompliance • Developmental and academic problems • Social cognitive difficulties (e.g., expression and recognition of affect; perspective taking; empathy, social problems solving) • Heightened aggression • Poor social skills • Conduct problems • Social withdrawal • Cognitive delays such as greater distractibility • Inconsistent school attendance • Fatigue • Low self-esteem • Difficulty trusting others • Trauma/stress-related symptoms • Poor conflict resolution skills • Poor affective expressive and recognition skills
III. Adolescence	• Failure to use age-appropriate child management strategies • Excessive attempts to control • Decreased ability to tolerate teenagers' moves toward autonomy • Poor ability to deal with emerging sexuality • Unrealistic expectations of taking on adult responsibilities	• Overrepresented among runaways, delinquents, and truants • Poor academic performance • Poor stress/anger management skills • Social skill and peer interaction problems • Conduct problems

rance & Twentyman, 1983), which in turn leads to more severe punishment (Dix, Ruble, & Zambarano, 1989). Moreover, the incidence of affective disturbances such as depression, which in and of itself may engender cognitive distortions (Beck 1963), appears to be higher among abusive parents (Susman, Trickett, Ianotti, Hollenbeck, & Zahn-Waxler, 1985; Zuravin, 1989). Finally, abusers appear to be poorer problem solvers in childrearing and nonchildrearing situations (Azar et al., 1984; Hansen, Pallotta, Tishelman, & Conaway, 1989), suggesting a more limited childrearing repertoire. Overall, these cognitive disturbances would act to increase frustration and aggression and detract from the positive aspects of parenting (e.g., feeling efficacy).

Along with cognitive disturbances, abuse appears to be associated with a variety of *deficits in parenting skills.* For example, mothers at risk for abuse make less use of explanation, engage in fewer positive interactions with children, are less contingent in their responses, and use more coercive and rigid control tactics than control mothers (Barnes & Azar, 1990; Oldershaw, Walters, & Hall, 1986).

Abusive parents also appear to have *difficulties managing stress* and may experience some events as more stressful than nonabusive parents. For example, studies have found that relative to controls, abusive mothers demonstrate greater physiological arousal in response to child and other stimuli (e.g., Casanova, Domanic, McCanne, & Milner, 1992; Wolfe, Fairbanks, Kelly, & Bradlyn, 1983). Because information processing capacities narrow under stress (Cohen, 1980), it may be that this greater subjective experience of stress impairs parents' information processing in childrearing situations and results in maladaptive responses.

Social support, which is helpful to parenting, appears to be lower for abusive parents. It has been posited that abusive parents *lack the social skills* necessary to build and maintain supportive social networks (Azar & Twentyman, 1986). Relative to nonmaltreating parents, maltreating mothers have been shown to view themselves as more isolated than others (Newberger, Hampton, Marx, & White, 1986) and possess fewer social relationships (Salzinger, Kaplan, & Artemyeff, 1983). Even within their families, abusive mothers have been found to initiate fewer verbal interactions, and these interactions tend to be negative in content (Burgess & Conger, 1978). There is also some evidence that their tendency toward overattributing responsibility to children for aversive events may be part of a more pervasive bias in perceiving the behavior of others (Miller & Azar, 1996), which may further frustrate and isolate them.

A final deficit area in abusive parents is in the *ability to inhibit impulsive behavior* (Azar & Twentyman, 1986). Abusive mothers appear to perform more poorly than control mothers on tasks requiring cognitive and motor inhibition (Rohrbeck & Twentyman, 1986). This fact, coupled with the hyperarousal pattern described earlier, may lead them to aggressive responses to children that would not provoke such responses in others (Knutson, 1978).

Although other parent-based problems, such as *substance abuse* (Famularo, Stone, Barnum & Wharton, 1986), *neurological problems* (Elliot, 1988), and *severe psychopathology* have been suggested as playing a role in maltreatment, the database supporting each is limited. For example, severe psychopathology may account for only 5 to 10% of cases (Steele, 1975).

Low intellectual functioning has also been linked to maltreatment, although more to neglect than abuse (Schilling & Schinke, 1984). The cognitive problems discussed above, however, are more common within low-functioning parents (Azar, 1991b) and these factors may account for this association.

Contextual stressors have also been found to impact abusers, acting to destabilize the family. These include *general life stress, child-based strain,* and *a history of trauma in the parent.* For example, heightened life stress, lack of community resources, and unfavorable socioeconomic conditions are associated with child abuse (Gelles, 1992; Steinberg, Catalano, & Dooley, 1981). Not all parents under high stress, however, abuse their children. Poor social skills and stress management may mediate the effects of these contextual factors.

Along with environmental stress, child characteristics (e.g., disabilities, heightened aggression) generally have been posited as playing an antecedent role to abuse (Oldershaw et al., 1986; Schmitt, 1987; Trickett & Kuczynski, 1986). Some of these aversive behaviors, however, may themselves be the results of living in a dysfunctional family (e.g., where violence is seen as an appropriate response to conflict).

One area of controversy in the field is the extent to which a parent's own history of maltreatment contributes to later abuse (Widom, 1989). Generally, such a history is less than a perfect predictor. Intergenerational transmission has been estimated to be approximately 25 to 35% (Kaufman & Zigler, 1987). It may be that experiencing abuse provides a script for inappropriate parenting, which may only be "activated" under certain contextual conditions.

In summary, whereas contextual factors need attention as activating events, each may be mediated by the cognitive disturbances and skills deficits outlined here and may be more directly addressed with work on these areas. A final note should be made regarding the fact that there is a general limitation in the literature reviewed. Most studies have focused on mothers. Less is known regarding abusive fathers. Thus, treatment efforts with them ultimately may require a different emphasis.

FACTORS DISTINGUISHING ABUSED CHILDREN AND ADOLESCENTS

Understanding the outcomes seen in abused children and adolescents is very complex. A bidirectional interaction of several factors determines child outcome, and both parent and child may contribute to the transactions that may shape it. Furthermore, outcome may not only relate to the abuse itself but also to other contextual factors associated with it (e.g., neglect of physical needs, low levels of stimulation, poverty, being placed in foster care, the stress of testifying in court against a caregiver; Ammerman, 1991; Azar, Barnes, & Twentyman, 1988). Our discussion will open with an examination of physical effects of maltreatment and then move to an exploration of other deficits, many of which parallel those found in abusive parents.

The most direct effects of abuse are *health-related* ones, such as physical trauma, including bruises, welts, burns, lacerations, and skeletal, and head and internal injuries. Severe blows to the head or back can result in CNS (central nervous system) damage. Although severe injury is less likely in teenagers, the health needs of older children should not be ignored (Azar, 1991c).

There are also *developmental effects* of maltreatment (Azar & Siegel, 1990; Crittenden & Ainsworth, 1989). It has been suggested that children who are forced to channel energy and attention, normally directed toward growth, into protection from abusive parents may experience lags in their development (e.g., motor skills, language development and socialization; Azar & Twentyman, 1986; Martin, 1976). Delays may also be due to CNS damage from abuse, medical or nutritional neglect, poor stimulation, or even congenital origins (Massachusetts Department of Social Services Report, 1986).

Abused children also may evidence *cognitive delays and disturbances,* such as greater distractibility and limited problem-solving ability, and are more likely to have *difficulties in school* (Hoffman-Plotkin & Twentyman, 1984; Smith, 1975). In a study of 420 maltreated children in grades K through 12, Eckenrode, Laird, and Doris (1993), for example, found that they had lower grades, more discipline referrals and suspensions, and performed more poorly on standardized tests than control children. Poor school attendance and poor care (e.g., fatigue, anemia, etc.) may play a role in these difficulties.

The *emotional effects* of abuse may be substantial, resulting in lower self-esteem and adversely effecting the development of healthy conceptions of self (Sirles, Walsma, Lytle-Barnaby, & Lender, 1988; Terr, 1991). Abuse during infancy, in particular, may disrupt the development of secure attachment (Crittenden & Ainsworth, 1989), affecting the child's ability to trust others and respond to positive attention and love. Trauma may also lead to the onset of posttraumatic stress disorder (PTSD) symptoms, including flashbacks of the traumatic event; repetitive behavior; trauma-specific fears; changed attitudes about people, life, and the future (e.g., depression); sleep problems; exaggerated startle responses; developmental regressions (e.g., clinging behavior); panic; irritability; and hypervigilance (Terr, 1991). Recent evidence suggests, however, that PTSD symptoms are seen more often in emotional and sexual abuse than physical abuse or neglect (Famularo, Fenton, & Kinscherff, 1993).

Abused children and adolescents also experience an enormous amount of stress. This overload to the system may affect the development of *stress management skills* and can lead to *poor anger control.* Emotionally and physically abused children can exhibit many negative behavioral outcomes, including overly compliant and passive behaviors; extremely aggressive, noncompliant, demanding, and rageful behaviors; conduct problems; and inappropriately adult and responsible behavior or extremely dependent behavior (Fantuzzo, 1990). In adolescence, greater risk for problems such as delinquency, running away, and truancy are also found (Azar & Siegel, 1990). One explanation is that in dysfunctional, stressful households, children may develop maladaptive coping mechanisms for self preservation (i.e., becoming overly compliant as an attempt to avoid confrontation with parents) or may model the poor interpersonal skills of their parents. Aggressive behaviors may also be caused by repeated frustration at parental inconsistency and neglected needs. These responses to the family may become the "mode of operation" for coping with the world outside the home.

Social development problems have also been observed among abuse victims, including social cognitive deficits and peer interaction problems (Azar, & Wientzen, 1993; Haskett, 1990). These disturbances may manifest themselves differently across developmental periods. For example, in infancy and in the preschool years, abused children show deficits in responsiveness (Crittendon, 1985), which in turn may create stress for caregivers (Azar & Twentyman, 1986). Preschool- and elementary-aged abused children have been shown to have problems with affective expressive and recognition skills, empathy, and perspective taking, as well as exhibit social withdrawal and be rejected by peers (Azar et al., 1988; Salzinger et al., 1993). Adolescents have also shown similar disturbances in social skills (Azar & Wientzen, 1993).

In summary, abused children and teenagers show a number of disturbances, many of which would also affect interpersonal transactions and impact group work. It should be pointed out again that the extra trauma associated with typical system interventions, such as foster care, can add to difficulties and may ultimately affect group work (e.g., changes in placements affect continuity of attendance and may decrease trust in adults even further).

PARENT/CHILD TRANSACTIONS: A DEVELOPMENTAL PERSPECTIVE

In conducting group work, one must consider not only the individual characteristics of children and parents but also the impact of family transactions, since the processes operating in abusive families are likely to replay themselves in groups. The tasks required of all parents across children's development will be used to highlight problems that might arise for abusive families (Azar & Siegel, 1990).

Infancy and Toddlerhood

Becoming a parent is stressful, requiring many new behaviors and coping strategies. Preexisting inadequacies may become even more apparent with the introduction of a child into an individual's life and may worsen with each additional child. The abusive parent has been shown to begin childrearing earlier than most parents (National Research Council, 1993), which itself may be associated with a host of factors that increase stress, such as poverty, single parenthood, closely spaced children, and larger family size. Over time, these issues may wear away at the parent and make typical stressors of childrearing less tolerable.

Poor stress management may occur when children exhibit behaviors "typical" to this period, such as prolonged crying, feeding and sleeping problems, and soiling, all of which are common antecedents of abuse (Herrenkohl, Herrenkohl, & Egolf, 1983). Unrealistic expectations during this period may include beliefs that children have perspective taking skills ("She knows I didn't get any sleep"), intentionality ("She wet on me on purpose"), and expectations of obtaining comforting from a child (i.e., role reversal). With social isolation, "corrective" feedback may not occur and alternative caregivers to relieve parents may be unavailable. Foster care, a common intervention during this period, may strain the attachment relationship between the parent and child, further disrupting transactions.

The reciprocal nature of parent/child transactions suggests that parental inadequacies may contribute to negative child responses, and these in turn may further exacerbate interactional problems. For example, supplying infants with cereal too early results in increased intestinal discomfort and greater irritability, and therefore, their general stressfulness. Infants with inadequate levels of stimulation may become unresponsive and less able to self-soothe and regulate affect, making them less engaging and more aversive.

Preschoolers and School-Aged Children

As children leave toddlerhood, some parental tasks decrease (e.g., basic care needs), others remain (e.g., need for responsive caregiving), and new ones emerge (e.g., active socialization). Before this period, self-regulation is not expected, and ideally, the major strategies to deal with children's aversive or dangerous behavior involve distraction, redirection, or environmental manipulation (e.g., baby-proofing the home). At this stage, limits are more quickly set on children. At the same time, vast shifts in language, social, and cognitive development also occur during this period, and children often resist such limit setting, as they make moves toward independence. All parents make greater use of physical punishment during this period (Wauchope & Straus, 1987). Thus, it is particularly risky for parents with impulse-control problems.

Overascribing negative intent to children may be more evident during this period. Common unrealistic expectations in the authors' experience include expecting 3-year-olds to "know enough" to stay away from parents when they are upset or expecting 8-year olds to get siblings dressed and off to day care. Again, child problems may exacerbate family stress. Self-regulation problems (e.g., bed wetting), noncompliance, and school problems are common antecedents of abuse (Herrenkohl et al., 1983).

Adolescence

Adolescent abuse has not received much attention (Azar, 1991c) and often goes unreported (Burgdorf, 1988). Teenagers are seen as less vulnerable than children. They may also engage more often in defensive aggression, and thus may be seen as a party to the violence. The other problems of adolescence (e.g., truancy) may overshadow abuse as a target of attention.

During adolescence, maltreatment experiences may be characterized by four patterns: (1) continuation of abuse that began in childhood; (2) maltreatment that occurred in childhood, ceased, and then began again in adolescence; (3) escalation of previously used forms of physical punishment; and (4) maltreatment that begins for the first time in adolescence (Pagelow, 1989). These patterns may determine treatment targets. For instance, abuse that emerges in adolescence may be linked to unique cues that emerge during this period (e.g., sexuality); whereas abuse that is a reemergence of earlier violence may relate to triggers common to both periods (e.g., autonomy moves).

Data regarding transactions between abusive parents and teenagers are limited. The developmental tasks of adolescence include separation from family, shifting to a sharing of allegiance with peers, and adjusting to emerging sexuality. Abusive parents may harbor inappropriate expectations and misinterpret teenagers' moves toward autonomy, viewing increased time with peers as a rejection. They also may fail to shift discipline strategies, continuing to use excessive control.

WORKING WITH ABUSIVE PARENTS IN GROUPS

Group approaches, especially social-learning theory ones, have been generally effective for parenting problems (Gordon & Davidson, 1991). Groups with abusive parents have used similar strategies, but added others (e.g., anger control). Empirical work in this area is still in its early phases and extensive outcome data are lacking. Federal funding has focused on establishing demonstration programs, but almost no emphasis has been placed on sophisticated evaluations of these efforts (Azar, Fantuzzo, & Twentyman, 1984; Knudsen, 1992). Thus, the material we present must be viewed with caution, as large-scale outcome studies of group treatment have not been done.

Whereas traditional group counseling has been used with abusing parents, the general conclusions of national evaluations point to it being ineffective in combating this problem (Berkeley Planning Associates, 1978; Daro, 1988). Social-learning theory-based and lay self-help groups have shown the most effectiveness, which may be due to the fact that these approaches address specific skill deficits and the social isolation found in abusive parents.

Once abuse has occurred, changing families may be more difficult; therefore efforts have also begun to be directed at prevention. At this point, however, society has been unwilling to commit the funds necessary for primary prevention (support for all parents). Secondary prevention is more common, where risk indicators are used to target smaller groups of parents. Currently, however, most targeting is crude (Wald & Woolverton, 1990).

Outcome studies have typically examined changes in mediators of abuse (e.g., parenting skill), not on abuse itself. Without data on this variable, there can be no certainty as to what works best. The limited literature examining effectiveness of group preventive and intervention approaches with parents is outlined below, followed by a discussion of specific techniques.

Interventions with Parents of Infants and Toddlers

Because parents with infants are less mobile, studies here have typically examined models of intervention with individuals (e.g., home visiting). Nonetheless, some group efforts have occurred, usually combined with individual work. Treatment goals include decreasing cognitive distortions; increasing infant stimulation, knowledge of child care, and child development; and improving stress coping.

As noted earlier, attachment problems may occur during this period. It has been suggested that attachment work should focus on changing parents' "representational models" of relationships (Egeland & Erickson, 1990), or in cognitive-behavioral terms, cognitive restructuring of their core relational schema. Group work is ideal for examining the messages parents have received in their own relationship histories, some of which may have involved threats to attachment (e.g., "If you do that again, I'm leaving for good"). Crittenden (1992) also recommends using videotaped interactions with infants to help parents identify their maladaptive interpretations of infant behavior and having therapists then challenge them. The efficacy of these approaches within this developmental era, however, has not yet been assessed.

Stress reduction can be an important goal during this period. Relaxation training and systematic desensitization have been used successfully with individual abusive parents to reduce negative reactions to infant crying or phobic-like responses to physical contact (Gilbert, 1976; Sanders, 1978). Stress reduction strategies may be adapted to group work.

In general, although home-based prevention seems to help both promote better mother-child interaction and reduce abuse, center-based programs (school or nursery program) appear to show better child and parent outcome results (Clewell, Brooks-Gunn, & Benasich, 1989). The modeling of caregiving by adults and social support available in such group settings may be crucial.

Group Interventions with Parents of Preschoolers and School-Aged Children

This age period has probably been the richest in terms of empirical work. Although the majority of the studies of cognitive and behavioral strategies have been aimed at individuals, a number of group-based packages have been studied.

One of the first efforts was that of Wolfe, Sandler, and Kaufman (1981). They used a multicomponent eight-session group treatment package with eight abusive families. The package included competency-based child management skills training (using role-plays, didactic instruction, problem solving, rehearsal) and self-control training. Adjunct, in-home implementation was also used.

McLeer, Atkins, Ralphe, & Foa, 1989). The chronicity of the abuse (developmental periods affected by abuse) and the related stresses (e.g., number of out-of-home placements, need for hospitalization, etc.) may moderate trauma symptoms (Famularo, Kinscherff, & Fenton, 1990; Terr, 1991). Many abused children are the victims of a series of traumas rather than a single traumatic event (Terr, 1991). Also, unlike other trauma, abuse victims may not only lack the support of loved ones in coping with the trauma, but the loved one may in fact be the perpetrator. This fact may engender greater withdrawal and mistrust in abused children relative to other victims of trauma.

In working with children and adolescents who have PTSD, Lipovksy (1991) emphasizes four treatment goals: education, facilitation of emotional expression, anxiety control, and controlled exposure to memories of the event. Clinicians may find that pursuit of some of these goals may be enhanced by group treatment, whereas others may be best attempted in individual work. In an individual setting, therapists must be sensitive to the possibility that abuse victims may be too fearful to confide quickly in adults (Aber & Allen, 1987; Steward et al., 1986). On the other hand, exposure to memories of the abusive event, through play therapy techniques or imaginal exposure may best be accomplished in an individual setting, because it is more difficult to monitor individual children's emotional reactions in a group setting.

In contrast, education goals that emphasize teaching children about normal reactions to stress and general coping strategies (Lipovsky, 1991) may be facilitated by a group. Seeing that other children share similar concerns, for example, may help to "destigmatize" the experience. Nonetheless, monitoring individual reactions is crucial. What may be an innocuous topic for one child may bring back painful memories for another.

With some exceptions, outcome studies for treatment of posttraumatic stress disorder have largely focused on adults and have suffered from methodological problems (McFarlane, 1989). Single-case design studies in the literature suggest, however, that symptoms of PTSD may be attenuated through the use of many of the methods described. For example, controlled exposure techniques have been used successfully to alleviate trauma due to other types of stressors in adults (McMillan, 1991; Richards & Rose, 1991) and children (Jones & Peterson, 1993). Anxiety management interventions such as biofeedback (Peniston, 1986) has also been used successfully with adults. Such approaches have begun to be adapted successfully for use with child sexual abuse victims.

Deblinger, McLeer, and Henry (1990), for example, examined the use of a treatment package for PTSD with nine sexually abused children that included gradual exposure, modeling, education, and coping and prevention skills training. Concurrent sessions with the nonoffending parent were provided to them with education regarding trauma responses and to reduce their inadvertently fostering the maintenance of the PTSD symptoms. These parent sessions also utilized cognitive behavioral coping strategies. The treatment produced reductions in PTSD symptoms. The use of these techniques in group work has yet to be demonstrated empirically, and thus must be approached with caution.

Social skills training has received a lot of attention in clinical group work with children (for reviews, see Goldstein & Goldstein, 1990; Guevremont, 1990; Schloss, Schloss, Wood, & Kiehl, 1986; Weissberg & Allen, 1986) and may be useful for abuse victims given their interpersonal skill deficits. Such training can include teaching children specific social skills (e.g., how to give a compliment) and more general cognitive strategies (e.g., how to problem solve) (Guevremont, 1990). Children are typically provided with opportunities to generalize and practice what they learn in other settings (e.g., home and school), and attempts are made to actively integrate the child into his or her peer group using a peer "tutor."

A carefully controlled group setting may allow abused children to practice specific social skills in a semi-naturalistic manner. The use of peer models rather than adult models has generally been found to have greater utility for children. Peer models may be especially important for abused children who may harbor mistrust of adults (Aber & Allen, 1987). In one of the only treatment studies with abuse victims, researchers paired maltreated children with an adult or child confederate who was trained to initiate social interactions with the child (Fantuzzo, Jurecic, Stovall, Hightower, Goins, & Schachtel, 1988). Children who were paired with peer confederates subsequently made more social overtures to playmates than those paired with adult confederates.

Although social skills training has been shown to be effective (Schloss et al., 1986), there is a paucity of data concerning the generalization of social skills. Programming for generalization may be crucial for abuse victims who may go home to poor role models who may not reinforce new skills and even may punish higher levels of social initiation. Effects on the parent/child relationship should be carefully monitored.

For adolescents, especially, successfully teaching them how to problem solve and how to deescalate conflict may be useful to alter parent-child interactions. In addition, for all victims of abuse, having better relationships with peers may moderate the effects of negative relationships at home, and ultimately the negative outcomes observed in this population.

Abused children and adolescents who exhibit aggression, conduct disorders, and social problems could benefit from *anger control training,* such as assertiveness training and stress inoculation (Fehrenbach & Thelen, 1981 Feindler & Ecton, 1986). Skills such as brief relaxation techniques and deep breathing, self-instruction (e.g., "keep cool," "chill out," "ignore it") and problem solving (e.g., "If I misbehave now, then what will happen?") can be taught and practiced within groups. (See Feindler & Scalley in Chapter 6 of this book.) Also, maladaptive social information processing patterns that may develop in response to harsh discipline, such as a heightened misattribution of negative intent to others, can be addressed through cognitive restructuring (Weiss, Dodge, Bates, & Pettit, 1992).

Some efforts have been directed at *primary prevention* of abuse with children. These have been of two types: ones focused on teaching children how to avoid abuse by others and ones directed at decreasing violence in youths. The latter hopes to have an impact on youth violence within the family and its occurrence long term when these youths start their own families. The former have mostly focused on sexual abuse, but many of the skills trained have implications for prevention of physical abuse as well, including assertiveness training, problem solving, and communications skills. Length of such programs varies from a single session of 30 minutes to an hour to several days. Length depends on goals. Longer programs teach skills like assertiveness and general personal safety skills, whereas shorter ones have a more circumscribed goal of teaching children protection from molesters.

Some evidence exists that programs that emphasize behavioral skills training (e.g., modeling of behavior, guided rehearsal, and reinforcement for approximations to the desired behavior) rather than only a didactic teaching approach are more effective. (See Miller-Perrin & Wurtele [1988] for a review.) At least one program has exposed children after training to simulated stranger situations and found good outcomes and retention at six-month follow-up. Booster sessions may be needed for children to retain skills learned. Older children also appear to benefit more than preschool and early elementary-aged children.

With an increase in violence in society, more programs have been directed toward preventing violence among youths. These programs may ultimately act to decrease violence when these youths start their own families. One such program is that of Hammond and Yung (1991) called Positive Adolescent Choices Training (PACT). The program's creators designed their program to meet the needs of African American youths. It emphasizes the use of behavioral modeling and feedback rather than just didactic instruction. Its goals include improving communication skills such as giving and receiving negative and positive feedback, problem-solving skills training, and negotiations skills training. Small-group training (10 to 12 high-risk middle-school youths) is carried out over 37 to 38 sessions of 50 minutes each. Students view videotaped vignettes and then students role-play responses, which are videotaped for discussion. Rewards for "success" are supplied using a "dollar" system that can be exchanged for t-shirts, cassette tapes, and so on. Initial findings based on ratings by teachers, participants, and independent raters suggest it is effective in improving the skills targeted. Other efforts of this type are currently underway and need further study.

Summary and Guidelines for Working with Abused Children and Adolescents in Groups

The empirical study of group treatments for child and adolescent victims has been relatively neglected. Some promising approaches, however, appear to be emerging (treatment of PTSD, peer initiation procedures). The field needs to focus attention on their evaluation and implementation, with special attention to the *adaptations* required for this population. Given the trauma experienced by such children and the continued risk they may experience while in parental custody, group work must be viewed cautiously.

Despite the limited data, some core issues can be highlighted for consideration in undertaking such groups. First, whether treating children in groups or individually, child safety should be first and foremost in therapists' minds. Clearly, the youngest children are the most physically vulnerable, but the safety needs of adolescents should not be ignored. Therapy will be of little use if the child must continue to devote energy to concerns regarding harm and survival. Clearly, concurrent work with parents in most cases should be required. Work with foster or adoptive parents may also be useful to help them cope with the children's response to their maltreatment and the contrast effect that may occur when these children are exposed to a more benign home context. For example, some abused children may be so accustomed to a negative and critical environment that they may experience discomfort and/or confusion when they are treated well and may "act out" to reproduce the negative environment with which they are more familiar. They may increase their risk of further abuse or, at the very least, rejection by caregivers.

Second, given the heterogeneity of problems shown by abused children, it is difficult to suggest high-priority treatment targets. Clearly, while they remain with abusive parents, reduction of aversive behavior (e.g., aggression, bedwetting) that may act as a trigger for maltreatment might be addressed first, followed by efforts to increase adaptive behaviors (e.g., social skills). Trauma symptoms (e.g., anger outbursts, dissociation) may also be a high priority as they may interfere with children's overall functioning.

The psychological maltreatment (e.g., rejection, humiliation, etc.) that often accompanies physical abuse gives rise to common themes in group work, including issues of trust, anticipation of rejection, feelings of loss, and fear of adult figures. Therapists must be vigilant regarding identification of these issues as they emerge in group work. This is especially important in treating PTSD symptoms, where extreme reactions may occur (e.g., dissociation, anger outbursts) that may interrupt the flow of group sessions.

THE ROLE OF THE FACILITATOR

Work with abusive families can be very stressful. As noted at the beginning of this chapter, recidivism rates are high, and thus the need to report maltreatment is likely to arise. Support from a co-therapist or treatment team can help in this regard. Mandatory reporting may be threatening to group processes and should be addressed early in group work. If reporting becomes necessary, the therapist should provide assistance to the client as they deal with agency responses (e.g., attend meetings with the parent, role-play what might take place during the investigation). These strategies may help to preserve the therapeutic relationship and group cohesion.

Values also become especially relevant when working with abusive families. As noted earlier, abusive parents may be seen as being on the periphery of what is considered normative in childrearing practices. This fact produces strain for therapists whose tasks are more than just "refining" minor skill problems, but tackling underlying belief systems. The clash in beliefs may produce extreme reactions on the part of therapists and group members.

Economically disadvantaged parents, in particular, have been under media attack lately, and abusive parents, as noted earlier in this chapter, may be particularly sensitive to criticism (Azar, 1996). Expectations of being devalued may increase resistance to attendance and interventions. Indeed, attrition rates have been high with abusive parents (Wolfe, Aragona, Kaufman, & Sandler, 1980). Similarly, parents may resist their children attending group sessions where interpersonal approaches that are disparate from their own are presented.

Incentives and behavioral contracts have been suggested as ways to increase compliance, as has court-ordered treatment (Azar & Wolfe, 1989). The latter, however, may introduce another source of resistance. One solution is to help parents reframe the "problem" in terms of day-to-day difficulties that the parent can identify. *Child noncompliance, poor ability to deal with stress, vocational difficulties,* and *lack of supports* may all be more easily accepted problem definitions than *abuse or neglect* for such parents. Openness to such redefinition and acceptance by the therapist of the parents' way of seeing their problem is crucial to reducing resistance for two reasons. First, it may reduce the parents' fear of being evaluated and labeled as "bad" parents by the therapist. Being labeled as persons who "have trouble handling their children" or as someone who "is very lonely" (e.g., without social supports) or "stressed" may be easier to accept. Second, such reframing may serve to differentiate the therapist from the referral source (e.g., child protective services or courts), whom the parents may see as the cause of their "trouble."

Care must be taken not to collude with the client that no problem exists. A delicate balance must be achieved. Some clients may initially be willing to accept only that they are "in trouble" and that the therapist may help them to learn ways to interact with their children to get "out of trouble." Lack of compliance with treatment may still occur despite such reformulations.

Therapists must also be careful of their own preconceived ideas about abusive parents and their victims. Abused children may inappropriately be "assumed" to be damaged, when they may be functioning well. Biases toward seeing pathology may result in a self-fulfilling prophecy.

Parents' and children's poor relationship skills further increase the difficulty of the group therapists' job. The adolescent who displays provocative behavior may be particularly difficult to handle in group therapy (as is the provocative parent). Vicarious trauma responses to dealing with traumatized clients and the real threats that may occur in working with this population all need to be monitored and addressed in supervision. Therapists who can consistently exhibit the kinds of interpersonal skills lacking in this population (i.e., maintain a calm, warm, nurturing, structuring, consistent, and positive style) will be the most helpful.

TREATMENT AGENTS

Intervention in child abuse tends to be interdisciplinary, including a myriad of professional and layperson groups. Separate literatures have emerged in medical, education, juvenile justice, social work, psychological, and psychiatric journals. The task of keeping up with such a wide literature is immense. An empirical literature examining differential effectiveness as to which professional group is best suited for working with this population has not emerged. Treatment studies have utilized psychologists or graduate student therapists, neither of which are the most common in practice. Thus, the generalization of findings of studies may be open to question. The agents most prominent in children's early years tend to be health care providers (nurses) or parent aides. Later in development, school, mental health, and criminal justice system professionals seem more common. The clinical literature on interventions with children has mainly used either school personnel (e.g., day-care providers) or psychotherapists (social workers or psychologists).

In prevention work with children in school settings, some discussion has occurred regarding whether using regular classroom teachers versus outside group leaders is more useful. It has been argued that teachers or day-care personnel have greater familiarity with their children and may be better able to structure training to meet their needs (Conte, Rosen, & Saperstein, 1986). Comparative work, however, has yet to be carried out.

LIMITATIONS OF GROUP INTERVENTION

One of the major limitation of group work with this population is difficulty monitoring risk. Although violence prediction is controversial, evaluating level of risk may have some utility (Grisso & Appelbaum, 1992). The empirical literature suggests that risk monitoring can be best done when the group one is making a prediction about has been clearly defined, the setting of the individual has limited parameters (e.g., on a hospital ward), and the time frame of prediction is short. Risk assessment must be an ongoing task in treatment. Only a very small literature, however, exists regarding predicting future harm in physical abuse cases (Wald & Woolverton, 1990). Gross screening procedures are still in their early stages of development and are methodologically flawed. A limited number of predictive instruments also exist such as the Child Abuse Potential Inventory (Milner, 1986), but the utility of these has also been questioned because they have high false-positive rates (Caldwell, Bogat, & Davidson, 1988) and are too cumbersome to be used on a continuous basis as is needed in therapy.

Kolko (1996) describes the use of weekly self-reports of behavioral risk indicators in treatment that may assist the therapist in determining therapeutic response and that may be useful for providing such ongoing monitoring. The assistance of other community professionals involved with the family (e.g., physicians, social workers, public health nurses) as monitoring agents is also crucial. Although vigilance is necessary for all families, it may be particularly important for families with infants and toddlers, where the outcome of violence may be fatal. Careful monitoring of abuse should also occur with adolescents, where abuse is less likely to leave visible evidence and can often be overlooked.

A second limitation of using group work with abusive populations is the fact that parents who lack the bare minimum of interpersonal skills may not be able to interact effectively enough to make group participation viable. Third, low cognitive functioning is common in abusive parents, and such individuals may have less ability to learn information presented didactically, have poorer attentional skills, and a high potential for misinterpretation of information. Individual work may be more appropriate for such parents.

A final limitation is that group work alone often cannot address the chaotic life-style and deprivation in some families. Such issues may preclude the active practicing of new strategies, consistent group attendance, and motivation. Rewards for compliance with treatment and for attempting to employ strategies may be helpful. Instability in children's caregivers (e.g., foster care) may also make continuity of treatment difficult. One program chose to maintain contact with whomever the child was currently placed (Steward et al., 1986). Yet, if consistent involvement from teachers and caregivers is required to produce change, focusing on those individuals involved in the current placement may not be enough.

FUTURE DIRECTIONS

Much remains to be done to understand what is effective in treating the members of an abusive family (National Research Council, 1993). There have only been beginning efforts at developing empirically validated treatments. Based on these early efforts, group approaches for treating abusive parents, however, do appear to hold promise and need to be explored more systematically. Large-scale evaluations examining these preliminary approaches need to be undertaken. Efforts at developing effective treatments for physically abused children have lagged behind, and although group approaches have been attempted clinically, outcome work has been almost nonexistent. Although physical safety needs of abused children and adolescents should be a primary concern, clinicians must become more aware of abused children's developmental and emotional treatment needs and how to effectively intervene. More treatment outcome research is desperately needed in this area. At present, most therapies in physical child abuse have targeted the parent, not the child. Although stopping parental violence is clearly a crucial first step, there is mounting evidence of the negative impact of physical abuse on children's outcomes. Group work that involves both parent and child might be explored, as well as groups for victims alone.

Many other issues plague treatment work in this area and require specific study, including how best to deal with low-functioning parents in group settings, monitoring risk to children, the relative effectiveness of different treatment agents, how to combat attrition and treatment noncompliance, and addressing the issues involved in providing parenting training to diverse groups.

Given the problems of waiting until abuse occurs to intervene, more emphasis also needs to be placed on primary prevention. Most prevention currently involves mothers only; increased study of the involvement of fathers is needed. Linking community services to form a supportive network for young parents also needs further study. Finally, preventive efforts that originate in the constants in children's lives (i.e., in the health care system for infants or the school system for older children) warrant more attention. Social policy efforts supporting funding for prevention work with all parents ultimately may be required to combat effectively this social problem affecting numerous children's and adolescents' lives.

REFERENCES

Aber, J. L., & Allen, J. P. (1987). The effects of maltreatment on young children's socio-emotional development: An attachment theory perspective. *Developmental Psychology, 23,* 406–414.

Ammerman, R. T. (1991). The role of children in physical abuse: A reappraisal. *Violence and Victims, 6,* 87–100.

Azar, S. T. (1986). A framework for understanding child maltreatment: An integration of cognitive behavioral and development perspectives. *Canadian Journal of Behavioral Science, 18,* 340–355.

Azar, S. T. (1989). Training parents of abused children. In C. E. Shaefer & J. M. Briesmeister (Eds.), *Handbook of parent training* (pp. 414–441). New York: Wiley.

Azar, S. T. (1991a). Models of physical child abuse: An metatheoretical analysis. *Criminal Justice and Behavior, 18,* 30–46.

Azar, S. T. (1991b, November). *Is the cognitively low functioning mother at risk for child maltreatment*? Presented at the annual meeting of the Association for Advancement of Behavior Therapy, New York.

Azar, S. T. (1991c, April). *Concern about the physical abuse of adolescents: A case of neglect.* Paper presented at the annual meeting of the Eastern Psychological Association, New York.

Azar, S. T. (1996). Cognitive restructuring of professionals' schema regarding women parenting in poverty. *Women & Therapy, 18,* 149–163.

Azar, S. T. (1997). A cognitive behavioral approach to understanding and treating parents who physically abuse their children. In R. McMahon, R. Peters, & D. A. Wolfe (Eds.), *Child abuse: New directions in prevention and treatment across the life span* (pp. 79–101). New York: Sage.

Azar, S. T., Barnes, K. T., & Twentyman, C. T. (1988). Developmental outcomes in physically abused children: Consequences of parental abuse or the effects of a more general breakdown in caregiving behaviors? *Behavior Therapist, 11,* 27–32.

Azar, S. T., & Benjet, C. L. (1994). A cognitive perspective on ethnicity, race, and termination of parental rights. *Law and Human Behavior, 18,* 249–268.

Azar, S. T., Fantuzzo, J., & Twentyman, C. T. (1984). An applied behavioral approach to child maltreatment: Back to basics. *Advances in Behavior Research and Therapy, 6,* 3–11.

Azar, S. T., Robinson, D. R., Hekimian, E., & Twentyman, C. T. (1984). Unrealistic expectations and problems solving ability in maltreating and comparison mothers. *Journal of Consulting and Clinical Psychology, 52,* 687–691.

Azar, S. T., & Rohrbeck, C. A. (1986). Child abuse and unrealistic expectations: Further validation of the Parent Opinion Questionnaire. *Journal of Consulting and Clinical Psychology, 54,* 867–868.

Azar, S. T., & Siegel, B. (1990). Behavioral treatment of child abuse: A developmental perspective. *Behavior Modification, 14,* 279–300.

Azar, S. T., & Twentyman, C. T. (1984, November). *An evaluation of the effectiveness of behaviorally versus insight oriented group treatments with maltreating mothers.* Paper presented at the annual meeting of the Association for Advancement of Behavior Therapy, Philadelphia.

Azar, S. T., & Twentyman, C. T. (1986). Cognitive-behavioral perspectives on the assessment and treatment of child abuse. In P. C. Kendall (Ed.), *Advances in cognitive-behavioral research and therapy* (Vol. 5, pp. 237–267). New York: Academic.

Azar, S. T., & Wientzen, J. (1993, March). *Abuse, social skills, and social support in adolescent runaways.* Paper presented at the biannual meeting of the Society for Research in Child Development, New Orleans.

Azar, S. T., & Wolfe, D. (1989). Child abuse and neglect. In F. J. Mash & R. A. Barkley (Eds.), *Treatment of childhood disorders* (pp. 451–489). New York: Guilford.

Barnes, K. T., & Azar, S. T. (1990, August). *Maternal expectations and attributions in discipline situations: A test of a cognitive model of parenting*. Paper presented at the annual meeting of the American Psychological Association, Boston.

Barth, R. P., Blythe, B. J., Schinke, S. P., Stevens, P., & Schilling, R. F. (1983). Self-control training with maltreating parents. *Child Welfare, 62,* 313–324.

Beck, A. T. (1963). Thinking and depression: Idiosyncratic content and cognitive distortions. *Archives of General Psychiatry, 9,* 324–333.

Berkeley Planning Associates. (1978). *Evaluation of child abuse demonstration projects 1974–1977.* Washington, DC: U.S. Department of Health, Education and Welfare.

Brunk, M., Henggeler, S. W., & Whelan, J. P. (1987). Comparison of multisystemic therapy and parent training in the brief treatment of child abuse and neglect. *Journal of Consulting and Clinical Psychology, 55,* 171–178.

Burgdorf, K. (1988). *Study of national incidence and prevalence of child abuse and neglect: 1988.* Washington, DC: NCCAN.

Burgess, R. L., & Conger, R. D. (1978). Family interaction in abusive, neglectful and normal families. *Child Development, 49,* 1163–1173.

Caldwell, R. A., Bogat, G. A., & Davidson, W. S. (1988). The assessment of child abuse potential and the prevention of child abuse and neglect: A policy analysis. *American Journal of Community Psychology, 16,* 609–624.

Campbell, R. V., O'Brien, S., Bickett, A. D., & Lutzker, J. R. (1983). In-home parent training of migraine headaches and marital counseling as an ecobehavioral approach to prevent child abuse. *Journal of Behavior Therapy and Experimental Psychiatry, 14,* 147–154.

Casanova, G. M., Domanic, J., McCanne, T. R., & Milner, J. S. (1992). Physiological responses to non-child-related stressors in mothers at risk for child abuse. *Child Abuse and Neglect, 16,* 31–44.

Cicchetti, D., & Rizley, R. (1981). Developmental perspectives on the etiology, intergenerational transmission, and sequelae of child maltreatment. *New Directions for Child Development, 11,* 31–56.

Clewell, B. C., Brooks-Gunn, J., & Benasich, A. A. (1989). Evaluating child-related outcomes of teenage parenting programs. *Family Relations, 38,* 201–209.

Cohen, S. (1980). After effects of stress on human performance and social behavior: A review of research and theory. *Psychological Bulletin, 88,* 82–108.

Cohn, A. (1979). Effective treatment of child abuse and neglect. *Social Work, 24,* 513–519.

Conger, R. D., Lahey, B. B., & Smith, S. S. (1981, July). *An intervention program for child abuse: Modifying maternal depression and behavior*. Paper presented at the Family Violence Research Conference, University of New Hampshire, Durham.

Conte, J. R., Rosen, C., & Saperstein, L. (1986). An analysis of programs to prevent the sexual victimization of children. *Journal of Primary Prevention, 6,* 141–155.

Crittenden, P. M. (1985). Maltreated infants: Vulnerability and resilience. *Journal of Child Psychology and Psychiatry, 26,* 85–96.

Crittenden, P. M. (1992). Treatment of anxious attachment in infancy and early childhood, *Developmental Psychopathology, 4,* 575–602.

Crittenden, P., & Ainsworth, M. (1989). Child maltreatment and attachment theory. In D. Cicchetti & V. Carlson (Eds.), *Child maltreatment* (pp. 423–463). Cambridge: Cambridge University Press.

Daro, D. (1988). *Confronting child abuse: Research for effective program design*. New York: Free Press.

Deblinger, E., McLeer, S. V., Atkins, M. S., Ralphe, D., & Foa, E. (1989). Post-traumatic stress in sexually abused, physically abused, and nonabused children. *Child Abuse and Neglect, 13,* 403–408.

Deblinger, E., McLeer, S. V., & Henry, D. (1990). Cognitive behavioral treatment for sexually abused children suffering from post traumatic stress: Preliminary findings. *American Academy of Child and Adolescent Psychiatry, 29,* 747–752.

Delgado, A. E., & Lutzker, J. R. (1985, November). *Training parents to identify and report their children's illness*. Paper presented at the annual convention of the Association for Advancement of Behavior Therapy, Houston.

DiGiuseppe, R. (1988). A cognitive-behavioral approach to the treatment of conduct disorder children and adolescents. In N. Epstein, S. F. Schlesinger, & W. Dryden (Eds.), *Cognitive-behavioral therapy with families* (pp. 183–214). New York: Bruner/Mazel.

Dix, T. H., Ruble, D. N., & Zambarano, R. J. (1989). Mothers' implicit theories of discipline: Child effects, parent effects, and the attribution process. *Child Development, 60,* 1373–1391.

Dumas, J. E., & Wahler, R. G. (1983). Predictors of treatment outcome in parent training: Mother insularity and socioeconomic disadvantage. *Behavioral Assessment, 5,* 301–313.

Eckenrode, J., Laird, M., & Doris, J. (1993). School performance and disciplinary problems among abused and neglected children. *Developmental Psychology, 29,* 53–62.

Egeland, B., & Erickson, M. F. (1990). Rising above the past: Strategies for helping new mothers break the cycle of abuse and neglect, *Zero to Three, 11,* 29–35.

Elliot, F. A. (1988). Neurological factors. In V. B. Van-Hasselt, R. L. Morison, A. S. Bellack, & M. Hersen (Eds.), *Handbook of family violence* (pp. 359–382). New York: Plenum.

Famularo, R., Fenton, T., & Kinscherff, R. (1993). Child maltreatment and the development of posttraumatic stress disorder. *American Journal of Diseases of Children, 147,* 755–760.

Famularo, R., Kinscherff, R., & Fenton, T. (1990). Symptom differences in acute and chronic presentation of childhood post-traumatic stress disorder. *Child Abuse and Neglect, 14,* 439–444.

Famularo, R., Stone, I., Barnum, R., & Wharton, R. (1986). Alcoholism and severe child maltreatment. *American Journal of Orthopsychiatry, 56,* 481–485.

Fantuzzo, J. (1990). Behavioral treatment of the victims of child abuse and neglect. *Behavior Modification, 14,* 316–339.

Fantuzzo, J. W., Jurecic, L., Stovall, A., Hightower, A. D., Goins, C., & Schachtel, D. (1988). Effects of adult and peer social initiations on the social behavior of withdrawn, maltreated preschool children. *Journal of Consulting and Clinical Psychology, 56,* 34–39.

Fehrenbach, P. A., & Thelen, M. H. (1981). Assertive-skills training for inappropriately aggressive college males: Effects on assertive and aggressive behaviors. *Journal of Behavior Therapy and Experimental Psychiatry, 12,* 213–217.

Feindler, E. L., & Ecton, R. B. (1986). *Adolescent anger control: Cognitive-behavioral techniques.* New York: Pergamon.

Fiske, S. T., & Taylor, S. E. (1991). *Social cognition.* New York: McGraw-Hill.

Flanagan, S., Adams, H. E., & Forehand, R. (1979). A comparison of four instructional techniques for teaching parents to use time out. *Behavior Therapy, 10,* 94–102.

Gelles, R. J. (1992). Poverty and violence toward children. *American Behavioral Scientist, 35,* 258–274.

Gelles, R. J., & Straus, M. A. (1987). Is violence toward children increasing? A comparison of 1975 and 1985 National Survey rates. *Journal of Interpersonal Violence, 2,* 212–222.

Gilbert, M. R. (1976). Behavioral approach to the treatment of child abuse. *Nursing Times, 72,* 140–143.

Goldstein, S., & Goldstein, M. (1990). *Managing attention disorders in children.* New York: John Wiley.

Gordon, S. B., & Davidson, N. (1991). Behavioral parent training. In A. F. Gurman & D. P. Kniskern (Eds.), *Handbook of family therapy* (pp. 517–555). New York: Brunner/Mazel.

Grisso, T., & Appelbaum, P. S. (1992). Is it unethical to offer predictions of future violence? *Law and Human Behavior, 16,* 621–633.

Guevremont, Wazzu D. (1990). Social skills and peer relationship training. In R. Barkely (Ed.), *Attention-deficit hyperactivity disorder: A handbook for diagnosis and treatment* (pp. 540–572). New York: Guilford.

Hammond, W. R., & Yung, B. R. (1991). Preventing violence in at-risk African-American youth. Conference: Pursuing the health and development of young African-American males. *Journal of Health Care for Poor and Underserved, 2,* 359–373.

Hansen, D. J., Pallotta, G. M., Tishelman, A. C., & Conaway, L. P. (1989). Parental problem-solving skills and child behavior problems: A comparison of physically abusive, neglectful, clinic, and community families. *Journal of Family Violence, 4,* 353–368.

Haskett, M. E. (1990). Social problem-solving skills of young physically abused children. *Child Psychiatry and Human Development, 21,* 109–118.

Herrenkohl, R. C., Herrenkohl, E. C., & Egolf, B. P. (1983). Circumstances surrounding the occurrence of child maltreatment. *Journal of Consulting and Clinical Psychology, 51,* 424–431.

Herrenkohl, R. C., Herrenkohl, E. C., Egolf, B., & Seech, M. (1979). The repetition of child abuse: How frequently does it occur? *Child Abuse and Neglect, 3,* 67–72.

Hoffman-Plotkin, D., & Twentyman, C. T. (1984). A multimodal assessment of behavioral and cognitive deficits in abused and neglected preschoolers. *Child Development, 55,* 794–802.

Jones, R. W., & Peterson, L. W. (1993). Post-traumatic stress disorder in a child following an automobile accident. *The Journal of Family Practice, 36,* 223–225.

Justice, B., & Justice, R. (1978). Evaluating outcome of group therapy for abusing parents. *Corrective and Social Psychiatry and Journal of Behavioral Technology, 24,* 45–49.

Kaufman, J., & Zigler, E. (1987). Do abused children become abusive parents? *American Journal of Orthopsychiatry, 57,* 186–192.

Knudsen, D. (1992). *Child maltreatment: Emerging perspectives.* Dix Hills, NY: General Hall.

Knutson, J. F. (1978). Child abuse as an area of aggres-

massage with lotion so that the mothers can learn ways of comforting their infants, particularly when they might see more negative expressions of affect, as well as offering containment and comfort through rocking and singing of lullabies.

Dyadic techniques with the mother center on empathizing with her feelings in the ongoing process. The therapist reflects with the mother about her feelings in relation to her young child's cues and behaviors. The therapist may also use wondering, coaching, and modeling with the mother to promote her ability to respond to her child's cues. Modeling is limited early in the relationship, to prevent feelings of inadequacy in the mothers. Therapists help to modulate emotions that may disrupt interactions and may intervene briefly if a mother appears to be overwhelmed. The therapist also amplifies the responsive behaviors and emotional expressions of the mother in order to respect, extend, and support her constructive initiatives and responses. Therapists also *wonder along* with mothers about the effectiveness of a particular approach.

During the mother-child dyadic group, therapists also amplify the child's emotional expressions and wonder along with the mother about how her infant may feel or what he or she may need. In doing so, the therapists assist mothers in reading and responding to their children. The therapist attempts to amplify the young child's communications by speaking for the child: "Oh, Mom, I really like it when you look at me that way!" The therapist also helps and supports the emerging language capacities of the young child to begin to convey his or her needs and wishes to the parents.

The appendix at the end of this chapter contains the weekly topics from the group curriculum and examples of weekly session guides for the mothers and dyadic therapy groups.

THERAPEUTIC OBJECTIVES

Therapeutic objectives can be described in the following manner:

1. Reduce the risk for maltreatment and neglect by involving parents in assessing their capacities to *recognize and respond* to their child's developmental and emotional needs. Provide specific strategies to assist these parents in increasing their sense of effectiveness in providing safe, nurturing environments for their children. Strategies for reducing potentially neglectful behavior include:
   - Attending to parents' perceived needs so they in turn can attend to their child's needs
   - Assisting parents in recognizing and responding to their child's cues, particularly distress cues by *speaking for the child*
   - Enhancing and amplifying positive interactions to increase their reinforcement value for the parent and child
2. Address and ameliorate maternal depressive symptoms. Identify negative thought patterns and provide cognitive-behavioral and interpersonal strategies for coping with depression, eliminating negative thought patterns, and increasing positive affective expression and regulation.
3. Assist parents in providing more empathic care for their child through recognition and discussion of their own experiences of being parented.
4. Involve parents in assessing their sources of stress and safety risk in their relationship with their child, their partner, and in their home and neighborhood.
5. Increase provision of safety in the home through *home visits* prior to group and involving parents in *assessing safety hazards* in their own home by use of a Safe Home Checklist.
6. Increase safe, positive parenting practices by building or enhancing feelings of competence in the parenting role through *positive commenting, empathic listening,* and so on, so that parents may take an active role in providing a safe environment for their child.
7. Provide peer support and reduce social isolation among group members by focusing on and discussing personal and parenting issues, common sources of stress, *exchange of ideas,* especially *sharing effective coping strategies by other parents.*
8. Improve parents' interactions with their child by teaching specific ways of interacting through *instruction, modeling, and observation* of videotaped interaction of themselves with their child in the parent/child interaction sessions. Involve parents in identifying and sharing for themselves and others

that which they have found effective and rewarding in interactions with their child.

TRAINING OF THERAPISTS AND ONGOING SUPERVISION

Therapists for these groups (which have been provided in cooperation with social services, the community mental health center, a community-based child abuse treatment program, and in our hospital-based clinic) include child psychiatry residents and psychology interns, postdoctoral fellows and students, volunteer therapists, and allied health professionals. The therapists are trained in a relational perspective and are given materials to further acquaint them not only with the identification and assessment of the risk factors for abuse but also with the meaning of these risk factors for the parents, for their young child, and for family relationships. The training includes information regarding child development during the first two years of life along with specific training in individual, group, and dyadic approaches. Specific training covers the dyadic work in depth. The shift from being the child's therapist to working with the dyad is complicated. It demands that the therapist become almost primarily involved with the mother in offering empathy and establishing the trust that will permit intensive therapeutic involvement.

Sessions are videotaped and supervisors observe behind a one-way mirror. Direct supervision then occurs immediately after each group session for 90 minutes, during which the therapists meet to process the events, discussions, and interactions for that particular session. During each supervision session, therapists focus on the emotional and relational issues for each mother, child, and family. Using their growing understanding of the family, therapists then develop individualized goals and strategies for therapeutic intervention focused on particular issues and needs related to future sessions.

EVALUATION RESULTS

The efficacy of this relationship-based group therapeutic model has been evaluated. Self-report and observational data were collected pre- and post-group and included mothers' levels of depressive symptoms, personality, parenting stress, and perceptions of their child's temperament and behavior. Children's developmental and psychosocial status and the quality of the mother-child interactions were also assessed pre- and postintervention or after 12 weeks for the control group.

This study included 30 women and their infants in a matched control group design with 15 depressed women and their children and 15 waiting-list control group research participants matched on demographic variables. The therapeutic group participants and matched control group participants were either referred for treatment by physicians, nurses, or other community agency professionals or were self-referred in response to advertisements and flyers in newspapers, diaper service newsletters, or Ob/Gyn, pediatrician's, or family practitioner's offices. Potential research participants were screened for depression by phone using a screener based on *DSM-IV* criteria, developed for this study. All of the participants reported depressive symptomatology within the clinical range on the Beck Depression Inventory (Beck, Ward, Mendelson, Mock, & Erbaugh, 1961). The mean age of the children in the study was 11 months, the mean age of the mothers was 31 years. The mean level of education for mothers in both groups was a college degree. The mean income for both of the groups was $29,000 to $30,000.

Separate analyses of covariance (ANCOVA), controlling for education, and pretest scores were conducted with the group (treatment vs. control) as an independent variable and the level of depressive symptoms (Beck Depression Inventory), parenting stress, perception of infant's temperament and quality of mother-infant interaction (6 PCERA subscales) as dependent variables. Mothers who had participated in the therapeutic group reported less depressive symptoms and lower levels of stress in the parenting role than mothers in the matched control group at posttesting . Specifically, the mothers who had participated in the therapeutic group reported seeing their infants as more adaptable and subsequently felt less stressed by their children. In analyses focusing on improvement in the quality of the mother-infant interaction, mothers who had completed the therapeutic group exhibited more positive, sensitive, and responsive behaviors with their infants and there was more mutuality and reciprocity observed in dyadic interactions than in the dyads in the control group (Clark, 1997).

Mothers who completed the therapeutic group were also asked to complete a client satisfaction questionnaire at the end of the 12 weeks. Group participants were provided with the goals they had set for themselves, their infant, and their relationship with their infant and asked the extent to which they felt they had achieved these goals. All mothers reported achieving their goals in each area, with most mothers' reporting a stronger sense of achievement and competence in the parenting role.

Additionally, mothers were asked which aspects of the adult and dyadic group they found most helpful. Mothers reported that sharing feelings about their own experience of being parented, about themselves as parents, discussing what they find difficult and enjoyable with their infants, and sharing feelings about their marital and other relationships were helpful (Clark et al., 1993).

LIMITATIONS AND DIRECTIONS FOR FUTURE EVALUATION RESEARCH

There are very few studies evaluating the effectiveness of preventive and early intervention approaches for supporting healthy mother-infant relationships. Little funding is available for evaluation research and the multirisk and at-risk populations pose difficulties for research of program effectiveness, including high attrition rates and high mobility reducing the possibility of follow-up assessment. In addition, matching groups on sociodemographic variables can be challenging, and ethical problems are posed by placing families in a control group when dyads are at high risk, especially for abuse. Also, more research is needed that identifies individual differences in terms of who benefits from what types of intervention for this population at risk. For example, we have found that mothers who have certain personality disorders have a difficult time being able to make use of a group due to issues of distrust and suspicion and often have difficulty sharing a therapist with one's child.

Another possible limitation as well as benefit of this approach is that it is not home based. Mothers with young children may have difficulty arranging child care and/or transportation; however, we have found that the social supports and one-to-one special time with the target child afforded by this approach is often unique to the mother's daily experience and can be quite therapeutic in itself. Follow-up studies are needed to determine the long-term benefits of this relationship-focused approach, including continued capacities for affective and behavioral regulation in both the mother and the young child, in the mother's ability to see the child as a separate individual and to respond to her or his changing developmental needs, as well as the mother's ability to make use of community resources in future times of stress.

APPENDIX: PARENT-INFANT AND EARLY CHILDHOOD CLINIC GROUP CURRICULUM

Sample Parent Group Session Guide

Session 2: Ambivalent Feelings—Love and Anger

Goals

To identify a range of human emotions that may be difficult for mother to experience or express

To learn on an individual level how members experience conflicting emotions or ambivalence (love and anger) towards their children and in other relationships

To recognize various ways of coping with ambivalent feelings

To recognize and accept children's expressions of love and anger towards parents

1. Check in.
   - How was the last session for you?
   - Review home activities and mothers' journals regarding how play times went for them.
   - Discuss any areas that need clarification.
   - How did the dyadic session feel?

2. Introduce and explain concept of ambivalence. Normalize feelings of anger toward those we love.
   - Discuss people we loved as a child and those whom we looked to for love.
     —Did you ever feel anger towards this person? How did you express it? How did you express loving feelings?
   - Have members write three adjectives that describe their relationship with those whom they looked to for love (e.g., their mother and their father).
   - Discuss each member's selection of words and what the meaning of these words is to members as women, mothers, and partners.
     —How easy or hard was it to come up with the adjectives?
     —Did anyone select words that are positive as well as negative?
     —Discuss ambivalence.
     —Are there people in your lives now whom you love but can also be angry with? How does that go?
     —With your children, do you feel anger and love at the same time? When is that likely to happen? How do you deal with it or express it?
     —Can you recognize when your child expresses loving feelings and angry feelings? Does he feel them at the same time? Can you help him to label the feelings and guide his behavior?
3. Bridge to dyadic session.
   - Observe children in developmental therapy group. Encourage mother to try to recognize different feeling states in their child. Talk about the idea of mixed feeling states in child (e.g., sad and angry) as well as themselves.
   - Encourage them to imagine what that might be like for themselves and for their child. Discuss how they can help their child understand how he feels by recognizing and labeling feeling states.

Home Activities

Continue play time with child.

Continue recording those sessions in journal.

Handouts

Plain Talk about Dealing with the Angry Child (Fried, 1978)

Helping Young Children Channel Their Aggressive Energies (Provence, 1985)

Sample Dyadic Group Session Guide

Session 2: Ambivalent Feelings—Love and Anger

Goals

To increase mothers' awareness of their child's range of emotion and their own

To increase mothers' comfort with their child's expression of both love and anger

To increase mothers' capacity to mirror and label their child's internal feeling states

Welcome Song

Song: "Come and Join the Circle"

Song: "Oh Here We Are Together" (2X)

Check In. Ask each parent to say:

1. One thing that makes (*child's name*) feel frustrated/angry
2. One thing that makes (*child's name*) feel happy

Activity 1. Song: If You're Happy and You Know It

"If you're happy and you know it,
clap your hands.

If you're happy and you know it,
give a smile.

If you're mad and you know it,
stomp your feet.

If you're surprised and you know it,
look surprised.

If you're happy and you know it,
wave your hands.

(Etc.)"

Facilitators. Encourage parents to model facial expressions for child(ren).

Bavolek, S. J. (1984). *A handbook for understanding child abuse and neglect.* Park City, UT: The Nurturing Program, Family Development Resources.

Bavolek, S. J. (1990). *Validation report of the nurturing program.* Park City, UT: The Nurturing Program, Family Development Resources.

Beck, A. T., Ward, C. H., Mendelson, M., Mock, J., & Erbaugh, J. (1961). An inventory for measuring depression. *Archives of General Psychiatry, 4*, 561–569.

Bowen, M. (1971). The use of family theory in clinical practice. In J. Haley (Ed.), *Changing families*. New York: Grune & Stratton.

Bowlby, J. (1968). *Attachment and loss: Attachment* (Vol. 1). New York: Basic Books.

Bowlby, J. (1973). *Attachment and loss: Separation* (Vol. 2). New York: Basic Books.

Bowlby, J. (1980). *Attachment and loss: Loss, sadness and depression* (Vol. 3). New York: Basic Books.

Braverman, J., & Roux, J. F. (1978). Screening for the patient at risk for postpartum depression. *Obstetrics and Gynecology, 52*, 731–736.

Bretherton, I. (1985). Attachment theory: Retrospect and prospect. *Monographs of the Society for Research in Child Development, 50*(1-2), 3–35.

Bronfenbrenner, U. (1979). *The ecology of human development: Experiments by nature and design*. Cambridge, MA: Harvard University Press.

Brown, G. W., & Davidson, S. (1978). Social class, psychiatric disorder of the mother, and accidents to children. *Lancet, 1*, 378.

Burns, D. D. (1989) *The feeling good handbook: Using the new mood therapy in everyday life*. New York: New American Library.

Campbell, S. B., & Cohn, J. F. (1997). The timing and chronicity of postpartum depression: Implications for infant development. In L. Murray & P. Cooper (Eds.), *Postpartum depression and child development* (pp. 165–197). New York: Guilford.

Campbell, S. B., Cohn, J. F., & Meyers, T. (1995). Depression in first-time mothers: Mother-infant interaction and depression chronicity. *Developmental Psychology, 31*(3), 349–357.

Campbell, S. B., Cohn, J. F., Flanagan, C., Popper, S., & Meyers, T. (1992). Course and correlates of postpartum depression during the transition to parenthood. *Development and Psychopathology, 4*, 29–47.

Cassidy, J., & Berlin, L. J. (1994). The insecure/ambivalent pattern of attachment: Theory and research. *Child Development, 65*, 971–991.

Cicchetti, D. (1987). Developmental psychopathology in infancy: Illustration from the study of maltreated youngsters. *Journal of Consulting and Clinical Psychology, 55*(6), 837–845.

Cicchetti, D., & Braunwald, K. G. (1984). An organizational approach to the study of emotional development in maltreated infants. *Infant Mental Health Journal, 5*(3), 172–183.

Clark, R. (1997). Efficacy of a therapeutic group approach for mothers with postpartum depression and their infants. Unpublished manuscript, University of Wisconsin–Madison.

Clark, R. (1994). *Postpartum depression group therapy for mothers and infants: A relational approach: Curriculum and manual.* University of Wisconsin–Madison.

Clark, R., Keller, A. D., Fedderly, S. S., & Paulson, A. W. (1993). Treating the relationships affected by postpartum depression: A group therapy model. *Zero to Three, 13*, 5–9.

Clark, R., Paulson, A., & Conlin, S. (1993). Assessment of developmental status and parent-infant relationships: The therapeutic process of evaluation. In C. Zeanah (Ed.), *Handbook of infant mental health* (pp. 191–209). New York: Guilford.

Cohn, J. F., & Tronick, E. L. (1983). Three month old infants' reactions to simulated maternal depression. *Child Development, 54*, 185–193.

Cohn, J. F., & Tronick, E. L. (1987). Mother-infant face-to-face interaction: The sequence of dyadic states at 3, 6, and 9 months. *Developmental Psychology, 23*(1), 68–77.

Cohn, J. F. & Tronick, E. L. (1989). Specificity of infant's response to mothers' affective behavior. *Journal of the American Academy of Child and Adolescent Psychiatry, 28*(2), 242–248.

Crittenden, P. M. (1995). Attachment and risk for psychopathology: The early years. *Developmental and Behavioral Pediatrics, 16*(3), 12–16.

Crowell, J. A., & Feldman, S. S. (1989). Assessment of mothers' working models of relationships: Some clinical implications. *Infant Mental Health Journal, 10*(3), 173–184.

Demos, V. (1982). The role of affect in early childhood: An exploratory study. In E. Z. Tronick (Ed.), *Social interchange in infancy: Affect, cognition, and communication* (pp. 79–124). Baltimore, MD: University Park Press.

Egeland, B., & Erickson, M. F. (1990). Rising above the past: Strategies for helping new mothers break the cycle of abuse and neglect. *Zero to Three, XI*(2), 29–35.

Emde, R. M. (1981). Emotional availability: A reciprocal reward system for infants and parents with implications for prevention of psychosocial disorders. In P.

Taylor (Ed.), *Parent-infant relationships*. New York: Grune & Stratton.

Erickson, M. F., Korfmacher, J., & Egeland, B. (1992). Attachments past and present: Implications for therapeutic intervention with mother-infant dyads. *Development and Psychopathology, 4*(4), 495–507.

Field, T. M. (1987). Affective and interactive disturbances in infants. In J. D. Osofsky (Ed.), *Handbook of infant development* (pp. 972–1005). New York: Wiley.

Field, T. M. (1992). Infants of depressed mothers. *Development and Psychopathology, 4*, 49–66.

Fraiberg, S., Adelson, E., & Shapiro, V. (1975). Ghosts in the nursery: A psychoanalytic approach to the problems of impaired infant-mother relationships. *Journal of the American Academy of Child Psychiatry, 14*, 387–421.

Fried, H. (1978). *Plain talk about dealing with the angry child*. Rockville, MD: U.S. Department of Health and Human Services.

Garbarino, J. (1990). The human ecology of early risk. In S. J. Meisels & J. P. Shonkoff (Eds.), *Handbook of early childhood intervention* (pp. 79–96). Cambridge: Cambridge University Press.

Garbarino J., & Kostelny, K. (1992). Child maltreatment as a community problem. *Child Abuse and Neglect, 16*(4), 455–464.

Gaudin, J. M., Polansky, N. A., Kilpatrick, A. C., & Shilton, P. (1993). Loneliness, depression, stress, and social supports in neglectful families. *American Journal of Orthopsychiatry, 63*, 597–605.

Goodman, S. H., & Brumley, H. E. (1990). Schizophrenic and depressed mothers: Relational deficits in parenting. *Developmental Psychology, 26*, 31–39.

Goodman, S. H., Radke-Yarrow, M., & Teti, D. (1993). Maternal depression as a context for child rearing. *Zero to Three, 13*(5), 16–23.

Greenspan, S. I. (1990). Comprehensive clinical approaches to infants and their families: Psychodynamic and developmental perspectives. In S. J. Meisels & J. P. Shonkoff (Eds.), *Handbook of early childhood intervention* (pp. 150–172). Cambridge: Cambridge University Press.

Greenspan, S., & Lourie, R. (1981). Developmental structuralist approach to the classification of adaptive and pathological personality organization: Application to infancy and early childhood. *American Journal of Psychiatry, 138*, 725–736.

Kashani, J. H., Anasseril, E. D., Dandoy, A., & Holcomb, W. R. (1992). Family violence: Impact on children. *Journal of the Academy of Child and Adolescent Psychiatry, 31*, 181–189.

Klerman, G. L., Weissman, M. M., Rounsaville, B. J., & Chevron, E. S. (1984). *Interpersonal psychotherapy of depression*. New York: Basic Books.

Kohut, H. (1971). The analysis of self. *The psychoanalytic study of the child monograph No. 4*. New York: Universities Press.

Landy, S. (1993). *Helping encourage affect regulation: A parenting program for parents of young children.* Toronto: Hincks Institute.

Lewis, M., & Goldberg, S. (1969). Perceptual-cognitive development in infancy: A generalized expectancy model as a function of the mother-infant interaction. *Merrill-Palmer Quarterly, 15*, 81–100.

Lyons-Ruth, K., Connell, D. B., & Zoll, D. (1989). Finding organization in disorganization: Lessons from research on maltreated infants' attachments to their caregivers. In D. Cicchetti & V. Carlson (Eds.), *Child maltreatment* (pp. 464–493). New York: Cambridge University Press.

Lyons-Ruth, K., Zoll, D., Connell, D., & Grunebaum, H. U. (1986). The depressed mother and her one-year-old infant: Environment, interaction, attachment, and infant development. *New Directions for Child Development, 34*, 61–82.

Main, M., & Hesse, H. (1990). Parents' unresolved traumatic experiences are related to infant disorganized attachment status: Is frightened and/or frightening parental behavior the linking mechanism? In M. T. Greenberg, D. Cicchetti, & M. E. Cummings (Eds.), *Attachment in the preschool years* (pp. 161–182). Chicago: University of Chicago Press.

McCurdy, K., & Daro, D. (1994). Child maltreatment: A national survey of reports and fatalities. *Journal of Interpersonal Violence, 9*(1), 75–94.

Mercy, J. A., Rosenberg, M. L., Powell, K. E., Broome, C. V., & Roper, W. L. (1993). Public health policy for preventing violence. Special Issue: Violence and the public's health. *Health Affairs, 12*(4).

Minuchin, S. (1974). *Families and family therapy*. Cambridge, MA: Harvard University Press.

National Center of Child Abuse and Neglect. (1981). *National study of incidence and severity of child abuse and neglect* (DHHS Publication No. OHDS 81-30325). Washington, DC: U.S. Department of Health and Human Services.

O'Hara, M. W. (1987). Post-partum "blues," depression and psychosis: A review. *Journal of Psychosomatic Obstetrics and Gynaecology, 7*, 205–227.

O'Hara, M. W. (1986). Social support, life events, and depression during pregnancy and puerperium. *Archives of General Psychiatry, 43*(6), 569–573.